The

SCHEMATICS

of

COMPUTATION

The
SCHEMATICS
of
COMPUTATION

Vincent S. Manis
Langara College

James J. Little
University of British Columbia

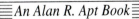
An Alan R. Apt Book

Prentice Hall, Englewood Cliffs, New Jersey 07632

Library of Congress Cataloging-in-Publication Data

Manis, Vincent S.
    The schematics of computation / Vincent S. Manis, James J. Little
        p.   cm.
    "An Alan R. Apt book."
    Includes bibiliographical references and index.
    ISBN 0-13-834284-9
    1. Scheme (Computer program language)   I. Little, James J.
II. Title.
QA76.73.S34M36 1995
005.13'3--dc20   94-21432
                                                           CIP

Publisher: Alan Apt
Project Manager: Mona Pompili
Developmental Editor: Sondra Chavez
Cover Designer: DeFranco Design Inc.
Copy Editor: Nick Murray
Production Coordinator: Lori Bulwin
Supplements Editor: Alice Dworkin
Editorial Assistant: Shirley McGuire

About the cover: Those who have advanced the sciences and arts have always used "schematic" methods to show their ideas. Christopher Wren's design for St Paul's Cathedral in London, Isaac Newton's reflector telescope, and Johann Sebastian Bach's score for the *Goldberg Variations* are all shown here in schematic form. Our computer programs are inspired by the schematic flavor of these works.

ISBN   0-13-834284-9

Prentice-Hall International (UK) Limited, *London*
Prentice-Hall of Australia Pty. Limited, *Sydney*
Prentice-Hall Canada, Inc., *Toronto*
Prentice-Hall Hispanoamericana, S.A., *Mexico*
Prentice-Hall of India Private Limited, *New Delhi*
Prentice-Hall of Japan, Inc., *Tokyo*
Simon & Schuster Asia Pte. Ltd., *Singapore*
Editora Prentice-Hall do Brasil, Ltda. *Rio de Janeiro*

This book is dedicated with love to my parents, Martin and Fay Manis. — VSM

*I dedicate this book to my mother, Marguerite,
and to my wife, Debra, and my children, Brendan and Hanna,
who endured my long absences in my study.* — JJL

Preface

The best laid schemes o' mice an' men
Gang aft a-gley.

— Robert Burns, "To a Mouse"

Students need an introductory course in computer science that exposes them to all of computer science. Computer science is not just about programming techniques. It rests on deep ideas and the nature of computation. We want students to understand these deep ideas, as well as grasp the practicality of computation and experience the pleasure of computing.

We wrote *The Schematics of Computation* for one reason—we wanted a book that presents the fundamental ideas of computer science in a way that students can understand. Introductory books in other fields such as physics introduce the areas of the field (mechanics, electricity and magnetism, and optics), while introductory computer science books often have chapters on how to use two-dimensional arrays.

We resolved to write a book that not only gives students essential programming skills, but also provides a vision of what computer science is about. We want to reach those individuals who are already committed to computer science, as well as those who plan to take computer science courses as part of a general education. We hope our enthusiasm for the field will encourage students to pursue advanced studies in computer science.

History and Objectives

This book had its genesis in a 1988 decision of the Department of Computer Science at the University of British Columbia to revitalize its introductory courses. A Scheme-based approach was adopted, and one of the authors (Little) set about teaching a prototype two-course sequence in 1989–90, using Abelson and Sussman's *Structure and Interpretation of Computer Programs*. We decided that we wanted a broader coverage of CS than Abelson and Sussman offers.

Since 1990, drafts of this book have been used at UBC, Langara, University College of the Okanagan, and the University College of the Cariboo, all in British Columbia, as well as at the University of Saskatchewan in Saskatoon, Saskatchewan. More recently, the book has been adopted by the University of Kansas and Vassar College.

Our model has been heavily influenced by the interim report of the ACM Task Force on the Core of Computer Science (CACM, January, 1989) and also by the ACM Curriculum '91 document.

The ACM Task Force Report identifies a number of areas in computer science, and develops three modes in which each of these areas can be studied, roughly corresponding to program design and implementation, empirical experimentation, and theoretical underpinnings. We have found this framework to be a useful way of designing a course that is effective in the classroom.

As we began planning this book, we identified several goals it had to satisfy.

- Whereas most texts give primary emphasis to programming skills, we give substantial weight to the analysis of programs and development of conceptual frameworks. We do not wish to shortchange the skills component of an introductory course. In fact, employers of students who have studied this material have told us that the students are *stronger* programmers than those who have taken the conventional Pascal course. However, we also want students to learn how to read programs and understand critical issues such as efficiency.

- The introductory course sequence offers a chance to recruit students into computer science. It should therefore offer a view of the questions a computer scientist studies, and the modes of inquiry that she or he would use. Even for students who plan no further studies in the field, we believe that a broad introduction to the ideas of computer science provides a strong foundation for acquiring further computing skills, as well as skills in other areas.

- Although it would be impossible to cover all of the areas identified by the ACM Task Force, we have given attention to important areas of computer science that are not studied in the traditional CS1/CS2 sequence. Databases, artificial intelligence, and logic programming are the most obvious examples.

- We wanted to show that a small number of powerful ideas underlies much of computer science, just as concepts such as "force" and "energy" underlie physics. We present a model of computation that can be used not only for Scheme, but for almost all languages.

- We wanted a presentation that was accessible to the average university or college student, requiring only Grade 12 mathematics.

Key Differences From Conventional Approaches

There are six ways in which this book differs from conventional introductions.

- **Features if necessary, but not necessarily features**
  Our philosophy is deliberately *minimalist*—we avoid introducing new features or concepts until they are absolutely necessary. This approach applies to our presentation of both the programming language and the applications.

- **Theory and Practice**
  We strongly believe in *balancing theory and practice*, and only presenting theory that is directly useful in solving problems. Each theoretical topic grows out of a practical problem that is being solved.

- **Experiential Learning**
  We emphasize *learning by doing*. This emphasis can be seen in the hundreds of exercises included in the book. These exercises have one major purpose—students should not read more than a page or two without being asked to apply what has been learned. The Laboratory Manual consists of a set of labs that ask students to apply a concept that has been covered in class.

- **System Prototypes**
  We follow a *schematic* approach by presenting prototypes of real, working software systems. It is not feasible for students to study a *real* relational database system or inference engine in an introductory course. But it *is* possible for students to understand a simplified database or inference engine. Our goal is not to study all of the complexity of the "real" versions of these systems. Instead, we want students to understand what such a system does, and the basic principles that underlie its implementation.

- **Broad View of Field**

  We present a *rich, broad view of computer science.* An introductory text is not a closed universe, but a starting-point. Sidebars present relevant applications, software tools, theoretical questions, and social issues.

- **Case Studies**

  The *Case Studies* located at the end of the chapters present extended examples of how software is developed and how it can be used to solve interesting, practical problems. Case Studies provide additional programming examples and demonstrate how the techniques covered in chapters have further application. We have chosen applications across a wide variety of endeavors including simulation, airline route planning, personal schedule planning, and client/server computing.

Instructional Support

The book is only a part of the comprehensive package we have developed to support the course. This package includes:

- A *Laboratory Manual* with approximately thirty different lab assignments keyed to the text, along with sidebars on such practical topics as debugging code.

- An *Instructor's Guide* that describes the pedagogy for each section of the book, as well as providing a number of resources such as a detailed Scheme manual and a tutorial on C++ for Schemers that can be distributed to students.

- A *Software Package* that includes a Microsoft Windows-based Scheme system, code to adapt other common Scheme systems to support this book, and all of the programs studied or used in the text or lab manual. The Software Package is provided in disk form with the Instructor's Guide, or it can be obtained in electronic form from the Internet (see Page *xvi* for details). The Internet version is preferred, because it may incorporate bug fixes and additions which have not yet reached the published version.

Choice of Programming Language

Almost nothing can arouse more controversy than the choice of introductory programming language (except perhaps which is the best text editor). Our approach is soundly based upon λ-calculus models that have been realized in many languages, and provide simple, consistent semantics. We have chosen to use *Scheme*, a lexically-scoped dialect of Lisp. Our choice was governed by several factors:

- minimal syntax to make learning fairly easy
- procedures as first-class objects
- support for a wide variety of programming paradigms including functional, imperative, object-oriented, and logic programming
- list processing capabilities (i.e., garbage collection)
- reasonably standardized implementations, especially for MS-DOS, Windows, Macintosh, and UNIX platforms

Even though Abelson and Sussman's *Structure and Interpretation of Computer Programs* influenced many of the ideas we explore, we certainly did not feel bound to use Scheme. Most other languages are bound too tightly to a single computational paradigm to be suitable for some of the areas we proposed to explore. In particular, our study of evaluators would have been seriously complicated if we had used a language with a great deal of syntax. The bottom line is that Scheme is a simple language that can be used in many interesting ways, and also allows us to produce sophisticated, complex software systems.

What about using a functional language? Most functional languages enforce a functional paradigm everywhere, whether or not it is appropriate. We agree that a database system can be modeled in a purely functional way, but don't agree that an introductory student will find such a model convincing. One outstanding exception, supporting all the paradigms we study in this book, is ML. The first six chapters of our book would suffer almost no changes if ML were used instead of Scheme. ML's syntax would most definitely complicate our discussion of evaluators. Most functional languages, including ML, have elaborate type systems. However useful these type systems may be to the experienced programmer, they are substantial barriers to the introductory student, and hence destroy the concept of a simple underlying model.

What about using an object-oriented language? We renew our objections to single-paradigm languages. More importantly, we want students to see that the language we study is well-founded (in a logic sense). It is easier to understand objects in terms of procedures and state than the reverse.

What about using an imperative, more "conventional" language like Pascal, Modula-2, or C++ as our teaching vehicle? Everything we do in this book could be done in one of these languages, though perhaps with great difficulty. Procedures as first-class citizens, and garbage collection make code much more perspicuous. We do not deny the importance of these languages (especially C++) for building sophisticated applications. However, we think that learning Scheme helps a student learn one of these languages.

We believe the ideas behind Scheme are not just academic curiosities, but are immensely practical. Scheme and Scheme-like languages have some industrial application. Further, many newer languages, ranging from ML and PostScript to NewtonScript and Dylan, use concepts that Scheme elegantly demonstrates. Scheme is already widely used as an introductory programming language.

Coverage and Topics

Although we were inspired by Abelson and Sussman's book, we chose different topics and a different organization. We include a sequence of topics that makes sense to students, provides strong programming skills, and gives a coherent picture of the field. We therefore adopted the following structure.

- Introduction to Programming (Chapters 1 through 3)

  — basic data types and programming concepts
  — computation as substitution
  — procedures and procedural abstraction
  — recursion
  — algorithmic complexity
  — distinction between value and effect
  — program organization
  — data abstraction

- List Processing (Chapter 4)

    — pairs and symbols
    — using pair structure to represent compound values
    — lists and list recursion

- State, Mutation, and Objects (Chapters 5 and 6)

    — mutating existing data structure
    — variables and assignment
    — how the environment model explains computation
    — how environments model objects
    — classes
    — delegation
    — object-oriented design

- Programming Languages (Chapter 7)

    — defining the syntax and semantics of programming languages
    — tree representation of programs
    — interpreters and compilers
    — a Scheme evaluator based upon the environment model

- Databases (Chapter 8)

    — relational table model
    — fundamental relational operators, select, project, and join
    — implementation of a simple database system
    — database analysis and design

- Algorithms (Chapter 9)

    — algorithms for searching (linear search, binary search trees) and sorting (insertion sort, Quicksort)
    — stacks and queues
    — application of stacks to implementing a graphics language based upon Postscript

- Rule-Based Computing (Chapter 10)

    — patterns and pattern matching
    — predicate calculus
    — logic programming languages
    — backward and forward chaining

- Machines and Evaluators (Chapters 11 and 12)

    — representation of data
    — a simple computer
    — programming in assembly language
    — building a Scheme evaluator for a conventional machine
    — introduction to operating systems

How To Use This Book

We have used this book in a number of ways at the University of British Columbia and at Langara College. Our original design was a two-course—CS1 and CS2—introductory sequence for science students (not necessarily CS majors). We have found little difference in the performance of students who have a programming background and those who do not.

We have also used this text in a one-semester course for students who have already taken CS1. Students in this course are primarily CS or Computer Engineering majors. Therefore, the course can be more intensive.

This text has been used in a course for students who are concurrently taking a conventional CS2 course. This course emphasizes the interrelations between the Scheme-based material and the C++-based content of the CS2 course. A similar course could be designed at the second year level for students with CS1 and CS2.

Regardless of the course design, *The Schematics of Computation* contains more material than can be covered. We have endeavored to provide a rich enough package of materials that instructors can tailor courses to their needs. We also want students to use this text as a reference, as well as a springboard to further study in CS.

Therefore, the book is divided into three parts:

- Chapters 1 through 7 are an integrated sequence that covers common programming paradigms: functional, imperative, and object-oriented.
- Chapters 8 through 10 provide an introduction to algorithms and data structures, through applications in data bases and logic.
- Chapters 11 and 12 introduce computer hardware and assembly-language programming, practical Scheme implementations, and operating systems.

In a two-semester course sequence, it is reasonable to cover the material right up to the imperative evaluator in Chapter 12. A one-semester course can go through the first two chapters much more quickly, and then cover Chapters 3 through 7 in depth. From there, the instructor has a number of choices:

- Proceed to Chapters 8, 9, and 10 if *algorithms* will be emphasized.
- Proceed to Chapters 11 and 12 if *machines* will be emphasized.
- A hybrid approach will go through Chapter 8 very quickly, and then cover Chapters 9 and 11 in depth, ending with the imperative evaluator in Chapter 12.

Many instructors will want to cover an additional language such as Modula-2, Pascal, C/C++, or Turing in the latter part of a two-course sequence. The Instructor's Guide contains a tutorial called *A Schemer's Guide to C++*, which can be distributed to students and used to introduce C++. The first part of the tutorial can be used with Chapter 7; the second part refers to Chapter 11.

To The Student

That lyf so short, the craft so long to lerne,
Th'assay so hard, so sharp the conquerynge.
— Geoffrey Chaucer, *The Parliament of Fowls*

We wrote *The Schematics of Computation* because we wanted to share our excitement about computer science with you. Programming languages, algorithms, and data structures are things of beauty. They are also immensely useful. Industries related to computing—such as information technology and software engineering—are in the process of becoming one of the biggest sectors in world economies. Things of beauty that can help us solve practical problems are rare indeed!

We want you to see how effective problem-solving techniques can help you plan useful programs, how a programming language can help you write those programs, how algorithms and data structures can help make those programs more efficient, and how conventional computers can help run programs.

We also want to introduce many of the current research areas of computer science. There are interesting and useful questions to ask in every area of the field: theory of algorithms, artificial intelligence and robotics, graphics, operating systems and networks, programming languages, data bases, and logic. Each of these areas has applications from designing sophisticated electronic circuits to making the computer systems in business, government, education, and elsewhere more responsive to the needs of their users.

It is important for you to understand that computer science, like all other fields of study, is based upon a few unifying ideas that recur over and over in computer science. One of our unifying ideas is the programming language we use—Scheme. This language is based upon a few fundamental ideas that can be combined in countless ways to produce interesting programming ideas. We will see a number of different programming styles, including functional, imperative, object-oriented, and logic programming.

$$* \quad * \quad *$$

The only way to learn computer science is to do it! We have scattered exercises throughout the text to help reinforce what has been covered. When you reach one of these exercises, *do it*! Then take a look at the answer in Appendix A.

At the end of each chapter, we have provided a list of the key words and Scheme features that have been covered in that chapter. Study these words and features until you understand them. We have included these lists not as something to be memorized, but rather as a measure of the important concepts you should be learning. We have also included some Problems for you to work on, a Self-Assessment (with answers in Appendix A) so you can see how effectively you have learned the basic chapter concepts, and some Programming Projects for you to investigate on your own.

Most chapters also end with a Case Study that explores ways in which the concepts you are learning can be used to solve complex problems. These Case Studies will repay your study of them.

Your instructor will give you lab assignments and programming projects to complete. The ideas and skills we show here will help you do interesting things and solve useful problems.

All of the programs we study are available electronically. Play with them! Try them out and modify them. You can learn a great deal about programming by studying the programs.

Although this is a large book, we only scratch the surface of computer science. Each chapter ends with a set of Suggested Readings that will let you explore further the topics raised in the chapter. The Bibliography at the end of the book lists all the books mentioned in the Suggested Readings, as well as many others that teach interesting programming languages, or cover other more advanced topics.

The only limit to what you can do with what you learn is your own creativity. There is an infinite variety of programs that have yet to be written. We can help to give you a start, but what you do with what you learn is up to you.

Acknowledgments

We owe thanks to those computer scientists who over the past fifty years have searched for a clear, understandable, basis of programming. In particular, we are indebted to those who have tried to use these models to introduce computing. The developers of Logo as a teaching tool showed us that students can learn to do interesting things with computers, when given a powerful programming environment. The culmination of this approach is Abelson and Sussman's *Structure and Interpretation of Computer Programs*.

We have also learned from Dennis Ritchie and Ken Thompson, whose original design for UNIX showed that power and simplicity need not be conflicting goals. The work of Donald Knuth has showed us the close relationship between mathematics and computer science, and between theory and practice.

The notes on which this book are based have been tested with many students, teaching assistants, and colleagues. These poor souls have reported numerous errors, obfuscations, and downright lies to us. We have endeavored to accommodate as many of their suggestions as possible.

Don Acton, Carl Alphonce, Art Boehm, Craig Boutilier, Roelof Brouwer, Dave Forsey, Murray Goldberg, Norm Hutchinson, David Kirkpatrick, Gerald Neufeld, Nick Pippenger, and George Tsiknis, the other instructors who have used this book, deserve our thanks. We owe a special debt to Nick, who several times drew attention to ways in which the manuscript could be substantially improved.

Our summer student helpers deserve much credit: Jason Holmes, Yaron Kiflawi, Cedric Lee, Carson Leung, Greg Reid, and Marko Riedel. Additional corrections and suggestions were provided by Adrienne Drobnies, Rick Gee, Joseph Manning, and Art Pope. We owe a particular debt of gratitude to Philip Greenspun who read and commented on an early draft of the book.

Dan Friedman provided us with a large number of suggestions and improvements.

Several reviewers for this book have influenced the current shape in ways too numerous to describe. One reviewer deserves special mention. Brian Harvey produced massive, detailed critiques of our work. Even that minority of his suggestions we couldn't adopt caused us to think carefully about what we were trying to do and why.

Our publisher, Alan Apt, and editor, Sondra Chavez, have pushed us to produce what we are convinced is a much better book than before. Mona Pompili, our project manager, worked with us very patiently as we typeset the book, and provided a number of suggestions that improved both the presentation and the content.

We owe all of these people our sincere thanks, but of course cannot hold them responsible for the final shape of the book.

We are particularly grateful to Maria Klawe and Bob Woodham of the Department of Computer Science, The University of British Columbia, and to Judy Boxler and Habib Kashani, Department of Computer Science, Langara College, for their strong moral support and encouragement of this project.

Support for this project was also provided by the Department of Computer Science, The University of British Columbia, and by Langara College.

How to Get the Software Package

The software covered in this book can be obtained from your instructor, or via Internet ftp. To obtain a copy via the Internet, you will require an Internet connection, and appropriate software. This discussion assumes you are using a character-based ftp program.

The Software Package consists of three files:

- `schmtics.zip`: the Scheme code presented in this book and the lab manual
- `winscm.zip`, a Microsoft Windows-based Scheme system for 386, 486, Pentium, and compatible computers
- `vslib.zip`, the "Schematics Adaptor Kit", a package that can be loaded into a standard Scheme system to add the extra features used in this book.

There is also a file `!Readme`, with late-breaking information about the software.

To get the software, you will need an Internet connection and an `ftp` program. The instructions given here assume a character-based `ftp` program; consult your documentation if you are using a Windows or Macintosh ftp program.

Start up your ftp program, and carry out the following steps (`ftp>` is a prompt from the program).

```
ftp> open ftp.cs.ubc.ca
ftp> cd pub/local/schematics
ftp> get !Readme
ftp> binary
ftp> get schmtics.zip
ftp> get winscm.zip
ftp> get vslib.zip
ftp> close
```

Once you have obtained these files, use PKZip or a similar program to unpack them, each into a separate directory. Each directory will contain a `!Readme` file with information on how to install the software.

Contents

The
SCHEMATICS
of
COMPUTATION

Chapter 1

Computers, Programs, and Scheme

Overview

Computer science is more than the study of how to use or program computers. It is about algorithms, methods of computing results, and automata—machines that follow instructions precisely. Our studies of computer science begin with algorithms and automata. We then examine Scheme, the programming language we use in this book. Scheme systems allow us to compute results using a consistent notation. We will build procedures that can be used with different data, and we will see how Scheme allows us to use names for both procedures and numbers. Any program that does something interesting must make decisions about its inputs. We will examine Scheme's decision-making features: Boolean data and procedures, and conditional forms. By the end of this chapter, we will have introduced virtually all of Scheme's key features. We end by developing a set of rules that tell us how to carry out the steps in a Scheme program.

> *We dissect nature along lines laid down by our native language. ... Language is not simply a reporting device for experience but a defining framework for it.*
> — Benjamin Whorf, *Thinking in Primitive Communities*

To begin our introduction to computer science, let us look first at who does computer science and how they do it. Before there were computers, there was **computation**,[1] the use of systematic methods for finding solutions to algebraic or symbolic problems. The ancient Babylonians, Egyptians, and Greeks developed a variety of methods for computing such things as the area of a circle or the greatest common divisor of two integers. In the nineteenth century, Charles Babbage envisioned a machine that could relieve humans of the tedium of computing and at the same time perform the calculations reliably.

The main motivation for many years in computing was developing accurate numerical computing. Computer science also grew out of the interest in formal systems for reasoning and the mechanization of logic, as well as business data processing. However, the real impact of computing came from the power of computers to represent, store, and transform information. Every aspect of the use of information has been affected by computing, from printing to accounting to communication. Computing has created many new areas of endeavor, such as electronic mail, desktop publishing, and multimedia.

As we learn computer science, we'll draw from all the sources of inspiration that have fostered computing over the years. Without deep mathematical and physical insights, the computer would not exist. Other insights have come from problems such as processing census data and business records.

The computer has made it possible not only to process data in useful ways, but to study computation. The computer allows us to express a computation as a computer program, and to try various methods of attack on a problem to find a

---

[1] Words in **boldface** are key words. Make sure you understand each of these words. A list of the key words introduced in each chapter appears at the end of the chapter. If you are not sure of the meaning of a key word, you can look it up in the Glossary at the end of the book.

good one. Solving real-world problems has required the study of how we do computations, how we make them efficient, and how we make them correct. In turn, this study has widened the range of problems that can be solved.

The computer programmer describes a method for solving a problem. The program can be run on a computer, either to test it, or to use it for processing real data. The program can also be studied by humans, either to gain insight into its workings, or to analyze defects or problems. Computer programs are a very rich field of study, as you will find.

The job of a computer programmer is to write a **program**, a set of instructions that tells the computer how to transform input data into the desired outputs. A program can be one line long, as in a request to add the numbers 3 and 5, or millions of lines long, as in a program to manage an air traffic control system. Computer programs are collectively called **software**, to distinguish them from the computer **hardware**. The computer programmer need not know much about the electronic details of the hardware, but must know how to analyze a problem and prepare a computer program to solve it.

We begin our study of computation by learning a programming language, Scheme. We'll learn how to use Scheme effectively to solve interesting and useful problems. We'll build a model of the language. That is, we'll state explicitly the rules that turn expressions (Scheme programs) into values. Later we will implement these rules in Scheme and build an **evaluator**—a program that reads a second program and carries out the operations specified by that program—for Scheme.

We emphasize how to write and understand correct programs. We're not the programming police, but training and practice are critical in any enterprise. We'll give you pointers on good technique. Programming is fun—it's creative and challenging, and the results are tools that can help us in many ways. It's more fun if you're not bogged down trying to figure out errors that could be prevented with a better understanding of computers, languages, and problem solving.

1.1   Setting the Stage

To err is human, but to really foul things up requires a computer.

— Anonymous

Your local bookstore probably has all sorts of books on word processors, spreadsheets, databases, accounting programs, on programming, and even the odd book that tells you how to build your own computer. Yet relatively few of these books will tell you anything about what computer scientists do.

Before we start doing computer science, let's define what computer science is. Computer science is *not* the study of how to use computer applications, nor is it the study of how to program a computer. Computer scientists use applications such as word processors, as do other professionals. Most computer scientists write large programs to test their ideas. They're interested in discovering the best way to find the solution to a particular problem. Many computer scientists have designed useful hardware and software. More than just getting a program to work, however, a computer scientist wants to understand the basic principles behind the program.

In fact, computer science isn't just about computers. One good definition of computer science follows.

> Computer science is the study of *algorithms* and *data*, and the *automata* that operate on them.

There are three critical words here:

1. An **algorithm** is a "recipe" for processing information—a series of steps that transform input to output.
2. **Data** is the particular information that is represented and organized for convenient processing by the algorithm.
3. An **automaton** is any device (a person or a computer) that can follow the instructions of the algorithm effectively to get the required result.

The algorithm and data together specify what processing needs to be done; the automaton actually does the work. Every automaton has a **language**, or system for writing the instructions the automaton will follow. Therefore, part of the programming task is to write the algorithm in the automaton's language.

Computer scientists study the whole computation process. They develop methods for solving various problems, and analyze those methods to show that they are correct and efficient. Some computer scientists are more interested in the automata. They design sophisticated computers and languages to make it easier to write fast, correct, understandable computer programs.

1.1.1   Algorithms

You are probably familiar with many problems that require you to compute values. For example, each spring, you may fill out an income tax return. A tax return is an algorithm for computing the amount of income tax you owe. It's extremely complicated and includes information on such matters as capital losses, political contributions, and university tuition. Let's look at a very simple algorithm for computing income tax.

Suppose your income tax is computed by subtracting $6,000 from your income and then taking 17% of the result. The only data we need is your income. The algorithm can be expressed according to the problem: subtract 6000 from the income, and multiply the result by 0.17. Unfortunately, this algorithm contains a **bug**, or error. If the taxpayer's income is less than $6,000, the government will end up paying money out (i.e., the income tax will be negative).

Grace Murray Hopper, one of the pioneers of modern computing, told a story of a time when the Harvard Mark II started misbehaving. After hours of checking through the machine's programming (a rat's nest of wires connected to plugboards), no errors could be found. All of the computer's components seemed to be working. The engineers were mystified, and took the machine apart. The cause of the problem turned out to be an insect that had found its way inside the machine and landed on an electrical switch. Its carbonized corpse had caused an electrical failure. "Bug" has had various nasty meanings at least since Shakespeare's day, and Thomas Edison used it in the sense of "defect". The log entry for the Mark II incident (1945 September 9), reading "1545 Relay #70 Panel F (moth) in relay. First actual case of bug being found", was the first use of the term in the sense used by a modern computer programmer.[2]

---

[2] There are many versions of this story, and there are amusing bugs in the different versions. You might refer to the "Jargon File", discussed in the Further Readings section at the end of the chapter, to find out about these bugs.

Computer malfunctions were common in earlier days, but today machines rarely fail. Sometimes we blame our computer or the software tools we're using when an error happens, but they are almost never at fault. Usually we ourselves have created the error. A large program has many opportunities for bugs, which means that programmers must be extremely careful in their work.

What's the problem with our income tax algorithm? There's an unspoken assumption in the problem statement—there is no tax if the net income, or the income minus $6000, is less than or equal to 0. Often a problem does not state these commonsense assumptions. It's up to us to dig them out and use them in the algorithm. We made this mistake in translating the problem statement into the algorithm.

☞ **Exercise 1-1**

➤   Answers to exercises are given in Appendix A.

What's the best way to keep mistakes out of your programs? ❏

To fix the bug, we need to develop a more complex algorithm, which is shown in Program 1-1.

Algorithm `income-tax`
Data: `income` is our name for the taxpayer's income; `net-income` is our name for the income after the $6,000 deduction.
Algorithm:

1. Let `net-income` be the result of subtracting 6000 from `income`.
2. If `net-income` is negative, then the income tax is 0.
3. If `net-income` is not negative, then the income tax is the result of multiplying `net-income` by 0.17.

Program 1-1   An algorithm for computing income tax

Algorithm `income-tax` is the first program in the book. Unlike most of our programs, it is not written in Scheme, the programming language we will use. Instead, we have written it in a form of English called **pseudocode**. Later we will also use a Scheme-like notation for pseudocode. An algorithm expressed in pseudocode isn't ready to be run on a computer; however, humans can easily follow a pseudocode algorithm.

☞ **Exercise 1-2**

Taxpayers are allowed to deduct their charitable donations, up to a maximum of $1000. Therefore, a taxpayer who made charitable donations of $1500 would only be able to get a $1000 deduction from income before the tax computation. Show the steps of the revised algorithm. ❏

☞ **Exercise 1-3**

Modify your algorithm from Exercise 1-2 so that charitable donations get a 100% deduction up to $1000, a 50% deduction from there to $2000, and no deductions over $2000. Thus, charitable donations of $1500 would get a $1250 deduction. ❏

Algorithms must often work with *collections* of data, such as student marks. Suppose we want to find the top student in a class, perhaps to give her an award. We're given a list of the students' names and marks.

This task is much trickier than the income tax problem. Imagine that the class included thousands of students. How would *you* go about finding the top student? One way is to write down the name and mark of the first student. Now look at every other student's name and mark. Whenever you find a student whose mark is higher, replace both the name and mark you have written down with the name and mark of the new student.

For example, suppose you're working with this class list:

```
Jennifer Lee      76
Bill Smith        65
Derek Kurich      81
Brenda Guzman     85
Fred Mueller      79
```

Start with Jennifer as the top student. Bill got a lower mark than Jennifer, so go to the next student. Derek's mark is higher than Jennifer's, so cross out her name and mark, and write in Derek's. After looking at all of the students, you'll see that Brenda is the top student. Program 1-2 shows the algorithm.

This method looks tedious. You probably looked at the list and saw instantly that Brenda had the top mark. Our method will work, however, for classes of any size at all (if you have enough patience).

Algorithm `find-top-student`

Data: the `name` and `mark`, for each student. We will also need to keep track of the name (`top-name`) and mark (`top-mark`) of the top student we have found so far.

Algorithm:

1. Let `top-name` be the name of the first student.
2. Let `top-mark` be the mark of the first student.
3. For each student except the first,
   If this student's `mark` is larger than `top-mark`,
      a.   Let `top-name` be this student's name.
      b.   Let `top-mark` be this student's mark.
4. When all students have been examined, the student named `top-name` has the highest mark.

Program 1-2   An algorithm for finding the top student in a class

---

Unfortunately, algorithm `find-top-student` contains an interesting bug: suppose two or more students both get the same top mark. As written, the algorithm says that the student with the top mark that appears first in the list will be considered the top student. Unlike the income tax bug, this one isn't a mistake in the preparation of the algorithm. Instead, the problem statement was insufficiently clear. We were told to find "the top student", incorrectly implying there is only one such student. Algorithm `find-top-student` will only work correctly when there is exactly one student with the top mark.

Computer programmers must not only develop a correct algorithm; they must also carefully study the description of the problem to be sure that they are solving the problem they were intended to solve. In this case, the problem statement should say either "Every student in the class has a different mark; therefore there will always be exactly one top student", or, more plausibly, "If more than one student obtains the top mark, list the name of each student with the top mark."

Practical Note

➤   This is the first "practical note" in the book. Practical notes suggest interesting programming techniques and warn you about problems you might encounter along the way. The icon we've chosen for practical notes is suggestive. A person is admiring the view, and nonchalantly about to walk off a cliff. She hasn't fallen yet; if she moves quickly, she can get back to safety.

Sometimes the problem has been carefully spelled out. For example, a programmer might be working for a customer who has said exactly what is needed. Often the problem is less clear. In fact, some aspects of the problem may not emerge until the programmer is well under way. Sometimes a new understanding of the problem gives you new insights into possible solutions, or even suggests other interesting problems to study. At other times, a new understanding of the problem just means that you must throw away the work you've done and start over.

Some people say you mustn't start solving a problem until you understand it in every detail. We don't agree. Sometimes the only way to understand a problem is to start trying to solve it, even if you have to throw away your first try. Even so, the effort you put into understanding a problem before you solve it is rarely wasted.

☞ **Exercise 1-4**

Which part of Algorithm `find-top-student` picks the first student in case of a tie? ❏

☞ **Exercise 1-5**

Find another case in which the statement of the problem is deficient. Hint: This is an extremely unlikely case. ❏

☞ **Exercise 1-6**

Modify Algorithm `find-top-student` to handle the case when there is more than one student with the top mark. ❏

On page 5, we said that an algorithm is a method for processing information by computing answers based upon some input data. The answers could be numbers, names, or whatever is required in a given problem.

We used the word *information* in the previous paragraph. Some people like to distinguish *information* from *data*. It is good enough for our purposes to say that information exists independently of the computer, and that data is information in a format suitable for computer processing. For example, the fact that Derek's mark is 81 is a piece of information. If we were to type that number into a spreadsheet of class marks, it would be a piece of data.

An algorithm must have the following characteristics:

1. It must be **correct**. It computes the answer it is supposed to.
2. It must be **feasible**. It doesn't ask you to do anything impossible, such as division by zero.

3. It must be **finite**. It doesn't go on forever. Each step of the algorithm should be of limited size, and the process should terminate in a finite number of steps.

In designing an algorithm, it's important to remember that the steps should be reasonable. In most computer algorithms, each arithmetic operation, such as multiplying or comparing two numbers, is one step. When we discuss algorithms for other processes, each step should be some simple operation like reading a ticket or examining a mark.

☞ **Exercise 1-7**

An airline charges for flights on the basis of flying distance, as follows. The ticket price is $0.75 per mile, with a minimum of 200 miles, plus a fixed charge of $25.00. Write an algorithm for computing the ticket price for a flight of *d* miles. ❏

☞ **Exercise 1-8**

On election day, voters can choose one of two candidates, A or B. After the polls close, election officials count the ballots. Give an algorithm for naming the winner. "Count all the ballots" is *not* a valid step. Break it down into more detailed steps. ❏

1.1.2 Computers

On page 5, we defined computer science as the study of algorithms and automata. An automaton is a device that is designed to automatically follow a predetermined sequence of operations. Both computers and thermostats are automata. A significant aspect of automata is that they react to the environment.

A thermostat gathers data from its environment by measuring the temperature. It responds to its environment by turning the furnace on and off, following a predetermined sequence of operations. The behavior of earlier thermostats was fixed by relays and switch settings.

Thermostats are examples of **cybernetic devices**.[3] A cybernetic device gathers data from its environment, determines (according to its program) what changes to make, and then makes those changes. The changes cause the environment to change, which in turn provides new input data to the device. The process is shown in Figure 1-1.

What separates the computer from the thermostat? A computer is a general-purpose machine. It can run any program specified in its language. The thermostat is narrow-minded. But both are cybernetic devices. The thermostat incorporates a thermometer to find the current temperature and a switch to turn the furnace on. The computer has connections that enable it to read data from the outside world and send results back. To learn how to use a thermostat, we learn how the controls work. If you learn how to program a computer, you can make it work for you. The generality of computers lets us use them effectively in place of special-purpose

---

[3] The term *cybernetics* comes from the Greek word for "steersman" (in a boat). Modern cybernetics—the study of devices that control their environment—is an interdisciplinary study that draws on computer science, control theory (a branch of electrical engineering), and other engineering disciplines. The *cyber* prefix has entered modern usage as meaning something vaguely like "high-tech", as in *cyberpunk* and *cyberschool*. We use it rather more precisely here.

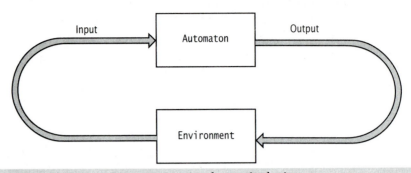

Figure 1-1   A cybernetic device

devices. These days a thermostat often contains a computer. Learning to program a computer allows you to create an enormous range of cybernetic devices.

Almost every program reads some information from an **input** device (e.g., a keyboard, mouse, or scanner). Suppose the computer is controlling an airplane. The data from the joystick or sliders on the screen will describe the settings for the controls of the aircraft. The computer uses the settings to specify, for example, the amount of throttle, to speed up or slow down the aircraft. Once the computer has decided what changes are needed, it sends commands to the control surfaces (the ailerons, flaps, and rudder) and to the engine in order to accomplish those changes. We call data sent from the computer to the outside world **output** data.

The computer has a **memory**, a large collection of devices that can remember data like numbers. The essential mechanism of the computer is the **central processing unit** that performs the steps of the program. Figure 1-2 shows the structure of a computer.

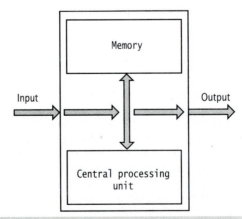

Figure 1-2   The structure of a computer

But where is the program itself? A computer is a physical thing, but a program is not physical. It's a set of instructions that tell the computer how to go from the input provided to the desired output. The early electromechanical computers used wires plugged into a board to specify the program. The big idea of the inventors of the modern general-purpose computer—Eckert and Mauchly, von Neumann, Turing, and Zuse among them—was that the program could be represented as data. Thus, different programs can be entered into the computer to perform different tasks, without rewiring the machines. Instead of producing a host of different cybernetic devices, a manufacturer can produce a single computer system that can be programmed for each task. Viewing programs as data gives us another benefit. It is possible to write a program that writes other programs, thus eliminating an enormous amount of clerical work for the human user of the program.

Although this idea was inherent in all of the early computer designs (Turing's 1937 paper had been based upon a hypothetical universal computer), John von Neumann has been given the credit. We speak of modern computers as being "von Neumann machines".[4]

In a von Neumann computer, the central processing unit fetches its commands from the memory. Some commands cause data to be input or output. Others perform arithmetic operations. Still others cause the computer to choose between two sequences of operations. To build a program, the programmer chooses a sequence of these commands that expresses the algorithm.

1.1.3   Programming Languages

The programs in early computers were written in **machine language**. A machine-language program looked like a long series of numbers. For example, to add the values 22, 31, and 44, a programmer would have to write something like this:

```
140900022
320900031
320900044
440900000
990000000
```

The first number might command the computer to place the number 22 in a temporary place. The next two instructions would command the machine to add first 31 and then 44 to that holding place. The next command tells the machine to print the contents of that holding place. The last command tells the computer to stop.

Programmers soon found that writing a large program as a series of numbers was extremely error-prone, not to mention boring! They began to write down their solutions to problems using their own notation. Those working on scientific problems used mathematical notation, whereas those working on data processing tended to use English. Both kinds of programmers worked much the way we did in the previous section. Once the algorithm was written down, it was translated—by hand—into a machine-language program.

Programmers discovered that, rather than "coding" the program into machine language, it was possible to write a program to do the same thing. At first, they used languages that were much like machine language. These **assembly languages** were

---

[4] Von Neumann's conception of the computer includes much more than this idea. In Chapter 11, we'll look at von Neumann computers in detail.

Computing Machines: Prehistory to Babbage

The history of computing machines begins with the abacus some 5000 years ago. The abacus is a manually operated storage device that aids a human calculator. Instead of writing down numbers during a calculation, beads are moved on rows of wires, each representing a decimal digit. The wires are divided into two sections: one has one bead, representing zero or five; the other has four beads representing units.

Even the word "calculate" has an ancient history, originating from the Latin word *calculus*, meaning small pebble, used in reckoning.

In 1617, John Napier, a Scottish mathematician who invented logarithms, built a device that did multiplication and division using mechanical rods, often made of ivory. Hence his device was called "Napier's bones". Napier's bones were eventually transformed into the slide rule, a computing device that was essential to scientists and engineers until the development of twentieth-century calculators and computers.

In 1642, Blaise Pascal developed a digital calculating machine that calculated by the action of geared wheels; data were entered on number dial wheels. A few of Pascal's machines were built, but they were too unreliable for general use.

Gottfried Leibniz designed (but did not build) a "Stepped Reckoner" in 1671. The Reckoner performed multiplication and division, and calculated square roots by using repeated addition. A working model was made in 1794, and a descendant achieved commercial success in the mid-nineteenth century. Leibniz was interested in the binary system, and showed the advantage of binary representation over decimal.

Automation was not restricted to calculation. Joseph-Marie Jacquard invented a loom in the early 1800s that used punched cards as instructions for weaving cloth, showing that coded data could represent instructions to a machine.

It is Charles Babbage, a British scientist, who can best be called the inventor of the modern digital computer. In 1821, Babbage designed a "Difference Engine" that could solve certain types of equations by a series of arithmetic operations. He labored for years, building various parts, but did not succeed in building a complete Difference Engine. Many people believe that the mechanical technology of his time wasn't sophisticated enough to build the complete Difference Engine. Recently, however, the Science Museum of London constructed a model.

Babbage's revolutionary contribution came in 1835 when he devised an "Analytical Engine" that combined arithmetic with the power to make decisions. This engine was a general-purpose machine that was programmed by punched cards containing data and instructions. His innovation was to use the data to control the sequence of calculations. Modern machines contain essentially the same components as his, but they use much different technology.

Ada Augusta, Lady Lovelace, the daughter of Lord Byron, became interested in Babbage's work and wrote the world's first computer program (it computed Bernoulli numbers) for the Engine. In the process, she invented many programming techniques, including conditional branches and self-modifying code.

The Analytical Engine was never completed. After Babbage's death in 1871, the British Association for the Advancement of Science appointed a committee to determine whether to invest funds in building an Engine. Although the committee was enthusiastic about the potential power of the Engine, they did not believe it could be constructed.

much easier to use than machine language. Here's our machine-language program translated into an assembly language.

```
loadi   22
addi    31
addi    44
print
stop
```

Assembly language made programming much easier, but what programmers really wanted was to use the mathematical, business, or other notation of the problem. As their skill increased, they wrote programs that could work with languages based upon these notations. Here's our machine-language program in FORTRAN:

```
integer x
x = 22 + 31 + 44
print *, x
end
```

Evaluators for these languages, named *compilers* or *interpreters*, depending upon their precise method of operation, allowed the programmer to forget about the numeric codes completely. Nowadays, it is common for highly skilled programmers not to know the details of the machine languages of the computers they use.

All languages have precise rules that define the **syntax** (what sorts of things we can write) and the **semantics** (what the programs we write mean).

The English sentence `Computer flavor red a catches` is completely ungrammatical (incorrect syntax), while `Colorless green ideas sleep furiously` is perfectly grammatical, but unfortunately makes no sense (incorrect semantics). If you want to be understood, you will take pains to make what you say or write grammatical (you'll get the syntax right) and mean something (you'll make sure that the semantics expresses what you mean to say).

Computer programming languages aren't like natural, or human, languages. A programming language is designed for one purpose only—expressing algorithms. This requires painstaking precision.

☞ **Exercise 1–9**

An author once gave Abraham Lincoln a copy of his very dull book. Lincoln wrote back "Many thanks for your kind gift. Please be assured that I shall lose no time in reading it."

Read the above story very carefully. Find an ambiguity in the way we've told it. ❏

☞ **Exercise 1–10**

Examine each of the following English sentences carefully. Identify each as being syntactically invalid, semantically invalid, or valid. Note: More than one description might apply.
   a. "When it is hot outside, it is cold."
   b. "Programmers are fungible."
   c. "John is play the game baseball."
   d. "I ain't going to school today."
   e. "The official language of France is Swedish." ❏

1.2 Scheme

we are for each other: then
laugh, leaning back in my arms
for life's not a paragraph
And death i think is no parenthesis — e. e. cummings, "since feeling is first"

Several *thousand* programming languages have been published (and many more unpublished languages have been developed). Most were only used by their authors. A few, notably ALGOL 60, BASIC, C, COBOL, FORTRAN, Pascal and Lisp, have been astonishingly influential.

1. FORTRAN, developed in the mid-1950s, was the first practical programming language (for scientific applications). The FORTRAN system developed at IBM could (under some circumstances) produce machine-language programs as efficient as those produced by a skilled human machine-language programmer.

2. COBOL, developed in the late 1950s, was designed for business programming. It was one of the first languages that worked on different makes of computers. Before this, languages had generally been designed for specific computers. Programs had to be rewritten for each new computer.

3. ALGOL 60 was developed around 1960 for scientific programming. Although ALGOL 60 never became a popular language in North America (it was popular in Europe), the ideas introduced into this language soon found their way into every other language, including Scheme.

4. BASIC was developed in the early 1960s for use by beginning programmers. The first implementation of BASIC was **interactive**, which meant that users did not have to punch their programs onto cards and wait hours for the program to be run. They could get their answers almost immediately.

5. Pascal was developed in the late 1960s as a teaching language. Based upon ALGOL 60, it influenced a number of popular languages.

6. C was developed at Bell Laboratories in the early 1970s. It was designed specifically for programs that had to be extremely efficient. C programs are often as efficient as their machine-language counterparts. A successor language, C++, has become widely popular.

In the 1950s, programmers developed languages for various types of computing. Scientific programming used algebraic notation. The name of the first widely used scientific language, FORTRAN, comes from "formula translator". Business data processing followed rules that were written in English. Business languages such as COBOL were also quite like English.

Researchers in artificial intelligence found neither of these approaches useful. A number of artificial-intelligence languages were developed, but none really caught on. A scientist in the MIT Research Laboratory of Electronics, John McCarthy, decided to develop a language that would be based upon solid concepts in logic and mathematics. Because his language worked primarily with lists of data, he called it Lisp (from "LISt Processor").[5]

---

[5] Detractors have called it "Lots of Irritating Spurious Parentheses". We aren't among them.

The Electronic Computer

George Boole in 1859 invented the Boolean algebra that formed the foundation of mathematical logic and led later to many uses in binary switching equipment.

Herman Hollerith, an American statistician, in 1886 devised a way of using punched cards to represent data for the 1890 U.S. census. Hollerith's machine used pins passing through holes in the cards into mercury-filled cups to sense the data. With Hollerith's machines, the 1890 census took one-third of the time of the 1880 census to tabulate. In following years he designed electromagnetic machines for sorting and punching. In 1911, Hollerith founded the Computing Tabulating Recording Company. By 1924, this company was under the direction of Thomas J. Watson Sr., who renamed it International Business Machines. By the 1940s, IBM had become an enormous company on the strength of its punched-card accounting machines, which were used in government, business, and education.

During the 1930s, many calculators were designed, including the Differential Analyzer, an analog mechanical computer developed by Vannevar Bush in 1932 to solve calculus problems, and the Atanasoff-Berry Computer (ABC), devised in 1939 by John V. Atanasoff with Clifford Berry for solving linear equations. Bush made another significant contribution to the development of computers in a 1945 article, "As We May Think", in which he imagined a device called a Memex that would not only hold books and other documents, but would allow people to make connections between documents as they saw fit. It took the technology 40 years to catch up with Bush's vision.

By 1945, Konrad Zuse and Helmut Schreyer, in Germany, had developed a series (Z1 . . . Z4) of general-purpose electronic digital calculators, culminating in 1941 with the Z4 fully programmable machine. Zuse also invented the first high-level programming language, the "Plankalkül".

Howard Aiken and Grace Murray Hopper, from 1939 through 1945 (working with IBM), designed the Harvard Mark I, a large electromechanical computing device. Although the Mark I was not a general-purpose computer, it was powerful enough to suggest to its designers the desirability of constructing a computer that could be programmed for many different tasks. The Aiken and Zuse machines could be used for practical calculations, but they were less powerful than Babbage's Analytical Engine design of the previous century.

Although Aiken's group eventually built a general-purpose computer (the Mark V), their machine was electromechanical. J. Presper Eckert and John W. Mauchly developed the University of Pennsylvania ENIAC (Electronic Numerical Integrator and Calculator) in 1946. ENIAC was the first general-purpose all-electronic computer. It was a thousand times faster than the Mark V.

Before World War II, Alan Turing, a British mathematician, had developed a formal model of a computing machine, the Turing Machine. Turing described it in 1937 in a paper on theoretical mathematics. During the war years, Turing designed and built the Colossus parallel computer at Bletchley Park, near London, to aid in decrypting German cyphers. Around 1946 he built the Pilot Ace machine at Teddington.

The U.S. mathematician John von Neumann independently developed the model of the stored-program computer. Following his model, he designed EDVAC, the Electronic Discrete Variable Automatic Computer, in 1945, and later built it.

Lisp was first used at MIT, but spread widely. Unlike some earlier artificial-intelligence languages, Lisp was clearly specified (so people could figure out how to use it). The original manual had quite detailed instructions on how to prepare a Lisp system for a computer.

Over the years, artificial-intelligence programming techniques were found to be useful in wide areas of computer science. Some of the most widely used applications written wholly or partly in Lisp include expert systems, text editors, and computer-assisted design programs. The language influenced the design of many popular programming languages, including Logo.

Industrial and research Lisp programmers normally use a version called Common Lisp, which is extremely powerful, but not easy to learn. We will use a dialect of Lisp called Scheme, which was developed at MIT by Guy Steele and Gerald Jay Sussman.[6] Scheme is a simple programming language; almost all of its major features are covered in this chapter. Nonetheless, Scheme is one of the most powerful languages available, which is why we use it.

Scheme systems have been prepared for almost every variety of computer. A Scheme system provides you with an evaluator that allows you to type in a Scheme program and see the result. Consult the manual for your Scheme system to find out how to use the evaluator.

When a user types in an expression in Scheme, the evaluator computes the result and displays it on the screen. This process is known as **evaluating** an expression. Here's a simple dialog with one Scheme system. The dialog on another Scheme system might look a bit different, but it will produce the same answers.

```
> (+ 2 2)
4
> (+ (* 3 7) 4)
25
> please tell me what the sum of 22 and 8 is
Error: variable please is not bound.
```

In this dialog, the Scheme system **prompts** for input with >. We first asked what $2 + 2$ is, and Scheme replied with 4. Then we asked Scheme to calculate $3 \times 7 + 4$, and again got the correct answer. Scheme, like many computer languages, uses the asterisk symbol * to denote the operation of multiplication. Using plain English with Scheme results in an error message. The error message was not *I didn't understand what you said.* Instead, the evaluator attempted to make sense of what we typed in its own terms. You don't have to understand this message right now. As you become more skilled with Scheme the error messages will become clearer.

We show expressions you type into Scheme like this, whereas we show the answers that Scheme produces *like this.* (Your Scheme evaluator will not usually show any difference.) Something you type into a Scheme evaluator is called a **form**, which is short for *formula*. A form is something that you are asking Scheme to evaluate, while an answer is a piece of data that is the result of evaluating a form.

---

[6] Scheme was one of a number of research languages developed for artificial intelligence in the early 1970s. These languages allowed the programmer to *plan* (i.e., to develop general strategies for solving complex problems). The first such language was called Planner, and the second, Conniver. Scheme was originally developed as one of these languages, and was hence called Schemer. Unfortunately, the ITS operating system on which the system was implemented only supported six-character filenames. The name therefore shrank to Scheme.

We'll call the answer that Scheme produces the **value** of the form. For the moment, all our values are numbers. The distinction between forms and values is one of the most important issues we will examine in this book.

For now, think of a form as the Scheme program for computing a value.

☞ **Exercise 1-11**

Identify each of the following as either a form or a value.
- a. (+ 3 7)
- b. 26
- c. *26* ❏

One minor piece of terminology: We often need to know what value we get if we evaluate a Scheme form. We can say, "the Scheme evaluator evaluates (+ 2 2) as *4*", but this is tedious. Instead, we will say, "Scheme evaluates (+ 2 2) as *4*."

Suppose we wanted to compute the area of an annulus, the doughnut-shaped region in Figure 1-3.

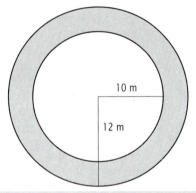

Figure 1-3   The doughnut: What is the shaded area?

The radius of the inner circle is 10 m, and the radius of the outer one is 12 m. The area of the shaded region can be computed by subtracting the area of the smaller circle from that of the larger one. We might write this in algebraic notation as

$$\pi 12^2 - \pi 10^2$$

In Scheme, we'd write it as follows:

```
(-
  (* 3.1415926 (* 12 12))
  (* 3.1415926 (* 10 10)))
```

The answer, according to the Scheme system we used, is *138.2300744*.

☞ **Exercise 1-12**

A circular track has been laid out as in Figure 1-3. A runner stands on the inside track, and a second runner stands on the outside. Each runs around the track once. Write a Scheme form that computes how much farther the outer runner ran than the inner runner. ❏

The annulus form may look a little cryptic, but actually Scheme's rules are extremely simple and consistent. In order to see how Scheme's syntax rules work, we need to remember functions and function notation. A **mathematical function** is a rule for giving an answer based upon some input values. So, for example, the function

$$f(x) = x^2 - 7$$

says that, for any given value x, $f(x)$ is computed by squaring x and subtracting 7. A mathematical function gives a specific answer for any given input value if the rule is valid for that input value. In the function

$$g(x) = 7/(x - 3)$$

$g(10) = 7/7 = 1$, but $g(3)$ is undefined.

(We use the phrase "mathematical function" because many computer programming languages use the word *function* to mean something very different.)

As mathematicians, we write a function such as sin or max together with the values to be used in the calculation, enclosed in parentheses:

$$\sin(30) \qquad \max(5,7)$$

We call these input values the **arguments** of the function.

The function notation developed by mathematicians gives the name of the function first, followed by a listing of the arguments, separated by commas and enclosed in parentheses. Mathematicians developed this notation because it was too cumbersome to think up symbols similar to + and − for these operators.

Mathematical notation uses two different systems. For arithmetic we use symbols such as + and ×. Most of these functions have two arguments. Trigonometric functions are written with function notation. There's really no particular reason for doing it this way, except that mathematicians have done it this way for centuries.

A programmer defines many different functions during the development of a program. For example, a program that controls a postage meter must be able to compute the postage for a letter of a given weight. Such a function would be of no use in a program that controls a microwave oven. The operations of arithmetic are just basic functions that we use as building blocks in our programs. Consistency suggests that we use function notation everywhere in our programs.

Once you've learned functional notation, writing a Scheme form is very simple: write $2 + 2$ as

```
(+ 2 2)
```

In other words, put the name of the function you want to use right after the open parenthesis rather than immediately before. Scheme adopts this rule because it makes the rules for evaluation very simple. In Scheme, unlike mathematical notation, we separate the arguments to a function by spaces, not commas.

When we get to more complex forms, such as

```
(* (+ 1 3) 7)
```

we must have rules about what to do first. The form (+ 1 3) must be done first:

```
(* (+ 1 3) 7)  ⇒   (* 4 7)  ⇒    28
```

We use the symbol ⇒ to mean "has the value". Scheme provides the arithmetic operations +,-,*, and /, corresponding to the operations of arithmetic.

Scheme notation has one major advantage over standard mathematical notation. When faced with a complicated mathematical formula such as $2 \times 3 + 8 \div 4 - 3 - 1$, it's difficult to know where to start. Mathematicians have evolved a large collection of rules (such as doing multiplications before additions, for example).

When you are asked to evaluate an algebraic formula, say $2 \times 3 + 4$, you expect that there is a "right answer". In mathematics, the evaluation of a formula always produces a specific answer, if such an answer exists. The formula $3/0$ can't be evaluated at all.

How do we evaluate formulas? With $2 \times 3 + 4$, we would do the multiplication first, giving $6 + 4$, and then do the addition, giving 10. Do we always do the operations from left to right? If we evaluate $2 + 3 \times 4$, we would still do the multiplication first, giving $2 + 12$, which then results in 14.

When they explain the rules of algebra, many high school math teachers talk about My Dear Aunt Sally, who apparently believes that you first do all the Multiplications, from left to right, then the Divisions, then the Additions, and finally the Subtractions.[7] Unfortunately, Aunt Sally is wrong. In fact, the evaluation rules for normal algebra are quite complex. They tell us to do multiplications and divisions first, and then additions and subtractions. However, that's not what Aunt Sally tells us to do. Expressions within parentheses are done first, according to the same rules. Then there are special rules for how we raise to a power, functions such as square root and logarithm, absolute values, minimum and maximum, and subscripts. These rules of algebra have evolved over hundreds of years, to suit the convenience of mathematicians. There isn't anything magic about them. Other rules could be used.

Unlike standard mathematical notation, Scheme follows a simple set of rules. For example, when evaluating

```
(* (+ 1 3) 7)
```

we had to do the addition first so we would have a number when we want to multiply by 7. We'll look at the exact Scheme rules later.

Practical Note

People often get confused about parentheses, especially if they have learned other programming languages. In many other languages, parentheses are used for grouping; programmers working in these languages often use extra parentheses to make their programs more readable.

In Scheme, parentheses have exactly one purpose—they tell us that what's inside is an expression involving a function (or a special form, which we'll look at later). We don't use parentheses randomly, but only where we're using functions. For example, (+ 2 3) ⇒ **6**, but (+ (2) 3) is an error (how do you "2" something?).

---

[7] The name is a mnemonic device, much like that of Roy G. Biv, the man who knows the colors of the spectrum, and "Every Good Boy Deserves Favor", which reminds us of the lines of the G clef in music.

☞ **Exercise 1–13**

Evaluate the following Scheme forms by hand. The answer might be "error". Explain why, if so.
  a. (+ 2 5)
  b. (* (- 5 3) 7)
  c. (/ (- 9 3) (+ 1 1))   (/ is Scheme-ese for ÷.)
  d. (/ 5 0)
  e. (+ (- (3) 4) 7) ❏

☞ **Exercise 1–14**

Convert each of the following algebraic formulas to a Scheme form.
  a. $2 + 3 \times 4$
  b. $2 \times 3 + 4$
  c. $(1 + 5) \times 6 - 12/3$ ❏

☞ **Exercise 1–15**

The government computes income tax as 17% of a taxpayer's income after deducting $6000. John worked at two jobs last year, earning $24,718 at the first and $14,284 at the second. Write a Scheme form that calculates John's income tax. ❏

1.2.1   𝕿𝖍𝖊 𝕽𝖚𝖑𝖊𝖘 (Version 1)

Since evaluation is at the heart of any programming language, the rules for form evaluation are important. One of Scheme's best features is that the set of rules for evaluation is very simple. All of the grouping is shown with parentheses. This simplicity is essential. Unlike algebraic formulas, Scheme forms are going to be evaluated by an automaton. The more special rules there are, the more complicated that automaton will have to be.

We're ready to introduce 𝕿𝖍𝖊 𝕽𝖚𝖑𝖊𝖘 (Version 1), which explains how Scheme evaluates forms. We haven't seen much of Scheme yet, so our rules will be quite limited. As we learn more Scheme features, we will improve our rules accordingly. Version 2 follows later in the chapter.

To start, let's take a look at the way we evaluate forms:

    (+ 3 (* 2 4)) ⇒ (+ 3 **8**) ⇒ **11**
    (+ (* 4 7) (+ 3 5)) ⇒ (+ **28** (+ 3 5)) ⇒ (+ **28 8**) ⇒ **36**

You might notice two aspects of the above evaluations. First, each step involves replacing a form with its value. (We call this replacement **substitution**.) Second, evaluation starts with a form, and ends up with a value. The intermediate steps aren't really forms, and aren't really values. Therefore, our rules must show *how we can go from a form to a value by using substitution.*

As you can see, we work by finding a simple form—one we can evaluate immediately—and replacing one form by another. Note the difference in font, in the first example, between (* 2 4) and **8**: the former is a *form*, whereas the latter is the *value* of the form, the data obtained by evaluating the form. We will be careful about this distinction. Scheme evaluates forms: It determines the values represented by the forms. Values are data inside the computer.

Looking at numbers should clear up the issue about forms and values. In a Scheme form there's no such thing as a number. Scheme forms instead contain

numerals, the written representations of numbers. Scheme reads a numeral and interprets it as a number in base 10. The decimal number 9 can be represented in many ways: as 9 in base 10, as 11 in base 8, or as IX in Roman numerals. All three numerals represent the same number to humans, though not to Scheme!

Remember that a form is either a numeral or something like

(*operation form form . . .*)

that is, (+ 2 3), (* (+ 1 2) 4), and so on. We call a form in parentheses an **application**, because we are "applying" the operation to the results of evaluating the other forms. An application generally has some forms following the operation. These forms are called the arguments of the application.

The operations of arithmetic are some of the **primitive** operations out of which the rest of Scheme is built.[8] Scheme has a large number of primitives. We'll be introducing them to you as we go. The "Scheme Summary" at the end of each chapter lists the features of Scheme introduced in the chapter; Appendix B explains each feature.

Program 1-3 shows our first version of 𝕿𝖍𝖊 𝕽𝖚𝖑𝖊𝖘 for evaluating the Scheme forms we've introduced so far. Each rule transforms a form or some part of a form into a value. As we apply the rules, we substitute the value for the form until we end up with a simple value. So far we only know about numbers, so the rules reduce forms to numbers.

---

1. [The 𝕹𝖚𝖒𝖇𝖊𝖗 rule] A numeral's value is a number, the numeral interpreted in base 10.
2. [The 𝕬𝖕𝖕𝖑𝖎𝖈𝖆𝖙𝖎𝖔𝖓 rule] An application is evaluated in two steps. First, evaluate all its arguments. Second, use the 𝕻𝖗𝖎𝖒𝖎𝖙𝖎𝖛𝖊 rule to compute the result.
3. [The 𝕻𝖗𝖎𝖒𝖎𝖙𝖎𝖛𝖊 rule] A primitive is applied by calculating the result for that primitive, given the arguments supplied.

Program 1-3   𝕿𝖍𝖊 𝕽𝖚𝖑𝖊𝖘, Version 1

Let's take a look at a few examples.

1. According to the 𝕹𝖚𝖒𝖇𝖊𝖗 rule, the value of the form 37 is **37**. You might ask what else could the value of 37 be. In fact there are a number of possible other answers. In many early versions of Lisp, 37 ⇒ **31**, because numbers were written in octal (base 8), so $37 = 3 \times 8^1 + 7 \times 8^0 = 31$. Fortunately, almost all modern languages use base 10, but we still need to say so.
2. The form (+ 2 2) is an application. We use the 𝕬𝖕𝖕𝖑𝖎𝖈𝖆𝖙𝖎𝖔𝖓 rule, which tells us to evaluate each of the arguments in turn. We get (+ **2 2**), and finally **4**.

The best way to show evaluation is in a tabular format. At each step, we show the rule that will be used to get the result on the next line (Figure 1-4). We've indented the middle lines of Figure 1-4 to show that we're evaluating arguments. Notice the pattern: We start with 𝕬𝖕𝖕𝖑𝖎𝖈𝖆𝖙𝖎𝖔𝖓 because we're

---

[8] The English word *primitive* may make you think of the Stone Age. In mathematics the word simply means "can't be defined in terms of anything simpler".

```
(+ 2 2)                          Application
  (+ 2 2)                        Number
  (+ 2 2)                        Number
  (+ 2 2)                        Primitive
4
```

Figure 1-4   Evaluating (+ 2 2)

evaluating a form in parentheses and we end with Primitive after having evaluated the arguments.

3. The form (+ 2 (* 3 4)) is also an application. We start with the Application rule to begin evaluating the application, and then move on to get (+ 2 (* 3 4)) using the Number rule. The second argument must be evaluated using the Application rule. Accordingly, we start working on the arguments using Number, and get (+ 2 (* 3 4)). Now we can use the Primitive rule to do the multiplication, giving (+ 2 12). Only now can we do the addition, giving 14. Figure 1-5 shows an evaluation of (+ 2 (* 3 4)).

```
(+ 2 (* 3 4))                    Application
  (+ 2 (* 3 4))                  Number
  (+ 2 (* 3 4))                  Application
    (+ 2 (* 3 4))                Number
    (+ 2 (* 3 4))                Number
  (+ 2 (* 3 4))                  Primitive
(+ 2 12)                         Primitive
14
```

Figure 1-5   Evaluating (+ 2 (* 3 4))

This may seem like a lot of work to do a computation all of us can do in our heads, but there's a reason for being so fussy. Our goal is to find out how Scheme works. To do this, we looked at a set of rules that gives a precise method of evaluating Scheme forms. In a surprisingly short time, these rules will become second nature to you.

Another concern comes from the Number rule. What's to stop us from generating Figure 1-6? The answer lies in the difference between 2 and 2: 2 is a numeral, a Scheme form, which can be evaluated, but 2 is just a value, and can't be evaluated any further. Each of the rules tells us how to evaluate a form (or at least something that still hasn't been simplified to just a value).

One question you might ask is, "Are the rules foolproof?" Or do we have to be careful of the order in which we use the rules? If we are computing (+ (* 2 3) (* 3 4)), which multiplication do we do first? This problem shows up when we consider (+ (* 2 3) (+ 4 7)). There are two ways of getting the answer 17, as shown in Figure 1-7.

As you can see, we get the same answer either way. The problem is that, as you're learning Scheme, you want to make sure you're evaluating correctly. We therefore adopt the following convention: *Work from left to right within a form, doing*

`(+ 2 (* 3 4))`	Application
`(+ 2 (* 3 4))`	Number
`(+ `**`2`**` (* 3 4))`	Number
`(+ `**`2`**` (* 3 4))`	Number
`(+ `**`2`**` (* 3 4))`	Number
`(+ `**`2`**` (* 3 4))`	Number
`...`	

Figure 1-6   A nonstop evaluation

`(+ (* 2 3) (+ 4 7))`	Application
`(+ (* 2 3) (+ 4 7))`	Application
`(+ (* 2 3) (+ 4 7))`	Number, Number
`(+ (* `**`2 3`**`) (+ 4 7))`	Primitive
`(+ `**`6`**` (+ 4 7))`	Application
`(+ `**`6`**` (+ 4 7))`	Number, Number
`(+ `**`6`**` (+ `**`4 7`**`))`	Primitive
`(+ `**`6 11`**`)`	Primitive
`17`	

(a) Evaluating from left to right

`(+ (* 2 3) (+ 4 7))`	Application
`(+ (* 2 3) (+ 4 7))`	Application
`(+ (* 2 3) (+ 4 7))`	Number, Number
`(+ (* 2 3) (+ `**`4 7`**`))`	Primitive
`(+ (* 2 3) `**`11`**`)`	Application
`(+ (* 2 3) `**`11`**`)`	Number, Number
`(+ (* `**`2 3`**`) `**`11`**`)`	Primitive
`(+ `**`6   11`**`)`	Primitive
`17`	

(b) Evaluating from right to left

Figure 1-7   Which order?

each form as soon as you can. This convention causes us to prefer the method of Figure 1-7 (a) to that of Figure 1-7 (b).

The Rules are a program for evaluating Scheme forms. If we feed a form into them, out comes the answer. They work on any valid Scheme form. In Chapter 2, we will study the Droid Model, which allows us to take shortcuts in using The Rules to evaluate forms. In Chapter 5, we will develop the Environment Model, an extension of the Droid Model, to provide a full explanation of evaluating Scheme forms. In Chapter 7, we will see how to turn the Environment Model into a Scheme program. We have taken the first steps.

☞ **Exercise 1-16**

Evaluate each of the following Scheme forms, and show the rules you used.
   a. `(+ 7 13)`
   b. `(- (* 2 14) 8)` ❑

1.3   Procedures and Definitions

A definition is the enclosing [of] a wilderness of idea within a wall of words.
— Samuel Butler, *Notebooks*

So far we've learned the elements of Scheme that let us write mathematical expressions in Scheme and compute their values. We need more than this if we are to write programs. In particular, we need to be able to create new "primitives" of our own. We call these primitives *procedures*. We also need to be able to name both numbers and procedures. Scheme provides a kind of form known as a *definition*, which lets us name things.

In this section, we will study procedures and definitions, and see how they work together to let us build programs.

1.3.1   Functions and Procedures

The ancient Egyptians found that each spring their farmland vanished under the floodwaters of the Nile. After a flood, they had to redetermine the boundaries of their fields. Surveyors discovered that a triangle with sides of relative lengths 3, 4, and 5 had a right angle, and could therefore be used to lay out a rectangular field.

The Greek mathematician Pythagoras and his students generalized this rule, resulting in the now-famous equality $a^2 + b^2 = c^2$. The Pythagoreans had gone from a specific triangle to a general rule that works for any right triangle.[9]

One way of looking at this equation is as a mathematical function that relates the inputs a and b to the output c:

$$f(a, b) = \sqrt{a^2 + b^2}$$

We could just as well look at the functions

$$g(b, c) = \sqrt{c^2 - b^2} \qquad \text{or} \qquad h(a, c) = \sqrt{c^2 - a^2}$$

which make a or b the output. In practice, however, the first form is the most useful.

On page 18 we said that a mathematical function is a rule for giving an answer based upon some input values. In mathematics, we have a number of ways to express a function. We can use a formula, as we did above, or we can write the set of all the values of a, b, and c that make the Pythagorean equation true. This set would include $(3, 4, 5)$ and $(6, 8, 10)$. Unfortunately, for the Pythagorean equation, the set is infinite and therefore can't be written down. A third way of specifying a function is by a graph.

In the Pythagorean example, the input values are the lengths of the two sides of the triangle; the function f gives the length of the hypotenuse. We could show this function with an equation (as we did above), or by a table of values for the

---

[9] Note that there exist integer values a, b, and c that satisfy this equation. The French mathematician Fermat believed that he had proved that no such integer values exist for the generalized equation $a^n + b^n = c^n$, where $n > 2$. Unfortunately, there is no room here to explain Fermat's reasoning, nor the reasoning of the more recent 200-page proof of Fermat's Theorem (yet to be verified) by A. Wiles.

three sides. (Drawing a graph would be difficult since it would have to be three-dimensional.)

We can write the form

```
(sqrt (+ (* a a) (* b b)))
```

to compute the length of the hypotenuse (sqrt is a Scheme primitive that computes the square-root of its input). But how do we link the names a and b to their values?

In the 1930s, the logician Alonzo Church asked: How was it possible that

$$f(a) = a + 1 \qquad \text{and} \qquad g(b) = b + 1$$

could both be the same function? (They clearly are: both f and g are functions that give us 1 more than their argument.) Church's answer was that it didn't matter what the names were, so long as they were used consistently. Church developed a system for saying what the arguments to a function are. John McCarthy used Church's ideas as the basis of Lisp. Scheme uses the same ideas, but without some substantial restrictions that were necessary in McCarthy's original version of Lisp.

To write a function, Scheme uses a lambda **form**, which consists of a form together with a specification of its arguments. The **parameters** of a lambda form are the names that act as placeholders for the arguments in the lambda form. Thus, for example, we can write a lambda form for the hypotenuse of a right triangle:

```
(lambda (a b)
  (sqrt (+ (* a a) (* b b))))
```

This is a lambda form that has two parameters, a and b, and computes a result according to the Pythagorean rule. The arguments are the values that substitute for the parameters when the lambda form is applied to them. We'll use these terms a lot, so get comfortable with them.[10]

In general, a lambda form consists of three parts:

1. The word lambda. Church's function notation used the Greek letter lambda (λ) for procedures. This notation was taken over by Lisp, and later Scheme. In hindsight, it would have been better to have used the word procedure. However, lambda is now so well entrenched that Scheme programmers have grown comfortable with it. You will too.

2. The names of the parameters, in parentheses.

3. A form to be evaluated when the lambda form is applied. This form is called the **body** of the lambda form.

Because the lambda form gives the names for the parameters, we can use any names we like. Thus, for example, we could have written the "Pythagoras" lambda form as

```
(lambda (x y) (sqrt (+ (* x x) (* y y))))
```

or even

```
(lambda (bob fred) (sqrt (+ (* bob bob) (* fred fred))))
```

---

[10] Different programming languages use the words *argument* and *parameter* in slightly different ways. Many programmers consider them to mean the same thing. We're using them in quite distinct senses here.

Practical Note

It doesn't matter to Scheme what names we use, as long as we're consistent. However, we should take care to use sensible names. Consider the lambda form

```
(lambda
  (fahrenheit-temperature)
    (+ (* fahrenheit-temperature 1.8)
       32))
```

which, from the name of the parameter, looks like it converts Fahrenheit to Celsius temperatures. The code, though, shows that it does exactly the opposite. Using a name in a misleading manner is worse than using a random name such as xyzzy.

The simplest way to use a lambda form is as follows:

```
((lambda (a b) (sqrt (+ (* a a) (* b b)))) 3 4)
```

In other words, we can use a lambda form in place of a primitive. Scheme evaluates an application involving a lambda form by matching the arguments (*3* and *4* in the above example) with the parameters (a and b). It then substitutes the arguments for the parameters in the body. The result gives us the form (sqrt (+ (* *3* *3*) (* *4* *4*))).

"Aha!" you say, "This is really stupid. I could just write

```
(sqrt (+ (* 3 3) (* 4 4)))
```

which is easier to read, and I don't have to learn the Greek alphabet!" In fact, in real Scheme programming, you'd never use a lambda form as we do here. Once we learn about definitions (in Section 1.3.2), we'll be able to give a lambda form a name and then just use it by name.

We know that the value of a numeral is a number. What's the value of a lambda form? The value of a lambda form is a **procedure**. The lambda form is the way the programmer expresses some operations performed on the arguments that returns a value. The procedure is Scheme's internal representation of the mechanism for implementing these steps. Once again, we make a distinction between a form (the lambda form) and a value (the procedure). This distinction is not important now, but will become crucial in Chapter 5.

When Scheme evaluates a lambda form and creates a procedure, we show the procedure in a different font, as we do with every other kind of value. So the value of (lambda (x) (+ 2 x)) is *(lambda (x) (+ 2 x))*. Scheme does not evaluate the elements of the body of the procedure when it evaluates the lambda form. When the body is applied to its arguments, Scheme evaluates the elements of the body.

How does Scheme evaluate an application of a procedure? First, it replaces the parameters as they occur in the body of the procedure with the arguments, and then it evaluates the body. We'll refer loosely to the body of the procedure when we mean the body of the lambda whose value it is. In addition, we'll often refer to the procedure that is the result of the lambda form while examining the lambda form.

Scheme procedures allow as many arguments as you want, but only one result. Allowing only one result sounds very restrictive, but Scheme has ways of getting around this requirement. We'll see some of those ways in Chapter 4.

One of the best ways to think about procedures is to imagine what happens in a bureaucracy, in which everything is done by writing down the information needed. For example, consider applying for admission to a college that has fixed criteria for admission (grades in specific courses, for example). You would have to write down information about the courses you have taken. This piece of paper is given to somebody who is responsible for processing the request. Eventually, an answer is given. Some of the information on the paper is provided by you (arguments). The admissions office looks in specific places (parameters) for information about you. Once the application form (pun intended) has been processed completely, information (results) is provided to you (a yes or no on whether you are admitted).

The admissions person follows a specific procedure in processing your application. The inputs to the procedure include courses taken, marks, and so on. Such information is often written in a document called a *Procedures Manual*.

This admissions procedure tells you how to compute an output value given the inputs. Procedures are nothing more than ways of specifying how to produce outputs from inputs. You might ask how a `lambda` form is different from a function in mathematics. A function describes what output corresponds to an input. On the other hand, the procedure represented by the `lambda` form expresses a *method* by which to compute the output from the input. For example, the square-root function outputs a number that, if multiplied by itself, gives the original input argument. There are many algorithms for computing square roots. We'll look at a general method for computing roots in Chapter 2.

It's important to understand that in order to use a procedure, you don't have to understand *how it works*, only *what it does*. There might be many ways of computing the result, but it doesn't matter which one you use as long as the procedure is correct. By comparison, imagine taking your car in for repairs. You normally don't tell the mechanic that the frammistan needs regrouting. Instead, you explain what's wrong with the car's behavior. The mechanic does whatever is needed in order to fix the problem. If the problem is fixed, you're happy.

We can thus distinguish between the **interface** and **implementation** of a procedure. The interface defines what the parameters are and what result the procedure is supposed to compute. The implementation defines the particular method that is used to compute the result. In our college admission example, the interface is the piece of paper, and the implementation is the particular method by which the successful candidate is chosen.

Interfaces only make sense when you think about the **client**, or user, of the procedure. If we are to build useful procedures, we must ensure that they can be used effectively. This means that the client has to know what inputs the procedure expects and what output it produces.

You can also think of a procedure as a "black box" (you can't see inside) into which you put the arguments and out of which comes a result, as in Figure 1-8.

The car-repair scenario is actually a good analogy for Scheme procedures. Just as there are many mechanics who will offer to repair your car, there are many ways of writing a Scheme procedure that computes a given result. Some mechanics will charge more than others. Some procedure implementations are more expensive (in computer time, for example) than others. Some mechanics are careful, but others are sloppy. Some implementations compute the result accurately, while others give only an approximation to the answer.

In Section 1.5, we will study precise rules for evaluating applications. For the time being, the following summary will give you enough to be able to do some practical work.

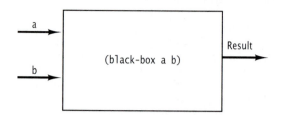

Figure 1-8   Procedures as black boxes

1. To evaluate an application, replace the parameters as they occur in the body of the procedure with the arguments, and then evaluate the body.
2. Match parameters with arguments on a strict left-to-right basis.
3. If there are nested applications, work by finding simple forms (ones that have no forms nested inside them) and evaluating them first.

For example, to evaluate

```
( (lambda (a b) (/ a b))
    (+ 17 3)
    ((lambda (x) (+ 3 x)) 2))
```

we must evaluate (+ 17 3) first and then do the inner application (((lambda (x) ...) 2)). This gives us the form (+ 3 2), or **5**. We substitute the argument values (**20** and **5**) for the parameters (a and b). The resulting form is (/ 20 5), not (/ 5 20), because we match arguments with parameters from left to right.

☞ **Exercise 1-17**

Evaluate each of the following Scheme forms.
   a. ((lambda (x) (+ x 2)) 5)
   b. ((lambda (x y) (+ x (* y 3))) 7 4)
   c. ((lambda (x) ((lambda (y) (* y 2)) (+ x 3))) 4) ❑

☞ **Exercise 1-18**

Write lambda forms that express the following algebraic formulas.
   a. $(x-32) \times (5/9)$
   b. $(x+3 \times y) \times (x-y)$ ❑

☞ **Exercise 1-19**

A carpet store computes the cost of installing wall-to-wall carpet in a rectangular room by multiplying the length and width of the room (in metres) by the cost of carpet in dollars per square metre, and adding a flat $50 service charge. Write a lambda form representing this computation. ❑

☞ **Exercise 1-20**

A student writes two midterm exams and a final exam. Write a procedure that computes the student's final mark. You will have to make some assumptions. Write them down before writing your procedure. ❑

1.3.2 Definitions

Linguists estimate that there are perhaps half a million different English words. No one person would know all of these words—the average person's vocabulary is a few tens of thousands of words. Why do we need so many words?

Words such as *neutron, electrocardiogram*, and *modem* were not needed before subatomic physics, medicine, and data communications technology developed the ideas. Conversely, words go out of usage. For example, a reader of Sherlock Holmes might be puzzled by references to gasogene, or wonder what that tantalus on the sideboard was used for. Language is a process. Words are created to express new ideas or to refer to new things. As our understanding of the world changes, so does our language.

In this respect, programming languages are similar to human languages. Once we have solved a problem, we'd like to be able to use our solution over and over. To do this, we need some way of giving names to values.

We can start by giving names to numbers. Scheme provides a `define` form for this purpose. For example, if we were using π in our computations, we could say

```
(+ (* 3.1415926 4) (+ 1 (* 3.1415296 6)))
```

but this is tedious and error-prone. Did you notice the typographical error?

It is much clearer to use a name.

```
(define pi 3.1415926)
(+ (* pi 4) (+ 1 (* pi 6)))
```

Note how the use of the name `pi` clarifies what we're doing. Since the numerical value only appears in the definition, the chances for error are much lower than with the earlier version. Of course, there is still a chance for error—nothing can take the place of careful proofreading!

In another example, consider calculating the total cost, including the sales tax, of a collection of purchases. Without definitions, we write

```
(* 1.07 (+ 24.95 32.95))
```

assuming the tax is 7%. However, sales taxes change, which means we must change the form each time. If, however, we define the sales tax as a name, then it's much clearer what might change. In fact, we can define both the tax and the purchase amount as names. We can also use the purchase amount for other purposes, such as computing a 5% rebate on purchases.

```
> (define tax-rate 0.07)
> (define amount (+ 24.95 32.95))
> (* (+ 1 tax-rate) amount)
61.953
> (* 0.05 amount)
2.895
```

Why would we do this? It certainly requires more writing than our original version. Yet this version is much clearer. We know which figure is the tax rate and which figure is the amount. We've broken the problem down into pieces: state the tax, state the amount, and then compute the total price.

A **definition** consists of three parts:

1. the word `define`

2. the name to be defined
3. any form that gives the `value`

A note on syntax here: A name can be any word or any sequence of characters that aren't treated specially by Scheme. Thus `salestax` and `sales-tax` are both names, as is ++. However, (((isn't a name, because parentheses have a special meaning to Scheme. Names can be of any reasonable length. (Appendix B describes the rules for forming names in Scheme.)

Practical Note

How do you pick the name? As with parameters, Scheme doesn't care, so we could have written the above code as

```
(define zxqwt 0.07)
(define bfxlsplt (+ 24.95 32.95))
(* (+ 1 zxqwt) bfxlsplt)
```

This version is harder to read, so mistakes will be harder to find. We are much better off with names that tell us what we're trying to do. Most Scheme programmers tend to use fairly long and descriptive names in their definitions, to help with readability. One of Scheme's primitive procedures is named `call-with-current-continuation`!

It's important to keep names, forms, and values clear in your mind. A name is a form. If you type a name into Scheme, you will get a value as an answer.

```
> (define pi 3.1415926)
> pi
3.1415926
> (define circle-multiplier pi)
> circle-multiplier
3.1415926
> (define two-pi (* 2 pi))
> two-pi
6.2831852
> (* two-pi 10)
62.831852
```

When we use a name in a Scheme form, Scheme replaces it with the value **bound** to it, or associated with it. We talk of a **binding** between the name and the value.

The words `lambda` and `define` *look* like names, but are used in **special forms**, forms in parentheses that start with a keyword; there is no `lambda` or `define` primitive. The difference between a special form and an application is that all of the arguments of an application are evaluated, whereas some of the arguments of a special form are not evaluated. There are about 30 types of special forms in Scheme. We will see many of them later. A list of all the special forms, and therefore the names that are reserved for Scheme's use, appears in Appendix B. Many Scheme evaluators define additional special forms (generally with quite strange names, which you are unlikely to use by accident). You can look in the manual for your Scheme system for a complete list of the names of additional special forms.

   You *might* get away with using define as a defined name, that is, (define define ...), on one Scheme system, but not on another. Regardless of whether you can get away with it, it's foolish to try. Even if the evaluator understands what you've written, your human readers won't.

   What is the value of a define form? It turns out that Scheme doesn't say what answer you should get back when you define, for example, (define foo 100). One Scheme system would give you back 100. Another would give you done. Yet a third might give you back ok or something similar. We use define to create new names, and because Scheme leaves the answer "unspecified", we won't rely on it. We follow the trend of some modern Scheme systems, which don't display any value when you enter a definition.

   The important element in a definition is the effect it has on how we compute after the definition has been evaluated. Afterwards, whenever Scheme encounters the defined name, Scheme substitutes the name's value in the form being evaluated.

Practical Note

If you have used other programming languages, you might be inclined to write things like:

```
> (define wrong! (+ 1 2))
> (define wrong! (+ wrong! 1))
```

This is not the purpose of define. A definition is used to establish a binding between a name and a value. You should use define only where the name is to be bound to a specific value, once and for all. Why does Scheme even allow you to redefine a name? Because you might have made a mistake, and have to do it again.

```
> (define pi 1.31415926)
> (define pi 3.1415926)  ; oops!
```

The quadratic equation gives us another example of using definitions.

$$ax^2 + bx + c = 0$$

has solutions given by the "Quadratic Formula":

$$x = \frac{-b \pm \sqrt{b^2 - 4ac}}{2a}$$

Assuming that real solutions exist (i.e., the "discriminant" $b^2 - 4ac$ is not negative), we can compute the solutions as shown in Program 1-4.

   The values are $-1/4$ and -1 for root1 and root2. How did this work? We created a series of defined names. First, we defined a, b, and c, the coefficients of the equation. Then we defined discriminant as the result of the form (- (* b b)

```
(define a 4)
(define b 5)
(define c 1)
(define discriminant
  (- (* b b) (* 4 (* a c))))
(define root1
  (/ (+ (- b) (sqrt discriminant))
     (* 2 a)))
(define root2
  (/ (- (- b) (sqrt discriminant))
     (* 2 a)))
```

Program 1-4   Calculating roots

(* 4 (* a c))), which turns out to be 9. Next, we defined root1, getting a value of -1/4, and root2, getting a value of -1.[11]

If you put the above sequence of definitions into a file (see the manual for your Scheme system), you have a rudimentary program. Then change the values for a, b, and c, and see the values for root1 and root2.

Scheme doesn't have a specific concept of "program". You can put forms together in whatever way makes sense to you, and then enter the whole collection into Scheme. We call such a collection of forms a program. The fact that Scheme doesn't require you to enter a complete program is a strength, because it means you can do things in small steps, trying things out as you go. Although we encourage you to plan your programs out, we also encourage you to try out specific things you're not sure about. Scheme systems make that process much easier than do systems that require you to create an entire program to try something out.

Let's go back to definitions. It's possible to imagine that the name pi would be known specially to Scheme. But what about discriminant? In the above example, how does Scheme know that the value of discriminant is 9?

To answer this question, we must introduce a new concept, the **environment**, which is a list of names and corresponding values. Just as we have an environment, so too does Scheme. Just as we react to things in our environment, so too does Scheme.

The quadratic equation problem would add the information shown in Figure 1-9 to the environment.

a	*4*
b	*5*
c	*1*
discriminant	*9*
root1	*-1/4*
root2	*-1*

Figure 1-9   Environment after quadratic equation

---

[11] Some Scheme systems will display the first value as -0.25.

Each time the evaluator sees a name, it looks up the name in the environment. For example, the form

```
(+ 2 a)
```

is evaluated by replacing the *name* a by the *value 4* (because that's the value associated with a in the environment). It would be evaluated as

$$(+ \ 2 \ a) \ \Rightarrow \ (+ \ 2 \ a) \ \Rightarrow \ (+ \ 2 \ 4) \ \Rightarrow \ 6$$

What about defining procedures? According to what we said about definitions, we can define a name in terms of any form. We should be able to define a name to have a lambda form as its value. For example, we can say

```
(define discr
   (lambda (pa pb pc)
      (- (* pb pb) (* 4 (* pa pc)))))
```

We added the name discr to the environment with the procedure as value, so now we can use discr as the name of a procedure:

```
(discr 4 5 1)  ⇒  9
```

Now the benefits of procedures should be apparent. We can define a procedure with a name, and then use the name whenever we wish to use that procedure. So why didn't we introduce definitions along with procedures? Because they are very separate concepts in Scheme. We have already seen definitions without procedures. In Chapter 3, we will see practical applications of procedures without definitions.

Once we've written discr, is it ready to use? Would you be willing to drive over a brand-new bridge that nobody had tested out? We need to **test** the procedure by applying it to specific inputs and checking that the output is correct. Once we have tested the procedure, we can then attempt to **debug** the program, by finding the cause of the errors.

☞ **Exercise 1–21**

In 1979, the U.S. Nuclear Regulatory Commission shut down a number of reactors because a protective earthwork around each reactor provided insufficient safety. The problem was tracked down to an error in a computer program; a + had been typed as a -. The program had, no doubt, been tested, but no inputs had been used that triggered this particular error.

Suppose we had accidentally typed

```
(define discr
  (lambda (pa pb pc)
    (+ (* pb pb) (* 4 (* pa pc)))))
```

We might test this procedure with several values for pa, pb, and pc. Show one set of data that would produce the correct results (i.e., it would appear as though the procedure was correct), and one set that would produce obviously incorrect results. Would you be convinced that a procedure was correct if it had been tested with a single set of arguments? ❏

It is instructive to look at the environment after discr has been defined, as shown in Figure 1–10.

Note that we have added one name, discr, to the environment. A look at discr's value is very instructive. It's a procedure. If you needed something to convince you that procedures are data, the fact that Scheme will bind a to a number

a	*4*
b	*5*
c	*1*
discriminant	*9*
root1	*-1/4*
root2	*-1*
discr	*(lambda (pa pb pc)*
	(- (* pb pb)
	(* 4 (* pa pc))))

Figure 1-10   Environment after defining discr

and `discr` to a procedure ought to do it. Keep in mind that if you try to evaluate `discr`, most Scheme evaluators won't respond by showing you *(lambda ...)*. For reasons we will explore in Chapter 6, procedures of this sort must be stored in a special way. Most Scheme evaluators will display a procedure as something like `#<procedure...>`.[12]

Note that the environment has entries for both `discriminant` and `discr`. `discriminant` has a number as a value, while `discr` has a procedure as a value. The fact that numbers and procedures are both kinds of data is an important aspect of Scheme.

We can write the definition for `root1` using our new `discr` procedure:

```
(define root1
  (/ (+ (- b) (sqrt (discr a b c)))
     (* 2 a)))
```

1.3.3   Defining Procedures

Our quadratic equation solver looks strange to an experienced Scheme programmer. It would make much more sense to have procedures that give the roots, rather than making names for the numbers. Our new version is shown in Program 1-5.

In this new version, `discr` is a **helper** procedure, which is a procedure that does a task on behalf of another procedure.

There are several benefits of splitting a procedure up into smaller pieces:

1. The independent pieces can be tested separately. In a big program, this is a lifesaver. Good programmers use a step-by-step process, in which they check each piece of the program on its own. At each step, they are looking at only a few lines of code that might have bugs.[13]

2. The resulting main procedure is much simpler to read, write, and test.

3. Intermediate values need not be recomputed, since they can be passed as parameters. This technique can make a substantial improvement in readability (since a complicated form need only be written once) and efficiency (since the program doesn't do the same calculation several times).

---

[12] Many Scheme systems use the word `closure` instead of `procedure`.

[13] We're not claiming the impossible here. Of course, a bug could sneak through the testing process and cause problems later on. Still, a systematic, piece-by-piece method reduces the number of bugs that are still present when the programmer puts the whole program together.

```
(define discr
  (lambda (pa pb pc)
    (- (* pb pb) (* 4 (* pa pc)))))
(define find-root1
  (lambda (pa pb pc)
    (/ (+ (- pb) (sqrt (discr pa pb pc)))
       (* 2 pa))))
(define find-root2
  (lambda (pa pb pc)
    (/ (- (- pb) (sqrt (discr pa pb pc)))
       (* 2 pa))))
```

Program 1-5   Quadratic equations using procedures

Helpers aren't part of the procedure's interface to the client (remember, a client is a form—either one you type in or one in another procedure—that calls a procedure), which doesn't care whether any helpers are used.

One of the important challenges in computing is to manage large systems of enormous complexity. One of the tools we use is **decomposition**: breaking large problems down into smaller, more manageable portions that can be understood on their own. The process of decomposing problems can continue through many levels. Our discr procedure moves down only one level from the starting problem, but in a large problem the process can continue for a long time.

By creating a procedure to solve a piece of a problem, we are engaging in abstraction (from the Latin words meaning "taking away"). In program design, it refers to suppressing irrelevant detail about the implementation of a piece of code, but specifying the interface completely. Once we have created a procedure to do something, we can use the procedure without thinking about the details of how the procedure is implemented. The procedure becomes a new primitive for a machine that we are customizing from the basic parts of Scheme. Procedures are like verbs in a language, and writing new procedures is like making new verbs. The skilled Scheme programmer builds a library of procedures that solve problems of interest. When one of these problems arises, a programmer does not have to solve it over again, but simply uses one of the procedures from the library.

Procedures and definitions together are the means by which we can build more complicated programs. By writing procedures, we can give rules for computing answers to various parts of a problem. Definitions allow us to give names to these rules. As we have seen, those names help us to understand what we're doing.

Suppose we want to compute the cost of painting a house. The best way to do this is to add up the cost for each room, assuming that the cost is a function of the dimensions of the room, as shown in Program 1-6 (length, width, and height given in metres).

If only we had a procedure named room-cost, then we could evaluate the above form. As it is, we can't do much with it.

Obviously, the cost of painting a room is going to be computed by taking the area of the walls and ceiling, dividing by the area covered by one can of paint, and then multiplying by the cost of a can of paint. Again, we'll do a bit of inventing, and pretend we have a procedure that gives us the area of the walls and ceiling for a room. For this procedure, we'll assume that a can of paint covers $15m^2$ and costs $10 (Program 1-7).

```
(+ (room-cost 4 5 3)           ; Living room.
   (+ (room-cost 3 4 3)        ; Dining room.
      (+ (room-cost 4 4 3)     ; Master bedroom.
         (+ (room-cost 3 4 3)    ; Second bedroom.
            (+ (room-cost 2 2 2)  ; Entrance hall.
            )))))
```

Program 1-6   Calculating total cost for rooms

```
(define coverage 15)
(define paint-cost 10)
(define room-cost
  (lambda (length width height)
    (* (/ (room-area length width height)
          coverage)
       paint-cost)))
```

Program 1-7   A procedure for computing surface area of a box

Finally, we need to calculate the area of the walls and ceiling. For this problem, let's pretend that each room is a box. Then the area of the walls and ceiling is $2lh + 2wh + lw$. A bit of algebra gives us a slightly simpler Scheme form than we would get by translating this form directly (Program 1-8).

```
(define room-area
  (lambda (length width height)
    (+ (* 2 (* height (+ length width)))
       (* length width))))
```

Program 1-8   Surface area of a room

Not only `room-cost` and `room-area`, but also `coverage` and `paint-cost` were defined in the environment. However, the former were defined with numeric values, while the latter were defined with procedural ones. In solving complex problems, it is common to have such a mix of numbers and procedures in one's programs.

One of the most common uses of procedures is as building blocks, to replace the collections of forms that often occur in programs. We might find it tedious to write `(+ 1 x)` whenever we add 1 to x, so we can write the procedures shown in Program 1-9. These are so useful that we'll assume they're part of Scheme's environment as built-in primitives.

```
(define add1
  (lambda (x) (+ x 1)))
(define sub1
  (lambda (x) (- x 1)))
```

Program 1-9   Adding and subtracting one

Often the building block we want is very generally useful. Recall the formula we wrote for the area of an annulus earlier in the chapter.

```
(- (* 3.1415926 (* 12 12))
   (* 3.1415926 (* 10 10)))
```

Let's write a procedure to calculate the area of an annulus. The inputs are the inner and outer radii, and the output is the difference between the area of the two circles. This formula twice calculates the area of a circle, so let's first write a procedure that computes the area of a circle:

```
(define circle-area
  (lambda (r)
    (* pi (* r r))))
```

We defined pi earlier. Now the procedure annulus-area should be easy:

```
(define annulus-area
  (lambda (inner outer)
    (- (circle-area outer) (circle-area inner))))
```

In a sense, the circle-area procedure is a helper to annulus-area, but it's so generally useful that we'll think of it as an element in our general toolbox of geometric procedures. When a programmer is working on a set of related problems, it's common to write a collection of procedures that solve frequently encountered problems. These procedures form a library of procedures that can be used by many programmers.

☞ **Exercise 1-22**

Show the environment created by the following series of definitions:

```
(define u 35)
(define v 17)
(define w (* u v))
(define x (+ v w))
(define f (lambda (a b) (+ a (* b 2))))
```

❑

☞ **Exercise 1-23**

Using the environment from the previous exercise, evaluate each of the following forms:
    a. u
    b. x
    c. f
    d. (+ u v)
    e. (f w u)
    f. ((lambda (f) (f 13 7)) -) ❑

☞ **Exercise 1-24**

Write a procedure named add2 that computes its argument plus **2**; thus (add2 5) ⇒ **7**, and (add2 93) ⇒ **95**. ❑

☞ **Exercise 1-25**

The primitive procedures add1 and sub1 allow you to express addition and subtraction by 1. For example (add1 2) ⇒ **3**, and (sub1 9) ⇒ **8**. Using only these procedures, and *not* the general primitives + and –, write a procedure that has a parameter n and computes

$$\sqrt{(n-1)/(n+1)}$$

❏

☞ **Exercise 1-26**

Write a procedure, `times2`, that computes its argument times 2. For example, `(times2 7)` ⇒ *14*. Using `times2`, *not* `*`, write `times64`, that computes its argument times 64. ❏

☞ **Exercise 1-27**

The area a of a triangle with sides of length x, y, and z can be computed by using the *semiperimeter* formula

$$a = \sqrt{s(s-x)(s-y)(s-z)}$$

where

$$s = (x+y+z)/2$$

We want to calculate s only once, not four times. Write a procedure to compute the semiperimeter from x, y, and z. Use that procedure in the procedure to calculate the area of the triangle. ❏

1.4   Decisions

> *'Beauty is truth, truth beauty,'—that is all*
> *Ye know on earth, and all ye need to know.*
> — John Keats, "Ode on a Grecian Urn"

So far, we have managed to make Scheme into a sort of giant calculator, dutifully carrying out the operations we command. If that were all Scheme could do, there would be no computer industry. Anything we can do in what we know of Scheme so far can be done more effectively on a calculator with a bit of memory and a ⌐Learn⌐ button. The user can enter a formula into such a calculator's program memory. When the user needs the same calculation, the calculator can repeat the steps.

We need to endow our computers with the ability to make decisions. This ability will let the program deal with different circumstances and repeat tasks when necessary, with the program deciding what is "necessary"—a very important point.

What exactly is a decision? For hundreds of years, writers have imagined "artificial humans". Legend has it that Rabbi Judah Löw, in medieval Prague, created a *golem*, or artificial human made of clay, that would obey him. Karel Čapek, a Czech writer of this century, wrote a play in 1917 entitled "R.U.R." in which androids Universal Robots eventually became self-aware and demanded an end to their slave status. Čapek coined the word *robot*, from the Czech word for "worker". Isaac Asimov wrote an extended series of stories about robots that are governed by the Three Laws of Robotics. These laws cause them to make extremely complex moral choices. Fredric Brown imagined a group of scientists who have just built the world's most powerful computer. They ask the computer, "Is there a God"? The machine replies, "There is now".

The Information Society

Who actually invented the modern computer? Babbage certainly laid the intellectual groundwork, but credit for the modern computer is divided among Eckert and Mauchly and von Neumann (U.S.), Turing (U.K.), and Zuse (Germany). If none of these individuals had designed computers, others certainly would have.

Computers were first used for producing mathematical tables. By 1947, there were enough computing enthusiasts to form a small society, the Association for Computing Machinery (ACM), which has grown to become the major worldwide scholarly organization for computer scientists.

The general public first became aware of the computer (or "Electronic Brain") in 1952, when CBS used one of the first commercial computers, UNIVAC I, to pick the winner of the U.S. Presidential election. By the mid-1950s, large organizations were using computers for business record-keeping and scientific computing. These early vacuum-tube machines were expensive and unreliable. By 1960, transistors made computers cheap and reliable enough that they could be used to provide remote-access services. American Airlines' Sabre system, which provided worldwide passenger reservations, used two mainframe computers, each with less computing power than a small desktop computer of 1994. In the 1970s, integrated circuitry lowered the cost of computers so that small companies and schools could afford them.

This cost reduction came about because more and more components could be placed upon a single integrated circuit chip. In the 1970s, semiconductor manufacturers developed the microprocessor, a single chip with all of the computing power of a small mainframe.

By the late 1970s, it was possible to buy a microprocessor-based computer for about the cost of a car. These early computers were slow and unreliable (as the early mainframes were), and came with little software, but people found uses for them. Soon, personal computers such as the Apple II and the IBM PC were developed. Non-programmers started buying these machines, and an industry appeared to write the necessary software. It soon became clear that computers were too hard to use, though. In 1984, Apple released the Macintosh, which uses a graphic user interface. Soon after, Microsoft released the first version of its Windows software package, which provides a graphic user interface on PCs.

The 1990s have seen the development of microprocessors with enormous computing power, such as the Intel Pentium and the IBM/Motorola PowerPC. Ready computing power has led to sophisticated computer networks and computers that can process voice and video data.

There has been a dramatic reduction in the size of computers. The 1960 mainframe required a large room and enormous supplies of power. A far more (computationally) powerful 1990s notebook computer can be carried in one hand and runs on a small storage battery. It has been said that if similar evolution had occurred in the aeronautical industry, a 747 would fit in the palm of one's hand, and cost a dollar!

Computers have become a part of the fabric of our society, from the cash machine at the convenience store to computer systems that can help disabled people to see or manipulate the environment. Along the way, there have been concerns about privacy or the quality of work or life when automated systems are used. Many of these political and ethical problems still require discussion and analysis to decide how to solve them most effectively in a democratic society.

The decisions we will study are considerably less grandiose than those of robot stories. Our programs won't have to decide whether or not to annihilate humanity, but only whether to skip or repeat particular parts of a computation. Therefore, we will think of a decision as asking a yes or no question, and then choosing an answer. The question will depend only on the values known to the computer and the result of some computation on the values. Decisions like these are determined by simple rules, not some insight or self-consciousness of the computer.

Example: "When people return to their country, Customs charges them duty on their purchases at a rate of 10%. If the person has been away for more than 48 hours, the first $100 of purchases is duty-free. If the duty owing is less than $2.00, it is not charged." The decisions here are:

- Has the person been away for more than 48 hours?
- Is the duty owing greater than or equal to $2.00?

Don't make the mistake of *anthropomorphizing* the computer. We aren't dealing with a machine that has consciousness or free will, but with a machine into which we can enter a set of rules that it will obey inflexibly. In that light, a computer is no more conscious or intelligent than a thermostat: both make "decisions" based upon their inputs.[14]

Let's take the Customs example and see how to write a procedure that calculates the duty owing. We'll break the problem down into procedures and subprocedures, for clarity, in Program 1-10.

```
(define duty-owing
  (lambda (num-hours-away total-purchases)
    (calculate-duty
       (if (< num-hours-away 48)
          total-purchases
          (- total-purchases 100)))))
(define calculate-duty
  (lambda (amount-dutiable)
    (charge-duty (* amount-dutiable 0.10))))
(define charge-duty
  (lambda (amount)
    (if (< amount 2.00) 0 amount)))
```

Program 1-10   Calculating duty owing

This solution uses two if forms. An if form is a type of **conditional** form, a special form that makes a decision, by selecting one or another form to evaluate. For example, (if (< x 3) 6 8) will select the value 6 if the value of x is less than 3, and 8 otherwise.

If you look at charge-duty, the procedure that decides how much duty to pay, you will notice that the lambda body is an if form. If the amount is less than $2.00, the answer is 0; otherwise, the answer is the value of amount. Similarly, duty-owing uses an if form to select the value to pass to calculate-duty, either total-purchases or (- total-purchases 100), depending upon the answer

---

[14] Whether artificial machines can develop consciousness or free will is a matter of current philosophical debate. We will examine this topic in Chapter 10.

to the question "Is the value of `num-hours-away` less than 48?" (Incidentally, an experienced Scheme programmer wouldn't need to write so many procedures to solve this problem. We'll see how to improve the style in Chapter 3.)

So far, we have seen two kinds of values: numbers and procedures. We say the numbers and procedures are two different **types** of data. We use the notion of type in everyday life. When we ask a question, we expect an answer of a particular type. If someone asks you your name, she will be very surprised if you answer "twelve." We tend to think of names and numbers as very different entities, and will not normally accept one where the other is expected.[15]

Types allow us to keep straight what sort of values we're working with. In Scheme, each value has a specific type. Many procedures and special forms insist that their operands be of specific types. For example, the form (+ 2 (lambda (x) x)) doesn't make sense, because we're trying to add a number and a procedure, which is a type error. On the other hand, (3 4) will also result in an error, because we can only apply procedures, not numbers.

We are going to add a third type to our collection, the so-called Boolean type, named for the 19th-century English mathematician George Boole, who was the inventor of modern mathematical logic. There are only two Boolean values, namely *true* and *false*.

Boole defined a number of operations upon Boolean values, of which we will consider three: and, or, and not. Since these words are so common in English, we must be careful about what we mean by them.

- The and operator means that *both* conditions must be true. For example, if we say, "Students must take English and mathematics", we mean, "Students must take English and students must take mathematics".

- The or operator means that at least *one* condition must be true. When we say, "Students may take computer science or mathematics", we will accept either one of the subjects. But what about a student who takes both? In fact, there are two flavors of or. If we allow the *both* case, then we are using *inclusive* or; it makes no sense to throw a student out for taking both computer science and mathematics. On the other hand, if one says, "Today I will go to the beach or do my homework", one normally assumes that the *both* case can't happen. The two conditions are then said to be *mutually exclusive*. This latter kind of or is known as *exclusive*: it *excludes* the *both* case. Computer languages, including Scheme, always use inclusive or as the meaning of or.

- The not operator is a denial that a condition is true. For example, by saying "John is not a computer science student", one is really saying "It is not true that John is a computer science student".

Any statement, however complicated, can be broken down into a set of simple conditions connected by and, or, and not. For example, if we say, "Mike is taking computer science, either physics or chemistry, and mathematics, but not biology," we can break it down into the following:

> (Mike is taking computer science) and ((Mike is taking physics) or (Mike is taking chemistry)) and (Mike is taking mathematics) and (not (Mike is taking biology))

---

[15] Unlike the ancient Romans, who gave boys names such as Quintus, Sextus, Septimius, Octavius, and so on.

Notice the use of parentheses here.

Let's turn our attention to Scheme now. In Scheme the two Boolean values *true* and *false* are written as #t and #f, respectively. Many Scheme systems will display #f as (). If yours does this, it's an historical aberration; just read it as #f.

Where do these values come from? There are a number of primitive procedures that yield Boolean results. For example, (< 5 6) ⇒ #t, because 5 < 6, while (> 5 6) ⇒ #f, because 5 ⊁ 6.

Practical Note

Scheme really only uses #f. Anything that is not #f is considered to be *true* for the purposes of an if form. If the value of the condition is not #f, the then-form is evaluated and returned. Thus, for example, (if 7 8 9) ⇒ **8**, though a good programmer would never write a form such as this. Why does Scheme work this way? Because it simplifies some sorts of Scheme forms. We'll see practical uses of this feature in Chapter 4. For the time being, take care to make the if condition evaluate to a Boolean value.

A procedure that yields a Boolean result is called a **predicate**. Think of it as a test. Scheme has the predicates <, >, =, <=, and >=, with the same meaning as in algebra. No *not equals* predicate is provided, but you can define one of your own (see Exercise 1–32).

Other predicates are named by words rather than mathematical symbols. For example, zero? yields #t when its argument is 0, and #f otherwise. For example,

        (zero? (- 3 (+ 1 2))) ⇒   (zero? (- 3 3)) ⇒   (zero? 0) ⇒   #t

By convention, predicates whose names are words end with a question mark. This reminds us that the outputs of such procedures are Boolean values. All of the predicates we have discussed so far take numbers as arguments, not procedures or Booleans. The names of the comparison operators are not words and so do not follow this convention. Thus, the less-than predicate is written as <, not <?.

Scheme has counterparts of the Boolean operations and, or, and not. The and form yields #t if *both* of its inputs are true, and #f otherwise. For example,

        (and (< 5 6) (> 9 8)) ⇒   (and #t #t) ⇒   #t

The or form yields #t if one or both of its inputs are true, and #f otherwise.

If you say "If $2 + 2 = 5$ and ...", you don't need to know what follows the and. The answer's obviously false. Similarly, "If $2 + 2 = 4$ or ..." is true, regardless of how the statement ends. Accordingly, and and or are not procedures, but special forms. Each of these forms evaluates only enough arguments to determine the answer. This fact has a practical application. Consider the form (and (> a 0) (> (/ 10 a) 5)). This form will always produce a Boolean result for any value of a. If and had been a procedure, it would always evaluate both arguments, even if a were zero. Instead of evaluating to #f, it would give an error (for dividing by zero). (Today, this way of doing and and or is pretty much universal in programming languages. It is often called "McCarthy and/or", after John McCarthy, who used it in the original version of Lisp.) not is an ordinary procedure.

Let's go back and look at if forms again. For example,

```
(if (< 5 6) 7 8)  ⇒   (if #t 7 8)  ⇒  7
```

while

```
(if (> 5 6) 7 8)  ⇒   (if #f 7 8)  ⇒  8
```

An if form has four parts:

1. the word if
2. a condition, a form yielding a Boolean value
3. a form to be evaluated if the condition yields #t (the *then-form*)
4. a form to be evaluated if the condition yields #f (the *else-form*)

The if form gives us the ability to make a procedure behave differently depending upon its input. For example, suppose we want to send a letter by courier. The courier company might charge $1.00 per 25 grams, with a minimum charge of $5.00 (125 grams). We could write a procedure to compute the postage:

```
(define courier-charge
  (lambda (weight)
    (if (< weight 125)
        5.00
        (/ weight 25))))
```

☞ **Exercise 1-28**

Write each of the following sentences using and, or, and not with simple conditions. For example, we can restate "Mary is taking mathematics and computer science" as "Mary is taking mathematics, and Mary is taking computer science".
 a. "Socrates is a Greek philosopher"
 b. "Mary is taking computer science instead of geometry"
 c. "John has taken neither computer science nor mathematics" ❏

☞ **Exercise 1-29**

Define a predicate called one? that yields a #t when its argument is 1, and #f otherwise. You may not use if, #t, or #f in your solution. ❏

☞ **Exercise 1-30**

Explain why evaluating (zero? (< 5 6)) will result in an error. ❏

☞ **Exercise 1-31**

Define a procedure (between? a x y), that yields #t if a is between x and y (including the equal cases), and #f otherwise. Hint: Use and. ❏

☞ **Exercise 1-32**

Define a *not equals* predicate procedure for numbers. This can be done in (at least) two ways, one using not, and the other using or. Do it both ways. ❏

☞ **Exercise 1-33**

Define <? with the same meaning as <. Your solution may not use the word lambda. ❏

☞ **Exercise 1–34**

The Post Office charges the following postage for a first-class letter, depending upon its weight:

- less than 30 grams, 15 cents
- 30 to 49 grams, 17 cents
- 50 to 99 grams, 22 cents
- 100 grams and over, 1 cent for each 4 grams

Write a procedure that is given the weight in grams and returns the postage in cents. Use `if`. There is a serious ambiguity in the statement of the problem. Find it. Explain what your program does in this case. ❏

1.5   The Rules (Version 2)

> *I had an aunt in Yucatan*
> *Who bought a Python from a man*
> *And kept it for a pet.*
> *She died, because she never knew*
> *These simple little rules and few;—*
> *The Snake is living yet.*
>
> — Hilaire Belloc, "The Python"

We've introduced procedures, definitions, and decisions, but given only an informal explanation of how the evaluator handles them. Let's add the necessary rules to our original rules to complete the description of the mechanism that evaluates Scheme forms. We will call our revised set of rules The Rules (Version 2).

First, let's look at definitions. We have two tasks: we must account for the `define` special form, and explain how the environment is managed. We will introduce a new Definition rule that tells us what to do with a definition, and a Name rule that tells us that names are replaced by their corresponding values from the environment.

- [The Name rule] A name is evaluated by looking it up in the environment.
- [The Definition rule] A form whose first element is the word `define` is handled specially: the second argument is evaluated in the normal way, but the first argument, which must be a name, is not evaluated at all. The binding between the name and value are added to the environment.

For example, if we ask Scheme to evaluate

```
(define answer 42)
answer
```

The Definition rule tells Scheme to evaluate the second argument (we obtain **42**, using the Number rule), and then to place a binding between the name answer and the value **42** into the environment. The second form can be evaluated by using the Name rule.

To evaluate forms such as (+ 2 2), the Primitive rule of The Rules (Version 1), told us to apply a primitive by calculating the result for that primitive, given the arguments supplied. Since then, we have learned that a primitive is a special kind of value. In most Scheme implementations, a primitive will be represented as a sequence of machine-language instructions.[16] Different Scheme systems will show a primitive in different formats. In this book we represent the value of a name such as + like this: ***#{plus}***. As a note of terminology, we generally use the word *procedure* to mean "user procedure" (i.e., one made from a lambda form).

- [The 𝔓rimitive rule] A primitive is applied by performing the machine-language instructions specified for the primitive, given the arguments supplied.

Next, let's write the rules for procedures. Clearly, procedures are evaluated when we have an application, such as

    ((lambda (a b) (- b a)) 3 5)

We intend the 3 to match with a, and 5 to match with b. In fact, we can evaluate the above form as follows:

    ((lambda (a b) (- b a)) 3 5) ⇒   (- 5 3) ⇒   2

What did we do? We replaced each parameter by the corresponding argument in (- b a), and then replaced the lambda form by the body. Then we evaluated the new body. Let's take a slightly more complicated example, and do it a bit more carefully.

    ((lambda (a b) (- b a)) 3 ((lambda (c) (+ 5 c)) 7))
    ⇒   (*(lambda (a b)* (- b a)) 3 (+ 5 7))
    ⇒   (*(lambda (a b)* (- b a)) 3 12)
    ⇒   (- 12 3) ⇒   9

In this example, we again worked from left to right, even though it doesn't look that way. We evaluated in turn the lambda form and 3. Then we evaluated the application ((lambda (c) (+ 5 c)) 7) and proceeded from there.

Thus there are two rules for procedures: 𝔏ambda tells us how to evaluate a lambda form, and 𝔓rocedure tells us how to apply a procedure.

- [The 𝔏ambda rule] The value of a lambda form is a procedure, which is the same as the lambda form, but written in ***value font***.
- [The 𝔓rocedure rule] A procedure application is evaluated in two steps:
    a. Replace, in the body of the procedure, each of the parameters by the corresponding arguments.
    b. Replace the entire application by the body.

Now, how do we put all of this together? We would like all applications to be handled in the same way. This means that we must revise the 𝔄pplication rule. In its new formulation, the 𝔄pplication rule says to evaluate all the arguments of an application, and only distinguish between primitives and procedures after the arguments have been evaluated. Because of the new 𝔓rocedure rule, an application now always has a name or lambda form in its first position.

- [The 𝔄pplication rule] An application is evaluated by evaluating each of its elements and then using the 𝔓rimitive rule, if a primitive is applied, or the 𝔓rocedure rule for a procedure.

---

[16] Many popular Scheme systems are actually written in higher-level languages such as C. However, the principle is the same as if machine language had been used.

As an example, consider evaluating ((lambda (x) (+ x 1)) 2). Scheme performs two applications. First, it applies the procedure *(lambda (x) (+ x 1))* to the number *2*. The Procedure rule causes this to be replaced with (+ *2* 1). Remember that + is a name bound in the environment. Scheme replaces this name with its value, *#{plus}*, and continues the evaluation, as shown in Figure 1–11.

((lambda (x) (+ x 1)) 2)	Application
((lambda (x) (+ x 1)) 2)	Lambda, Number
((lambda (x) (+ x 1)) 2)	Procedure
(+ *2* 1)	Application
(+ *2* 1)	Name, Number
(#{plus} 2 1)	Primitive
3	

Figure 1–11   Evaluating a procedure application

This example shows the pattern for performing an application. We use the Application rule first, which causes us to evaluate all of the arguments. Once the arguments have all been evaluated, the Application rule tells us to use the appropriate rule—either Procedure or Primitive—to finish things off.

Even as simple a form as (sqrt 4) can't be evaluated according to these rules unless we show how sqrt can appear in the environment. We therefore added an Initialization rule, to specify the names predefined in the environment. Different Scheme implementations provide different sets of primitives. We will assume that all of the standard arithmetic primitives are provided in Scheme.

There are also three special forms related to Booleans: if, and, and or. We therefore need If, And, and Or rules. (These rules appear with all our new rules, in The Rules, Version 2, shown in Program 1–11.)

The value of an if form is either the then-form or the else-form, depending upon whether the condition is *true* or *false* (remember that in Scheme *true* is anything but #f). When we evaluate, using The Rules,

```
(define number 12)
(if (> 19 number) 3 4)
```

we get

(if (> 19 number) 3 4)	If
(if (> 19 number) 3 4)	Application
(if (> 19 number) 3 4)	Name, Number, Name
(if (*#{greater} 19 12*) 3 4)	Primitive
(if *#t* 3 4)	Number
3	

Confusing

Once the condition has been evaluated, the then-form or else-form is immediately evaluated, depending on whether the condition is *true* or *false*.

Let's do a slightly more complicated example. Program 1–12 computes the monthly interest on a bank balance. If the balance is less than a minimum, the interest is 0.0. Figure 1–12 shows how Scheme evaluates (monthly 125).

1. [Initialization] Initially, the environment is initialized to contain only the built-in primitive procedures.
2. [The Number rule] A numeral's value is a number, the numeral interpreted in base 10.
3. [The Name rule] A name is evaluated by looking it up in the environment.
4. [The Lambda rule] The value of a lambda form is a procedure, which is the same as the lambda form, but written in **value font**.
5. [The Application rule] An application is evaluated by evaluating each of its elements, and then using the Primitive rule, if a primitive is applied, or the Procedure rule for a procedure.
6. [The Primitive rule] A primitive is applied by performing the machine-language instructions specified for the primitive, given the arguments supplied.
7. [The Procedure rule] A procedure application is evaluated in two steps:
   a. Replace, in the body of the procedure, each of the parameters by the corresponding arguments.
   b. Replace the entire application by the body.
8. [The Definition rule] A form whose first element is the word `define` is handled specially. The second argument is evaluated in the normal way, but the first argument, which must be a name, is not evaluated at all. The name and value are added to the environment.
9. [The If rule] A form whose first element is the word `if` is handled specially. Such a form must have three subforms: a *condition*, a *then-form*, and an *else-form*. The condition is evaluated. The `if` form's value will be that of the then-form or the else-form, depending upon whether the condition's value was *true* or *false*, respectively. By *false* we mean \#f; by *true* we mean anything else.
10. [The And rule] An and form is evaluated by evaluating each argument in turn. If all of the arguments evaluate to true, the form has the value of the last argument. Otherwise, the value is **#f**.
11. [The Or rule] An or form is evaluated by evaluating each argument in turn. The value of the first true (not **#f**) argument is the value of the or form. If no argument evaluates to true, the form has the value **#f**.

conditional?

Program 1-11   The Rules, Version 2

☞ **Exercise 1-35**

Suppose that you evaluate the following:

```
(define what 33)
(define my-procedure (lambda (x) (+ what x)))
(my-procedure 2)
```

Show the sequence of evaluations performed. ❏

```
(define minimum-balance 100)
(define interest-rate 0.03)
(define monthly
  (lambda (bal)
    (if (> bal minimum-balance)
        (/ (* interest-rate bal) 12.0)
        0.0)))
```

Program 1-12   Calculating monthly interest

(monthly 125)	𝔄pplication
(monthly 125)	𝔑ame,𝔑umber
((lambda (bal) ....) 125)	𝔓rocedure
(if (> **125** minimum-balance) ...)	𝔍f
(if (> **125** minimum-balance) ...)	𝔄pplication
(if (> **125** minimum-balance) ...)	𝔑ame,𝔑ame
(if (**#{greater}** 125 100) ...)	𝔓rimitive
(if **#t** (/ (* interest-rate **125**) 12.0) 0.0)	𝔄pplication
(... (/ (* interest-rate **125**) 12.0) ...)	𝔑ame
(**#{divide}** (* interest-rate **125**) 12.0)	𝔄pplication
(**#{divide}** (* interest-rate **125**) 12.0)	𝔑ame,𝔑ame
(**#{divide}** (**#{times}** **0.03 125**) 12.0)	𝔓rimitive
(**#{divide}** **3.75** 12.0)	𝔑umber
(**#{divide}** **3.75 12.0**)	𝔓rimitive
0.3125	

Figure 1-12   Scheme evaluation of (monthly 125)

In an if form only one of the then-form or the else-form is evaluated. The form

```
(if (< 5 7) 8 (/ 7 0))
```

evaluates to **8**, even though evaluating the else-form would result in an error.

Practical Note

An if form doesn't need to have the *else-form*. If there is no *else-form* and the value of the condition is #f, the value of the if form is unspecified, which will cause disastrous results when it is used as a value. The form (+ 3 (if (< 4 5) 7)) has the value **10**, but (+ 3 (if (> 4 5) 7)) has no value, and will generate an error, Argument not a number, in most Scheme systems.

There are uses for "elseless" ifs—which we will study in Chapter 3—for forms such as this, but for now they are best avoided.

Case Study: Clock Calculations

Let's consider how to calculate the angle between the hands of a clock, given the time of day. The input will be the time of day, in hours, minutes, and seconds. Our output will be the angle between the minute and hour hands in degrees. So our procedure should look like this:

```
(lambda (hours minutes seconds) ...)
```

The code to compute the angle is a series of steps:

1. Find the position of the hour hand.
2. Find the position of the minute hand.
3. Compute the difference.

Each hour, the hour hand moves 30 degrees. So the expression for the hour hand is (* hour 30), where 30 degrees represents one o'clock. But what about twelve o'clock? Our expression gives us 360 degrees, but we'd really like to have 0 degrees for twelve o'clock. So we'll use (if (= hour 12) 0 (* hour 30)).

Each minute, the minute hand moves 6 degrees. So the expression for the minute hand is (* minute 6). The result is the difference between the two angles: (- (if (= hour 12) 0 (* hour 30)) (* minute 6)). This expresses the number of degrees the minute hand must rotate clockwise to get to the hour hand.

This won't always work. We've made an assumption here that usually isn't true—that the minute and hour hands move in discrete jumps every minute or hour. Some clocks do this, but on most clocks, the minute and hour hands seem to move continuously even though the second hand may jump. This means the expression for the location of the minute hand should include the seconds and the expression for the hour hand should include the minutes as well as the seconds.

Our new expression for the hour hand is

```
(+ (+ (* (if (= hour 12) 0 hour) 30)
      (* 0.5 minute))
   (* seconds (/ 0.5 60)))
```

How did we get this expression? On a twelve-hour clock, the hour hand moves 30 degrees per hour, and thus 2 degrees per minute, or 1 degree each 30 seconds.

Our new expression for the minute hand is

```
(+ (* minute 6) (* seconds 0.1))
```

since the minute hand moves 6 degrees in 60 seconds.

The full procedure appears in Program 1–13 (a).

We've filled in all of the details now. We've created two procedures, one for the jumping clock and one for the smoothly moving clock. We can put them together, first listing the description of the procedure and the assumptions that lead up to the implementation. Program 1–13 (b) shows a procedure that computes the angle in degrees between the hour and minute hands. It assumes that it is a 12-hour clock, that clock hands move clockwise, and that the clock has a minute hand.

The switch jump? is an extra parameter in our new clock procedure. Note our assumptions. Most clocks you see have only twelve hours, but military clocks have twenty-four hours, and most railway and airplane timetables are given in twenty-four hour times. The second assumption is unusual, but Grace Murray Hopper had an anticlockwise clock!

```
(define clock-distance
  (lambda (hour minute seconds)
    (-
      (+
        (+
          (* (if (= hour 12) 0 hour) 30)
          (* 0.5 minute))
        (* seconds (/ 0.5 60)))
      (+ (* minute 6) (* seconds 0.1)))))
```

(a) Angle of the minute hand

```
(define clock-distance
  (lambda (hour minute seconds jump?)
    (if jump?
      (-
        (* (if (= hour 12) 0 hour) 30)
        (* minute 6))
      (-
        (+
          (+
            (* (if (= hour 12) 0 hour) 30)
            (* 0.5 minute))
          (* seconds (/ 0.5 60)))
        (+ (* minute 6) (* seconds 0.1))))))
```

(b) Angle between hour and minute hand

Program 1-13   Two versions of `clock-distance`

Let's examine what we've done here. We began with a brief problem statement, to find the angle between the hands of a clock. We proceeded to write out a series of possible programs that gradually became more general and gave more complete answers to the problem. We were teasing out, step by step, the underlying structure of the problem. When we were done with this process, we had the original problem and a set of assumptions that describe how various details omitted from the original problem could affect the solution. The result was a **specification** for a program: a clear statement of the inputs, outputs, assumptions and the relation between the inputs and outputs. If the specification is clear enough, what remains is to specify the data and operations that compute the desired output. Getting the specification right is a large part of the problem. Of course, much of the creativity and play come in designing the data structures and writing the code, but there is enormous creativity in designing the specification. Most problems are even more nebulous than the simple one we've given here, and defining the problem is itself a challenge!

☞ **Exercise 1-36**

Many modern clocks violate our assumptions. Describe how they do this. ❏

Summary

This chapter lays the foundation for understanding computing. We began by intro-ducing you to algorithms, data, and computers. We continued by starting to learn the language Scheme, which allows us to express algorithms for evaluation on our computer. Scheme uses a notation similar to function notation in mathematics, so we looked at the two ways of writing down formulas. Scheme has simple syntax that we used first to write forms that express arithmetic calculations. We learned how to name the results of computations, so that they could be used in other com-putations. Then we began our introduction to the deep idea of writing a procedure, a form that expresses a general way of computing an output from a set of inputs. We increased our power of expression by using if forms to make decisions based upon the value of conditions.

Underlying all this is a model of how Scheme operates to transform the Scheme forms we write into values. The Rules is an algorithm, expressed in English, for taking forms in Scheme and, step by step, replacing individual pieces of the forms with simpler forms. Eventually, a form is reduced to applications of primitives and finally to simple values. The Rules is a tool for understanding how to write Scheme forms as well as a way of seeing how the forms produce values.

Further Readings

An interesting book to read is *The Analytical Engine* by Rick Decker and Stuart Hirshfield—it combines a broad introduction to tools in computing with hands-on experience.

A number of books have been published on the history of computers. *The Origins of Digital Computers*, edited by Brian Randell, reprints some of the classic papers in the field. *The Computer from Pascal to von Neumann*, by H. Goldstine, is also a valuable source. For a biography of Alan Turing, see *Alan Turing: The Enigma*, by Andrew Hodges.

The Little Lisper, by Dan Friedman and M. Felleisen, is a rich, enjoyable dis-cussion of the basics of Scheme programming and λ-calculus, the mathematics of lambda forms. Another Scheme book is Michael Eisenberg's *Programming in Scheme*. Another book—a classic in the field—is H. Abelson and G. Sussman's *Structure and Interpretation of Computer Programs*.

The Internet provides a large number of resources. Many schools provide In-ternet access; if your school does not provide Internet access, you may have a FreeNet or a commercial Internet access point in your city. The software in this book is available at ftp.cs.ubc, in /pub/local/schematics. The "Scheme repository", at ftp.cs.indiana.edu, in /pub/scheme-repository, provides Scheme systems, exam-ples, and utilities.

One of the most fruitful sources of information is the so-called Jargon File, available on the Internet (prep.ai.mit.edu, in pub/gnu/jarg300.txt.gz), and pub-lished as *The New Hacker's Dictionary*, edited by Eric S. Raymond.

The risks of computing (and other technology) are discussed in an Internet mailing list, Risks. If you have Usenet news access, you can access this mailing list by reading comp.risks.

comp.lang.scheme is a Usenet newsgroup dedicated to Scheme. Participants range from Scheme beginners to the gurus of the Scheme community.

Key Words

Here are the *key words* introduced in this chapter. Make sure you understand what each one means.

abstraction	definition	numeral
algorithm	environment	output
application	evaluate	parameter
argument	evaluator	predicate
assembly language	feasible	primitive
automaton	finite	procedure
binding	form	program
bound	hardware	prompt
body	helper	pseudocode
bug	`if` form	semantics
central processing unit	implementation	software
client	input	special form
computation	interactive	specification
conditional	interface	substitution
correctness	`lambda` form	syntax
cybernetic device	language	test
data	machine language	type
debug	mathematical function	value
decomposition	memory	

Scheme Features Introduced in This Chapter

Primitive Procedures

`+`	`-`	`*`	`/`
`<`	`>`	`=`	`<=`
`>=`	`add1`	`not`	`sqrt`
`sub1`	`zero?`		

Special Forms

`and`	`define`	`if`	`lambda`
`or`			

Cumulative List of Data Types

number, boolean, procedure

Problems

1. A medical researcher has conducted trials of a new drug. A double blind test was administered, in which the subjects were divided into two groups. One received the drug, and the other received a placebo (an inert substitute). Neither the subjects nor the experimenters knew which group a subject was in. Before and after administering the drug, the experimenters measured the subject's blood pressure. The experimenters were looking for a significant change in blood pressure, where *significant* was defined as 10% or more (they don't care about direction; all they want to see is whether or not this drug causes a change

in blood pressure). We need a program to analyze the data by determining the percentage of each group that experienced a significant blood-pressure change.
   a. Identify the information that we need from each subject.
   b. How should the results be displayed?
   c. Write an algorithm (maybe with some subalgorithms) for doing this processing.

2. Joel User types the following form into his Scheme system: (+ (< 2 3) (< 5 6)). What happens? Why?

3. The government has set new fines for speeding, as follows:
   - If the motorist was traveling less than 40% above the speed limit, the basic fine is $50.
   - If the motorist was traveling 40% above the speed limit or more, the basic fine is $100.

   The actual fine is computed as the square of the number of speeding tickets in the past three years times the basic fine. Thus, a motorist traveling 70 km/hour in a 50 km/hour zone, with three prior speeding tickets, will pay $100 * 3^2 = $900. (The hope is that motorists will stop speeding or, if not, the government's financial problems will be solved forever!)

   Write a Scheme procedure (maybe with helpers) that computes the actual fine, given the appropriate data.

4. In the metric system, a car's gasoline-consumption rate is called its *metrage*, and is measured by computing the number of litres of gasoline required to drive 100 km. Many people still measure gasoline consumption in miles per gallon, which is even more confusing, since there are two kinds of gallons. The *imperial gallon* is equivalent to 4.56 litres, and the U.S. gallon is equivalent to 3.79 litres. Write a *single* procedure that can take as arguments the mileage, number of gallons used, and the number of gallons per litre, and compute the metrage. One kilometre is equal to 0.62 miles.

5. Scheme's trigonometric functions, sin, cos, and so on, take their arguments in radians, where 1 radian = $180/\pi$ degrees. Write a procedure to compute the secant of an argument given in degrees, where $\sec x = 1/\cos x$, using a helper procedure. (Hint: Your helper should be useful in writing other related trigonometric functions.)

6. In the game of craps, the player throws two dice. A player who throws "snake eyes", (2) has "crapped out". Write a procedure snake? that accepts two numbers representing the die values and returns #t if the player has thrown snake eyes, and #f otherwise.

Self-Assessment

➤   Answers to Self-Assessment problems are given in Appendix A.

1. A library sends out overdue notices for each book that is more than one week overdue.
   a. What data does the library need for this procedure?
   b. Give an algorithm (*not* Scheme code) for solving this problem.

2. A political scientist has conducted a survey in which she asked several thousand people about a number of controversial issues. Her questionnaire contained 25 questions, one for each issue, and asked for a response of 1 ("not interested at all") to 5 ("this issue is extremely important to me"). For confidentiality, no names appear on the questionnaire; identification numbers are used instead.

   The researcher has asked you to write a program that provides a list of all the subjects who are likely to be activists. She defines "likely to be an activist" as meaning that the person has answered 4 or 5 to 10 or more questions.

   Identify the data needed to solve this problem, and write an algorithm (*not* a Scheme program) for this task. Note that the researcher might change her definition of *activist*.

Accordingly, your algorithm should be structured so that it is easy to find what must be changed in your algorithm to satisfy her needs. *Hint:* Break the problem down into pieces, and write a separate algorithm for each part as well as a main algorithm for the whole task.

3. Susan got 86% in Computer Science, 78% in English, and 91% in Mathematics. Write a Scheme form that calculates her average grade.

4. The surface area of a cylinder of height *h* and diameter *d* is given by πdh. Write a procedure that accepts the height and radius of a cylinder and returns its surface area.

5. Evaluate, according to **The Rules**, the following:

```
( (lambda (x) (* 2 x))
    ( (lambda (y) (+ y 1))
      3))
```

6. Write a procedure that computes the cube of its argument: thus, (cube 3) ⇒ **27**, and (cube -2) ⇒ **-8**.

7. According to relativity theory, objects moving at speeds close to the speed of light, *c*, experience time more slowly. The factor of time as experienced by the observer to that experienced by a stationary observer is computed by the Lorentz formula

$$\sqrt{1 - v^2/c^2}$$

where *v* is the object's velocity and *c* is 299,800,000 metres per second. Write a Scheme procedure for computing the Lorentz formula.

8. Joel User has been assigned the job of writing a predicate that takes as argument a number representing a voltage from a piece of scientific equipment and returns #t if the number is "in range", and #f if the number is "out of range". The correct range is two intervals: greater than −5 and less than −3, and greater than 2 and less than or equal to 4. After several weeks(!) of effort, Joel produces the following procedure:

```
(define in-range?
  (lambda (x)
    (if (> x -3)
        (if (<= x 4)
            (if (> x 2)
                #t
                #f))
        (if (< x -5)
            #f
            #t))))
```

He rushes to show his solution to Ima Schemer, but Ima is not impressed. "This procedure could be written much more readably if only you didn't use if". Show the procedure the way Ima might have written it.

Programming Problems

1. The *geometric mean* of two numbers *a* and *b* is defined as $\sqrt{ab}$. The familiar *average*, or *arithmetic mean*, is defined as $(a + b)/2$. Write a procedure that computes the difference between the arithmetic mean and the geometric mean of two values.

2. In the game of blackjack, a player is dealt cards, and the goal is to get as high a score as possible without going over 21. Aces count as either 1 or 11, at the player's choice; kings, queens, and jacks count as 10. The player can choose to be dealt another card ("hit me"), or to "stand". One simple strategy is to stand if the current score is 16 or more, and to ask for another card otherwise.

    Write a procedure (with some helpers) that is given the player's current score and the value of the next card to be played. The procedure should decide whether to stand or ask for another card. It should return the new score (taking due account of aces). Needless to say, it would be cheating to look at the next card's face value until *after* determining whether to stand.

Chapter 2

Recursion

Overview

In Chapter 1, we saw most of the basic features needed to build Scheme programs. We have not seen any particularly useful programs, though, because we need to see how the operations in a program can be repeated many times. A technique known as *recursion*—calling a procedure from its own body—lets us write compact procedures that repeat a task as many times as necessary. To understand recursion, we will need to develop a more compact way than 𝕿𝖍𝖊 𝕽𝖚𝖑𝖊𝖘 of explaining how forms are evaluated. The Droid Model, which we'll study first, does exactly this.

Once we have the basic idea of recursion, we will use it for various tasks, such as approximating the roots of mathematical functions, playing a lunar-landing game, and calculating the number of ways of getting a flush in poker. Whereas the procedures in Chapter 1 took only a few milliseconds of computer time, some of the procedures we'll look at in this chapter can take minutes, hours, or years to run. Efficiency is therefore an important issue. We'll show a technique known as *big-oh notation* for comparing the relative execution time of procedures based on different algorithms. Finally, we'll look at how you can test and debug a recursive procedure.

Even the longest journey begins with a single step.   — Chinese proverb

So far we have looked at Scheme forms that do simple calculations. if forms added the capability of making decisions. The programs we have written so far take only milliseconds to evaluate. Yet these programs took time and effort to write. As we've seen it, Scheme is no more than a calculator with a very elaborate interface. The programs we've written may be faster than doing the calculation by hand, but it's clear that we're not using the full power of a machine that can perform millions of operations per second. Any program in Chapter 1 takes thousands of times longer to write than to evaluate!

Where computers excel is at being able to repeat operations over and over again. For example, a computer analyzing weather data will have data representing temperature, humidity, and other variables, all measured at a large number of locations. Meteorologists have developed models of weather changes. These models operate by examining the current data and computing new values according to the model. The calculations themselves are very simple, but we must apply these calculations to millions of points. It is not feasible to do these calculations by hand. Even the fastest computer, capable of hundreds of millions of operations per second, takes hours to produce a weather forecast. The efficiency of the program becomes an issue. There's no point in an accurate 24-hour forecast that took 28 hours to calculate!

To get full use of a computer, we need a way to specify that operations are to be repeated many times. It might take us a long time to specify the particular computation to be performed, but the first million repetitions will justify our having taken that time. The term **loop** is often used for a programming structure that specifies repetition, because early techniques for diagraming programs made a loop structure look like a loop of string.

Conventional programming languages such as Pascal or C++ have evolved a number of ways to specify repetition. The Pascal or Modula keywords FOR, WHILE, and REPEAT specify repetition. Other languages have similar looping keywords. On the other hand, Scheme uses no keywords to specify that operations be repeated. Instead, we use procedures.

Once we know how to write loops in Scheme, we will be able to use procedures to solve more complex problems that involve exploring many possible solutions.

We won't need to use a new element of the syntax of Scheme, but we will use what we know in a different way. In this sense, this chapter is as much about problem solving as it is about a computer language. We will solve a wide range of problems here.

Computer science gives us the analytical tools to understand how our algorithms behave with changing inputs. We're interested in how much time and space an algorithm takes, depending on the size of the input. Such tools let us decide which algorithm is best for solving a particular problem.

Finally we'll get some more concrete experience in testing and debugging a procedure. A small error in a procedure that is repeated many times can easily produce results that are complete nonsense. Therefore, we need some effective tools for ensuring that our code is correct.

2.1   Recursive Procedures

> *GLENDOWER: I can call spirits from the vasty deep.*
> *HOTSPUR: Why, so can I, or so can any man;*
> *But will they come when you do call for them?*
>
> — William Shakespeare, *Henry IV, Part 1*

Many programming languages have been designed by adding many different features together. Scheme is based on one overriding idea—the supremacy of procedures. Guy Steele, Scheme's original designer, wrote a series of papers in which he systematically showed how each feature of even complex programming languages is in reality just a special use of procedures.[1] Scheme has evolved since its original design, but at each step the designers of the language have been careful to define each new feature in terms of the existing ones. Therefore, if we understand procedures, we will understand how our computer language works.

Long before Steele's work, it was known that repetition is equivalent to a particular pattern of procedure usage, in which a procedure is applied in its own body. Even for repetition, we will use procedures.

Given the importance of procedures, it's a shame that using procedures with 𝕿𝖍𝖊 𝕽𝖚𝖑𝖊𝖘 is so clumsy. Line after line of 𝕬𝖕𝖕𝖑𝖎𝖈𝖆𝖙𝖎𝖔𝖓, 𝕹𝖚𝖒𝖇𝖊𝖗, 𝕻𝖗𝖔𝖈𝖊𝖉𝖚𝖗𝖊, and so on must be written for each procedure call. 𝕿𝖍𝖊 𝕽𝖚𝖑𝖊𝖘 is a valuable way of learning how to evaluate Scheme forms. Now that we understand it, we need a shorthand notation. In this section, we will create a new model for evaluating Scheme forms. This "Droid Model" doesn't replace 𝕿𝖍𝖊 𝕽𝖚𝖑𝖊𝖘; it merely makes it easier to understand the way procedures are called.

Then we turn to the central idea of the chapter—how to understand procedures that call themselves. We'll use such procedures to implement repetition in Scheme. We will see how we can define procedures that duplicate Scheme's arithmetic primitives, in terms of very simple operations: adding or subtracting one, or multiplying or dividing by two. Finally, we will use our new power in Scheme to implement a lunar lander, a procedure that calculates whether a lunar vehicle can land on the moon.

---

[1] Many of Steele's examples were already known. His achievement was in organizing and communicating them. He also showed how to build an efficient Scheme evaluator.

2.1.1   The Droid Model

Consider the following procedures.

```
(define foo
  (lambda (x)
    (- (bar (add1 x)) 5)))
(define bar
  (lambda (y)
    (* y 2)))
```

When Scheme evaluates (foo 3), it must also evaluate (bar 4), which in turn evaluates to 8. Think of procedure foo as saying, "OK, I'll compute $x + 1$ and then send that result on to bar." In turn, bar says, "I'll take my argument, multiply it by 2, and return the result."

Practical Note

Most of the time, programmers want to name a procedure in a way that describes the procedure's task. Sometimes, though, a programmer will write a procedure not to do a task, but to illustrate a programming point, as we've done above to show how procedures call each other. Nobody would want to confuse procedures such as this with the real thing!

Therefore, a custom has grown of giving such procedures nonsense names, such as foo, bar, baz, mumble, glorp, and so on. The Jargon File has a colorful list of the most common such names (see the entry for foo).

What does it mean to apply a procedure? The Rules say to replace the parameters by the arguments in the body, and then evaluate the body, but as we've seen, the individual steps in this process are tedious. For us, procedures are the fundamental "stuff" of computing. If we must use The Rules each time we see a procedure application, and therefore go through a tedious sequence of substitutions and evaluations, we will get lost. What we need is a way of working with procedures without having to concentrate upon every step.

The Rules isn't necessarily the only model we can devise for Scheme. We can look at procedures in quite a different way, using a new model that we call the **Droid Model**.[2] In our model, each time a procedure is applied, a **droid** is created to evaluate the application. Two droids are depicted in Figure 2-1: the top holds the name of the procedure, the parameters and the arguments appear in the body, and the arrow points to the droid that called the droid.

The first step a droid carries out is to make a table showing the relationship between the parameters and the arguments. Then the droid evaluates the body using The Rules, as well as the table of arguments where necessary. The last event in a droid's life is to give back the answer to whoever requested it, which is why the droid must also know what to do after it has finished.

---

[2] The word *droid* appears to have originated in George Lucas' *Star Wars* films, as a shorter version of *android*, which means a machine in the shape of a human.

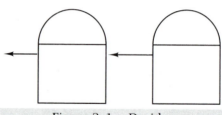

Figure 2-1   Droids

For example, when Scheme evaluates (foo 3), it uses the 𝒩ame rule to find that foo is bound to *(lambda (x) (- (bar (add1 x)) 5))*. Since it's about to apply this procedure to the argument *3* (again evaluated, this time using the 𝒩umber rule), a droid is created that knows x is bound to *3*. In turn, this eventually applies add1 to 3. (Is a droid created when we apply a primitive such as add1? Yes, but it's not worth drawing. The droid created when Scheme applies a primitive immediately does its job and returns its result.) A droid is now created to evaluate the application of bar, which returns *8*, and therefore the droid returns *3* as the final result.

Often we term the process of applying a procedure **calling** the procedure. You might call a person by name and get the person to do something for you. So instead of saying "the application of bar", we could say the "call of bar", or "calling the procedure bar". Another word often used to say "call a procedure" is *invoke* a procedure; calling a procedure is termed an **invocation**. *Call* is a specific word with a technical meaning. In the form (+ 2 x), we don't speak of calling x, although we do call +, or, to be precise, the primitive named +. The only things we can call are procedures and primitives.

Note how important it is that droids remember who asked them to do the job. The arrow between droids in the **droid diagram** in Figure 2-2 shows the "who called me" information.

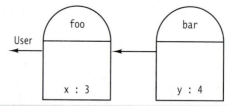

Figure 2-2   Droids for foo and bar

It isn't sufficient for a droid simply to compute an answer; it must also communicate that answer to the droid that asked for the answer. The bar droid returns the value *8* along the arrow to the foo droid. Any computation, no matter how complex, consists of a large number of droids, each of which is working on a particular part. At any given time, only one droid is doing any work.[3] All of the other droids are dormant, waiting for answers to be returned to them.

---

[3] In Scheme, anyway. Researchers have developed Schemelike languages in which many droids can be working at once. This turns out to be a good way of using multiprocessor computer systems.

The Droid Model isn't in conflict with a straight application of 𝕿𝖍𝖊 𝕽𝖚𝖑𝖊𝖘. Every form we've seen will give the same answer, no matter whether we use droids or rules. It's just a matter of convenience to use droids. One of the major advantages of the Droid Model is that we don't have to write down the whole computation at each step. If we were just using 𝕿𝖍𝖊 𝕽𝖚𝖑𝖊𝖘, we would have to write down complex lambda-expressions and applications for each step. With droids, we don't have to copy any code; we only need to draw droids for each application. We will still use 𝕿𝖍𝖊 𝕽𝖚𝖑𝖊𝖘 for such things as numbers, names, and special forms such as if.

Figure 2-3 shows the result of evaluating (foo 3) by using 𝕿𝖍𝖊 𝕽𝖚𝖑𝖊𝖘.

```
(foo 3)                                          Application, Name, Number
((lambda (x) (- (bar (add1 x)) 5)) 3)            Procedure
(- (bar (add1 3)) 5)                             Application, Name
(#{minus} (bar (add1 3)) 5)                      Application, Name
(#{minus} ((lambda (y) (* y 2)) (add1 3)) 5)     Application, Name
(#{minus} ((lambda (y) (* y 2)) (#{add1} 3)) 5)  Primitive
(#{minus} ((lambda (y) (* y 2)) 4) 5)            Procedure
(#{minus} (* 4 2) 5)                             Application, Name, Number
(#{minus} (#{times} 4 2) 5)                      Primitive
(#{minus} 8 5)                                   Primitive
3
```

We haven't indented the rules on the right-hand side for space reasons.

Figure 2-3   Evaluating (foo 3) with 𝕿𝖍𝖊 𝕽𝖚𝖑𝖊𝖘

This is the last use of 𝕿𝖍𝖊 𝕽𝖚𝖑𝖊𝖘 in this book. It has served its purpose. From now on, we can use the Droid Model to show how procedures are called and applied, without having to go through a detailed explanation of each step.

We can also stop making so much fuss about the difference between forms and values. We've been showing values *like this*, but by now you should be able to tell the difference between the two without needing the "value font". From now on, we'll show both forms and values like this.

2.1.2   Repetition

Now, what about repetition? Suppose we want to write a procedure that computes the *factorial* function in mathematics. The factorial of a number n is written as $n!$, and computed according to the following rule:

$$n! = n \times (n-1) \times \ldots \times 1$$

The factorial function is particularly useful. For example, the number of arrangements of n distinct items is $n!$—there are n possible choices for the first position, $n-1$ choices for the second, and so on. $n!$ grows very quickly: $5! = 120$, $10! = 3,628,800$, and $20! = 2,432,902,008,176,640,000$.

Another way of writing the rule for factorial follows:

$$0! = 1$$

$$n! = n \times (n - 1)!$$

These rules say that we can follow a straightforward algorithm to compute factorial. If you want to compute 6!, you can write that as 6! = 6 × 5! using the second rule. Now you can write 5! as 5 × 4! and so forth, down to 1! = 1 × 0!. The whole process stops at the next step, because we find that 0! = 1, using the first rule. The entire expression is then:

$$6! = 6 \times 5 \times 4 \times 3 \times 2 \times 1 \times 1$$

The second rule simplifies the problem, by reducing the problem size by one. For factorial, that means converting 6! to a multiplication of 6 and 5!. 5! is simpler since it involves only five multiplications, while 6! involves six. Multiplication is a primitive, so it's as simple as we can get. The first rule stops the whole process—it says that you needn't do any further work for 0!. We know that answer.

If we switch off our minds and write the rules for factorial in Scheme, we get

```
(define factorial
  (lambda (n)
    (if (= n 0)
        1
        (* n (factorial (sub1 n))))))
```

What seems surprising is that this procedure works! If you evaluate (factorial 6), you will get 720 (= 6 × 5 × 4 × 3 × 2 × 1). But how can factorial work? How is it possible that we can have a procedure call itself? Isn't this simply circular reasoning?[4]

The critical point to notice is that there's a way out. If n equals 0, then factorial returns the value 1 without going through the whole process again. Only if n is nonzero does factorial try to do the multiplication.

Let's try computing (factorial 3) by informally replacing each (factorial n) expression with the corresponding body of factorial. We've omitted the if forms because the test condition is almost always false:

```
(factorial 3)
⇒   (* 3 (factorial 2))
⇒   (* 3 (* 2 (factorial 1)))
⇒   (* 3 (* 2 (* 1 (factorial 0))))
⇒   (* 3 (* 2 (* 1 1)))
⇒   6
```

Similarly, if we compute (factorial 1000), we end up evaluating

```
(* 1000 (* 999 (* 998 ... (* 2 (* 1 1))...)))
```

Even though our procedure is only five lines long, it has the potential of specifying an enormous computation, depending upon the value of n we choose.

We can certainly evaluate forms such as (factorial 3) with The Rules, even though it is tedious. The Droid Model makes things much easier. Figure 2-4 shows what happens by the time we've hired four droids.

---

[4] The computer scientist Donald Knuth once wrote a book in which the index contained the entries "Circular Definition, *see* Definition, Circular," and "Definition, Circular, *see* Circular Definition."

There are several interesting aspects of this diagram. We name each of the droids by the order in which they were created; *factorial$_i$* is the name we use for the ith droid, counting from 0. One procedure has created four droids, and will end up creating 1001 droids to compute (factorial 1000). Each droid uses its own copy of n. The other droids not shown will lie to the right, on the arrow outside the picture. The value for (factorial 996) will be returned along that arrow. We've not shown the values returned along the arrows for two reasons. First, this is a snapshot while the droids are being created, and second, the values are enormous numbers with about two thousand decimal digits each!

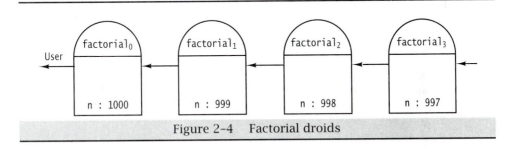

Figure 2-4   Factorial droids

☞ **Exercise 2-1**

Use 𝒯𝒽𝑒 𝑅𝑢𝑙𝑒𝑠 to evaluate (factorial 3). Show each step. Compare this with the evaluation in Figure 2-4. ❏

☞ **Exercise 2-2**

Suppose we've defined

```
(define count
  (lambda (n)
    (if (<= n 0)
      0
      (+ 2 (count (- n 3))))))
```

and we now evaluate (count 7). Draw a droid diagram for this computation. ❏

Suppose we want to compute z^n (i.e., to raise z to the nth power). We'll assume n is a positive integer. A little thought will convince you that if

$$z^n = \overbrace{z \times z \times \cdots \times z}^{n \text{ times}}$$

then another way we could write it is

$$z^n = z \times z^{n-1}$$

But what if $n = 0$? Well, $z^0 = 1$, since $z^n \times z^{-n} = 1$, and $z^n \times z^{-n} = z^0$. Putting this together, we can define the procedure in Program 2-1.

The method we've been looking at is called **recursion**. What we're doing is calling the procedure again, but with a simpler value. Eventually, we get to a value

```
(define power
  (lambda (x n)
    (if (= n 0)
      1
      (* x (power x (sub1 n))))))
```

Program 2-1   Calculating powers

for which we know the answer. At this point we can give the known answer. For power, the complete result is a long multiplication built up from the case at which we stop (when $n = 0$) combined with the other multiplications from the previous calls to power.

The Droid Model is a particularly good way of thinking about recursion. Notice that we can have many droids using the same procedure in their work. Each droid uses its own arguments; therefore, even though humans might get confused about "the value of n", droids won't. In Figure 2-4, it's clear that each droid knows its own value of n, and doesn't care what another droid might think n is.

So how do you design a recursive procedure? Look again at the formula for computing factorials. This formula tells us two things:

- There is one number whose factorial is known ($0! = 1$).
- If you know $(n - 1)!$, you can compute $n!$: $n! = n \times (n - 1)!$.

Now look at the procedure we wrote:

```
(define factorial
  (lambda (n)
    (if (= n 0)
      1
      (* n (factorial (sub1 n))))))
```

If we don't know the factorial immediately, we then break the problem into two simpler ones: compute $(n - 1)!$, and multiply the result by n.

For the moment, all recursive procedures will have the framework we used in both factorial and power, in which the procedure body itself consists of an if form. The if divides the calculation into a **base case**, for which we know the answer, and a **recursion step**, in which we apply the procedure to a somewhat simpler problem. For example, notice that in both factorial and power, the recursion step uses (sub1 n), which gets us closer to the case when n is zero.

The goal of any recursive procedure is to get us to the base case; each recursion step should get us a bit closer to the base case. In the factorial example, our goal is to get n equal to 0. If n is greater than zero, we can break the computation down into two pieces: first compute (factorial (sub1 n)), and then multiply that answer by n.

What if we tried factorial with n equal to a negative number? In this case, the recursion step gets us *farther away* from the base case. This is known as an **infinite recursion** or an **infinite loop**, and is a programming error that has bedeviled programmers since the dawn of computers. Since the computation never stops, something external, such as the user telling the evaluator to stop, has to intervene.

Before we move on to more complex examples, let's make sure we understand the basic idea of recursion. What if we wish to compute the sum of the first n squares, that is, the sum of i^2 for i from 1 to n? Most languages have an explicit construct to do such a repetition, but with Scheme we can just write a recursive procedure. You write some code to compute the ith square and add it to a sum. When we write this procedure, we'll count down from the original n, until n reaches 1, adding the square of the current value to the sum of squares up to n-1. sumsquares is shown in Program 2-2.

```scheme
(define sumsquares
  (lambda (n)
    (if (= n 1)
        1
        (+ (* n n) (sumsquares (sub1 n))))))
```

Program 2-2   Procedure to sum squares

Again, we have a procedure that is divided into a base case (the sum of the squares up to 1 is 1), and a recursion case (the sum of squares up to n is $n^2 +$ the sum of squares up to $n - 1$). The recursion step uses a simpler value of n, one closer to the base case.

☞ **Exercise 2-3**

Use the Droid Model to evaluate (power 7 3). You don't have to show all the steps. ❏

☞ **Exercise 2-4**

Pretend the "multiply" primitive * is "broken" on your Scheme evaluator (i.e., it calculates the wrong answer). Everybody knows that multiplying $a \times b$ is just repeated addition, so long as b is an integer

$$a \times b = \overbrace{a + a + \cdots + a}^{b \text{ times}}$$

Write a procedure, (mult% a b), that calculates $a \times b$. Hint: The framework is just like power. When we write a procedure that replaces a Scheme procedure foo, we will use a convention that the name of the replacement will be foo%. We use the name mult% for our version of *, the multiply primitive. *% is too hard to read. ❏

In Exercise 2-4, we asked you to imagine that the * primitive was broken, and to write your own procedure using just addition and subtraction. But what if these latter primitives are also broken?

In real programs, additions and subtractions are often by 1. However, if + is broken, we might be able to manufacture a new addition procedure add% using only the simpler primitives add1 and sub1.

The names add% and mult% are significant. Often we will want to show how a Scheme primitive works. The best way to do this is to write our own version (our versions may sometimes not be as general or flexible as the Scheme primitives, but will show you the basic idea). To avoid confusion, we give our procedure a different name by ending the name with a percent sign, %. You probably won't want to call our procedure (Scheme primitives are often faster and more flexible), but you will want to study it to see how it works.

A bit of algebra shows us the way. There are two cases:

- $a + b = (a + 1) + (b - 1)$, provided that $b > 0$.
- $a + 0 = a$.

We now have the two cases we need for a recursive procedure:

- [Base case] (add% a 0) = a.
- [Recursion step] (add% a b) = (add% (add1 a) (sub1 b)), provided $b > 0$.

The translation into Scheme is fairly straightforward (Program 2-3). If we try it, we find that (add% 3 5) $\Rightarrow$ 8.

```
(define add%
  (lambda (a b)
    (if (= b 0)
      a
      (add% (add1 a) (sub1 b)))))
```
Program 2-3   Addition by repeatedly adding 1

Most Scheme systems have ways of allowing you to ask for a particular procedure to be **traced** and to stop tracing a procedure. In many Scheme systems, we can trace add% by evaluating the special form (trace add%), and turn off the tracing of add% by evaluating (untrace add%). trace doesn't do anything immediately, but each time thereafter that Scheme evaluates a form that uses add%, a message is written to the screen. The output of evaluating (add% 3 5) appears in Figure 2-5.

```
call add%: 3 5
| call add%: 4 4
| | call add%: 5 3
| | | call add%: 6 2
| | | | call add%: 7 1
| | | | | call add%: 8 0
| | | | | return from add%: 8
| | | | return from add%: 8
| | | return from add%: 8
| | return from add%: 8
| return from add%: 8
return from add%: 8
```
Figure 2-5   Tracing (add% 3 5)

The trace output shows the arguments each time we call the procedure add%. The last line shows the value returned by the call. The indentation each time shows that a recursive call has been made. The vertical lines connect the call with the corresponding return. (This trace output resembles the output of our Scheme system. Your system might produce slightly different output; check your manual.)

Each application of add% results in another one, until eventually we reach (add% 8 0), the base case. At that point, add% returns the value of a.

Unfortunately, add% has a serious bug. While a can be any number, b must be a positive integer, or add% won't stop. Exercise 2-7 asks you to investigate this bug.

Any version of + we might write can be made as general as the Scheme + primitive. It will be a lot of work, because + handles many different kinds of numbers. add% will be slow compared to + because computers have machine instructions that add integers at much higher speeds than repeated addition by 1.

☞ **Exercise 2-5**

Compare the trace for (add% 3 5) with what you'd get if you had followed 𝔗𝔥𝔢 𝔎𝔲𝔩𝔢𝔰. ❑

☞ **Exercise 2-6**

By using traces, show why (add% 1 2.5) and (add% 1 -1) won't stop. ❑

☞ **Exercise 2-7**

Write a procedure (add-negative a b) that uses only add1 and sub1 to add the integers a and b, assuming b is negative. Then write a non-recursive procedure add-integer that uses add% and add-negative to add any pair of integers together. In hindsight, it would have been better to have used the name add-positive instead of add%. ❑

☞ **Exercise 2-8**

Write a procedure count-even that counts the number of even digits in the decimal representation of a positive number. You can use two new Scheme primitives: quotient and remainder, which perform division on integers, returning the result and the remainder, respectively, as an integer. ❑

2.1.3   An Example: A Lunar Lander

One of the first computer games that became popular was Lunar Lander, a program for landing a lunar exploration vehicle on the moon. You find yourself in a vehicle falling toward the moon. You know its velocity, its height, and the amount of fuel it has. The challenge is to use your fuel wisely to brake your fall toward the moon. You try to control the retro rockets and the left and right thrusters to land on the a nice smooth part of the moon, not on the tip of a lunar mountain.

Our lander will be simpler than the real Lunar Lander. The vehicle will only move up and down. The challenge will be to land on the moon without crashing. lander is a recursive procedure that requires the initial velocity, height, and fuel. We control the lander by setting the fuel-rate and the duration of the rocket firing. If we're correct, the lander arrives at height 0 with zero velocity. Because we can't get the velocity exactly, the game specifies a maximum safe landing velocity.

A description of the interface to the procedure lander follows. Programmers find that it's helpful to write down a description of what the procedure is to do before they decide how to implement the procedure.

Purpose: lander takes the specifications of the lunar lander and a duration of rocket firing, and determines whether the vehicle will crash, land, escape, or just complete its burn. The simulation computes the change in velocity and height for each second, and terminates when the time is out, the lander has landed, or has crashed.

Inputs: The first three inputs specify the lander; the last two control the vehicle. vel is the initial velocity, height the distance above the ground, fuel the total fuel, fuel-rate the fuel burn rate, and seconds the duration of the burn.

Output: lander outputs a numeric code signifying the status of the landing. For a safe landing, the output is 1, for an escape 2, for a crash 0, and if the lander runs out of fuel -1.

Assumptions: All inputs are numbers and must be physically meaningful.

Some of the important details of the lander are included as definitions:

```
(define mass 1000)           ;;; mass of the vehicle in kg
(define gravity 2.04)        ;;; m/s*s
(define escape -2400)        ;;; m/s
(define max-safe-velocity 5) ;;; m/s
```

We have used a new Scheme feature to annotate our definitions: **comments**. When Scheme encounters a ";" in its input, it ignores the rest of the input line. Scheme programmers use that part of the input file to write comments, text intended not for Scheme but for a human reader of the program.

Sample runs of the lander are shown in Figure 2-6 (a). Positive velocity is toward the surface of the moon, so the escape velocity is negative (meaning upwards). Most of the simplification occurs in the physics. In the real universe, the force of gravity changes with distance from the moon, and the mass of the vehicle changes as it burns fuel, but we keep them both constant. A trace of the last run appears in Figure 2-6 (b). (We omitted all the "return from" lines in the trace of lander.)

```
(lander 10 100 100000 2000 100)  ⇒   0
(lander 10 100 100000 2200 100)  ⇒   0
(lander 10 100 100000 2300 100)  ⇒   0
(lander 10 100 100000 2400 100)  ⇒   0
(lander 10 100 100000 2500 100)  ⇒   1
```

(a) : Several sample runs

```
> (lander 10 100 100000 2500 100)
call lander: 10 100 100000 2500 100
| call lander: 9.54 90 97500 2500 99
| | call lander: 9.08 80.46 95000 2500 98
| | | call lander: 8.62 71.38 92500 2500 97
| | | | call lander: 8.16 62.76 90000 2500 96
| | | | | call lander: 7.70 54.60 87500 2500 95
| | | | | | call lander: 7.24 46.90 85000 2500 94
...
1
```

(b) : Tracing the last run

Figure 2-6   Running the lunar lander

Program 2-4 shows lander. The velocity increases at the rate of gravity each second, while it decreases by the fuel-rate divided by the mass. Everything is simplified by the fact that we compute every second; the height decreases by the velocity—positive is toward the ground. We could make the computation more realistic by including the reduction of mass due to fuel burning.

lander is a complex procedure. Unfortunately, it is not easy to break it apart into smaller procedures. The complications come from all the different cases we must consider. Is the time 0? Has the lander reached the Moon's surface? Is the lander out of fuel? These conditions interact; for example, if the lander is at the Moon's surface with zero velocity, it doesn't matter if there's no fuel (until takeoff,

```
(define lander
  (lambda (vel height fuel fuel-rate seconds)
    (if (= seconds 0)
      (if (= height 0)
        1
        (if (< height 0)
          0
          (if (< vel escape) 2 -1)))
      (if (< height 0)
        (if (<  vel max-safe-velocity) 1 0)
        (if (<= fuel 0)
          -1
          (if (< vel escape)
            2
            (lander (- (+ vel gravity) (/ fuel-rate mass))
              (- height vel)
              (- fuel fuel-rate)
              fuel-rate
              (sub1 seconds))))))))))
```

Program 2-4　The lander procedure

at least!). The order that lander checks each condition must be carefully chosen so that an "Out of fuel" error isn't reported in this case.

Once you have learned input/output in Chapter 3, you can, if you want, build an interactive Lander program based on lander.

2.2 Designing Recursive Procedures

> *'Tis a lesson you should heed*
> *Try, try again.*
> *If at first you don't succeed,*
> *Try, try again.*
> — W. E. Hickson, "Try and Try Again"

In this section we develop solutions to further computing problems using the mechanisms of recursive procedures we have studied. We have chosen these problems to show a number of different ways that recursion can be used. The insights we get from attacking them lead to solutions for wide range of related problems.

2.2.1　Finding Roots

We are going to write a procedure that gives us $\sqrt[3]{a}$. To put it another way, we want to write a procedure that calculates $f(a) = y$ such that $a = y^3$. Scheme has a procedure to compute $\sqrt{a}$, called sqrt (everybody pronounces this "squirt"). Few languages have procedures to compute higher roots.

We need some way of approximating $\sqrt[3]{x}$. Let's pretend we already have a guess at the value. If we can find a formula that gives a better approximation, then

Numbers in Scheme

Scheme primitives such as + and / take any sort of number and produce appropriate answers. Thus, (+ 2 3) ⇒ 5 and (+ 2.0 3.0) ⇒ 5.0. The rules of Scheme arithmetic are quite complex. Fortunately, that complexity makes Scheme arithmetic work pretty much as we would expect. Scheme's number system was designed to avoid surprises. It's still worth knowing a bit about Scheme's different types of numbers.

Scheme has four basic types of numbers: complex (3+4.7i), floating-point (3.14), rational (3/4), and integer (-2871). Not all Scheme systems support all four kinds of numbers; some extremely limited ones may only support integers in the range from −65536 to 65535. As with all of Scheme's types, these numeric types have Boolean procedures that identify them. For example, the procedure integer? returns #t only for integers, similar to number?, boolean? and procedure?.

For the most part, you don't have to worry about what kind of number you have, provided the operation you want to perform makes sense for that kind of number. For example, since it's nonsense to ask whether 42.5 is an odd integer, in most Scheme systems, (odd? 42.5) ⇒ *error*. However, each kind of number has its own area of use.

Complex numbers are used in many kinds of scientific and engineering problems (e.g., electronic circuits). Generally, a problem will state specifically that it needs complex numbers.

Floating-point numbers, often called **floats**, are best used for *measuring* things; whenever you write a real number, you're expressing a degree of approximation. You can write a float with an optional power-of-10 exponent (e.g., 1.732E9), which means 1.732×10^9.

Rationals are best used to express an exact ratio. For example, if you want to say that a PC video screen has 800 dots horizontally and 600 vertically, you will say its "aspect ratio" is 3/4. If you described that value as 0.75, you're leaving open the possibility that the true value might be 0.7513.

Integers are used for counting. Some very limited Scheme systems will limit the range of integers, but all good ones will support integers with thousands of digits.

Scheme allows you to say that any number—real or not—is either exact or inexact. Normally, integers are exact, and floats are inexact. These facts are not normally important unless you're a numerical analyst, but are significant to the average programmer in one case. Suppose you want an integer that is the rounded-off value of a float. The primitive round gives you a rounded-off integer, but it's flagged as inexact. For many Scheme systems, this means that integer? will return #f in such a case. If you really care about making a number into an integer, use something like

```
(define round-to-integer
   (lambda (x) (inexact->exact (round x))))
```

The Scheme primitive inexact->exact takes an inexact argument and returns the argument value flagged as exact.

we can feed our guess into the formula and use the result as a better guess. We can turn the crank on our approximation machine as many times as are necessary. Eventually, we'll have the answer.

Mathematicians have developed a number of approximation methods for computing roots. One method is called **bisection**. Suppose we want to find $\sqrt[3]{a}$. Suppose further that we have two values x_0 and x_1, and we know $x_0 \leq \sqrt[3]{a} \leq x_1$. Another way of saying this is $x_0^3 \leq a \leq x_1^3$. Then we can chop the interval in half, picking $m = (x_0 + x_1)/2$. Now we look at m^3. There are three cases:

- $x_0 = x_1$. We have found the answer, so we stop. (Since $x_0 \leq m \leq x_1$, if $x_0 = x_1$, then $m = x_0 = x_1$. It doesn't matter which one we pick.)
- $m^3 > a$. We look in the range from x_0 to m.
- $m^3 < a$. We look in the range from m to x_1.

Figure 2-7 shows the case where $m^3 < a$. The next subrange to examine is from m to x_1, and s identifies the point where $s^3 = a$.

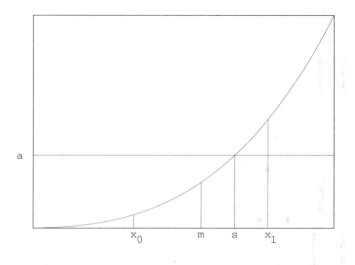

Figure 2-7   Bisection for cube roots

We'll need a helper here to compute x^3:

```
(define cube
  (lambda (x) (* x (* x x))))
```

"Looking in the range" is obviously a recursive operation. We'll write a Scheme procedure `cube-root-solve` that uses bisection to find the root in Program 2-5.

We've written 2.0 instead of just 2, so the answer will come out as a number with decimal places. Scheme sticks to integers or fractions as long as you don't include a real (floating-point) number. Once a real number enters the calculation, Scheme uses real numbers throughout.

`cube-root-solve` takes three arguments: a, the number whose cube root we're computing, and x0 and x1, the lower and upper limits of the search range. Although there are two applications of `cube-root-solve` in the procedure, only one of them is used at any one time. The second `if` form determines which case is relevant (by

```
(define cube-root-solve
  (lambda (a x0 x1)
    (if (= x1 x0)
        x0
        (if (> (cube (/ (+ x0 x1) 2.0)) a)
            (cube-root-solve a x0 (/ (+ x0 x1) 2.0))
            (cube-root-solve a (/ (+ x0 x1) 2.0) x1)))))
```

Program 2-5   A cube-root procedure

comparing m^3 to a), and then recursively calls cube-root-solve with the appropriate arguments.

Unfortunately, this procedure has a serious flaw. The Pythagoreans we discussed back in Chapter 1 studied triangles. One of the triangles they investigated had sides 1, 1, $\sqrt{2}$. To their horror, they discovered that $\sqrt{2}$ could not be expressed as the ratio of two numbers, each with a finite number of decimal places.[5] This discovery created a tremendous scandal among the Greeks. However, they had to accept the fact that some numbers are irrational, meaning they can't be expressed as the ratio of two finite integer numbers, and therefore can't be represented by two numbers, each with a finite number of decimal places.

Even more problematic is the fact that computers represent real numbers with limited precision, perhaps 30 places right of the decimal point. Even numbers that can be represented in a finite number of places are not exactly represented if the number of places is larger than the limit. This means our test $x_0 = x_1$ can lead to problems. For almost all numbers, we will never reach that point. What may happen is that (/ (+ x0 x1) 2.0) may equal either x0 or x1. Then we're stuck—we never reach equality! It's really surprising that it's possible on a computer when $a > 0$, $b > 0$ that $a + b = a$.

We can use the idea of a **limit** to solve the problem. We can keep doing a calculation until the difference gets so small that it doesn't matter. Mathematicians use the Greek letter ϵ (epsilon) for a quantity so small that it makes no difference.[6] You can think of ϵ as being short for "error", the maximum amount by which the answer may differ from the true answer.

In our rewritten procedure, let's get rid of the unnecessary parameters. If we just want to compute a cube root, all we should have to specify is a. Expecting a user to specify the range for the arguments and an initial guess is simply unreasonable. We can set up an initial range and guess, and then our cube-root procedure can compute the rest. This gives us the following cube-root procedure:

```
(define cube-root
  (lambda (a)
    (cube-root-solve a 1 a)))
```

---

[5] Many people misuse the word *finite* to mean "small". We don't mean it this way. Even if we were to write $\sqrt{2}$ to a trillion places, there would still be round-off. A number with a trillion places still has a finite number of places.

[6] Epsilon has entered computer science slang. For example, a programmer might say that their program is "within epsilon of working". Sounds great, but having a program within epsilon of working isn't the same as having one that actually works!

This procedure doesn't seem to do anything. In fact, what it does is to calculate initial values of x_0, x_1, and m, and then call a procedure cube-root-solve. We know $\sqrt[3]{a}$ must lie between 1 and a, for any $a > 1$. The initial value of m is then $(1 + a)/2 = a/2$. Thus cube-root is the procedure the user applies. cube-root-solve is not intended to be called by the user, but only by cube-root. As we saw in Chapter 1, we call such a procedure a *helping* procedure, or helper. The pattern of a main procedure that sets things up and a recursive helper is very common.

The whole package, along with the comments that help a human reader make sense of the program, now looks like Program 2-6. In the rest of this text, we will omit comments from the programs we present, for the sake of brevity. The programs will be adequately explained in the text. A program outside the text, such as any in the software package, however, will contain many comments.

```
;;; Change this value to get more or less accurate answers.
(define epsilon 0.005)
;;; This is the main cube-root procedure. It is given the
;;; value whose cube root is to be computed. It produces
;;; an answer correct to within epsilon if a >= 1.0.
(define cube-root
  (lambda (a)
    (cube-root-solve a 1.0 a)))
;;; This procedure is a helper for cube-root. It is given
;;; three arguments: a is the value whose cube root is
;;; to be computed. x0 and x1 are the limits of the range
;;; in which the cube root is to be found.
(define cube-root-solve
  (lambda (a x0 x1)
    (if (< (- x1 x0) epsilon)
        (/ (+ x0 x1) 2.0)
        (if (> (cube (/ (+ x1 x0) 2.0)) a)
          (cube-root-solve
            a x0 (/ (+ x0 x1) 2.0))
          (cube-root-solve
            a  (/ (+ x0 x1) 2.0) x1)))))))
```

Program 2-6   Cube root program

We've defined epsilon to be quite large. If we wanted extreme accuracy, we might pick epsilon equal to 0.0000000000000001, assuming that the computer we're using stores that many places. The smaller the value of epsilon, the longer the result will take to compute.

We ran this example and traced cube-root and cube-root-solve. The output is shown in Figure 2-8. Notice that cube-root is only applied once to get things started at the beginning.

```
> (trace cube-root)
> (trace cube-root-solve)
> (cube-root 3)
call cube-root: 3
call cube-root-solve: 3 1 3
| call cube-root-solve: 3 1 2.0
| | call cube-root-solve: 3 1.0 1.5
| | | call cube-root-solve: 3 1.25 1.5
| | | | call cube-root-solve: 3 1.375 1.5
| | | | | call cube-root-solve: 3 1.4375 1.5
| | | | | | call cube-root-solve: 3 1.4375 1.46875
| | | | | | | call cube-root-solve: 3 1.4375 1.453125
| | | | | | | | call cube-root-solve: 3 1.4375 1.4453125
| | | | | | | | | call cube-root-solve: 3 1.44140625 1.4453125
| | | | | | | | | return from cube-root-solve: 1.443359375
| | | | | | | | return from cube-root-solve: 1.443359375
| | | | | | | return from cube-root-solve: 1.443359375
| | | | | | return from cube-root-solve: 1.443359375
| | | | | return from cube-root-solve: 1.443359375
| | | | return from cube-root-solve: 1.443359375
| | | return from cube-root-solve: 1.443359375
| | return from cube-root-solve: 1.443359375
| return from cube-root-solve: 1.443359375
return from cube-root-solve: 1.443359375
```

Figure 2-8   Trace of cube root procedures

☞ **Exercise 2-9**

Suppose you were using a bargain-basement computer that only stored numbers to four decimal places. What could happen if you picked epsilon to be $1.0e - 6$? ❏

☞ **Exercise 2-10**

Modify the second version of cube-root to work correctly with numbers between 0 and 0.9999 . . . . You won't make any changes to cube-root-solve. ❏

☞ **Exercise 2-11**

$\sqrt[3]{a} = -\sqrt[3]{-a}$. What happens if you try to apply our new cube-root procedure (the one that handles any number greater than zero) to a negative number? What went wrong? How can you fix this? Hint: (abs x) computes the absolute value of x, i.e., x if $x > 0$ else $-x$. ❏

☞ **Exercise 2-12**

Write a procedure that computes the sum of the digits of a nonnegative integer. For example, (sum-digits 1248) ⇒ 15.

☞ **Exercise 2-13**

Write a procedure collect-evens that takes a positive integer and returns a positive integer composed of only the even digits in the original integer. For example

(collect-evens 12345) ⇒ 24

```
(collect-evens 0123450)  ⇒   240
```

❏

Practical Note

We've used comments in the cube-root program to specify the interface to the procedure, that is, the arguments to the procedures, what kind of values they should be, and their meaning. We also indicate what kind of output the procedure will produce. Comments are also useful for annotating the procedures with their purpose—why and when they should be used.

Another important use of comments is to write down the assumptions underlying the procedures. We may be justified in assuming that the input is always positive. If so, we record that assumption with the procedure, so that anyone using the code later is forewarned not to use negative numbers.

We don't usually employ comments to explain *how* the code computes its results. Well-written code should be understandable. Some programmers write comments to explain the clever tricks they use in their code—tricks that might not be understood by lesser programmers. That practice usually leads to trouble, because even the cleverest programmer can forget how the trick worked. It is better to avoid this use of comments by avoiding unnecessary tricks in the first place.

When you change a program, make sure you remember to make corresponding changes to the comments. Incorrect comments are worse than useless.

2.2.2   Multiway Recursion

Let's look at as more general form of recursive procedure. Every recursive procedure we've examined has only one call to itself. Problem decomposition has consisted of simplifying by one step and then recursing on the rest. `factorial` multiplies with the current value and recurses on a problem one less in size.

Some problems are best solved by dividing them into several parts, solving each subproblem separately, and then putting the results together. Many computer science algorithms **divide and conquer** a problem. The algorithm divides the problem into *subproblems*, conquers (solves) the subproblems, and combines their solutions. We'll see more of divide and conquer in Chapter 9. Algorithms that consider alternatives also use divide and conquer.

We must consider alternatives in the kind of problem where we count the number of different ways we can do something, for example, the number of ways of storing a given amount of material in a set of containers of different sizes. Many counting problems look different on the surface, but rely on the same techniques for solution.

Let's consider the problem of counting the number of ways to get a spade flush in poker. The game of poker uses a *deck* of fifty-two cards divided into four *suits* of clubs, diamonds, hearts, and spades. Each suit has thirteen cards: ace, two through ten, and three "face" cards, jack, queen, and king. Each *hand* of poker usually contains five cards drawn randomly from the deck. In a *flush*, all cards belong to the same suit. A good poker player has an understanding of the probability of getting a flush, as well as other types of hands, such as a *straight*, where the cards can be arranged sequentially.

To understand these probabilities, we need to count the number of different ways to select five cards from the thirteen cards in the spade suit, among other problems. We already know how to count the number of different arrangements of *n* cards, which is *n*!. Here we need to count how many different sets of *k* cards can be selected from *n* cards.

To represent the cards, we can identify the cards with the numbers one through thirteen. Here is the representation and some example flushes.

the cards:	A 2 3 4 5 6 7 8 9 10 J Q K
the numbers:	1 2 3 4 5 6 7 8 9 10 11 12 13
some flushes:	1 2 4 10 13 = A 2 4 10 K
	2 7 9 11 12 = 2 7 9 J Q

To count the number of different sets of five spades, we can step through the thirteen cards, one by one. There are two kinds of flushes: ones that include the ace, and those that don't. Card number 1 is either in or out. When there are two alternatives, we *add* the number of sets using the first alternative to the number of sets using the second alternative.

Let's call the number of ways to have a flush of size m in n cards $flush(n, m)$. There are two alternatives in selecting a flush of size m from a suit of size n. For a particular card, the number of possible flushes using that card is the number of ways to get a flush one smaller, $m - 1$, from a suit of one less, $n - 1$, or $flush(n-1, m-1)$. The other alternative is not to use the card. The number of ways to get a flush of size m is then the number of ways to get a flush of size m from a suit without that card, and so of size $n - 1$, or $flush(n - 1, m)$. So the total number of ways is the sum of the two alternatives, or

$$flush(n, m) = flush(n - 1, m - 1) + flush(n - 1, m)$$

This recursive formula is unlike those we've studied before: the right-hand side of the formula has two occurrences of the recursive function. There are three base cases:

$$flush(0, 0) = 1 \text{ and } flush(n, 0) = 1 \text{ and } flush(0, m) = 0$$

There is only one way to select 0 cards from any number of cards, including zero cards, and there is no way to select $m > 0$ cards from a deck of zero cards.

Let's translate our *flush* equation into Scheme, as shown in Program 2-7.

When flushes has reduced size to zero, a flush has been completed, so it returns 1. All the rest of the computation occurs by reducing the problem size. What this code does is *try all possibilities*!

In the example in Figure 2-9, the first three recursive calls to flushes explore the possibility of getting a flush by not using the 3, then not using the 2, and then not using the 1. flushes runs out of cards before it runs out of spaces in the hand (cards is zero before size equals zero). So the result is zero—no flush. The very next line, call flushes: 0 1, follows from (flushes 1 2). flushes is trying to construct a flush of size two from one card so the result is also zero. The successful flushes

```
(define flushes
  (lambda (cards size)
    (if (= size 0)
        1
        (if (= cards 0)
            0
            (+ (flushes (sub1 cards) (sub1 size))
               (flushes (sub1 cards) size))))))
```

Program 2-7   Computing the number of flushes

```
> (flushes 3 2)
call flushes: 3 2
| call flushes: 2 2
| | call flushes: 1 2
| | | call flushes: 0 2
| | | 0
| | | call flushes: 0 1
| | | 0
| | 0
| | call flushes: 1 1
| | | call flushes: 0 1
| | | 0
| | | call flushes: 0 0
| | | 1
| | 1
| 1
| call flushes: 2 1
| | call flushes: 1 1
| | | call flushes: 0 1
| | | 0
| | | call flushes: 0 0
| | | 1
| | 1
| | call flushes: 1 0
| | 1
| 2
3
3
```

Figure 2-9   Trace of flushes in action

come from the cards 3,2 and 3,1 and 2,1. For example, the card choice 3,1 comes from the calls: (flushes 3 2), (flushes 2 1), (flushes 1 1), (flushes 0 0).

If you've studied mathematical probability, you've come across the idea of counting different ways to arrange objects or to select them from various collections. The numbers of ways to select *k* objects from a set of *n* objects is called *n choose k* and is written as

$$\binom{n}{k} = n!/(k! \times (n-k)!)$$

Program 2-8 shows the procedure to compute this (in terms of flushes).

```
(define compute-flushes
  (lambda (cards size)
    (if (> size cards)
        0
        (/ (factorial cards)
           (* (factorial size) (factorial (- cards size)))))))
```
Program 2-8   Calculating the number of flushes

Each time `flushes` calls itself, it creates two droids: one to compute the number of flushes when the card is used in the flush, and one to count the number when it is not used in the flush. Two droids get created, in no particular order, and *only one is active at a time*. A good model is that the second only gets created when the other has finished its work and has returned its value to its creator. Figure 2-10 shows the droid for (`flushes 3 2`) getting values from both (`flushes 2 2`) and (`flushes 2 1`). Each of these droids in fact creates several more droids—just look at Figure 2-9 to see how many.

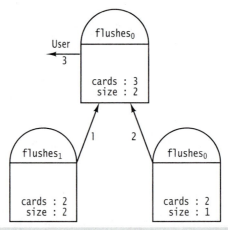

Figure 2-10   Procedure `flushes` creates two droids at recursion

The numbering of droids 1 and 2 in Figure 2-10 is arbitrary, since different Scheme systems will create them in different orders.

☞ **Exercise 2-14**

Write a procedure `compute-straights` to count the number of straights (see page 76) of length `size` in a set of n consecutive cards. ❏

Another problem where we must consider many alternatives arises when we're given a number of jars of varying size, and we want to count the number of ways we can store a quantity of liquid in those jars. This is a counting problem just like finding the number of flushes. The alternative at each step is either to use the jar, or not to use any jars of that type. We count a success when we run out of liquid. Otherwise, we count the number of ways, both using the jar, and not using the jar. Program 2-9 is a solution to this problem.

```
(define store
  (lambda (amount nh nf nt no)
    (if (= amount 0)
        1
        (if (and (> nh 0) (>= amount 100))
            (+ (store (- amount 100) (sub1 nh) nf nt no)
               (store amount 0 nf nt no))
            (if (and (> nf 0) (>= amount 50))
                (+ (store (- amount 50) nh  (sub1 nf) nt no)
                   (store amount nh 0 nt no))
                (if (and (> nt 0) (>= amount 10))
                    (+ (store (- amount 10) nh nf (sub1 nt) no)
                       (store amount nh nf 0 no))
                    (if (and (> no 0) (>= amount 1))
                        (store (- amount 1) nh nf nt (sub1 no))
                        0)))))))))
```

Program 2-9   The number of ways to store milk in jars

The difference between `store` and `flushes` is that `store` must check before it deducts the amount for a particular jar—is there enough liquid left to use this type of jar, and are there any jars of this type left? Otherwise they are essentially the same. `store` must count four different kinds of jars. The following examples shows how we can use `store`.

```
(store 25 0 0 2 5) ⇒ 1
(store 25 0 0 5 5) ⇒ 1
(store 50 0 1 5 5) ⇒ 2
(store 50 0 1 2 5) ⇒ 1
(store 55 0 1 6 60) ⇒ 7
```

If you don't believe this works, count the number of ways to store 55 litres, as shown in Figure 2-11. Each row shows how many jars of each capacity are used. The final column enumerates the alternatives.

store turns out to have many uses. It is also a procedure to make change—`store` will tell you how many different ways there are of making change for `amount`. The interpretation doesn't matter—the procedure just counts alternatives.

These procedures present a new form of recursion that we've termed **multiway recursion**, since the recursive procedure calls itself more than once each time it recurs. This is more difficult, but still there is only one droid active at a time. It's important to see that multiway recursion depends on reducing the problem size at each step, as do all kinds of recursion. Unlike the simple recursions in `power` and `factorial`, there is more than one way to reduce the problem. The multiway recursive procedures we've studied create lots of droids. The first one may create two or more, and the rest create multiple copies. The pattern of droids for (`flushes 3 2`), as we saw in Figure 2-10, branches out and resembles an upside-down tree when fully drawn. Hence, multiway recursion is often termed tree recursion.

Jars	50	10	1	#
	1	0	5	1
	0	0	55	2
	0	1	45	3
	0	2	35	4
	0	3	25	5
	0	4	15	6
	0	5	5	7

Figure 2-11   The number of ways to store 55 litres

`flushes` and `store` combine the solutions of the subproblems by addition. When we show in Chapters 7 and 9 how to represent more complex data such as trees, we will see the importance of this way of attacking problems.

2.3   Measuring the Cost of a Computation

To choose time is to save time.

— Francis Bacon, *Essays*

So far we haven't paid much attention to the efficiency of Scheme programs. You might feel that our attitude is reasonable. After all, computers are fast and becoming faster. In 1980 a computer that could perform one million instructions per second was considered a mainframe. Such a computer is said to be capable of 1 **MIPS**, or millions of instructions per second. In 1990 a computer 10 times as fast is sold in a discount computer store as a personal machine at 2% of the 1980 price.

We can't ignore efficiency. Some tasks simply take too long, no matter how fast the computer operates. For example, consider the game of chess. A chess-playing program can be written in a few pages of code. The program will consider each square on the board, each possible response by the opponent, then each possible response to each response, and so on. Unfortunately, even if we have a computer that can examine a response in a fraction of an attosecond,[7] it would take longer than the expected lifetime of the universe for this program to make its first move. Why? There are an enormous number of possible chess games. Unless the program limits how many moves it considers, the computer would have to examine them all!

There are chess programs that play well; some of them have beaten grand masters. These programs search many positions, and drop some lines of play by reasoning that there are better ways of playing. Researchers at a number of places, including MIT and Bell Labs, have built "chess computers" that provide a number of hardware features to examine positions very rapidly.

We therefore need some method of describing how efficient a program is. Our method should allow us to ignore such matters as how fast the computer is, how much memory the computer has, and how efficiently Scheme is executed on the computer. Our method must let us ignore even the language being used. If Program A is run on a highly optimizing Scheme compiler, and Program B is run on a slow Basic interpreter, we could not necessarily claim Program A as the winner.

---

[7] One attosecond is 10^{-15} seconds. The fastest computer in 1994 takes more than a million attoseconds to execute one instruction.

Parallelism and Multiprocessing

All of our traces show that only one droid is active at any given time. While a droid is waiting for an answer from a second droid, it is suspended, doing nothing.

Recursive procedures that call themselves more than once suggest that both droids could compute at the same time. This is not just a wild suggestion, but an important style of computing called **parallel computation**. The way we have written programs up to now lends itself to solution in parallel, meaning the droids do not work one after another ("serially"), but rather at the same time ("in parallel"). Droids can proceed in parallel when the result of one does not depend on the result of the other. All sorts of computation could in theory be done in parallel, but only with recursion is the computation complex enough to make it worthwhile.

factorial, as we've written it, cannot be run in parallel—the results of (factorial n) depend on (factorial (sub1 n)). But the recursive invocations of the flushes procedure *can* be run in parallel. The two calls to flushes in the body of flushes do not depend on each other. Each can be computed without interference from the other.

Parallel computation is particularly useful in areas such as computer vision, in which a program analyzes what it sees through a camera. The program takes as input a huge grid of pixels (picture elements), and attempts to determine what it sees. One part of the program must look at the actual pixels. This part can benefit from parallelism because there are perhaps millions of pixels in a single image, and they each require the same processing. Another part of the program must attempt to determine what's in the picture. For example, if the camera is pointed at a set of parts being assembled by a robot arm, the program must determine which parts are in the picture, and how they are positioned. This requires considering a large number of alternatives (much as our flushes procedure had to consider a large number of alternatives). Again parallelism allows many alternatives to be considered at the same time.

Many modern computers can be configured with more than one processor. In other words, more than one droid can compute at the same time. Sometimes computer systems have thousands of processing units. These "massively parallel" machines are ideal for problems like computer vision and weather prediction.

A central problem in modern computer science is to map out the range of problems that can be subdivided in such a way that a collection of droids can compute independently on subparts of the problem. The critical issue is how to communicate the results of many droids to each other, so that they can continue computing. Many computer scientists believe that parallel computing is essential to modern computing.

Coding Program A in Basic and Program B in Scheme might well reverse the outcome. Therefore, what we want is *a method of comparing two programs that compute exactly the same result, without regard to the speed of the underlying evaluator.*

We refer to such a measure of a program's efficiency as its algorithmic **complexity**. There are many complexity measurements we might want to examine. Most commonly, we are interested in how quickly the program executes and how much memory it needs during execution.[8]

---

[8] We haven't talked much about memory. As we'll see later, some computations require us to use additional storage within the computer, as we would a scratch pad if we were working by hand.

Suppose we have a procedure foo. How should we talk about its algorithmic complexity? Few recursive procedures always have the same behavior regardless of the arguments. It's the arguments that determine how much computation is to be performed; the further the initial arguments are from the base case, the more recursion steps must be performed. After all, we would agree that arranging five names in alphabetical order is much less work than arranging five million names. Thus, if foo is defined as

```
(define foo
  (lambda (n) ...))
```

the value of n should be what affects the running time. Therefore, we should be able to describe the procedure's running time as a function of n.

Often, we want to determine the complexity of a procedure because we have several different algorithms that all produce the same results and want to find the fastest method. We'll look at a method for finding a formula that describes how the time a procedure takes changes with growing input size. Then we'll see how we can use that formula to rate various procedures that do the same thing.

2.3.1   Time Complexity

There are at least three ways to multiply integers.

1. the primitive *
2. the procedure mult%1

```
(define mult%1
  (lambda (a b)
    (if (= b 1)
        a
        (+ a (mult%1 a (sub1 b))))))
```

3. the procedure mult%2

```
(define mult%2
  (lambda (a b)
    (if (= b 1)
        a
        (+ (mult%2 (double a) (halve b))
           (if (not (even? b)) a 0)))))
```

If you time these on large numbers (say by squaring 10,000), you will find that * is extremely fast, mult%1 is extremely slow, and mult%2 is quite fast. But what does that mean?

Many Scheme systems perform * by executing a single machine-language instruction. Computer instructions take about the same amount of time to execute (about 50 nanoseconds, or 5×10^{-8} seconds, on a typical desktop computer). Thus, for all intents and purposes, we say the time to evaluate * is constant for integers and floating-point numbers. Scheme can also represent numbers of essentially unlimited size, but these don't take constant time to multiply! Complexity analysis of algorithms usually ignores such issues, but they are of great practical importance.

mult%1 is a standard recursion that you wrote in Exercise 2-4, using a recursive loop based upon the identity

$$a \times b = a + a \times (b - 1) \qquad (b > 0)$$
$$a \times b = a \qquad (b = 1)$$

mult%2 is known as the **Egyptian peasant** method of multiplication.[9] Egyptian peasants, it was said, multiplied numbers by doubling one and halving the other. For example, to multiply 17 by 13, we would do the following calculation:

$$17 * 13 = 34 * 6 + 17 = 68 * 3 + 17 = 136 * 1 + 68 + 17$$

There are three cases when we use the Egyptian peasant method to multiply $a \times b$.

$$a \times b = 2a \times \frac{b}{2} + a \qquad (b \text{ odd}, b > 1)$$
$$a \times b = 2a \times \frac{b}{2} \qquad (b \text{ even}, b > 1)$$
$$a \times b = a \qquad (b = 1)$$

mult%2 depends upon two helper procedures, shown in Program 2-10.

```
(define double
  (lambda (a) (* a 2)))
(define halve
  (lambda (a) (quotient a 2)))
```

Program 2-10   mult%2's helpers

These procedures appear to use multiplication and division, which is the very operation we're trying to implement! However, doubling and halving positive integers are special operations that every computer supports in hardware, whether or not it has a general multiplication operation. Many high-performance Scheme systems provide these operations as primitives. Look in the manual for your Scheme system for the names of these operations. (They are often called *shifts*.)

If we run mult%1 and mult%2, we'll see that they both get the same answer. For small values of a and b, they both seem to be pretty fast. Yet tracing them shows a rather different story (Figures 2-12 and 2-13).

In fact, various examples show that if $b = 1$, the two procedures do about the same amount of work, but if b is large, then mult%2 will do much less work than mult%1. The amount of work doesn't seem to depend upon a.

Implicitly, we've been measuring the amount of work by the amount of output produced by a trace. This is a reasonable definition when we consider that each line of output corresponds either to a call of a procedure or to a value being returned by a procedure. In fact, counting only the actual call lines is good enough.[10]

---

[9] Also known as the Russian peasant method. Sources agree that peasants from *somewhere* discovered it. Presumably the aristocrats had time to kill, and used mult%1.

[10] An old joke has a train passenger counting cattle by counting the legs and dividing by four. Each call line in the trace corresponds to a returned value line somewhere later on.

```
> (trace mult%1 mult%2 *)
(mult%1 mult%2)
> (mult%1 17 13)
call mult%1: 17 13
| call mult%1: 17 12
| | call mult%1:: 17 11
| | | call mult%1: 17 10
| | | | call mult%1: 17 9
| | | | | call mult%1: 17 8
| | | | | | call mult%1: 17 7
| | | | | | | call mult%1: 17 6
| | | | | | | | call mult%1: 17 5
| | | | | | | | | | call mult%1: 17 4
| | | | | | | | | | | call mult%1: 17 3
| | | | | | | | | | | | call mult%1: 17 2
| | | | | | | | | | | | | call mult%1: 17 1
| | | | | | | | | | | | | return from mult%1: 17
| | | | | | | | | | | | return from mult%1: 34
| | | | | | | | | | | return from mult%1: 51
| | | | | | | | | | return from mult%1: 68
| | | | | | | | | return from mult%1: 85
| | | | | | | | return from mult%1: 102
| | | | | | | return from mult%1: 119
| | | | | | return from mult%1: 136
| | | | | return from mult%1: 153
| | | | return from mult%1: 170
| | | return from mult%1: 187
| | return from mult%1: 204
| return from mult%1: 221
return from mult%1: 221
221
```

Figure 2-12 Tracing mult%1

```
> (mult%2 17 13)
call mult%2: 17 13
| call mult%2: 34 6
| | call mult%2: 68 3
| | | call mult%2: 136 1
| | | return from mult%2: 136
| | return from mult%2: 204
| return from mult%2: 221
return from mult%2: 221
221
```

Figure 2-13 Tracing mult%2

Therefore, our question about the computational cost of a procedure reduces to this:

> How many calls (and therefore how many lines of trace output) will a procedure foo generate, as a function of its arguments?

For example, we would expect the number of calls for factorial to be a function of n. With both mult%1 and mult%2, the number of calls will be (technically) a function of a and b, although only b will actually count.

We're not asking, "How many calls are made when we evaluate (factorial 5)?" but saying, "Give me a function of n that tells how many calls are made in (factorial n)." The difference is crucial because we're only interested in an answer when n gets large. If n is small, then the overall running time of the procedure will be too small to care about.

Let's apply this analysis to our multiplication procedures. mult%1 operates by calling itself with $b - 1$ each time. This means that if we evaluate (mult%1 a b), a grand total of b recursive calls will be made.

mult%2 is a little more complicated. On the first recursive call, the value $\frac{b}{2}$ will be used. On each successive recursive call, the value of b is halved. How many calls will we need to get b down to 1? The answer requires using the $\log_2 b$ function or the logarithm base 2, often written as $\lg b$. Recall that if $x = a^b$ then $\log_a x = b$, which is the logarithm of x in base a. The logarithm operation and the operation of raising to a power are inverse operations. In other words, the logarithm of a number x in, say, base 2, is the power to which you have to raise 2 in order to get x. The logarithm of 4 in base 2 is 2, and the logarithm or log of 16 is 4. We will usually use base 2, as do most computer scientists.

Let's take an example. Suppose we want to evaluate (mult%2 17 256). The steps are shown in Figure 2-14.

This example required nine calls. (We couldn't show you a trace of (mult%1 17 256); it would take three or four pages.) Computing (mult%2 17 512) requires only one extra step. In general, to compute (mult%2 a 2^n), we will need $n + 1$ calls.

The difference between the two versions is dramatic. If we want to multiply 239,712 by 16,777,216, mult%1 requires 16,777,216 recursive calls, but mult%2 needs only $\lg 16777216 + 1 = 25$ recursive calls. We assume that our doubling and halving procedures take a constant amount of time. Even if that's not strictly true, it really doesn't alter the analysis very much.

For most procedures, the running time is not so easy to compute. Often a procedure will have some small start-up cost, or some of the steps might be a bit more complicated. There is, however, a mathematical notation that allows us to throw away a lot of the small variations. We can write that mult%1 has complexity (computational cost) $O(b)$. This means that the number of calls is "on the order of" b (we read this as **"big-oh** of b"). By "on the order of," we mean that some small variations might be present, but nothing worth paying too much attention to when b is large. Similarly, we say that mult%2 has cost $O(\lg b)$, meaning that the cost can be approximated by the logarithm of one of the arguments. Figure 2-15 (a) shows the growth of time required by mult%2, compared with mult%1 and *. At this scale, only mult%1 shows, so Figure 2-15 (b) shows them with mult%1 scaled.

This means little when n is small, but as n gets large, the $O(\dots)$ notation tells us what happens to the running time of the procedure. Double b and the running time of mult%1 will double, but mult%2 will take only one more repetition. You can

```
> (trace mult%2)
> (mult%2 17 256)
call mult%2: 17 256
| call mult%2: 34 128
| | call mult%2: 68 64
| | | call mult%2: 136 32
| | | | call mult%2: 272 16
| | | | | call mult%2: 544 8
| | | | | | call mult%2: 1088 4
| | | | | | | call mult%2: 2176 2
| | | | | | | | call mult%2: 4352 1
| | | | | | | | return from mult%2: 4352
| | | | | | | return from mult%2: 4352
| | | | | | return from mult%2: 4352
| | | | | return from mult%2: 4352
| | | | return from mult%2: 4352
| | | return from mult%2: 4352
| | return from mult%2: 4352
| return from mult%2: 4352
return from mult%2: 4352
4352
```

Figure 2-14   The number of calls of `mult%2`

see this by noting that if you call (`mult%2 2n b`), it will immediately call (`mult%2 n b`), thus taking one more call. Mathematically, $\lg 2^{n+1} = \lg(2^n \times 2^1) = \lg 2^n + \lg 2 = \lg 2^n + 1$.

In general, simply counting the number of recursive calls will give you a very messy formula. $O(\dots)$ notation allows you to concentrate on the important terms. Suppose that you found that a certain procedure did $5n^3 + 17n^2 + 12n + 4$ recursive calls. As n gets large, n^3 will be very much larger than n^2. For example, if $n = 100$, $n^3 = 1,000,000$, but n^2 is only $10,000$. Therefore, throwing away the n^2 term results in less than 4% error. We can approximate the running time of our procedure as $5n^3$. But the coefficient is again somewhat arbitrary. One could simply buy a computer that was five times faster. We would therefore write a "big-oh" approximation to $5n^3 + 17n^2 + 12n + 4$ as $O(n^3)$.

Fundamentally, what "big-oh" notation tells us is what happens to the running time when n is really large. If we say that procedure `foo` has $O(n^2)$ running time, what we mean is that if n is large and you double it, the procedure will take four times as long to run. In other words, "big-oh" notation doesn't say anything absolute about the running time. Instead, it tells us how quickly the running time grows.

Sometimes a computation takes constant time. We would write this as $O(1)$ time. If you eliminate all but the most important term in the expression c and strike out the coefficient, you're left with 1. It doesn't matter whether the computation takes 1 second, 1 minute, or 1 millennium. The time is constant, and that's all "big-oh" notation tells us.

☞ **Exercise 2–15**

Joel User has done an analysis of a procedure he wrote, concluding that it has running time $O(n!)$. Is it likely that he's right? Why or why not? ❏

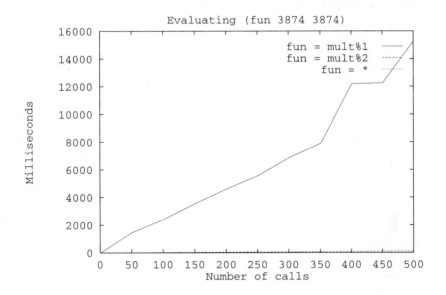

(a) : Unscaled comparison

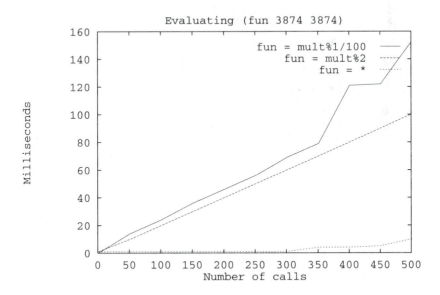

(b) : `mult%1` scaled by 0.01 for comparison

Figure 2-15   Time complexity of `mult%1`, `mult%2`, and `*`

Hard Problems

Computer science has developed algorithms for many problems. Some problems have simple descriptions, while others are much more difficult to describe. It's perplexing that some problems are simple to describe but require lots of computation to solve.

Earlier we saw an algorithm to compute the number of ways to make a flush of m cards out of a suit of n cards. What is the complexity of flushes? Each application of flushes calls flushes twice. The number of calls depends on n, which must be larger than m. A simplified, but wrong, analysis might conclude that flushes has $O(n)$ time complexity, since a path to a solution has length n. But there are many paths! Instead, we should multiply the number of calls at each level (which is 2) n times, since each application of flushes independently creates two new calls to flushes. Thus, flushes has time complexity $O(2^n)$. When the complexity of an algorithm is described by a constant raised to some power, we say that it has **exponential complexity**. If each application of flushes takes one nanosecond (1.0^{-9} second), an application of (flushes 50 49) would take just slightly more than 13 days! (The answer is 50.)

Exponential algorithms are therefore quite impractical. Although the solution is not difficult to program, the running time makes them almost useless except for small problems. But real problems can have $n = 1000$ or larger.

One of the most challenging issues in computer science has been to understand exactly which *problems* have exponential algorithms and which problems have practical algorithms. A *practical* algorithm has *polynomial* complexity, that is, $O(n^k)$ for some k. An $O(n^3)$ algorithm is barely practical. For example, an $O(n^3)$ algorithm that operates on an image with a million elements (the size of a computer screen) at one nanosecond per step would take 11,574 days. Even so, the difference between exponential and polynomial complexity is huge, as shown in the following figure.

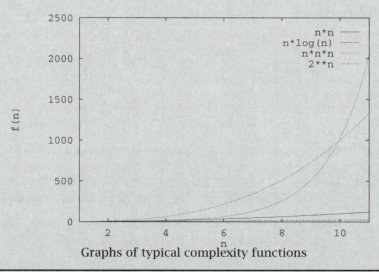

Graphs of typical complexity functions

Many algorithms we will study have complexities described by n^2 and $n \lg n$, as shown in close-up in the following figure.

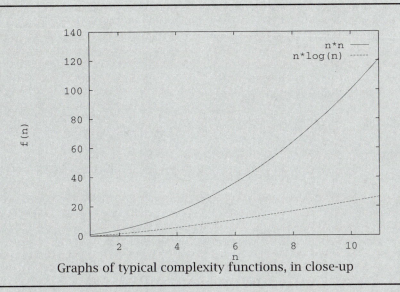

Graphs of typical complexity functions, in close-up

Another exponential problem is the "traveling seller" problem. Suppose a seller must make sales calls in several cities, but wants to visit each city only once. The procedure is easy to write (we solve a similar problem in the Case Study in Chapter 4), but it has exponential complexity. This problem might only be of interest to the seller's manager, but related problems, such as laying out the components on an integrated circuit chip so as to minimize the distance between them, are of immense practical value.

The following problem has, as far as we know, exponential complexity. Given a set of n numbers, $s_1, s_2 \ldots s_n$, find the subset of them whose sum is largest, subject to the condition that the sum is less than k. This is the **knapsack** problem—the numbers are the sizes of objects, k is the capacity of your knapsack, and you're trying to maximize the total size of the objects in your knapsack. This problem has significant practical value. Lumber-processing companies find it interesting because it will help to write programs that determine the optimal way of sawing apart a tree in order to get as much good-quality wood.

Even though we can state the knapsack problem simply, it is hard to solve exactly and efficiently. In 1971, Steven Cook showed that there is a class, called *NP*, of problems like this. (A problem in *NP* can be solved by a non-deterministic computer that guesses a solution and then checks whether the guess is correct. On a normal computer a problem in *NP* will take exponential time, to the best of our knowledge.) The class of problems that have polynomial algorithms called *P*. Over twenty years after Cook's work, we are still trying to determine whether $P = NP$; if $P = NP$, the problems in *NP* have polynomial solutions. Most computer scientists believe that $P \neq NP$, but it has not been proved. That such simple questions have resisted solution is very tantalizing. Many other deep problems remain to be solved in computing. Whether $P = NP$ is particularly interesting because it affects the way we solve many practical problems.

☞ **Exercise 2-16**

Give a running-time estimate for the following procedure:

```
(define foo
  (lambda (x)
    (if (< x 0)
        5
        (foo (- x 3))))))
```

❏

☞ **Exercise 2-17**

Write an $O(1)$ procedure that does the same as foo in Exercise 2-16. ❏

☞ **Exercise 2-18**

We have two procedures, p1 and p2; p1 is $O(n)$ and p2 is $O(1)$. Under what circumstances, even for some large n, would p2 run more slowly than p1? ❏

☞ **Exercise 2-19**

Give a running-time estimate for procedure bar. This one is quite hard! Hint: Break the problem into pieces.

```
(define bar
  (lambda (n) (bar1 n n n)))
(define bar1
  (lambda (a b c)
    (if (= a 0)
        c
        (bar1 (sub1 a) b (+ c (bar2 b))))))
(define bar2
  (lambda (x)
    (if (< x 1)
        0
        (+ 1 (bar2 (/ x 3.0)))))))
```

❏

☞ **Exercise 2-20**

You are approached by a smooth-talking software salesman who offers to sell you a procedure mult%3 that performs multiplication on numbers of any size, even numbers having thousands of digits, in $O(1)$ time. What's your response? ❏

2.3.2 Space Complexity

If we're going to do a serious job of comparing procedures, we ought to look at more than just the execution time. The amount of computer memory used in a computation is also a concern. So far, we haven't stored any complex data structures in the computer. However, our programs do take up memory, and we ought to be careful about how much we use.

You might challenge us on this point. After all, memory is one of the only commodities that has been getting cheaper every year. If you draw a graph of memory price versus cost since 1960, you will find that memory prices have dropped by a factor of 2 approximately every two years. In 1965 a 128K computer was a mainframe; each large university had one. In 1980 a 128K computer was a top-of-the-line desktop unit and might have been used to store the records of a small business. A 128K computer now fits in a shirt-pocket and is used as an electronic appointment book.

Even the largest computer has a limited amount of memory, however. Both memory and time are resources, but they have one important difference. Time isn't an absolute limit: if a program needs more time, it can have it. The situation is different with memory. A program that runs out of memory simply dies. You can run it on a computer with more memory, but you usually have to start all over again. As programs grow, they become slower, since they can't fit into the computer's real memory and must be brought in from disk.

How do our programs use memory? Obviously, some amount of memory is needed to store the program, but the amount required, except for an extremely large program, is not a serious constraint. However, each time we call a procedure, we use a little bit of memory. Since a reasonably fast computer can execute hundreds of thousands of calls per second, those little bits of memory can amount to all the memory available on a supercomputer, unless we're careful.

What is the purpose of this "little bit of memory" consumed each time we call a procedure? Each procedure call creates a droid. Droids need a bit of memory to store the information they must remember, such as the values of the arguments and who receives the answer. We assume the procedure body is shared by all droids.

Consider, for example, the procedure `fact1` of Program 2-11. The output from a traced call on `fact1` is shown in Figure 2-16.

```
(define fact1
  (lambda (n)
    (if (= n 0)
        1
        (* n (fact1 (sub1 n)))))))
```
Program 2-11   Simple factorial procedure

`fact1` operates in two separate phases. It first breaks the factorial problem into a set of multiplications. Then, as each call returns, it does the multiplications. Scheme must create a new droid for each recursive call. Now compare `fact1` with Program 2-12. Tracing `(fact2 5)` gives us Figure 2-17. `fact2-helper` does all the real work; all `fact2` does is start things off by calling `fact2-helper`.

There's a radical difference between the behavior of the two factorial procedures. All of the return values are the same this time. `fact2-helper` has completed the calculation by the time it's called with first argument 0. Now look at the code for the two versions. The recursion step in `fact1` consists of

```
(* n (fact1 (sub1 n)))
```

whereas in `fact2` it is

```
(fact2-helper (sub1 n) (* n a))
```

```
> (fact1 5)
call fact1: 5
| call fact1: 4
| | call fact1: 3
| | | call fact1: 2
| | | | call fact1: 1
| | | | | call fact1: 0
| | | | | return from fact1: 1
| | | | return from fact1: 1
| | | return from fact1: 2
| | return from fact1: 6
| return from fact1: 24
return from fact1: 120
120
```

Figure 2-16   Trace of `fact1`

What's the difference? In `fact1`, we compute the factorial of (`sub1 n`) first and only then multiply it by n. On the other hand, in `fact2-helper` we do the multiplication first and then the recursive call. This seemingly trivial difference is crucial to the efficiency of the calculation. Because we've already done the multiplication first in `fact2-helper`, the recursive call is the last step of the procedure.

```
(define fact2
  (lambda (n) (fact2-helper n 1)))
(define fact2-helper
  (lambda (n a)
    (if (= n 0)
        a
        (fact2-helper (sub1 n) (* n a)))))
```

Program 2-12   Tail-recursive factorial

`fact2-helper` uses a special kind of recursion known as **tail recursion**. In tail recursion, the recursion step is the absolute last step in a procedure (the tail), with consequent savings in computer memory. Offsetting this savings is the need to introduce a second parameter, a so-called **accumulator**. The parameter a is an accumulator, because it accumulates the multiplied value so far during recursion. Each call of `fact2-helper` multiplies its a by its n, and sends the new value on to the next call. A tail-recursive procedure uses less memory because it completes all its computations before it calls itself recursively.

Some Scheme implementations trace procedures to make it clear that a tail-recursive procedure uses less memory. One implementation we use, *Chez Scheme*, traces `fact2` and `fact2-helper` in a different way, as shown in Figure 2-18.

In this form of trace output, the tracer does not indent recursive calls to `fact2-helper`. The lack of indentation indicates there's no new droid created and no work left to do when `fact-helper` returns. Thus, the current droid can compute the next call to `fact2-helper`. Tracing does not show the result being returned through each of the 11 calls to `fact2-helper`. This shows that the result is essentially returned directly from the last call (`fact2-helper 0 3628800`) to the first call, and then it's

```
> (fact2 5)
call fact2: 5
call fact2-helper: 5 1
| call fact2-helper: 4 5
| | call fact2-helper: 3 20
| | | call fact2-helper: 2 60
| | | | call fact2-helper: 1 120
| | | | | call fact2-helper: 0 120
| | | | | return from fact2-helper: 120
| | | | return from fact2-helper: 120
| | | return from fact2-helper: 120
| | return from fact2-helper: 120
| return from fact2-helper: 120
return from fact2-helper: 120
120
```

Figure 2-17   Tracing fact2

returned by fact2. The first 120 is the trace of the procedure's return, and the second is the procedure's result.

```
> (fact2 5)
(fact2 5)
(fact2-helper 5 1)
(fact2-helper 4 5)
(fact2-helper 3 20)
(fact2-helper 2 60)
(fact2-helper 1 120)
(fact2-helper 0 120)
120
120
```

Figure 2-18   Chez trace of fact2

In a tail-recursive procedure, the droid evaluates the body of the procedure and encounters the recursive call. It realizes it has nothing left to do after the recursive call. The droid doesn't need to recruit another droid, but can process the new call itself. Each time Scheme creates another droid, it uses some memory to store the arguments of the procedure. Avoiding the creation of new droids substantially reduces the amount of memory required.

It should be clear that the tail-recursive solution is much less tidy than the recursive one. We needed a helper procedure and an accumulator. On the other hand, tail recursion is faster and uses less computer memory. You should, therefore, not worry about tail recursion when first writing a procedure. Only if the procedure uses too much memory should you attempt to rewrite it. In fact, not all recursive procedures can be rewritten tail-recursively, in the sense that their memory use does not increase with the number of times they're called recursively.

Conventional programming languages such as Pascal have special **iteration**, or looping, statements. Scheme, in its essential parts, has none of these statements. Here, we're restricting ourselves to the essentials of Scheme, sufficient to express all other parts of Scheme, sort of an "Econo-Scheme", a lean and mean Scheme.[11] Iteration in Scheme is just a specialized form of recursion. We leave it up to the Scheme evaluator to implement tail recursion efficiently (a topic we'll return to in later chapters).

☞ **Exercise 2–21**

Look back at the add%, mult%1, and mult%2 procedures in previous sections. Classify each as either tail-recursive or non-tail-recursive. ❏

It is possible to write several different procedures that compute the sum of the numbers from 1 to *n*. Note: For maximum learning effectiveness, do the following three exercises in the order shown.

☞ **Exercise 2–22**

Write a recursive (but non-tail-recursive) version. Hint: Compute the sum of the numbers from 1 to *n* − 1. ❏

☞ **Exercise 2–23**

Write a tail-recursive version. Hint: Look carefully at the two factorial procedures. ❏

☞ **Exercise 2–24**

(For mathematicians) When the mathematician Carl Friedrich Gauss was in school, he was asked to add up the numbers from 1 to 100 by hand. Gauss was both brilliant and lazy, and came up with a formula for the sum of the integers from 1 to *n* which involved no repetition. Duplicate Gauss' achievement.[12] ❏

2.4   Designing, Testing, and Debugging

Program testing can reveal the presence of bugs, but not their absence.
— E. W. Dijkstra

Recursion allows us to do thousands of repetitions in the blink of an eye, but if the procedure is wrong, we might end up with a thousand-repetition disaster. How do we know whether our procedure is correctly written?

Before we make any claims that a procedure is correct, we need to have some evidence to back up those claims. Because some bugs are surprisingly hard to find, we must develop some systematic ways of establishing the correctness of our procedures.

---

[11] Actually, it is possible for an advanced Scheme programmer to define loop forms, and most Scheme implementations define special forms such as while and do. Many Scheme programmers who started off with Pascal or similar languages use these programmer-defined loop forms because they are familiar with them. Scheme purists frown on the use of loop forms, considering them, as the MIT computer scientist Hal Abelson said, to be the computational analog of putting ketchup on caviar. In Chapter 7 we will discover how to improve the flavor of caviar.

[12] For daring to find a better method than the teacher knew, Gauss was beaten by his teacher. Teaching methods have changed in the past two centuries.

There are two basic stages in determining that a procedure is correct: testing and proof. We looked at testing in Chapter 1. We can test a procedure by feeding it inputs and seeing whether it behaves correctly. Testing will be our primary correctness method. Proving a procedure correct is much like proving a mathematical theorem correct—one analyzes the procedure logically and demonstrates that the sequence of steps in the procedure must produce the required results. **Proof** is a complex enough technique that we will only be able to hint at it, in Chapter 10.

Both testing and proof require a clear statement of what the inputs are supposed to be, and what the corresponding outputs must be. For example, in our cube-root procedure, it makes no sense to ask whether the procedure is correct unless we say what the output is supposed to be, and what inputs are valid.

To test a procedure, we feed it inputs and, without using the procedure, determine what output is supposed to be produced for each. We run the procedure for each input, and then check the output for each input. But which inputs should we use? On many computers, there are as many as 2^{64}, or about 10^{30}, possible floating-point numbers, so testing each one is completely out of the question.

Many programmers do a sloppy job of testing because they don't like finding errors. For example, if you evaluate (incorrect-square-root 4), given

```
(define incorrect-square-root
  (lambda (x)
    2))
```

it will indeed give the "correct" answer. Some programmers feel vindicated as soon as their code works correctly in one case, and immediately declare their program correct.[13]

A good programmer gives considerable thought to developing a set of **test cases** along with the code. A test case is a set of inputs to the procedure, along with the value the procedure will produce if it is correct. To test the code, we run the procedure with the test case inputs and check whether the result was correct. If *we have prepared a good set of test cases* and the program passes all the test cases, then we have good reason to believe that the program is correct. Of course, we can't be certain, which is why our testing is only as good as the test cases we prepared.

For cube-root, we might pick the following cases:

- A number larger than 1, say 27. The cube root will be 3.
- A number smaller than 1, say 0.125. The cube root will be 0.5.
- 0. The cube root will be 0.
- 1. The cube root will be 1.
- A very large number, say 1,000,000. The cube root will be 100.
- Some negative numbers. The same cases will apply, with the opposite sign.

The first two cases are typical, in that there's nothing special about either 27 or 0.125, but there are two cases, since the main procedure treats $x > 1$ differently from $x < 1$. This is a case of **glass-box testing**, where we choose tests based on knowing what's in the box, versus standard **black-box testing**. Zero and 1 are

---

[13] If you're like this, imagine the following scenario. You're in a terrible accident and come back to consciousness connected to all sorts of life support equipment. You notice that the software in this equipment uses procedures you've written. It's a bit late now to wish that you'd tested the code a bit more carefully!

boundary cases. Zero is the absolute smallest number that has a nonnegative cube root, and it is at 1 that we must change our method of computing the initial guess. It's worth checking very large numbers because our handling of error tolerance may not be as good as it should be. Finally, it's worth trying an invalid input, so we can see what will happen.

These cases were carefully chosen; if cube-root works correctly for them, it will probably work correctly for all other inputs. But that's where thought is necessary. What if a case that we hadn't thought about occurs in practice? We'd better be sure that our test set is comprehensive.

Let's apply this to another problem. You've deposited n dollars in an interest-bearing savings account that gives p percent interest per time period. You'd like to be able to compare Acme National's new account and its yield with what you're getting from Zaphod Securities in your current account. You've decided to write a procedure interest that will compute your final balance, as in Program 2-13.

```
(define interest
  (lambda (dollars rate time-units)
    (if (< time-units 0)
      dollars
      (interest (* rate dollars)
        rate)
        (sub1 time-unit))))
```

Program 2-13   An incorrect interest procedure

After you've typed this into your Scheme evaluator, you get back

```
Error in if:
 invalid syntax (if (< time-units 0) dollars
    (interest (* rate dollars) rate) (sub1 time-unit)).
```

What's going on here? You check your program and find that you've put a parenthesis after rate in the second-to-last line of the procedure. Text editors can do automatic parenthesis checking, which reduces (though never completely eliminates) the likelihood of mismatched parentheses.

Practical Note

In Program 2-13, we were able to discern the intent by looking at the indentation. Although Scheme evaluators use the parentheses, the indentation provided by the programmer gives a clearer indication of what was intended. If you are lucky enough to have an auto-indenting editor—one that indents each line for you, based upon the current parenthesis depth—use it (see your Scheme system manual for details). If you make a parenthesis error, an auto-indenting editor will indent to the wrong position, thus giving you a clue that you have made an error.

Program 2-14 shows our next attempt.

```
(define interest
  (lambda (dollars rate time-units)
    (if (< time-units 0)
      dollars
      (interest (* rate dollars)
        rate
        (sub1 time-unit)))))
```

Program 2-14   Second try at the interest procedure

Now when you try

```
> (interest 100.0 100.0 1)
Error: variable time-unit is not bound.
```

you get an error: another typo. When you change `time-unit` to `time-units`, Scheme doesn't complain.

Let's devise a set of test cases before we start testing our program. What should we test?

1. When the dollar amount is 0, the value remains 0.
2. 1 percent of `100.0` for one year returns `101.0`.
3. 100 percent of `100.0` for one year returns `200.0`.

Let's start our testing of the program with one test case.

```
(interest 0.0 1.0 1) ⇒ 0.0
```

A sloppy programmer might say, "The program produced a correct answer, and I got no error messages from Scheme. Therefore, the program is correct." Not so fast!

```
(interest 100.0 1.0 1) ⇒ 100.0
```

Something's wrong with this! It gives the wrong answer. How did you know this was incorrect? When writing the program, you begin with an informal specification of the input, output, and the transformation between the two. You have an expectation about what the output will be, especially for certain inputs. You may not know exactly how much you should have for any input, but you do know that you should have more money at the end of one time-unit than when you started! Debugging often begins with these insights about what the expected output should be.

Debugging is the next step after testing. Once we know that program works incorrectly, debugging begins. Debugging is the detection of errors followed by correction of the errors. It's an exciting and challenging part of programming, and can be lots of fun. There's nothing so satisfying as the flash of insight that explains why your program is working the way it does, rather than the way it should! Debugging is interwoven with testing, because each new hypothesis about the source of the error needs to be tested. New evidence leads to new testing and new hypotheses.

What must be fixed in `interest`? One common mistake is to forget that a *percentage* must be converted into a fraction, and you made that mistake. Before multiplying `rate` by `dollars`, you should divide by `100.0` to get a fraction:

```
> (define interest
    (lambda (dollars rate time-units)
      (if (< time-units 0)
```

```
                dollars
                (interest (* (/ rate 100.0) dollars)
                  rate
                  (sub1 time-units)))))
    > (interest 100.0 1.0 1)
    0.01
```

Ouch, this is worse! Of course, you should add the fraction to 1.0—the interest is added to the original amount. Changing the fifth line to

```
    (interest (* (+ 1.0 (/ rate 100.0)) dollars)
```

gives us

```
    (interest 100.0 1.0 1) ⇒ 102.01
```

That's more like it, but it's still not right. After one time-unit, your original 100.0 units is slightly increased, but by too much. Let's use another test case for which we know the answer. If the interest is 100.0 percent, our money should double in one year.

```
    (interest 100.0 100.0 1) ⇒ 400.0
```

We're not out of the woods yet! Let's trace `interest` to see what's up.

```
    > (trace interest)
    (interest)
    > (interest 100.0 100.0 1)
    call interest: 100.0 100.0 1
    | call interest: 200.0 100.0 0
    | | call interest: 400.0 100.0 -1
    | | return from interest: 400.0
    | return from interest: 400.0
    400.0
```

Ah, now there's the problem—`interest` went one step too far. The **termination test** should be (= time-units 0). Now let's see what you get.

```
    (interest 100.0 100.0 1) ⇒ 200.0
    (interest 100.0 1.0 1) ⇒ 101.0
```

Now you can use `interest` to compare your two banks.

Acme is offering 4.98 percent compounded quarterly, while Zaphod is currently giving you 5.0 percent compounded semi-annually. The difference in time periods means that when you use `interest` to compute the new amount, you must divide the percentage by the number of periods per year, *and* multiply the time by the same number. Thus,

```
    (interest 100.0 (/ 5.0 2.0) 2.0) ⇒ 105.06249999999997
    (interest 100.0 (/ 4.98 4.0) 4.0)) ⇒ 105.07377581502752
```

You have discovered that it might be better to get a slightly lower rate and compound it more often. It's even slightly better at 4.95 percent compounded monthly

```
    (interest 100.0 (/ 4.95 12.0) 12.0)) ⇒ 105.06386171982437
```

Those who know something about compound interest may be surprised in the other direction. Compounding more frequently doesn't make *that* large a difference.

To summarize, we discovered a bug in the code by testing it. Then we became detectives, looking for the bug. If you can't see the bug logically, then tracing one or more procedures can give you data on what the procedure is doing.

☞ **Exercise 2-25**

Give a comprehensive set of test values that would convince you that `mult%2` works correctly. ❏

Case Study: Predators and Prey

A major use of computers in science and engineering is for *simulation*: exploring the behavior of a real-life system using a mathematical model. A classic example is modeling population change using the Predator-Prey model. Originally developed to model the fluctuation in fish populations in the Adriatic Sea, it can be applied to many other problems as well.

Imagine an area in the northern part of North America populated only by wolves and caribou. Some people claim that there are too many wolves, and that they will eat all the caribou. Others claim that there are too many caribou, and they will overfeed and destroy grazing lands. Let's suppose that we have obtained some estimates of wolf and caribou population over several years. Is there any way to predict what will happen to the populations?

According to the Predator-Prey model w_{n+1} and c_{n+1}, the populations of wolves and caribou in year $n + 1$ can be determined from the populations in year n by the following equations:

$$c_{n+1} = Ac_n - Bc_nw_n$$

$$w_{n+1} = Cw_n + Dc_nw_n$$

where A, B, C, and D are experimentally determined coefficients (i.e., people go out and count the number of wolves and caribou each year). Each new population is proportional to the old one (a bit larger or smaller, depending on the natural growth rate—so A and C should be close to 1—wolves and caribou have few children). The chance that a caribou will be eaten depends on the number of wolves and the probability that a wolf will eat a caribou that it encounters. The overall loss in caribou population is proportional to the product of the number of wolves and caribou. Likewise, the increase in wolf population depends on the food supply, which is represented by the same product of the wolf and caribou populations. Hence B and D should be positive but small.

For example, if $A = 1.1$, $B = 0.02$, $C = 0.9$ and $D = 0.015$, and there were 10 caribou and 10 wolves, then according to the model there would be 9 caribou and 10.5 wolves next year. Does the model predict that there would be half a wolf (a semiwolf)? Or does this mean that the number of wolves is about 10 or 11? You ought to sensibly interpret the numbers you get from a computer—in this or any other problem.

How shall we write this program? The inputs are the four coefficients, the initial populations of wolves and caribou, and the number of years for which we want to run the simulation. We can write a recursive procedure, pops, that will compute population after n years. What do we need? Since we must perform this estimate every year for n years, the procedure will be a tail-recursive procedure and call itself recursively with the new populations of wolves and caribou. It should be straightforward to write the expressions for the new populations. For caribou, the formula is

```
(- (* a caribou) (* b wolves caribou))
```

For wolves, it is

```
(+ (* c wolves) (* d wolves caribou))
```

Let's define our interface as

```
(define pops
  (lambda (a b c d wolves caribou n)
```

We call the population procedure with new populations for each year, decreasing the number of years left. So the body of our procedure will be an if form.

```
(define pops
  (lambda (a b c d wolves caribou n)
    (if (= n 0)
      --done--
      --call again--)))
```

To call our procedure again, we need to plug in the new values for the wolf and caribou population (Program 2-15).

```
(define pops
  (lambda (a b c d wolves caribou n)
    (if (= n 0)
      --done--
      (pops a b c d
        (+ (* c wolves) (* d wolves caribou))
        (- (* a caribou) (* b wolves caribou))
        (sub1 n)))))
```

Program 2-15   Computing populations

We're facing a slight difficulty here. When we're done (at $n = 0$), we have *two* values to report. We'd just return it if it were one value. Of course, Scheme has ways to package up more than one value; we'll discuss them in Chapter 4. For now, we'll introduce a procedure, output-wc, that will display two values for us on the screen. We will write output-wc in Chapter 3; for now, we'll write 0 as its body and use tracing to get output. Our recursive procedure appears as Program 2-16.

The output of our simulation using our original example, $A = 1.1$, $B = 0.02$, $C = 0.9$ and $D = 0.015$, is given in Figure 2-19.

We now have a procedure that will run our simulation for n years and report the result at the end of that period. One of the more interesting uses of this model is to watch the growth and decline of the two populations year by year for a long time. We evaluated our model after 1, 10, and 20 years, rerunning it each time.

```
(define pops
  (lambda (a b c d wolves caribou n)
    (if (= n 0)
      (output-wc wolves caribou)
      (pops a b c d
        (+ (* c wolves) (* d wolves caribou))
        (- (* a caribou) (* b wolves caribou))
        (sub1 n)))))
(define output-wc
  (lambda (wolves caribou)
    0))
```

Program 2-16   Procedure pops

```
> (pops 1.1 .02 .9 .015 10 10 1)
call output-wc: 10.5 9.0
return from output-wc: 0
> (pops 1.1 .02 .9 .015 10 10 10)
call output-wc: 9.251799698484708 3.044413011656412
return from output-wc: 0
> (pops 1.1 .02 .9 .015 10 10 20)
call output-wc:  9.251799698484708 3.044413011656412
return from output-wc: 0
```

Figure 2-19   Wolves and caribou output

How will we watch the change in population? Let's use our output procedure to display the values every k years—we'll need to check before going on whether we need to print out the value. Note how and sequences two operations. and evaluates its arguments in order left to right, and only stops when the value of one of them is #f. If all of its arguments return something other than #f, and evaluates each of the arguments in left-to-right order. We wrote output-wc so that it displays the number of wolves and caribou. Thus, to perform two operations in order, we gave them as arguments to and, ensuring that output-wc always returns #t and that the if form returns #t in the else-part. We'll see Scheme's better way of doing this in Chapter 3. The revised procedure, popsk, that runs the wolves-caribou model for n years and outputs its results every k years, appears in Program 2-17.

Displaying the results every year gives information on the slow decline of the caribou population and the gradual increase of the wolf population (Figure 2-20).

The trace output has been edited to show only the calling arguments. The result of output-wc is always 0. Interestingly, if we run the model longer, the caribou population increases! Figure 2-21 shows a snapshot every ten years for 100 years.

Figure 2-22 shows the output from years eleven to thirty. We've annotated the output where the wolf population reaches a maximum (year twelve) and the caribou population reaches a minimum (year twenty-nine).

Notice the fluctuations. The caribou population sometimes increases, resulting in an increased wolf population, and finally a decreased population. These results are hard to predict without using the model. Of course, the model itself must be verified. Ecologists have developed complex population models, and verify

```
(define popsk
  (lambda (a b c d wolves caribou n k)
    (if (= n 0)
        (output-wc wolves caribou)
        (and
          (if (= 0 (remainder n k))
              (output-wc wolves caribou)
              #t)
          (popsk a b c d
            (+ (* c wolves) (* d wolves caribou))
            (- (* a caribou) (* b wolves caribou))
            (sub1 n) k)))))
```

Program 2-17   Procedure popsk

```
> (popsk 1.1 .01 .9 .02 10 10 7 1)
call output-wc 10 10
call output-wc 11.0 10.0
call output-wc 12.100000000000001 9.9
call output-wc 13.285800000000002 9.6921
call output-wc 14.532566043600003 9.3736369782
call output-wc 15.803769408328456 8.948770691475774
call output-wc 17.051878637417435 8.42940467566244
call output-wc 18.22143448397719 7.834973288077934
```

Figure 2-20   The first simulation run

```
> (popsk 1.1 .01 .9 .02 10 10 100 10)
call output-wc 10 10
call output-wc 20.711384214109003 5.866399725237211
call output-wc 15.93713321103512 2.101324526612264
call output-wc 8.200978277665882 1.6891136120570782
call output-wc 4.365709921574937 2.4502200553334834
call output-wc 3.05661652536691002 4.549062818890679
call output-wc 3.909302471319726 8.78086614913315
call output-wc 12.029799809716321 12.484912140306877
call output-wc 26.90504110233412 4.038942586858527
call output-wc 15.015638889731909 1.1008188666804017
call output-wc 6.513960150808835 1.0298769253395146
```

Figure 2-21   Every ten years for a hundred years

them by confirming that the model accurately predicts populations. Our model is oversimplified, and does not include the effects caused by other animals, climatic change, or human activities.

Is there a better way of using this model? If we could draw a graph showing the populations as they change over time, we could see patterns in the shape of the graph that might not be apparent from the numbers. We'll see how to draw graphs with Scheme in Chapter 3.

```
> (popsk 1.1 .01 .9 .02 10 10 100 1)
. . .
call output-wc 21.0702709659 5.23802711113
call output-wc 21.17057688053 4.65816331665        Wolf Max
call output-wc 21.02583928482 4.13781960215
call output-wc 20.66327795523 3.68159026292
call output-wc 20.11842461811 3.289012060013
call output-wc 19.42997698024 2.95621585404

. . .
call output-wc 10.80822030411 1.67417493581
call output-wc 10.08929530438 1.660643914055
call output-wc 9.41546031082 1.659161037017
call output-wc 8.78634957761 1.66885949178         Caribou Min
call output-wc 8.20097827766 1.689113612057
```

Figure 2-22   From year eleven to year thirty

Summary

This chapter introduces recursive procedures, the fundamental means for express-ing repetition in Scheme. We have learned how recursive procedures express a way of reducing a problem in size in each recursive call until the base case is reached. We were introduced to several basic ways to use recursion, from mathematical func-tions like factorial and power to simple repetitions. The Lunar Lander example showed how to use a recursive procedure to compute the repetitive steps in a phys-ical computation. Then we looked into bisection, a recursive solution technique for mathematical equations. Multi-way recursion offered a way of exploring multiple alternative subproblems and combining the results. To understand how algorithms use time and space resources, we introduced ideas of time and space complexity. This led us to investigate tail-recursive procedures that use no extra space to com-pute recursively. Finally, we explored ways of testing and debugging programs.

Further Readings

George Polya's classic book *How to Solve It* contains many insights into simplifying problems to aid their solution. This book is out of print, but can be found in libraries.

Although we did not introduce any new Scheme features (apart from a few primitives, and the tracing forms) in this chapter, the Scheme references in Chap-ter 1 are very useful for more examples of recursion.

Key Words

Here are the *key words* introduced in this chapter. Make sure you understand what each one means.

accumulator	Droid Model	loop
base case	Egyptian peasant method	MIPS
"big-oh" ($O(\ldots)$) notation	exponential complexity	multiway recursion
bisection	floating point	parallel computation
black-box testing	glass-box testing	proof
calling a procedure	infinite loop	recursion
comment	infinite recursion	recursion step
complexity	invocation	tail recursion
divide and conquer	iteration	termination test
droid	knapsack problem	test case
droid diagram	limit	trace

Scheme Features Introduced in This Chapter

Primitive Procedures

abs	boolean	integer?	inexact->exact
number?	procedure?	quotient	remainder
round			

Special Forms

trace	untrace

Cumulative List of Data Types

number (complex, floating-point number, rational, integer), boolean, procedure

Problems

1. Write a procedure, `reverse-digits`, to take a positive integer n written in decimal form as abcde ... m and return another integer that is written in decimal form as m ... edcba. For example,

   ```
   (reverse-digits 7) ⇒ 7
   (reverse-digits 123) ⇒ 321
   ```

2. Write a procedure, `shuffle`, that takes two positive integers a and b, written in decimal as bcd ... e and mno ... p and returns a new integer that shuffles the two numbers together—bmcndo ... ep:

   ```
   (shuffle 12 34) ⇒ 1324     (shuffle 123 456) ⇒ 142536
   ```

3. Suppose we've defined

   ```
   (define funny
     (lambda (n)
       (if (<= n 0)
           0
           (if (odd? n)
               (+ 2 (funny (- n 3)))
   ```

```
(add1 (funny (funny (- n 4))))))))
```

and we now evaluate (funny 9). Draw a droid diagram for this computation.

4. Write a procedure, add-odd, that adds up the digits at odd positions (counting from the right, with the one's digit at position 1) in the decimal representation of a positive number. For example, (add-odd 1248) ⇒ 10.

5. Write a procedure, count-even-odd, that counts the number of even digits at odd positions (counting from the right, with the one's digit at position 1) in the decimal representation of a positive number.

6. Write a procedure, sum-ax+b, that takes four arguments, a b from to, and evaluates the sum of $ax + b$ for x from from to to. Thus:

```
(sum-ax+b 1 0 1 10) ⇒ 55
(sum-ax+b 2 0 1 10) ⇒ 110
(sum-ax+b 2 1 1 10) ⇒ 120
```

7. Write a version of power that raises z to the power n that uses only log n multiplications.

8. Write a predicate, (find? x n), that returns #t if the digit x occurs in the decimal representation of n, and otherwise returns #f.

9. Generalize find to handle the case when x is a two-digit decimal number.

10. Write a procedure, (nth-digit n x), that takes a nonnegative integer n and a positive integer x, and returns the nth from the *left* of x, counting from 0. For example,

```
(nth-digit 0 10) ⇒ 1.0    (nth-digit 0 1234) ⇒ 1.0
(nth-digit 3 1234) ⇒ 4.0
```

11. Write a recursive procedure, (digit-0 x), to return the index (counting from 0) of the first digit from the right that is 0 in the number x. If no digit is 0, then return -1.

```
(digit-0 0) ⇒ 0
(digit-0 1) ⇒ 0
(digit-0 1) ⇒ 1
(digit-0 101) ⇒ 1
(digit-0 1011) ⇒ 2
```

Self-Assessment

1. Give the value of the last form in the following sequence:

```
(define a
  (lambda (n)
    (if (< n 2)
        0
        (+ n (b (sub1 n))))))
(define b
  (lambda (n)
    (if (< n 1)
        1
        (* n (a (- n 2))))))
(a 5)
```

2. Give the value of the last form in the following sequence:

```
(define f
  (lambda (n)
    (g n 1)))
(define g
  (lambda (n e)
    (if (> (expt 3 e) n)
        e
        (g n (+ e 1)))))
(f 27)
```

3. Write a recursive procedure, product-of-even, that takes an argument n and returns the product of the first n even integers. For example, (product-of-even 4) should evaluate to $2 * 4 * 6 * 8 = 384$.

4. Write product-of-even in tail-recursive form.

5. Write procedure kth-digit that takes a nonnegative integer k and a positive integer n, and returns the kth digit from the right of n, counting from 0. For example,

```
(kth-digit 0 4321) ⇒ 1
(kth-digit 3 4321) ⇒ 4
```

6. The recursive procedure power-close-to is as follows:

```
(define power-close-to
  (lambda (b n)
    (power-iter b n 1)))
(define power-iter
  (lambda (b n e)
    (if (> (expt b e) n)
        e
        (power-iter b n (+ e 1)))))
```

What is the value of the expression (power-close-to 2 32)? Express the time complexity of power-close-to in terms of its parameters, b and n.

7. Write the recursive procedure (0-digit x) to return the index (counting from 0) of the first digit from the right that is 0 in the number x

```
(0-digit 0) ⇒ 0
(0-digit 1) ⇒ 1
(0-digit 101) ⇒ 1
(0-digit 1011) ⇒ 2
```

Programming Problems

1. Funarg Corporation marks each of its cartons with a numeric code to indicate the number of items of each type inside the carton. The code consists of triples of digits. Each triple consists of two digits specifying the type of item, followed by one digit specifying the number of that item. There can be any number of different items. For example 128934 specifies that there are 8 items of type 12 and 4 items of type 93. Write the procedure

(`count-of-items code type`) that returns the number of items of kind `type` specified in `code`. Return `-1` if there are no items of that kind.

2. A financial institution accepts term deposits over periods of several years. An initial deposit of p dollars is made. At the end of each year, interest is credited at a rate of $r\%$ (on the total, principal plus deposits). The deposit is held for n years, where n is an integer (thus there will always be exactly n interest deposits, with the last coming on the day the deposit matures). The best interest procedure is tail-recursive.

   Write a procedure that calculates the final deposit amount, using the values p, r, and n. Your procedure will be recursive (on which argument?). Try your procedure out (by hand) with the values $p = 1000$, $r = 0.1$, and $n = 5$ (the answer should be $\$1610.51$).

3. A *perfect number* is one that is equal to the sum of its divisors. For example, $6 = 1 + 2 + 3$ and is therefore perfect. (We include 1, but do not include the number itself.) The next perfect number is $28 = 1 + 2 + 4 + 7 + 14$. If a number has the same divisor more than once, we only include it once.

   In this problem, you are to write a predicate `perfect?` that takes an integer argument and returns true if it is perfect and false if it is not. Use decomposition to build your solution. Once you have completed the code, analyze it to obtain a time complexity estimate, in $O(\dots)$ notation.

Chapter 3

Building Programs

Overview

This chapter introduces text processing by adding two new data types: *characters* and *strings*, which are collections of characters. To handle string data structures, we will learn new recursion techniques that process each character in a string one by one. We explore input and output in Scheme, and then graphic output. Input and output force us to consider how to sequence a set of computations. We next learn how to write procedures that take procedures as arguments. Using procedures as arguments, we can write generalized procedures. Finally, we see how to organize programs. Within procedures, we can control how variables are bound to values. We also introduce *modules*, a way of organizing procedures so as to hide the names of auxiliary procedures, to help us build readable programs.

Give us the tools and we will finish the job.   — Winston Churchill

In Chapters 1 and 2, we saw enough of Scheme to write sophisticated programs. In fact, the programming capabilities we've already seen in Scheme are more complete than those of many early programming languages. Procedures and recursion allow us to divide programs into manageable pieces and write loops. Many early languages didn't give the programmer so much power. Many versions of languages such as FORTRAN and BASIC used in the 1980s didn't have general recursion.[1]

Yet there is more to programming than we've seen. We need tools that let us represent information effectively, and we need tools that allow us to create and organize larger programs.

We need to represent data such as people's names or addresses, or the names of books. *Characters* and *strings* represent textual information. Strings, collections of characters, require new recursion methods.

Any useful language must allow us to read or write a data value in a program. Sometimes we are satisfied with writing data in textual form. At other times, we want to display our program's results graphically. Input/output and graphics require us to be more careful about specifying what it means to evaluate a Scheme form.

No matter how useful more Scheme features might be, what's most important is to improve our skills at abstraction and program design. The skills a programmer might need to write a large program are of a different order than those needed for a quick little procedure. We'll see how to structure larger programs by using techniques based on abstraction. We'll see how to generalize a procedure by using procedures as arguments. We'll also see that abstraction can be used to create new kinds of data.

Scheme provides a number of features for structuring larger programs. One of them, scope, allows us to limit the range in which a name is known. The `let` special form allows us to use scope to create better-structured programs. Finally, we'll study modules, which allow us to group related procedures and data together.

---

[1] The "jars" problem from the previous chapter would require a substantial amount of code in such languages.

3.1   Text Processing

There are strings in the human heart that had better not be wibrated [sic].
— Charles Dickens, *Barnaby Rudge*

 The code presented in this section can be found in file `string.scm`.

Computers can process many sorts of data, but so far we have seen only three types: numbers, Booleans, and procedures. These data types are very powerful, but more are needed. A brief look at some common computer applications will show that we need more than numbers. Spreadsheets work with numbers, but any good spreadsheet will have labels. A column of numbers without any explanation is useless. Many computer applications, such as word processing, are not about numbers at all.

We will extend our repertoire of Scheme data types by adding two *text* data types: characters and strings. These data types represent data such as words, people's names, and other text. New data types require new programming styles, and we will develop new recursion techniques and new problem-analysis techniques to exploit strings fully.

3.1.1   Characters

Almost every computer has a keyboard containing between 80 and 100 keys. Each key sends a single piece of data to the computer. Almost all the data entered into computers comes, eventually, from pressing these keys.[2] Many keys are labeled with capital letters, such as ⒜. Others are labeled with function codes, such as the F1 key on the keyboard that we used for entering this paragraph.

When you press the ⒜ key, you get a value that is of Scheme's **character** data type. We write the value obtained by pressing ⒜ as #\a. It is conventional for keyboards to be labeled with capital letters. To enter a capital letter, however, one must press two keys, Shift ⒜, which enter the character written in Scheme as #\A. There isn't a one-to-one relationship between characters and keys, since there are many more characters than keys. Standard keyboards use so-called modifier keys, such as Shift, Ctrl, and Alt, to allow users to enter characters by combinations of keystrokes.[3]

---

[2] Most computers also have a *mouse* that allows (x,y) positions on the screen to be selected. *Pens* allow users to enter sketches and handwritten data. Many computers have *scanners* that allow graphic images to be entered. None of these devices has replaced the keyboard yet.

[3] The term *bucky bits* is often used for the Ctrl and Alt shift modifier keys, and for the bits they add to a character. The Jargon File (*The New Hacker's Dictionary*),edited by Eric Raymond, MIT Press) says, "It has long been rumored that 'bucky bits' were named for Buckminster Fuller during a period when he was consulting at Stanford. Actually, bucky bits were invented by Niklaus Wirth when *he* was at Stanford. He first suggested the idea of an EDIT key to set the 8th bit of an otherwise 7-bit ASCII character. This was used in a number of editors written at Stanford or in its environs (TV-EDIT and NLS being the best known). Some sources claim that 'Bucky' was Niklaus Wirth's nickname at Stanford, but Wirth himself does not recall this."

Scheme provides primitive procedures to check whether a value is a character and to compare two characters.

```
(char? #\A) ⇒ #t
(char? 5) ⇒ #f
```

The predicate char? accepts any value as an argument and returns #t if and only if the value is a character, like the number?, boolean?, and procedure? primitives we have already seen.

Characters are a genuinely new type in Scheme. This can be confusing, because some of the keys on a keyboard appear to enter numbers. Nonetheless, the characters these keys enter are indeed characters, not numbers.

```
> (+ 5 2)
7
> (+ #\5 #\2)
Error in +: #\5 is not a number.
```

The Scheme primitive +, like all Scheme primitives, can identify that \#5 is not a number, but a character. Chapter 11 discusses how numerals are converted from sequences of characters to numbers.

☞ **Exercise 3-1**

What type is the value of each of the following forms?
  a. #\t
  b. #t
  c. t □

Characters can be compared for equality using the char=? primitive. We must have a new primitive here, because our familiar = primitive is designed to work only with numbers.

```
> (= #\A #\B)
Error in =: #\A is not a number.
> (char=? #\A #\B)
#f
> (char=? #\A #\A)
#t
```

Like most predicates, char?'s name ends with a question mark, following our style rule for naming predicates. The numeric comparison procedures such as = are exceptions to this rule, and then only for historical reasons (these names preceded the rule).[4]

```
(char=? #\A #\B) ⇒ #f
(char=? #\A #\a) ⇒ #f
```

---

[4] People often think that languages ought to be thoroughly consistent. Unfortunately, what makes sense from a logical viewpoint may not match what people have been doing historically. As a result, any language, including Scheme, has a number of features that might have been different had the whole language been designed at once, rather than over a period of over 30 years. Sometimes consistency is crucial, but not always. On this topic Ralph Waldo Emerson is often misquoted. He really said, "A *foolish* consistency is the hobgoblin of little minds".

In many contexts (e.g., in dictionaries and indexes), we would consider #\A and #\a to be equal. We therefore need a second method of comparing characters that is *case insensitive*; Scheme provides the primitive char-ci=?.[5]

```
(char=? #\A #\a) ⇒ #f
(char-ci=? #\A #\a) ⇒ #t
```

Program 3-1 shows a procedure that determines whether a character is a vowel.

```
(define vowel?
  (lambda (ch)
    (or
      (char-ci=? ch #\A)
      (char-ci=? ch #\E)
      (char-ci=? ch #\I)
      (char-ci=? ch #\O)
      (char-ci=? ch #\U))))
```

Program 3-1   Determining whether a character is a vowel

☞ **Exercise 3-2**

We can remember the standard list of colors in the spectrum by using the mnemonic "Roy G. Biv" (red, orange, yellow, green, blue, indigo, violet). Write a predicate that tells whether a character representing a color is one of these seven. ❏

Scheme provides primitives to convert between upper- and lowercase: char-upcase converts to uppercase, and char-downcase converts to lowercase.

☞ **Exercise 3-3**

Write char-ci=?%, your own version of char-ci=?. ❏

Characters are represented in the computer by numeric codes. The primitive procedure char->integer accepts a character argument and returns its numeric code. integer->char does the reverse. (The symbol -> in a procedure name tells the programmer that the procedure accepts one type of argument and returns a similar value of a different type. Such procedures are called **conversion procedures**.)

```
(char->integer #\A) ⇒ 65
(integer->char 97) ⇒ #\a
(char->integer #\2) ⇒ 50
```

The numeric code for #\2 isn't 2.

---

[5] *Case* is an old printing term. Typesetters used to work, before computer typesetting, or even the early Linotype machines, with pieces of metal type, each containing one character. A typesetter wishing to set the word *and* would take one piece from the *a* box, one from the *n* box, and one from the *d* box, and would clamp these pieces together in a frame that was then used for the actual printing. The boxes for the small letters were organized in a case, as were those for the capital letters. Because a typesetter needed many more small letters than large ones, the small-letter case was placed below the capital-letter case, hence the names lower- and uppercase.

The numeric codes actually define how characters work. `char=?` returns `#t` if and only if its two arguments have the same numeric code. The other character comparison procedures, `char<?`, `char<=?`, `char>?`, and `char>=?`, as well as case independent versions (`char-ci>?`, for example) are also provided.

Each of the manufacturers of the first computers assigned its own codes to characters. Many early computers were designed to work with sets of as few as 48 characters. This arrangement meant that it was not possible to use both upper- and lowercase letters. Hence, computer printers were often designed with uppercase only, leading to the idea that documents produced by computers HAD TO BE IN CAPITAL LETTERS. Names such as FORTRAN (FORmula TRANslator) are remnants of this tradition.

In the early 1960s, a number of computer manufacturers became concerned that character data could not be easily moved from one computer to another because each machine used its own character-coding system. These companies developed a standardized coding system that eventually became approved as a national standard. The system was named ASCII, the American Standard Code for Information Interchange. ASCII was a great improvement on earlier coding systems. It allowed 128 different characters, enough for upper- and lowercase letters, digits, a generous selection of punctuation marks, and 32 **control characters**, which were intended to be used in data communications. Data communications techniques have improved to the point that most of the control characters are no longer needed for this purpose. Programs use them instead for signaling special situations. The Esc key, for example, is often used to cancel an operation.

Unfortunately, ASCII only works well in the United States. Other countries have other needs for special characters, including accented characters, special currency signs, and so on. The International Standards Organization developed versions of ASCII that provide these characters, but many special characters had to be removed to accommodate them. ASCII doesn't support at all alphabets such as Cyrillic, used in Russia, Ukraine, and a number of other Slavic countries, not to mention Chinese, Japanese, Korean, and other alphabets. In the 1990s, a new coding system, Unicode, was developed to accommodate all of these characters. Most Scheme systems still use ASCII.[6]

Regardless of the coding system, the character-comparison primitives work in the same way. We compare characters by comparing their codes: (`char<? #\a #\b`) ⇒ `#t` because the ASCII character code for a, 97, is indeed less than that for b, 98. This fact isn't a law of nature, but all commonly used coding schemes arrange the letters in the order in which they appear in the alphabet. On the other hand, (`char<? #\0 #\a`) might result in `#t` on one machine and `#f` on another, depending upon the relative code values for 0 and a. On all machines, though, the digits are consecutive (e.g., 48 through 57 for 0 through 9). In ASCII (though not in some other coding systems) the letters are also consecutive.

☞ **Exercise 3–4**

Using `char->integer`, write a procedure named `letter->number` that returns the number of a character within the alphabet, for example, (`letter->number #\A`) ⇒ 0, as does

---

[6] Another coding system, EBCDIC, is based upon punched card codes. EBCDIC has traditionally been used on large IBM mainframes, but its use is decreasing. Even desktop computers made by IBM don't use EBCDIC anymore, so character data must be converted from EBCDIC to ASCII when it is sent from an IBM mainframe to an IBM desktop computer.

(letter->number #\a), and (letter->number #\Z) ⇒ 25. Your procedure should return -1 if the argument isn't a letter. Note especially that we've chosen Scheme's technique of counting from 0. ❏

☞ **Exercise 3-5**

Write the opposite procedure, number->letter, which returns the (lowercase) letter corresponding to a number between 0 and 25. For any other numeric argument, return a + character. ❏

Some characters don't have a printable representation. In Scheme, we can write these characters with our familiar #\... notation, except that we use a mnemonic word instead of the character itself. For example, we can write #\space instead of #\ , which would be unclear. One character that occurs frequently (once per line!) is the character #\newline. This character, which is invisible on a screen or printout, forces the computer to go to the beginning of the next line. You generate a newline by pressing the ⎡Return⎤ or ⎡Enter⎤ key on your keyboard.

3.1.2   Strings

Characters by themselves are useful, but we need a way to work with groups of characters. Scheme provides the **string** data type for this purpose. A string is a sequence of characters in a particular order. We write string literals as characters surrounded by quotation marks (e.g., "cat's cradle"). Like our other data types, strings come with a type-checking predicate, string?.

```
(string? 5) ⇒ #f
(string? #\5) ⇒ #f
(string? "five") ⇒ #t
```

Scheme has several primitive procedures for working with strings. string-append returns a new string formed by joining, or *catenating*, the strings given as arguments, and string-length returns the number of characters in its argument.

```
(string-append "abc" "def") ⇒ "abcdef"
(string-length "eggplant") ⇒ 8
```

People are often surprised that it is possible to have a string with no characters. We call this string the **null string**. It's not really that astonishing. It's just a string with length 0. Appending the null string to a string x produces a new string with the same characters as x. The null string is used as the starting point in recursions that build up strings by appending strings.

```
(string-append "zilch" "") ⇒ "zilch"
(string-length "") ⇒ 0
```

In Scheme, a string is a collection of boxes, each containing a character. The string "PICKLE" can be visualized as in Figure 3-1.

Each box is labeled with a number called the **position** of the box. Positions start at 0. Thus the character #\C can be found in box number 2. It's box 2, but it's the *third* one in the string, since Scheme always counts from zero. There are good reasons for this choice, which we will see in Chapter 11.

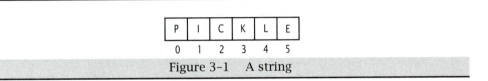

Figure 3-1   A string

We can access the contents of the box at a particular position with the primitive `string-ref`: `(string-ref "PICKLE" 2)` ⇒ `#\C`. It stands to reason that `string-ref` returns a character, rather than a string: each box in a string stores a character.

The `string=?` primitive determines whether two strings have the same contents.

```
(string=?  "PICKLE" "pickle") ⇒ #f
(string=?  "pickle" "pickle") ⇒ #t
```

To help understand strings, let's write `string=?%`, our own version of `string=?`. How will we determine if two strings are equal? First, they must be the same length; second, the characters in corresponding boxes of the strings must be identical. The first condition is easy to test. To handle the second, we need to write a recursive procedure that can examine each of the characters in the string, in order, one after another. This pattern of recursion for strings is called **string recursion**.

The idea of string recursion is to keep track of both the current box number and the total number of boxes in the string. We'll call these two arguments `pos` (for position), and `len` (for length). Program 3-2 presents a string-recursive procedure for testing the equality of two strings.

```
(define string=?%-help
  (lambda (str1 str2 pos len)
    (if (>= pos len)
        #t
        (if (char=? (string-ref str1 pos)
                    (string-ref str2 pos))
          (string=?%-help str1 str2 (add1 pos) len)
          #f))))
```

Program 3-2   String-recursive procedure to determine equality

`string=?%-help` checks the equality of characters at position `pos` in `str1` and `str2`. If the characters are equal, recursion continues until `pos` is equal to `len`, when the verdict is that the strings are equal. `string=?%` tests the first condition (lengths equal) and then calls the helper (Program 3-3).

Inside a string, the backslash character is used for a number of purposes. A backslash or quotation mark can be written by preceding it with a backslash.

3.1.3   Encryption

Throughout history, people have searched for methods of keeping information secret. When few people could read or write, writing down a message was sufficient. As literacy spread, however, people looked for ways to write messages that only the intended recipient could understand. Two basic methods of encryption were

```
(define string=?%
  (lambda (str1 str2)
    (if (= (string-length str1) (string-length str2))
        (string=?%-help str1 str2 0 (string-length str1))
        #f)))
```

Program 3-3   Procedure for computing string equality

developed: a **cipher** refers to a method of substituting characters, whereas a **code** refers to a word-by-word substitution. Encryption and computers have gone hand-in-hand. One of the first designers of the modern digital computer, Alan Turing, worked on decrypting the German Enigma encryption system during World War II.

When a Caesar died, the Romans would go through his private papers, looking for anything that might be of advantage to them, or even just juicy gossip. Anticipating this, Caesars would encrypt their papers, to prevent people from reading them. The effectiveness of this technique can be judged by the work of the Roman historian Suetonius, who often comments upon the particular encryption method a Caesar used. He mentions that Augustus encrypted his papers by replacing every letter by the next, except for *X*, which was replaced by *AA*. This technique is even easier to break than the "secret decoder rings" that used to be included in cereal boxes.

Julius Caesar, it is said, used a cipher in which each letter was replaced by the letter three letters farther on; *X*, *Y*, and *Z* were replaced by *A*, *B*, and *C* respectively. Can we write a procedure that will encrypt a string using the Caesar cipher?

Let's start by trying to write a procedure that will encrypt a single character. You might think of writing a huge if form: "If the character is *a*, the answer is *d*, and if the character is *b*, the answer is *e*; . . .". There's an easier method, however.

We can use the procedures that we wrote in Exercise 3-4 to convert between letters and "letter-numbers". Once we have a numeric code, we can add 3. The result is in the range 3 to 28. Before converting that code to a number, we must bring it back into the range 0 to 25 by computing its remainder after dividing by 26, as shown in Program 3-4.

```
(define caesar-rotate-char
  (lambda (ch)
    (number->letter
      (remainder
        (+ (letter->number ch) 3)
        26))))
```

Program 3-4   The Caesar character cipher

Let's try this procedure out:

```
(caesar-rotate-char #\a) ⇒ #\d
(caesar-rotate-char #\z) ⇒ #\c
(caesar-rotate-char #\*) ⇒ #\c
```

This procedure works well, except that the characters #\z and * give the same result. We'll have to check for nonletters, therefore, before calling this procedure.

Because we encrypt a whole string letter-by-letter, our helper, shown in Program 3-5, must go through the string, looking at each character in turn, using string recursion. Program 3-6 shows the main procedure that calls the helper.

The recursion here is on pos. In the base case, the procedure has processed all of the boxes; hence, pos is no longer less than len. (You might think that we should process the box in position len; however, remember that we're counting from zero. The last box of the string is numbered len-1.)

```
(define caesar-encrypt-string-helper
  (lambda (str pos len)
    (if (>= pos len)
        ""
        (string-append
          (caesar-encrypt-char
            (string-ref str pos))
          (caesar-encrypt-string-helper
            str (add1 pos) len)))))
```
Program 3-5   A helper for encrypting a string with Caesar cipher

```
(define caesar-encrypt-string
  (lambda (str)
    (caesar-encrypt-string-helper str 0
      (string-length str))))
```
Program 3-6   Encrypting a string using Caesar cipher

In the base case, the procedure returns a null string. In the recursion case, the procedure returns a string by catenating two pieces: a single-character string that is the result of caesar-encrypt-char (which we'll handle momentarily), and the string coming back from a recursive call of caesar-encrypt-string-helper.

Figure 3-2 shows a trace of this procedure.

```
> (caesar-encrypt-string-helper "help" 0 4)
call caesar-encrypt-string-helper: "help" 0 4
| call caesar-encrypt-string-helper: "help" 1 4
| | call caesar-encrypt-string-helper: "help" 2 4
| | | call caesar-encrypt-string-helper: "help" 3 4
| | | | call caesar-encrypt-string-helper: "help" 4 4
| | | | return from caesar-encrypt-string-helper: ""
| | | return from caesar-encrypt-string-helper: "s"
| | return from caesar-encrypt-string-helper: "os"
| return from caesar-encrypt-string-helper: "hos"
return from caesar-encrypt-string-helper: "khos"
```
Figure 3-2   Trace of caesar-encrypt-string-helper

How do we encrypt a single character? Here we must be careful about strings and characters. string-ref delivers us a *character*, but string-append wants a *string.* To convert between the two types, we use the primitive procedure `string` that accepts a single character and returns a string consisting of that character. What about nonletters? We can use the primitive `char-alphabetic?` to tell us whether a character is a letter or not.[7] Our character-encryption procedure appears in Program 3-7.

```
(define caesar-encrypt-char
  (lambda (ch)
    (if (char-alphabetic? ch)
      (string (caesar-rotate-char ch))
      "")))
```
Program 3-7   Encrypting a character

So far we've processed strings to produce Booleans (`string=?%`) or strings of the same size (`caesar-encrypt-string`). To extract part of a string, we use the `substring` primitive: (`substring str from after`) returns a new string composed of the characters in `str` from position `from` to position `after`-1.

```
(substring "PICKLE" 0 4) ⇒ "PICK"
(substring "Mississippi" 6 9) ⇒ "sip"
```

We can develop another style of recursion on strings by using `substring`. We'll demonstrate **substring recursion** by writing another version of `caesar-encrypt-string` (Program 3-8).

```
(define caesar-encrypt-string-s
  (lambda (str)
    (if (string=? str "")
      ""
      (string-append
        (caesar-encrypt-char
          (string-ref str 0))
        (caesar-encrypt-string-s
          (substring str 1 (string-length str)))))))
```
Program 3-8   Recursion using substrings

Since we don't have to keep track of position, we don't need a helper. Each step encrypts the first character in the string into a one-character string that is appended to the recursive result. The argument to the recursive call is the input string, omitting the character at position 0.

You might wonder why we don't use substring recursion instead of the method of string recursion we first saw. After all, there's no need for a helper. There are two reasons: the cost of calling `string-length` each time (although one could pass

---

[7] You might ask why we didn't modify `caesar-rotate-char` to check for this case. It would certainly have been possible, but it would have complicated an already complicated procedure. Sometimes it's convenient to check for special cases as we go, and other times it's better to check for them before we start. This seems to be an example of the latter case.

the length) and the cost of creating a new string at each step. For small problems, however, these costs are relatively insignificant, and both styles of recursion are acceptable. The next chapter introduces data structures whose recursion techniques strongly resemble substring recursion.

☞ **Exercise 3-6**

Evaluate

```
(string-append
  (substring "clay bricks" 5 9)
  (string-append
    "-a-"
    (substring "abracadabra" 1 5)))
```

❏

☞ **Exercise 3-7**

Write `string-upcase`, a procedure that uses `char-upcase` to convert every character in a string to uppercase. ❏

3.1.4 Palindromes

Another interesting problem is to find out whether a string is a *palindrome*, that is, whether it reads the same backwards as forwards, ignoring punctuation, case and blanks. For example, the first sentence Eve heard, "Madam, I'm Adam", is a palindrome, as is Napoleon's lament on his island of exile, "Able was I ere I saw Elba". "Level" is a palindrome, but "lever" isn't.

Writing a procedure to identify a palindrome is fairly complicated, because we have to skip over punctuation, and treat upper- and lowercase letters the same, as well as actually checking whether we have a palindrome.

A simple solution strategy would be to check the beginning and end of the word or phrase. If they're not the same, we know the string isn't a palindrome. If they are the same, our string might be a palindrome. We use recursion to look at the second and second-to-last letters. In pseudocode, we can write the algorithm shown in Program 3-9.

```
(define palindrome?
  (lambda (str first-pos last-pos)
    (if (all the characters have been looked at)
        #t
        (if (first character differs from last character)
            #f
            (palindrome? str (add1 first-pos) (sub1 last-pos))))))
```

Program 3-9   Pseudocode for a palindrome checker

This looks pretty good, and it works on some strings, but it won't work properly on such strings as "Madam, I'm Adam.". There are punctuation marks and spaces, and some characters are in different cases.

Faced with this problem, some programmers simply plunge in and try all the cases, writing something like the monstrous procedure shown in Program 3-10. This procedure will work, but it's the wrong way to go about solving the problem. Why? Because it mixes up many separate tasks in a single procedure. If we want to add even one trivial change to the input, we must redesign the whole thing.

```
(define palindrome?
  (lambda (str first-pos last-pos)
    (if (all the characters have been looked at)
        #t
        (if (first character is a punctuation character or space)
            (palindrome? str (add1 first-pos) last-pos)
            (if (last character is a punctuation character or space)
                (palindrome? str first-pos (sub1 last-pos))
                (if (first character is differs from last character)
                    #f
                    (palindrome? str (add1 first-pos) (sub1 last-pos)))))))))
```
Program 3-10   Initial palindrome program

Good programs are made of **cohesive** procedures; that is, each procedure does exactly one thing. Such procedures tend to be short, often no more than a few lines. They are easy to read and understand, because their tasks are well stated. To design a program that consists of cohesive procedures, we examine the problem carefully, and notice how it decomposes into subtasks. Before writing any code, we develop a strategy for the program as a whole.

The best way to organize this problem is to start from the top (that's why we call it **top-down programming**). The top, in this case, is a general description of the problem. The bottom is the set of programming tools for solving our problem, in this case Scheme's set of primitives, along with any procedures we've already written to solve other problems. The process of solving a problem with top-down programming begins with trying to write a solution in a few lines of code. To do this, we must imagine one or more procedures that will do the various tasks. Once we've written this simple solution, we can apply the same top-down principle to each of the procedures we've imagined.

As an analogy, suppose you are planning an air trip to visit a friend. You can break the problem down into three phases: how to get to the airport, which flight to take, and how to get from the destination airport to your friend's home. You'd probably work on choosing the flight first, since it's probably the hardest part of the problem. You might even arrive at the destination airport without having found out how to get to your friend's home, relying on a telephone call when you arrive.

Top-down programming doesn't *guarantee* a good solution; however, it is a useful way of solving many sorts of problems. How can we apply top-down programming to the palindrome problem? We can divide the task into two separate subtasks: eliminate nonletters from a string, and find out whether a string composed of only letters is a palindrome. Let's write a procedure that calls two others: `filter-nonletters` will give us a string containing only letters, and `palindrome1?` will determine whether the resulting string is a palindrome. Our `palindrome?` procedure can just call these two helpers.

```
(define palindrome?
  (lambda (str)
    (palindrome1? (filter-nonletters str 0 (string-length str)))))
```

The procedure `palindrome1?` will be defined in terms of a helper that uses string recursion to process the pairs of characters, first and last, then next-to-first and next-to-last, and so on, of the string, pretty much as in our original pseudocode (Program 3-11).

```
(define palindrome-helper?
  (lambda (str pos1 pos2)
    (if (>= pos1 pos2)
        #t
        (if (char-ci=? (string-ref str pos1)
              (string-ref str pos2))
            (palindrome-helper? str (add1 pos1) (sub1 pos2))
            #f))))
```

Program 3-11   Palindrome program

We can build a fairly simple procedure to call the helper:

```
(define palindrome1?
  (lambda (str)
    (palindrome-helper? str 0 (sub1 (string-length str)))))
```

The third argument to `palindrome-helper` is not the length of the string, but the second position to be checked for equality. The value of `pos1` increases during recursion, while `pos2` decreases.

Before we proceed, we need to define `filter-nonletters`, but we can try what we've done, provided that we write a **stub procedure** for `filter-nonletters`. A stub is a version of a procedure that doesn't do anything, which usually means returning the input unchanged. As long as our stub conforms to the specifications of the real procedure, we can try out the rest of the code.

```
> (define filter-nonletters (lambda (str pos len) str))
> (filter-nonletters "Help!" 0 5)
"Help!"
```

The procedure just returns the input string, but we can use it to test our palindrome code, as shown in Figure 3-3.

```
(palindrome? "level") ⇒ #t
(palindrome? "abcdefgfedcba") ⇒ #t
(palindrome? "abcdefggfedcba") ⇒ #t
(palindrome? "liver") ⇒ #f
(palindrome? "Madam, I'm Adam") ⇒ #f
```

Figure 3-3   Testing `palindrome?`.

This code seems to work (except, of course, for the stub, which gave incorrect results for the last test). Now let's turn to the real version of `filter-nonletters` (Program 3-12).

```
(define filter-nonletters
  (lambda (str pos len)
    (if (>= pos len)
        ""
        (if (char-alphabetic? (string-ref str pos))
            (string-append
              (string (string-ref str pos))
              (filter-nonletters str (add1 pos) len))
            (filter-nonletters str (add1 pos) len)))))
```

Program 3-12   Removing characters that are not letters

Note how characters extracted by (`string-ref str pos`) must be made into a string before being appended. `filter-nonletters` is an example of the important idea of filtering, that is, selecting and returning a subset of the elements of a collection. We will see more of filtering in the next chapter.

Practical Note

Sometimes beginning programmers think they have to understand a problem completely before they can start writing code. In the palindrome problem, we started with an incomplete algorithm, that gradually evolved into our final design.

The best way to begin solving a problem is to start with a "normal case", whatever you think that might be. In the palindrome problem, the normal case is all letters, without punctuation. We added the other element, removing punctuation, later.

A Scheme system evaluates forms you type in, but *you* must evaluate the success of your approach after developing an algorithm. A case you haven't thought of may destroy your whole approach. Still, see what you've learned from that approach before trying another solution.

The *worst* thing to do is to try to think of all the error cases. There's no point in trying to write bullet-proof code before you've solved the problem at hand. Force yourself to bullet-proof your code *after* you've got the normal cases working correctly.

☞ **Exercise 3-8**

Write procedure `palindrome-n?` that checks whether a number is a palindrome. A number is a palindrome if the sequence of digits in the decimal representation of the number is a palindrome. You may not convert the number to a string and use `palindrome?`. Hint: Write procedures `number-ref` and `number-length`, analogous to the string procedures. ❏

☞ **Exercise 3-9**

Write `string-rotate`, a procedure that creates a new string in which the character at

position pos is the one position pos+k in the input string. (k is nonnegative.)
(string-rotate "abc" 0) ⇒ "abc"   (string-rotate "abc" 2) ⇒ "cab" ❑

3.2 Input/Output and Graphics

> *Pictures are for entertainment, [but] messages should be delivered by West-*
> *ern Union.*   — Samuel Goldwyn, *attributed*

Any useful programming language lets you not only compute results, but also interact with the outside world. By *outside world* we mean human users, as well as storage devices and other computers. So far, we've used Scheme to compute results. Now we need to see how it can present those results to a user, and how it can obtain input from a user.

Languages have varying views of input/output. Some, such as COBOL, consider input/output to be of prime importance. Others, such as Prolog, view it as an unfortunate blemish on a mathematically elegant language. The Prolog viewpoint has some merit—adding input/output to a language turns out to violate some of the principles we've established in the past two chapters (look at the discussion on page 125). On the other hand, input/output is an important job in real programs. A language must do more than manage values inside a computer; it must read and write, too.

3.2.1   Reading

Suppose we want to write a program that reads in a series of student marks and calculates the average. To solve this problem, we must remember the formula for the average, $\bar{x}$, of a set of values $x_1, x_2, \ldots, x_n$:

$$\bar{x} = \frac{\sum_{i=1}^{n} x_i}{n}$$

in which n is the number of marks.

To solve this problem, we need to sum the marks and, at the same time, count how many there are. After processing the marks, we divide the sum by n (assuming $n > 0$, of course) for the result. This leads to a two-pronged approach: first compute the sum and number of marks, and then compute the average. The second part is shown in Program 3-13; compute-average returns -1 if n is 0.

```
(define compute-average
  (lambda (sum n)
    (if (> n 0)
      (/ sum n)
      -1)))
```

Program 3-13   Computing the average, given the sum and the count

We've chosen -1 as a return value to indicate that we couldn't compute the average, because there was no data. We could have just tried to divide by zero, relying upon Scheme to flag the error, but the code shown seems cleaner.

There's a hidden assumption in our choice of -1 as an error result from compute-average. We're assuming that the average of a real set of data can never be -1. This works for a set of student marks, which we can assume are nonnegative. But what if we were measuring voltages, or company profitability values, or anything else that can be negative? *Always spell out those hidden assumptions clearly in comments at the beginning of your procedure.*

To get to compute-average?, we must be able to add a set of marks. What we need is a way of **reading** input values while our program is running. We must be able to make the program stop, wait for the user to type a value, and then use that value in further computation.

We need a new primitive procedure, read, that gets a value from an input device. If you're running Scheme interactively, the input device is your keyboard (consult your Scheme system's documentation for the exact rules—they vary from system to system). When read is called, your program stops, and waits for you to type an input value, which can be a number, a Boolean, or any other Scheme value. If the input is any other Scheme form, such as an application, lambda form, or special form, read does not evaluate the form; it just returns it. In later chapters we'll learn how to handle these unevaluated forms.

read takes no arguments, which should tell you that it's different from anything we've studied so far. The value of (read) is the value of the next item of input. The use of read gives us the code in Program 3-14 (compute-average was defined above). average reads in a set of data items and returns their average; it returns the average, or -1 if there was no data.

```
(define average
  (lambda ()
    (average-helper 0 0 (read))))
(define average-helper
  (lambda (sum n next)
    (if (not (number? next))
      (compute-average sum n)
      (average-helper (+ next sum) (add1 n) (read)))))
```

Program 3-14   Computing the average of a set of input numbers

---

average takes no arguments. We could have designed it to accept n, the number of items, but this would have been poor user-interface design. If we have a large number of items, we can't expect humans to count them. Counting more than a few items is unlikely to produce the correct answer. On the other hand, computers are very good at counting. We can therefore write code to read as many items as the user provides, with the requirement that the last item be followed by a special item telling us that all items have been read. We call a value used to end an input sequence a **sentinel**.[8] We must choose our sentinel carefully, because it must be a

---

[8] In normal English, a *sentinel* is a person who acts as a guard. A sentinel in a military encampment warns against attacks. Our sentinel warns us that we have finished processing all of the data.

value that cannot occur in the input. In this example, anything that is not a number makes no sense as input. Thus, we just have to check that we don't have a number. We will use #f as our sentinel. average-helper gets the next value as its argument next. If next is #f, it calls compute-average; otherwise, it calls itself, adding the value of next, incrementing n and getting the next value.

Running average is instructive:

```
> (average)
78
92
70
#f
80
```

Our program waited for us to type each input value. When we input the #f value, it called compute-average to produce the final output, 80. (No, the output isn't very user-friendly! We'll fix this soon.)

read is extremely useful; however, using it reveals one of the important aspects of programming-language implementations. Consider the following:

```
> (- (read) (read))
27
14
```

What value should be displayed? You might try it on one Scheme system and get the value 13. On another, you would get -13. Which one is correct?

Actually, neither is correct. The correct result is "The value of this form is undefined". The specification of the Scheme language insists that an evaluator be allowed to evaluate the arguments of a procedure call in any order it chooses. Even on a particular evaluator, the arguments can be evaluated from left to right one time (which would give us 13 in the above example), and right to left another. Why? Because some Scheme evaluators can do a particularly efficient job if they are allowed to choose a particular evaluation order. (We will see how and why this is true in Chapter 12.) Scheme evaluators are not required to give you an error message when you use a form whose value is undefined, and most don't.

We have never had to worry about this issue before, because read is the first procedure we've seen that produces an **effect** in addition to computing a value. read does something to the outside world: it accepts a value from the keyboard. In simple cases of read, the effect is intended. Sometimes, however, an effect is unintended and can produce problems. We call such effects, or misuses of effects such as (- (read) (read)), **side effects**.[9] read not only returns a value, but also accepts an input value. Sometimes an effect does not appear to be a side effect except when we are considering another part of the program, and we forget that the effect is happening. The effect of accepting the input is central when total is reading the input, but as part of computing an average value, the effect of the read is a side effect.

---

[9] "Well, Mr Bloggins, I don't see what you're complaining about. My miracle pill has cured your baldness. The tentacles, green skin, and scales are just side effects."

3.2.2   Output

Unfortunately, our average program isn't very user-friendly. How does a user know that the program wants input? The program simply stops and waits, with no indication that the user is supposed to do anything. Students learning to program with read often assume that the program has gone off in an infinite loop!

We need to have some way of **prompting** the user, by displaying a message saying what the user is supposed to do. Thus, we also need procedures that perform output. (These terms, *input* and *output*, are from the program's viewpoint.)

Scheme provides two output routines: display and newline. display takes an argument that is displayed on the screen (or elsewhere; see your Scheme system documentation for a complete description of how to use display on your system). newline moves the screen cursor to the beginning of the next line.

Both display and newline are new to us. Until now, a procedure has been a rule for computing a value. We provide it with argument values, and it provides us with an answer. display is different. It computes no useful value. Instead, display actually causes something to happen on the screen. We call a procedure such as display a **command**—its purpose is to *produce an effect*.

Every procedure in Scheme, however, must return a value. Different Scheme systems will return different values for commands. The trend in more modern systems is to return a special **void** value, a sort of "no value" value, from commands. Modern Scheme systems often don't print out the void value; they just prompt for the next form to evaluate instead. The form (void) returns the void value, which we'll simply term *void*.

Even looking at a transcript that uses display can be confusing (Figure 3–4).

```
> (+ 2 3)
5
> (display (+ 2 3))
5
> (* (+ 2 3) 4)
20
> (* (display (+ 2 3)) 4)
5
Error: #<void> is not a number.
```

Figure 3-4   Transcript of display output

It's important to realize that whereas (+ 2 3) returns a value, (display (+ 2 3)) doesn't. We can use the value of (+ 2 3) in another form, but display returns no useful value, and certainly not one that can be multiplied by 4.[10] The Scheme system we use shows the void value as #<void>.

display prints out strings. When we include backslashes in a string so that we can have quotation marks or backslashes in it, Scheme shows the backslashes when it prints the value of the string. display, however, omits the backslashes:

---

[10] As we said, some older Scheme systems have display primitives that return other values. Obviously, if display has to return a value, its argument is a good choice. On such a system, the fourth form won't cause an error, but it's still wrong. It's not valid in Scheme to depend upon the return value from a command. We'll finesse the whole issue by always assuming that commands return void.

```
> (display "This space intentionally left blank.")
This space intentionally left blank.>
. . .
> "\"Use the backslash\", she said. It looks like this: \\  "
"\"Use the backslash\", she said. It looks like this: \\  "
> (display
  "\"Use the backslash\", she said. It looks like this: \\  ")
"Use the backslash", she said.---It looks like this: \ >
```

Note how the prompt character > appears at the end of the string, because the string does not include anything to cause the output to move to the next line.

☞ **Exercise 3-10**

newline is actually unnecessary. Write your own version, newline%, which uses display to write out a newline. (Hint: Look back at the definitions of character and string literals.) ❏

We'd like to use display in our average program to prompt the user, but we have a second problem. How do we ensure that the prompt appears before the user is expected to type in the next value? Again we must compromise our principles. We have always been able to assume that the order of evaluation didn't matter. We've already seen that read gives us a problem here. Displaying values to the screen makes it essential that we have some way of **sequencing** our program.

The Scheme special form begin allows us to specify that a series of forms be evaluated in a strict sequence:

```
(begin
  (display "Hello, ")
  (display "world!")
  (void))
```

will always display Hello, world! on the screen. A begin form may contain any number of forms. It evaluates these forms in strict order, from first to last, and returns the value of the last form. (void) returns void, as the name suggests. If display on your system already returns void, the last form isn't necessary.

☞ **Exercise 3-11**

Write a procedure that takes two arguments, a and b. It should display the sum and product of these two values, and then return the larger of a and b. ❏

We can use begin and display to write out a table of the numbers and their squares (Program 3-15). A trace of this procedure is instructive (Figure 3-5).

But how exactly does squares-version1 return void? There is no call to (void) in the code. The if form doesn't have an else part! An if form without an else part never made sense when we were working only with values. With commands, it makes perfect sense to say, "*If* this condition is true, do such-and-such, and if not, don't do anything at all". The value of doing nothing at all is, of course, void.

Although squares-version1 is correct, it is not very readable. All of those display calls give us a long-winded procedure. Can we simplify the code? Scheme itself gives us no help with the problem of displaying output conveniently. Most Scheme systems, however, come with a **library**, an organized collection of useful procedures and program packages that are written in Scheme. There's nothing special about them, except that they perform tasks that are useful in a wide range of problems. We will use a number of library procedures in this book. Consult your Scheme

```
(define squares-version1
  (lambda (i n)
    (if (<= i n)
      (begin
        (display i)
        (display " * ")
        (display i)
        (display " = ")
        (display (* i i))
        (newline)
        (squares-version1 (add1 i) n)))))
```

Program 3-15   Procedure `squares-version1`

```
> (squares-version1 1 5)
call squares-version1: 1 5
1 * 1 = 1
| call squares-version1: 2 5
2 * 2 = 4
| | call squares-version1: 3 5
3 * 3 = 9
| | | call squares-version1: 4 5
4 * 4 = 16
| | | | call squares-version1: 5 5
5 * 5 = 25
| | | | | call squares-version1: 6 5
| | | | | return from squares-version1: #<void>
| | | | return from squares-version1: #<void>
| | | return from squares-version1: #<void>
| | return from squares-version1: #<void>
| return from squares-version1: #<void>
return from squares-version1: #<void>
```

Figure 3-5   Tracing `squares`

system documentation for details on the library available. Many Scheme programmers use a library procedure named `format`, which helps to produce formatted output. `format` takes at least two arguments. The first must be #t, and the second must be a **format string**, which says how to display the remaining arguments.[11]

Figure 3-6 shows several uses of `format`. In the first example, the format string is "a0 is ~a, a1 is ~a, and a3 is ~a". Ordinary text in a format string is taken as is. The tilde character ~, however, means that the next character or characters are a code saying how to display the next argument.

We'll use very few format codes in this book. ~a means that the next argument is to be displayed as an ASCII string, and ~% says to write out a newline. The second example shows how strings can be output to produce text. The number of codes in

---

[11] Many Scheme procedures, especially primitive procedures, take a variable number of arguments. We will see how to write such procedures in Chapter 4.

```
> (format #t  "a0 is ~a, a1 is ~a, and a3 is ~a~%" 3 6 12)
a0 is 3, a1 is 6, and a3 is 12
> (format #t
    "Friends, ~a, and ~a~%Lend me your ~a"
    "Romans" "countrymen" "ears.~%")
Friends, Romans, and countrymen
Lend me your ears.
```

Figure 3-6   Using format

the format string indicates how many remaining arguments there must be. Every occurrence of ~a needs another Scheme value for output. format complains when there are not enough arguments. Format strings can be quite sophisticated; you can specify how many character positions are to be used to display a value, for example. Consult your Scheme system documentation for details.

With format, our squares procedure becomes much simpler:

```
(define squares-version2
  (lambda (i n)
    (if (<= i n)
      (begin
        (format #t "~a * ~a = ~a~%" i i (* i i))
        (squares-version2 (add1 i) n)))))
```

Now we can make our average procedure much more user friendly by prompting the user for input (Program 3-16).

```
(define average
  (lambda ()
    (average-helper 0 0 (read-value))))
(define average-helper
  (lambda (sum n x)
    (if (not (number? x))
      (compute-average sum n)
      (average-helper (+ x sum) (add1 n) (read-value)))))
```

Program 3-16   Procedure average

The procedure read-value prompts the user for input and then error-checks the resulting value. To do the latter, it calls a helper, which, if the data value is not valid, displays an error message, and then calls read-value again to try for another value (Program 3-17).

Procedures such as read-value and read-value-helper exhibit **mutual recursion**: each calls the other. As soon as a valid data value has been read, read-value-helper returns it.

You may notice something unusual about read-value: its body contains two forms. Scheme treats any sequence of forms in the body of a procedure as if they were enclosed in a begin form, and evaluates them in order. Thus we say that there is an **implicit begin** in the body of a procedure.

```
(define read-value
  (lambda ()
    (display "Enter an input value, or #f to end: ")
    (read-value-helper (read))))
(define read-value-helper
  (lambda (x)
    (if (or (boolean? x)
            (and (number? x)
                 (>= x 0)
                 (<= x 100)))
        x
        (begin
          (format #t "Sorry, the input must be either a number~%")
          (format #t "between 0 and 100 or a Boolean.")
          (format #t "Please try again.~%")
          (read-value)))))
```

Program 3-17   Reading values

Practical Note

Designing useful user dialogs is not easy. Here, we've assumed that the user needs step-by-step guidance on how to use the program. The program prompts for each data value, and tells the user how to end the input. An experienced user of such a program would probably find this irritating, and would prefer just to enter the data, perhaps without any prompting at all. There is a fine line between building a program that helps users, on the one hand, and building one that underestimates their knowledge or intelligence.

The best way to design a user dialog is to imagine who the users will be (programmers? children? bank customers?), and to attempt to decide what messages would be the most useful to *them* .

Our error message told the user what the program was expecting. Error messages such as Invalid input can leave the user completely mystified. It seems malicious for the programmer to know what the user did wrong but not to display a clear message saying what it was. On the other hand, producing a screenful of output ("You have made a mistake . . . Please don't worry! . . . ") is unhelpful.

☞ **Exercise 3–12**

Our quadratic equation procedure roots from Chapter 1 doesn't produce a clear explanation of its results. Build a quadratic equation solver that displays clear output showing what happened; for example,

```
> (quadratic 1 -2 -8)
1x^2 + -2x + -8 = 0 has two real roots, -2 and 4.
```

Use format. ❏

3.2.3 Graphics

We deal every day with all sorts of sensory inputs: vision, sound, smell, taste, and touch. Everyone, even those with impaired vision or hearing, can easily be bombarded with more sensory data than they can manage. Of all the data we encounter, almost none is presented in the sort of textual, character-string format we've been using so far. The reason is simple. In many cases, it is much harder to *describe* than it is to *show*.

Early computer systems began with nothing more than character input and output devices. Over the years, graphic input and output devices, as well as algorithms for processing graphic data, have evolved to the point that many movies and low-cost television programs incorporate elaborate computer-graphic effects.

Nowhere is the use of graphics more important to science than in visualization, the process of presenting information in graphic form. A complex relationship between variables might be hard to understand, but when that relationship is shown in pictorial form, it becomes clear and obvious. Graphs are one example of visualization techniques. With the advent of the computer, however, many different techniques for presenting data have been developed.

Scheme has no graphics facilities, but many Scheme systems do have elaborate packages of graphics procedures. We will use a simple graphics package in this book. Consult your system documentation for details on the graphics procedures available in your version.

An artist might work with a pen on paper. We too will work with a pen, but we'll use a screen rather than paper. Our screen will be divided into a large number of points, or *pixels* ("picture elements"), each of which can show a color. Inexpensive displays allow a grid of 640 (horizontally) by 480 (vertically) pixels, each of which can display 2 or 16 colors. Expensive displays allow as many as 1280 by 1024 pixels, in 16,777,216 (2^{24}) colors. Our Scheme graphics procedures treat the screen as a 500-by-500 grid, with the origin in the lower left corner.[12]

There is also a pen. At any given time, the pen has an (x, y) position, and you can move the pen to another position, (x_1, y_1). In doing so, you can choose whether the pen is down (drawing) or up (not drawing). The pen can also draw text to label a picture.

Our package consists of the following graphics procedures:

- (draw-clear)
  Erases anything on the screen and prepares for a new drawing. The pen moves to $(0, 0)$.
- (draw-move x_1 y_1)
  Moves the pen (without drawing anything) to point (x_1, y_1).
- (draw-line x_1 y_1)
  Moves the pen, drawing a line, to point (x_1, y_1).
- (draw-text *string*)
  Draws the string at the current point, but doesn't move the point.

This is not a high-performance graphics package, but it will satisfy our needs. If you want more graphics facilities, you can look at the code for these procedures (on most systems, they're generally written in Scheme) and consult your Scheme system documentation.

---

[12] One pixel in the Scheme package may or may not correspond to a screen pixel.

Back to visualization. One of the most basic things we can do is to plot a graph from some data. We can start by writing a package that reads in (x, y) data and plots it (Program 3-18). The structure of `plot-data` is a bit strange. It goes to great lengths to split up the reading of the x and y values—tasks that seem as if they should be done together. The specification would be "Read in the x and *y* coordinates of a point and return them, or return (void) to indicate that there is no more data". Our design is shaped by our need to ensure that the two values are read in the correct order. We can only force two values to be read in order by creative use of procedure calling. `begin` won't help us here, because the steps of a `begin` form are done strictly in order, and all of the values are thrown away except the last. `plot-data` successively reads pairs of numbers. If anything but a number appears as the first item of a pair, it stops and returns void.

```
(define plot-data
  (lambda ()
    (plot1 (read) #f)))
(define plot1
  (lambda (x pendown)
    (if (not (number? x))
      (void)
      (plot2 x (read) pendown))))
(define plot2
  (lambda (x y pendown)
    (if pendown
      (draw-line x y)
      (draw-move x y))
    (plot1 (read) #t)))
```

Program 3-18   Graphing program: `plot-data`

The structure of `plot-data` might be necessary, but it certainly isn't pleasant. The procedure `plot1` seems somewhat arbitrary. It doesn't do any specific task, but only exists to ensure that x has been read before y. At present, using a procedure like `plot1` is the only way we know to ensure a specific order of evaluation. Fortunately, there are a number of Scheme forms and program design techniques to help us write sequenced code. We will see some of them later in this chapter.

☞ **Exercise 3-13**

Many graphics problems can be solved by top-down programming. Write a procedure that draws a house, shown as a rectangle with a triangle on top of it, by writing rectangle and triangle procedures. Hint: You could keep track of the coordinates of the pen before and after drawing each figure. A good way to do this is to move the pen at the beginning of each subfigure. That way you won't have to assume anything about the pen position in the rectangle and triangle procedures. ❏

3.3   Procedures as Arguments

We hold these truths to be self-evident, that all men are created equal, that they are endowed by their Creator with certain unalienable rights, that among these are life, liberty, and the pursuit of happiness.
— Thomas Jefferson, *The Declaration of Independence*

Early programming languages had elaborate rules about where certain sorts of data could be used, and even whether certain sorts of data were permissible. One early PL/I compiler would allow Boolean expressions but not Boolean variables. Early versions of FORTRAN required that character data masquerade as integers or even floating-point numbers.

Scheme has as few of these rules as possible. In Scheme, you can use a value anywhere it makes sense. It doesn't make sense to add two Booleans, or to compute the logical and of two numbers, but both numbers and Booleans can be passed to procedures and returned as the results of procedures. We call values that can be passed as arguments, returned as results, and used as the values of variables **first-class citizens**. Such values are entitled to all of the rights and responsibilities that all values are entitled to. Early languages were aristocratic, granting the rights of first-class citizens to few if any data types. Modern languages are more egalitarian, granting them to all, or almost all, data types.

One data type that has traditionally not been treated as a first-class citizen is the procedure. In Scheme, however, procedures are first-class citizens, and can be passed as arguments to other procedures, or returned as values from other procedures. This allows us to write very general procedures, and gives Scheme much of its flavor.

Let's take a look at the Caesar cipher again. The program we built was capable of exactly one cipher. But perhaps we want a more flexible cipher. Do we have to write new procedures for that new cipher?

One way to make our procedures more general is to endow them with additional parameters. We could include a parameter that tells us how many positions to rotate in the alphabet, but then the procedure is still specialized for encryption by rotating characters.   What we need is a way to write a general rule for encryption, leaving the details of exactly how characters are encrypted to the time when we need to encrypt. We can then use whatever rule we want.

Program 3–19 presents `encrypt-string`, a general-purpose encryption procedure. Now we can use `caesar-encrypt-char` as our procedure (Figure 3–7).

A quick look at `encrypt-string` and its helper reveals no calls to `caesar-encrypt-char`, yet the procedure is certainly being called! `caesar-encrypt-char` is defined to be the name of a procedure. We pass that procedure as an argument to `encrypt-string`, which in turn passes it on to its helper, where the procedure, bound to `proc`, is called. Any procedure that accepts a character and returns a string would do as an argument to be bound to `proc` in `encrypt-string-helper`.

We should be careful about our terminology. Procedures don't really have names. Procedures are values created by evaluating `lambda` forms. `caesar-encrypt-char` is a *variable* whose value is a procedure. Just as we can define names for numbers and Booleans, we can define names for procedures. Just as we can pass Booleans and numbers to our procedures, so we can pass procedures.

```
(define encrypt-string
  (lambda (proc str)
    (encrypt-string-helper
      proc str 0
      (string-length str))))
(define encrypt-string-helper
  (lambda (proc str pos len)
    (if (>= pos len)
        ""
        (string-append
          (proc (string-ref str pos))
          (encrypt-string-helper proc
            str (add1 pos) len)))))
```

Program 3-19   Encryption

```
> (trace caesar-encrypt-char)
> (encrypt-string caesar-encrypt-char "abc")
call caesar-encrypt-char: #\a
return from caesar-encrypt-char: "d"
call caesar-encrypt-char: #\b
return from caesar-encrypt-char: "e"
call caesar-encrypt-char: #\c
return from caesar-encrypt-char: "f"
"def"
```

Figure 3-7   Encrypting

☞ **Exercise 3-14**

Usenet users sometimes send messages encrypted using a code known as ROT13, in which characters are rotated 13 positions in the alphabet. The string "abcno" is encrypted as "nopab"—the alphabet is taken to wrap around, with *a* following *z*. Nonletters are left unchanged. ROT13 isn't much good as a code, especially since people who use it tend to say so at the beginning of the message. It *is* useful for hiding the punchline to a joke, for example.

Write a procedure that performs ROT13 on a single character, and use it in a call to `encrypt-string` to encode the message "How many earth people does it take to change a light bulb?". Don't change the code of `encrypt-string` or its helper. ❏

Many of the problems we did with string recursion seem to follow the same pattern: we look at each character in the string, and do something with it. This pattern cries out for a generalized procedure, which we call `string-map`, shown in Program 3-20. We can use `string-map` in a number of interesting ways:

(string-map rot13 "Secret") ⇒ "frperg"

(The version of `rot13` provided as a solution to Exercise 3-14 returns characters in lowercase.)

We can think of any character cipher (coding on a character-by-character basis) as being a form of string mapping.

```
(define string-map
  (lambda (proc str)
    (string-map-helper proc str 0 (string-length str))))
(define string-map-helper
  (lambda (proc str pos len)
    (if (< pos len)
      (string-append
        (proc (string-ref str pos))
        (string-map-helper proc str (add1 pos) len))
      "")))
```

Program 3-20   Processing strings

Another use of `string-map` is to convert a string to uppercase. The primitive `char-upcase` will do this for a single character, but we have no built-in way of doing this for a whole string. One line of code suffices:

```
(string-map
  (lambda (ch) (string (char-upcase ch))) "koala") ⇒ "KOALA"
```

Here we have used an anonymous procedure as an argument. We haven't used anonymous procedures since we introduced `define`. You may have thought that they were not useful, but here's a counterexample. Any time you have a procedure that exists solely to be an argument, you might want to use an anonymous procedure.

Procedure arguments are useful in other applications. Let's revisit our plotting package. Often, in plotting, we find that the raw data doesn't fill the graph properly. For example, the function $f(x) = 0.001x$ looks like a horizontal line on a 500-by-500 grid. To make the graph of the function legible, we can **transform** the data by using a formula to compute a display y value from an actual y value. For our example function f, we can transform y by multiplying by 250, which gives a new value in the range 0 to 500, if x is in the same range. For functions that grow quickly, such as x^2, a logarithmic transform is suitable.

What we'd like to do, then, is to pass a transform function as one of the arguments of `plot-data`. The transform function takes as an argument the actual y value, and returns an integer between 0 and 500 that is used as the y coordinate. Program 3-21 shows our new plot package.

There's another problem with our current plotter: we must type all the data at the console. For a small amount of data, this is reasonable, but what if we wanted to plot a function at 500 points? We might even have another program that produces the data (say by obtaining values from a lab instrument). Is that program supposed to display the values it obtained on the screen? We can't expect the user to copy the data values from the screen into a notebook, and then type them into the plotter.

Fortunately, Scheme provides primitives for accessing files on disk. Many of the detailed rules are beyond the scope of this book, but we can use two simple primitives to read or write data from files. In our case, we want to read our plotting data from a file, but we'd like to avoid rewriting our plotting procedures to use specialized file-reading procedures.

Suppose we have prepared a file named `plot.dat` containing the squares of the numbers between 0 and 500. We will need a transform procedure that divides

```
(define plot-data-transform
  (lambda (xform)
    (plot1-x xform (read) #f)))
(define plot1-x
  (lambda (xform x pendown)
    (if (not (number? x))
        (void)
        (plot2-x xform x (read) pendown))))
(define plot2-x
  (lambda (xform x y pendown)
    (if pendown
        (draw-line x (xform y))
        (draw-move x (xform y)))
    (plot1-x xform (read) #t)))
```

Program 3-21   Plotter package

the y coordinate by 500, in order to fit the plot onto the screen. To set up so that reading takes input from the file, we do the following:

```
(with-input-from-file "plot.dat"
  (lambda ()
    (plot-data-transform (lambda (x) (/ x 500)))))
```

with-input-from-file is a primitive procedure that has two arguments: a filename and a procedure with no arguments. When the procedure argument is evaluated, read and other input operations will refer to the file plot.dat. After the procedure is evaluated, with-input-from-file restores input to the keyboard. If you run this form, you will notice a slight pause while the plot is being drawn, and then input will revert to the keyboard.

A similar procedure, with-output-to-file, can be used to write to a file.

```
(with-output-to-file "myfile.dat"
  (display "Hello, world!"))
```

creates a file named myfile.dat containing Hello, world!.

Procedures with no arguments, such as the one passed to with-input-from-file, are called **thunks**. A thunk can be thought of as a way of packaging a form so that it isn't executed right away, but only when the called procedure wants to evaluate it.[13] The code for with-input-from-file% looks something like this:

```
(define with-input-from-file%
  (lambda (filename thunk)
    ...arrange that read reads from the file named filename...
    (thunk)
    ...restore input to the keyboard...))
```

---

[13] The word *thunk* appears to have been coined by Peter Ingerman, a member of the team that developed the programming language ALGOL 60. At one point in the proceedings, the language designers needed a technique similar to that used in with-input-from-file. It was very late at night, and nobody could think of a name. Ingerman, it is said, remarked that this was just something they'd "thunk" up. The name stuck.

Software Engineering

In the 1950s, there was a spate of films about mutations caused by atomic radiation, capitalizing on the Cold War fears of the audience. One of the best of these was *Them*, in which the atomic tests in New Mexico cause ants to grow to a gigantic size. The ants initially menace the inhabitants of New Mexico, and then move to Los Angeles. In a terrifying climax, the U.S. Army battles them in the storm sewers under the city.

The ants in *Them* are truly frightening. Unfortunately, an elementary law of physics, the square-cube law, renders them completely impossible. The strength of an ant's (or a human's) skeleton is proportional to the cross-sectional area of the bones or other supports. The mass, on the other hand, is proportional to the volume. If we multiply the ant's length, width, and height by a constant factor k, the cross-sectional area will go up by a factor of k^2, but the volume will go up by a factor of k^3. The result is that an ant magnified 100-fold would not have the strength even to stand up, let alone menace soldiers.

Similar problems of scale have bedeviled computer programmers right from the beginning. In the 1950s, programmers wrote programs comparable to those we have studied and made them work. But our programs have been small in scale. With the crude computers of the time, a program had to be keypunched, left in a tray for an operator to pick up and then run (perhaps overnight), and the output delivered a day or two later. Getting even a small program to run at all was a major achievement, let alone worrying whether it was doing the right thing!

The success of programmers in those early days gave rise to false confidence. By the 1960s, many software projects involved large teams of programmers. Projects with ever-grander scope were attempted, until programmers suddenly became aware that they were being less and less successful.

One of the grandest of these projects was OS/360, an "operating system" for the IBM System/360 computers introduced in 1964. (An operating system controls which programs are being run on behalf of which users at any given time; we will discuss operating systems in Chapter 12. OS/360's descendant, MVS, is still in use on IBM mainframe computers. Other well-known contemporary operating systems include MS-DOS and UNIX.) OS/360 had very ambitious goals, attempting to go far beyond any operating system designed up to that point. The OS/360 design team consisted of thousands of programmers and other technicians, scattered at IBM research facilities all over the world.

The manager of the OS/360 project, F. P. Brooks, wrote a book (*The Mythical Man-Month*) about his experiences. With each release of the system software, thousands of errors were corrected, but thousands more were introduced. OS/360 was finally completed, but at great cost, and long after IBM had promised it. Brooks discovered many surprising facts about software development. The best known of these is "Brooks' Law": Adding new people to an overdue software project just makes it worse.

The OS/360 experience, and many similar ones, gave rise to the perception of a "software crisis". Whereas computers were constantly becoming faster, more reliable, and cheaper, software still seemed to be expensive and not particularly reliable. By 1970, air-traffic control and banking, among many other fields of endeavor, were wholly dependent on computers and programs. Computer users and programmers became increasingly afraid that their software would fail mysteriously.

At the time, software was often written in low-level machine languages, frequently taking advantage of specific capabilities of the computer being used. Reprogramming an application for a different computer was difficult and often introduced new bugs. The programs were so complicated that only the original author could really make sense of them. As a result, finding bugs was a hit-and-miss process, and programmers dreaded it.

At a conference in 1968, academics and practitioners discussed the problems they were encountering and their fears regarding the future of software projects. The participants agreed that the fundamental problem wasn't really the languages or other programming tools, but the methods being used.

Software design at the time was a haphazard process. There was no organized way to ensure that a program was relatively bug-free, and often even the most trivial changes required redesigning the program, with a consequent rash of new bugs. In general, we do not expect any real program to contain zero bugs (or that, even if it did, we would know it). A program consisting of millions of lines of code is not easy to prove completely bug-free. If the program is tested adequately, however, we should be able to eliminate bugs that impair its use substantially, and if a program is well-designed, we should be able to fix any bugs we find without introducing new ones.

Software engineers must confront a broad range of problems. During her or his career, a software engineer might write programs for analyzing and displaying medical imaging data, for carrying data safely across a network, and for cataloging books in a library. The problems that a software engineer solves have much less to do with each other than do those a designer of physical artifacts solves.

To build a useful program, software engineers must try to find out what the user needs. Often the user doesn't know what is needed, or what will be needed after the program has been used for a few years. Software engineers use methods of *requirements analysis* to give as exact a specification as possible of the needs a program will satisfy.

Another factor complicates the software engineer's life: programs must live in a world of change. Software developers must constantly change their programs to satisfy new requirements. Airlines, for example, often change their prices rapidly to respond to a competitor's actions, giving programmers only a few hours' notice. Somehow, by the next day, the program must work with the new prices, so that the airline won't lose business. Usually it's not just prices for flights that change, but also the way in which tickets are booked (seven, fourteen or twenty-one days in advance).

If we are going to design a program that does something useful in the real world, such as handling travel arrangements or modeling the aerodynamics of a new airplane, we must accommodate the most noticeable aspect of the real world, namely, change. Ticketing rules affecting the airline will change, or a plane may suddenly have to be redesigned because of safety concerns. Then, of course, there are the bugs. With most real programs, much more work is expended after the program has been put into service, fixing bugs and making requested changes, than is expended during the actual development process.

Software engineering is now an established discipline that covers techniques of designing, implementing (coding), and testing programs. In this book, we use software engineering principles to design our programs. Most Computer Science programs include software engineering courses, which allow you to study those principles in depth.

A procedure can also be returned as the value of a procedure. This feature of Scheme (not found in most programming languages) lets us write some very interesting programs, and even leads to object-oriented programming. We'll revisit the topic of procedures as returned values in Chapters 5 and 6.

☞ **Exercise 3–15**

You have been given a file of data giving the high and low temperatures (in that order) for a city for each day of the past year. The file looks something like this:

```
37  22
35  23
...
#f
```

(the end-of-file sentinel is #f.)

Write a procedure that reads this file and produces a new file showing the temperature range (the difference between high and low) for each day. The output file would be

```
15
12
...
```

Your procedure should accept as arguments the names of the input and output files. ❏

3.4 Program Organization: Variables, Values and Interfaces

Not so much a programme, more a way of life
                                    — BBC television series title, 1960s

We're now in a position to write substantial programs. Our plotting program could be elaborated into a package that allows for plotting and labeling axes, fitting curves, and doing other tasks. We could define an entire "command language" to specify which actions the program would take on a given data set.

But a complex plotting program will have many procedures. Some will be important, but many will be helpers. Some, for example plot1, will only exist because we need to sequence input/output operations. As the program becomes more complicated, you will have more and more difficulty finding your way through it. If a colleague works on the program with you, what is to stop each of you from choosing the same procedure name?

We need a technique for building large programs that include many small pieces. We'll see some Scheme forms that help us create variables inside procedures and hide procedures inside programs. We'll also introduce data abstraction, a program design method for larger programs.

The tools we provide for program design are methods for **programming in the small**, for managing abstractions by a single programmer. Designing software in larger groups is more complex (it's called **programming in the large**) and has led to the development of methods and tools not only for managing programs but also for communication among programmers, called **software engineering**.

3.4.1   `let` **and scope**

Many people who have studied the problem of building a space habitat have argued for a cylindrical shape. For one thing, the habitat must spin in order to simulate gravity. The cylinder will be hollow, and we might therefore reasonably ask, for a habitat of given size, how much material (by volume) is needed to form the walls?

The best way to compute the volume of the walls is to imagine that the habitat is a solid cylinder whose radius is the outside radius of the habitat, and then imagine removing a volume whose radius is the inner radius of the habitat. The thickness of the wall represents the difference in radius between the inside and outside cylinders. The annulus problem, in Chapter 1, was similar.

It's clear how we should program this:

```
(- (cylinder radius height)
   (cylinder (- radius thickness)
     (- height (* 2 thickness))))
```

We use a helper named `cylinder`. Perhaps we need to compute the volumes of lots of cylinders, but maybe we don't. We need a way to make `cylinder` an explicit helper of our procedure; that is, we want to prevent programmers who use our main procedure from calling, or even seeing, the helper.

People often think that hiding procedures has something to do with keeping code secret. On the contrary, we want people to read other people's code. The last thing we want to do is to encourage you to keep your code secret. But if other people are to use your code, they must know that it will work correctly with their program. Hiding helpers is one important way of doing this.

The `let` special form in Scheme gives us a way of creating a temporary variable in a piece of code. For example,

```
(let ((a 1))
  (+ a 47))
```

defines the value of the variable a as 1 in the body of the form. The binding of the variable is the association between the name of the variable and its value. We speak of the variable being bound to its value. Once the `let` has been evaluated, the binding is forgotten:

```
> (let ((a 1)) (+ a 47))
48
> a
Error: unbound variable: a
```

With a `let` form, we can introduce a variable name and be confident that its use will not interfere with code outside the form. The variable is *local* to the `let` form and unavailable outside the `let`. Not only does the `let` form introduce a variable; it also gives the variable a value. (It is impossible, in Scheme, to create a variable with no value. It is possible in other languages and is a common source of bugs.)

A `let` form has the following syntax:

```
(let ((name value)) body)
```

where *name* is any variable name, *value* is a Scheme form that is evaluated to produce an initial value for the variable, and *body* is any form. Within the form, the variable is bound, but once the form is completely evaluated, the variable binding is forgotten. We speak of the **scope** of a variable as the region of the program in which that variable is known. The scope of the binding in a `let` is the body.

☞ **Exercise 3-16**

Evaluate

```
(let ((x 3)) (+ x x))
```

❏

☞ **Exercise 3-17**

Evaluate

```
(let
  ((foo (lambda (x) (* x 3))))
  (+ (foo 4) (foo 7)))
```

❏

Program 3-22 shows our procedure for calculating the volume of material needed for the space habitat from its dimensions.

```
(define habitat-material
  (lambda (height radius thickness)
    (let
      ((pi 3.1415926))
      (let
        ((cylinder
          (lambda (r h)
            (* h (* pi (* r r))))))
        (-
          (cylinder radius height)
          (cylinder (- radius thickness)
                    (- height (* 2 thickness)))))))))
```

Program 3-22   Volume needed to build space habitat

The `habitat-material` procedure uses two nested `let` forms: one to define the variable `pi`, and one to define `cylinder`. (Thus the body of the first `let` form is the second `let`.) By the time we get to the `(- ... )` form, both `pi` and `cylinder` have been bound, and we can therefore use them. Once we have finished a call to `habitat-material`, both variables are forgotten, as shown in Figure 3-8. (A space habitat 1000 metres in height and 500 metres in radius, with 7-metre thick walls would require 32.5 million cubic metres of material for its walls. Not cheap.)

In each application of `habitat-material`, Scheme first binds the variable `pi` and then the variable `cylinder`. Then the body is evaluated, and then Scheme forgets about first `cylinder` and then `pi`.[14]

---

[14] Don't be too concerned about the cost of binding and forgetting variables. High-performance Scheme evaluators use clever tricks to make the cost essentially zero, except for the cost of evaluating the initialization expression.

```
> (habitat-material 1000 500 5)
+23327110.45315
> pi
Error: unbound variable:  pi
> cylinder
Error: unbound variable:  cylinder
> (habitat-material 1000 500 7)
+32527063.320324
```

Figure 3-8   Using `habitat-material`

`let` forms can be used to introduce more than one variable:

```
> (let
    ((a 3)
     (b 2))
    (+ a b))
5
```

Can we use the same structure with `habitat-material`? Thinking so, you might try to write Program 3-23.

```
(define habitat-material
  (lambda (height radius thickness)
    (let
      ((pi 3.1415926)
       (cylinder
        (lambda (r h)
          (* h (* pi (* r r))))))
      (-
       (cylinder radius height)
       (cylinder (- radius thickness)
                 (- height (* 2 thickness)))))))
```

Program 3-23   Incorrect use of `let`

When you run this code, you'll get an error message about the variable `pi` not being known. But it *is* known! It's right there, just above the definition of `cylinder`. To find out why `pi` isn't known, we must look at the inner mechanisms of Scheme. `let` forms are, in reality, an optical illusion. The Scheme evaluator actually translates a `let` form into a procedure call!

Consider again the form above, `(let ((a 3) (b 2)) (+ a b))`. The Scheme evaluator translates this form into `((lambda (a b) (+ a b)) 3 2)`. Scheme creates an anonymous procedure whose parameters are the variables being bound and whose body is the body of the `let` form. It then applies the anonymous procedure to the expressions given as the values of the variables being bound.

More formally, the equivalent of

```
(let ((name1 value1))
     ((name2 value2))

        . . .
```

> ((*namen valuen*))
> *body*)

is

> ((lambda (*name1 name2 . . . namen*) *body*)
> *value1 value2 . . . valuen*)

This presentation demonstrates the difference between let and the equivalent lambda. let brings the names and values together, while the lambda separates the names and values by the distance of the body.

☞ **Exercise 3-18**

Translate (let ((w 3)) (let ((x 4)) (/ w x))) into procedure calls. ❏

☞ **Exercise 3-19**

Rewrite the following using let:

```
( (lambda (x)
   ( (lambda (y)
      (+ (* 2 y) x)) ( + x 3))) 5)
```

❏

Now consider (let ((a 4) (b (add1 a))) (+ a b)). This should evaluate to 9, but instead it produces an error. Why? Because the translation into a procedure call reads like this: ((lambda (a b) (+ a b)) 4 (add1 a)). If you look at the call to (add1 a), you'll see that it's not inside the procedure. In other words, the variable a is not in the scope of the binding of a.

Program 3-24 shows two let forms, one inside the other, or **embedded** in the other. We also say that the inner let is *nested* inside the outer let.

```
(let
  ((x 4)
   (y 7))
  (let
    ((u (add1 x))
     (v (sub1 y)))
    (* u (+ x v))))
```

Program 3-24   Embedded let forms

The scope of x and y is the body of the outer let, whose body is itself another let. The scope of u and v is the form (* u (+ x v)). Whenever a variable is bound with let or lambda, the scope of that variable is the body of the let or lambda.

We might use the same variable name several times in a large program. In a large program, however, you can't spend time thinking up new variable names (variable names should be as descriptive as possible). We often do want to use the same name to identify different variables. We might, for example, want to have several procedures all taking a height parameter.

☞ **Exercise 3–20**

Is there any reason not to use pos as the name of the position in two string-recursive procedures that call each other? ❏

How do you identify the value of a variable, given its name? Scheme uses a very simple rule, known as **static scoping**:

- Start from the place where the name is used, and read backwards.
- Skip over completely nested let and lambda forms. Anything bound in one of these forms does not affect the name.
- When you find a binding for the variable, stop.
- If you don't find a binding by the time you reach the beginning of the top-level form you're in, look in the global environment.
- If you still don't find it, the program's in error.

For example, consider

```
(define a 1)
(define times-2-add-a
  (lambda (x)
    (let ((y (* 2 x)))
      (add-a y))))
(define add-a
  (lambda (x) (+ x a)))
```

This example includes two variables named x. The first is bound by the procedure named times-2-add-a, and the second is bound by the procedure named add-a. The body of times-2-add-a contains a let form that binds y. The static scoping rule states that we find the binding of x in the line above. When times-2-add-a calls add-a, x is bound as a parameter, and a is bound in the global environment.

Another name for static scoping is **lexical** scoping, from the Greek word *lexis*, for "word". This name emphasizes that we can determine the value of a name just by inspecting the text of the program.

☞ **Exercise 3–21**

What is the value of

```
(let ((x 5))
  (let ((x 3)
        (y (* 2 x)))
    (+ x y)))
```

❏

Now back to (let ((a 4) (b (add1 a))) (+ a b)). Translating it into procedure calls gives us

```
((lambda (a b) (+ a b))
  4 (add1 a))
```

If we use the static scoping rule, we will scan all the way to the beginning of the form without finding a binding for a (remember, we skip over lambda forms and let forms). Unless we find a in the global environment, it's an error.

There's actually a simple way to remember how `let` works. The expressions that determine the values to which the names are bound are evaluated in the scope enclosing the `let`. In (`let ((a 4) (b (add1 a))) (+ a b)`), this rule tells us that (`add1 a`) is evaluated in the scope outside the `let`. If there's no binding for a in that scope (which is the global environment), then a is unbound.

In our plotting example, we needed to read the x and y values in separate procedures. As shown in Program 3-25, the `let` form helps us to write our code more cleanly. This version eliminates `plot2-x` by using `let` to bind first x and then y prior to doing the drawing operation.

```
(define plot-data-transform-let
  (lambda (xform)
    (plot1-x-let xform #f)))
(define plot1-x-let
  (lambda (xform pendown)
    (let
      ((x (read)))
      (if (boolean? x)
        (void)
        (let
          ((y (read)))
          (if pendown
            (draw-line x (xform y))
            (draw-move x (xform y)))
          (plot1-x-let xform #t)))))))
```

Program 3-25   Plot examples

Suppose we just wanted to read in x and y, and then do some operation on them. You might write

```
(let
  ((x (read))
   (y (read)))
  (do-something-with x y))
```

However, as we know, this doesn't guarantee that x is bound to the first value and y to the second. Because the `let` form is equivalent to ((lambda (x y) (do-something-with x y)) (read) (read)), and because the arguments of procedure calls are evaluated in an unspecified order, the `let` may or may not work as you had planned.

As we did in `plot1-x-let`, we can use nested `let`s to ensure that the intended sequence of reading operations is performed:

```
(let
  ((x (read)))
  (let
    ((y (read)))
    (do-something-with x y)))
```

This structure is so common that a separate special form is provided:

```
(let*
  ((x (read))
   (y (read)))
  (do-something-with x y))
```

A let* form is entirely equivalent to the nested let form shown above. It isn't necessary; it's merely a convenience. We can use let* to break up a complicated expression into pieces, as in Program 3-26.

```
(let*
  ((pi 3.1415926)
   (r 10)
   (h 20)
   (circle-area (* pi r r))
   (cylinder-volume (* h circle-area)))
  (format #t
    "a cylinder of radius ~a and height ~a has volume ~a~%"
    r h cylinder-volume))
```

Program 3-26   Using let*

☞ **Exercise 3-22**

What is the value of

```
(let ((x 5))
  (let*
    ((x 3)
     (y (* 2 x)))
    (+ x y)))
```

❏

We can bind procedures in a let form, as we did in Program 3-23. but trying to do so with a recursive procedure results in a shock.

```
> (let
    ((fact
       (lambda (n)
         (if (= n 0) 1 (* n (fact (sub1 n)))))))
    (fact 3))
Error: unbound variable: fact
```

How can fact be unbound? We've bound it right here! A translation into procedure calls demonstrates the problem:

```
((lambda (fact) (fact 3))
  (lambda (n)
    (if (= n 0) 1 (* n (fact (sub1 n))))))
```

The recursive call to fact isn't actually within the scope of the binding of the name fact, so Scheme can't find the binding.

Because `let*` is just a way of writing some `let` forms more conveniently, it's not surprising that `let*` doesn't help us much here. Scheme has a special form, `letrec`, for binding recursive procedures in a `let`:

```
(letrec
  ((fact
    (lambda (n)
      (if (= n 0) 1 (* n (fact (sub1 n)))))))
  (fact 3))
```

We can't explain how `letrec` works just yet. Think of it, for now, as a trick for solving the problem of binding a recursive procedure. In Chapter 5 we'll see how to implement `letrec`.

In Program 3-2 we defined the helper for `string=?%`. Let's embed the helper (Program 3-27).

```
(define string=?%
  (lambda (str1 str2)
    (letrec
      ((help
        (lambda (str1 str2 pos len)
          (if (>= pos len)
            #t
            (if (char=? (string-ref str1 pos)
                        (string-ref str2 pos))
              (help str1 str2 (add1 pos) len)
              #f)))))
      (if (= (string-length str1) (string-length str2))
        (help str1 str2 0 (string-length str1))
        #f))))
```

Program 3-27　　`string=?%` with an embedded helper

We've simply inserted the helper into the main procedure. We can use a simpler name as a result. But things can be simplified further. Let's look at the helper. `str1` and `str2` occur throughout the procedure. Since these variables are in the scope of the bindings of the parameters to `string=?%`, they don't need to be passed as arguments to `help`. A **shared variable** is a variable used in an inner `let` or `lambda` that occurs in an enclosing scope. The value of the variable must be the same in both scopes. Because the value is the same, we don't have to bind it again as an argument to `help`. The resulting procedure appears in Program 3-28.

Actually we can make this simpler still. If we bind `len` using a `let`, we won't have to pass it to the helper, either. Our final version appears in Program 3-29.

It's important to remember why we identify shared variables and remove them as arguments to embedded procedures—to simplify the code. We are not primarily concerned with efficiency, but with ease of programming and correctness. Simplifying the parameters of an embedded procedure clarifies the relation between the inner procedure and the enclosing bindings. Any remaining parameters change each time the procedure is called.

```
(define string=?%
  (lambda (str1 str2)
    (letrec
      ((help
         (lambda (pos len)
           (if (>= pos len)
             #t
             (if (char=? (string-ref str1 pos)
                         (string-ref str2 pos))
               (help (add1 pos) len)
               #f)))))
      (if (= (string-length str1) (string-length str2))
        (help 0 (string-length str1))
        #f))))
```

Program 3-28   `string=?%` with a helper and some shared variables removed

```
(define string=?%
  (lambda (str1 str2)
    (let
      ((len1 (string-length str1))
       (len2 (string-length str2)))
      (letrec
        ((help
           (lambda (pos)
             (if (>= pos len1)
               #t
               (if (char=? (string-ref str1 pos)
                           (string-ref str2 pos))
                 (help (add1 pos))
                 #f)))))
        (if (= len1 len2) (help 0) #f)))))
```

Program 3-29   `string=?%` with shared variables

Practical Note

It may seem that `letrec` and `let*` are the same. In fact, we could rewrite our last version of `string=?%` as follows:

```
(define string=?%
  (lambda (str1 str2)
    (letrec
      ((len1 (string-length str1))
       (len2 (string-length str2))
       (help
         (lambda (pos)
           (if (>= pos len1)
             #t
             (if (char=? (string-ref str1 pos)
```

```
                    (string-ref str2 pos))
            (help (add1 pos))
            #f)))))
    (if (= len1 len2) (help 0) #f))))
```

We've converted our `letrec` embedded inside a `let` into a single `letrec`. `letrec` allows use of the names by procedures defined in its scope. But `letrec` is no substitute for `let*`. Consider the following:

```
> (let* ((a (sqrt 3)) (b (sqrt a))) b)
1.3160740129524924
```

The names a and b are defined in sequence, so a has a value when (sqrt a) is evaluated. Using `letrec`, however, the following occurs:

```
> (letrec ((a (sqrt 3)) (b (sqrt a))) b)
Error: unbound variable: a
```

`letrec` makes no guarantee about the order of evaluation of the name-value pairs. Using `letrec` this way can lead, in some Scheme systems, to very subtle and hard-to-discover bugs. Use `let*` when you need sequential evaluation. Better still, don't be afraid to use nested `lets`. Tailor the scopes you are creating to your understanding of the problem. Don't waste your time compressing all scopes into one.

☞ **Exercise 3–23**

Write a `let*` form that reorganizes procedure `discr` by binding b^2 and then $4ac$, computing their difference, and then returning the root of the difference. ❏

3.4.2   Modules

As programs get larger, programmers find it harder and harder to organize them. A large program might have hundreds or thousands of procedures. It would be impossible to keep track of the interactions among several thousand procedures.

Programmers normally don't think of a large program in terms of the procedures that compose it. Instead, they think of a program as a collection of **subsystems**, each of which is a set of procedures that, collectively, have one specific function. For example, a program that runs an on-board aircraft computer might be divided into the following subsystems:

- Gather data from aircraft sensors.
- Gather data from air traffic control stations.
- Process data to get information on airspeed, nearby aircraft, and so on.
- Display data on pilot consoles.
- Respond to pilot commands.

Programmers have discovered that there is a tremendous difference between programming-in-the-small (writing a small program to do one specific task) and programming-in-the-large (writing a large software system to handle complex information processing). Niklaus Wirth, the designer of Pascal, decided in the early 1970s to study the problems of writing large programs. He eventually designed a language, Modula-1, that allowed programmers to organize procedures into packages. Wirth's next language, Modula-2, refined these concepts and influenced many languages.

What Wirth did was to define a **module** as a collection of definitions (and other things, in Modula-2) that perform some set of **services** for the programmer. Modules keep some definitions **private**. Private definitions include procedures and other definitions that are not intended to be called by the outside world, but only by other procedures in the module. Other definitions are **exported** (made visible to the rest of the program) and may be used freely there.

Scheme has no facilities for managing modules, although some experimental Scheme implementations have provided them. A skilled Scheme programmer, however, can define modules, and we have done so. To add our module features to your Scheme system, refer to the instructions in the Software Package.

A module is a special form that looks like this:

```
(module module-name
  (export name1 name2 . . . namen)
  definition . . . )
```

Program 3-30 shows our plotting package, written as a module.

```
(module plotter
  (export plot-data-transform-mod)
  (define plot-data-transform-mod
    (lambda (xform) (helper xform #f)))
  (define helper
    (lambda (xform pendown)
      (let ((x (read)))
        (if (boolean? x)
          (void)
          (let ((y (read)))
            (if pendown
              (draw-line x (xform y))
              (draw-move x (xform y)))
            (helper xform #t)))))))
```

Program 3-30   Plotter module

Figure 3-9 shows that `plot-data-transform-mod` can be called, but `helper` can't, since it hasn't been exported. This is just as well, as `helper` is just a helper and is not intended to be called except by `plot-data-transform-mod`. The module name, `plotter`, isn't bound to a procedure at all; it is just some bookkeeping information about the module.

A `module` form is evaluated by evaluating its definitions, but then throwing away all of the names except those that have been exported. Any definition can be exported, whether or not it names a procedure. The result is to create an **abstraction barrier**, an interface that hides internal structure but allows the exported names to be used. This has two major effects:

- Helper procedures that were not intended to be called directly are not accessible outside the module.

```
> (plot-data-transform-mod (lambda (x) x))
1 200
10 200
50 201
#f
void
> helper
Error: unbound variable:  helper
> plotter
(module plotter exports (plot-data-transform-mod))
```

Figure 3-9   Plotter example

- The same name may be freely defined in several modules, provided that at most one of the modules exports it.

The second effect is useful: we don't have to create new names for each helper. Instead, we put the helpers in a module, and don't export them.

For small programs, modules aren't needed. You can just use `letrec` to hide helpers. In larger programs, you might want to share a helper between two procedures, without making the helper generally visible. If nothing else, modules show that a group of definitions belong together.

3.4.3   Abstract Data Types

Suppose we're processing map data, for example, the coordinates of various locations on the earth. We might wish to find the distance d between two locations, c_1 and c_2, as in Figure 3-10.[15]

On the surface,[16] this problem is trivial (Program 3-31).

Program 3-32 shows another way of doing the same thing. Both versions of `distance` have the same *interface*, but their *implementations* are different. They both compute the correct result, but they're not what we want. We would like to process our location data (`c1` and `c2`). The `distance` procedures demand that we supply them with (x, y) coordinates of the locations in question, not locations.

A general distance procedure for locations can't depend on being handed (x, y) coordinates. Not all location data is recorded in rectangular (x, y) coordinates. Data might just as easily be recorded in degrees, minutes, or seconds, or as map references (e.g., a4). The data might not even use rectangular coordinates at all. Polar coordinates, which locate points by reference to an angle and distance, are often useful. For example, the navigator on an airplane thinks of a city as being 125 miles away on a heading of 35 degrees.[17]

We want to write our code without knowing how the data is recorded, so as to hide the **representation**, the internal structure that corresponds to some information.

---

[15] We're calculating distance as if the earth were flat. It isn't, and sometimes we use latitudes and longitudes as coordinates, not some general map positions. It's all to make things simpler, we hope.

[16] Pun intended.

[17] We normally measure everything in metric, but the air-traffic system uses feet and miles.

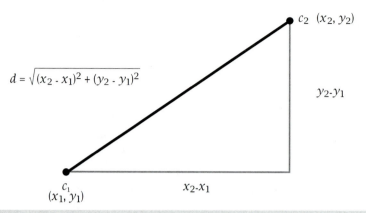

$$d = \sqrt{(x_2 - x_1)^2 + (y_2 - y_1)^2}$$

Figure 3-10   The distance between two points

```
(define distance
  (lambda (x0 y0 x1 y1)
    (let ((square (lambda (x) (* x x))))
      (sqrt
        (+ (square (- x1 x0))
           (square (- y1 y0)))))))
```

Program 3-31   Computing distance in the plane (1)

```
(define distance
  (lambda (x0 y0 x1 y1)
    (let
      ((x (- x1 x0))
       (y (- y1 y0)))
      (sqrt (+ (* x x) (* y y))))))
```

Program 3-32   Computing distance in the plane (2)

Still, we *must* have x and y coordinates if we're going to do this distance calculation. But why should the `distance` procedure know how to get them? Why not pass `distance` the two locations themselves, and provide procedures that give the coordinates of a city? In other words, why not think of a city's location as a piece of data, just like numbers, Booleans, and procedures. We speak of the set of data that works in a certain way as a *data type.* Thus, in addition to Scheme's built-in *number, Boolean,* and *procedure* data types, we are going to define our own *location* data type. Program 3-33 shows a `distance` procedure whose inputs are values of type *location.*

Locations aren't useful as values by themselves, but we can use auxiliary procedures `location-x` and `location-y` to get the coordinates of a location. Note also that this procedure exemplifies the style of embedding helper procedures using `let`. We can type in numbers, Booleans, and procedures directly, but since Scheme doesn't know about locations, we'll have to write a procedure that creates a location. We can call this "constructor" procedure `make-location`.

```
(define distance
  (lambda (c1 c2)
    (let ((square (lambda (x) (* x x))))
      (sqrt (+ (square (- (location-x c2)
                          (location-x c1)))
               (square (- (location-y c2)
                          (location-y c1)))))))))
```

Program 3-33   Procedure `distance` with location input

```
> (define riverdale (make-location 200 50))
> (define pleasantville  (make-location 4300 75))
> (distance riverdale pleasantville)
4100.076218803743
```

☞ **Exercise 3-24**

Write a Scheme form that finds the distance between location $(147, 223)$ and $(308, 14)$, using the above `distance` procedure. ❏

These "location" procedures can be used for many other purposes, for example, in this code for determining whether one location is farther west than a second one:

```
(define farther-west?
  (lambda (c1 c2)
    (< (location-x c1) (location-x c2))))
```

or this procedure that gives the southernmost of two locations:

```
(define southernmost
  (lambda (c1 c2)
    (if (< (location-y c1) (location-y c2)) c1 c2)))
```

We're practicing **data abstraction**: we're using locations, without worrying about exactly what sort of data they are. Data abstraction specifies an interface to data by describing a set of procedures that build the data structure and provide access to its elements. However, nothing is promised about how the data is stored. Just like procedural abstraction, data abstraction depends on the interfaces described by procedures and their parameters.

We're treating the `location` type as an **abstract data type (ADT)**. In effect, we are pretending that, along with numbers, Booleans, and procedures, Scheme knows about locations. Just as we have procedures (e.g., +) that know about numbers, and procedures (e.g., not) that know about Booleans, and procedures (e.g., `string-map`) that know about procedures, we will have procedures that know about locations.

The name *abstract data type* turns out to be somewhat unfortunate. *Abstract* means that our view of the data won't be conditioned by what's easy for the computer, but by the kinds of data we're thinking about. Thus the spectrum from abstract to concrete is from the computer's point of view, not from ours. For us, the more abstract the type is, the better, because we have less to worry about regarding the way the computer will store values of that type.

Some technical terms are useful here. We refer to a procedure such as `make-location` as a **constructor** (because it constructs a new location value), and to a procedure such as location-x as an **accessor**. An accessor can access a part of the data that's not even explicitly stored, as we'll see later when we build ADTs with several constructors. Our convention is that the constructor for the student ADT, for example, is named make-student and the accessors for the name and gpa parts are student-name and student-gpa.

Figure 3-11 is an ADT specification for the type location. When we design the interface for an ADT, we will provide a table in this form showing each of the procedures, and what it does. You can think of this specification as a "contract" between the implementor of the ADT and programmers who use it.

Constructors

- (make-location *x y*)
  Create a new location with coordinates *x* and *y*.

Accessors

- (location-x *loc*)
  Return the *x*-coordinate of location *loc*.

- (location-y *loc*)
  Return the *y*-coordinate of location *loc*.

Figure 3-11   **Abstract Data Type:** location

We will always implement ADTs as modules; the module name will be the ADT name. By convention, we will break up the export list into the same categories that comprise the ADT specification.

Our first implementation assumes that no coordinate can be greater than 999 (Program 3-34). In this version, we're storing a pair of coordinates such as $(148, 275)$ as the number 148275. In the general case, we store the location (x, y) as $1000x + y$. The built-in operations quotient and remainder let us extract the information we need.

```
(module location
  (export make-location location-x location-y)
  (define make-location
    (lambda (x y)
      (+ (* 1000 x) y)))
  (define location-x
    (lambda (c)
      (quotient c 1000)))
  (define location-y
    (lambda (c)
      (remainder c 1000))))
```

Program 3-34   Location module

☞ **Exercise 3-25**

Give some values of x and y that will cause our current version of make-location to fail, i.e., to create an incorrect location. ❏

Our implementation of the `location` ADT is not very good. However, it does let us process location data, so long as we're careful to error-check the inputs to `make-location`. In chapter 4, we'll see how data structures can help us to implement data types such as `make-location` more effectively.

3.4.4 Summary

This section has introduced important tools for organizing program elements. `let`, `let*`, and `letrec` allow us to create temporary bindings (other than the parameters) inside procedures. We can simplify embedded helper procedures by eliminating shared variables. A module collects related procedures into a unit, and hides the internal procedures. Finally, abstract data types let us abstract the interface to data without knowing the implementation.

Case Study: Visualization

Much of what scientists do requires considerable leaps of intuition. There is a famous story of the chemist August Kekulé, who was attempting to find the structure of the benzene molecule. No method of attack was successful, until one day Kekulé was dozing in front of a fire. He dreamt of a snake with its tail in its mouth. When he awoke, the image was so vivid that he attempted a circular structure, which turned out to be correct.

Part of intuition involves pictures. Symbols, such as words, equations, and columns of figures don't really give much insight into what is going on in a problem, whereas a picture can do the job quickly. Often, a simple picture will bring out patterns and relationships among data that no column of figures can make clear.

The program we wrote in the Chapter 2 Case Study can tell us what happened over several years in a wolf/caribou population, but it doesn't really help us visualize what's going on. Anyone working with the program would appreciate some graphic output, rather than columns of numbers.

Our first attempt is to draw two graphs: one for wolves and one for caribou. It would make no sense to draw these graphs separately; we want to see what effect a change in one population has on the other.

Let's start by just cleaning up `popsk` and making it a simple module. We did a number of things in Chapter 2 to force sequencing, and so on. Now we can use `begin` and `if` without `else` to write cleaner code, as shown in Program 3–35. This version is functionally the same as the one in Chapter 2. The module has the effect of hiding `output-wc`, which, in this version, just writes out a line of output.

To modify this code to produce a graph, we must modify `output-wc`. Each year, it must draw two small line segments: one for the wolf population and one for the caribou population. Because we're computing new values for each population each year, we can't simply draw one graph and then go back and draw the other. Instead, we must draw one line segment for each population, which requires that we know the old values for each population, passed in as parameters `oldw` and `oldc`. This gives us a new version of `output-wc` (Program 3–36).

We've used two more procedures, `draw-move-scaled` and `draw-line-scaled`, because the (x, y) values we draw are likely to be small (we might have just 20 or so wolves, with a y range of 0 to 500). These procedures magnify the (x, y) values

```
(module predator/prey
  (export popsk popsk-demo)
  (define popsk
    (lambda (a b c d wolves caribou n m)
      (if (= n 0)
          (output-wc m wolves caribou)
          (begin
            (output-wc (- m n) wolves caribou)
            (popsk a b c d
              (+ (* c wolves) (* d caribou))
              (- (* a caribou) (* b (* wolves caribou)))
              (sub1 n) m)))))
  (define output-wc
    (lambda (n w c)
      (format #t "year: ~a wolves: ~a caribou: ~a~%" n w c)))
  (define popsk-demo
    (lambda ()
      (popsk 1.1 0.01 0.9 0.02 10 10 100 100)))
) ; end of module
```

Program 3-35   Population simulator

```
(define output-wc
  (lambda (n w c oldw oldc)
    (format #t "year: ~a wolves: ~a caribou: ~a~%" n w c)
    (draw-move-scaled n oldw)
    (draw-line-scaled (add1 n) w)
    (draw-move-scaled n oldc)
    (draw-line-scaled (add1 n) c)))
```

Program 3-36   output-wc with previous values as input

```
(define scale 2)
(define draw-move-scaled
  (lambda (x y) (draw-move-x (* x scale) (* y scale))))
(define draw-line-scaled
  (lambda (x y) (draw-line-x (* x scale) (* y scale))))
```

Program 3-37   Scaling factors in graphic output

by an amount given as a scaling factor, which can easily be changed. The program appears in Program 3-37.

Unfortunately, when we run the resulting package, we find that our graph makes no sense. We don't know which line corresponds to wolves, and which to caribou. The solution, shown in Program 3-38, is to label each line.

After making these changes, we can run the resulting module and get a picture like that in Figure 3-12. This gives us a clear idea of what's happening over time: the caribou are slowly dying out.

What if we're less interested in what's happening over time than in the relation between the two populations? The model computes new populations simply in terms of the current populations (which may be too simple a model). Thus, regard-

```
(define popsk
  (lambda (a b c d wolves caribou oldw oldc n m)
    (if (= n 0)
      (begin
        (output-wc m wolves caribou oldw oldc)
        (label m wolves "wolves")
        (label m caribou "caribou"))
      (begin
        (output-wc (- m n) wolves caribou oldw oldc)
        (popsk a b c d
          (+ (* c wolves) (* d caribou))
          (- (* a caribou) (* b (* wolves caribou)))
          wolves caribou
          (sub1 n) m)))))
(define label
  (lambda (x y str)
    (draw-move-scaled x y)
    (draw-text str)))
```

Program 3-38   Simulator with labels

Figure 3-12   Graph of predator/prey run

less of the way we reached a specific combination of populations, the next year's populations would be the same.

One way to visualize this is known as a *phase diagram*, in which the x and y coordinates correspond directly to the two population values. Time isn't shown explicitly in a phase diagram, though we can follow the path to see successive years. A phase diagram is an excellent way to show what happens in particular circumstances. For example, we might have an explosive growth of wolves, followed by a sharp collapse of caribou populations, followed in turn by wolf extinction. You might be surprised to learn that phase diagrams are easier to program than graphs. We only need to draw the given (x, y) values.

Which way is better? Both pictures give us useful information. The graph shows the sequence of events, and is useful in picking out cyclic patterns, or delays (e.g., consistent increase in the caribou population followed by a wolf increase three years later). The phase diagram lets us see, more directly, the behavior of the model. Accordingly, we will keep both versions. Our final version has a Boolean flag, phase-diagram, that tells us which picture to produce (Program 3-39).

Running this version produces the picture shown in Figure 3-13. Note how

```
(module predator-prey
  (export
    popsk popsk-demo)
  (define popsk
    (lambda (a b c d wolves caribou oldw oldc n m draw-phase)
      (if (= n 0)
        (begin
          (output-wc m wolves caribou oldw oldc draw-phase)
          (if (not draw-phase)
            (begin
              (label m wolves "wolves")
              (label m caribou "caribou"))))
        (begin
          (output-wc (- m n) wolves caribou oldw oldc draw-phase)
          (popsk a b c d
            (+ (* c wolves) (* d caribou))
            (- (* a caribou) (* b (* wolves caribou)))
            wolves caribou
            (sub1 n) m
            draw-phase)))))
  (define output-wc
    (lambda (n w c oldw oldc draw-phase)
      (format #t "year: ~a wolves: ~a caribou: ~a~%" n w c)
      (if draw-phase
        (draw-line-scaled w c)
        (begin
          (draw-move-scaled n oldw)
          (draw-line-scaled (add1 n) w)
          (draw-move-scaled n oldc)
          (draw-line-scaled (add1 n) c)))))
  (define label
    (lambda (x y str)
      (draw-move-scaled x y)
      (draw-text str)))
  (define scale 2)
  (define draw-move-scaled
    (lambda (x y)
      (draw-move-x (* x scale) (* y scale))))
  (define draw-line-scaled
    (lambda (x y)
      (draw-line-x (* x scale) (* y scale))))
  (define popsk-demo
    (lambda (draw-phase)
      (draw-clear)
      (popsk 1.1 0.01 0.9 0.02 10 10 0 0 100 100 draw-phase)))
) ; end of module
```

Program 3-39   Simulator with phase diagram output

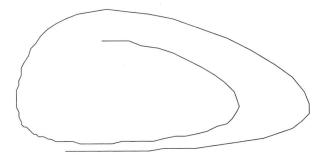

Figure 3-13   Graph of predator/prey phase diagram

our final version uses modules effectively. All of the helpers are hidden; only the demonstration procedure and popsk are visible.

☞ **Exercise 3-26**

The pictures we produce are fairly sparse. There are no axes, for example. Write a second module that draws labeled axes. Note: You'll need to write a procedure that writes the characters of a string vertically in order to label the *y* axis. Scheme has no such primitive, but you can do it with string recursion. ❏

Summary

We began this chapter with a simple view of Scheme. All we could do was write simple recursions on numeric arguments. This chapter has made our programming world more interesting in three ways. First, strings and characters let us represent textual information. Processing strings introduced us to new forms of recursion. String recursion is based on position in the string. Substring recursion processes the remainder of a string after handling the first character. Input/output and graphics allow us to write programs that interact with the environment. Unlike most computations, they produce effects as well as values. To handle input/output properly, we learned new techniques for sequencing operations. Finally, we introduced methods for organizing programs. We learned about let and its variants and the use of scope in programs. Modules let us organize related procedures into units. Lastly, abstract data types let us operate on data types independently of implementation.

Further Readings

The Scheme references in Chapter 1 are useful as a reference on the new Scheme features we have introduced in this chapter.

    See *The Mythical Man-Month: Essays on Software Engineering* by Frederick P. Brooks, for software engineering.

The Visual Display of Quantitative Information, by Edward R. Tufte, shows how to communicate quantitative information clearly by using graphics.

Your Scheme system probably has additional features for dealing with strings, as well as for I/O and graphics. Consult your Scheme manual for more information.

Key Words

Here are the *key words* introduced in this chapter. Make sure you understand what each one means.

abstract data type (ADT)	format string	sequencing
abstraction barrier	implicit begin	service
accessor	lexical	shared variable
character	library	side effect
cipher	module	software engineering
code	mutual recursion	static scoping
cohesive	null string	string
command	position	string recursion
constructor	private	stub procedure
control characters	programming in the large	substring recursion
conversion procedures	programming in the small	subsystem
data abstraction	prompting	thunk
effect	read	top-down programming
embed	representation	transform
export	scope	void
first-class citizens	sentinel	

Scheme Features Introduced in This Chapter

Primitive Procedures

`char->integer`	`char-ci<=?`	`char-ci<?`	`char-ci=?`
`char-ci>=?`	`char-ci>?`	`char-downcase`	`char-upcase`
`char<=?`	`char<?`	`char=?`	`char>=?`
`char>?`	`char?`	`display`	`draw-clear`
`draw-line`	`draw-move`	`draw-text`	`format`
`integer->char`	`newline`	`read`	`string`
`string-append`	`string-length`	`string-ref`	`string=?`
`string?`	`substring`	`void`	`void?`

Special Forms

`begin`	`let`	`let*`	`letrec`
`module`			

Cumulative List of Data Types

Starting in this chapter, we will give a table for the datatypes we have studied. Although the table has entries for constructors and accessors, they are not applicable (—) for the simple data types. As we introduce more types, we will extend this table.

Name	Constructor	Accessors	Predicate
Boolean	—	—	boolean?
character	integer->char	char->integer	char?
number	—	—	number?
procedure	lambda	—	procedure?
string	string	string-ref	string?
void	void	—	void?

Problems

1. Evaluate

   ```
   (string-append
     (substring "syllabub" 0 (string-length "this"))
     "og"
     (substring "strabismus" 5 8))
   ```

2. Children sometimes use a code called pig Latin, which has nothing to do with Caesar ciphers, except that it is far easier to break! To convert a word to pig Latin, put the first letter of the word at the end, followed by ay. Thus dog becomes ogday, and noodle becomes oodlenay. If the word starts with a vowel, the pig Latin is just the original word followed by yay (e.g., antyay). (This description is incomplete; in real pig Latin, we would put the first *sound* at the end. Our system will convert shoe to hoesay, whereas the correct translation is oeshay.)

   Write a procedure that takes a string representing a word and translates it to pig Latin.

3. Write a procedure that gives you the reverse of a string. Thus, (string-reverse "antithesis") should evaluate to "sisehtitna".

4. Using string-map, write a procedure that accepts a string as an argument, returning a string with the same length as the original, but with 1 in place of any letters, d in place of any digits, and _ in place of anything else. Thus, (classify-chars "ralph 12c41+") ⇒ "11111_dd1dd_".

5. Convert the following let forms into lambda forms:
   a. (let ((a 1)) (add1 a))
   b. (let ((x "hello") (y "world")) (string-append y x))
   c. (let ((w +)) (let ((z 3)) (w z 5)))

6. Give some advantages and disadvantages of using letrec for helper procedures, rather than just using define.

7. Compare and contrast the letrec and module forms.

8. Write substring%, using string primitives string-append, string-ref, and string.

9. Write a more efficient version of caesar-encrypt-string-s, the procedure that uses substring recursion, by eliminating the repetitive call to string-length.

Self-Assessment

1. Write a procedure that counts the number of spaces in a string.

2. Write a procedure that "zips" two strings together. Its return value is a new string that contains the characters of the original strings in alternate order. For example, (zip "hello" "world")⇒ "hweolrllod". Assume that the two strings have the same length.

3. Write a procedure that scans for one string within another, returning the index number of the first occurrence of the first string in the second, or –1 if the first string doesn't appear. For example,

```
(scan-string "foo" "foobar")⇒ 0
(scan-string "is" "mississippi")⇒ 1
(scan-string "gp" "eggplant")⇒ 2
(scan-string "xx" "zucchini")⇒ -1
```

4. Write a Scheme form (or forms) that prints the values of x, y, and z as follows:

```
The values are:  x: 2  y: 5  z: 10
```

Assume that x is 2, y is 5, and z is 10.

5. What is the value of

```
(define f (lambda (x) (- x 3)))
(define g
  (lambda (y)
    (let
      ((f
        (lambda (z)
          (if (= z 0)
            2
            (f (- z 1))))))
      (f y))))
(g 5)
```

6. Rewrite the following, using lambda:

```
(let
  ((a 4)
   (b 9)
   (c 2))
  (let ((disc (- (* b b) (* 4 (* a c)))))
    (/ (+ (- b) (sqrt disc))
      (* 2 a))))
```

7. Joel User has written the following Scheme form. Assuming that the two input values it reads are 7 and 3, in that order, what is its value? Why?

```
(let
  ((a (read))
   (b (read))
   (c (add1 a)))
  (/ a (+ b c)))
```

8. The following procedure and its helper compute

$$\sum_{i=0}^{n} f(i) = f(0) + f(1) + \cdots + f(n)$$

```
(define sum-series
  (lambda (f n)
    (sum-series-helper f 0 n 0)))
(define sum-series-helper
  (lambda (f i n acc)
    (if (> i n)
        acc
        (sum-series-helper f (add1 i) n (+ acc (f i))))))
```

Rewrite this code, using `letrec` (the resulting helper must still be tail-recursive). Your helper procedure should have as few arguments as possible.

9. Write a procedure named `string-tail-map` that operates in much the same way as `string-map`, except that, instead of calling its procedure argument with each *character* of the string, it calls the procedure with each *tail* of the string, where the *n*th tail of a string is the substring starting with the *n*th character position. For example,

```
> (string-tail-map (lambda (x) (display x) (newline)) "Scheme")
Scheme
cheme
heme
eme
me
e
```

Is your `string-tail-map` useful in implementing `scan-string`, above? Why or why not?

Programming Problems

1. Modify the data visualization program to make it more useful:
   - Draw axes, with labels and tick marks.
   - Allow both *x* and *y* axes to be transformed.
   - Allow more than one curve to be drawn on the same graph, with each curve being labeled.

   You will have to change the format of the data file to accommodate these modifications.

2. Telephone companies provide directory assistance, which allows callers to ask for a person by name and get the person's phone number. Given the volume of calls, it isn't possible to ask every caller to spell the person's name (even if the caller knows the exact spelling). In addition, many names have different spellings: for example, Smith, Smythe, and Smithe, or Macrae, McRae, and Macree.

   The solution is obvious: ignore the exact spelling, and use phonetics. Get all of the names that sound about the same. If there's more than one, the operator can ask for the address in order to find the desired number.

One method that has been used for decades is called *Soundex coding*.[18] The Soundex method transforms any string (of letters only, though it is trivial to modify the algorithm to exclude punctuation) into a four-character string, of which the first character is a letter, and the remaining three characters are digits, as follows:

   a. Translate the first letter of the name to uppercase.

   b. Remove all occurrences of the letters a, e, h, i, o, u, w, and y from the string (in other than the first position).

   c. Any remaining letters should be translated to numeric codes, as follows:

- b, f, p, v → 1
- c, g, j, k, q, s, x, and z → 2
- d, t → 3
- l → 4
- m, n → 5
- r → 6

   d. If two or more adjacent code values occur, drop all but the first.

   e. The Soundex code consists of the original first letter followed by three numeric code values. If there are more than three code values, take only the first three. If there were fewer than three code values, add code 0 characters at the right.

For example, `Micawber` is translated first to MCBR, and then to M216. `Boz` is translated first to BZ, then to B2, and finally to B200. `Chuzzlewit` is translated first to C2243 and then to C243 (the duplicated z is dropped).

Directory-assistance computer systems can use Soundex coding to bring up all the names that sound the same, and let the operator and caller determine which is the right one. (In practice, a directory-assistance system uses any additional information the caller provides, such as street or neighborhood, in order to limit the number of names it brings up.)

Write a Scheme predicate, with helpers, to determine whether two strings sound the same, using Soundex.

Hints: Write a separate procedure for each of the steps shown above, and then write a procedure named `soundex-code` that puts them all together. To avoid massive nests of `if`s, you might find it useful to create and use strings such as `"cgjkqsxz"`.

3. At the end of Chapter 1, you were asked to write a procedure that looked at a blackjack player's score and determined whether to stand or to ask for another card. Review that procedure, and use it as the basis for a blackjack-playing program. In this program, the user will choose whether or not to stand, and the program will (if desired) deal another card and report the player's score. The program will play a hand itself; the user and the player will alternate play. When both the program and the user have declined any more cards, the program will determine the winner and keep track of the number of games won by the user and by the program. (We don't necessarily endorse gambling, so our assumption is that the user will play merely for the joy of it.)

Your program should interact with the user, showing the player both the card it has dealt the player, and the one it has dealt itself.

Note: In an actual blackjack game, cards are dealt from a deck (or, in Las Vegas, a pair of decks), and the same card can't be dealt more than once (twice in Las Vegas, because there are six decks). A clever player can count the cards that have been played, in order to assess the probabilities of getting particular cards. Unfortunately, we haven't yet studied

---

[18] Donald Knuth, in volume 3 of *The Art of Computer Programming*, credits Margaret Odell and Robert C. Russell, in two patents dated 1918 and 1922. This description is taken from Knuth.

techniques for keeping track of which cards have been dealt (that will come in Chapter 5). Therefore, your program may deal the same card many times. If anybody complains, tell them you reshuffle the whole deck before each hand!

4. Write a procedure that compresses a string by eliminating unnecessary blanks (i.e., those blanks at the beginning or end of a string, as well as more than one blank between words). Thus, (compress "   Ad   astra   per   aspera") ⇒ "Ad astra per aspera", and (compress "foo") ⇒ "foo" (it isn't an error if the string contains no spaces.

5. Write a procedure that returns the nth word of a string, assuming words are separated by spaces. Thus (word-ref " Sic transit gloria mundi" 2) ⇒ "gloria" (words are counted from zero; leading and trailing blanks are ignored). *Hint:* Use substring.

6. It is possible to use bisection to solve a simple guessing game. The user thinks of a number between 1 and 100, and the program attempts to guess it. For each guess, the user responds with one of three strings: "high", "low", or "correct". (The quotation marks are necessary. We'll see how to do without them by using a new data type in the next chapter.) A simple dialog with this program might look like this:

```
> (guessing-game)
I guess 50
"high"
I guess 25
"low"
I guess 37
"high"
I guess 31
"correct"
Hey!!! It only took me 4 guesses.
```

Chapter 4

Structures and Collections

Overview

This chapter introduces the simple and powerful ideas that underlie data structures in Scheme, as well as the procedures that support the data structures. We begin by introducing *pairs*, Scheme's facilities for treating two values as a unit. Scheme lets us enter structured data directly in the form in which it displays the data, using *quoting*. Once we can quote input to Scheme, we introduce a new Scheme data type, *symbols*, for representing names. Quoting lets us enter structured data, and we see how Scheme displays such data. We will see how pairs, and structures made from pairs, provide an excellent way to implement abstract data types. One extremely important kind of pair structure, known as a *list*, lets us work with *collections* of data. Scheme has a rich set of primitives that manipulate and operate on structures composed of pairs. We explore many different ways to operate on structures and collections. Procedures as first-class citizens allow us to work with lists in systematic ways such as *mapping*, *filtering*, and *reduction*.

If we take in our hand any volume; of divinity or school metaphysics, for instance; let us ask, Does it contain any abstract reasoning concerning quantity or number? No. Does it contain any experimental reasoning, concerning matter of fact and existence? No. Commit it then to the flames: for it can contain nothing but sophistry and illusion.

— David Hume, *An Enquiry Concerning Human Understanding*

So far, procedures have been our principal tool for organizing computations. This chapter introduces composite data structures and the procedures that handle them. Previous chapters have introduced the ideas of procedural and data abstraction, both powerful tools for constructing effective programs, but there has to be more than that. Many things cannot be easily modeled with the types we have studied so far, such as numbers, Booleans, procedures, characters, and strings.

Programs that do useful things must work with many different types of data. For example, if you wanted to catalog your CD collection, you'd need to be able to represent such things as a composer's or performer's name. In fact, you'd need to be able to represent a whole collection of things (unless you only have one CD, of course!). Therefore, we need to represent various sorts of data if we are to write useful programs. We have seen how abstract data types extend the range of data that we can represent in Scheme. In this chapter, we'll put ADTs to practical use.

This chapter introduces ways of representing real-world objects that have rich structure. First, we will see how to use Scheme to represent structured data. Programs that represent complex objects having parts or several properties need a way to treat several values as a single value. To represent data that has component parts, we will introduce *pairs*, Scheme's data type for representing structured data. Pairs are flexible and essential for programming in Scheme.

We will also extend the range of data types by introducing *symbols*, a Scheme data type for directly representing names. At the same time, we show how Scheme uses *quoting* to let us enter data containing pairs and symbols.

Pairs also let us build data structures for collections of objects. *Lists* use pairs to build structures with an arbitrary number of elements. Scheme has a rich set of primitives that manipulate and operate on structures composed of pairs.

Finally, we will explore how to use Scheme's powerful data and procedural abstraction tools in building programs with list structures. *Mapping* techniques simplify the process of writing programs that manipulate collections. Sometimes we don't want all of the elements in a collection, but want to select a subset of the elements. *Filtering* is a general process for selecting elements from a collection. Something as specific as finding the total of the elements in a collection is actually an example of a more general idea, *reduction*, where we apply an operation to all elements of a collection to get a single result.

4.1 Structures

With a name like yours, you might be any shape, almost.
— Lewis Carroll, *Through the Looking Glass*

The implementation of `make-location` in Chapter 3, shown in Program 4-1, has some serious limitations.

```
(module location
  (export make-location location-x location-y)
    (define make-location
      (lambda (x y) (+ (* 1000 x) y)))
    (define location-x
      (lambda (c) (quotient c 1000)))
    (define location-y
      (lambda (c) (remainder c 1000))))
```
Program 4-1   The initial location module

If we define `loc1` as `(make-location 1 -3)` and `loc2` as `(make-location 0 997)`, then

`(location-x loc1)` ⇒   0, and `(location-x loc2)` ⇒   0
`(location-y loc1)` ⇒   997, and `(location-y loc2)` ⇒   997

Clearly this implementation only works for numbers in a limited range. We tried to cheat by representing two values with only one number. Unless the range of inputs is limited, we were bound to fail.

We need a method of packing two items into one value, to condense them into a unit that Scheme can treat as a single value. The data type we need is Scheme's **pair** data type, which stores two values. We can use a pair to store the (x, y) coordinates.

Scheme has a number of procedures that manage pairs. `cons` creates a pair containing the two values given as its arguments, `car` returns the first element of a pair, and `cdr` returns the second.

Just as we presented the constructor, accessors, and predicates for abstract data types, we will present the appropriate interfaces for **primitive data types** or PDTs (Figure 4-1). The specification for PDTs is determined by Scheme, unlike ADTs, which we define ourselves. We present these to collect information about a primitive in one place. Using the pair **data structure**, we can rewrite the location ADT as shown in Program 4-2.

What exactly does `cons` do? A pair is nothing more than a composite object with two boxes, which we call the **car** and **cdr**. Each box can hold any value in

Constructor

- (cons *a b*)

  Make a new pair, and put *a* in the first box and *b* in the second.

Accessors

- (car *pair*)

  Return the first value of the pair.

- (cdr *pair*)

  Return the second value of the pair.

Predicates

- (pair? *x*)

  Return #t if *x* is a pair, and #f if *x* is anything else.

Figure 4-1   Primitive Data Type: pair

```
(module location
  (export make-location location-x location-y)
    (define make-location
      (lambda (x y) (cons x y)))
    (define location-x
      (lambda (c) (car c)))
    (define location-y
      (lambda (c) (cdr c))))
```

Program 4-2   The location module using pairs

Scheme, unlike boxes in strings, which are restricted to characters. The pair merely joins the two boxes into a single unit that Scheme treats as a single value. Since the pair is one object, it can be the value bound to a name. A Scheme programmer would diagram the pair created by (cons 3 1) as shown in Figure 4-2. The pair is shown as two squares (the boxes) next to each other. The left holds the car and the right holds the cdr of the pair.

To a Scheme programmer, the words "car" and "cdr" have two meanings: either one of the boxes of a pair, or the primitive that gets the value in that box. Similarly, we often use the word "cons" as a verb: we **cons** two values to produce a pair.[1] Using our naming conventions for procedures associated with a data type, cons should have been called make-pair, car should have been called pair-first, and cdr should have been called pair-second, but Lisp and Scheme tradition is strong enough to preserve the original names.

For example, the form

```
(let ((a (cons 1 2))
      (b (cons 4 8)))
  (+ (car a) (cdr b)))
```

[1] Pairs can be implemented extremely efficiently on a computer. On the first computer to implement Lisp (the IBM 7090, circa 1960), a pair corresponded to a machine word, which, on that computer, was composed of an Address part and a Decrement part. One component was the Contents of the Address part of a Register, and the other was the Contents of the Decrement part of a Register. cons is short for "*cons*truct a pair."

Figure 4-2   The value of (cons 3 1)

creates two pairs for no purpose at all, as shown in Figure 4-3. The car of the first is 1, and the cdr of the second is 8, giving a result of 9. Of course, this form *is* silly! There's no point in creating a pair unless you intend to use it *as a pair*.

Figure 4-3   Creating two pairs

Pairs are a general storage mechanism. Although it may seem limiting to be constrained to two components, two is enough to allow us any sort of data structure we need. There are no restrictions on the type of value stored in the car and cdr of a pair. We can write (cons "hat" (cons 1 #t)), a pair whose car is "hat" and whose cdr is (cons 1 #t). This generality is what makes pairs so powerful. We can also apply car to the result of cdr (provided it's a pair) and vice versa.

```
(car (cdr (cons "hat" (cons 1 #t))))  ⇒  1
```

☞ **Exercise 4–1**

Evaluate:
 a. (car (cons 1 2))
 b. (cdr (cons 1 2))
 c. (car (cdr (cons 1 (cons 2 3)))) ❏

☞ **Exercise 4–2**

Without using lambda, define the "sensible" synonyms for the pair operations: cons should have been called make-pair, car should have been called pair-first, and cdr should have been called pair-second. ❏

Pairs are so important as a data structure in Scheme that Scheme has a special notation for printing pairs called **dot notation**.

```
(cons 1 2)  ⇒  (1 . 2)
```

We call (1 . 2) a *dotted pair*. Like most notations, dot notation is a shorthand for something that could be written in a more complex form. A dotted pair is a representation of the pair; Scheme could just as well have used (cons 1 2) itself as the representation, but the dotted pair is more compact. While (1 . 2) is the output for a pair, this notation leads to a problem on input:

```
> (define foo (1 . 2))
Error: invalid application syntax (1 . 2).
```

The printed representation of a pair looks like an application, but it isn't. In Section 4.2.1 we will see how a Scheme construct called quote solves this problem.

☞ **Exercise 4-3**

Evaluate (cons (cdr (cons 1 2)) (cdr (cons 3 4))). ❏

4.1.1   A More Elaborate location Module

Why should we bother with the three procedures above, make-location, location-x, and location-y? Why not use car, cdr, and cons directly in our distance procedure? The answer is that the rectangular coordinates we've been using aren't the only representation of a location. Rectangular coordinates are good when using a map, but they're clumsy when trying to plot a course from one location to the other. In this case, we'd normally use polar coordinates, which represent a location by a distance from the origin ρ, and a heading angle, θ.

We can build a more sophisticated location module that lets us specify a location in either polar or rectangular coordinates and get either rectangular or polar coordinates for any location, regardless of the way it was originally constructed.

Before we begin, let's review some trigonometry. The rectangular and polar coordinates of a point are related by the following equations:

$$x = \rho \cos(\theta) \qquad y = \rho \sin(\theta)$$

from which it follows that

$$\rho = \sqrt{x^2 + y^2} \qquad \theta = \arctan(y, x)$$

Figure 4-4 shows the relation between the two coordinate systems.

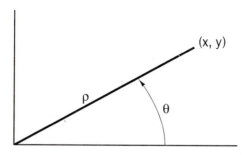

Figure 4-4   The relation between polar coordinates and rectangular coordinates

We need a procedure for finding the arctangent (arctan $a = \theta$ if tan $\theta = a$). We associate the tangent with the slope of the line from the origin to a point. Since tan $\theta = y/x$, $\theta = \arctan y/x$. We can compute arctan(y/x) by the Scheme primitive (atan y x). atan takes separate arguments because, if $x = 0$, the division is undefined, but in that case the arctangent is very well defined, namely $\pi/2$ when x is positive, and $-\pi/2$ when x is negative. Even though the tangent is infinite for $x = 0$, the arctangent is well defined. Of course, (atan 0 0) is undefined.

Program 4-3 shows our solution. We don't care which system represents locations within the module. We can access the coordinates of any location using either system, as needed. The procedures in the module hide the information about the representation of locations. Using a module allows us to keep the interface constant but alters the underlying representation.

```
(module location-rect-polar
  (export make-location-rectangular make-location-polar
    location-x location-y location-rho location-theta
    location-display-rectangular location-display-polar)
  (define make-location-rectangular
    (lambda (x y) (cons x y)))
  (define make-location-polar
    (lambda (rho theta)
      (cons (* rho (cos theta))
        (* rho (sin theta)))))
  (define location-x
    (lambda (loc) (car loc)))
  (define location-y
    (lambda (loc) (cdr loc)))
  (define location-display-rectangular
    (lambda (loc)
      (format #t "x: ~a y: ~a ~%"
        (location-x loc) (location-y loc))))
  (define location-rho
    (lambda (loc)
      (let
        ((x (car loc))
         (y (cdr loc)))
        (sqrt (+ (* x x) (* y y))))))
  (define location-theta
    (lambda (loc)
      (atan (cdr loc) (car loc))))
  (define location-display-polar
    (lambda (loc)
      (format #t "rho: ~a theta: ~a ~%"
        (location-rho loc)
        (location-theta loc)))))
```

Program 4-3   Rectangular and polar coordinates

The make-location procedure has been replaced with two constructors, the first for rectangular data, (x, y) locations, and the second for polar data, (ρ, θ). Display procedures for both formats have been included also. The display procedures use the accessors—if the representation were to change again, these procedures would not need to be modified.

Exercise 4-4

Write a version of the location module that represents all points using polar coordinates, while still providing the same procedure interfaces. ❏

4.1.2   Diagramming pairs

The code presented in this section can be found in file ch04.scm.

We saw how we can draw a pair as two adjacent boxes: the car on the left, and the cdr on the right. Nothing prevents us from constructing a pair whose cdr is itself a pair, such as (cons 1 (cons 2 3)). We diagram such a complex structure in Figure 4-5 (b). The cdr of the structure (cons 1 (cons 2 3)) is (cons 2 3), so it is drawn inside the right-hand box of the pair.

In fact, nothing prevents us from having as many levels of pairs as we want. No matter how much data we have, we can use pairs whose car and cdr possibly contain other pairs to organize the data.

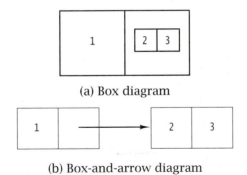

(a) Box diagram

(b) Box-and-arrow diagram

Figure 4-5   Diagramming (cons 1 (cons 2 3))

Figure 4-6 shows that drawing boxes inside boxes is fine for one box but if we put boxes inside those inner boxes, the pictures become very complicated (and the innermost boxes become very small!). The purpose of these diagrams is to help us visualize the structures; a diagram with boxes within boxes within boxes is worse than useless, because it may leave us even more confused than before!

Pair diagrams are much easier to read if we move the contents of some of the boxes outside the pair. For example, we usually draw (cons 1 (cons 2 3)) as shown in Figure 4-5 (b).

In the **box-and-arrow diagram** representation, we show a pair as two adjacent boxes, the left for the car and the right for the cdr. The rules for drawing box-and-arrow diagrams are as follows:

- If a box contains another pair, the pair is drawn outside the box, and an arrow connects the first box to the pair contained in it.

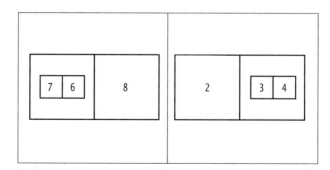

Figure 4-6   Box diagram of (cons (cons (cons 7 6) 8) (cons 2 (cons 3 4)))

- If a box contains any other Scheme value, the value is shown inside the box, if it fits. Otherwise, the value is drawn outside the box, connected by an arrow.

Figure 4-7 shows the value of (cons (cons 3 "foo") (cons 6 "bar")). The structure is a pair whose car and cdr are themselves pairs.

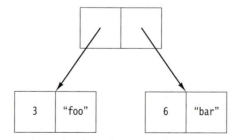

Figure 4-7   Box-and-arrow diagram of (cons (cons 3 "foo") (cons 6 "bar"))

We saw that (cons 1 2) displays as (1 . 2). How does Scheme display a more complex structure, such as (cons 1 (cons 2 3))?

(cons 1 (cons 2 3)) ⇒ (1 2 . 3)

The rule for printing a pair follows: (cons *x y*) prints as (*x . y*). The rule implies that (cons 1 (cons 2 3)) prints as (1 . (2 . 3)), but Scheme uses a more compact notation. Scheme omits the dot and the enclosing parentheses when the item to the right of the dot is a pair. This rule really pays off in examples such as:

(cons 1 (cons 2 (cons 3 4))) ⇒ (1 2 3 . 4)

which we would have had to write as (1 . (2 . (3 . 4))). The two representations are equivalent. Section 4.3 gives a complete explanation later when we study another Scheme structure that uses pairs. You can check to see how (1 2 3 . 4) is the shorthand way of writing down (1 . (2 . (3 . 4))) by simplifying it using the rule: Omit the dot and the following parentheses when the item to the right of the dot is a pair.

```
(1 . (2 . (3 . 4)))    simplifies to
(1 2 . (3 . 4))        which simplifies to
(1 2 3 . 4)
```

☞ **Exercise 4-5**

Draw a box-and-arrow diagram of (cons (cons 37 (cons 52 91)) (cons 52 91)). ❏

4.1.3 Abstract Data Types for Cities

In Chapter 3, we introduced abstract data types. An abstract data type hides the representation of a data value, but provides procedures that allow us to work with the value. Chapter 3's ADTs were hindered by the lack of any data structuring features. We had to use a trick (combining the x and y values of a location into one number) in order to do it at all.

We now know how to create complex data structures, using pairs. Let's use a concrete example to see how to express a complex ADT by using pairs. What if we want to represent information about a set of cities? First, we should define an ADT that represents a city. To do this, we need to know what information is necessary to solve the problem at hand. If we are interested in populations, we will need to store different information than what we'd store if we were interested in cities with teams in a sports league.

Suppose we are only interested in the population and physical location of each city. In that case, we would assume that a city consists of a name, a population, a latitude, and a longitude. (Of course, real cities have many more attributes.)

Figure 4-8 shows our city ADT specification. We have treated the latitude and longitude as separate quantities. We could have used the location ADT we studied earlier, but we avoided it to simplify things.

Suppose we want to work with the data for several cities. After gathering the data, we can write the following Scheme form to compute the combined population of Vancouver and Leipzig:[2]

```
(let
  ((vancouver (make-city "Vancouver" 1500 49 123))
   (leipzig (make-city "Leipzig" 545 51 -12))
   (vladivostok (make-city "Vladivostok" 648 43 -131))
   (perth (make-city "Perth" 1200 -31 -115)))
  (+ (city-population vancouver) (city-population leipzig)))
```

Now, how do we represent cities? The representation in Program 4-4 uses a structure of pairs. Because we so frequently need to access items in a chain of pairs, we often use the following procedures:

```
(define first (lambda (x) (car x)))
(define second (lambda (x) (car (cdr x))))
```

---

[2] Population figures (in thousands) are circa 1993. Latitudes are positive for N and negative for S; longitudes are positive for W and negative for E. Both values are in degrees. Vancouver is in Canada; Leipzig is in the Federal Republic of Germany (in the former German Democratic Republic); Vladivostok is in the far east of the Russian Federation; Perth is in Australia.

Constructor

- (make-city   *city-name city-pop city-lat city-long*)
  Make a city with name *city-name*, population *city-pop*, and location (*city-lat*, *city-long*).

Accessors

- (city-name   *city*)
  Return name of *city*.
- (city-population   *city*)
  Return population of *city*.
- (city-latitude   *city*)
  Return latitude of *city*.
- (city-longitude   *city*)
  Return longitude of *city*.

Output procedure

- (show-city   *city*)
  Display the name, population, latitude, and longitude of *city*.

Figure 4-8   **Abstract Data Type:** city

```
(define third (lambda (x) (car (cdr (cdr x)))))
...
(define first-tail (lambda (x) (cdr x)))
(define second-tail (lambda (x) (cdr (cdr x))))
(define third-tail (lambda (x) (cdr (cdr (cdr x)))))
...
```

up to tenth and tenth-tail. The box-and-arrow diagram for the value of (make-city "Vancouver" 1500 49 123) appears in Figure 4-9.

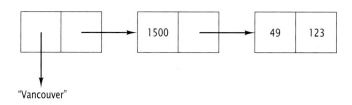

"Vancouver"

Figure 4-9   Box diagram of (make-city "Vancouver" 1500 49 123)

This implementation makes name easiest to access, then pop, then lat, and finally long. We measure ease of access in a pair chain by counting the number of cdr operations needed to get to the desired pair from the first pair in the chain.

☞ **Exercise 4-6**

Write a procedure, (farther-north? city1 city2), that returns #t when city1 is farther north than city2. Use the city procedures, not direct pair manipulation. ❑

```
(module cities
  (export make-city city-name city-population
    city-latitude city-longitude)
  (define make-city
    (lambda (name pop lat long)
      (cons name
        (cons pop
          (cons lat long)))))
  (define city-name
    (lambda (city) (first city)))
  (define city-population
    (lambda (city) (second city)))
  (define city-latitude
    (lambda (city) (third city)))
  (define city-longitude
    (lambda (city) (third-tail city)))
)
```

| Program 4-4   Implementing the city ADT |

☞ **Exercise 4-7**

Why did we organize the city ADT structure the way we did? Suppose we mostly need populations, occasionally need locations, and rarely need city names. Redo the city ADT so that the information needed most often is the easiest to access.

Even though all procedures in the module will be changed from the original version, no program that uses the city ADT will notice any difference, except that the program might run more quickly. ❏

☞ **Exercise 4-8**

Write a display procedure named show-city for the cities module, so that

```
> (define vancouver (make-city "Vancouver" 1500 49 123))
> (show-city vancouver)
City Vancouver at lat: 49 long: 123 has 1500000 people
```

❏

☞ **Exercise 4-9**

We have been representing latitudes and longitudes as numbers. Normally, these values are given in degrees, minutes, and seconds. Implement an angle ADT with the interface shown in Figure 4-10 (descriptions have been omitted, since they are straightforward). ❏

Constructor

- (make-angle *degrees minutes seconds*)
  Make an angle specified by *degrees, minutes,* and *seconds.*

Accessors

- (angle-degrees *angle*)
  Return the degree component of *angle.*

- (angle-minutes *angle*)
  Return the minutes component of *angle.*

- (angle-seconds *angle*)
  Return the seconds component of *angle.*

Output procedure

- (show-angle *angle*)
  Display the *angle* as degrees, minutes, and seconds.

Figure 4-10 **Abstract Data Type:** angle

4.2 Quote and Symbols

> *Every quotation contributes something to the stability or enlargement of the language.* — Samuel Johnson, *A Dictionary of the English Language*

Pairs are the foundation of Scheme's way of representing structured data. We have seen how to use the primitives that construct and access pairs, how to diagram them, and how Scheme prints them out. To enter pairs directly, we need to learn a new feature of Scheme: quoting. Quoting lets us enter structured data as is, without having to use cons. At the same time, knowing how to use quoting lets us learn about symbols, which is Scheme's way of representing names.

4.2.1 Quoting

Can we enter the dotted pair that Scheme uses to represent (cons 1 2)?

```
> (1 . 2)
Error: invalid application syntax (1 . 2).
```

We should have expected this. The Scheme evaluator thinks everything enclosed in parentheses is either an application or a special form, to which it can apply 𝕿𝖍𝖊 𝕽𝖚𝖑𝖊𝖘. Nothing in the syntax of Scheme allows periods to appear in applications. We need a way of telling the evaluator *not* to apply 𝕿𝖍𝖊 𝕽𝖚𝖑𝖊𝖘 to something we want to treat as a plain unevaluated structure of pairs.

In English we often use quotation marks around words to show that we are referring to the words and not their meaning. We can state that a chair is a piece of furniture, but we state that "chair" is a noun. The instance of the word in quotation marks brings our attention to the word itself, and not what it names.

In ordinary English, we also distinguish between sentences in quotation marks and sentences without quotation marks. For example, if a newspaper article says of Politician X that "X is a criminal and a liar", the reader assumes there is evidence to prove this. If, on the other hand, an article says "Politician Y said, 'X is a criminal and a liar'", the reader knows that what is being reported is not the fact of X's criminality, but rather what Y said about it. The quotation marks show that the speaker is reporting the words literally, without any interpretation of them.[3]

In Scheme, **quoting** serves a similar purpose. We can write

```
(quote (1 . 2)) ⇒ (1 . 2)
```

The quote form tells Scheme not to try to evaluate (1 . 2), but simply to create exactly the structure as described.

Because we have to do a lot of quoting, Scheme provides a shorthand. We can write (quote (1 . 2)) as

```
'(1 . 2)
```

The apostrophe is Scheme shorthand for a quote form. When Scheme sees 'x, it treats it as if it were (quote x), where x can be any Scheme form. This shorthand is an artifact of read, the Scheme procedure that reads what you type. By the time the evaluator sees it, such a form will have been turned into a quote form.[4]

Practical Note

What must be quoted? We could, if we wanted, quote every piece of data, writing forms such as (zero? '2) or (if '#t '3 '4). However, no Scheme programmer would bother quoting numbers. The rules are fairly straightforward:

- You *must* quote pairs.
- You *must not* quote Scheme forms, including lambda forms.
- You may quote numbers, strings, and Booleans if you wish, but it makes no difference. Most programmers don't.

4.2.2   Symbols

To keep track of city names, we have used strings. We can also represent names in Scheme with the *symbol* type. A symbol is like a name, for example, vancouver or scheme. Any sequence of characters that is a legal name is also a legal symbol. Symbols give us a non-numeric data type that we can use anywhere in our program.

Since we have symbols, where earlier we wrote (cons (cons 3 "foo") (cons 6 "bar")), we can now write (cons (cons 3 'foo) (cons 6 'bar)). Why do we have to quote symbols in this context?

```
> (define thecity vancouver)
Error: variable vancouver is not bound.
> (define thecity 'vancouver)
```

---

[3] In English, quotation marks often imply sarcasm, as when an opposition politician speaks of the government's "fiscal responsibility". Scheme has no features to support this use.

[4] We speak of ' as the shorthand of quotation marks, even though in normal English usage " and " are called *quotation marks*. This is a historical anomaly. Do not confuse the apostrophe ' with the *backquote* `.

```
> thecity
vancouver
> (define name-pop '(vancouver . 1500))
```

Unless the symbol is quoted, Scheme tries to evaluate it as a name, which may or may not have a value. We assumed in the example just given that we had not defined a variable named vancouver. The last form in the example shows that you don't need to quote a symbol inside a quoted form. Scheme already knows that the structure is to be created as-is. Using quoting, we could make a city using symbols like this:

```
(define vancouver (make-city 'vancouver 1500 49 123))
```

☞ **Exercise 4-10**

Try to evaluate each of the following expressions; some may be illegal.
  a. (+ '2 2)
  b. ('+ 2 2)
  c. () ❏

☞ **Exercise 4-11**

Assume that you have entered

```
(define a 'b)
(define b 3)
```

into Scheme. Evaluate each of the following:
  a. a
  b. b
  c. 'a
  d. 'b
  e. ''a ❏

There is a big difference between symbols and strings. A symbol stands for itself. Scheme considers the symbols fred and fred1 to be completely unrelated. On the other hand, a string is a collection of characters. There are Scheme primitives for joining, pulling apart, and comparing strings (we discussed these in Chapter 3). Use symbols when you want to give names for things; use strings when you want to manipulate the data. Strings can be decomposed into smaller pieces; symbols can't.

Practical Note

To display a message, we would write, for example,

```
> (begin (display "Hello, world!") (newline))
Hello, world!
```

Case is not significant in symbols: blob, bLOb, and BLOB are the same symbol, whereas "blob", "bLOb", and "BLOB" are different strings (try displaying each of these values). It's interesting to try to produce the same printed output from symbols as from strings:

```
> (begin (display 'hello) (display 'world) (newline))
helloworld
```

The symbols are printed one after another with no spaces! Don't try to use commas anywhere in Scheme except in strings until you're expert with macros, since commas have a special meaning to read. We'll see macros in Chapter 7.

There is a way to take symbols as input and get close to what we want:

```
> (format #t "~a, ~a!~%" 'hello 'world)
hello, world!
```

but we can still cannot force Scheme to capitalize the "h".

People often get confused about when to use strings and when to use symbols. You should use strings when you want to think of data as being a set of characters. Generally, tasks that are primarily input and output call for strings. For example, a person's name, the title of a book, and the caption for a drawing should all be represented as strings.

Use symbols when you want to specify a value that is chosen from a set of alternatives. Suits in cards, departments in a college or company, and chemical elements are all examples in which symbols are useful. Other languages such as Pascal, Modula-2, and C++, have "enumerated types" that serve a similar purpose. Scheme's symbols differ from enumerated types in that you do not have to state in advance the list of symbols that you will be using in a specific problem.

Symbols are useful when we want to represent something that has a name, as well as other data. For example, we could represent cards in a deck of playing cards as numbers from 1 to 52, but for most purposes it's more convenient to record the rank in each suit from 1 to 13, and to record the suit (i.e., hearts, clubs, diamonds, spades). First, we should define an ADT for cards (Figure 4-11). The particular ADT we design will depend upon the rules of the game. We can make a very general ADT, or we can design one that is more useful in playing a specific game. We have chosen an ADT that lets us create a pair with a specific rank and suit. The implementation in Program 4-5 uses pairs to represent cards. We could store either the rank as it is given to make-card, or convert it to an integer between 1 and 13.

With this implementation, we represent a card as a pair and manipulate each card as a unit, without having to invent a code for each of the suits. Symbols let us directly represent the names.

```
> (define acard (make-card 'heart 11))
> (show-card acard)
heart j
```

Symbols play a limited but useful role. We can test to see whether two symbols are the same, and display symbols, but not much else. Other types are more flexible. Booleans are essential for conditionals; characters and strings are essential for input and output; procedures implement computations; and numbers are essential for numerical computation. We know how to test equality for characters, strings, and numbers: char=?,string=?, and =, respectively. Logic defines the equivalence of Booleans, which we can implement as follows:

Constructor

- (make-card *suit rank*)
  Make a card with suit *suit* and rank *rank*, a number from 1 to 13.

Accessors

- (card-suit *card*)
  Return the suit of card.

- (card-rank *card*)
  Return the rank of the card as a number.

Output procedure

- (show-card *card*)
  Display the suit and rank, translated into card names for face cards and the ace.

Figure 4-11   Abstract Data Type: cards

```
(module cards
  (export make-card card-suit card-rank show-card)
  (define make-card
    (lambda (suit rank) (cons suit rank)))
  (define card-suit
    (lambda (card) (car card)))
  (define card-rank
    (lambda (card) (cdr card)))
  (define show-card
    (lambda (card)
      (format #t " ~a ~a~%" (card-suit card)
        (show-card-rank card))))
  (define show-card-rank
    (lambda (card)
      (let ((rank (card-rank card)))
        (if (= rank 1)
          'A
          (if (< rank 11)
            rank
            (if (= rank 11)
              'J
              (if (= rank 12)
                'Q
                'K)))))))))
```

Program 4-5   A representation for cards

```
(define equivalent?
  (lambda (a b)
    (or (and a b) (and (not a) (not b)))))
```

Equality of procedures is both simple and much more complex. We haven't yet had a reason to worry about this issue; we will return to it in Chapter 5.

How do we tell whether two symbols are the same? Standard Scheme does not have a predicate specifically to test equality of symbols, so we add the predicate symbol-equal?. In addition, just as we have predicates that identify types, such as number?, and boolean?, we have symbol?. Figure 4-12 shows the symbol PDT.

The conversion procedures string->symbol and symbol->string convert back and forth between symbols and strings. By catenating strings and converting, we can produce new symbols in our programs. (You will rarely need these primitives.)

Constructor

- Symbols are usually created during input (e.g., when read encounters foo it returns the symbol foo).

- string->symbol
  Create a symbol whose name is the same as the string.

Accessors

- (symbol->string *symbol*)
  Returns the name of *symbol* as a string.

Predicates

- (symbol? *x*)
  Return #t if *x* is a symbol, and #f otherwise.

- (symbol-equal? *x* *y*)
  Return #t if *x* and *y* are the same symbol, and #f otherwise.

Figure 4-12   **Primitive Data Type:** symbol

We can also implement type-checking predicates for our own ADTs by using symbols. If we implement make-city as follows,

```
(define make-city
  (lambda (name pop lat long)
    (cons 'city (cons name (cons pop (cons lat long))))))
```

we can implement a city? predicate:

```
(define city?
  (lambda (city) (symbol-equal? (car city) 'city)))
```

We must also redefine all the other elements of the ADT.

Before we leave symbols, we must add them to our list of forms that must be quoted. If you don't quote a symbol, Scheme will treat it as a variable.

Practical Note

Consider the difference between (zero? 2), (zero? '2), and ('zero? 2). The first of these is a normal Scheme form, with no quoting. The second quotes the number 2. The third, on the other hand, is illegal: it asks us to apply the *symbol* zero? to 2. We can only apply procedures (either primitive or programmer-defined). It makes no sense to apply a symbol: zero? is a name that is defined (by the Scheme evaluator) to have a procedure value; 'zero? is a form whose value is zero?; and "zero?" is a string that has nothing to do with the procedure or the symbol.

4.3   Collections

> *The true University of these days is a collection of books.*
> — Thomas Carlyle, *On Heroes, Hero Worship, and the Heroic*

Chapter 2 showed us how to write recursive procedures. There, we used recursion to compute numerical results. Many problems require us to collect data about a large number of individuals. The need for repetition arises because we must process a collection: students, customers, employees, library books, cities, or airplane parts. We may want to find the top student, or compute the total salary paid to all employees.

In Section 4.1, we saw that the location ADT can be represented as a pair, an association of two objects that can be extracted by the car and cdr procedures. When we use pairs to build structured data, we find that we can't use them to represent collections with an arbitrary number of elements (i.e., collections where the number of elements is not fixed when the collection is first created). This section introduces *lists* and list programming to let us manage collections. We will see how to find an item in a collection, how to join collections, and how to reverse the order of items in a collection. Recursive programs that operate on lists match the recursive structure of lists.

4.3.1   Lists

What if we want to store not just a single location, but information about a whole collection of locations? We can try to use cons to construct collections of items. Let's call a collection of items consed together a *clump*.

```
(define sum-clump
  (lambda (c)
    (if (pair? c)
        (+ (car c) (sum-clump (cdr c)))
        c)))
(define a-clump (cons 1 (cons 6 (cons 2 3))))
(sum-clump a-clump) ⇒  12
```

This is our first recursive procedure on pairs. The cars of the clump structure hold the data, just like the chain of pairs in Figure 4-9. If c is a pair, sum-clump adds its car to the result of applying sum-clump to the cdr. The recursion terminates when c is no longer a pair, in which case it returns c. Recursion over chains of pairs is similar to substring recursion, which we saw in Chapter 3. We process the first element and then pass all but the first to the recursive call; a trace shows what's happening.

```
> (trace sum-clump)
> (sum-clump a-clump)
call sum-clump: (1 6 2 . 3)
|  call sum-clump: (6 2 . 3)
|  |  call sum-clump: (2 . 3)
|  |  |  call sum-clump: 3
|  |  |  return from sum-clump: 3
```

```
|  |  return from sum-clump: 5
|   return from sum-clump: 11
return from sum-clump: 12
```

Practical Note

Often the first attempt at producing a data representation suffices for the application we have in mind at the time. Can we use the representation under slightly different circumstances? Ask yourselves this question when designing a data structure, not only because you might want to use it for something else, but also because you will often not completely grasp the subtleties of the specification the first time.

Let's look at clumps. They seem to work for items that are not pairs. What if we want to store pairs, with numbers in their cars, as the items in the clump?

```
> (define p-clump
    (cons '(1 . a) (cons '(6 . f) (cons '(2 . b) '(3 . c)))))
> (define sum-p-clump
    (lambda (c)
      (if (pair? c)
        (+ (car (car c)) (sum-p-clump (cdr c)))
        c)))
> (sum-p-clump p-clump)
Error in car: 3 is not a pair.
> (trace sum-p-clump)
> (sum-p-clump p-clump)
call sum-p-clump: ((1 . a) (6 . f) (2 . b) 3 . c)
|  call sum-p-clump: ((6 . f) (2 . b) 3 . c)
|  |  call sum-p-clump: ((2 . b) 3 . c)
|  |  |  call sum-p-clump: (3 . c)
|  |  |  |  call sum-p-clump: c
|  |  |  |  c
Error in car: 3 is not a pair.
```

The trace shows the story. sum-p-clump went one step too far; it didn't recognize the distinction between a pair that's an item in the clump and the pairs that represent the clump—a fatal confusion. There's really no way to construct a general collection without some way to signal the end of the collection. For this reason, Scheme has a special marker, **null**, which we write as (). The Scheme data type for representing collections is called a **list**.[5] We signify the end of a list by making the cdr of the last pair contain null. In our code, we can test for null using null?.

A list is defined as follows:

---

[5] In common English, the word *list* means something like "a whole bunch of things". Here, we are using the word in a technical sense. Thus, for example, location pairs are not lists, in our sense of the word.

> - Null is a list.
> - If a is a list, then (cons x a) is also a list. The term x can be any Scheme form.

Note that this is an **inductive definition**, which means that it starts from the base case and builds up in simple steps. cons is fundamental to the list data type. We can read (cons x a) as "Make a new list whose first item is the value of x and whose remaining items are those found in a".

Lists are clumps with one special difference: the cdr of the last pair must be null. Null, (), is the end-of-list marker that we needed in clumps. Null is written like a list, and is a list, but it is not a pair. Only lists with one or more items are constructed out of pairs. Therefore pair? returns #t for all lists but null. Since null is not a pair, it's an error to apply either car or cdr to null.

The clump data structure is called an **improper list** to distinguish it from a chain of pairs terminated by null.

Scheme provides a number of primitives that operate upon lists. Some of the most important are shown in Figure 4–13.

Practical Note

When we want a list with no items, we write '(). The set of parentheses, (), is not a valid form in Scheme, although some older implementations treat () as null. This doesn't really make sense, because Scheme uses parentheses to mark special forms and applications. The use of unquoted () for null is a holdover from Lisp; you should not use it. Null should remind you of the null string; both have no items. Do not confuse null with void, a nonprinting object.

To create a list with one item, say 4, we follow the inductive definition.

```
(cons 4 '())  ⇒   (4)
```

A one-item list is a pair whose car contains the item and whose cdr contains null.

Things get interesting when we want several items. Suppose we want a list of two items, 3 and 4, in that order:

```
(cons 3 (cons 4 '()))  ⇒   (3 4)
```

We build the list of two items by consing 3, the first item, onto (cons 4 '()), a list containing 4. The list containing 3 and 4 is not written as (cons (cons 3 4) '()). That results in a list with just one item, the pair (cons 3 4).

Recall that (cons x y) prints as (x . y). Therefore, (cons 3 (cons 4 '())), by this rule, would be represented in dot notation as (3 . (4 . ())). The rule for simplifying dot notation ("Omit the dot and the following parentheses if the cdr of the pair is a pair") reduces this to (3 4 . ()).

The abbreviated notation for pairs is really for lists. Scheme has one additional rule: If the cdr of a pair is null, omit the dot and the null. The result is (3 4).

When we make a list, x, with three items, we write

```
(define x (cons 'a (cons 'b (cons 'c '()))))
x ⇒  (a b c)
```

Constructors

- (list *item1 item2 ... itemn*)
  Make a list containing the evaluated arguments in the given order.
- (cons *a b*)
  Make a new pair and put *a* in the first box, and *b* in the second.
- (append *list1 list2*)
  Returns a list consisting of the elements of *list1* followed by the elements of *list2*.

Accessors

- (car *any-list*)
  Return the first value of the pair.
- (cdr *any-list*)
  Return the second value of the pair.
- (list-ref *any-list pos*)
  Return the element at position *pos* in *any-list*.
- (list-tail *any-list pos*)
  Returns the sublist of *any-list* obtained by omitting the first *pos* elements.
- (length *any-list*)
  Return the number of items in *any-list*.

Predicates

- (list? *x*)
  Return #t if *x* is a list, and #f otherwise.

Figure 4-13   **Primitive Data Type:** list

Let's examine the pairs in this list. The first item is a, which is (car x). By the inductive definition, the cdr of the first pair in the list is also a list:

    (cdr x) ⇒   (b c)

car picks out the *first* element in a list, and cdr picks out another list that is the *rest* of the original list.

We write a list by writing a left parenthesis, the elements themselves, and a right parenthesis. This looks like a Scheme form, but we must quote it to prevent evaluation. Writing (define foo '(a b c)) will bind foo to the list (a b c). Without quote, Scheme would try to apply a to the arguments b and c, which would result in an error unless a variable a exists and is bound to a procedure.

List notation, like the use of the apostrophe as a shorthand for quote, is merely a convenience; a list with the elements a, b, and c can be written as (a b c) or as (a . (b . (c . ()))).

Sometimes the elements of a list must be computed. To make a pair of the values of (+ 1 1) and (+ 2 1), we use (cons (+ 1 1) (+ 2 1)) ⇒ (2 . 3). If we wanted a list of the values of 1, (+ 1 1), and (+ 2 1), we could write out the conses:

    (cons 1 (cons (+ 1 1) (cons (+ 2 1) '()))) ⇒   (1 2 3)

Quoting the forms will not give us what we want:

    '(1 (+ 1 1) (+ 2 1)) ⇒   (1 (+ 1 1) (+ 2 1))

quote doesn't evaluate the form; it returns exactly the structure specified. The Scheme primitive list is what we need. The list procedure makes a list out of its arguments: (list 1 (+ 1 1) (+ 2 1)) ⇒ (1 2 3).

You can provide any number of arguments to list. cons creates a pair from its two arguments; list conses all its arguments into a list. These and other list operations are described in Figure 4-13.

We will see some elements of the list PDT later in this section: append joins two lists into a single list, and list-ref and list-tail access items in lists by position.

Exercise 4-12 asks you to write list?, the type-checking predicate for lists. We typically operate on lists as pairs, since that is what really makes up lists. In list processing, we'll use most of the elements of the PDT but we'll usually just use car and cdr to access parts of lists.

We can modify sum-clump to work with lists. We gave an inductive definition for constructing lists. To analyze lists, we'll use a **recursive definition** of lists. A recursive definition for *x* specifies the definition of *x* in terms of a simpler kind of *x*, ultimately reducing the definition to a base case that need not be defined in terms of anything else.

A list, defined recursively, is either one of the following:

- null
- a pair whose *car* is the first element of the list, and whose *cdr* is a list

---

To sum the elements of a list, we need to organize the recursion around the two cases: If the list is null, return 0; otherwise, add the car of the list to the result of summing the cdr of the list, as shown in Program 4-6.

```
(define sum-list
  (lambda (x)
    (if (null? x)
      0
      (+ (car x) (sum-list (cdr x))))))
;; alternative: mimic sum-clump:
(define sum-list
  (lambda (x)
    (if (pair? x)
      (+ (car x) (sum-list (cdr x)))
      0)))
```

Program 4-6   Summing a list

We prefer the first of the two forms of sum-list, because it closely matches the recursive definition.

☞ **Exercise 4-12**

Write list? in terms of other more basic primitives. If a list has *n* elements, how many operations does it take to determine whether it is a list? ❏

☞ **Exercise 4-13**

Explain the difference between (cons 1 2) and (list 1 2). ❏

☞ **Exercise 4-14**

Define the following using `list`:
  a. `(cons 1 (cons 2 (cons 3 '())))`
  b. `(cons 1 (cons 2 (cons 4 '())))`
  c. `(cons (cons  1 (cons 2 '())) (cons 2 '(3)))` ❑

☞ **Exercise 4-15**

Evaluate each of the following expressions; some may be illegal.
  a. `'(+ 2 2)`
  b. `'(lambda (x) (+ 2 3))`
  c. `'()`
  d. `''()`
  e. `'(1 (2 3))`
  f. `'(1 '(2 3))`
  g. `(+ (* 3 4) 5)`
  h. `(+ '(* 3 4) 5)`
  i. `'(1.2)` ❑

4.3.2   Diagramming Lists

Lists are pair structures with one very special difference. When there is a long string of pairs, the cdr of the last pair must be null. A Scheme programmer would diagram the list (a b c) as shown in Figure 4-14.

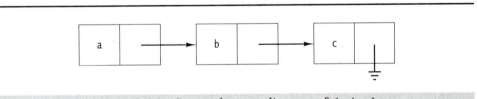

Figure 4-14   Box-and-arrow diagram of (a b c)

We would use a structure like that of Figure 4-14 to represent a list of student's grades, for example, (79 83 74 91 88).

To handle lists as well as other structures composed of pairs, we must add a rule about null to our previous rules about pairs:

- If a box contains another pair, the pair is drawn outside the box, and an arrow connects the first box to the pair contained in it.
- If a box contains any other Scheme value, the value is shown inside the box if it fits. Otherwise, the value is drawn outside the box, connected by an arrow.
- Null is shown as the electrical "ground" symbol: a vertical line above three horizontal lines of decreasing width.

These diagrams reveal the essential similarity of lists and other structures composed of pairs. Sometimes, we will use the term *list structure* informally to refer to any data structure composed of pairs, even though lists are strictly those objects that adhere to the recursive definition given above. Clumps, for example, are often called list structure even though they are not lists.

What if we need to represent the grades of several students? The grades of one student are represented as a list; the grades of several students form a collection of grades. We'll represent the collection of grades as a list in which the elements are themselves lists, like this: ((79 83 74 91 88) (69 78 72 85 79) (85 95 91 88 86)). Lists containing lists can be drawn with the existing rules; Figure 4-15 shows the diagram for the list ((a b) (c d)).

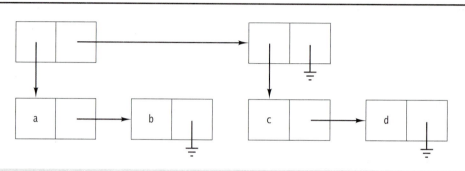

Figure 4-15   Box-and-arrow diagram of ((a b) (c d))

((a b) (c d)) is a list containing two elements, (a b) and (c d). At the **top level**, the list has just these two elements. The top level of a list is the set of elements contained in the cars of all the cells in a direct line from the cell at the beginning of the list and all the cdrs until the end of the list. That is, the top level contains all elements that can be accessed by an operation of the form (car (cdr ... (cdr x))), where there are zero or more cdr operations. Thus the elements at the top level of (a (1 2) b (c (d))) are a, (1 2), b and (c (d)). When we speak of the items in a list, we mean the elements at the top level.

We can identify an item at the top level of a list by the position of the pair that stores it. The first pair holds the item at location 0, and the second pair is at location 1. To compute the location of an item, count the number of cdr operations you need before you apply car to get the item.

The Scheme primitive list-ref selects list elements by location, for example, (list-ref thelist n) returns the item at the nth location, counting from zero. (Thus n corresponds to the number of cdr operations that must be performed.) Program 4-7 shows our version of list-ref.

We used the parameter name any-list here, because list-ref% will work on any sort of list. All we're doing is "navigating" through the list, using car and cdr, and not actually doing any computation with the list elements. You might be tempted to use the name list in place of any-list, but this could lead to problems, because list is the name of a primitive procedure. If there were other procedures inside the body of list-ref% that used the name list, they would expect list to be bound to the Scheme primitive, but the binding introduced by using list as a parameter name would hide the Scheme primitive and produce a very surprising bug. (There is a bug in our version of list-ref; Exercise 4-17 asks you to fix it.)

list-ref should remind you of string-ref, which takes a string and a position and returns the character at that position in the string. Strings are collections, so they could easily be represented as a list where the items are restricted to characters. We could do without strings as long as we create a Scheme procedure to

```
(define list-ref%
  (lambda (any-list n)
    (if (zero? n)
        (car any-list)
        (list-ref% (cdr any-list) (sub1 n)))))
```

Program 4-7   Our version of `list-ref`

display lists of characters as strings. Otherwise we could use list operations to perform all the string manipulation we would need. Strings are convenient for most programming, however, so they are included in Scheme as a useful abstraction, as in most languages.

The concept of the top level of a list is important; the way we usually recurse over lists is to look at the car of the list, then loop on the cdr of the list. Processing the list this way is called *cdring* down the list. The cars of the lists that a recursive procedure sees while cdring down a list form the top level of the argument list.

Practical Note

Diagrams are helpful for determining the value of expressions like (cdr (car x)), where x is a complex list structure. Suppose x is bound to ((a b) (c d)), as shown in Figure 4-15. To get the result of (cdr (car x)), first find the car of x, which is the pair (a b). The cdr operation selects the value in the right box, b. car and cdr move around in list structures. The best way to understand the result, for complex list structures, is to draw the diagram and follow the arrows.

Box-and-arrow diagrams are especially helpful when we write procedures to process complex structures. We'll use pair structures for ADTs and in the next section, we'll see how lists represent collections of values, each of which may be a complex structure having lists as parts. *When in doubt, diagram.*

☞ **Exercise 4-16**

Give box-and-arrow diagrams for the following:
   a. (a b c)
   b. (a (b . c) d)
   c. ((a . b) . (c . d)) ❏

☞ **Exercise 4-17** ·

`list-ref%` will cause an error if n is negative or greater than the length of the list. Fix it. ❏

4.3.3   Processing List Elements

Suppose we are storing populations for various locations. We might write our location information as follows:

```
(define locs '(400 1000 900))
```

in which the population (in thousands) is recorded for Riverdale, Pleasantville, and Happyvale respectively. For this list, the value for Riverdale, 400, is the car, and the cdr is (1000 900). For the list (1000 900), the car is the population of Pleasantville, 1000, and the cdr is the list for Happyvale, (900). The population of Happyvale, 900, is the car of this list, and the cdr is null, ().

There's a significant difference between a list with one element, such as (1000), and the element itself, 1000. If we want to use the element in a singleton list, we must take the car of the list. On the other hand, taking the car of an ordinary value such as 1000 is completely meaningless. What a difference a pair of parentheses makes!

Earlier we defined `sum-list` to sum the elements of a list:

```
(define sum-list
  (lambda (x)
    (if (null? x)
        0
        (+ (car x) (sum-list (cdr x))))))
```

`sum-list` will compute the total population from the list.

We can sum the values in the cars of a list of pairs, using a method similar to `p-clump`.

```
(define p-list
  '((1 . a) (6 . f) (2 . b) (3 . c)))
(define sum-p-list
  (lambda (c)
    (if (null? c)
        0
        (+ (car (car c)) (sum-p-list (cdr c))))))
(sum-p-list p-list) ⇒ 12
```

`p-list` is a list of pairs, and `sum-p-list` is exactly like `sum-list`, except that it adds the cars of the items.

☞ **Exercise 4-18**

Write a list that causes an error in `sum-list`. ❏

☞ **Exercise 4-19**

Write a procedure that is given a list of nonnegative numbers and finds the largest element. Use the primitive `max` for finding the larger of two numbers. ❏

☞ **Exercise 4-20**

Write procedure `length%`, which finds the number of elements in a list given as its argument. ❏

We can mix different types of data in a list. For example, we could have a list of symbols and numbers,

```
(define locations
  '(riverdale 400 pleasantville 1000 happyvale 900))
```

in which the car is the symbol riverdale, and the car of the cdr is Riverdale's population. To find the total population for a "new-style" location list, we write the code shown in Program 4-8.

```
(define total-population
  (lambda (population-list)
    (if (null? population-list)
      0
      (+ (car (cdr population-list))
        (total-population
          (cdr (cdr population-list)))))))
```

Program 4-8   Totaling a mixed-data population list

We now have to apply the cdr procedure twice to get to the next city name. As with some of our earlier procedures, this procedure will fail if the list is malformed.

list-tail is a Scheme primitive analogous to list-ref. Whereas list-ref picks out the nth element in a list, list-tail returns the nth sublist. A **sublist** is a list that is part of another list. Since it's a list, it starts at an element and continues until the end of the list. Program 4-9 shows the code for list-tail.

Now we can redefine our "*n*th" procedures, first, second, and so on.

```
(define first (lambda (x) (list-ref x 0)))
(define first-tail (lambda (x) (list-tail x 1)))
```

```
(define list-tail%
  (lambda (x n)
    (if (= n 0)
      x
      (list-tail (cdr x) (sub1 n)))))
```

Program 4-9   Our version of list-tail

We often need to create a new list based on the values in an input list. Suppose we want to compute the money due to a city from the federal government in a per capita funds-distribution program. Assume that each city gets $2 per person. Let's compute a list of money due to each city for a simple population list like (400 1000 900):

```
(define due
  (lambda (pop-list)
    (if (null? pop-list)
      '()
      (cons
        (* 2 (car pop-list))
        (due (cdr pop-list))))))
```

The result of evaluating (due locs) is (800 2000 1800). Each time due is called, it takes the first element of the list and creates a new list whose first element is twice the car and whose cdr is the recursive result. due builds up the result by consing onto the recursive results. Figure 4-16 (a) shows the creation of the first pair of the resulting list. Figure 4-16 (b) shows the next pair added to the result.

(The conses actually occur as due returns from the recursive calls. The figures intend to show that the resulting list is being computed as due cdrs down pop-list.)

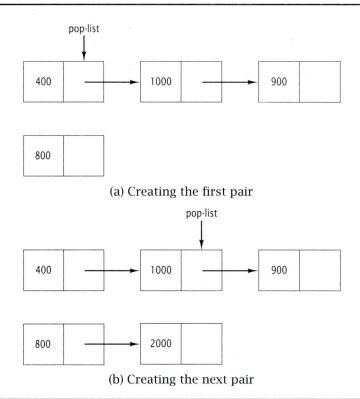

(a) Creating the first pair

(b) Creating the next pair

Figure 4-16   Pairs being created cdring down a list

☞ **Exercise 4-21**

Write a procedure, population-list-ref, that gets the population for the nth city in a "new-style" population list (i.e., one with the population names included). Remember that position is counted from 0. ❏

☞ **Exercise 4-22**

Write a procedure that finds the population of one of the cities in a "new-style" city list. Your procedure will be called as (population-find *city-name city-list*). Assume that the named city does in fact appear in *city-list*.

4.3.4   Equality

How do we decide whether two data structures are equal? You might already have discovered that = doesn't work for pairs (it only works for numbers). There are a number of other procedures for testing whether things are equal; string=? tests whether two strings are equal, and we introduced symbol-equal? to decide whether two symbols are equal.

The most general way of testing whether two objects are equal is equal?; it handles numbers, strings, symbols, and even list structures. Once we can test equality of list structures, we can do all sort of interesting things. For example, here's how we define the null? primitive:

```
(define null?%
   (lambda (an-object) (equal? an-object '())))
```

equal? tests whether two structures have the same shape and contain the same values. The code for equal?% appears in Program 4-10.

```
(define equal?%
   (lambda (a b)
     (if (and (pair? a) (pair? b))
       (and
         (equal?% (car a) (car b))
         (equal?% (cdr a) (cdr b)))
       (if (and (number? a) (number? b))
         (= a b)
         (if (and (symbol? a) (symbol? b))
           (symbol-equal? a b)
           (if (and (string? a) (string? b))
             (string=? a b)
             (and (null? a) (null? b)))))))))
```

Program 4-10   equal?%

equal?% omits many details that are found in Scheme's equal? primitive. Our main purpose here is to demonstrate that when both a and b are pairs, equal?% needs to call itself recursively, testing both the cars and cdrs of the pairs. Otherwise, equal?% must test to see if the arguments are both the same type and perform the appropriate test. It should include tests for all of Scheme's data types, but we omitted several for brevity; this version may produce wrong answers for those types. When equal?% has determined that its arguments are not the same type, it can return #f, since it knows the arguments can't be equal if they are different types.

4.3.5   Finding an Element in a List

We often want to find out whether an item is in a list. For example, we might have a list of city names, and we want to know whether a particular city name already appears in the list. Scheme provides a primitive procedure named member for this purpose:

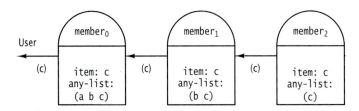

Figure 4-17   Droids evaluating (member 'c '(a b c))

```
(member 'a '(a b c))  ⇒   (a b c)
(member 'c '(a b c))  ⇒   (c)
(member 'd '(a b c))  ⇒   #f
```

If the first argument is found in the list, member returns the sublist starting with that element. If the element is not found, member returns #f. (Older Scheme implementations return null in this case. There are a few programs that will not work correctly on older implementations, but nothing we show will suffer from this problem.) In the city list example, where cities is (seattle vancouver montreal boston), we would write

```
(member 'montreal cities)  ⇒   (montreal boston)
```

member returns a list when it succeeds, and a Boolean, #f, when it fails. Therefore, we can't count on the return value being a list. This style of computing is extremely useful. In Chapter 1 we saw that anything other than #f is considered to be true, and member shows the wisdom of this choice. When the value of the condition in an if form is anything but #f, the then-form is evaluated. Consequently member can be used as the condition predicate in an if form, as follows:

```
(if (member item any-list)
  ...
  ...)
```

member% can be defined as:

```
(define member%
  (lambda (item any-list)
    (if (null? any-list)
      #f
      (if (equal? item (car any-list))
        any-list
        (member% item
          (cdr any-list))))))
```

which uses eqv? instead.

It's important to understand that member only considers elements of the top level of the list. Thus (member 'b '(a b c)) ⇒ (b c), while (member 'b '((a b) (b c))) ⇒ #f and (member '(b c) '(a b c)) ⇒ #f. The best way to understand a recursive procedure like member% is to trace it; Figure 4-17 shows droids evaluating (member 'c '(a b c)).

Practical Note

You might ask what happens if #f is one of the elements in the list:

```
(member #f '(a #f b)) ⇒  (#f b)
(member #f '(a b c)) ⇒  #f
```

If #f is found in the list, a *list* is returned. It doesn't matter that the first element of that list happens to be #f. When member fails, it returns #f, which is not a list.

One common programming style using member follows:

```
(let ((x (member y z)))
  (if x
    (do-something-with x)
    (handle-case-where-not-found)))
```

Binding the result in the let keeps the value to be tested and then used. Of course, handle-case-where-not-found can't use the value of x.

4.3.6   Joining Lists

We might want to join lists together. Suppose that two of your colleagues have done censuses of the populations of locations in British Columbia and Washington State. You might have two lists defined as follows:

```
(define bc-populations ...)
(define washington-populations ...)
```

To produce a consolidated list for both regions, you can use the primitive procedure append:

```
(define north-western-populations
  (append bc-populations washington-populations))
```

The concept of appending two lists should be familiar from our treatment of string-append in the last chapter.

```
(define append%
  (lambda (x y)
    (if (null? x)
      y
      (cons (car x) (append% (cdr x) y)))))
```

The trace shows that append% calls itself with successive cdrs of the first argument, until it reaches null.

```
> (append% '(a b c) '(d e))
call append%:  (a b c) (d e)
|  call append%: (b c) (d e)
|  |  call append%: (c) (d e)
|  |  |  call append%: () (d e)
```

```
|   |   |   return from append%: (d e)
|   |   return from append%: (c d e)
|   return from append%: (b c d e)
return from append%: (a b c d e)
(a b c d e)
```

☞ **Exercise 4-23**

Evaluate (append '(a (b c) d) '(e)). ❑

☞ **Exercise 4-24**

Evaluate (append '() '(x y z)) ❑

☞ **Exercise 4-25**

How many `cons` operations does `append%` perform in appending a list of length m to a list of length n? ❑

☞ **Exercise 4-26**

Write a procedure, using just the `city` ADT; that finds the name of the city in a list of cities with the largest population. For example, suppose that `NA-cities` is bound to a list of all the major cities in North America. `(largest-population NA-cities)` ought to return `Mexico-City`. If the list is null, return `#f`. ❑

☞ **Exercise 4-27**

Evaluate each of the following. If there is an error, say why.
   a. (append% '(x y) '(z z y))
   b. (append% '(x y z) '())
   c. (append% 'foo '(bar))
   d. (append% '(foo) 'bar) ❑

4.3.7   Representing Airline Flight Information

The code presented in this section can be found in file `airline.scm`.

List structure is useful for representing almost any sort of information. In this section, we'll study the problem of representing information about airline flights between different cities. We'll look at an ADT for representing an airline flight. Our ADT will have some limitations, but it will allow us to write procedures that use the flight information in useful ways.

The data we need comes from timetables of flights. Figure 4-18 shows an extract from one timetable.[6]

The first entry (Vancouver to Seattle) isn't complicated. We have, in order, departure time, arrival time, and flight number; times written `like this` are A.M.; times written *like this* are P.M.

The next entry in the timetable (Vancouver to Seoul) demonstrates how complicated things can get. Not only are multiple flights involved (the 6:05 flight is

---

[6] United Airlines, effective September 9, 1992.

```
Vancouver, BC
TO
Seattle, WA

 605  650  1483
 810  900  856
1130 1220  1011
 300  347  355
 544  631  1929


Vancouver, BC
TO
Seoul, Korea

 605  705+1  1483/853/803
      Above Sched. Eff. 9/20
 810  635+1  856/1777/807
      Above Sched. Disc. 10/24
 810  735+1  856/1715/807
      Above Sched. Eff. 10/25
```

Figure 4-18   A timetable of flights

routed through Seattle, San Francisco, and Tokyo; the 8:10 flight goes through Seattle and San Francisco), but flight times are changed throughout the year. In addition, the flight arrives on a second day, indicated by the +1 annotation on the time.

We had better define what *we* mean by *flight*. Doing so will be critical to the design of the whole program. We might think of a flight as being our trip from one city to another; yet that is not what an airline means: there are three separate flights on our trip from Vancouver to Seoul. Not even the plane always stays the same: flight UA807 operates on a DC10 from Chicago/O'Hare to San Francisco, and then on a Boeing 747 from there to Seoul and Manila.

We're going to take a fairly narrow view of the word *flight*: it consists of a trip from one airport to another, with no stops in between. Thus, for example, flight UA807 consists of three flights: the first is from Chicago/O'Hare to San Francisco, the second is from San Francisco to Seoul, and the third is from Seoul to Manila.[7] This leads to an abstract data type for flights, shown in Figure 4-20.

Figure 4-19 shows a form that creates a list representing a collection of flights, each represented as a list. The first flight in our database connects Vancouver (YVR) to Seattle (SEA) on Alaska Airlines (AS). Others go to Anchorage (ANC), Fairbanks (FAI), Missoula (MSO), San Francisco (SFO), Oakland (OAK), Redding (RDD), Chicago (ORD), Newark (EWR), and London/Heathrow (LHR), via Northwest Airlines (NW) and United Airlines (UA). Origin and destination are not cities, but airports.

☞ **Exercise 4-28**

Write the procedures for the flight ADT. ❏

---

[7] Airlines give each flight a different number. If we wanted to preserve this rule, we could number our flights 807A, 807B, and 807C, respectively. This is an unnecessary complication for us.

```
(define flights
  (list
    ;;        airline orig dest flt# dprt arrv
    ;;
    (make-flight 'AS 'YVR 'SEA 2039 0930 1020)
    (make-flight 'AS 'SEA 'YVR 2126 1220 1310)
    (make-flight 'AS 'SEA 'ANC   85 1150 1430)
    (make-flight 'AS 'ANC 'FAI   93 1530 1620)
    (make-flight 'NW 'SEA 'MSO 2199 1700 2025)
    (make-flight 'UA 'YVR 'SEA 1483 0605 0650)
    (make-flight 'UA 'ANC 'FAI 1744 2220 2314)
    (make-flight 'UA 'SEA 'ANC 1760 1410 1636)
    (make-flight 'UA 'SEA 'SFO 1203 0630 0835)
    (make-flight 'UA 'SEA 'SFO 1764 1130 1334)
    (make-flight 'UA 'SEA 'OAK 1143 1228 1444)
    (make-flight 'UA 'SEA 'ORD  154 0700 1248)
    (make-flight 'UA 'SFO 'SEA 1706 1030 1234)
    (make-flight 'UA 'SFO 'RDD 7005 1420 1535)
    (make-flight 'UA 'SFO 'EWR   12 0800 1622)
    (make-flight 'UA 'RDD 'SFO 7014 0645 0800)
    (make-flight 'UA 'EWR 'LHR  906 1855 0645)
    (make-flight 'UA 'ORD 'EWR  362 1330 1648)
))
```

Figure 4-19   A collection of flights

☞ **Exercise 4-29**

Write a procedure that finds all flights for a given airline. ❏

4.3.8   Reversing a List

Often we need a list that is the *reverse* of an existing one. The Scheme primitive reverse does just that:

```
(reverse '(a z c y e x))  ⇒  (x e y c z a)
```

How do we write reverse%? We know that we build up a result by consing onto a recursive call, as in due. Our first attempt is based upon the kind of recursion we used with append%.

```
(define first-reverse%
  (lambda (l)
    (if (null? l)
        '()
        (cons (car l) (first-reverse% (cdr l))))))
(first-reverse% '(a x c y e z)) ⇒ (a x c y e z)
```

No luck here. Somehow we have to put the first element in the last place, but first-reverse% takes the first element off and puts it at the beginning of the result. If we want to build a list up from the end, we must start with the null list and then

Constructor

- (make-flight *carrier origin destination flight-no depart arrive*))
  Create a new flight object with the specified carrier (airline), originating airport, destination airport, flight number, departure, and arrival times. Carriers are specified by standard ICAO (International Civil Aviation Organization) two-letter codes; airports are specified by standard ICAO three-letter codes. Departure and arrival times are given in local time (this is a mistake).

Accessors

- (flight-carrier *flt*)
  Return the carrier of the flight.
- (flight-origin *flt*)
  Return the city of origin of the flight.
- (flight-destination *flt*)
  Return the destination city of the flight.
- (flight-no *flt*)
  Return the flight number.
- (flight-depart *flt*)
  Return the departure time of the flight.
- (flight-arrive *flt*)
  Return the arrival time of the flight.

Output procedure

- (display-flight *flt*)
  Display a flight object in a readable form, for example,
  UA906 Origin: EWR Destination: LHR Depart: 1855 Arrive: 645

Figure 4-20   Abstract Data Type: flight

cons onto it. The only efficient way to do that is to use a helper procedure that *accumulates* the result, beginning with null.

```
(define reverse%
  (lambda (l)
    (letrec
      ((helper
         (lambda (in out)
           (if (null? in)
               out
               (helper (cdr in) (cons (car in) out)))))))
      (helper l '()))))
```

The benefit of using an accumulator is obvious. We start with null and build up the result. Figure 4-21 (a) shows the droids created during (reverse% '(a b c)), and Figure 4-21 (b) shows the three conses during (reverse% '(a b c)).

There is another way to write reverse%, using append:

```
(define a-reverse
  (lambda (l)
    (if (null? l)
```

```
'()
(append (a-reverse (cdr 1)) (list (car 1))))))
```

This works! The essential operation is putting an element x on the end of a list lst by (append lst (list x)). Its time complexity, however, is $O(n^2)$ (see Exercise 4-25). The average length of the list is $n/2$, and each of the n times a-reverse is applied, append must cdr down a list of length $n/2$. This is very expensive for long lists, so we prefer the tail-recursive version.

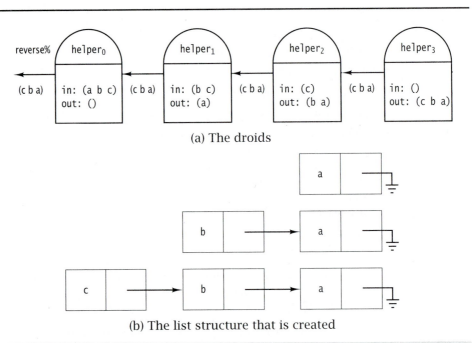

(a) The droids

(b) The list structure that is created

Figure 4-21   Evaluating (reverse% '(a b c))

☞ **Exercise 4-30**

Joel User decides to use the accumulator style in all his list procedures, to make his procedures tail-recursive. What happens when he runs his version of append%?

```
(define new-append%
  (lambda (x y)
    (if (null? x)
        y
        (new-append% (cdr x) (cons (car x) y)))))
```

❑

4.3.9   Input and Output of List Structures

Input and output procedures have two major tasks. They must transfer data between the computer and the outside world, and they must convert between the computer's representations and those of the outside world.

We have seen two ways of representing pairs and lists: as a box-and-arrow diagram, and as a sequence of characters in parentheses. The box-and-arrow diagram is very close to the actual computer representation of list structure, as we will see in Chapter 12. Here we'll examine how a Scheme system converts between this representation and the character form. Again, we'll use our recursive definitions to design procedures, this time for reading and writing lists.

4.3.9.1   Reading a list   We can't use left or right parentheses, (or), in our input procedures. These are special to the Scheme input process. Once Scheme sees (on input, it continues to read until it encounters), and then evaluates the application or returns the list structure, if the parenthesized form is inside a `quote`. Scheme will read symbols and return them. We only need to select two symbols to mark out the beginning and end of lists, that is, to act as **delimiters**, which we pass to the list-reading procedure, shown in Program 4-11.[8]

`read-lists` reads a sequence of Scheme values. When `read-lists` encounters the symbol {, it begins reading the elements of a list, consing them onto the rest of the list. When it encounters }, it returns null. If, in reading the elements of the list, it sees {, it calls itself recursively.

```
(define read-lists
  (lambda (list-begin list-end)
    (letrec
      ((innerlist
        (lambda ()
          (let ((new (read)))
            (if (symbol-equal? new list-begin)
              (let ((first (innerlist)))
                (cons first (innerlist)))
              (if (symbol-equal? new list-end)
                '()
                (cons new (innerlist))))))))
      (let ((in (read)))
        (if (symbol-equal? in list-begin)
          (innerlist)
          in)))))
```

Program 4-11   Reading lists

We have selected { and } as delimiters. Scheme will treat characters separated by spaces as symbols; special characters like { and } are not allowed in names, so they don't need to be separated by spaces, as shown in Figure 4-22.

---

[8] It is possible to use the parentheses as list delimiters, but only if we read character-by-character. We leave this as a nontrivial programming project for you, once you have read Chapter 11 on the input/output of numbers.

```
> (read-lists '{ '} )
{a b}
(a b)
> (read-lists '{ '} )
{z {a b} {{ c }}}
(z (a b) ((c)))
```

Figure 4-22 Using `read-lists`

We know that Scheme will read in an entire form as one value:

```
> (define foo (read))
(1 2 3 4)
> foo
(1 2 3 4)
```

4.3.9.2 Displaying a list Scheme uses the following rule to display lists: Omit the dot and the following parentheses when the item to the right of the dot is a pair. `display-lists`, a procedure that prints list structures, appears in Program 4-12. `display-lists` prints lists according to this rule, using a helper, `display-list-cdr`. `display-lists` begins by displaying the car of the form, and `display-lists-cdr` prints the pair without parens or a dot when the pair is the cdr of a cons. `display-lists-cdr` needs to be separate, since it knows that it's printing out something that is the cdr of a pair, and therefore shouldn't display parentheses or dots. `display-lists-cdr` applies `display-lists` to the car of the pair, and itself to the cdr. When the cdr is null, `display-lists-cdr` displays). Only when it encounters a non-null, nonpair cdr does it output dot, the final value, and the closing parenthesis.

```
(define display-lists
  (lambda (s)
    (if (pair? s)
      (begin
        (display "{")
        (display-lists (car s))
        (display-lists-cdr (cdr s)))
      (display s))))
(define display-lists-cdr
  (lambda (tail)
    (if (null? tail)
      (display "}")
      (if (pair? tail)
        (begin
          (display " ")
          (display-lists (car tail))
          (display-lists-cdr (cdr tail)))
        (format #t " . ~a)" tail)))))
```

Program 4-12 Procedures for printing lists

4.3.9.3   The repl   Scheme has carefully been defined so that Scheme forms look like list structure. (Most Scheme systems don't actually represent a form as a list, though.) With our ability to read and display lists, we can write a "master control program" for Scheme, using three Scheme primitives: read, eval, and display.

read converts the characters we type into Scheme data. The evaluator, eval, is the primitive that evaluates a list representing a Scheme form and returns its value. We have given you a specification of a part of that process in 𝕿𝕳𝕖 ℜ𝔲𝔩𝔢𝔰, and we'll see how to implement eval in Chapters 7 and 12. display is the primitive that displays the values to the user. display-lists is the portion of display that handles display of list structure.

We can envision Scheme's master control loop as a *read-eval-display* loop that repeatedly reads in a list, evaluates it, and displays the result. For historical reasons, this last part is often known as "printing", and thus we speak of a "read-eval-print" loop, or **repl** (pronounced "repple"). Program 4–13 shows a simple repl. Many Scheme systems have elaborate repls that provide a history of recent operations, give online help, or in other ways assist the programmer.

```
(define repl%
  (lambda ()
    (display "What? ")
    (display (eval (read)))
    (newline)
    (repl%)))
```

Program 4–13   A basic read-eval-print loop (repl)

☞ **Exercise 4–31**

Describe what would happen if we wrote badshow, in which display-lists-cdr applies itself each time to the car of its argument, as well as to the cdr, as in the following example: (badshow (cons 1 (cons (cons 2 3) 4))) ❏

Practical Note

We have shown various ways to join elements into pairs and lists. Since there are so many ways to create list structures, it's important to know how the list-processing procedures work, so that we know when it's appropriate to use each of them.

cons creates a pair. To put an element at the beginning of a list, cons it to the front of the list; (cons item list) creates a new list with item as its first element and the elements of list following. The arguments to cons can be anything. Unless the second argument is a list, the result will not be a list.

list constructs a list with all of its arguments at top level. The arguments to list can be anything—there is no restriction.

append constructs a new list from two lists. The arguments to append must *both* be lists. The elements in the result of (append list1 list2) are the elements of list1 in the order they appear in list1, followed by the elements of list2 in the order they appear in list2. Thus (append '(1 2) '(5 6)) results in (1 2 5 6).

A simple way to make a list with the item x on the end of the list l is (append l (list x)). This is very inefficient when l is long, since append must step down the list to find its end.

Finally, let's clarify the status of these three primitives: cons must be a primitive, but list and append can be written in terms of cons.

Lists are an extremely useful basic data structure for representing collections of objects. Based on a special marker, null, marking the end of a list, and the cons operation, they can be used in many ways. We can pick an item from a list by its position, using list-ref. We also learned how to perform operations on an entire collection, such as summing the elements of a population list. Our tour of list processing introduced us to append, which joins together lists; member, which identifies the sublist, if any, starting with a particular item, and reverse, which returns a list with its elements in reverse order. We also explored how Scheme reads and writes values such as lists.

4.4   Mapping, Filtering, and Reduction

A great deal of misapprehension arises from the popular use of maps on a small scale. As with such maps you are able to put a thumb on India and a finger on Russia, some persons at once think that the political situation is alarming and that India must be looked to. If the noble Lord would use a larger map—say one on the scale of the Ordnance Map of England—he would find that the distance between Russia and British India is not to be measured by the finger and thumb, but by a rule.
— Lord Salisbury, British House of Commons, 11 June 1877

In the previous section, we saw a core set of primitives that let us reverse lists, append them together, and build them step-by-step. Those primitive procedures are useful in many different tasks. We also saw how we could build procedures to do custom tasks such as finding data about a specific city in a list of cities. You may have noticed that many of these procedures had similar elements. Many of them process each item, and call themselves on the cdr, until they reach a null list.

This section introduces three general ideas about handling collections of data: mapping, filtering, and reduction. The procedures that implement these abstractions all take procedures as arguments.

A list contains *many* data items. We often want to apply the same procedure to all the elements in the list, either to create a new list with the results of the application or to produce some output for each item in the list. *Mapping* applies a procedure to all elements in a list; it is a *many-to-many* operation.

We may not want all the elements in a list. *Filtering* returns a new list of those elements in a list that satisfy some predicate. Like mapping, filtering is a *many-to-many* operation. In both mapping and filtering, the result is a list.

Sometimes we want to compute a total result depending equally on all the elements in a list. *Reduction* takes the many elements in the list and computes *one* result; it is a *many-to-one* operation.

To write procedures that have a variable number of arguments, we introduce the syntax of *variadic* procedures.

4.4.1 Mapping

We often must perform the same operation on each element of a list. Suppose we are building a simple module to store information about cities. We might revive our city ADT, using a somewhat more elegant implementation, as shown in Program 4-14.

```
(module cities
  (export make-city city-name city-population
    city-latitude city-longitude)
  (define make-city
    (lambda (name pop lat long)
      (list name pop lat long)))
  (define city-name (lambda (c) (car c)))
  (define city-population (lambda (c) (car (cdr c))))
  (define city-latitude (lambda (c) (car (cdr (cdr c)))))
  (define city-longitude (lambda (c) (car (cdr (cdr (cdr c)))))))
;;; Now we can make a list of cities:
(define cities
  (list
    (make-city 'Vancouver 1500 49 123)
    (make-city 'Leipzig 545 51 -12)
    (make-city 'Vladivostok 648 43 -131)
    (make-city 'Perth 1200 -31 -115)))
```
Program 4-14   A new city module

Program 4-15 shows a procedure to list the population of each city. `list-of-city-names`, also shown in Program 4-15, gets the names of the cities.

```
(list-of-city-populations cities) ⇒  (1268 565 550 844)
(list-of-city-names cities)
   ⇒  (vancouver leipzig vladivostok perth)
```

These populations and names procedures look similar. Once you had written `list-of-city-population` and `list-of-city-names`, you could write a procedure to give the latitudes of the cities with little effort. So why not write a general procedure for this kind of job? Indeed, Scheme has such a primitive, named `map`:

```
(map city-name cities) ⇒  (vancouver leipzig vladivostok perth)
```

`map` is a primitive procedure that applies its first argument, a procedure, to each of the elements in its second argument, a list. So the result of

```
(define foo (lambda (x) .....))
(map foo '(45 17 22 93))
```

```
(define list-of-city-populations
  (lambda (city-list)
    (if (null? city-list)
        '()
        (cons
          (city-population (car city-list))
          (list-of-city-populations (cdr city-list))))))
(define list-of-city-names
  (lambda (city-list)
    (if (null? city-list)
        '()
        (cons
          (city-name (car city-list))
          (list-of-city-names (cdr city-list))))))
```

Program 4-15   Finding populations or names in a city list

is equivalent to (list (foo 45) (foo 17) (foo 22) (foo 93)).

Suppose we want to produce the squares of a list of numbers:

```
(map (lambda (x) (* x x)) '(45 17 22 93))
  ⇒   (2025 289 484 8649)
```

Scheme makes no guarantees about the order in which map evaluates the elements of the list. A particular evaluator can choose to do it left to right or right to left, for convenience. This is only a problem when the procedure does a (read) or some other operation that has an effect:

```
> (map (lambda (x) (+ x (read))) '(1 2))
3 6
(7 5)
```

It appears that the evaluator for this example applied the procedure to the list from right to left, effectively producing (list (+ 1 6) (+ 3 2)). Don't use procedures with effects as arguments to map! The results will vary from system to system.

Regardless, the result will appear in the proper order—the element at position k in the result is the value returned by the procedure argument applied to the element at position k in the list argument to map. This was true even in the (unpredictable) case above: the first result depended on 1, and the second on 2. Only the results of (read) were used in a surprising order.

The general idea of applying a procedure to each element of a list and returning a list composed of the results of these applications, is called **mapping**. map isn't the only mapping procedure one can write; string-map, from Chapter 3 returns a string that is the result of applying a procedure to each element of a string.

We'll now write our own version of map, which is a bit more limited than the version built into Scheme:

```
(define map%
  (lambda (proc x)
    (if (null? x)
        '()
        (cons (proc (car x)) (map% proc (cdr x))))))
```

The similarities between map% and our earlier list-of-... procedures should be obvious. All we have done is abstract out the procedure applied to the car of the list at each step. In map%, that procedure is an argument.

```
(map% city-name cities) ⇒  (vancouver leipzig vladivostok perth)
(map% city-population cities) ⇒   (1500 545 648 1200)
```

The procedure in Program 4-16 produces a report showing the information for each city in the list.

```
(define report-cities
  (lambda (city-list)
    (if (null? city-list)
      (void)
      (let ((city (car city-list)))
        (format #t "Loc: ~a, Population: ~a000, Location: (~a,~a)~%"
          (city-name city)
          (city-population city)
          (city-latitude city)
          (city-longitude city))
        (report-cities (cdr city-list))))))
```

Program 4-16   Reporting cities

Now we can call report-cities:

```
> (report-cities cities)
Loc: vancouver, Population: 1500000, Location: (49,123)
Loc: leipzig, Population: 545000, Location: (51,-12)
Loc: vladivostok, Population: 648000, Location: (43,-131)
Loc: perth, Population: 1200000, Location: (-31,-115)
```

What's wrong with report-cities as we've written it? Two different tasks are being done in the same procedure: going through the city list and printing the information for a particular city. To change the report format, we'd have to wade through a very complicated procedure. Part of that complication could be eliminated through careful comments, but it's better to redesign the procedure.

The procedure shown in Program 4-17 displays one city.

```
(define report-city
  (lambda (city)
    (format #t "Loc: ~a, Population: ~a000, Location: (~a,~a)~%"
      (city-name city)
      (city-population city)
      (city-latitude city)
      (city-longitude city))))
```

Program 4-17   Displaying the report for one city

The display we get follows:

```
> (define leipzig (car (cdr cities)))
> (report-city leipzig)
City: leipzig, Population: 565000, Location: (51,-12)
```

We can now use map to produce the report.

```
> (map report-city cities)
Loc: perth, Population: 1200000, Location: (-31,-115)
Loc: vladivostok, Population: 648000, Location: (43,-131)
Loc: leipzig, Population: 545000, Location: (51,-12)
Loc: vancouver, Population: 1500000, Location: (49,123)
(#<void> #<void> #<void> #<void>)
```

Two things are odd. First, the output came out in the wrong order. Second, map returned a list made up of four void objects. report-city returns a void object as its result (that's what format returns), and map consed them together. Each cons operation causes the machine to do some work and to consume some storage: in this case, the conses are really just wasted motion.

For problems like this, Scheme has a for-each primitive that applies the specified procedure to each element of a list, in the order of their appearance, but does nothing with the results (the value for-each returns is unspecified).

```
>  (for-each report-city cities)
Loc: vancouver, Population: 1500000, Location: (49,123)
Loc: leipzig, Population: 545000, Location: (51,-12)
Loc: vladivostok, Population: 648000, Location: (43,-131)
Loc: perth, Population: 1200000, Location: (-31,-115)
```

The output came out in the correct order, but now the return value is not specified. (The Scheme system we use returns void.)

Mapping restricts the application of the procedure argument to the *top level* of the list argument. When we need to apply the procedure to all the elements of the list structure, we can use deep-map, a version of map that operates on all levels of the input list. For example,

```
(deep-map add1 '(1 (2 3) 4 (5 6))) ⇒  (2 (3 4) 5 (6 7))
```

What's the result of (map add1 '(1 (2 3) 4 (5 6)))?

```
Error in add1: (5 6) is not a number.
```

deep-map is another example of tree recursion. Unlike our examples in Chapter 2, the argument is a list, not a number, but the principle is the same. deep-map, shown in Program 4-18, applies itself recursively to the car and cdr of any pairs in its arguments. Only when it runs into an element that is not a pair does it actually apply its procedure argument.

Many Scheme implementations include subst, a procedure that replaces all occurrences of an item with another item:

```
(subst 'one 1 '(1 2 3 4 1)) ⇒  (one 2 3 4 one)
(subst 'one 1 '(1 2 (1 2) 3 4) ) ⇒  (one 2 (one 2) 3 4)
```

We read (subst 'one 1 '(1 2 3 4)) as "Substitute one for all occurrences of 1 in (1 2 3 4)". subst% is easy to write using deep-map:

```
(define subst%
```

```
(define deep-map
  (lambda (proc x)
    (if (null? x)
        '()
        (if (pair? x)
            (cons (deep-map proc (car x))
                  (deep-map proc (cdr x)))
            (proc x)))))
```

Program 4-18   A tree-recursive mapping procedure

```
(lambda (to from in)
  (deep-map (lambda (x) (if (equal? x from) to x)) in)))
```

We might have written map-subst% with map:

```
(define map-subst
  (lambda (to from in)
    (map (lambda (x) (if (equal? x from) to x)) in)))
(map-subst 'one 1 '(1 2 (1 2) 3 4)) ⇒ (one 2 (1 2) 3 4)
```

We can implement a related procedure, subsplice, that splices in a list argument wherever a specified item occurs:

```
(subsplice '(one two three) 1 '(1 2 3 4 1))
    ⇒   (one two three 2 3 4 one two three)
```

map isn't useful here; it produces one output element for each input element. foreach produces no output elements at all. subst also doesn't work.

```
(subst '(one two three) 1 '(1 2 3 4 1))
    ⇒   ((one two three) 2 3 4 (one two three))
```

Program 4-19 shows subsplice. The important operation is appending either the inserted list to or (list (car in)) to the recursive result.

```
(define subsplice
  (lambda (to from in)
    (if (null? in)
        '()
        (append
          (if (equal? (car in) from)
              to
              (list (car in)))
          (subsplice to from (cdr in))))))
```

Program 4-19   Splicing in substitutions

☞ **Exercise 4-32**

Evaluate
(subst% 'wisdom 'stupidity '(wisdom and stupidity are not the same)). ❑

☞ **Exercise 4-33**

Evaluate
```
  a. (map add1 '(2 5 8 9))
  b. (map (lambda (x) (cons x 'foo)) '(a b c))
```

☞ **Exercise 4-34**

Write a procedure, for-each%, that duplicates the for-each primitive.

The following exercises implement procedure let-to-lambda, which converts a list structure in the form of a let to a list that represents the corresponding lambda. We are operating on lists here, not code. The similarity between Scheme code and lists is not accidental! (We will exploit it in Chapter 7.)

```
(let-to-lambda
  '(let ((n1 v1) (n2 v2) (n3 v3)) (+ n1 n2 n3)))
  ⇒   ((lambda (n1 n2 n3) (+ n1 n2 n3)) v1 v2 v3)
(let-to-lambda
  '(let ((foo 1) (bar (+ x 2)))
      (+ (add1 foo) bar)))
  ⇒   ((lambda (foo bar) (+ (add1 foo) bar)) 1 (+ x 2))
```

☞ **Exercise 4-35**

In order to write let-to-lambda, we need a utility procedure, unzip, that takes a list of names and values and collects the names into one list and the values into another. unzip returns a pair whose car is a list composed of the names and whose cdr is a list of the values.

```
(define result (unzip '((n1 v1) (n2 v2) (n3 v3))))
(car result) ⇒  (n1 n2 n3)
(cdr result) ⇒  (v1 v2 v3)
```

Write unzip. You can assume the input is a list in the proper form.

☞ **Exercise 4-36**

let-to-lambda has the following form:

```
(define let-to-lambda
  (lambda (letf)
    (let
      ((names-values
        (unzip (car (cdr letf)))))
      (--A--
        (cons 'lambda
          (--B--
            (car names-values)
            (--C-- (--D-- letf))))
        (cdr names-values)))))
```

Fill in the blanks.

4.4.2 Filtering

Suppose we want to list those populations that are greater than 200 in our population list. `big-populations`, shown in Program 4-20, selects such items.

```
(define big-populations
  (lambda (population-list)
    (if (null? population-list)
        '()
        (let ((pop (car population-list)))
          (if (> pop 200)
              (cons pop
                (big-populations (cdr population-list)))
              (big-populations (cdr population-list)))))))
```

Program 4-20   Selecting big populations

The null case is straightforward: we return null (we have to quote null). Otherwise, we have two cases, depending upon the population. If the car of the population list is large, we have to include its value in the new list. If not, we go on to the rest of the list.

`big-populations` creates a list of all items in its input list that satisfy the test "greater than 200". It **filters** its input based on the predicate `(lambda (x) (> x 200))`.

☞ **Exercise 4-37**

Evaluate `(big-populations '(50 250 400 225 75 900))`. ❑

We can generalize `big-populations`: `filter`, shown in Program 4-21, takes the predicate `test` and a list, and returns a list of the items in the original list where `(test item)` succeeds (i.e., it returns something other than #f).

```
(define filter
  (lambda (test lst)
    (if (null? lst)
        '()
        (if (test (car lst))
            (cons (car lst) (filter test (cdr lst)))
            (filter test (cdr lst))))))
```

Program 4-21   Filtering a list

Using `filter`, we write `(big-populations '(50 250 400 225 75 900))` as

`(filter (lambda (x) (> x 200)) '(50 250 400 225 75 900))`

We can now take the next step with our airline example. In the Case Study, we'll develop a program to find all routes between an origin and a destination. The first step is to use the database to find all direct flights between the two cities. `find-routes-direct` filters all the flights in the `flights` database, looking for each flight whose origin and destination match the origin and destination of the flight.

Program 4-22 shows how `filter` can be used to find airline flights. The database is the list of flights that we described in Section 4.3.7. We select those flights that have the appropriate origin and destination. In this case, a route is just a single flight. The Case Study includes routes consisting of one or more flights.

```
(define find-routes-direct
  (lambda (origin destination)
    (filter
      (lambda (f)
        (and (same-city? origin (flight-origin f))
             (same-city? destination (flight-destination f))))
      flights)))
```

Program 4-22   Filtering direct routes

`same-city?` checks whether two cities are the same. Therefore, the result is

```
(find-routes-direct 'yvr 'sea)
  ⇒  (((ua yvr sea 1483 605 650)) ((as yvr sea 2039 930 1020)))
```

`filter` selects *all* elements in the collection that satisfy some predicate, but often we only need the first element in the list that satisfies some condition. `find-first`, shown in Program 4-23, finds the first element that makes a predicate true.

```
(define find-first
  (lambda (test? lst)
    (if (null? lst)
      #f
      (if (test? (car lst))
        (car lst)
        (find-first test? (cdr lst))))))
```

Program 4-23   Finding the first satisfactory element

`find-first` assumes that we don't want to find an element that is `#f`. We can't tell whether we failed to find an element satisfying `test?` or we found `#f`. There are ways around this, but the solution would complicate `find-first`.

☞ **Exercise 4-38**

Evaluate `(filter list? '(1 (2 3) 4 9 (8 7) ((2))))`. ❑

☞ **Exercise 4-39**

Write the procedure `delete` that returns a copy of its second argument (a list) with all instances of its first argument deleted.

```
(delete 1 '(1 3 4 7)) ⇒  (3 4 7)
(delete 3 '(a 3 b 4 c 6 a 7 z 3)) ⇒  (a b 4 c 6 a 7 z)
(delete '(a 1) '((b 4) z (q (a 1)) (a 1) (d 2)))
  ⇒  ((b 4) z (q (a 1)) (d 2))
```

❑

4.4.3 Reduction

Often we have a list that contains values, and we want a total, or some other value depending on all the values in the list. **Reduction** is computing a function that depends on all members of a list. For example, we might want to find the total population of the locations in our list of populations, using `sum-list`.

```
(sum-list (map city-population cities)) ⇒ 3227
```

Notice how we first produce the list of populations and then add them! We usually want to avoid conses that do not appear in the final result. Doing so wastes storage.

We can generalize procedures of this sort. Program 4-24 shows `reduce`, a procedure that can be used to apply any binary operation to all the elements of a list. The second parameter, `base`, is the base element in the recursion (for arithmetic and logical operations, `base` is typically the base element for the binary operation `op`). Here's how `reduce` is used:

```
(reduce + 0 (map city-population cities)) ⇒ 3227
(reduce * 1 '(33 17 22 19 85)) ⇒ 19932330
(reduce cons '() '(hello world how are you))
  ⇒ (hello world how are you)
```

```
(define reduce
  (lambda (op base x)
    (if (null? x)
        base
        (op (car x) (reduce op base (cdr x))))))
```

Program 4-24   Reduction

`reduce` is useful in computing totals over collections. We can compute the average for a student with grades (79 83 74 91 88) by computing the total,

```
(reduce + 0 '(79 83 74 91 88)) ⇒ 415
```

and then dividing by the number of elements in the list:

```
(/ (reduce + 0 '(79 83 74 91 88)) (length '(79 83 74 91 88)))
  ⇒ 83
```

We can write `total-population` as a reduction:

```
(define total-population
  (lambda (population-list)
    (reduce + 0 population-list)))
```

We can use `reduce` to find the minimum or maximum of a collection:

```
(reduce max -1 '(79 83 74 91 88)) ⇒ 91
(reduce min 101 '(79 83 74 91 88)) ⇒ 74
```

We started with a base value that is outside the expected range of the values 0–100, so that the actual maximum or minimum is returned.

We can extend the notion of reduction. So far, reduce applies an operation combining the elements of the list. reduce-map, shown in Program 4-25, combines the results of applying a procedure to each element of the list.

```
(define reduce-map
  (lambda (op fun identity x)
    (if (null? x)
        identity
        (op (fun (car x))
            (reduce-map op fun identity (cdr x))))))
```
Program 4-25   Reduction and mapping combined

reduce-map has features of both reduce (its combining power) and map (applying a procedure to each element of the list). It can be used to determine whether every element of a list satisfies some property. Figure 4-23 shows every?, which uses reduce-map and an auxiliary procedure, mand, to compute whether every element of a list satisfies a predicate, pred?.

```
(define mand
  (lambda (a b) (and a b)))
(define every?
  (lambda (pred? any-list)
    (reduce-map mand pred? #t any-list)))
(every? odd? '(1 3 5 7)) ⇒  #t
(every? odd? '(1 3 4 7)) ⇒  #f
```
Figure 4-23   Using reduce-map

Problem 7 at the end of the chapter asks you to write, using reduce-map, a companion procedure, some, that determines whether at least one element of a list satisfies pred?.

reduce-map lets us improve our total of city populations. Before we used (reduce + 0 (map city-population cities)), but this creates a new list structure, using map, before applying reduce. Instead we can use

(reduce-map + city-population 0 cities) ⇒ 3227

This is not only more compact but more efficient because we don't create the unnecessary list structure.

As well as being useful in ordinary programming, reduce is an important tool in numerical linear algebra (computer methods for solving linear equations). Linear equations can be represented as lists of the coefficients (the constants in the equations). Thus,

$$2x + 3y + 4z = 10$$

$$9x - 6y + 5z = -4$$

can be represented by the two lists (2 3 4) and (9 -6 5) for the left hand sides of the equations.

The basic operations of linear algebra can be written using `reduce` and similar procedures, operating on the list of coefficients. These procedures can be adapted to *parallel* computers, which have many processors and allow reductions of collections of *n* elements to be performed in $O(\log n)$ time. Some Lisp dialects have been designed that allow programmers to use such machines effectively.

☞ **Exercise 4–40**

Why did we have to write `mand`? ❏

☞ **Exercise 4–41**

Write the filter procedure `only` that takes as arguments a list of routes and an airline carrier code. The filter procedure should give a list of those routes that consist only of flights on that carrier. Your best bet is to use procedure `filter` as part of the code.

Deciding whether a route consists only of flights on a certain carrier is a matter of reducing the route to a Boolean by testing each flight to see whether it is on the carrier. This suggests using a reduction procedure. Use one we have shown, or write your own. ❏

☞ **Exercise 4–42**

Evaluate `(reduce (lambda (x y) (+ x (* 2 y))) 5 '(17 22 11))`. ❏

4.4.4 Variadic Procedures

All the procedures we have designed up to now take only a specified number of arguments. For example, `cons` takes two arguments, whereas `car` takes one. Technically, we call a procedure that takes one argument *monadic* (from the Greek word for "one"), a two-argument procedure *dyadic*, and so on. We write the procedures with a particular number of parameters. When the procedure is applied, Scheme matches the arguments and parameters one-to-one.

We have seen some procedures, however, such as `format` and `list`, that take a variable number of arguments. In fact, many Scheme primitives do, including +, -, *, /, >, <, and =, and most numeric comparison predicates.[9] Most have the obvious interpretation, so (+ 1 2 3 4 5) is the sum of all five numbers, and (* 1 2 3 4 5) is the product. These procedures are described as **variadic**, meaning they take a variable number of arguments, zero or more.[10]

A variadic procedure cannot be written with the syntax for parameters that we know. Unlike our standard procedures, in a variadic procedure we want all the arguments collected into a list and passed to the procedure. We will use the Scheme syntax for a variadic procedure in writing a version of `list`:

```
(define list%
  (lambda x
    x))
```

---

[9] Consult a Scheme reference manual for the meaning of these primitives when they have zero or one arguments.

[10] Purists dislike a word such as *variadic*, because it comes from mixed Greek and Latin roots. One of the authors is a purist, and the other isn't, so we don't take a stand on whether *variadic* is a desirable word. In any case, the battle to keep our etymology pure has long since been lost; had it been won, we would have been driving ipsemobiles!

In this procedure, the parameter is not a name or names enclosed in parentheses, but is simply a name. This signals Scheme to assemble all the arguments to list% into a list and binds x to the list. Thus the result of list% is simply x.

Both map and for-each are variadic. For example,

```
(map + '(3 7 11 16 22) '(1 2 3 4 5))
  ⇒  (4 9 14 20 27)
```

Exercise 4-44 challenges you to write map in variadic form.

As our first substantial variadic procedure, let's write +%, our own variadic version of +. Since + is itself variadic, we'll use add, a binary version of +:

```
(define add (lambda (a b) (+ a b)))
```

+% must cdr down its list of arguments, adding the car of the list to the result of applying +% to the rest of the arguments, which is the cdr of the list. When +% hits the end of the list, it returns 0. For our first try, we have

```
(define +%
  (lambda x
    (if (null? x)
        0
        (add (car x)
          (+% (cdr x))))))
```

The only catch is that this version of +% goes into an infinite loop when we evaluate (+% 1 2 3). Let's trace it:

```
call +%: (1 2 3)
| call +%: ((2 3))
| | call add%: (())
| | | call add%: (())
```

The first time +% calls itself, the argument is (2 3), but Scheme delivers that argument in a list: x is bound to ((2 3)). The next recursive call puts (), the cdr of ((2 3)) as the argument, so x is bound to (()). Then we're caught in a loop: x will always be (()). We need a way of telling Scheme to apply the procedure +% to a list of arguments (arg1 arg2 ... argn) as if Scheme were evaluating (+% arg1 arg2 ... argn).

The secret is the Scheme primitive apply, which applies a procedure to a list of arguments:

```
(apply + '(1 2 3 4)) ⇒  10    (apply cons '(2 3)) ⇒  (2 . 3)
```

(apply foo '(a b c)) is effectively the same as (foo a b c). This is certainly not the same as (foo '(a b c)).

apply is useful for writing variadic procedures without a helper. Here's +% using apply:

```
(define +%
  (lambda x
    (if (null? x)
        0
        (add (car x)
          (apply +% (cdr x))))))
```

```
(+% 1 2 3 4) ⇒  10
(+% 1) ⇒  1
```

Sometimes we would like to specify that a procedure has at least a certain number of arguments. Scheme's syntax lets us create a pattern for the arguments using the parameter list. For example, the Scheme primitive subst takes three arguments: (new old in), where new replaces old wherever it occurs in in. Program 4-26 shows a version of vsubst that accepts several sets of substitutions. We'll need to reorder the parameters so that all the variation happens at the end. We would like to write arguments as follows: (vsubst in new1 old1 new2 old2 ... newn oldn).

```
(define vsubst
  (lambda (in . oldnews)
    (if (null? oldnews)
        in
        (apply vsubst
          (subst (car oldnews) (car (cdr oldnews)) in)
          (cdr (cdr oldnews))))))
```

Program 4-26   Implementing subst with a variable number of arguments

---

vsubst works as follows:

```
> (vsubst '(1 2 3 4 3 2 1) 'one 1)
(one 2 3 4 3 2 one)
> (vsubst '(1 2 3 4 3 2 1) 'one 1 'two 2)
(one two 3 4 3 two one)
> (vsubst )
Error: incorrect number of arguments to #<procedure vsubst>.
```

The parameter list (in . oldnews) says "Bind the first argument to in and the rest of the arguments, as a list, to oldnews". The parameter list (par1 par2 ... parn . rest) specifies that the first n arguments are bound to the parameters as given, and any remaining arguments are collected into a list and bound to rest. Scheme will complain if there aren't as many arguments as there are parameters before the dot. (vsubst does not check whether there is an even number of old-new arguments.) If there are n arguments, in this last case, rest is bound to null.

We have also used the second form of apply in vsubst.

   (apply *proc arg1* . . . *argn arg-list*)

is equivalent to

   (apply *proc* (append (list *arg1* . . . *argn*) *arg-list*))

We can also write variadic procedures by immediately calling a helper:

```
(define +% (lambda x (add-em x)))
(define add-em
  (lambda (nums sum)
    (if (null? nums)
        0
        (+ (car nums) (add-em (cdr nums))))))
```

The helper expects a list of numbers as its argument. +% now only serves to package the numbers into a list and then call add-em.

☞ **Exercise 4-43**

Suppose we want to know if one of several items is in a list. Write vmember so that (vmember '(m e m b e r) 'e 'f) ⇒ (e m b e r), (vmember '(m e m b e r) 't 'f 'b) ⇒ (b e r) and (vmember '(m e m b e r) 't 'f 'g) ⇒ #f. ❏

☞ **Exercise 4-44**

[Challenging] The real Scheme primitives map and for-each take any number of list arguments, for example,

```
(map
  (lambda (x y) (* x y))
  '(2 4 6 8 10)
  '(1 2 3 4 5))
⇒   (2 8 18 32 50)
```

Write a procedure, map-variadic%, that duplicates map. ❏

Case Study: An Airline Trip-Planning Program

The code presented in this section can be found in file airline.scm.

Anyone who has flown in a commercial aircraft knows the complexity of planning a specific route. Sometimes airlines offer nonstop flights. Frequently, though, traveling between two cities requires more than one flight. It is often impossible to use one airline throughout.

We need a program that will plan airline trips for us. The program will consult a database, containing all of the flight information, and produce a list of all the routes between two cities. The user can examine this list, and choose the route that best satisfies her needs, such as preferred airlines, departure and arrival times, and number of stops.[11]

Analysis should start with the schedules provided by the airlines. We'd like to be able to use a database of flights, derived from the schedules, to find flights between cities. We've already discussed the structure of a database of flights in Sections 4.3.7 and 4.4.2; see page 200 for the data we're using. Here's how we'd interact with our route finder:

```
> (display-routes (find-routes 'yvr 'sea))
Route:
UA1483 Origin: YVR Destination: SEA Depart: 605 Arrive: 650
Route:
AS2039 Origin: YVR Destination: SEA Depart: 930 Arrive: 1020
```

---

[11] No attempt will be made to deal with prices. Airlines base their prices not on the costs of the individual flights, but on the air distance between the two cities, along with market factors such as prices charged by competing airlines. It is not feasible to add price data to the program we are developing here.

Our database had two flights between Vancouver and Seattle: United Airlines Flight 1483 and Alaska Airlines Flight 2039.

We want to plan a trip through a number of connecting cities, for example, from Seattle (SEA) to London/Heathrow (LHR) (Figure 4-24). To do this, we look at each of the cities to which we can fly. If the one we're testing is the destination city, we're done; otherwise, the problem is to find a route from the new city to the destination. To get from Seattle to London, we can look at all the cities we can get to from Seattle (Anchorage, Vancouver, Missoula, and San Francisco, in our database). Now see, recursively, whether there is a route from any of these cities to London.

```
> (display-routes (find-routes 'sea 'lhr))
Route:
UA154 Origin: SEA Destination: ORD Depart: 700 Arrive: 1248
UA362 Origin: ORD Destination: EWR Depart: 1330 Arrive: 1648
UA906 Origin: EWR Destination: LHR Depart: 1855 Arrive: 645

Route:
UA1764 Origin: SEA Destination: SFO Depart: 1130 Arrive: 1334
UA12 Origin: SFO Destination: EWR Depart: 800 Arrive: 1622
UA906 Origin: EWR Destination: LHR Depart: 1855 Arrive: 645

Route:
UA1203 Origin: SEA Destination: SFO Depart: 630 Arrive: 835
UA12 Origin: SFO Destination: EWR Depart: 800 Arrive: 1622
UA906 Origin: EWR Destination: LHR Depart: 1855 Arrive: 645
```

Figure 4-24   Routes

The program was able to find three routes: one via Chicago and Newark, and the other two via San Francisco and Newark. The last two are impractical because the San Francisco connection requires an overnight stay. Filtering out routes with impractical connections is left as a project for you!

Now that we know *what* the program is supposed to do, we need to decide *how*. We begin with the database described in Section 4.3.7. From that definition of flights and routes, we can now define the top level of our program. We will write a procedure called find-routes, which accepts the originating and destination airport codes, and returns a *list* of routes between them. Each route is a list of flights. The result of find-routes is therefore a list whose elements are lists of flights. A flight is itself (in our implementation) a list! By using abstraction, we can avoid getting lost in this morass of lists.

We are ready to write the program. The flight ADT and data base are straightforward. Two auxiliary procedures, same-city?, and display-routes, appear next. The Boolean procedure same-city? determines whether two airports are in the same city. It uses equal?, and hence only identifies whether two airport codes are the same. Chicago/O'Hare and Chicago/Midway are two airports in Chicago, but same-city? reports that they are not in the same city. Hence a route that involves an arrival at O'Hare and a connection at Midway will be rejected. Exercise 4-46 asks you to remedy this defect.

The meat of the program is the procedure find-routes. We use a method called **stepwise refinement** to develop it. Rather than doing the whole thing at once, we write a simple procedure that does part of the job. We then see if we can improve it. This allows us to break our development of the program into "mind-size" steps, so at each step we can comprehend how we got there and what we gained. Therefore, there are three `find-routes-...` procedures, named `find-routes-direct`, `find-routes-exhaustive`, and `find-routes-remember`. To use `find-routes-exhaustive`, you can write

```
(define find-routes find-routes-exhaustive)
```

One of the most important aspects of stepwise refinement is keeping the interface for all of the versions the same. Thus, all three of our procedures accept origin and destination arguments, and all three return a list of routes (even though each route will be a list of a single flight, in the case of `find-routes-direct`). Our goal is to improve the implementation.

In a real production program, we wouldn't show the earlier steps. We would include only the code for the last step, since the earlier steps are just our first efforts. Because our goal in this Case Study is to show you how the program is built, we *have* included the earlier steps.

`find-routes-direct` in Section 4.4.2 is a good first attempt at a route-finder, but it's too conservative. We also need to consider routes with two or more flights. Our exhaustive route-finder will iterate over all flights, looking for a flight leaving the origin. If there is one, our route-finder will return the result of tacking this flight onto all flights from its destination to the problem destination.

The main procedure appears in Program 4–27. What is the termination case? The simplest method is to think of the termination case as the one where the origin and destination are the same. In this case, the value should be `(())`, a list containing one route, the null route: the route from a place to itself involves no flights and `find-routes` must return a list of routes, so its answer is `(())`. If the result were null itself, `()`, that would indicate that there are no routes, which is not at all the same thing.

```
(define find-routes-exhaustive
  (lambda (origin destination)
    (if (same-city? origin destination)
        '(())
        (map-each-flight-from-origin  origin destination))))
```
Program 4-27   Procedure `find-routes-exhaustive`

This choice of the termination case fits together with the way we construct routes (Program 4–28).

`map-each-flight-from-origin` uses a technique we call *ansing*, using an argument named ans. Its helper loops over all the flights. When a flight starts at the origin, it appends all the routes that `try-route-from-flight-destination` finds to ans. When the helper runs out of flights, it returns the answer.

Procedure `try-route-from-flight-destination` (Program 4–29), takes a flight and calls `find-routes-exhaustive` recursively to get a list of routes from the destination. We get back a list of routes from this destination city to the final destination. Now we can cons our original flight to the beginning of each of these routes. The null routes returned by `find-routes-exhaustive` make sense now, because when we cons a flight onto null, we create the list of flights that will constitute a route. Remember, `find-routes-exhaustive` can return null, indicating that there is no route to the final destination. In this case, `map` does nothing, and just returns null.

```
(define map-each-flight-from-origin
  (lambda (origin destination)
    (letrec
      ((helper
        (lambda (flts ans)
          (if (null? flts)
            ans
            (helper
              (cdr flts)
              (if (same-city? origin (flight-origin (car flts)))
                (append
                  (try-route-from-flight-destination (car flts)
                    destination)
                  ans)
                ans)))))
      (helper flights '()))))
```

Program 4-28   Procedure `map-each-flight-from-origin`

```
(define try-route-from-flight-destination
  (lambda (flt destination)
    (map
      (lambda (x) (cons flt x))
      (find-routes-exhaustive
        (flight-destination flt)
        destination))))
```

Program 4-29   Procedure `try-route-from-flight-destination`

Unfortunately, `find-routes-exhaustive` has a fatal design error. Suppose that we want to plan a trip from Seattle to Fairbanks. There is no direct flight, so we must look at all of the cities that can be reached from Seattle: Anchorage, Missoula, Vancouver, Chicago, and San Francisco. For each, we attempt to find a route to Fairbanks. We quickly succeed from Anchorage. But when we try to find flights from Vancouver, we start looking at all the cities that can be reached from Vancouver. There is only one, namely, Seattle. So we start looking at cities reachable from Seattle. Needless to say, this is an infinite loop. This procedure doesn't actually solve our problem, but its design is a useful step on the path toward a final route-finder.

The remedy for this design error is to keep track of the cities you have visited on your way to the city you're currently in, and reject any flight that leads to one of those cities (such a flight would close the loop). This change brings us to our third version, called `find-routes-remember`, which is very similar to `find-routes-exhaustive`, except that what was the main part of the procedure has been moved into a helper named `check-flights`, so that we can add an extra argument, the cities that have been visited. The result is shown in Program 4-30. Instead of calling `find-routes-remember` recursively, we call `check-flights` recursively, consing the current `origin` city onto the `visited` argument. One other change must be made to `check-flights`: if the origin has already been visited, we just return null. There cannot be any cycles in our routes.

Most of the procedures are the same, except that they pass along the list of visited cities as well as their other arguments. For example, `r-map-each-flight-from-origin` is the same as `map-each-flight-from-origin` with the addition of the `visited` parameter. `check-flights` just checks to see whether the city has been visited, and fails if it has; otherwise it continues as before.

```
(define check-flights
  (lambda (origin destination visited)
    (if (member origin visited)
        '()
        (if (same-city? origin destination)
            '(())
            (r-map-each-flight-from-origin
              origin destination visited)))))
```

Program 4-30   Procedure `check-flights`

We have come a long way. We have built a fairly complicated procedure that does something interesting. It's time to take stock. First, although our program works, it is too slow to be usable. With the trivial database in this study, it runs with no appreciable pause (on a 386/25, using PC Scheme and an experimental Windows Scheme, neither of which is very fast). Therefore, we would expect that if we were to build a complete database, it might be slower, but still usable.

Unfortunately, on a serious database (the Official Airline Guide, which lists every scheduled flight for every commercial air carrier), the program, even on the fastest computer in existence, using a high-performance Scheme compiler, would be too slow to be usable. The problem is that `find-routes-remember` has exponential complexity, that is, it runs in $O(n^n)$ time. For 1000 flights ($n = 1000$), the program would blindly try every flight and attempt to find routes from each destination to the final destination. Adding just one flight causes the program to consider that flight each time it examines any route. Adding one flight to a database with 1000 flights will cause the program to take (in theory) 1000 times as long.

There are much better algorithms than the one we've considered here, but they are more difficult to describe. They consider distance and try to find short routes, not all routes. Our program considers cities that are completely irrelevant (flying from London to Paris via Brisbane, for example), which is a profound waste of time. From a performance point of view, therefore, `find-routes-remember` is the beginning of the road, rather than the end.

☞ **Exercise 4-45**

The routes found by `find-routes`, our Case Study program, from San Francisco (SFO) to Missoula (MSO), are

```
(find-routes 'sfo 'mso)
  ⇒  (((ua sfo sea 1706 1030 1234) (nw sea mso 2199 1700 2025)))
```

Draw a box-and-arrow diagram of the resulting data structure. ❏

☞ **Exercise 4-46**

Some cities have more than one airport. For example, the San Francisco Bay Area is served by San Francisco International (SFO), Oakland International (OAK), and San Jose International (SJC). Modify `same-city?` to support this. Don't write special-case code for multiple airports; instead, design a data structure that `same-city?` can consult. If an airport is not in this data structure, assume that it is not in the same city as any other airport. ❏

Summary

This chapter has introduced Scheme data structures: pairs and lists, how they are constructed and manipulated, how to diagram them, and how to program using them. Pairs form the basis of data structures, and are the components for lists, also. Pairs are sufficient for representing structures with a fixed number of elements. Once we need collections with an arbitrary number of items, we turn to lists. Lists in particular can be described recursively as either null, (), or a pair whose cdr is a list. This powerful recursive definition leads to many useful list-manipulation procedures, including append, `member`, `reverse`, and many others. In turn, we generalized list processing to include procedures that operate on all elements of a list either to produce a new result list, a single value or effects.

Further Readings

Our standard Scheme references, *Scheme and the Art of Programming*, by G. Springer and D. P. Friedman, and *Programming in Scheme*, by M. Eisenberg , both have excellent discussions of the use of pairs and lists and many interesting exercises using them.

Key Words

Here are the *key words* introduced in this chapter. Make sure you understand what each one means.

box-and-arrow	list	recursive definition
delimiter	mapping	reduction
dot notation	null	sublist
filtering	pair	top level (of list)
improper list	primitive data type (PDT)	variadic
inductive definition	quote	

Scheme Features Introduced in This Chapter

Primitive Procedures

append	apply	car	cdr
cons	eighth	eighth-tail	equal?
fifth	fifth-tail	first	first-tail
for-each	fourth	fourth-tail	length
list-ref	list-tail	map	member
ninth	ninth-tail	null?	reverse
second	second-tail	seventh	seventh-tail
sixth	sixth-tail	tenth	tenth-tail
third	third-tail		

Special Forms

quote

Cumulative List of Data Types

Name	Constructor	Accessors	Predicate
Boolean	—	—	boolean?
character	integer->char	char->integer	char?
list	list	car, cdr	list?
number	—	—	number?
pair	cons	car, cdr	pair?
procedure	lambda	—	procedure?
string	string	string-ref	string?
symbol	string->symbol	—	symbol?
void	void	—	void?

Note: there is no actual data type list in Scheme. As far as the Scheme evaluator is concerned, lists are just pair structures. Most Scheme programmers regard lists as a separate type, though.

Problems

1. Write a tail-recursive version of append%.

2. Consider (define addtocar (lambda (x) (add1 (car x)))). Explain the difference between the result of (addtocar '(map add1 '(1 2 3))) and that of (addtocar (map add1 '(1 2 3))).

3. Write a procedure, collect-evens, that takes a list of integers and returns a list containing only the even integers in the original list. For example,

   ```
   (collect-evens '(1 2 3 4 5))    ⇒   (2 4)
   (collect-evens '(1 2 3 4 5 0))  ⇒   (2 4 0)
   ```

4. Write collect-evens by using filter.

5. Write deep-reverse, a version of the Scheme primitive reverse that reverses all lists occurring in the list structure.

   ```
   (deep-reverse '(1 (2 3) 4  (5 6)))  ⇒   ((6 5) 4 (3 2) 1)
   ```

```
(deep-reverse '(1 (2 3) (4 (5 6))))  ⇒  (((6 5) 4) (3 2) 1)
```

6. The procedure `flatten` creates a list of all the simple elements (i.e., those that are not pairs), of its input:

```
(flatten '(1 (2 (3 (4 5) ((6) 7)))))  ⇒  (1 2 3 4 5 6 7)
```

This is an example of tree recursion. We have to flatten both the car and the cdr of any pair we might encounter during the recursion. Since `flatten` returns a list, we have to use the correct procedure to combine the results of flattening the car and of flattening the cdr.

7. Write a procedure, `some`, that determines whether at least one element in a list satisfies `pred?`. Use `reduce-map`.

```
(some odd? '(1 3 4 7))  ⇒  #t     (some odd? '(2 4 6))  ⇒  #f
```

8. Write a procedure, `last`, that returns the last element in a list.

```
> (last '(1 2 3 4))
4
> (last '())
Error in last: No elements in list.
```

9. Write a procedure, `butlast`, that returns the list except for its last element.

```
> (butlast '(1 2 3 4))
'(1 2 3)
> (butlast '())
Error in butlast: No elements in list.
```

10. Write `subst%` without using `deep-map`.

Self-Assessment

1. What is the value of the last form in each of the following sequences of Scheme forms?
   a. `(define a (list (cons 'a 'b) 'c))`
      `(define b (list 'b a)))`
      `b`
   b. `(define a (list '(a 'c) 'b))`
      `(define b (cons a a))`
      `b`

2. What is the value of this form?

```
(begin
  (define p
    (append (list 'b 'c)
      (cons '((d) e) (cons 'a '()))))
  (car (cdr (cdr p))))
```

3. Draw the box-and-arrow diagram for p in the previous question.

4. Here are three of our tries to produce a correct version of `reverse`. Each is missing the constructor for building the reversed list from the recursive call. One of the three, `append`, `cons`, or `list`, fits in each of the following procedures in the empty space. When the correct one is there, the procedure produces the output shown afterward. Replace the sequence of dashes in each procedure by `append`, `cons`, or `list`.

```
(define rev1
  (lambda (lis)
    (if (null? lis)
        '()
        (------- (rev1 (cdr lis)) (car lis)))))
(rev1 '(1 2 3 4)) ⇒  (((((() . 4) . 3) . 2) . 1)
(define rev2
  (lambda (lis)
    (if (null? lis)
        '()
        (------- (rev2 (cdr lis)) (list (car lis))))))
(rev2 '(1 2 3 4)) ⇒  (4 3 2 1)
(define rev3
  (lambda (lis)
    (if (null? lis)
        '()
        (------- (rev3 (cdr lis)) (car lis)))))
(rev3 '(1 2 3 4)) ⇒  (((((() 4) 3) 2) 1)
```

5. You've written `reverse` and `deep-reverse`. Now write `odd-reverse`, a procedure that reverses only the odd levels of a list, not the even.

```
(odd-reverse '(1 2 3)) ⇒  (3 2 1)
(odd-reverse '((a b c) z x)) ⇒  (x z (a b c))
(odd-reverse '((a b (d e f)) b c)) ⇒  (c b (a b (f e d)))
```

You can use `reverse` in writing this. Hint: It's easy to write this if you use `map`.

6. Define a procedure, `flipper`, that takes a list as an argument. It should return a new list, where the elements in a at even-numbered positions appear in reverse order, and the ones at odd positions appear in the original order. The position of an element is counted from 0. Hint: Treat the elements at even-numbered positions and odd-numbered positions separately.

```
(flipper '()) ⇒  ()
(flipper '(0)) ⇒  (0)
(flipper '(0 1 2 3 4)) ⇒  (4 1 2 3 0)
(flipper '(0 1 2 3 4 5 6)) ⇒  (6 1 4 3 2 5 0)
```

7. Write `reverse-r` using `list-ref`. What is its complexity in terms of n, the length of its input?

8. Write `delete` using `filter`. (See Exercise 4-39.) ❏

Programming Problems

1. We are having a hard time remembering the CDs we have and who the composers and artists are. Design a CD ADT that describes the composer, artist and year for each CD.

   Then build software to manage a list of CDs (each represented by the CD ADT). The procedures should let us create a new CD, and add it to the list, and search the list for all CDs by a certain composer or artist. Try to think of other utilities for your CD collection.

2. In poker, a hand is a collection of cards, selected at random from the deck of 52 cards.

Cards are chosen from four suits: clubs, diamonds, hearts, and spades. The numbers from 1 to 13 represent the values ace, 2 through 10, then jack, queen, and king. In order to play poker, we'll need procedures to determine whether certain configurations of cards are in a hand. Write procedures, using our card ADT, to determine whether the hand is all of the same suit (a flush), or can be arranged in an ascending sequence of numbers (a straight). Write procedures for other configurations of interest: for example, in a hand of five cards, a full house consists of 2 cards of one number, and 3 cards of another.

3. A linear cellular automaton is a machine that stores a set of values arranged as points on a line. It computes new values recursively. At each step, the value at a point is a function of the value at that point and the values at the two adjacent points. The most famous of these automata is a 2-d automaton that implements the game Life. We'll use a list of zeroes and ones to represent the input values to a linear cellular automaton.

The input to our automaton is a list of values and a rule for generating the new values. The rule is in the form (`rule a b c`) where its arguments are zero or one—its output is a zero or one. Here's an example of a linear automaton:

```
> (run-auto '(0 1 0 1 0 1 0 1 0 1 0) brule 6)
(0 1 0 1 0 1 0 1 0 1 0)
(0 0 1 0 1 0 1 0 1 0 0)
(0 0 0 1 0 1 0 1 0 0 0)
(0 0 0 0 1 0 1 0 0 0 0)
(0 0 0 0 0 1 0 0 0 0 0)
(0 0 0 0 0 0 0 0 0 0 0)
(0 0 0 0 0 0 0 0 0 0 0)
```

Write the procedure `run-auto` that runs the automaton, with initial input values as specified, using procedure `brule` to generate new values, for 6 "generations".

In each generation, `run-auto` displays its input, produces a new list of values, using the rules, and calls itself recursively. Here we used:

```
(define brule
   (lambda (a b c) (if (> (+ a b c) 1) 1 0)))
```

4. An alternative to filtering the result of `find-routes` is to give `find-routes` an extra argument (i.e., change the interface) that is a filter procedure. Each route is passed to the filter procedure, and is only included in the result if the filter procedure returns #t. Design and implement the necessary changes so that `find-routes-remember` will support this filter-procedure argument.

5. This question derives from the Case Study. Because the departure and arrival times for flights are given as local times, it is very difficult to compute the flying time of a flight. We would therefore like to store all times internally as Universal Time which was, until 1977, known as Greenwich Mean Time). For each airport, we can store the number of minutes' difference from UTC. We have to store the difference in minutes because some cities are in time zones that are not an integral number of hours away from UTC: Newfoundland, for example, is UTC-3:30.

Some flight times are shown in schedules as "Depart 2105, Arrive 0700+1" (leave at 9:05 **P.M.**, arrive at 7:00 **A.M.** the next day). We will therefore standardize on a system in which a day's difference is shown as a multiple of 24 hours. Thus the above example would have a departure time of 2105 and an arrival time of 3100.

Describe the necessary data structures for airport time differences, and the necessary time conversion procedures. Then write a one-line `flight-time` procedure that gives the flying time for the flight. (If this procedure isn't trivial, you've done something wrong.) Remember: The next minute from 1159 is 1200!

Chapter 5

Mutation and State

Overview

If computation is the art of modeling the world in a program, then our view of computation is incomplete, because it does not allow us to express *change*. We must extend our view to ensure that our programs are accurate models. We will look at two related concepts: the *state* of a computation and *mutation* of data. We look first at the simplest kind of mutable data, a *box* into which we may place different values at different times. We will see how Scheme's pairs can be mutated. Finally, our exploration of mutating variables will lead us into a fundamentally different model of the way in which a Scheme system works. Procedure applications are the basic unit in the new model. Each application creates a *frame* to bind the procedure's arguments to its parameters. This new model of computation allows us to understand procedures as returned values and procedures that maintain state. The new model also explains definitions and `letrec`.

> *That's a pretty bad state for a State to be in!*   — Tim Rice, *Evita*

> *Mutate now—avoid the post-bomb rush!*   — Vancouver graffito, circa 1985

The last four chapters have presented Scheme programming in terms of applying transformations to data. If we add 1 to a value, we get a new value; if we cons two values together, we get a pair. In our view, values exist eternally, and computation consists of applying procedures to these values in order to produce new ones. We have followed what is generally known as a functional, or applicative approach. We have designed procedures that have been intended to produce a result.

We have sometimes used `define` or `letrec` to create variable bindings, or `display` to write things to the screen, but we have not discussed exactly what was happening with procedures and forms such as these. In fact, `define` and `display` are evaluated not for the *value* they return (which is unspecified), but for the *effect* they cause. Compare them with +, which simply returns a value. After we define or display something, new variable bindings exist, or the screen has changed. We call such changes *effects*.

Languages such as Pascal encourage programmers to design their programs around effects; Scheme lets us write significant programs without effects (apart from input/output). We call languages such as Pascal imperative: instead of evaluating expressions, the programmer commands the computer to produce an effect.[1] A program in an imperative language is organized as a sequence of commands that are performed in the order specified by the programmer. The most fundamental imperative language is the machine language of most computers (see Chapter 11), whose operations look like `add a and b and put the result in c`. The designers of many programming languages, including Pascal, C++, and Ada have used machine language as a model.

While it is sensible for computer designers to use an imperative model, the argument for imperative programming languages is much weaker. Many traditional languages have been imperative, but tradition isn't always the best justification.

---

[1] *Imperative* comes from the same Latin root as *emperor*.

Studies of software engineering projects show that overuse of imperative features detracts from the readability and reliability of programs.

Some languages have abandoned imperative features completely. Scheme's designers were unwilling to do so, because imperative programs do one thing well: they allow us to model *state*. The Oxford English Dictionary defines **state** as "combination of circumstances or attributes belonging for the time being to a person or thing". One word is crucial in that definition: *time*. The state of a person or thing can change over time.

In the real world, objects have many characteristics that vary with time: employees are hired, students receive grades, and robot arms pick up parts on an assembly line. If we want to write computer programs that deal with employees, students, and robots, we must consider the state of these objects.

Many problems are best solved with applicative programs, but most complex problems require us to think about the states of various entities. In this chapter and in Chapter 6, we will look at the concept of state and see how it gradually evolves into object-oriented programming.

5.1   Balances and Boxes

> *Little boxes, on the hillside*
> *Little boxes made of ticky-tacky*
> *Little boxes, little boxes, little boxes, all the same*
> *There's a green one, and a pink one, and a blue one, and a yellow one*
> *And they're all made out of ticky-tacky*
> *And they all look just the same.*
> *And the people in the boxes*
> *All go to the University*
> *And they all get put in boxes,*
> *Little boxes, all the same*
> *And there's doctors, and there's lawyers, and business executives;*
> *And they're all made out of ticky-tacky*
> *And they all look just the same.*   — Malvina Reynolds, "Little Boxes"

The concept of state can be made more real for us by visiting a bank. Bank customers make deposits to and withdrawals from their accounts. Each time they do so, they change the account balance.

If the balance never changed, we could represent the customer's balance by a number. But how do we talk about a balance that is $120.00 in the morning and $250.00 in the afternoon? We must introduce the element of time. In the applicative framework, to bind a name, say `balance`, to two different values, we would have two different `balance`s. In the real world, however, there's only one account; it just *changes* from time to time.

So far, we have resisted discussing time except when dealing with input and output. Applicative Scheme is like a glorified calculator. Input and output varied this slightly, but we were still able to say, "Each time you start a given computation *with given inputs*, you get the same results." That isn't what happens in a bank. Making two deposits for a given amount does not yield the same balance as one deposit for the same amount. A value such as a balance has state that can change over time as a result of transactions such as deposits, withdrawals, interest payments, and service charges. Figure 5-1 shows our starting point: a `balance` ADT that supports deposits and withdrawals.

Constructor

- (make-balance *initial-deposit*)
  Create a new `balance` with value *initial-deposit*.

Accessor

- (balance-amount *balance*)
  Return the current amount on deposit.

Mutators

- (balance-deposit! *balance n*)
  Increase the amount on deposit by *n*.

- (balance-withdraw! *balance n*)
  Decrease the amount on deposit by *n* unless the amount on deposit is already less than *n* (this would be an attempt to overdraw the account).

Figure 5-1   Abstract Data Type: `balance`

As an example,

```
(define joe (make-balance 100))
(balance-amount joe) ⇒ 100
(balance-deposit! joe 50)
(balance-withdraw! joe 20)
(balance-amount joe) ⇒ 130
```

The `balance` ADT introduces a new class of operations, **mutators**, that change a value's state. We call changing a value's state **mutation**, which comes from the Latin word meaning "to change". We call values whose state can be changed **mutable**. Values whose state cannot be changed are called **immutable**. Most of the primitive data types we've studied are immutable. Procedures, numbers, characters, and Booleans are all immutable; only strings and pairs are mutable.[2]

A Scheme procedure or special form that mutates a value generally has a name ending with an exclamation point to remind us that it does something unusual.

5.1.1   Boxes

How do we implement balances? If a balance did not change over time, we could represent it as a number. But balances do change over time, and numbers don't. Therefore, we need a new primitive type for our `balance` implementation.

Scheme allows you to create a value that can be mutated. We call such values **boxes**.[3] We can envision a box as a container for a value. We create a box, using

---

[2] See Orwell's *1984* for an argument that truth is mutable.

[3] Boxes aren't a formal part of Scheme, though they may easily be added. Consult your Scheme manual for details on boxes. Some Scheme systems may display boxes as pairs. Because we never need to display boxes, except for debugging, you can ignore the output format your Scheme system uses.

make-box, with an initial value. At any time, we can obtain the value in the box using box-ref. Most importantly, we can replace the contents of the box with another value using box-set! Figure 5–2 shows the interface for boxes.

Constructor

- (make-box *initial-value*)
  Create a box with the specified initial value, and return it.

Accessor

- (box-ref *box*)
  Return the current value of the *box.*

Mutator

- (box-set! *box new-value*)
  Change the value of *box* to *new-value.*

Predicate

- (box? *anything*)
  Return #t if *anything* is a box, and #f otherwise.

Figure 5–2   **Primitive Data Type:** box

At any given time, a box contains a specific value (the initial value, or the last value placed in it). box-set! allows us to put a new value in the box. Boxes in Scheme and in the real world have similar properties. A box can contain one thing; take that thing out, and you have room to put something else into the box.

```
(define mybox (make-box 40))
(box-ref mybox) ⇒ 40
(box-set! mybox 38)
(box-ref mybox) ⇒ 38
```

Consider a box as an *internal* value. It doesn't make sense to read or display a box, but it makes perfect sense to read or display the value *contained* in a box.

We can draw a box-and-arrow diagram showing what happened in the above example. Figure 5–3 (a) shows what happens before the box-set!, and Figure 5–3 (b) shows what happens after.

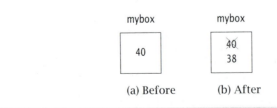

(a) Before   (b) After

Figure 5–3   Boxes at work

There is one crucial difference between box-set! and the forms we've used up to now (except input/output). The value of (box-ref mybox) can change; that's exactly why we use it. Mutation complicates reasoning about programs, but it is critical for real computing systems. To understand programs with mutation, we'll need to know the history of the computation.

☞ **Exercise 5-1**

Suppose we execute the following code:

```
(define w (make-box 2))
(define f (lambda (a) (+ (box-ref w) a)))     (f 4) ⇒   ???
(set-box! w 3)                                (f 4) ⇒   ???
```

What values are displayed as the results of the two applications of f? Why? ❏

☞ **Exercise 5-2**

Draw a diagram showing what happens in the following code:

```
(let
  ((a (make-box 23))
   (b (make-box 57)))
  (let
    ((c (box-ref a)))
    (box-set! a (box-ref b))
    (list (box-ref a) (box-ref b) c)))
```

What is the returned value? *Hint*: c's value isn't a box. ❏

Sometimes, we want to mutate a box by using a new value computed on the basis of the old value that was in the box.

```
(define x (make-box 30))
(box-set! b (+ (box-ref b) 22))
(box-ref b)  ⇒   52
```

It is essential to use a strict order in evaluating a sequence of forms with effects. The form (box-ref b) yields different values at different times, depending on what is in the box. We've run into this problem before when we studied input/output. Experience shows that programmers are more likely to be sloppy about the order of evaluation when dealing with mutation than when doing input/output.

☞ **Exercise 5-3**

Two Scheme programmers are arguing about the value of the following form:

```
(let ((a (make-box 3)))
  (- (box-ref a) (begin (box-set! a 2) (box-ref a))))
```

What is the value of this form? ❏

5.1.2   Using Boxes to Implement Balances

Boxes have uses beyond writing unreadable versions of applicative code. The prime use for a box is to represent data that changes over time, for example, a balance, as shown in Program 5-1. make-balance creates a box that contains the amount initially deposited, and balance-deposit mutates this amount after checking that the deposit value is valid. We have included a fair amount of error-checking code in this example. Good programs include error-checking code, but we won't generally do so in our examples, because it takes too much space.

```
(module balance
  (export make-balance balance-amount
    balance-deposit! balance-withdraw!)
  (define make-balance
    (lambda (amt)
      (check-number amt)
      (make-box amt)))
  (define balance-amount
    (lambda (bal)
      (check-bal bal)
      (box-ref bal)))
  (define balance-deposit!
    (lambda (bal amt)
      (check-bal bal)
      (check-number amt)
      (box-set! bal (+ (box-ref bal) amt))))
  (define balance-withdraw!
    (lambda (bal amt)
      (check-bal bal)
      (check-number amt)
      (if (< (box-ref bal) amt)
        (error 'balance-withdraw! "Overdrafts aren't allowed"))
      (box-set! bal (- (box-ref bal) amt))))
  (define check-bal
    (lambda (bal)
      (if (not (box? bal))
        (error 'balance "Balance expected"))))
  (define check-number
    (lambda (amt)
      (if (not (number? amt))
        (error 'balance "Number expected"))))
) ;; end of module
```

Program 5-1   A balance implementation

☞ **Exercise 5-4**

A claim of bulletproof error-checking should always be taken with a grain of salt. In this case, the error-checking is definitely incomplete. What invalid data could be supplied to the procedures in this module to allow an unscrupulous user to cheat? How should you fix these bugs? ❏

☞ **Exercise 5-5**

Modify the balance implementation to count the total number of transactions for all accounts. Provide a procedure that returns this number. ❏

5.2 Mutating Data Structures

If we want things to stay as they are, things will have to change.
— Giuseppe di Lampedusa, *The Leopard*

A fussy programming-language designer might decree that boxes should be the only mutable data type. Scheme allows a number of other data types to be mutable, however, including strings and pairs. We can mutate the characters of a string; we can also mutate the car or cdr of a pair. We won't often use mutable strings (though they can make practical programming much more convenient), but mutable pairs allow us to build complex mutable data structures.

5.2.1 Accounts

No credible financial institution would model customer accounts simply as balances. Accounts are identified by account numbers; names, addresses, and phone numbers are other essential pieces of information. Taxation authorities require reports on interest payments, so the bank must store a taxpayer identification number, such as a Social Security Number (SSN) in the United States, or a Social Insurance Number (SIN) in Canada. The balance itself is not sufficient to answer queries about the account status. If the balance isn't what the customer expects, we must be able to provide a list of the transactions that have been processed.

The `account` ADT represents simple bank accounts, along with a small amount of information about the customer. We've left out information such as address and phone number to simplify things, and our code, shown in Figure 5-4, omits the necessary error-checking, to make the code more compact.

There is a certain degree of arbitrariness in the specification of an ADT such as this. We might have much more information available to us. A real bank account is a complex data structure, including such things as interest payments, multiple addresses (as the customer moves), and so on. A substantial amount of analysis must be done to decide what information should be kept. This analysis (known variously as **systems analysis** and **database design**) is complex, and requires a good understanding of the problem. We'll take a brief look at systems analysis in Chapters 6 and 8.

How do we implement `accounts`? If it were not for mutation, we could represent an `account` as a list such as (*name address* ...); however, almost everything in this structure is mutable. One solution is to store everything that is mutable in a box. We would then have a list that included some boxes, which could be mutated at any time. Unfortunately, using boxes in this way would result in code that was almost unreadable. All the clutter of `box-ref` and `box-set!` make it impossible to discern the algorithms and data structures being used.

The solution is clear: we need to be able to mutate the contents not only of boxes, but also of pairs. Therefore, Scheme provides two additional procedures, `set-car!` and `set-cdr!` for this purpose. As the name suggests, `set-car!` mutates the car of a pair, and `set-cdr!` mutates the cdr. For example, consider the following code:

```
(define a (cons 1 2))
```

Constructor

- (make-account *name SSN/SIN*)
  Create a new account for a customer with a specified name and taxpayer number.

Accessors

- (account-number *account*)
  Return the account number for the specified account.
- (account-name *account*)
  Return the name of the account holder.
- (account-amount *account*)
  Return the current amount on deposit.
- (account-tax-number *account*)
  Return the SSN or SIN for this account.

Mutators

- (account-set-name! *account name*)
  Change the account holder's name to *name*.
- (account-set-tax-number! *account tax-number*)
  Change the account's SSN/SIN to *tax-number*.
- (account-deposit! *account n*)
  Increase the amount on deposit by *n*.
- (account-withdraw! *account n*)
  Decrease the amount on deposit by *n*, unless the amount on deposit is already less than *n* (this would be an attempt to overdraw the account).

Display procedures

- (account-display *account*)
  Display the name, account number, taxpayer number, and current balance of the account.
- (account-display-history *account*)
  Display, in reverse order, the transactions for this account.

Figure 5-4   **Abstract Data Type:** account

```
a ⇒ (1 . 2)
(set-car! a 3)
(set-cdr! a 4)
a ⇒ (3 . 4)
```

Figure 5-5 shows that neither set-car! nor set-cdr! is evaluated for a result; the only purpose of calling either of these primitives is to mutate an existing pair.

We saw how list-ref was a useful way to access a given list element. list-set!, its mutator counterpart, which mutates the *n*th element of a list, is not provided with Scheme, but it can be written as follows:

```
(define list-set!
  (lambda (x n v)
    (set-car! (list-tail x n) v)))
```

We will consider list-set! to be a primitive. Scheme provides a mutator for strings, string-set!, that replaces the character at the specified position.

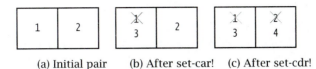

(a) Initial pair   (b) After set-car!   (c) After set-cdr!

Figure 5-5   Pair mutation

We will represent an account as a list of five elements, as follows:

1. the account number
2. name
3. current balance
4. taxpayer number
5. a list of transactions

The implementation is shown in Program 5-2 and Program 5-3.

```
(module account
  (export make-account account-number account-name
    account-amount account-tax-number
    account-set-name! account-set-tax-number!
    account-deposit! account-withdraw!
    account-display account-display-history)
  (define next-account-number (make-box 0))
  (define make-account
    (lambda (name SSN/SIN)
      (box-set! next-account-number
                (add1 (box-ref next-account-number)))
      (list (box-ref next-account-number)
            name 0 SSN/SIN (make-box '()))))
  (define account-number
    (lambda (account) (list-ref account 0)))
  (define account-name
    (lambda (account) (list-ref account 1)))
  (define account-amount
    (lambda (account) (list-ref account 2)))
  (define account-tax-number
    (lambda (account) (list-ref account 3)))
  (define account-log
    (lambda (account) (list-ref account 4)))
```

Program 5-2   account implementation: constructor and accessors

☞ **Exercise 5-6**

Why is it important for set-balance! to be private? ❏

The current balance is in fact redundant. An account need not record the current balance; it could "replay" the transaction list to recompute the balance

```
(define account-set-name!
  (lambda (account name) (list-set! account 1 name)))
(define account-set-tax-number!
  (lambda (account tax-number) (list-set! account 3 tax-number)))
(define set-balance!
  (lambda (account amount) (list-set! account 2 amount)))
(define account-deposit!
  (lambda (account amount)
    (set-balance! account (+ (account-amount account) amount))
    (log-transaction account 'deposit amount)))
(define account-withdraw!
  (lambda (account amount)
    (if (< (account-amount account) amount)
        (error 'account-withdraw! "Overdrafts aren't allowed")
        (begin
          (set-balance! account (- (account-amount account) amount))
          (log-transaction account 'withdraw amount)))))
(define log-transaction
  (lambda (account trans amount)
    (let ((log (account-log account)))
      (box-set! log
        (cons (list (timestamp) trans amount) (box-ref log))))))
(define account-display
  (lambda (account)
    (let
      ((show
         (lambda (label value)
           (format #t "~a ~a~%" label value))))
      (show "Account:" (account-number account))
      (show "Name:" (account-name account))
      (show "SSN/SIN:" (account-tax-number account))
      (show "Balance:" (account-amount account)))))
(define account-display-history
  (lambda (account)
    (for-each
      (lambda (trans)
        (format #t "~a~%" trans))
      (box-ref (account-log account)))))
) ;;; end of module
```

Program 5-3   account implementation: mutators and displays

whenever we needed it. There is a practical reason for including the current balance: we need to know the balance frequently (e.g., when we need to determine whether we can honor a withdrawal). Recomputing it each time would be time-consuming.

Our make-account specification leaves no room for specifying the account number. This is deliberate: we don't want humans to specify the account number. The consequences of assigning the same account number to two different accounts are potentially disastrous. Instead, we can assign account numbers as we create accounts. All we need is a box, next-account-number, that contains the next account number; each time we call `make-account`, we mutate this box.

It might also be surprising that we use a box to contain the transaction log. We could mutate the account list itself, using `set-cdr!`. We have chosen not to do so, in order to make the code a bit clearer. Many people who attack this problem try to mutate the transaction list itself. To convince yourself that this won't work, remember that the transaction list is initially null; it is an error to `set-cdr!` null. We leave the removal of the unnecessary box as a project for you.

The procedure `timestamp` is not shown here. Its job is to produce a string showing the current time and date. Unfortunately, Scheme doesn't have a standardized way of doing this; the designers of each Scheme system have therefore provided their own time and date primitives. Consult your Scheme system's manual for the information you'll need to write `timestamp` for your system.

5.2.2   Structural Mutation

We've seen several uses for the `set-car!` primitive. There is a `set-cdr!` primitive as well, with many uses. From one point of view, the car and cdr of a pair are symmetric. If, for example, we want a value to represent the position of a mouse, we can store the *x* coordinate in the car, and the *y* coordinate in the cdr. As the user moves the mouse, the car and cdr are mutated appropriately. If we're working with list structure, though, there is no symmetry. The car of a pair in a list contains a value, and the cdr contains an arrow to the next pair. Mutating the cdr, then, doesn't change the *values* in the list; it changes the *structure*.

Scheme programmers have learned to treat structural mutation very cautiously. Careless use of `set-cdr!` can create tangled data structures. Still, appropriate use of structural mutation can help, in some situations. We'll look at two: destructive list operations, and circular lists.

In Chapter 4, we presented a number of useful procedures for list manipulation. All of these procedures were applicative: they didn't mutate the list itself but created a new list. Sometimes, though, we do want to alter a list, especially if it represents something with state. For example, if we have a list of a student's courses, we may need to add or delete entries as the student registers in or withdraws from given courses. We could handle such operations by making a new list and mutating a box or pair to contain the new list, but this might be impractical, especially if the list is large.

Suppose we need to insert items into a list of numbers arranged in ascending order. Program 5-4 (a) shows an applicative version that makes a new list, doing $O(n)$ conses in the process.

Cons operations are somewhat costly, because each cons call creates a new pair, which takes up memory. Scheme manages memory, so your programs seldom run out of space, but it takes more time to run them if they create lots of extra pairs, rather than reusing existing ones. A **destructive** list operation mutates an existing list. If we were concerned about doing a lot of consing, we might write a destructive version, as shown in Program 5-4 (b).

The only difference between `insert-applicative` and `insert-destructive!` is what happens in the last line, that is, in how the result of the recursive call is connected to the beginning of the list. `insert-destructive!` does only one cons, at the point where it inserts the new element. All the interesting work happens in the `set-cdr!` call. If we haven't reached the right place, we call `insert-destructive!`

```
(define insert-applicative
  (lambda (x element)
    (if (null? x)
        (cons element '())
        (if (< element (car x))
            (cons element x)
            (cons (car x) (insert-applicative (cdr x) element)))))))
```

(a) Applicative insertion

```
(define insert-destructive!
  (lambda (x element)
    (if (null? x)
        (list element)
        (if (< element (car x))
            (cons element x)
            (begin
              (set-cdr! x (insert-destructive! (cdr x) element))
              x)))))
```

(b) Destructive insertion

Program 5-4   Two methods of list insertion

recursively, and mutate the current pair's cdr to hold the result (the result will either be the same cell, or one of the base-case cons calls).

At first, insert-destructive! appears to be correct, but we soon find that it does not work in some cases.

```
(define z (list 10 20 30))
(insert-destructive! z 15) ⇒   (10 15 20 30)
(insert-destructive! z 40) ⇒   (10 15 20 30 40)
(insert-destructive! z 5) ⇒   (5 10 15 20 30 40)
(insert-destructive! z 3) ⇒   (3 10 15 20 30 40)
```

The 5 inserted in the second-to-last call doesn't show up in the list after the insertion of 3. You might think that the 3 is overwriting the first element, but a look at the code for insert-destructive! reveals no call of set-car!. We can solve this problem by asking what the value of z is at the end of this series of insertions.

```
    z ⇒   (10 15 20 30 40)
```

The value of z is unchanged by insertions at its front. (The insertions at the middle and end worked properly.) If we insert at the front of the list, we create a new pair and return it without doing any mutation at all (this new pair might be created by either of the two base cases).

We could solve this problem by passing insert-destructive! a box containing the list, but this approach clutters up the code with box-ref and box-set! calls. The alternative is to use a box for the result of insert-destructive!:

```
(define z-box (make-box z))
(box-set! z-box (insert-destructive! (box-ref z-box) 5))
(box-set! z-box (insert-destructive! (box-ref z-box) 3))
(box-ref z-box) ⇒   (3 5 10 15 20 30 40)
```

Variables, which we'll see later, provide a slightly cleaner way of doing this job.

☞ **Exercise 5-7**

Draw a box-and-arrow diagram showing what happens as the list z is built. ❏

Scheme has a number of built-in applicative list-manipulation procedures. Earlier Lisp dialects (but not Scheme) generally provide some matching destructive list-manipulation procedures. We can write our own. For example, we can write append!%, a destructive version of append that mutates the cdr of the last pair of the first list, shown in Program 5-5.

```
(define append!
  (lambda (x y)
    (if (null? x)
        y
        (begin
          (if (null? (cdr x))
              (set-cdr! x y)
              (append! (cdr x) y))
          x))))
```

Program 5-5   Mutating version of append

The first test is necessary to append a null first list to another list. The *else* part of the if form checks whether we've found the last pair. If so, it mutates the cdr to the list y; otherwise, it applies itself to the cdr of x. append! thus finds the last pair of the list and then mutates its cdr.

Again, we must use a box when we call this procedure, to account for the fact that it does no mutation in the null case.

```
> (define a (make-box ...))
> (box-set! a (append! (box-ref a) (list 1 2 3)))
```

Practical Note

Newcomers to Scheme, especially people with a Pascal or C background, tend to overuse destructive operations. Generally, you should use a destructive procedure only when it is absolutely necessary: either you are modeling some aspect of state, or you have an extremely large list. Good programmers get an applicative version of their program working *before* attempting to use destructive procedures.

We can use structural mutation to produce some rather interesting "lists".

```
(define a (list 1 2 3))
(set-cdr! (list-tail a 2) a)
```

This seems pretty innocuous, until you try to evaluate a:

```
a ⇒  (1 2 3 1 2 3 1 2 3 ...)
```

The box-and-arrow diagram in Figure 5-6 shows the list structure. The last cdr has been set to point to the first one. All `display` does is to follow cdrs. In this case, we can follow as many cdrs as we like, but we'll never reach the null that is `display`'s base case. We call a structure in which the cdr of the last pair contains an arrow to the first pair a **circular list**.

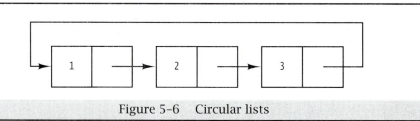

Figure 5-6   Circular lists

Circular lists have some uses. For example, many text editors (including the GNU Emacs and Epsilon editors used by the authors) allow the user to edit many files at once. Such editors often provide an "edit next file" operation. The editor keeps a circular list of all the files that the user was editing; a box contains an arrow to the pair whose car describes the current file. Suppose we call this box `current-file`, and the circular list `all-files`. All the editor must do is

```
(box-set! current-file (cdr (box-ref current-file)))
```

If the user does this operation enough times, the editor will be back at the first file, without needing to check for reaching the end of the list.

☞ **Exercise 5-8**

Assuming that you have a procedure `lastcdr` that returns the last pair of a non-null list, rewrite `append!`. ❏

☞ **Exercise 5-9**
  a. Is a circular list a list?
  b. A circular list has one restriction not required for regular lists: a circular list must contain at least one element. Why?
  c. Write a procedure that finds the number of elements in a circular list. ❏

5.2.3   Another Look at Equality

We can put the values we've studied so far into two classes: atomic and composite values. We call values such as numbers, characters, procedures, Booleans, null, and symbols **atomic**: they can't be broken down into simpler values.[4] Strings, boxes, and pairs are called **composite**, since they contain values within them.

---

[4] The term *atomic* comes from the Greco-Roman philosophy of Democritus and Lucretius, which asserted that matter was made up of small, indivisible particles called *atoms*, which comes from Greek for "can't be cut". This idea was revived in the 19th century, and by the time that it was found that real atoms consist of smaller particles, the name was too entrenched to change. Computer science usage comes from mathematical logic, which ignores new-fangled particles such as electrons.

To determine whether two values are **equal**, we use equal?, even if we know that the two values are numbers or characters. Sometimes, however, we choose one of the specialized equality predicates: for numbers, =; for strings, string=? and string-ci?; for characters, char=? and char-ci=?; and for symbols, symbol-equal?. One reason we use other equality predicates is efficiency: if all equal? does with numbers is to apply = to them, it seems like a waste of time to use equal?. Another reason is that sometimes we need a different definition of equality: char-ci=? for characters, or approximate equality ((< (abs (- x y)) tolerance)) for numbers. If we're dealing with lists and pairs, however, we're going to use equal?. Accordingly, it's worth trying to duplicate equal?, to see how it works. This task requires a careful look at values and equality.

As well as the type-oriented primitives such as =, Scheme provides eqv? (from "equivalent"), which tells us whether any two atomic values are equal. There is also an eq? procedure, which provides a restricted (but extremely efficient) equality test called **identity**. eq? will return #f in some cases where we would expect it to return #t. These restrictions on eq? are imposed in the name of efficiency; we will avoid using eq?.

Scheme's rules about the equality of procedures are complex. Scheme only guarantees that eqv? will return #t if the two procedures are the result of the same definition.

```
(define foo (lambda (x) 1))
(define bar foo)
(eqv? foo bar) ⇒  #t
```

Scheme implementations are free to return #f in any other case. In general, you will have little need to compare procedures.

One way of understanding eqv? on composite values is to think about mutation. If two values are equivalent, then mutating one results in mutating the other.

```
(define a (cons 1 2))
(define b (cons 1 2))
(define c a)
(equal? a b) ⇒  #t
(eqv? a b) ⇒  #f
(eqv? a c) ⇒  #t
(set-car! a 'ork!)
a ⇒  (ork! . 2)
b ⇒  (1 . 2)
c ⇒  (ork! . 2)
```

a and b are different pairs, but c is the same pair as a. Initially a, b, and c are all equal, but mutating a affects c as well. eqv? lets us discover that, even before the mutation occurs.

How do equivalence and equality appear in box-and-arrow diagrams? We've tended to show atomic values as being inside boxes. To be strict, we should show any value as being an arrow to the actual value. Then we'd show any atomic value just *once*. How does this relate to atomic values? Atomic values can't be mutated. Whether there is one or many doesn't matter.

When we diagram composite values, we must identify whether two values are equivalent. *Two values are* **equivalent** *if their arrows lead to the same place.* Notice that we said *values*, not *atomic values*. This definition applies to any kind of value.

Two values might not be equivalent, but might still be related in such a way that mutating one mutates the other.

```
(define x (cons 1 2))
(define y (cons 0 x))
(eqv? x y) ⇒  #f
(set-car! x 'foo)
y ⇒  (0 foo . 2)
```

Mutating x results in y being mutated; we say that x and y **share storage**. The box-and-arrow diagram in Figure 5-7, showing how x and y are mutated, should clarify matters.

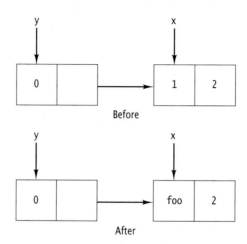

Figure 5-7   Box-and-arrow diagrams and sharing storage

Practical Note

Unintended sharing can lead to disaster. As long as you don't mutate shared values (i.e., you just use applicative operations), you don't need to worry. If you start mutating structures, however, be sure to draw pictures of the data structure to make sure you understand what sharing is going on, and whether it is desirable. Where possible, though, avoid using mutating or destructive operations. If you do use sharing, some comments can help make your code easier to understand.

Some Scheme primitives create shared structures. append, for example, returns a result that it shares with its last argument:

```
(define x (list 32 17 41))
(define y (append (list 66 14) x))
(set-car! x 91)
y ⇒  (66 14 91 17 41)
```

Be careful when mutating lists built this way.[5]

We created the pair in Figure 5-5 with a call to `cons`. Writing the pair literally (using `quote`) would have caused a problem:

```
(define a '(1 . 2))
(set-car! a 3)
```
Something bad may happen, depending on your Scheme system.

The problem is that a pair created with `quote` is immutable, because Scheme creates only *one* constant (1 . 2); if you specify more than one, they share storage. If Scheme let you mutate one of the constants sharing storage, the other would change, with disastrous consequences. For technical reasons, it is not feasible for most Scheme systems to report an attempt to mutate data created via `quote`; the results vary from system to system, but they are always surprising.

Students often try to resolve problems like these by testing the code in question on their Scheme system. When no error message appears, and perhaps even a sensible result—(the vast majority of Scheme evaluators will simply display (3 . 2), with no error message)—they say, "See? There's nothing wrong with my code"! The fact that one Scheme system fails to detect an error does not mean that another won't fail miserably when evaluating the same code. We all want to write **portable** code (code that can run on any implementation of its source language), so don't write code that can fail in these ways.

Before we can write `equal?%`, we need a predicate to tell us whether a value is atomic, so we've written `atomic?`. Many Scheme systems provide a procedure named `atom?`. Unfortunately, there isn't a clear agreement as to which are the atomic types. For example, the inclusion of procedures as an atomic type is debatable.

We can now write our version of `equal?`, which we'll call `equal?%`, using `atomic`, as shown in Program 5-6. We can write `equal?` recursively. For atomic types, we use `eqv?`. For each of the composite types, we use a different strategy. For strings, we check types and use `string=?`. For boxes, we recurse on the contents; for pairs, we recurse on the cars and cdrs of the pairs.

`equal?` lacks one property that `eqv?` has. Whereas `eqv?` is an $O(1)$ operation,[6] the time taken by `equal?` depends upon the number of arrows that must be followed. In particular, a circular list has an *infinite* number of arrows; `equal?` will therefore go into an infinite loop when applied to a circular list.

Since we can't use `equal?` on circular lists, what do we do? We can't prohibit circular lists, which are too useful for many problems. Instead, we must know in advance that we're dealing with a potentially circular list and develop an equality procedure appropriate to our needs. Writing such a predicate requires techniques beyond the scope of this book.

---

[5] Sharing corresponds to the beliefs of many so-called primitive peoples, who believe that two objects may be linked so that actions done to one object have effects on the other. For example, burning the hair clippings of an individual will cause that person to suffer pain. "Primitive" magic relies on sophisticated concepts!

[6] Scheme allows whole numbers with no limit on magnitude. To represent them it essentially uses a list of standard integers. Testing equivalence of such number requires time proportional to the number of digits in the number. Other values can be tested for equivalence in constant time.

```
(define atomic?
  (lambda (x)
    (or (number? x)
        (char? x)
        (boolean? x)
        (symbol? x)
        (procedure? x)
        (null? x))))
(define equal?%
  (lambda (x y)
    (if (and (atomic? x) (atomic? y))
        (eqv? x y)
        (if (string? x)
            (and (string? y) (string=? x y))
            (if (box? x)
                (and (box? y)
                     (equal?% (box-ref x) (box-ref y)))
                (and (pair? y)
                     (equal?% (car x) (car y))
                     (equal?% (cdr x) (cdr y))))))))))
```

Program 5-6   Implementing `equal?`

☞ **Exercise 5-10**

We say that two lists are *structurally equal* if they contain the same arrangement of pairs, even if the atomic data in those pairs is different. Two boxes are also always structurally equivalent, as are two strings. For example, (a b (c d)) is structurally equivalent to (1 2 (3 4)), but not to (a b c d). Write a predicate that returns #t if its two arguments are structurally equal, and #f if they are not. ❑

☞ **Exercise 5-11**

In the previous exercise, we defined *structural equality*. Can there be such a thing as *structural equivalence*, according to our definitions? Why, or why not? ❑

5.2.4   Dictionaries

In many problems, we must search for data in a collection. For example, we are unlikely to write a program to manage just one bank account; we would probably want to keep track of an entire collection of accounts, using the customer's *account number* to search for the correct account. We refer to the account number as a **key**, because it "unlocks" the specific data value desired.

Searching is a common problem in computer science. Dictionaries are an ADT for storing data so that it may be searched conveniently. The method shown in this chapter is too slow to be practical with large collections of data (e.g., 100,000 bank accounts), but it's satisfactory for small amounts of data. We return to this problem in Chapter 9, and look at some methods of managing large collections of data.

We will specify (see Figure 5-8) and implement a data type called a *dictionary*. A real dictionary is a collection of keys (words) and associated values (the meanings of the words).

Constructor

- `(make-dictionary)`
  Make and return an empty dictionary (i.e., a dictionary with no keys or values).

Accessor

- `(dictionary-search` *dict key*`)`
  Search dictionary *dict* for a key equal to *key*. Return the associated value (if the key was found) or displays an error message (if the key wasn't found).

Predicate

- `(dictionary-found?` *dict key*`)`
  Return #t if *key* is found in *dict*, and #f otherwise.

Mapping procedure

- `(dictionary-for-each` *dict proc*`)`
  Apply *proc* to each item in the dictionary. *proc* must take one argument that is a pair whose car is the key and whose cdr is the value associated with the key.

Mutator

- `(dictionary-insert!` *dict key value*`)`
  Insert the key *key* with value *value* into dictionary *dict*. If the key was already in the dictionary, replace the value.

Figure 5-8   **Abstract Data Type:** `dictionary`

```
(define foo (make-dictionary))
(dictionary-insert! foo 'one 'ein)
(dictionary-insert! foo 'two 'zwei)
(dictionary-search foo 'one) ⇒ ein
(dictionary-insert! foo 'one 'odin) ⇒ odin
(dictionary-search foo 'one) ⇒ odin
```

In this example, we made a new dictionary and then inserted the key one with value ein ("one" in German). Next we inserted key two with value zwei (again a German translation). When we searched for one, we retrieved ein, as expected. Then we changed the value for one to odin ("one" in Russian). Sure enough, a search for key one retrieves odin.

We can implement a dictionary in many ways that vary widely in efficiency. An **association list**, or **alist**, works well for small collections of data (e.g., no more than about 10 items), and is widely used in Scheme. In Chapter 9, we'll look at techniques for implementing large dictionaries efficiently. An association list is a list of pairs of the form (*key* . *value*), for example,

((one . odin) (two . dva) (three . tri) (four . chetireh))

The cars of the pairs are the keys, and the cdrs are the corresponding values. In this example, the keys are English number words, and the values are the corresponding Russian number words.

It is important to understand that Scheme doesn't treat alists in any special way. The only significance of an alist is that its structure makes it easy to search. We can search an alist using the Scheme primitive assoc:

```
(assoc 'Sartre
       '((Mann . Germany) (Sartre . France)
         (Proust . France) (Wells . Britain)
         (Faulkner . USA) (Laurence . Canada)))
    ⇒   (sartre . france)
(assoc 'Galsworthy
       '((Mann . Germany) (Sartre . France)
         (Proust . France) (Wells . Britain)
         (Faulkner . USA) (Laurence . Canada)))
    ⇒   #f
```

The keys are the names of writers, and the values are the names of the countries in which they were born. (We would expect the keys to be unique, but it's reasonable for the values to be duplicated. Two writers could both be born in France, but one writer could not have been born in two different countries.)

assoc returns the pair whose car was equal to the search key. If no such pair exists, assoc returns #f.

☞ **Exercise 5-12**

Why was assoc designed to return the pair rather than the value itself? ❏

assoc is easy to write; the only reason it is primitive in Scheme is programmer convenience:

```
(define assoc%
  (lambda (key alist)
    (if (null? alist)
        #f
        (let ((item (car alist)))
          (if (equal? key (car item))
              item
              (assoc% key (cdr alist)))))))
```

☞ **Exercise 5-13**

What will happen if you try to evaluate

```
(assoc% 'clef
        '((gaudeamus . igitur)
          higamus hogamus))
```

❏

Often, the keys in an association list are merely symbols, in which case equal? is overkill. Another Scheme primitive, assv, is defined to be the same as assoc, except that it uses eqv? in place of equal?

Program 5-7 provides an implementation of our dictionary ADT. We've stopped after the first three procedures, because what we've written is riddled with bugs that need to be eliminated.

- dictionary-search will fail if given a key that is not in the dictionary (it will try to take the car of null, which is an error condition).
- dictionary-insert! was supposed to handle the case of duplicates, but it doesn't check for duplicate keys.

```
(define make-dictionary
  (lambda ()
    '()))
(define dictionary-insert!
  (lambda (dict key value)
    (cons (cons key value) dict)))
(define dictionary-search
  (lambda (dict key)
    (car (assoc key dict)))))
```

Program 5-7　　Dictionary implementation

- Most important, insertions never actually happen. We cons the new key and value together, and cons them onto the list, but never actually mutate the alist! A careful reading of the code reveals no exclamation points. No mutation is taking place. (Remember that cons doesn't mutate anything.)

In our new implementation we will generate the error ourselves, using error, rather than letting Scheme detect the error, thus producing a more useful error report. We will handle the second bug by replacing the value of a duplicated key. Of these bugs, the third is by far the most serious. What good is an empty dictionary into which we can make no insertions? What can we do about it?

We had the same problem before with transaction logs in accounts. Each dictionary needs a separate alist. We can't just start with null and mutate it, since set-car! and set-cdr! only operate on pairs. A solution to this problem is to represent a dictionary as a box that *contains* the alist. Then we can use box-set! when we add something to the dictionary, as shown in the module in Program 5-8. We've taken advantage of the fact that anything except #f is considered to be true: (not item) is true if item is #f, and false otherwise.

This section has shown how structural mutation works in Scheme, and how and why we use it. We saw the set-car! and set-cdr! primitives. We saw how they could be used to create structures that grow or change over time, as well infinite structures such as circular lists. Understanding how some of these structures worked required us to think carefully about how values are stored in memory, and to understand sharing and equivalence.

The techniques we examined in this chapter are powerful enough to be dangerous. But if you use abstraction effectively, as we did with our account and dictionary types, you can design a mutable data structure, and isolate the state-dependent part of your code into the modules that actually need mutation.

5.3　Variables that Vary

> *The use of Clothes continues, though the Fashion of them has been mutable.*
> — Sir Richard Steele, *Tattler, no. 39*

To a mathematician, a variable is something whose value changes. When we write an equation such as $y = 3x + 2$, we think of x as being "any value at all", and y as being "whatever value is determined by computing $3x + 2$". Scheme's view of

```
(module dictionary
  (export make-dictionary dictionary-insert!
          dictionary-search dictionary-found?
          dictionary-for-each)
  (define make-dictionary
    (lambda ()
      (make-box '())))
  (define dictionary-insert!
    (lambda (dict key value)
      (let ((item (assoc key (box-ref dict))))
        (if (not item)
            (box-set! dict
              (cons (cons key value) (box-ref dict)))
            (set-cdr! item value)))))
  (define dictionary-search
    (lambda (dict key)
      (let ((item (assoc key (box-ref dict))))
        (if (not item)
            (error 'dictionary-search "Key not found")
            (cdr item)))))
  (define dictionary-found?
    (lambda (dict key)
      (assoc key (box-ref dict))))
  (define dictionary-for-each
    (lambda (dict proc)
      (map proc (box-ref dict))))
)
```

Program 5-8   Dictionary implementation using boxes

variables has been quite different. We have considered a variable such as x to be a binding of the name x to a value. Such bindings are created either by define or by procedure application (including the use of let). So far we have treated variables as if they were immutable: once we create a variable, the name stays bound to the value for the lifetime of the variable. We know that we can mutate data structures, but can we mutate variables themselves?

5.3.1   The set! Form

Must we be able to mutate variables? In short, no. Given boxes (or other mutable values), we can represent any value that needs state, so variable mutation is not strictly necessary. Overusing boxes, however, clutters code with calls to box-set! and box-ref so much that the programmer's intent becomes unclear.

Scheme therefore allows you to mutate the value of a variable; it provides a special form called a set!, or an **assignment**.[7]

```
> (let ((x 1))
    (format #t "x = ~a~%" x)
```

---

[7] The term *assignment* is used because a set! form *assigns*, or gives, a new value to the variable.

```
      (set! x 2)
      (format #t "x = ~a~%" x))
  x = 1
  x = 2
```

The set! form takes two arguments:
- the name of a variable, *which must already be bound*
- a form that is evaluated to obtain a new value for the variable.

Practical Note

Don't confuse let and set!. let creates a new variable binding; set! mutates an existing variable. This can be confusing, because some languages (especially early versions of BASIC) use let where we use set!.

The problem with set! is not in *learning* how to program with it. The problem is in *reading, understanding,* and *debugging* programs that use it, because the value of a variable that has been mutated depends on its history.

set! doesn't provide anything more than boxes do, other than making code a bit clearer. The general rule for using it correctly is *use set! when your program needs to keep track of state*. For example, a vending machine needs to keep track of state. Since most vending machines are controlled by microprocessors, it is reasonable for a program to control the vending machine.[8]

Our vending machine will have a slot for money, and a number of buttons that select the items. If the customer has deposited enough money, the machine returns the selected item and change (if needed). The procedure (vend-deposit *n*) records the deposit of *n* cents; the procedure (vend-choose *n*) performs the action selected by pressing button *n*. In a real vending machine, these procedures would be called by hardware: vend-deposit would be triggered by a coin sensor, and vend-choose by the closing of a switch. For our purposes, we'll call these procedures in the normal way, from a read-eval-print loop, or from Scheme code.

Figure 5-9 shows the code. Two variables record state: amount contains the current amount deposited, and items contains a list of the items that are currently for sale. Each item is a list of three elements: the item's name, price (in cents), and quantity. The name, price, and quantity comprise the product's state: prices change, and the machine's owners will probably load different items at different times. Each time somebody buys something, the quantity must be decreased by one.

We haven't used any boxes in this program; we use a variable to record the amount on deposit, and we use list mutation to keep track of the number of each item. (We can't use a variable for this purpose, because we need to keep track of each item separately.)

---

[8] To be truthful, such programs are not often written in Scheme. They are in fact often written by people who are not expert programmers and do not know how to write structured code. The program is made to work by extensive testing and patching, but is hardly readable. Nobody cares too much about vending machines, but when the same techniques are applied to elevators and on-board airplane computers, some genuine concerns arise. A great deal of effort is being expended in trying to produce standards for the development of software for so-called embedded systems (computer systems used as control elements in other machines).

```
(module vending-machine
  (export vend-deposit vend-choose)
  (define amount 0)
  (define items
    (list
        ;;    ...name...                    ..price..  ..number..
        (list "Simulated cheese food"       75          10)
        (list "Potato-style chips"          80          10)
        (list "Orange drink (1% orange juice!)" 80 10)))
  (define vend-deposit
    (lambda (x)
      (set! amount (+ amount x))
      (format #t "You have deposited ~d cents.~%" amount)))
  (define vend-choose
    (lambda (n)
      (if (< n (length items))
          (dispense (list-ref items n))
          (display "Tilt!~%"))))
  (define dispense
    (lambda (item)
      (if (> (list-ref item 2) 0)
        (if (>= amount (list-ref item 1))
          (begin
            (format #t "Here's your ~a, and your ~d cents change.~%"
                  (list-ref item 0)
                  (- amount (list-ref item 1)))
            (set-car! (list-tail item 2)
                  (sub1 (list-ref item 2)))
            (set! amount 0))
          (display "Sorry, I want more money!~%"))
        (display "Sorry, please choose another item.~%"))))
)
```

Figure 5-9   The vending machine program

☞ **Exercise 5-14**

Write a procedure vend-load that allows a maintenance person to load a new item. The procedure should take as arguments the name, price, and number on hand of an item, and the number of the button that selects it. ❏

☞ **Exercise 5-15**

Some vending machines have gimmicks to encourage people to buy things; for example, an extra item might be given periodically. How would you modify vend-choose to give a free package of Simulated Cheese Food to every 50th customer? ❏

5.3.2   `set!` **in Depth**

`set!` is more complicated than it seems. Let's consider code to exchange (**swap**) the values of two variables.

```
(define a 'first)
(define b 'second)
(set! a b)
(set! b a)
(cons a b) ⇒  (second . second)
```

As you can see, it's wrong, because the first `set!` obliterates the value of a, without saving it first. The right way to do this is to introduce a **temporary variable**, a variable used to hold a value for a short period of time.

```
(define a 'first)
(define b 'second)
(let
   ((temp a))
   (set! a b)
   (set! b temp))
(cons a b) ⇒  (second . first)
```

Normally variables introduced by `let` are not intended to be mutated, and a programming style that depends on mutating temporary variables can lead to inscrutable programs. Swapping values requires temporary variables, but avoid unnecessary use of them.

You might be tempted to write a procedure to swap the values of two variables.

```
(define swap
   (lambda (a b)
     (let
        ((temp a))
        (set! a b)
        (set! b temp))))
(define x 1)
(define y 2)
(swap x y)
(cons x y) ⇒  (1 . 2)    Wrong!!!
```

When Scheme passes arguments to a procedure, it passes their *values*. We can mutate parameters all we like, but that has no effect upon the arguments. We will introduce a new model of Scheme evaluation in Section 5.4 to explain how this happens.

Let's take a closer look at the `set!` form. First, unlike the other mutators we've seen in this chapter, `set!` isn't a procedure, but a special form. The reasons for this lead to some useful insights about variables.

So far, we have praised Scheme for making everything a first-class citizen. We have argued that arbitrary restrictions on values are annoying to the programmer, with no benefit except perhaps a marginal improvement in program efficiency. Given the increasing costs of software development and the decreasing costs of computer power, any choice that improves the productivity of the programmer is important. Making variables first-class introduces many problems, for both the Scheme programmer and the person writing the Scheme evaluator. The majority of programming languages have some second-class citizens. Variables in Scheme are not values. All you can do with a variable is create it (by means of `define`, `lambda`, or a `let` form), and access its value (by writing its name as a form).

To see why variables are second-class, we must look at them more closely. A **variable** is a binding of a **name** to a value. We can't create variables whenever we want (there's no `make-variable` primitive), but only in a procedure application or `define` (`let` and its friends are, of course, syntactic sugar for `lambda` forms). We can't put variables into data structures: (`cons x #f`) creates a pair whose car contains not the variable x but the *value* of the variable x. We can't return variables from a procedure: (`lambda (x) x`) returns the *value* of x, not the variable itself.

Second-class variables and static scoping are directly related. Scheme's designers wanted the programmer to be able to determine, by reading the program, which variable is mutated. Therefore the name of the variable *must* appear in the `set!`. If `set!` were a procedure, the name of the variable could be the result of some complex form;[9] therefore, `set!` is a special form that requires the programmer to give a specific name.

What if we need a variable as a first-class value? If we need a way to create a list of variables, we can use boxes! A box *is* a first-class citizen, and can therefore appear in a data structure. The disadvantage of boxes is the clutter of `box-ref` and `box-set!` calls in box-oriented code. The advantage is that we can use boxes freely, without regard to special forms and variable scoping.

☞ **Exercise 5-16**

Examine the following form:

```
(let
  ((a 'constantinople)
   (b 'istanbul)
   (c 'byzantium))
  ...
  (display (list a b c)))
```

The intention is to display the list (`byzantium constantinople istanbul`). Write a *single form*, using one or more `set!`'s, to replace the ellipsis .... Your form must mutate these variables appropriately (not using quoted data, of course!). ❏

---

[9] Languages such as Pascal and C++ that support reference (VAR, in Pascal) parameters lose the simplicity of simple assignment.

5.4   From Substitution to Environments

> *O! Swear not by the moon, the inconstant moon,*
> *That monthly changes in her circled orb,*
> *Lest that thy love prove likewise variable.*   — Shakespeare, *Romeo and Juliet*

We've seen many examples that show the usefulness of state in solving problems. What is less apparent is that all computations, even those in a purely applicative style, go through a sequence of states.

In Chapter 2, we described droids being created and destroyed as computation moved from one application to another. The droids record the state of the computation. In this chapter, we have added state to our toolbox. Boxes and mutable pairs make state explicitly visible to the programmer. We have seen what it means to mutate a box or the car or cdr of a pair, but what does it mean to mutate a variable? We've already seen that variables aren't first-class.

In Chapter 1, Scheme operated just as algebra did. The Rules were designed deliberately to mimic algebra. When we applied a procedure, we substituted parameters for arguments in exactly the way we evaluate an algebraic expression. Droids, as we saw in Chapter 2, show the process of evaluation by focusing on procedure applications, not on each form.

A number of phenomena, however, don't fit into this framework. When we introduced mutation, we violated some of the assumptions in The Rules. The relationship with algebra seems completely gone now. In a form such as

```
(let ((a 1))
  (display a)
  (set! a 2)
  (display a))
```

a is replaced at one point by 1, and at another by 2. Nothing in algebra corresponds to this; algebraic evaluation is static, while mutation alters the value of a variable over time.

What happens when a procedure mutates its parameters?

```
(define x 3)
(define add2 (lambda (y) (set! y (+ y 2))))
(add2 x)
x ⇒  3
```

The value of x hasn't changed! But when x is a list, we get the following:

```
(define x (list 3 4))
(define add2 (lambda (y) (set-car! y (+ (car y) 2))))
(add2 x)
x ⇒  (5 4)
```

The mutation has affected the argument. We need a clear picture of the workings of Scheme to understand the differences between the two cases. This section introduces the *environment model* to explain these effects.

If, instead of introducing a new model, we want to keep a simple model for computation, we could simply abandon mutation. We could argue that it seems nice, but it's difficult to understand how it works. Many functional programming languages have done exactly that, but they are not sufficiently fast nor expressive to be widely popular.

Mutation is an important feature of most common languages. Furthermore, object-oriented programming, which needs procedures with state, is an increasingly important aspect of software design, precisely because people actually do think in terms of things in the world, of state and change. Therefore we will develop a new model of lambda evaluation and application so that we can understand how to write programs with state. This model is not restricted to Scheme. Almost all languages use a similar mechanism to handle procedure invocation, so your understanding of procedures in Scheme will carry over to the next language you learn. Moreover, the model is realistic enough to use in Chapter 7, where we write an evaluator for Scheme in Scheme. Our knowledge of data structures will let us see how the abstract model can be translated into a working program.

This section shows that procedures create structures, called *frames*, that hold the bindings of the parameters of the procedures to the arguments of the procedure application, as well as information about how the procedure is called and what names are accessible. Frames are the basis of the environment model. The relations among frames record which procedures call other procedures and where procedures are created. To explain these relations, we introduce *snapshots*: diagrams that depict the connections between frames. Like photographs, snapshots record the frames at an instant; unlike photographs, they change over time.

5.4.1   Introduction to Environments

Scheme creates new bindings frequently. In the global environment, we used `define` to create global bindings. Each binding is an association between a name and a value, accessible anywhere, except where the name introduced by a `lambda` form takes precedence over a binding in an enclosing scope. Each `lambda` form creates new bindings for its parameters. `set!` changes the value associated with a name by altering the record in the environment.

After evaluating

```
(define a 3)
(define b 2)
```

the global environment looks like Figure 5–10. The diagram shows two **frames**. A frame is a structure created at procedure application, containing variable bindings and housekeeping information about the call to the procedure. In the diagram, one frame contains bindings for the primitives, and a second contains the new variables we've just defined. The first frame, the *primitive frame*, is created by the Scheme system when it starts; the second, the *user* frame, is the frame of the read-eval-print loop (repl). Together they represent the global environment.

Initially, Scheme creates the global environment frame. Whenever a procedure is applied, Scheme creates a new frame and attaches it to the appropriate frame. How and where a frame connects to other frames depends on where the procedure was created and where (in which frame) the application occurred. Frames and environments form the basis of our new model, the **environment model**, which is a computational model of Scheme based on frames and procedure application. The model explains how bindings are created and how procedures interact.

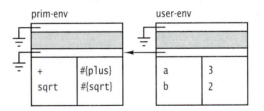

Figure 5-10   The global environment

The diagrams we use to illustrate frames and their connections are an important aspect of the environment model. Like all diagrams, they are not an end in themselves, but are meant to explain and communicate. We call them **snapshots** to emphasize that they describe the state of a computation at a particular point in the computation.

Practical Note

The two global environment frames are the center of a Scheme computation. Ultimately, anything you type into a read-eval-print loop must be defined here. Mutating variables at this level can affect the whole Scheme evaluator. For example, consider evaluating (set! car 'edsel)! Some Scheme systems make it hard for you to mutate variables defined in the primitive frame, for precisely this reason. Though there are legitimate reasons for mutating variables defined in the primitive frame, it is so uncommon that most attempts to do so are probably errors.

The user frame's contents are indeed chosen by you (though library packages such as format might also define things here), and it is therefore much harder to break the system by mutating variables in the user environment frame. A **global variable** is a variable defined in the user frame. Mutating a global variable can affect your whole program. The chances of creating bugs by misusing global variables are so great that most programmers avoid global variable mutation except in special circumstances.

Procedure application creates a frame. A frame has four significant components, as shown in Figure 5-11:

1. a **dynamic link** to a **calling frame** that tells Scheme what to do with the value computed by the present procedure
2. a **resume point** showing what piece of code was responsible for the creation of the frame
3. a **static link** to a **parent frame** that tells Scheme how to get values for names not found in the new frame
4. the bindings, a set of *names* corresponding to the lambda parameters, and a matching set of *values* bound to these names. (These values are the arguments to the procedure.)

The name user-env isn't part of the frame; it allows us to refer to the frame in our discussion.

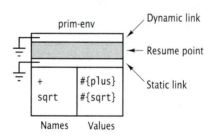

Figure 5-11   A frame

The static and dynamic links of prim-env are null because this frame is the most basic one. The static link of user-env leads back to prim-env. Static links are used to identify variable bindings. If we can't find a name in user-env, we try prim-env. The resume points of both frames are null, which we show as grayed out (resume points aren't arrows, so we can't use our familiar ground symbol).

Applying a procedure creates a new frame that binds the formal parameters to the arguments. Then the body of the procedure is evaluated in the new frame. The parent frame is the environment in which the procedure was created by evaluating a lambda form. In Figure 5-10, there is no parent frame for the primitive frame, so its static link is null.

The environment is now more complex than the global environment we knew before. Now when we say environment, we mean the current frame and all the other frames that are parents of the current frame.

5.4.2   Rethinking Lambda

Consider defining the procedure double:

```
(define double
  (lambda (n)
    (* 2 n)))
```

define adds double to the global environment, as shown in Figure 5-12.

Figure 5-12 introduces another new element of snapshots: procedures. We show a procedure as an ellipse divided into two parts. The left side contains an arrow indicating the parent frame. The right side shows the lambda form that created the procedure, put there to describe the operation of the procedure. From now on, we'll just put the parameter list of the procedure in the right side, to avoid clutter.

Evaluating (double 3) requires searching through the global environment for a binding of double, and then substituting the value (the procedure) in place of it. At this point, the environment model begins to depart from the substitution model.

A procedure application is evaluated by doing the following:

1. creating a new frame connected to the parent frame by the static link and to the caller by the dynamic link
2. evaluating the body of the procedure in the new environment
3. discarding the frame when evaluation is complete
4. using the dynamic link to go back to the calling procedure

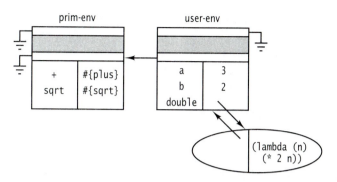

Figure 5-12   Defining `double`

The frame created for the parameters of `double` (Figure 5-13) has both a static link and a dynamic link that point back to the global environment. Why? The static link points to the user frame because `double` was created in the global environment. The static link of each frame points to its parent (except for the primitive frame, which has none). The dynamic link of `double` also connects to the user frame for a different reason. We treat each form evaluated in the repl as originating in the user frame. Because `double` was applied in the user frame, its dynamic link connects to the user frame. The dynamic link is equivalent to the arrow connecting a droid to its caller. `double` is called from the repl and returns its value to the repl for printing. Our convention in naming frames is to write the name of the procedure above the frame, followed by a subscript indexing the number of its occurrence over time, starting from 0.

When Scheme looks for the binding of a name, it looks first in the current frame. If the name isn't bound there, Scheme follows the static link, and thus looks in the parent frame. This process continues recursively up to the primitive frame, where Scheme reports an `Unbound variable` error if the name isn't there. So the value of a name in a form comes from the first occurrence of the name in the chained set of frames from the current frame back to the global environment. Thus, in `double`, the `n` in (`* 2 n`) gets its value from the frame created by the application of `double`. When we speak of the "environment of `double`", we mean the chain of frames that begins with the frame for `double`, and extends through the static links until the primitive frame `prim-env` is reached.

The frame for `double` has a non-null resume point. The frame $double_0$ was created by a call to the procedure `double`. Each frame has a resume point showing what to do after the current computation is complete. We show the exact spot at which control will resume by a small black box. In this example, we have typed in (`double 3`), so the resume point is in the repl, once (`double 3`) completes.

The environment model explains lexical scope.

```
(define n 6)
(define double
    (lambda (n)
        (* 2 n)))
(double 3)
```

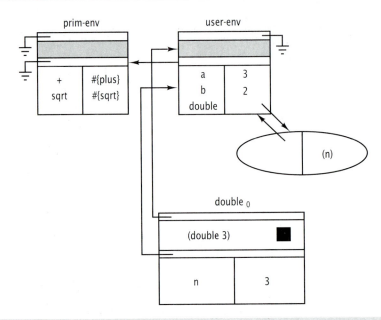

Figure 5-13 Evaluating (double 3)

While Scheme is evaluating the body of double, the n in the global environment does not exist, since the n in the parameters of double is encountered first when searching the chain of frames, as in Figure 5-14. The n in the frame of double **shadows** other occurrences of n in the environment. We stop looking as soon as we reach a definition for a variable, following the chain of static links. Hence the definition of n in user-env isn't seen.

Free names, that is, names not bound in the current frame, must be found somewhere in the chain of frames. Otherwise, the program is in error. Consider:

```
(define pi (add1 2.1416))
(define circumference
  (lambda (diameter)
    (* pi diameter)))
```

Evaluating (circumference 10) produces the snapshot shown in Figure 5-15. Notice that the form (add1 2.1416) does not appear anywhere. We have omitted the primitive frame in this and all following snapshots, replacing it by the name prim-env at the end of the static link from user-env. In this situation, the value for diameter comes from the local frame of the procedure, and that of pi from the global environment.

Variable binding in the environment model completely matches our rules for lexical scoping in Chapter 3. These rules aren't specific to Scheme, and in fact most programming languages use lexical scope. Therefore, the environment model is useful not just for Scheme, but for most other languages.

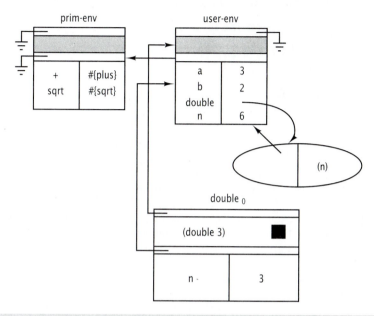

Figure 5-14   Evaluating (`double` 3) with another n

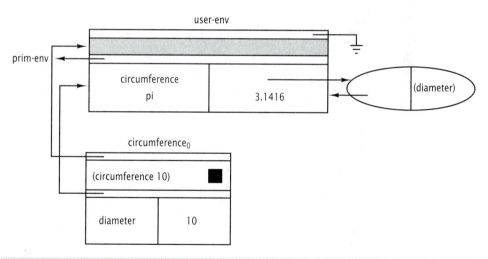

Figure 5-15   Environments and `circumference`

5.4.3   Relations between Procedures

When Scheme evaluates the following code:

```
(define double-and-add3
  (lambda (x)
    (add3 (* 2 x))))
(define add3
  (lambda (x)
    (+ 3 x)))
```

it adds two procedures to the global environment. Let's trace the way frames are created when (double-and-add3 3) is evaluated. First, a frame for double-and-add3 is created and linked, both statically and dynamically, back to the global environment, where double-and-add3 was created and applied. In the new frame, x is bound to 3. Then the body of double-and-add3, (add3 (* 2 x)), is evaluated.

This is another procedure application, so the argument (* 2 x) is evaluated to 6 in the environment of double-and-add3, and another frame is created that is connected statically to the global environment, where add3 was created. This frame's dynamic link connects to double-and-add3, since that's where add3 was applied. In the frame created by add3, x is bound to 6, and then the body of add3 is evaluated.

Note how this works: the two frames of the procedures are separate, as shown in Figure 5-16, so there is no confusion about the name x, which occurs in both procedures.

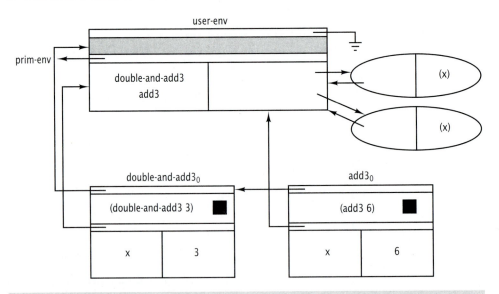

Figure 5-16   Environments of add3 and double-and-add3

5.4.4   Static Scoping Revisited

We explained that bindings created by a `lambda` remain in effect for the body of the `lambda`. How is that represented using the snapshots we have developed? Let's look at an example in Program 5-9, where we use a `let` to create local names.

```
(define score
  (lambda (field-goal free-throws treys)
    (let ((fg (* 2 field-goal))
          (tp (* 3 treys)))
      (+ fg free-throws  tp))))
```
Program 5-9   A `let` creating local names

What does (`score 12 11 4`) compute? Followers of basketball will recognize the three categories of scoring events, worth two, one, and three points respectively. The total scoring for a game is the sum of all three types of scoring events; `treys` is just a cute name for a three-point basket.

Program 5-10 shows a snapshot after expanding the `let` into a `lambda`.

```
(define score
  (lambda (field-goals free-throws treys)
    ((lambda (fg tp)
       (+ fg free-throws tp))
     (* 2 field-goals)
     (* 3 treys))))
```
Program 5-10   Expanded `let` creating local names

Each of the `lambda`s in `score` creates a frame. `score` is defined in the global environment, so its parent is the global environment, as shown in Figure 5-17, while evaluating (`score 12 11 4`), just as `score` is called and before its body is evaluated. The frame $score_0$ binds the three parameters of `score`.

Something new happens with the `lambda` resulting from the `let`. The `let` produces a procedure in the environment of `score`, and that procedure is applied to the two forms that were the right-hand sides of the `let` variables. We call a procedure generated by a `let` or a direct application, like ((`lambda (x) (+ 2 x)) 3`), an **anonymous procedure**. The parent of the anonymous procedure is `score`, where the `let` was evaluated. When we draw the frame for this new procedure, its static and dynamic links both point back to the frame for `score` as in Figure 5-18. Notice that no name is bound to the anonymous procedure.

Compare this with the snapshot in Figure 5-16. The new frame (labeled let_0) of the anonymous procedure in `score` connects via its static link to the frame of `score`, because it was created inside the environment of `score`. Its dynamic link also points there, because it was applied there.

`diff-times-sum` presents a more complicated example, in which the `let` binds a procedure, as shown in Program 5-11 (a).

Before drawing a snapshot, we expand the `let` into a `lambda`, as shown in Program 5-11 (b). When evaluating (`diff-times-sum 2 3`), the snapshot looks like Figure 5-19.

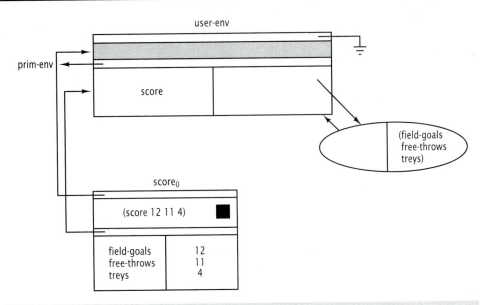

user-env

prim-env

score

(field-goals
free-throws
treys)

$score_0$

(score 12 11 4) ■

field-goals	12
free-throws	11
treys	4

Figure 5-17   Initial environment on application of score

We add only one new procedure to the global environment: diff-times-sum. When (diff-times-sum 2 3) is evaluated, its frame is attached by both its static and dynamic links to the global environment, and a and b are bound to the values 2 and 3. The body of diff-times-sum is a let form. Since a let is a lambda in disguise, Scheme creates a procedure within the frame of diff-times-sum. In this example, this procedure will create the environment that contains the binding of times. The evaluation of that let begins by evaluating the form whose value will be bound to times. Since this procedure is created in the frame of diff-times-sum, its arrow connects the procedure to the frame of diff-times-sum. Then Scheme creates the frame let_0, where times is bound to the procedure just created.

The body of the let is (times (- a b) (+ a b)). This application creates a third frame. By convention we label this frame with the name to which it's bound, as if it were defined in the global environment. The static link of the frame for times points to the frame for diff-times-sum, where times was created, not to the let. The dynamic link of times, however, connects to the let because that is where times was applied. The body of times refers directly only to its arguments. What if the body of times were (* (- c a) (/ d 2.0))? In this form, the name a does not occur in times's environment, but it can be found by following the chain of environments back to the previous environment containing the parameters of diff-times-sum, where a is bound. The complete snapshot appears in Figure 5-20.

We explained static scoping by nesting of lambda forms in Chapter 3. Here we see that it is a direct consequence of the way in which environments are created by procedure application. When a name is encountered in the body of a procedure, the evaluator finds its value by looking in the the frame of the procedure. If the evaluator doesn't find it there, it looks in the chain of frames found by following the static links. Now consider

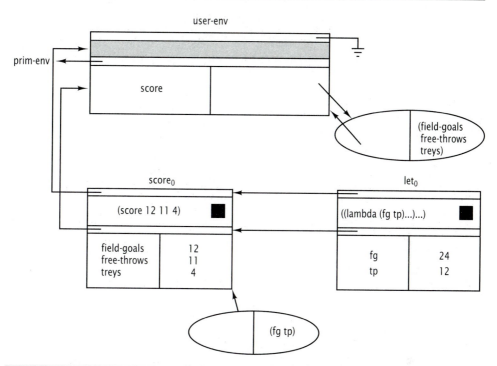

Figure 5-18   Snapshot of `score` and an anonymous procedure

```
(define diff-times-sum
  (lambda (a b)
    (let
     ((times
       (lambda (c d) (* c d))))
     (times (- a b) (+ a b)))))
```

(a) The original procedure

```
(define diff-times-sum
  (lambda (a b)
    ((lambda (times)
       (times (- a b) (+ a b)))
     (lambda (c d) (* c d)))))
```

(b) After expanding lets

Program 5-11   A procedure with an embedded helper

```
(define confusing
  (lambda (a)
    ((lambda (a) (+ a 7)) (+ a 2))))
```

Within the body of confusing, there are two bindings of a. In ((lambda (a) (+ a 7)) (+ a 2)), the last a is free, but it's bound by the parameter of confusing. The a in (+ a 7) is bound by the enclosed lambda, so it is separate.

☞ **Exercise 5-17**

Draw the snapshot for (confusing 4). ❏

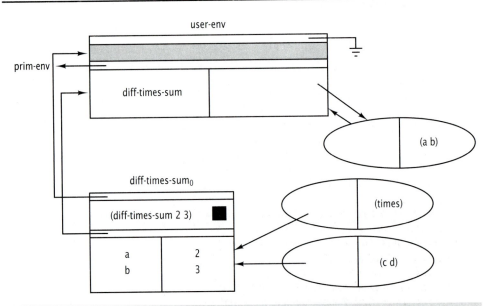

Figure 5-19   Environments and diff-times-sum

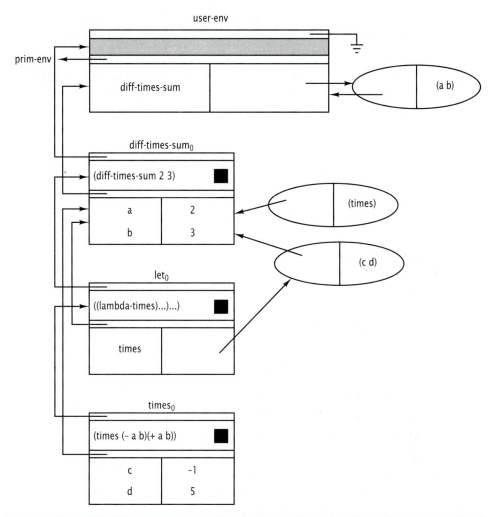

Figure 5-20   Complete environment for `diff-times-sum`

5.4.5   Recursive Procedures

Recall the `fact` procedure, a recursive procedure that computes $n!$:

```
(define fact
  (lambda (n)
    (if (= n 0)
        1
        (* n (fact (- n 1))))))
```

`fact` is defined at top level, so the snapshot during evaluation of `(fact 4)` looks like Figure 5-22.

The frames are not connected to each other because the parent environment of a procedure is found at the frame where the procedure is defined. fact was defined in the global environment, so all the frames that it creates must connect to the global environment. The snapshot shows how the procedures return values to each other through the dynamic links. Compare the snapshot with the corresponding droid diagram in Figure 5-21. The two representations are similar, especially in that the droids connect via arrows that we now know are the dynamic links between frames.

☞ **Exercise 5-18**

Two procedures that call each other are called *mutually recursive*. Here are two mutually recursive procedures:

```
(define alphonce
  (lambda (n)
    (if (<= n 0)
        2
        (+ 1 (gaston (- n 1))))))
(define gaston
  (lambda (n)
    (if (<= n 1)
        1
        (+ 2 (alphonce (- n 2))))))
```

Of course, (gaston 11), (gaston 12) and (gaston 13) all evaluate to 13. Draw the snapshot just after alphonce has called gaston the first time in (gaston 13). ❏

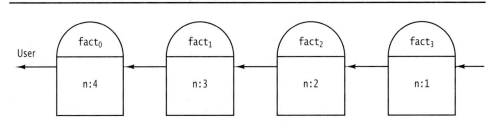

Figure 5-21   Droid diagram for (fact 4)

5.4.6   Procedures as Returned Values

We've described how to construct procedures that return numbers, Booleans, lists and all other Scheme data types as their values, except procedures. We also said that Scheme treats procedures as first-class citizens, so it should not be surprising that we can write a procedure whose value is another procedure. We need the environment model to explain how the resulting procedure can refer to the parameters of the procedure that created it.

As a simple example of a procedure returned as the value of a procedure, we'll write a procedure with one argument, n. Its value is a procedure that adds n to its argument:

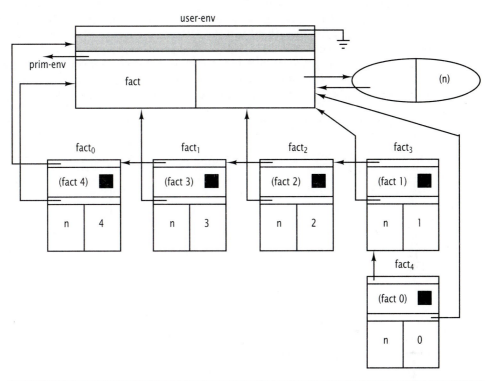

Figure 5-22   Environment during evaluation of (fact 4)

```
(define make-adder
  (lambda (n)
    (lambda (y) (+ n y))))
```

If we bind the result of (make-adder 3) to the name add-three, we can apply it to any argument:

```
(define add-three (make-adder 3))
(add-three 7) ⇒ 10
(add-three 21) ⇒ 24
```

We can also use the result as an anonymous procedure:

```
((make-adder 3) 7) ⇒ 10
```

Even better, we can hand the result of (make-adder k), for some k, to map

```
(map (make-adder 3) '(1 3 5 7)) ⇒ (4 6 8 10)
(map (make-adder 6) '(1 4 9 25)) ⇒ (7 10 15 31)
```

We call a procedure that produces another procedure as its result a **factory**. A factory generalizes procedures—we write a factory to create a large set of procedures that differ only in some small way, which we specify by the arguments to the factory. Here we are generating adder procedures. How can a procedure result refer to the arguments of its factory? The Rules defines the result of a lambda form as a procedure that is the same as the lambda form. There is no place in the procedure, as defined under The Rules, to record the arguments to its creator. The environment model explains make-adder easily.

When make-adder is applied to 3, Scheme creates a frame, make-adder_0, to bind n to 3. When the lambda form is evaluated, the resulting procedure's parent frame is make-adder_0, as shown in Figure 5-23.

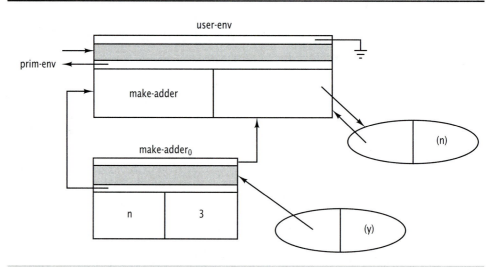

Figure 5-23   Creating the result of (make-adder 3)

Once add-three is bound to the resulting procedure, we can apply it. Figure 5-24 shows the snapshot for (add-three 6), which includes something unusual. The dynamic link from frame add-three_0 points to user-env, bypassing frame make-adder_0, but the static link connects add-three_0 to make-adder_0. The make-adder_0 frame is **captured** by the procedure add-three, that is, the frame remains after the procedure has returned and serves only to record bindings that are accessible to add-three. The make-adder_0 frame is now merely a data structure that holds bindings; it is not connected via a dynamic link to any frame.

Previously we said that Scheme discards the frame when evaluation is complete, but now we must amend that. Scheme keeps the frame if a procedure captures it. A procedure returned as a value captures all frames between it and the user frame (i.e., on the chain of frames from the procedure to the user frame). During the evaluation of the body of add-three; that is, (+ x n), the bindings of the three names in that expression come from three different frames: + from the primitive frame, n from the frame left behind by make-adder, and x from the local frame of add-three.

Let's return to the topic of using procedures as returned values. We can make new procedures with procedural building blocks; thus, the input to a factory can be a procedure. The resulting procedure can use the procedural argument in a variety of ways. make-adder had a number argument. We could generalize make-adder by writing make-binary, which takes two arguments—a procedure that implements a

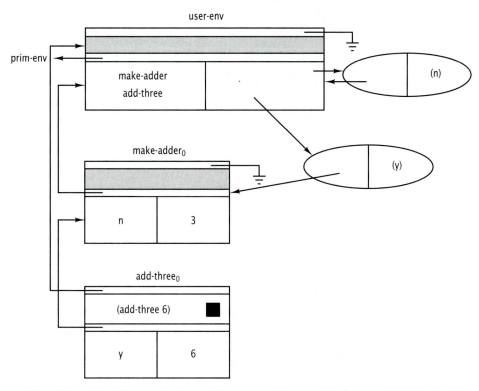

Figure 5-24   Snapshot of `(add-three 6)`

numerical binary operator, and a number—and returns a procedure with one numerical parameter. Here's an example:

```
(define make-binary
  (lambda (op n)
    (lambda (m)
      (op m n))))
```

We can write a procedure that multiplies its argument by 2 as `(make-binary * 2)`. We now have three ways to write a procedure to add 3 to its arguments.

```
(define add-three
  (lambda (x) (+ x 3)))
(define add-three (make-adder 3))
(define add-three (make-binary + 3))
```

`make-binary` generalizes `make-adder` in the simplest way, by using one procedural parameter.

Assume that we have a generalized function-graphing system. We can write a procedure `plot-function` for drawing any function described by a procedure. `plot-function` takes three arguments: `from-x`, `to-x`, and a function to plot. If we want to graph many mathematical functions, we could implement each one by writing a

Scheme procedure that would compute it. For example, for $f(x) = 2x + 7$ we'd write (define f (lambda (x) (+ (* 2 x) 7))). Our work would be easier, though, if we could build functions from more elementary functions, for example, if we could add the functions $g(x) = 2x$ and $h(x) = 7$ to get $f(x)$, instead of creating each from scratch.

Let's write a procedure, combine, that takes three arguments: a binary operator (a procedure that takes two numbers and returns one number), and two functions, each a procedure with one argument. We'll ignore for now the distinction between a mathematical function and the procedure that implements it, and refer to such procedures as *functions*. We'll use combine to generate a whole set of possible functions; it returns a procedure that implements the function f(x) op g(x).

```
(define combine
   (lambda (op f g)
      (lambda (x)
         (op (f x) (g x)))))
```

For example, we can combine a procedure to implement $x + 2$ and a procedure to implement $x + 3$ to get one that implements $2x + 5$:

```
((combine + (make-adder 3) (make-adder 2)) 9) ⇒  23
((combine + (make-adder 5) add1) 9) ⇒  24
((combine + - +) 9) ⇒  0
((combine + add1 sub1) 9) ⇒  18
```

To plot the difference of two functions f and g over the range 1 to 5, we need only write

```
(plot-function 1 5 (combine - f g))
```

All of combine's arguments are procedures. Scheme makes writing procedures like combine easy.[10] By treating procedures as first-class values, Scheme opens up a whole new way of computing, without abandoning many of the nice features, like block structure, found in other programming languages.

Let's return to combine. We can use combine to construct many other combinations of functions, such as the maximum or minimum of two functions, or the sum, product, or quotient, just by varying the binary operation argument:

```
minimum: (combine min f g)
product: (combine * f g)
quotient: (combine / f g)
```

To write more complicated expressions involving several combinations of functions, we supply the result of a combination (a procedure) as one of the arguments to combine. To plot the function $h(x) \times (f(x) + g(x))$, we write

```
(plot-function 1 5
   (combine * h (combine + f g)))
```

The expression (combine + f g) returns a procedure that evaluates $(f(x) + g(x))$, which is then combined with h to get their product.

---

[10] On-the-fly construction of procedures is only possible in languages such as Lisp and Scheme. Popular languages such as BASIC, C, or Pascal lack this flexibility.

Can we describe, for example, the function $2f(x)+g(x)$? (See Exercise 6-1.)

☞ **Exercise 5-19**

Write `k-function`, a procedure with one argument, k, a number, so that (`combine * f` `(k-function k))` produces a procedure of one argument, x, giving the value of $kf(x)$. ❑

☞ **Exercise 5-20**

Assuming we have function `k-function`, as described in Exercise 5-19, write the expressions using `combine` that give the functions $3f(x) - 2g(x)$ and $4f(x) \times g(x)$. ❑

☞ **Exercise 5-21**

Just as we can compose functions, we can compose procedures, provided we make sure that the data types and numbers of arguments match. Assuming that f and g are numerical procedures with one numerical argument, write `compose` so that (`(compose f g) x`) implements $f(g(x))$. ❑

☞ **Exercise 5-22**

`compose` comes in handy when we have a collection of procedures for processing some data type, such as strings, and want to create a new procedure easily out of the procedural building blocks. Let's say we have two procedures, `string-upcase` and `no-spaces`, that change a string to uppercase and remove space characters from a string, respectively.

```
(string-upcase "a b cd e f") ⇒ "A B CD E F"
(no-spaces "A B CD E F") ⇒ "ABCDEF"
```

Use `compose` to create `upcase-no-spaces`, a procedure that does both of these operations:

```
(upcase-no-spaces "a b cd e f") ⇒ "ABCDEF"
```

❑

When we write a procedure that returns a procedure as its value, we are using an important and special aspect of Scheme. Few languages treat procedures as returned values, just like any other value. This flexibility in Scheme leads to interesting programming techniques that are unavailable in many other languages.

5.4.7   Procedures with State

Now that we understand how procedures can capture frames, we see how the captured frames let us write procedures that have state. Consider writing `squares`, a procedure to generate a sequence of values, such as the set of squares of integers. It's well known that $n^2 = (n-1)^2 + (2n+1)$. That is, we generate the sequence of squares by starting at 0 and then adding to the last square successive odd numbers. Here's how `squares` acts:

```
(squares) ⇒ 1
(squares) ⇒ 4
(squares) ⇒ 9
```

`squares` must maintain state, because it has no input, and the value it returns changes on each application. It must keep track of two values: the current odd number and the previous square, so we write a `let` form enclosing the `lambda` to hold these values. The code for `squares` appears in Program 5-12.

squares needs no arguments, since its state is in the bindings of the enclosing `let`. The first time squares is called, it assigns 1 to sum and 3 to n. Its value is 1. The next time it's called, it mutates sum to 4, n to 5, and returns 4. Figure 5-25 shows the bindings in the `let` around squares.

```
(define squares
  (let ((n 1)
        (sum 0))
    (lambda ()
      (set! sum (+ sum n))
      (set! n (+ 2 n))
      sum)))
```
Program 5-12   Computing squares by sums of odd numbers

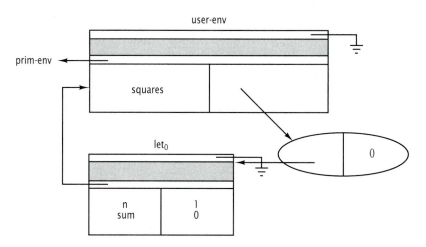

Figure 5-25   Snapshot for `squares`

The frame let_0 is *not* discarded after squares is created. To function properly, squares needs access to the binding in that frame; squares has *captured* the frame created by the `let`. We can also write squares as the result of a procedure, as shown in Program 5-13. We write squares as (sums 1 0). The frames are exactly the same, with the exception that the let_0 frame is now labeled $sums_0$.

The structure of the frames during evaluation of both versions of squares shows an important pattern: Procedures with state must connect to a frame before the frame created by the procedure's application. The procedure captures the preceding frame. It doesn't matter whether the frame comes from the procedure whose body returned the procedure with state, or whether it comes from a `let` enclosing a `lambda`, as in our first version of square. We describe the pattern where the `let` encloses the `lambda` as let **over** `lambda`. When a procedure returns a procedure, the

```
(define sums
  (lambda (n sum)
    (lambda ()
      (set! sum (+ sum n))
      (set! n (+ 2 n))
      sum)))
```

Program 5-13   A procedure to create squares

pattern is lambda **over** lambda. Both result in the same structure of frames, since the let turns into a lambda.

One useful application of procedures with state is the generation of random numbers. In several exercises, we've seen how random numbers are useful for such tasks as playing games. In Chapter 9, we'll use random numbers to simulate a ticket office. What is a random number? Is 7 a random number? How about 42? It doesn't make sense to say that a number by itself is random, but it does make sense to say that the sequence 7, 32, 81, 58, 67, 46, ... appears to be random. We say that a sequence is **random** if its elements can't be predicted from the previous ones. Besides game-playing and simulation, random numbers are useful in polls (pollsters want to make sure they get a random sample of the public), and several advanced mathematical techniques.

A typical computer can't easily generate genuinely random numbers. Everything a computer does is deterministic, which by definition means not random. Fortunately, statisticians have developed the concept of pseudorandomness. If a sequence appears to be random (using various statistical techniques), but is generated by an algorithm, we say it is **pseudorandom**.

One of the earliest pseudorandom number generators employs the *linear congruence method* developed by D. Lehmer in 1951. We start with a value known as a **seed**, x, or starting value for the sequence. Each time, we generate a new value by computing $(ax + 1) \bmod n$, where a is a constant that is chosen with great care, and n is a value specified by the user. The result is a pseudorandom value between 0 and $n - 1$. The linear congruence method is easy to implement in Scheme, as Program 5-14 shows.

```
(define random-const 31415821)
(define random-integer
  (lambda (n seed)
    (remainder (add1 (* random-const seed)) n)))
```

Program 5-14   Generating random numbers

Each time random-integer is called, it is given as arguments the value of n and the old seed. Its return value is used as the seed for the next call. The need to retain the seed makes this version clumsy to use.

Program 5-15 shows a better way. In this version, we call random-integer to get back a procedure whose environment has captured the variable seed. Each time this procedure is called, it mutates seed and returns the appropriate value. Life is easier for the user, and accidental damage to the seed (e.g., passing the wrong value to the first version) is avoided.

```
(define random-const 31415821)
(define random-integer
  (lambda (seed)
    (lambda (n)
      (set! seed
        (remainder (add1 (* random-const seed)) n))
      seed)))
```

Program 5-15   Generating random numbers with retained state

```
(define r (random-integer 19322143))
r ⇒  #<procedure>
(r 1000) ⇒  404
(r 1000) ⇒  685
(r 1000) ⇒  386
(r 1000) ⇒  907
```

We cannot conclude a discussion of random number generators without a note of caution. Many people have written random number generators, and many of them have been anything but random. The computer scientist Donald Knuth once wrote a random number generator that took most of a page to express in pseudocode. Unfortunately, with the first seed that he tried, it began to repeat itself after seven iterations! Knuth warns, "Random numbers should not be generated with a method chosen at random".

☞ **Exercise 5-23**

Design remember, a procedure that accepts a number as input and then returns the sum of the current argument and its previous argument. To do this, remember must store its last input.

```
(remember 1) ⇒  "First time"
(remember 2) ⇒  3
(remember 3) ⇒  5
(remember 4) ⇒  7
```

Write remember. ❑

5.5   Definitions and modules

In the beginning and in the end the only decent
Definition is tautology: man is man,
Woman woman, and tree tree.
                              — Louis MacNeice, *Plain Speaking*

The environment model gives us a good way to understand how define and letrec forms work. Analyzing these forms will help us explore the environment model further, and will also shed some light on define and letrec.

5.5.1 Recursive Definitions

Our examples in the previous section made frequent use of define. From those examples, you should see that define works as follows:

1. Evaluate the *value* argument.
2. Place the resulting value into the global environment.

Step 2 is an act of mutation. In fact, definitions can be done more than once, in which case the second and subsequent definitions act as a set!. This feature is ugly from a theoretical viewpoint, but necessary from a practical point of view. Most Scheme systems allow the user to edit a file containing definitions and load it into the system several times (the so-called "edit-load-test" cycle that you are probably accustomed to). Preventing the user from redefining procedures would be an intolerable restriction.

From the snapshots, you will notice that procedures give rise to a circular structure: there is an arrow in the variable binding to the procedure, and the procedure's environment part contains an arrow back to the frame in which it was created. Just as circular list structures are created via mutation, circular environment/procedure structures also require mutation. The structure being created can't refer to itself, since it isn't yet created. You must change it after it's created. This is essentially the problem that letrec remedies.

Program 5-16 shows the factorial procedure in tail-recursive form, using a helper procedure. This works quite well at top level, since all names are defined in the global environment. We got burned when we embedded fact-helper using a let in Program 5-17. This didn't work. Let's first look at the expanded form using lambda in Program 5-18.

```
(define fact
  (lambda (n)
    (fact-helper n 0 1)))
(define fact-helper
  (lambda (n count acc)
    (if (= count n)
        acc
        (fact-helper
          n (add1 count) (* (add1 count) acc)))))
```

Program 5-16   Tail-recursive fact with a helper

Consider what happens while evaluating (fact 4), just as Scheme begins the first application of fact-helper. Figure 5-26 presents the snapshot. which shows why using let doesn't work: the name fact-helper is not bound on the chain of frames coming from the bottom frame where count and acc are bound. An error occurs because Scheme can't find the binding of fact-helper.

What happens in the snapshot when we do the right thing and use letrec, as shown in Program 5-19 (a)? Let's first look at the expanded form in Program 5-19 (b). Figure 5-27 shows the snapshot corresponding to this new, expanded form just after fact-helper has been bound to #f. Immediately after this, the let creates a new frame binding fact-helper-new. This new procedure is created in the environment of the let binding fact-helper, so its parent is the frame binding

```
(define fact
  (lambda (n)
    (let
      ((fact-helper
         (lambda (count acc)
           (if (= count n)
             acc
             (fact-helper
               (add1 count)
               (* (add1 count) acc))))))
      (fact-helper 0 1))))
```

Program 5-17   A helper embedded with `let`

```
(define fact
  (lambda (n)
    ( (lambda (fact-helper) (fact-helper 0 1))
      (lambda (count acc)
        (if (= count n)
          acc
          (fact-helper
            (add1 count)
            (* (add1 count) acc)))))))
```

Program 5-18   Expanded helper

`fact-helper`. The full snapshot is shown in Figure 5-28 at the first application of `fact-helper`.

What about `let*`? Consider the following:

```
(let*
  ((i 5)
   (j (add1 i))
   (k (* j 3)))
  k)
```

Any `let*` form can be rewritten as a nest of `let` forms:

```
(let
  ((i 5))
  (let
    ((j (add1 i)))
    (let
      ((k (* j 3)))
      k)))
```

Figure 5-29 shows what the snapshot for the `let*` looks like. So that each successive binding can refer to the previous bindings, Scheme must create a series of frames, each connected to the previous one.

☞ **Exercise 5-24**

Where will the other frames created by the applications of `fact-helper` lie in the snapshot of Figure 5-28? ❏

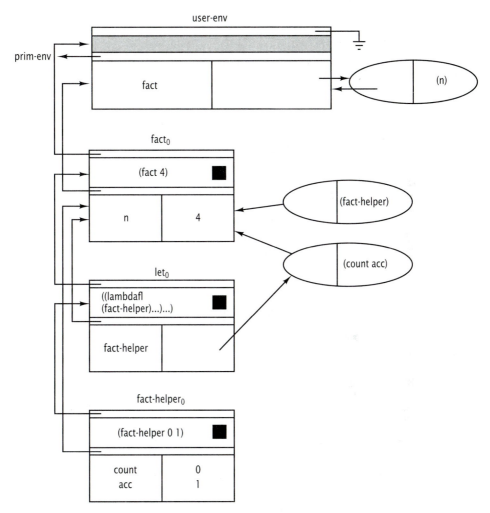

Figure 5-26 Environment during (fact 4) using let

5.5.2 Modules and the Environment Model

The environment model explains how modules are implemented. Recall that modules collect a set of procedures and variables into a package from which only a portion of the names are exported to the outside world of the global environment. How is this done? The challenge is to hide names from the global environment, yet use them in the definitions. We will use our factorial procedure, implemented in a module, to explain how module meets this challenge.

There are two components to a module definition: the exported names and the definitions (Program 5–20 (a)). We can see the definitions as a collection of name-value pairings, much like the bindings in a let. The module form conveniently lets us use the define syntax.

```
(define fact
  (lambda (n)
    (letrec ((fact-helper
               (lambda (count acc)
                 (if (= count n)
                     acc
                     (fact-helper
                       (add1 count)
                       (* (add1 count) acc))))))
       (fact-helper 0 1))))
```

(a) With letrec

```
(define fact
  (lambda (n)
    (let ((fact-helper #f))
      (let ((fact-helper-new
              (lambda (count acc)
                (if (= count n)
                    acc
                    (fact-helper
                      (add1 count)
                      (* (add1 count) acc))))))
        (set! fact-helper fact-helper-new)
        (fact-helper 0 1)))))
```

(b) After expanding letrec

Program 5-19   Procedure fact with letrec

When module processes its arguments, it creates a set of definitions for the exported names, initially binding the names to #f. These definitions occur in the global environment. In this case, fact is bound to #f. The module can use letrec to create the definitions given in the module.

The values of the definitions that are being exported to the global environment must be transported back to the names defined in the first step. Mutation must occur. Moreover, any definitions hidden within the module, whether of procedures or other values, are state that must be kept by the module. Within the innermost frame created by the letrec, the names exported by the module appear as the programmer defined them. The names must also appear the same to the global environment. It would make no sense, though, to write (set! fact fact) within the letrec. because only the local binding would be mutated.

The trick that makes this work is that module places a let form between the global environment and the inner letrec to create artificial names that Scheme can generate, initially bound to #f. Program 5-20 (b) shows the code equivalent of the module. (This code is not actually what is generated by module, but it generates frames that have the same relations as those generated by the actual code.)

The body of the letrec in the module code then mutates the binding of the generated name, for example, *g0*, to the value of the inner binding: (set! *g0* fact). Then, within the let, it mutates the outer binding to the inner binding: (set! fact *g0*).

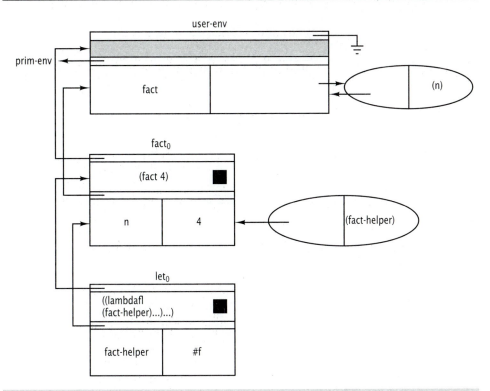

Figure 5-27   Environment during `(fact 4)` using `letrec`

Figure 5-30 shows the snapshot after the `factor` module has been defined. Note how `fact` as defined can refer to `fact-helper`, which is hidden in the module. The binding for `*g0*` remains, as well as the bindings of `f-new`, `f-h-new`, and `fact-helper`, but none of these bindings is available in the global environment.

Another example shows how the state retained by a module can itself be explicitly mutated. What if we only want to have one random number generator? Program 5-21 implements a module whose internal state includes the definitions of the two exported procedures, the random constant, and the seed. The value of `seed` is mutated each time `random-integer` is applied.

☞ **Exercise 5-25**

Draw the snapshot for `randoms` after

```
(set-random-seed! 12091)
(random-integer 102)  ⇒  62
```

❏

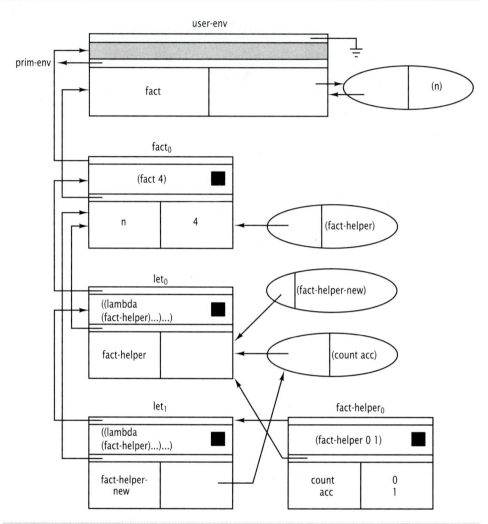

Figure 5-28   Final environment during (fact 4) using `letrec`

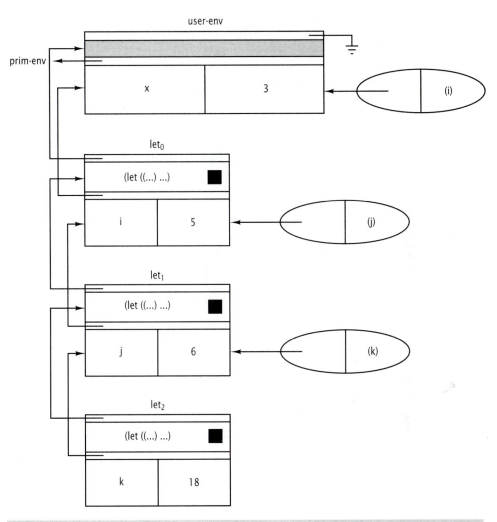

Figure 5-29   Environment of `let*`

```
(module factor
  (export fact)
  (define fact
    (lambda (n)
      (fact-helper n 1)))
  (define fact-helper
    (lambda (n acc)
      (if (= 0 n)
          acc
          (fact-helper (sub1 n) (* n acc))))))
```

(a) Using <code>module</code>

```
(begin
  (define fact #f)
  (let ((*g0* #f))
    (letrec
      ((fact
         (lambda (n) (fact-helper n 1)))
       (fact-helper
         (lambda (n acc)
           (if (= 0 n) acc (fact-helper (sub1 n) (* n acc))))))
      (set! *g0* fact))
    (set! fact *g0*))
```

(b) After expanding <code>module</code>

Program 5-20   A factorial module

```
(module randoms
  (export random-integer set-random-seed!)
  (define random-const 31415821)
  (define seed 0)
  (define set-random-seed!
    (lambda (s)
      (set! seed s)))
  (define random-integer
    (lambda (n)
      (set! seed
        (remainder (add1 (* random-const seed)) n))
      seed)))
```

Program 5-21   A module for random integers

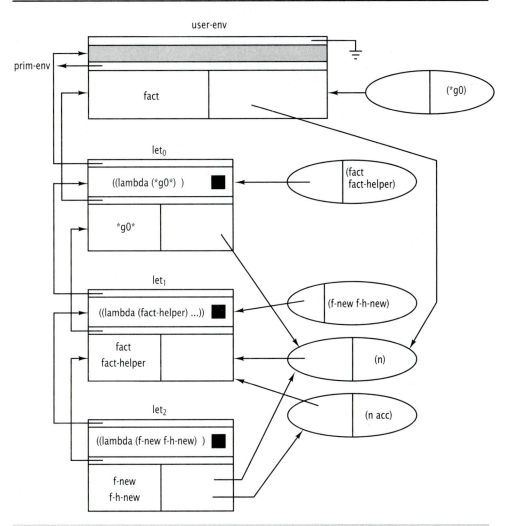

Figure 5–30　　Snapshot of `factor` module

Case Study: An Airline Reservation System

We've seen how an airline can build a computer system to manage its route database, and how that database can be used to answer a variety of questions. We also saw that many of the "obvious" algorithms for answering these questions are useless because of their exponential complexity.

Once an airline establishes flights between cities, the next step is to sell seats on those flights. It is generally *not* desirable to sell the same seat to two passengers. There are many complexities in this problem. Airlines don't just sell their own seats: travel agents and other airlines also make reservations. In addition, people who make airline reservations also make reservations for hotel and car rentals. A good reservation system is very important to an airline. One of the first on-line systems was American Airlines' SABRE system, which went into operation in the early 1960s. Our example system will be overly simplified. We want to be able to book passengers on flights, and get a list of the passengers on a flight.

One of the most important tasks confronting the designer of a reservation system is the development of a **user interface**, which determines how the user interacts with the system. We will limit our example to the simple text interface provided by read. You are probably familiar with Graphical User Interface environments such as Windows and the Macintosh. Such complex systems are not a standard part of Scheme. We could build a complex text interface, with lots of help and interaction; however, fancy interfaces aren't always the right choice.

The users of our system are typically reservations clerks who are not necessarily fast typists. Therefore we don't want to have long commands or require clerks to type large amounts of information. Though the clerks may not know much about computers, they *do* know a great deal about their job. Some reservations tasks are quite complicated, involving complex sequences of connecting flights and discounted fares. Reservation clerks are often under great pressure to get tasks done as quickly as possible.

Accordingly, we should build a system that allows tasks to be done with a minimum of typing. Cryptic codes can help get the task done more quickly, but the system should help clerks to identify the less common codes and commands that they might not remember.

Here's a simple dialog with our system:

```
> (reservations-agent)
Command? help
Invalid command; please try again (enter H for help).
Command? h
Available commands:
   R flt date name
   M flt date
   Q
   H
```

Our on-line help is somewhat primitive. There are four commands: Reserve a flight for a passenger, display the passenger Manifest (the list of passengers on a particular flight), Quit, and display Help.

```
Command? r 77 Jul7 "Frodo Baggins"
Please select a craft for flight (77 . jul7)
```

```
? b-77
Passenger manifest for flight 77, date jul7, craft b-77
  Seat 3B, passenger Frodo Baggins
End of manifest
```

We now make a reservation for Frodo Baggins. Since passengers might make reservations as much as a year in advance, we might not yet have any passengers for a particular flight on a particular day. On the first reservation for a new flight, the program prompts the clerk for the type of craft to be used (different craft have different seating arrangements); we've selected a B-77.

```
Command? r 77 Jul7 "Peregrin Took"
Passenger manifest for flight 77, date jul7, craft b-77
  Seat 3A, passenger Peregrin Took
End of manifest
Command? r 77 Jul7 "Meriadoc Brandybuck"
Passenger manifest for flight 77, date jul7, craft b-77
  Seat 2B, passenger Meriadoc Brandybuck
End of manifest
```

Frodo's friends Peregrin and Meriadoc make reservations on the same flight. No craft is allocated.

```
Command? r 77 Jul9 "Sauron"
Please select a craft for flight (77 . jul9).
? dc-0
Passenger manifest for flight 77, date jul9, craft dc-0
  Seat 2B, passenger Sauron
End of manifest
```

Sauron makes a reservation for the same flight, but on a different day. Again a plane must be allocated: this time, we choose a DC-0.

```
Command? m 77 Jul9
Passenger manifest for flight 77, date jul9, craft dc-0
 Seat 2B, passenger Sauron
 Seat 2A, passenger <none>
 Seat 1B, passenger <none>
 Seat 1A, passenger <none>
End of manifest
Command? m 77 Jul7
Passenger manifest for flight 77, date jul7, craft b-77
 Seat 3B, passenger Frodo Baggins
 Seat 3A, passenger Peregrin Took
 Seat 2B, passenger Meriadoc Brandybuck
 Seat 2A, passenger <none>
 Seat 1B, passenger <none>
 Seat 1A, passenger <none>
End of manifest
Command? q
End of session.
```

We now display the manifests for the two flights and log out.

One interesting design question is why we didn't ask first whether there are any free seats, and then reserve one separately. We could do this in our example system, but it would be a disaster in a real reservation system. Many clerks access the same manifests in a real system, and may attempt to make reservations at the same time. Thus, the free-seat count might be inaccurate as different clerks attempt to make reservations simultaneously. Doing inquiry and reservation at the same time assures us that the reservation has been made. If the passenger doesn't really want the reservation, it can easily be canceled. An airline reservation system is a classic example of **concurrency**, the simultaneous performance of several tasks. Concurrent systems require us to perform some actions as **indivisible tasks** (one action is processed completely before working on another). The design of concurrent systems is an area of major interest in computer science.

Our "no-nonsense" user interface is designed to support the needs of the clerks. There is little typing, and little chatter to clutter up the screen. When the clerk makes a mistake, a brief message is displayed, but no on-line help is shown unless the clerk asks for it.

We can now look at the design of the program. There are four modules:

- the *craft inventory* manager (Program 5-22), which keeps track of the available types of planes, and their seating arrangements
- a *manifest ADT*, which represents the reservations on a particular flight on a particular day
- a *reservation manager*, which keeps track of the collection of manifests, and retrieves the manifest for a particular flight
- a *user interface*, which centralizes most of the input and output between the user and the system

```
(module inventory
 (export craft-inventory add-craft find-craft)
 (define craft-inventory (make-dictionary))

 (define add-craft
   (lambda (kind seating)
     (dictionary-insert! craft-inventory kind seating)))
 (define find-craft
   (lambda (kind)
     (dictionary-search craft-inventory kind)))
 ) ;;; end of module
(add-craft 'B-77 '("1A" "1B" "2A" "2B" "3A" "3B"))
(add-craft 'DC-0 '("1A" "1B" "2A" "2B"))
```

Program 5-22   Airline reservation: the craft inventory

The craft inventory module keeps track of the various aircraft used by the airline. For each type of plane, the inventory keeps a list of the seating arrangements. (We have assumed that all planes of each type have the same seating arrangement; this is not true in a real airline.) Our two airplane models have somewhat limited seating!

For each flight on a given day, an airline builds a *passenger manifest*, showing the passengers reserved on this flight, so we need an ADT to represent manifests.

Our ADT supports three operations: we can make a new manifest, we can display a manifest, and we can add a passenger to the manifest, as shown in Program 5-23. (Our system chooses the passenger's seat because it's simple to program, but that wouldn't be acceptable in a real system!)

```
(module manifest
  (export make-manifest manifest-display manifest-add-passenger)
  (define make-manifest
    (lambda (flight date craft-name)
      (let ((seating (make-dictionary)))
        (map
         (lambda (seat)
           (dictionary-insert! seating seat #f))
         (find-craft craft-name))
        (list flight date craft-name seating))))
  (define manifest-display
    (lambda (manifest passenger)
      (format
       #t
       "Passenger manifest for flight ~a, date ~a, craft ~a~%
       (list-ref manifest 0)
       (list-ref manifest 1)
       (list-ref manifest 2))
      (dictionary-for-each
       (list-ref manifest 3)
       (lambda (seat)
         (if (or (eqv? passenger #t)
                 (equal? passenger (cdr seat)))
             (format #t " Seat ~a, passenger ~a~%"
               (car seat) (if (cdr seat) (cdr seat) "<none>")))))
      (format #t "End of manifest~%")))
  (define manifest-add-passenger
    (lambda (manifest passenger)
      (let ((seated #f)
            (seats (list-ref manifest 3)))
        (dictionary-for-each
         seats
         (lambda (seat)
           (if (not seated)
               (if (not (cdr seat))
                   (begin
                     (dictionary-insert! seats (car seat) passenger)
                     (set! seated #t))))))
        seated)))
) ;;; end of module
```

Program 5-23   Airline reservation system: manifests

`manifest-display` gives us two choices: we can display the entire manifest (use #t for the passenger), or the seating arrangement for a particular passenger.

Note our use of dictionaries in both of the modules we've looked at. A small set of extremely useful data structures is used repeatedly. The tools of computing include many such important data structures. We will encounter more of these structures as we study more applications, especially in Chapter 9.

The reservations manager is responsible for retrieving the manifest for a given flight and day and making the reservation, as shown in Program 5-24. If there is already a manifest for this flight, it is mutated accordingly; if not, a new flight must be created. Creating a flight isn't trivial, because we must decide which plane to use. It should not be the job of a reservations manager to do this. Even though our method of creating flights is pretty straightforward, we've made it a separate procedure.

```
(module reservation-manager
  (export find-manifest reserve)
  (define reservations (make-dictionary))
  (define add-manifest
    (lambda (flight date craft-name)
      (dictionary-insert! reservations (cons flight date)
                          (make-manifest flight date craft-name))))
  (define find-manifest
    (lambda (flight date)
      (let ((key (cons flight date)))
        (if (not (dictionary-found? reservations key))
            (add-manifest flight date
                          (allocate-craft key)))
        (dictionary-search reservations key))))
  (define reserve
    (lambda (flight date passenger)
      (let ((m (find-manifest flight date)))
        (manifest-add-passenger m passenger))))
) ;;; end of module
```

Program 5-24   Airline reservation system: reservation management

The user interface module does most of the interaction between the user and the system (the only exception is the displaying of manifests). By centralizing this code, shown in Program 5-25, we achieve two benefits. First, we avoid cluttering up our other modules with input/output, which can easily obscure what we're trying to do in those modules. Second, we make the user interface easy to change. Many reasons to change user interfaces might arise, including the need to add new commands and to allow clerks to use languages other than English. Again, it is wise to put the user interface into one module.

```
(module airline-user-interface
  (export reservations-agent allocate-craft)
  (define reservations-agent
    (lambda ()
      (display "Command? ")
      (let ((val (read)))
        (if (eqv? val 'R)
          (let* ((flight (read))
                 (date (read))
                 (passenger (read)))
            (reserve flight date passenger)
            (manifest-display
             (find-manifest flight date) passenger)
            (reservations-agent))
          (if (eqv? val 'M)
            (let* ((flight (read))
                   (date (read)))
              (manifest-display
               (find-manifest flight date) #t)
              (reservations-agent)))
            (if (eqv? val 'Q)
              (display "End of session.~%"))
              (if (eqv? val 'H)
                (begin
                  (display "Available commands: ~%")
                  (display "   R flt date name~%")
                  (display "   M flt date~%")
                  (display "   Q~%")
                  (display "   H~%")
                  (reservations-agent))
                (begin
                (display
"Invalid command; please try again (enter H for help).~%")
                (reservations-agent)))))))
  (define allocate-craft
    (lambda (key)
      (format #t "Please select a craft for flight ~a.~%? " key)
      (read)))
) ;;; end of module
```

Program 5-25   Airline reservation system: user interface

Summary

In this chapter, we've seen how mutation allows us to write programs that change data over time. First with boxes, then with pairs, and finally with variables, we saw how mutation allows us to model state. Variable mutation required us to rethink the concept of what a variable was. This led to the environment model, which gave us a way to specify what happens with any Scheme computation. We elaborated the environment model with snapshots: diagrams of the current state of the frames created by procedure application to record bindings and specify control relations among procedure applications.

Further Readings

The following books all have extensive exercises on using list and variable mutation: George Springer and Daniel P. Friedman, *Scheme and the Art of Programming*, (McGraw Hill, 1990); Michael Eisenberg, *Programming in Scheme*, (Scientific Press, 1988); and Harold Abelson and Gerald Jay Sussman, with Julie Sussman, *Structure and Interpretation of Computer Programs*, (McGraw-Hill, 1985). Our discussion of snapshots was inspired by Abelson, Sussman and Sussman, but differs significantly from theirs.

Key Words

Here are the *key words* introduced in this chapter. Make sure you understand what each one means.

alist	equivalent	pseudorandom
anonymous procedure	factory	sequence
assignment	free name	random sequence
association list	frame	reference arguments
atomic	global variable	resume point
box	immutable	seed
calling frame	indivisible task	shadowing
captured frame	key	share storage
circular list	lambda over lambda	snapshot
composite	let over lambda	state
concurrent tasks	mutable	static link
database design	mutation	swap
destructive	mutator	systems analysis
dynamic link	name	temporary variable
environment	parent frame	user interface
environment model	portable	variable

Scheme Features Introduced in This Chapter

Primitive Procedures

```
box-ref      box-set!      eqv?        make-box
set-car!     set-cdr!
```

Special Forms

set!

Cumulative List of Data Types

Name	Constructor	Accessors	Predicate
Boolean	—	—	boolean?
box	make-box	box-ref	box-set!
character	integer->char	char->integer	char?
list	list	car, cdr	list?
number	—	—	number?
pair	cons	car, cdr	pair?
procedure	lambda	—	procedure?
string	string	string-ref	string?
symbol	string->symbol	—	symbol?
void	void	—	void?

Problems

1. Some old-fashioned light switches have two buttons, labeled ON and OFF. Pressing the ON button switches the light on if it was off, but has no effect otherwise. The OFF button is similar. Write a procedure (switch x) that simulates such a switch. You'll need a global variable (a box) to contain the state.

2. Many houses have more than one switch that controls the same light. Flipping any of the switches turns the light on if it was off, and off if it was on. (Such systems are often used on stairs, with one switch at the top and one at the bottom.) Write a procedure named flip that models such a switch. You'll need a global variable (a box) to contain the state.

3. Write a procedure that accepts as an argument a list, x, each of whose items is a number, and adds 1 to each item of the list, mutating the list.

4. Write a procedure that displays a circular list in some format of your choice.

5. Draw a snapshot showing how the following form is evaluated:
```
(let
  ((a 3))
  (let
    ((foo (lambda (x) (* x a))))
    (foo 7)))
```

6. Draw the snapshot after evaluating the following forms:
```
(define make-thing
  (lambda (sort)
    (lambda (in1 in2)
      (let ((memory '()))
        (if (eqv? in1 'insert)
          (set! memory (cons in2 memory))
          (if (eqv? in1 'show)
            memory))))))
(define odd-make-thing
  (lambda (x)
```

```
      (make-thing (if (odd? x) 'even 'odd))))
(define one-of-them (odd-make-thing 3))
```

7. Your summer job involves updating the technical dictionary at your employer's business. They don't want to rewrite the whole dictionary, so they need `dictionary-update!`, a procedure that finds an item in the dictionary and changes the associated term. Write `dictionary-update!` for the dictionary implementation in this chapter. Signal an error by using `error` if the key is not found.

8. Write `subsplice!`, a list-mutating version of `subsplice`, which we saw in Chapter 4.

```
(define x '(1 2 3 4 1))
(subsplice! '(one two three) 1 x) ⇒  (one two three 2 3 4 one two three)
```

9. The procedure `compose`, defined below, takes two procedures as arguments: `op1` is a binary numerical operator and `f` is a numerical procedure with one argument; the value returned by `compose` is a numerical procedure that takes one argument.

```
(define compose
  (lambda (op f)
    (lambda (x)
      (op (f x) (f (f x))))))
```

We use `compose` to create the following procedure:

```
(define add-add
  (compose + add1))
```

a. What is the value of `(add-add 2)`?
b. Draw a snapshot of evaluation of `(add-add 9)` just before `(op (f x) (f (f x)))` is evaluated. Include in the snapshot both `compose` and `add-add`.

Self-Assessment

1. Evaluate the following form:

```
(let
  ((a (make-box 2)) (b (make-box 9)) (c (make-box #f)))
  (box-set! a 6)
  (box-set! c (make-box (box-ref b)))
  (box-set! (box-ref c) 8)
  (list (box-ref a) (box-ref b) (box-ref c)))
```

2. Some Scheme systems don't provide boxes as a primitive data type. Suppose we have a program that makes extensive use of boxes. Is there a way to run the program on such a system *without modifying the code*?

3. Evaluate the following form:

```
(let
  ((a (list 1 2))
   (b (list 3 4)))
  (set-car! b a)
  (set-car! a 5)
  a)
```

4. What property of the following code might lead to errors?

```
(define a (list 1 2 3 4))
(define b (cdr (cdr a)))
(set-car! (cdr b) 7)
```

5. Write a procedure that deletes all the odd numbers in a list of numbers. The procedure should alter the input list, not return a new list. For example,

```
(define x '(1 2 3 4))
(set! x (delete-odd! x))
x ⇒  (2 4)
```

6. The following procedure was written by a programmer who refuses to believe that imperative programs are often harder to read than functional ones. Rewrite it as a functional procedure (the procedure should of course do exactly the same thing!).

```
(define tiberius
  (lambda (n)
    (let ((x 0))
      (letrec
        ((helper
          (lambda (m)
            (if (< m n)
                (begin
                  (if (> (remainder m 5) 3)
                      (set! x (+ x m)))
                  (helper (add1 m)))))))
        (helper 1)
        x))))
```

7. What is the value of the last form?

```
(define bluff
  (lambda (x)
    (let ((count 0))
      (set! count (+ x count))
      count)))
(bluff 2)
(bluff 3)
```

8. Draw the snapshot while evaluating (bluff 3).

9. Write a procedure, remember-all, that remembers every input it has received and returns the whole list of inputs each time it's called.

```
(remember-all 1) ⇒  (1)
(remember-all 2) ⇒  (2 1)
```

10. Write a procedure of three arguments a, b, and c, named linear-combination that returns as its value a procedure with three arguments x, y, and z that computes $ax + by + cz$. For example, ((linear-combination 1 2 3) 4 5 6) should evaluate to 32.

11. Write a procedure make-sequence, with two arguments a and b, that returns a procedure with no arguments. When that procedure is applied, it returns the next number in the sequence of numbers $ai + b$, starting with $i = 1$.

```
(define make-sequence (lambda (a b) .......))
(define plus1 (make-sequence 1 1))
(plus1) ⇒  2
(plus1) ⇒  3
(plus1) ⇒  4
(define evens (make-sequence 2 0))
(evens) ⇒  2
(evens) ⇒  4
```

You may not use global variables.

12.

```
(let ((x 1))
   (let ((x 2))
     (+ x 3)))
```

What is the value of this form? Draw a snapshot to prove that your answer is right.

13. Joel User is calculating a long expression that he breaks up into several subexpressions. He writes the subexpressions down in the following code, which causes a Scheme error:

```
(letrec
   ((x (* a 42))
    (y (+ b x))
    (z (* c (+ x y))))
   (* x (- z y)))
```

a, b, and c are defined in an enclosing scope. Where did Joel User go wrong?

Programming Problems

1. Yale Technologies has devised a french-fry dispensing machine. You deposit your money, and the machine makes fresh hot french fries and delivers them to you in a small cardboard box. The requirements for delivery are that you have deposited enough money (they're cheap, at 50 cents per box), and that the machine has enough fry-mix, fat, salt, and boxes to produce fries. Implement a `fry-machine` as a list containing the money deposited, the fry-mix, fat, salt, and box counts for the machine. Write a procedure, `make-fries`, that takes a `fry-machine` and an amount of money as its arguments. If the previous money plus the current deposit exceeds the price, `make-fries` checks the supplies against the necessary amounts, and if they are sufficient, it deducts the appropriate amounts and delivers your crispy hot fries.

   By implementing a machine as a list argument to the procedure, we can have several machines operating at the same time.

2. ABC Corporation needs to manage its inventory. It has a variety of items that it wants to store, arranged in order of arrival at the business, the latest first. Each item has two pieces of information: its type (a symbol), and its arrival date (a number). The types are known beforehand. Write a procedure, `make-inventory`, to accept the list of types and produce an inventory data structure. Choose a data structure for the inventory that allows you to take an item and insert it in the list for its type, in the correct position determined by its time of arrival, using procedure `enter-item`. `remove-item` takes the most recently arrived item of a given type out of the inventory.

3. Write a simple daily manager procedure, `daily`. The procedure should accept a series of simple commands, such as C for create, E for enter, and D for display. When you input E, it reads an event, consisting of a time (a number), a kind (a symbol) and a description (a string). Keep the list of events in a global variable.

   `daily` should list the events in order by time when you input D. `daily` should also accept an L command that asks for further input of a kind, and should list all of the events of a certain kind in its list of events.

Chapter 6

Object-Oriented Programming

Overview

Object-oriented programming is a powerful way of designing and writing programs. An object is an entity in a program with both state and procedures. Programmers have found that working with objects often results in programs that are easier to read and modify than those designed with either procedural or data abstraction.

We will look at objects and classes, and see how we can write object-oriented programs in Scheme using a new special form, `define-class`. This special form is in turn a logical consequence of environments; all of `define-class`'s features are applications of the basic principles of the environment model. Finally, we'll study object-oriented design, an abstraction technique that builds on data abstraction to produce good object-oriented programs.

6.1 **A World of Objects**

6.2 **Implementing Classes with Procedures**

6.3 **Object-oriented Design**

Summary, Further Readings, Key Words

Problems, Self-Assessment, Programming Problems

My object all sublime
I shall achieve in time—
To let the punishment fit the crime—
The punishment fit the crime.
And make each prisoner pent
Unwillingly represent
A source of innocent merriment—
Of innocent merriment.

— W. S. Gilbert, *The Mikado*

Early computer programs contained a few hundreds or thousands of lines of code. Today, programs are millions of lines long. Indeed, there are programs whose listings, reduced to microfiche, are taller than a human being! How can such a complicated program be written, tested, or debugged?

A good way to start answering this question is to ask *why* programs are so complicated. The most obvious answer—the one that programmers like to believe is the only cause—is that we are now trying to solve much more complicated problems than before. In the 1960s, a business would write a program to manage its inventory, keeping track of when items were received or shipped. A 1990s inventory system monitors the demand for items, generates orders to be shipped to specific stores (rather than a central warehouse), generates electronic payments for shipments that have been received in good order, and does many things that would have been unimaginable 30 years ago. This sophistication may sometimes be directly responsible for the company's profitability.

Nowhere has the increasing sophistication of computer software been felt as strongly as in user interfaces. In the 1960s, a computer user prepared a sequence of commands using a command language that required specific characters in specific columns of a punched card. Later, the user received a thick printout that contained, somewhere, the required information. In the 1990s, users expect a **graphic user interface**, or **GUI**, that allows them to work directly with items on the screen. Windows, the Macintosh operating system, Motif, and NeXTStep are well-known GUIs.

Unfortunately, it is difficult to program for these GUIs. Programmers need to deal with many different conditions. Each GUI provides hundreds of different procedures that the programmer must call in specific circumstances. As a result, many programmers find it difficult to write useful GUI programs.

The complex nature of modern software is not *always* a result of complex problems. The development of much modern software is driven by "featuritis", the desire of a company to provide all of the features that its competition has. Many spreadsheets have spelling checkers. Word processors come with built-in drawing packages. Drawing programs often incorporate word-processing features, including spelling checkers. Rather than designing a set of programs that work effectively with each other, some programmers build ever bigger programs that integrate all the features users might want. What we want instead is a collection of smaller, well-designed programs that work effectively together.

This "software bloat" has dramatic results. One early Pascal compiler worked effectively and productively on a 128K PC with only floppy disks. This compiler, with many useful additional features, but with much additional bloat, now requires a multimegabyte 386 computer and many megabytes of space on a hard disk.

Writing good programs requires careful design and analysis. We must develop techniques that are useful for building large programs, and we need a way to design programs that relates to the real world, so that our programs make more sense. Whether you're writing a banking system for thousands of users, or a game for your own use, the structure of the program should mirror the structure of the problem.

Unfortunately, while procedural and data abstraction are extremely useful in solving smaller problems, they aren't as helpful in large problems. As programs become larger, more and more details must be addressed, with the result that programs become less and less modular. This decrease in modularity makes programs harder to change as the users' requirements change.

Object-oriented programming is a technique that is particularly effective in the design of programs that solve real-world problems. Object-oriented programming is based not on procedures that compute results, but on objects: values that represent real-world entities such as students, bank accounts, and airplane parts. These values are sent messages, and reply with appropriate values. An object contains variables that represent state. For example, a bank-account object's state would include the customer's name and balance. A library book's state would include the author's name, the book's title, and the name of the current borrower (if any). Object-oriented programming is the next step after data abstraction; it unites the procedures that work on data with the data that represent the object's state.

Object-oriented design helps us break a problem into parts that make sense. Each part deals with a specific part of the overall problem. For example, a game program can have objects that represent game pieces. A game piece can behave in various ways: it can move somewhere else on the board, capture another piece, and so on. An object-oriented design for this problem would create an object to represent a game piece. The object would contain internal state to indicate, for example, where on the board it is. Another part of the program could send a message to the piece, asking where it is.

An object in a computer program contains state and procedures. Objects in the real world also have state and can perform various operations for other objects. For this reason, we speak of object-oriented programs as simulating the real world. Because object-oriented programs are easier to change than those designed with procedural or data abstraction, they serve the needs of the user more effectively. Further, an object-oriented program need not have every feature thrown into it from the start. Because object-oriented programs are modular, new features can be added to them as desired.

One key benefit of object-oriented design is that many object-oriented programs are built out of **reusable** components. For example, a bank-account object can be used in many different banking problems. Reusable components can be used in many different programs and specialized (tailored) to the specific needs of the programmer. Reusable code lets the programmer concentrate upon how this problem is different from others that have been solved previously, rather than having to rewrite the same code repeatedly.

Object-oriented programming is not a solution to all of the world's programming problems. Properly used, however, it can help you to solve problems that would be difficult with other techniques. Object-oriented approaches do use procedural and data abstraction where these older techniques are appropriate.

Although object-oriented programming has been around for a long time (the earliest language with specific object-oriented features, Simula-67, was developed in 1967), its usefulness only became apparent in the late 1970s. Today, most large software systems that are developed from scratch use object-oriented programming techniques. In fairness, we should observe that most large software systems *aren't* developed from scratch. Many are revisions of existing systems, and thus must use obsolete programming languages, program design techniques, and operating systems. This **legacy code** is an endless source of frustration to programmers.

Object-oriented programmers don't generally like working with legacy code. Object-oriented code is modular, so that individual pieces can be used again in new programs. Much legacy code is not at all modular, and is therefore difficult to modify or adapt to new situations.

This chapter focuses on object-oriented programming. We'll see how to write object-oriented programs in Scheme. Then we'll see how all of the object-oriented features are really just specialized uses of procedures with state. In fact, Scheme has no specific object-oriented features; everything we will study in this chapter is a consequence of the environment model. Once we understand how object-oriented programming works, we'll look at object-oriented design.

6.1   A World of Objects

> *Art thou pale for weariness*
> *Of climbing heaven, and gazing on the earth,*
> *Wandering companionless*
> *Among stars that have a different birth,—*
> *And ever changing, like a joyless eye*
> *That finds no object worth its constancy?*   — P. B. Shelley, "To the Moon"

In Chapter 5, we saw how to use data abstraction to represent an `account` ADT. Now imagine that you must write a software system to process data for a bank. The bank has customers, and each one might have several accounts (savings account, checking account, retirement account). There are several special types of accounts:

- A child's account is a savings account that allows only one withdrawal a month.
- A senior's account is a savings or checking account that has no service charges.

- A business checking account has no service charges, but pays no interest.

A customer can make deposits in person or through a teller machine. Withdrawals can be made in person, by check (for checking accounts), or through a teller machine (for savings or checking accounts, but not other kinds of accounts). Each month the bank mails each customer a statement showing the account activity.

Faced with this description of the problem, you might be nervous about how to build this software system. When you realize that the description is extremely oversimplified, and that real banks have many additional kinds of accounts, as well as responsibilities (reporting interest income to the government, for example), your nervousness may turn to outright apprehension.

The traditional approach to this problem has been to use procedural abstraction. Most business programmers have studied a special form of procedural abstraction known as **structured analysis**. A structured analysis of a bank would yield a set of tasks such as withdrawals, deposits, and statement preparation. Each of these tasks would be broken down further into subtasks.

Structured analysis leads to a single task, `process-withdrawal`, that must include special-case code for each kind of account. The result is a program that is a rat's nest of `if`s. All of the special-case code obscures the actual processing of data. Such programs are hard to read and tend to contain many errors.

There is another way to think about this problem. Why not think about the problem from the customer's viewpoint? The customer walks into the bank, presents appropriate identification to the teller, and requests money from an account. The teller responds by deducting the amount from the account balance, and giving the money to the customer.

If we address the problem from the customer's viewpoint, we can write a part of the program that deals with specific kinds of accounts. The client code is more modular than in the structured approach. To process a withdrawal, we just "ask" the account to do the job. All of the rules about whether a withdrawal is permitted, service charges, and interest are managed by the account. The teller code need not know any of these things. The bank can even create new kinds of accounts. The teller part of the program only needs to know that to take money out of an account, the account must be asked for it.

This section shows what objects are, how we can use them to simplify the bank problem, and how we can use objects in Scheme.

6.1.1   Introduction to Objects

We can think of the account as an **object**, a value to which **messages** may be sent. The customer says to the teller, "I would like to withdraw $100 from account 137125." In an object-oriented view, the teller passes this request to the account, which determines whether to permit the request. (Is there enough money on deposit? Does this kind of account permit withdrawals?) If the withdrawal is permitted, then the account adjusts the balance appropriately, and gives the teller permission to give the customer the money. Figure 6-1 shows the process.

It is not the *teller* who makes the decision to authorize the transaction, but the *account*. The teller's job is to transmit the customer's request to the account, and give the customer the money. This task is easily automated. (Of course, many other teller tasks are complex. Automated teller machines rarely perform all of the tasks that tellers are asked to do. In any case, many customers still prefer dealing with a human.)

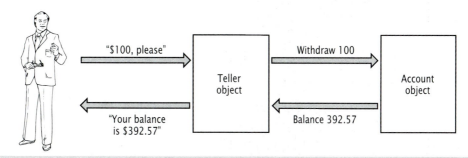

Figure 6-1   Bank objects

You may have felt uncomfortable with our account-based description. We spoke as though an account was an active entity that could respond to messages, rather than just some place in the bank's records for keeping track of a customer's deposits. Yet that is exactly how bank customers speak. "I want an account that pays high interest". "Will this kind of account let me make as many withdrawals as I want"? "What sort of service charges does this account have"? These are typical questions that a customer might ask. Customers know that accounts don't actually do these things, but they find it useful to speak as if they did.

We can therefore describe an object as having three characteristics:

1. a state, such as the account balance
2. a **behavior**, which is a set of messages the object can respond to
3. an identity, which distinguishes objects with the same state and behavior

In the bank-account example, the state of an account consists of its balance and the sequence of deposits and withdrawals that have occurred this month. The behavior is the set of operations for the account, which includes requests to deposit to and withdraw from the account, and requests for the balance of the account. Each account must have an identity, because two accounts that happen to have the same state and behavior are still not the same account. We've talked about sharing before; we say that two objects are identical if mutating one mutates the other.[1]

We make a distinction between the concepts of message and **method**. A message is a request to an object to do something, whereas a method is the procedure that the object uses to carry out the request.

☞ **Exercise 6–1**

Why is it essential to make the sequence of transactions part of the bank-account state? What additional message or messages is/are needed as a result? ❏

☞ **Exercise 6–2**

You have been asked to write a program to process student grades, and have decided to use an object-oriented approach. At the end of each semester, instructors send a grade list

---

[1] Scheme makes a distinction between identity (tested by the primitive eq?), and equivalence (tested by eqv?). In Chapter 5 we discussed equivalence. Identity is a bit fussier than equivalence; in many Scheme systems, numbers might be equivalent without being identical, for example. This distinction is unimportant for our purposes.

to the college administration. Students are sent a transcript, a list of course grades, that includes their cumulative grade-point average for all the semesters they have attended the college. What state and behavior would `student` objects need? ❏

6.1.2   Classes

Imagine what the world would be like if we didn't classify information. Each situation would be completely new, and we would have to think up a new response. Even the information flowing from your eyes to your brain would not make any sense, because you would have no abstract concepts. Not only would concepts such as "chair" and "table" be meaningless, but so too would "shape" and "color".

At birth, we make few distinctions. Perhaps "comfortable" and "uncomfortable" are the only ones a newborn baby makes. As a baby learns about the world, it develops categories such as "mother", "warm", and "hungry". As we mature, we become masters of more sophisticated classification systems, such as those found in school, in various sports, and on the job.

Our previous discussion of objects was incomplete, because we treated each object as an independent entity. Objects indeed have state, behavior, and identity, but they are too low-level a concept to serve as the basis for a programming style. Who wants to write a program for Mary Jones' bank account, and another program for Rick Chan's, and another for Tom Singh's, and so on? What we really want is a program that defines how bank accounts work.

We therefore need an abstraction for our objects, so we must group them into **classes**. Each class consists of objects that have the same behavior, the same set of messages. For example, the class of bank accounts is the set of objects that all have a bank balance (a state variable), and have `deposit` and `withdraw` methods. In a library circulation system, the class of books is the set of objects that have author, title, call number, and borrower-name information (the state variables), and have `check-out`, `check-in`, and `inquire` methods. An object is often called an **instance** of its class. For example, Edward Gibbon's *Decline and Fall of the Roman Empire* is an instance of the class `book`, but not of the class `employee`. We use the word **instantiate** to describe the process of creating a new instance of a class.

Don't confuse a class with a collection. A class is not a data structure. The library might have a list (or other data structure) of all its books, but that isn't the class `book`. A class is like a type. The program uses the class to make new instances; these instances, in turn, respond to messages that the program sends to them. People often think that a class takes some responsibility for the instances, but this isn't true. If we were writing a library circulation system, we would have a class `book`, but the book objects, once created, would still have to be put into some sort of list structure in order to keep track of them.

In almost all object-oriented programming languages, the programmer's main concern is the creation of classes. For the banking system, the programmer creates a class of bank accounts, and decides which messages a bank account understands, that is, which methods it implements.

The big question in object-oriented programming is therefore, "What classes are needed to solve a particular problem"? Whereas with procedural abstraction we look for tasks and subtasks, in object-oriented programming we need to identify useful classes. As such, object-oriented programming is an extension of data abstraction. We will come back to this question in Section 6.3.

6.1.3   Object-oriented programming in Scheme

The code presented in this section can be found in file `bank1.scm`.

We're now ready to apply our object-oriented framework to Scheme. We need to define a class of bank accounts. Each account will have **instance variables** to hold the customer name, current balance, and the transaction history. If we were building a full banking system, we would also create a class of tellers. A teller would be a **user interface object** that allowed the user to enter information and see responses. The teller object converts user commands into messages that it sends to the account. We won't implement tellers here, but one of the programming projects asks you to investigate this problem.

The official Scheme language doesn't have any specific features for object-oriented programming, but makes it easy for an advanced programmer to define whatever features are needed. A number of object-oriented programming packages have been developed for Scheme. Ours is simplified, and not as powerful as some of the most sophisticated packages, but is still useful.

Figure 6-2 presents a brief session showing transactions for two customers of the Pickfair Bank. The first step is to create two objects named mary and doug. As with abstract data types, we use constructors to make new types. However, we don't write the constructor; instead, we create a new instance by sending the message make to the *class*. For the moment, this is the only message we will send to a class; all other messages are sent to individual objects.

```
> (define mary (account1 'make "Mary" 200))
> (define doug (account1 'make "Doug" 150))
> (mary 'balance)
200
> (doug 'balance)
150
> (mary 'deposit 100)
300
> (mary 'balance)
300
> (doug 'balance)
150
> (mary 'withdraw 75)
225
> (doug 'withdraw 160)
Customer Doug: sorry, overdrafts aren't permitted.
150
```

Figure 6-2   Using account objects

You can think of the class's object constructor as a factory that makes new objects. These objects in turn can be sent messages commanding them to do things. You might order a computer from a factory, but once you get it, you use it. You only interact with the factory when something goes wrong with the computer.[2]

---
[2] Our classes do not have service departments, though!

Unlike using ADTs, where we call a procedure to carry out a particular task, we use an object by sending it a message. In our package, messages are symbols. First we ask `mary` for her balance, by sending the message `balance` to `mary`. Figure 6-3 shows this message being processed.

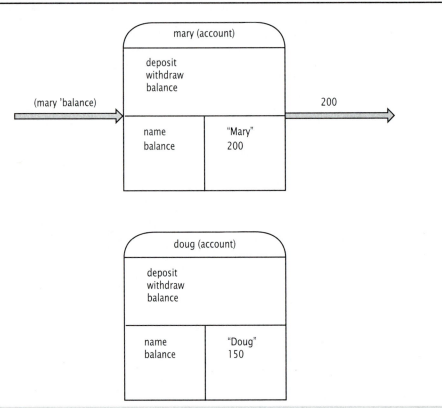

Figure 6-3   An object receiving a message

Subsequently, we tell `mary` to deposit $100. We get back her new balance, but, being unsure, we ask both `mary` and `doug` for their balances. `mary`'s has changed, but `doug`'s stayed the same. We now attempt to withdraw from both accounts. The withdrawal from `mary`'s succeeds, but that for `doug` fails, and his balance is unchanged.

This first attempt at a bank-account class is shown in Program 6-1. To run this example, you must make sure that the `define-class` special form has been loaded into Scheme; consult your local documentation for more information.

The form `define-class` is complex. We will see more of its features in later examples. In Program 6-1, we are defining a class named `account1`. Every class has a built-in constructor procedure. All we have to do is to specify the arguments, using the `constructor-arguments` clause, and `define-class` writes the constructor procedure for us. The constructor procedure for `account1` takes the arguments `name` and `balance` (Figure 6-2, above, shows how these arguments are used).

The main part of a `define-class` form is a sequence of methods. Each method consists of a symbol, in parentheses, followed by the body in implicit `begin` format.

```
(define-class account1
  (constructor-arguments name balance)
  (methods (message . args)
    ((withdraw)
     (let ((amount (get-argument args 0)))
           (if (> (- balance amount) 0)
               (set! balance (- balance amount))
               (format #t
                 "Customer ~a: sorry, overdrafts aren't permitted.~%"
                 name))
       balance))
    ((deposit)
     (let ((amount (get-argument args 0)))
       (set! balance (+ balance amount))
       balance))
    ((balance)
       balance)))
```

Program 6-1   First version of account class

All methods get the same parameter list, which means that almost all class definitions define the methods using a variadic parameter list.

   The simplest method is that for obtaining the balance.

```
((balance)
   balance)
```

The first line contains the message symbol to activate this particular method, and
the second contains the body to be evaluated when this message is received.

   A more interesting method is used to process a deposit.

```
((deposit)
 (let ((amount (get-argument args 0)))
   (set! balance (+ balance amount))
   balance))
```

Here the keyword is `deposit`, and the body is the `let` form. The method parameters are named `(message . args)`. The first argument is the message symbol—not
used directly in our code—and succeeding arguments are packed together into the
list `args`. The utility procedure `get-argument` gets an item from a list and generates
a more useful error message than `list-ref` would produce if not enough arguments
are given.

```
(define get-argument
  (lambda (args n)
    (if (< (length args) n)
      (error 'get-argument "Invalid number of arguments")
      (list-ref args n))))
```

   Finally, the withdrawal method ensures that sufficient funds are on deposit.

```
((withdraw)
 (let ((amount (get-argument args 0)))
```

```
(if (> (- balance amount) 0)
   (set! balance (- balance amount))
   (format #t "Customer ~a: sorry, overdrafts aren't permitted.~%"
     name))
 balance))
```

Each `account1` object's balance is encapsulated in the object. You can't get at it directly; you only get it by sending the object a message. This restricts your programming freedom, but on the other hand it means that you're less likely to make sloppy mistakes (for example, forgetting to check for sufficient funds when processing some other kind of withdrawal). By centralizing the checking in the `withdraw` method, you make your code more readable—you don't have to write the error check in each place, or even call a procedure—and you are less likely to have bugs.

The syntax of `define-class`, as we've seen it thus far, follows:

```
(define-class class-name
  (constructor-arguments names)
  (methods (message . args)
    ((keyword)
     body)
    ((keyword)
     body)))
```

☞ **Exercise 6–3**

Write a method for `account1` that returns the customer's name. ❑

☞ **Exercise 6–4**

Write a method for `account1` that credits a $5.00 bonus to an account. ❑

☞ **Exercise 6–5**

Write a procedure that accepts a list of accounts and returns the account (not its balance or customer name) with the largest balance. ❑

Our original problem statement included a feature that this version doesn't support—producing a list of transactions. This ability requires an additional `define-class` feature, namely slots. A **slot** is an instance variable that is not a constructor argument. Slots are initialized to values determined by the programmer when an object is created. `define-class` supports a `slots` clause to list the slots of an object, in a format similar to a `let` form.

In Program 6-2, we have added a `transactions` slot (initialized to null), and methods for manipulating the list of transactions. `clear` resets the transactions list to null, and `process-transactions` maps the supplied procedure onto the list of transactions. You might ask why we didn't provide a method to get the transactions list directly. There are two reasons:

1. We might want to change the way transactions are stored. For example, we might decide to store them in a file. If we did, the implementation of `account2` would have to be substantially changed. However, code that sends messages to an instance of `account2` would not care.

2. Returning the actual transactions list could result in some bugs that would be hard to track down. What if client code mutated the list in some way? By

```
(define-class account2
  (constructor-arguments name balance)
  (slots (transactions '()))
  (methods (message . args)
    ((withdraw)
     (let ((amount (get-argument args 0)))
          (if (> (- balance amount) 0)
             (begin
               (set! balance (- balance amount))
               (set! transactions
                 (cons
                   (cons 'withdraw amount) transactions)))
             (format #t
               "Customer ~a: sorry, overdrafts aren't permitted.~%"
               name))
       balance))
    ((deposit)
     (let ((amount (get-argument args 0)))
       (set! balance (+ balance amount))
       (set! transactions
         (cons (cons 'deposit amount) transactions))
       balance))
    ((clear)
     (set! transactions '()))
    ((process-transactions)
     (for-each (get-argument args 0) transactions))
    ((balance)
       balance)))
```

Program 6-2   Second version of account class

breaking things down as we have done, we make it less likely that an error will creep in to a part of code that has already been tested and debugged.[3]

Returning the transactions list would violate data abstraction. The outside world shouldn't have to know the data structure used by instances of account2.

Figure 6-4 shows a dialog that uses account2. Instances of account2 accept the same messages as do instances of account1, with the addition of process-transactions (and clear, which isn't used in this dialog). The additional state information is kept in the slot transactions.

Code that uses account2 doesn't really care what kind of account it handles, as long as it responds to messages such as deposit, withdraw, and so on. We can use this fact to create a checking-account class that responds to the same messages. Checking accounts at Pickfair Bank allow an overdraft of $1000 (i.e., a customer's account can be as low as $-1000), but charge $0.25 per check. Pickfair's checking accounts treat checks and over-the-counter withdrawals the same. Program 6-3 shows the code, and the dialog follows.

---

[3] "Less likely", not "impossible". Don't get the idea that object-oriented programming will make testing and debugging unnecessary!

```
> (define mary (account2 'make "Mary" 200))
> (define doug (account2 'make "Doug" 150))
> (mary 'deposit 100)
300
> (mary 'withdraw 75)
225
> (doug 'withdraw 160)
Customer Doug: sorry, overdrafts aren't permitted.
150
> (define print-transaction
    (lambda (trans)
      (format #t
        "action: ~a amount: ~a~%" (car trans) (cdr trans))))
> (mary 'process-transactions print-transaction)
action: withdraw amount: 75
action: deposit amount: 100
> (doug 'process-transactions print-transaction)
>
```

Figure 6-4   Using account2

```
> (define bill (checking-account 'make "Bill" 200))
> (bill 'deposit 100)
300
> (bill 'withdraw 500)
-200.25
> (bill 'withdraw 1000)
Customer Bill: sorry, you're over your limit.
-200.25
```

In the dialog, bill is created as an instance of class checking-account. Although a different constructor is used (because we send the make message to a different class), bill responds to the same messages as instances of account2 do. As the dialog shows, however, the withdraw method for checking accounts can't be the same as in account2.

Class checking-account illustrates a crucial aspect of object-oriented programming. It doesn't matter what class an object is a member of, so long as it responds to the desired messages. We have already seen **polymorphic** procedures, procedures that can respond to different types of arguments (equal? is an example). Objects introduce a second kind of polymorphism. Several classes can be written so that they respond to the same messages, but in different ways. We can add many different bank-account classes, each with different methods for the same messages. Client code doesn't care at all; it just sends the appropriate message to each object.

☞ **Exercise 6-6**

Exercise 6-5 asked you to write a procedure that found the account with the largest balance. Suppose you had a list that contained some account2 instances and some checking-account instances. What changes would you have to make to your solution to that exercise to handle this list? ❑

```
(define-class checking-account
  (constructor-arguments name balance)
  (slots (transactions '()))
  (methods (message . args)
    ((withdraw)
     (let ((amount (get-argument args 0)))
       (if (> (- balance amount) -1000)
           (begin
             (set! balance (- balance amount 0.25))
             (set! transactions
             (cons
               (cons 'withdraw amount) transactions)))
             (format #t
               "Customer ~a: sorry, you're over your limit.~%"
               name))
         balance))
    ((deposit)
     (let ((amount (get-argument args 0)))
       (set! balance (+ balance amount))
       (set! transactions
         (cons (cons 'deposit amount) transactions))
       balance))
    ((clear)
     (set! transactions '()))
    ((process-transactions)
     (for-each (get-argument args 0) transactions))
    ((balance)
     balance)))
```

Program 6-3   Checking accounts

☞ **Exercise 6-7**

You have been asked to write a class for an account for young children. This account allows any number of deposits, but only two withdrawals per month, and no withdrawals larger than $10.00. The way to write this class is to make a copy of account2 and make some changes to the copy. What are the changes? ❏

A final evolution in our account class allows interest to be paid. Each kind of account will have a different rate, which the bank can set from time to time. This means that we must somehow create a variable that is accessible to all of the instances of the class.

The constructor arguments and slots of an object are most definitely *not* such variables. We don't want to share balance information or names among accounts. The whole point of encapsulation is to organize this information so that each account has access to precisely its own instance variables. What we need is the ability to define **class variables** that any instance of a class may access (or change, where that makes sense).

If there are class variables, are there class methods? Yes: a **class method** is defined for the whole class. With define-class, you activate a class method by sending the appropriate message to the class, rather than to an instance.

Figure 6-5 shows account, our final class, at work. We create two accounts as before, and then send the message compute-interest, which applies the current interest rate to the balance. A quick calculation shows that the initial interest rate must be 5%. To change the rate, we must send the message set-rate to the class account. (This is a class message; sending it to mary or doug would generate an error.) After setting the rate, we compute interest for mary and doug. Note how both of these accounts now use the new interest rate.

```
(define mary (account 'make "Mary" 200))
(define doug (account 'make "Doug" 150))
(mary 'compute-interest) ⇒ 210.0
(mary 'deposit 90) ⇒ 300.0
(account 'set-rate 0.07)
(mary 'compute-interest) ⇒ 321.0
(doug 'compute-interest) ⇒ 160.5
```

Figure 6-5   Class methods and interest rates

Program 6-4 shows account. The class-variables clause specifies one or more class variables, in the same format as slots; note the initialization of interest-rate. The class-methods clause gives the methods of the class, which in this case is set-rate.

6.1.4   Using define-class

```
(define-class class-name
  (class-variables bindings)
  (class-methods (message . args)
    ((keyword)
     body)
    ((keyword)
     body)
    ...)
  (constructor-arguments names)
  (slots bindings)
  (methods (message . args)
    ((keyword)
     body)
    ((keyword)
     body)
    ...))
```

Figure 6-6   The syntax of define-class

Now that we have seen all the features of define-class, let's put what we've studied into perspective. Figure 6-6 shows a full summary of define-class, with all of its clauses. There are two parts to a class definition: class methods and variables, and instance variables and methods. The class-methods and class-variables clauses

```
(define-class account
  (class-variables (interest-rate 0.05))
  (class-methods (message . args)
    ((set-rate)
     (set! interest-rate (get-argument args 0))))
  (constructor-arguments name balance)
  (slots (transactions '()))
  (methods (message . args)
    ((withdraw)
     (let ((amount (get-argument args 0)))
          (if (> (- balance amount) 0)
             (begin
               (set! balance (- balance amount))
               (set! transactions
                     (cons
                       (cons 'withdraw amount) transactions)))
             (format #t
               "Customer ~a: sorry, overdrafts aren't permitted.~%"
               name))
       balance))
    ((deposit)
     (let ((amount (get-argument args 0)))
       (set! balance (+ balance amount))
       (set! transactions
             (cons (cons 'deposit amount) transactions))
       balance))
    ((clear)
     (set! transactions '()))
    ((process-transactions)
     (for-each (get-argument args 0) transactions))
    ((compute-interest)
     (set! balance (* balance (+ interest-rate 1.0)))
     balance)
    ((balance)
       balance)))
```

Program 6-4   The final account class

define the behavior and state of the entire class, and the constructor-arguments, slots, and methods clauses define the behavior and state of individual instances.

☞ **Exercise 6-8**

Suppose we are building a class to represent pieces in a game similar to checkers. Each piece has a position (row and column number) on the board. Pieces are given an initial position (by the player) when they are put on the board. They can be moved in three directions: "ahead" (n rows forward), "diagonal-right" (n rows forward and n columns to the right), and "diagonal-left" (n rows forward and n columns to the left); the value of n depends upon the part of the game we're currently in, and can be changed by the rest of the program.

Write a class definition for the class piece, with appropriate class and instance variables and methods. Don't worry about going off the edge of the board. ❏

☞ **Exercise 6-9**

In Exercise 6-7 you were asked to write a class for children's accounts. The solution we gave used "magic numbers" for the maximum withdrawal amount and number of withdrawals.

- Modify the class to pay interest (at an initial rate of 5%) and to support class messages for setting these magic numbers.
- Modify the `withdraw` method to use these class variables. ❏

6.2 Implementing Classes with Procedures

I could have had class. I could have been a contender.
— Budd Schulberg, *On The Waterfront* (line spoken by Marlon Brando)

In Section 6.1, you saw how the `define-class` special form works. You have enough information to be able to use all of the features that it provides. Even though `define-class` doesn't include as many advanced object-oriented features as many other object-oriented programming packages for Scheme, it provides enough so that you can write powerful and useful programs.

To understand `define-class`, we must investigate how it fits into the environment model. There are two reasons for doing this: first, we want to demystify `define-class`—so that you can use it with more confidence—and second, implementing `define-class` gives us a chance to see more implications of the environment model. Many of these implications have practical uses not related to object-oriented programming.

When we send a message to an object, we write something like

```
> (define mary (account 'make "Mary" 200))
(mary 'deposit 100) ⇒ 300
```

The value of `mary` is an object. Yet a glance at the above form suggests that we are actually calling a procedure. (Remember, in Scheme, a form in parentheses is either a procedure application or a special form. Since `mary` is not the keyword of a special form, it must be the name of a procedure value.) Similarly, `account` must be bound to a procedure. How else could we call it with arguments like `make`, `"Mary"`, and `200`?

`define-class` must therefore create procedure values to represent classes and objects. We have already learned (in Chapter 5) all the techniques we need to understand how this is done. Now we merely need to harness those techniques.

6.2.1 Using Factories

Imagine that you must process a collection of meteorological data in the format shown in Figure 6-7 (a). The data consists of city names, each followed by any number of temperatures.

This format is a poor choice. It is difficult to do anything useful with the data, because the only way to know that the data from one city has ended is to blunder into the name of the next city. It may surprise you that anyone would design a data format like this, but people who lay out data formats often do choose representations that are hard to process.

```
(   "Vancouver"       17 19 23 18 20
    "Seattle"         18 22 19
    "London"          15 12 12 16
    "Novosibirsk"     8 11
    "Pretoria"        25 27 24 29
    "Kyoto"           14 11 19          )
```
(a) Raw data

```
(   ("Vancouver"      17 19 23 18 20)
    ("Seattle"        18 22 19)
    ("London"         15 12 12 16)
    ("Novosibirsk"    8 11)
    ("Pretoria"       25 27 24 29)
    ("Kyoto"          14 11 19)         )
```
(b) Converted data

Figure 6-7   Temperature data

Rather than make each program that processes this data deal with this format, we can write a procedure to convert from this format into one more suitable for processing. The obvious choice is a list of lists, each representing the data for one city, as in Figure 6-7 (b). It probably occurred to you to define a meteorological-data ADT, in which case we can consider the converted data to be a list of meteorological-data values.

We can't use mapping or any similar technique to write this procedure, because its output will have one item for each *group* of input values. We only know that we have processed all the data for one city when we run into the name of the next city, or when we run off the end of the list. One way *not* to do this job is to write a procedure that is full of calls to car and cdr. There are enough special cases that it's easy to make errors, either attempting to take the car of the empty list, or losing some data.

A good breakdown of this problem yields two parts. We need one part that keeps track of where we are in the original list, and a second that produces the new list. One way to get this breakdown is by means of a **dispenser**, a procedure that encapsulates a list and delivers the items one by one.

A dispenser can perform two different operations. The caller can get the next item or peek at the next item. The difference between getting and peeking is that successive get operations yield successive elements of the list, whereas successive peek operations yield the same element. When a dispenser reaches the end of its list, it returns the symbol end-of-data.

Our implementation of dispensers is shown in Program 6-5. make-dispenser is a factory procedure that returns a new dispenser, in which any-list is bound to the original list argument. The dispenser takes a symbol, which is used to determine whether a peek or get operation is intended. Our version is somewhat sloppy, in that any argument other than 'peek is taken as meaning get. It also allows any number of gets at the end of the list. It is debatable whether it is worthwhile to check for these cases.

A dispenser works by mutating the variable any-list. As we saw in Chapter 5, each dispenser has its own binding for any-list. Each time the dispenser is asked to get, it mutates any-list appropriately.

```
(define make-dispenser
  (lambda (any-list)
    (lambda (operation)
      (if (eqv? operation 'peek)
        (if (null? any-list)
          'end-of-data
          (car any-list))
        (begin
          (if (null? any-list)
            'end-of-data
            (let ((x (car any-list)))
              (set! any-list (cdr any-list))
              x)))))))
```

Program 6-5   Dispensers

☞ **Exercise 6-10**

Suppose we write the following:

```
(define d1 (make-dispenser '(john paul george ringo)))
(define d2 (make-dispenser '(curly larry moe)))
(d1 'get) ⇒ john
```

Draw a snapshot of the environment after the dialog. ❑

We can use dispensers effectively to solve the data-format conversion problem, as Program 6-6 shows. process-one-city takes advantage of dispensers to peek at each item. If it is a number, it is included in the current city's data, and the dispenser is advanced to the next item. If it is not a number, then no get is performed, and hence the next get (in helper) returns city-name again.

Practical Note

This code has two minor unrealistic aspects. First, if we're processing a large amount of data, we will probably want to rewrite it using tail recursion. Second, this code is easily confused. If, through an error, a non-number appears in an unexpected place, the result may be meaningless. For example, the input

```
( "Lublin" 14 q3 18
  "Melbourne" 26 28   )
```

produces the following result:

```
( ("Lublin" 14)
  (q3 18)
  ("Melbourne" 26 28) )
```

(A look at any keyboard will suggest that the second value for Lublin was probably intended as 13.) If the data format contained counts, such an error could easily result in total confusion, and possibly crash the conversion program. (This is the reason

```
(define convert-data
  (lambda (orig-list)
    (let ((d (make-dispenser orig-list)))
      (letrec
        ((helper
           (lambda ()
             (let ((city-name (d 'get)))
               (if (eqv? city-name 'end-of-data)
                 '()
                 (let ((this (cons city-name (process-one-city d))))
                   (cons this (helper))))))))
        (helper)))))
(define process-one-city
  (lambda (d)
    (let ((next-value (d 'peek)))
      (if (number? next-value)
        (begin
          (d 'get)
          (cons next-value (process-one-city d)))
        '()))))
```

Program 6-6   Data format conversion

that import and export procedures in popular programs such as word processors and spreadsheets are often unreliable.) There's not much that we can do about this problem; the fault is in the original data format.

6.2.2   Dispensers as Objects

Dispensers are a practical example of how procedures encapsulate state. Each dispenser acts like an object. Dispensers even receive messages, such as get and peek. We can use our basic dispenser design as the basis for instance variables and methods.

The significant thing about factory procedures is that they use a pattern of nested lambda forms that we call "lambda over lambda". A factory returns a procedure that has captured the factory's arguments. This is exactly the same mechanism we proposed for objects: an object generally has some constructor arguments, which correspond to the factory arguments.

What about methods? We've spoken of them as if they were procedures. However, a method is really just a sequence of forms that is run in response to a message. If we consider messages to be symbols, an if form to select the appropriate method is sufficient.

To show how dispensers really correspond to objects, we can write dispensers as a class, as shown in Program 6-7, in which any-list has become a constructor argument. There are two methods: get and peek. What do we mean by saying, "We can write dispensers as a class"? As it happens, define-class will translate the class definition into almost the same format as in Program 6-5. For our purposes, the factory version and the class version are identical. We prefer the class version

```
(define-class dispenser
  (constructor-arguments any-list)
  (methods (operation)
    ((peek)
     (if (null? any-list)
         'end-of-data
         (car any-list)))
    ((get)
     (if (null? any-list)
         'end-of-data
         (let ((x (car any-list)))
           (set! any-list (cdr any-list))
           x)))))
```

Program 6-7   The dispenser class

because it is much easier to read, but if we didn't have define-class, we could get its effects by careful use of factories.

☞ **Exercise 6-11**

The class dispenser isn't exactly the same as the factory make-dispenser. Identify the differences. ❏

☞ **Exercise 6-12**

Following is the code for class location, which represents a position on a two-dimensional plane. Rewrite this code without using define-class (i.e., using factories).

```
(define-class location
  (constructor-arguments x y)
  (methods (message . args)
    ((move)
     (set! x (+ x (get-argument args 0)))
     (set! y (+ x (get-argument args 1))))
    ((distance-from-origin)
     (sqrt (+ (* x x) (* y y))))))
```

❏

6.2.3   Processing Messages

Objects receive messages and respond to them by invoking the appropriate methods. In our examples of dispenser and location (from Exercises 6-11 and 6-12) we have done the analysis of messages with an if. However, if forms can become extremely complex when more than two or three alternatives are necessary. Maybe we need some alternatives to if itself!

Scheme has two additional forms that check conditions. The case form is the one that solves our present problem. An extremely general conditional form, cond, is discussed in Chapter 7. Neither is necessary; each form can be replaced with corresponding ifs, but using them appropriately can make programs much more readable.

A sample case form is shown in Program 6–8. If x is the symbol up, a message is displayed, and the floor number incremented. If x is the symbol down, the floor number is decremented. Any other value for x results in the Help! message being displayed.

```
(case direction
  ((up)
   (display "Going up!")
   (set! floor (add1 floor)))
  ((down)
   (display "Going down!")
   (set! floor (sub1 floor)))
  (else
   (display "Help! This elevator only goes up and down")))
```

Program 6-8   The case form

The syntax of the case form is shown in Figure 6–8. case evaluates the first form and then tests whether its value is equivalent to any of the keys, in the order they appear. If the value is equivalent to a key in one of the lists, Scheme evaluates the forms following that list of keys, as if they were in an implicit begin. If none of the keys matches, then the forms following else are evaluated.

```
(case form
  ((key1 key2 ...)
   form ...)
  ((key1 key2 ...)
   form ...)
  ...
  (else
    form ...))
```

Figure 6-8   case format

Scheme uses eqv? to make the comparison. According to our discussion of equality in Chapter 5, this means that the key can be a symbol, a number, or a string, but not a pair or list. In practice, symbol and number keys are the most common.

We can use case to write a form that converts a symbol representing a day of the week, in either English or French, to an integer between 1 and 7.

```
(case weekday-name
  ((sunday dimanche) 1)
  ((monday lundi) 2)
  ((tuesday mardi) 3)
  ((wednesday mercredi) 4)
  ((thursday jeudi) 5)
  ((friday vendredi) 6)
  ((saturday samedi) 7)
  (else -1))
```

If we had written this form using `if`, it would be hard to read; there would be fifteen alternatives! The `case` form provides a compact way to write such forms.

The `case` form exists not because it is theoretically necessary, but because `if`s of this form are common. In the interests of compactness and readability, `case` forms are special-purpose. The only forms that are evaluated are the form after `case`, and the forms in the selected clause, the one that has a key match. In particular, the keys aren't evaluated. If you want keys to be evaluated, you must use `if` (or, as we will see in Chapter 7, `cond`).

☞ **Exercise 6-13**

Joel User has decided to write `symbol-equal?` using `case`.

```
(define joel-symbol-equal?
  (lambda (symb1 symb2)
    (case symb1
      ((symb2) #t)
      (else #f))))
```

Study this solution. Give an example where it correctly returns `#t`. Give another example where it correctly returns `#f`. Is it correct? Why or why not? ❑

☞ **Exercise 6-14**

Is it possible to use `case` to see whether a form evaluates to the symbol `else`? If so, is there any confusion with the `else` clause? ❑

The Scheme manual states that the `else` clause is optional. According to the rules, if the key doesn't match and there is no `else` clause, the results are "unspecified". A Scheme system might report an error, return a default value such as void, or do something else. (A poorly written Scheme system might even crash.) Most Scheme programmers make a practice of putting an `else` clause into each `case`, at the very least to report an error.

 Practical Note

Many programs have "this can't happen" cases; given the input values, the `else` case is impossible. For example, in our "day of the week" case, we might already know that the symbol is valid. In such situations, you might be tempted to leave the `else` off. It is astonishing how often a "can't happen" case actually does happen, because of errors in input data or in another part of the program. It costs little to write a line of code to report an error in this case, and you might find bugs you would otherwise not notice. `define-class` inserts an `else` clause that reports an error if you don't write your own `else`.

6.2.4   Slots, Class Variables and Methods

We have seen the basic framework for implementing `define-class`: a class can be written as a factory with a `case` for selecting the appropriate method. Now we need to see how the remaining features of `define-class` are implemented.

Slots are straightforward. The slot declarations look like `let` variable bindings, and indeed we can implement slots with "`lambda` over `let` over `lambda`". The outer `lambda` implements the account constructor, the `let` binds the slots, and the inner `lambda` implements the methods and is the returned procedure that captures the two enclosing frames.

If we want a `transactions` slot, for example, we can write

```
(define make-account
  (lambda (name balance)
    (let ((transactions '()))
      (lambda (message . args)
        ...))))
```

Each time the factory is called (that is, each time the class is instantiated), a frame is created in which `transactions` is bound. The procedure that is returned captures this frame.

☞ **Exercise 6-15**

Suppose we do the following:

```
> (define nick (make-account "Nikolai Rimski-Korsakov" 100))
> (define mili (make-account "Mili Balakirev" 150))
```

Draw a snapshot of the resulting environment. ❏

Class variables fit into this framework, which we now call "`let` over `lambda` over `let` over `lambda`". The `class-variables` clause in `define-class` looks similar to the `slots` clause. Therefore, we should be able to use a second `let`. If we want a class variable `interest-rate`, we can write

```
(define make-account
  (let ((interest-rate 0.05))
    (lambda (name balance)
      (let ((transactions '()))
        (lambda (message . args)
          ...)))))
```

Class methods present more of a problem. We need to have the instance created as a result of the `make` message, which leads to the final version of `account`, shown in Program 6-9. Figure 6-9 shows the snapshot of the frames holding the information for the class.

6.2.5 Putting `define-class` Together

We have shown how constructor arguments, slots, and class variables can be accommodated with appropriate nestings of `let` and `lambda` forms. We have also seen how methods can be structured as `case` clauses. Yet this is not sufficient to write `define-class`. Although we have built a package of object-oriented programming techniques, we have no way to write `define-class` itself, because it isn't a procedure, but a special form. Almost all Scheme systems provide ways of adding such special forms, or macros, to the system, but we're not ready to do this yet. In Chapter 7, we will see how macros work in Scheme.

```
(define account
  (let ((interest-rate 0.05))
    (let
      ((the-constructor
        (lambda (name balance)
          (let ((transactions '()))
            (lambda (message . args)
              ...)))))
      (lambda (message . args)
        (case message
          ((make)
           (apply the-constructor args))
          ((set-rate)
           (set! interest-rate (get-argument args 0)))
          (else
           (error 'account "Invalid class message")))))))
```

Program 6-9   Implementing class methods

6.3   Object-oriented Design

> *Guidelines for bureaucrats: (1) When in charge, ponder. (2) When in trouble, delegate. (3) When in doubt, mumble.*
> — James H. Boren

We've seen how to use `define-class`, and we've seen how classes and objects fit into the environment model. But how do we *program* effectively with objects and classes? Computer scientists have tried in many ways to find a so-called magic bullet that will slay the monster of difficult programming problems. Various bullets have been proposed: new programming languages, new data types, new loop structures, new programming environments, new ways to organize programming projects, and so on. Hopeful programmers tried these bullets and sometimes found them useful, but none of them slew the monster. Complicated problems are inherently hard to solve, and no matter how many tools a programmer has, there is no substitute for clear thinking and careful planning.

Objects and classes give us powerful weapons against the monster, but there's no point in using techniques like `define-class` without really thinking in object-oriented terms. Our goal in object-oriented programming is to write a program whose structure matches that of the problem. We need a way of "thinking with objects", a technique of planning a program so that the classes will be as similar as possible to the real world. Techniques of **object-oriented design** have been developed to help us plan a program in object-oriented terms. These techniques aren't a magic bullet, but at least they can make the monster uncomfortable!

This section presents some of the techniques of object-oriented design. We'll see how to identify the classes in a problem, and how to relate classes to each other. In the process, we'll look at a powerful programming technique, delegation, that lets us define classes in terms of other existing ones. We'll use these concepts to help solve the banking problem from Section 6.1.

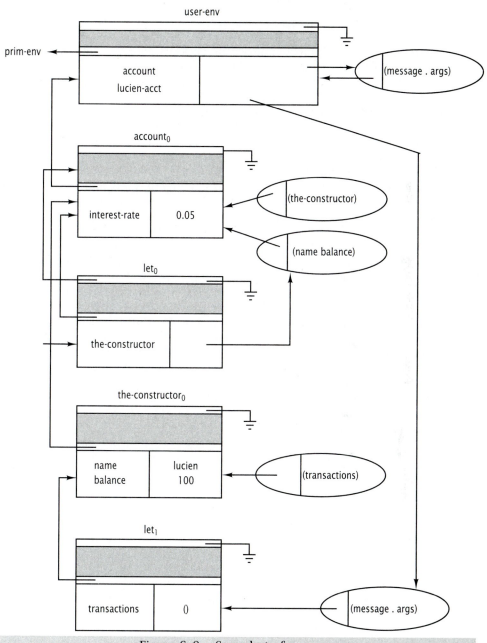

Figure 6–9   Snapshot of account

6.3.1   Finding classes

The task of **finding classes**, or identifying the classes needed in a problem, is often extremely difficult. The real world is a complicated place. If our programs are to be understandable, we must eliminate unnecessary complications and keep those that are part of the problem we're trying to solve.

Imagine that you're building a software system to manage a library's records. These records include the catalog, the list of books that have been ordered, and the circulation list, which shows who has checked each book out. A library system allows users to ask for books on a particular subject, to ask whether a given book is in the library or checked out, and to request that a particular book be ordered.

To use object-oriented design in this problem, we must make a list of classes that might be useful. The most obvious classes are book and user (borrower), but this isn't enough. A library usually has many kinds of items in its collection (including CDs, videotapes, maps, pamphlets, and magazines). Each of these might have its own kind of borrowing rules, might be stored in a different place, and might have its own cataloging rules. How *do* we classify things in a library?

In North America, there are two main systems of classification: the Dewey Decimal System and the Library of Congress System. Melvil Dewey (1851–1931) was interested in promoting public libraries. He developed a cataloging system that was intended to be easy to learn and use, even by nonexperts. The United States Library of Congress system was developed to organize collections that include many government publications. The different purposes of these systems are revealed by their major classifications. For example, military science, a minor topic in the Dewey Decimal System, has two major subject headings in the Library of Congress System.

These systems are relatively hard to change. Neither the Dewey nor Library of Congress system has a major category for computer science. In both systems, many books on programming and computing are cataloged under "mathematical aids to computation" (e.g., books on how to use a slide rule). Others appear under electronics, bookkeeping, or typesetting.

Since our program is supposed to tell us where a book is located in the library, locations should depend upon how an item is cataloged. Many public libraries ignore the Dewey call number when they shelve books, placing them instead on shelves labeled "Fiction", "Young Readers", and "Large Print Books".

The complexity of the problem raises many questions:

- What are the classes, and how do they relate?
- How do we decide what objects are in a class?
- How do we avoid the problem of making our classes too general (e.g., thing-found-in-library) or too specific (book-on-scheme-programming)?
- When we've identified a set of useful classes, how do we know that our classification system is right?

There are no "right answers" to these questions. A good analysis will produce a set of classes that is useful in thinking about the problem. A poor analysis will produce strange classes with many special cases. The whole point of the object-oriented approach is to provide tools for modeling the real world. Therefore, we want a classification system that makes sense to librarians and library users.

One basic way to identify classes is known as the **narrative method**. We ask our client (a librarian, for example) to give a detailed description of the problem.

As we read this description, we regard any noun in the description as the name of a possible class. Our librarian might give the following description of the problem.

> The library has two kinds of items in its collection, books and magazines. Books are placed on the shelves according to the Dewey Decimal System. Magazines are divided into volumes, each bound separately, and shelved in the Magazine Area.
>
> Any user may check books out for a period of time that depends upon the type of book and the demand for that book. When a user checks a book in, it is placed back on the shelves. If a book is overdue, a notice is sent to the user.
>
> Books can be ordered by users. When an ordered book is received, a notice is sent to the user.

Analysis of this description yields the following possible classes, in order of their appearance:

- `library`
- `item`
- `collection`
- `book`
- `magazine`
- `shelf`
- `Dewey-Decimal-System`
- `volume`
- `Magazine-Area`
- `user`
- `notice`

If you tried this yourself, you might have a slightly different list. You might have included such classes as "time", for example. It's a good idea to make this first step, listing all of the nouns as possible classes, as general as possible.

Our next step is to delete from our set of classes those that don't seem to be useful in solving the problem, for example, classes that have only one instance, and classes that don't seem to relate to objects in the real world. (Again, the definition of *useful* will depend upon the problem.) Our next list is slimmed down somewhat, and ordered alphabetically.

- `book`
- `item`
- `magazine`
- `notice`
- `shelf`
- `user`
- `volume`

The final step is to categorize our classes into groups of related classes. For example, a volume is a kind of book; they're both physical objects that can be put onto a shelf and checked out. Books and magazines are items. This categorization gives us a final list of classes.

- `item, book, magazine, volume`
- `notice`
- `shelf`
- `user`

What about the verbs in the description? The verbs often correspond to the messages passed between the objects. For example, a borrower "checks a book out", which would lead to a `check-out` message for the library.

Let's apply the narrative technique to the bank problem. A discussion with the bank staff results in this description of the problem.

> Pickfair Bank has customers with two kinds of accounts, savings and checking. A customer may have one or many accounts. The differences between the account types are in the interest rate and service charges. Customers may make deposits and withdrawals at the bank on each kind of account. Checks may also be written on checking, but not savings, accounts. At the end of the month, a statement is mailed to each customer, showing all of the transactions on each account.

A study of this description yields the following classes.
- `Pickfair-Bank`
- `customer`
- `account`
- `savings-account`
- `checking-account`
- `interest-rate`
- `service-charge`
- `deposit`
- `withdrawal`
- `check`
- `statement`
- `transaction`

Again, we can eliminate some classes. The interest-rate and service-charge classes seem to be nothing but straightforward numbers, and Pickfair Bank would be a class with one instance. It's not stated in the problem, but deposits, withdrawals, and checks are kinds of transactions.

The resulting set of classes is
- `account, savings-account, checking-account`
- `customer`
- `statement`
- `transaction, deposit, withdrawal, check`

Well-chosen classes represent entities in the real world. Generally, a correct classification should enable you to explain your classes to an expert in the problem (a librarian, for example) even if that person knows nothing about computers.

The set of classes should include the following:
- people, places, things
- documents
- external entities

An **external entity** is a device or person that provides data to the system or receives data from the system. The class of customers is an example of something that is both a person and an external entity. A remote computer on a network is an example of a device that is an external entity.

The set of classes should *not* include
- classes with only one instance (a bank, for example)
- classes with only a single piece of state and no behavior (an interest rate)

☞ **Exercise 6–16**

You have been asked to write the software for a system that controls the environment in a large building. The system consists of

- a central computer
- a large number of sensors, such as thermometers (for measuring heat) and photocells (for measuring light intensity)
- a number of devices, such as heaters, the air conditioning system, and lamps

The system should turn devices on and off as necessary to maintain adequate heat and light levels, and should produce reports on its activities that are given to the maintenance staff. Periodically, the maintenance staff will enter schedules into the system (e.g., to switch off sets of lights after midnight).

What classes would you expect in this system? ❏

6.3.2   Class Relationships

It seems reasonable to assume that once we've identified some classes in a problem, we can start designing those classes. But classes can't be designed in isolation. Classes interact; they have various kinds of relationships. The records of a library or bank aren't just a random collection of objects. A library user has some books on loan; a bank account is subject to various rules, depending upon the kind of account. Therefore, we must identify the relationships among classes, relationships among objects, and relationships among classes and objects.

Look again at the library example. A user can have one or more books on loan. The set of books for a user must be part of the user's state, and will change over time as books are returned and new ones borrowed. We say that a user has-a set of checked-out books.

The has-a relation between two objects is often called **containment**. An object contains a second object if the first object has the second as part of its state. In particular, the first has the second as the value of an instance variable. In the library example, containment indicates possession: the borrower has the books. Other kinds of containment don't necessarily indicate possession. For example, in the banking system a monthly statement contains a set of transactions. When we say that "a statement has-a transaction", we mean "has as parts".

We define the **cardinality** as the number of objects that are part of an object's state. For example, we can say that each customer has-a account. If each customer can only have one account, we say that the relationship's cardinality is **one-to-one**. If each customer can have any number of accounts, we say that the relationship's cardinality is **one-to-many**.

Let's apply has-a to the banking example. Recall that we identified the following classes:

- account, savings-account, checking-account
- customer
- statement
- transaction, deposit, withdrawal, check

If Pickfair Bank allows each customer to have any number of savings and checking accounts, then customer has-a savings-account and customer has-a checking-account, both having one-to-many cardinality. (*Many* includes zero, so there's no requirement that a customer have both kinds of accounts.) Sometimes the bank staff must handle a "problem" transaction (for example, a check with insufficient funds), and must identify the customer with that account. Accordingly, account has-a customer—one-to-one. Each account records the transactions on it, and therefore account has-a deposit, account has-a withdrawal, and account has-a check—again one-to-many. If the bank sends out a single statement for each account, statement has-a account has a one-to-one cardinality.

Class and object relationships are complicated enough that it's useful to diagram them. Figure 6-10 shows a diagram of the classes at Pickfair Bank.

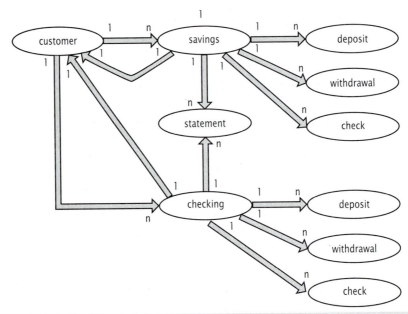

Figure 6-10   The set of has-a relationships at Pickfair Bank

Each arrow represents a has-a relationship; each arrow shows the cardinality (1–1 (one-to-one) or 1–n (one-to-many) of the relationship). Even though the diagram appears to show relationships between classes, has-a applies only to objects. We mean, for example, that *each* account has-a *single* customer.

Figure 6-10 is not about *messages*, such as withdraw. We haven't yet begun to design the messages that each object receives. First we must plan out the *classes*, such as withdrawal.

☞ **Exercise 6–17**

Suppose that you are building a data structure to contain information about the parts of a car. Give one example each of a one-to-one has-a relationship, and of a one-to-many has-a relationship. ❑

What about the classes account and transaction? They seem to have vanished from the bank analysis. Recall, however, that has-a is a relationship between two specific *objects*. For example, customer John Smith has-a account 124837. To include these two classes, we need a comparable relationship between *classes*.

The relationship between classes is called is-a. For example, we can say that any `checking-account` is-a `account`. We saw that has-a is called containment; is-a is called **specialization**, and means that the first class is a specialized version of the second. When we say that a `checking-account` is-a `account`, we mean that each instance of `checking-account` is a specialized version of an `account`. To understand specialization, consider that both savings and checking accounts are kinds of accounts. They both permit withdrawals and deposits, and both record transactions.

Figure 6-11 shows both kinds of relationships. The gray arrows, as before, indicate has-a relations. The black arrows indicate is-a relations. You can read the is-a arrow, from tail to head, as "specializes to". Notice how specialization simplifies the diagram. There are only four main classes in this version: `customer`, `account`, `transaction`, and `statement`. The is-a relations show the different kinds of accounts. The most appealing aspect of this revised class structure is that we can add many different kinds of accounts without complicating the relationship between accounts and transactions. Whereas the "has-a-only" approach of Figure 6-10 requires relationships between each kind of account and each kind of transaction, adding is-a lets us have *one* relationship between accounts and transactions.

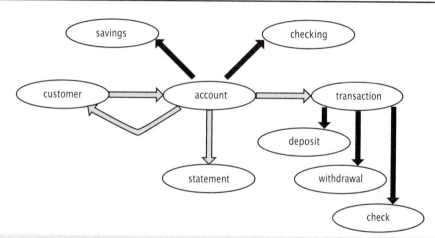

Figure 6-11   The has-a and is-a relationships at Pickfair Bank

People often get containment and specialization confused. Containment is a form of state; an object contains other objects. Specialization isn't about state. When we say that one class is a specialization of another, we are saying that each instance of the specialized class contains the instance variables of and has the methods of the general class.

One way to see this distinction is to consider mutability. Containment is obviously mutable. For example, customers can open and close accounts as desired. We don't have to be able to mutate every instance variable; we might not allow the account number to be mutated. In theory, however, any containment relation can be mutated.

Specialization is immutable. Once an object has been created, its class membership is fixed. A bank account cannot suddenly turn into a customer, or a library user into a book. If class membership is immutable, then specialization must also be immutable. When we say that `savings-account` is-a account, we are saying that *every* `savings-account` has the state and methods defined by account.

It is no accident that we identified has-a before is-a relationships. The has-a relationship is a tool for connecting different kinds of objects; is-a is a tool for simplifying complex relationships of classes.

☞ **Exercise 6–18**

Refer to the final description of the library classes on page 327. Identify the has-a and is-a relationships, and their associated cardinalities. ❏

6.3.3   Implementing Class Relationships in Scheme

We have only one remaining issue in implementing our banking system. How do we represent the class relationships has-a and is-a? The has-a relationship is straightforward. Saying that an `account` has-a `customer` means that an `account` contains an instance variable to hold a customer. Even cardinality can be handled within this framework. For example, `customer` has-a `account`, with cardinality one-to-many. This can be implemented by using a list (or one of the other data structures that we'll study in later chapters, such as trees and vectors) as an instance variable.

Program 6-10 shows a simplified `customer` class. We could have used either a slot or a constructor argument (perhaps a list of existing accounts) to specify the accounts. We chose a slot because most banks do not allow an account to be created without a customer, nor to they give an account away to another customer.

```
(define-class customer
   (constructor-arguments name address)
   (slots (accounts '()))
   (methods (message . args)
     ((new-account)
      (set! accounts (cons (get-argument args 0) accounts)))))
```
Program 6-10   The `customer` class

What about specialization? A specialized class consists of the state and methods of the general class, along with some additional state, additional methods, or both. Many object-oriented languages, for example, C++ and Smalltalk, use a specialization technique known as **inheritance**, in which the system automatically redirects messages sent to an object of a specialized class to the general class if the specialized class has no corresponding method.

Unfortunately, inheritance doesn't fit easily into the environment model.[4] However, there is another technique for implementing specialization, known as **delega-**

---

[4] The original ideas for object-oriented programming in Lisp-based languages followed an ice-cream metaphor, because many of the original Lisp object-oriented designers frequented an ice-cream parlor in Somerville, Massachusetts, named Steve's. One early object-oriented package for Lisp was called Flavors. What we call *classes* were called *flavors* in this system. A general version of a specialized class was known as a *vanilla* class. One version of specialization was called a *mixin* (much like peanuts and chocolate chips). A similar package for Scheme was called Scoops. The Common Lisp Object System, which evolved from Flavors, incorporates a sophisticated type of inheritance. The techniques for implementing inheritance are beyond the scope of this book.

tion. We can use an instance variable of the specialized class to hold an instance of the general class. Any message that is not defined for the specialized class can be redirected to the delegate object.

We can see delegation at work by looking at a design for savings and checking accounts. Both kinds of accounts accept deposits and withdrawals, but the rules for withdrawals are different for each kind of account. Savings accounts have a $1.00 service charge and no overdraft. Checking accounts have a $0.50 service charge, and a $1000 overdraft limit. We won't show all of the machinery for accounts, but only those parts that illustrate delegation (the following version is essentially a simplified version of the account class in Program 6-1).

Program 6-11 shows the class. No check is made to see if there are sufficient funds on deposit, and there are no service charges. This version doesn't show transaction logging; you can adapt the techniques we showed in Program 6-2 to add it.

```
(define-class general-account
  (constructor-arguments balance)
  (methods (message . args)
    ((withdraw)
     (let ((amount (get-argument args 0)))
       (set! balance (+ balance amount))
       balance))
    ((deposit)
     (let ((amount (get-argument args 0)))
       (set! balance (+ balance amount))
       balance))
    ((balance)
      balance)))
```

Program 6-11 Generalized account class

Obviously we will not allow customers to open general-accounts. Instances of general-account are intended to be delegates of specialized kinds of accounts. Program 6-12 shows how the savings-account class uses an instance of general-account as a delegate.

The only method in savings-account is withdrawal. Since a savings-account doesn't contain a balance directly, the withdrawal method sends a message to its delegate to get the balance. If there are sufficient funds, two messages are sent to the delegate: one to withdraw the requested amount, and one for the service charge.

A savings-account uses an else clause to catch all messages that it doesn't explicitly recognize. These messages are forwarded to the delegate, using apply with more than one argument after the procedure. The expression (apply proc arg1 arg2 ... argn rest) is equivalent to (apply proc (cons arg1 (cons arg2 ... (cons argn rest)))). The first n arguments to proc are specified one by one, and the remaining arguments are drawn from rest, which must be a list.

6.3.4 A Retrospective

Object-oriented design can lead us from a problem statement to a program that solves the problem by the following steps:

```
(define-class savings-account
  (constructor-arguments balance)
  (slots (delegate (general-account 'make balance)))
  (methods (message . args)
    ((withdraw)
     (let ((amount (get-argument args 0)))
       (if (< (delegate 'balance) amount)
           (format #t "Sorry, overdraft not permitted.~%")
           (begin
             (delegate 'withdraw amount)
             (delegate 'withdraw 1.00)))))
    (else
     (apply delegate message args))))
```

Program 6-12   Using delegation to implement `savings-account`

1. Read the problem statement carefully.
2. Build a list of the classes that might appear in the problem.
3. Identify the has-a and is-a relationships.
4. Using the has-a relationships, identify the instance variables for each class.
5. Write a set of classes corresponding to the original problem. Test and debug as usual.

This is definitely *not* a recipe for instant programs without work. Mistakes can occur with any method of analyzing and solving problems. The problem statement itself might be incorrect or incomplete. Nevertheless, it is a good way to solve many complex problems, and leads to programs that are understandable and reusable.

Can you use these techniques without using object-oriented programs? To a limited extent, yes. If your problem doesn't require a great deal of polymorphism or specialization, you can represent classes as ADTs. This technique is sometimes known as **object-based design**, and is suitable if you are programming in a language such as C, which has no object-oriented features. On the other hand, most modern programming languages (and many that aren't so modern) have object-oriented features.

We don't use object-oriented approaches much in the rest of the book. Object-oriented approaches are best for large problems, ones that are larger than the limit of a few hundred lines for those programs that we will study. For truly large problems, object-oriented design is essential.

Case Study: An Object-Based Implementation of a Calendar

The code presented in this section can be found in file `calendar.scm`.

Many computers can manage a personal appointments schedule or a calendar. In this Case Study, we'll implement a calendar. A full-blown calendar would need many kinds of events, including daily, weekly, monthly, and even irregular events, but we will only implement weekly events and one-time appointments.

The first thing a calendar must do is record the dates of appointments for specific days. The other main task of a calendar is to record the ongoing regular weekly appointments. In this calendar, we have implemented weekly appointments that occur on a particular day of the week (e.g., Monday). Let's assume that the user will ask the calendar what's scheduled for a time period. To simplify things, we'll specify all days by number from the beginning of the month. Weekly events will be specified by the day of the week, and all events will take place in one month. We've assumed that events begin and end on the same day. Another important simplification is that queries will only be about events on one day. These two simplifications eliminate any concerns about boundaries between one day and the next.

We've used the methods of object-oriented design to design the classes in this Case Study, but we won't show the steps. Before reading the results, you should review the process. Program 6-13 shows the class definition for a simple event. Program 6-14 shows the class definition for a weekly appointment.

```
(define-class event
  (constructor-arguments
    day time-begin time-end kind annote with at)
  (methods
   (message . args)
   ((about) annote)
   ((begin) time-begin)
   ((day) day)
   ((day-of-the-week)
    (weekday-from-day-of-month day))
   ((print-if-overlap)
    (if (overlap (list-ref args 0) (list-ref args 1)
                 (list-ref args 2)
                 day time-begin time-end)
        (print-event day time-begin time-end kind)))
   ((end) time-end)
   ((kind) kind)
   ((print) (print-event day time-begin time-end kind))
   ((where) at)
   ((whom) with))))
```

Program 6-13   Class definition for events

A weekly appointment differs only slightly internally from a standard event, but it is used differently. A weekly event knows its day of the week, while a standard event calculates the weekday on which it occurs by counting from the day `first-of-month`, specified globally. Internally, the weekly event is represented as an event whose date is zero. The calendar itself separates weekly and daily appointments.

The calendar will be an object that takes four messages: add-event, whatsup, print, and list-free. The add-event method interactively asks the user to fill in the data for a particular event. Queries ask for the events in a time period; for example, (calendar 'whatsup) prints the events that occur, either wholly or partially, in a time period. The calendar begins a dialog that asks for a date (day, hour, and minute) and then a time of the day (hour and minute). print displays all the events in the calendar. list-free is the complement of whatsup; it lists the free time in a time period. Program 6-15 shows the class definition for the calendar.

First, we make a calendar:

```
(define-class weekly
  (constructor-arguments
    day time-begin time-end kind annote with at)
  (slots
    (event (event 'make 0 time-begin time-end kind annote with at)))
  (methods
  (message . args)
  ((day) day)
  ((day-of-the-week) day)
  ((print) (print-event day time-begin time-end kind))
  (else (apply event (cons message args)))))
```

Program 6-14   Class definition for weekly appointments

```
> (define cal (make-calendar 'jim))
```

The name of the calendar is jim. We enter an event:

```
> (cal 'add-event)
Starting time: Enter day, hour, and minute: 1 12 20
Ending time: Enter hour and minute:   13 30
Enter annotation, whom with, where:
 "lunch" vincent Trekkers
```

The dialog asks for the day: a number specifies a day of the month, so the event is an appointment; otherwise, the input is a symbol, so the event is a weekly meeting.

Time is the complicated issue in calendars. We need to organize events so that the calendar can easily determine whether a particular time slot is full or not, on input, and can respond to questions about particular time periods. Representing events is also important. Another critical decision is whether to organize the calendar around events, as we've done, or days of the month. A calendar organized around days, like an appointment book, would need a collection of days. Each day would be a collection of events. An appointment occurs on one day, but a weekly event is distributed over at least four days in a month.

We chose to manage events, not days, so information is more centralized. But weekly and appointment events are different. A weekly event occurs every week; it has a day of the week but not a date. The calendar must manage the two different types of events separately. Appointments are kept in a list. Since weekly events are associated with weekdays, a calendar has a slot for weekly events, an alist whose keys are the weekdays and whose values are the lists of events on a weekday.

The calendar maintains events in both lists in order of time of occurrence. It is essential that no two events overlap in time. put-in-place, shown in Program 6-16, takes an event and a list of events and returns a new list of events in which the new event is inserted in its proper place. Most important, it checks whether two events overlap in time and warns when "Events conflict!"

The add-event shows the important activities of the calendar. First it creates a new event using the create-event input procedure. It then treats the event as an appointment or a weekly. For weekly events, it finds the weekday in the weekly list, and puts the event in the correct place in the list. put-in-place will check for any conflict with an existing event. Appointments are handled differently; they must be compared with the events on that day, and also with the weekly events that occur on the day of the week corresponding to the date.

```
(define-class calendar
  (constructor-arguments name)
  (slots (wevents (weeklies)) (events '()))
  (methods (message)
   ((add-event)
    (let ((event (create-event)))
      (case (event 'kind)
        ((weekly)
         (let ((pair (assv (event 'day-of-the-week) wevents)))
           (set-cdr! pair (put-in-place event (cdr pair)))))
        ((appointment)
         (let ((weekday (assv (event 'day-of-the-week) wevents)))
           (if (or (null? weekday)
                   (no-overlap? event (cdr weekday)))
               (set! events (put-in-place event events)))))))))
   ((list-free)
    (format #t "Time period? ")
    (let* ((date-from (input-date))
           (to-time (begin (display "to ") (input-time))))
      (show-free
        (date-time date-from)
        to-time
        (cdr (assv (weekday-from-day-of-month (date-day date-from))
               wevents))
        events)))
   ((whatsup)
    (format #t "Time period? ")
    (let* ((date-from (input-date))
           (to-time (begin (display "to ") (input-time))))
      (for-each
        (lambda (x)
          (x 'print-if-overlap (date-day date-from)
            (date-time date-from) to-time))
        events)
      (newline)
      (for-each
       (lambda (day)
          (for-each
           (lambda (x)
             (x 'print-if-overlap 0 (date-time date-from) to-time))
          (cdr day)))
       wevents)))
   ((print)
    (for-each (lambda (x) (x 'print)) events)
    (for-each
      (lambda (day) (for-each (lambda (x) (x 'print)) (cdr day)))
      wevents))))
```

Program 6-15   Class definition for calendars

```
(define put-in-place
  (lambda (event events)
    (if (null? events)
        (list event)
        (let ((res (e-overlap event (car events))))
          (if (eqv? res 'less)
              (cons event events)
              (if (eqv? res 'grtr)
                  (cons (car events)
                        (put-in-place event (cdr events)))
                  (begin
                    (display "Events conflict!") (newline)
                    (display "New: ") (event 'print)
                    (display "Existing: ")
                    ((car events) 'print)
                    events)))))))
```

Program 6-16   Inserting an event in temporal order

e-overlap determines whether the time periods of events overlap, comparing the beginning and ending times of two events. It returns one of three symbols: less, grtr, and over. Using these three values, put-in-place can order events in an event list. Chapter 9 presents similar comparison procedures to handle the general problem of organizing data in order.

Figure 6-12 shows a dialog using the calendar. The four message types are demonstrated, as well as the calendar's ability to check for conflict among events.

☞ **Exercise 6-19**

Add a delete-event message to the calendar object. ❏

Summary

This chapter has introduced object-oriented programming and design. The world can be modeled as a set of objects that interact by sending each other messages, and we can organize these objects into classes. We studied define-class as an example of an object-oriented extension to Scheme, and we saw how define-class can be implemented in terms of the environment model.

Object-oriented programming isn't enough to write complex programs. Object-oriented design allows us to study a problem, identify relationships between classes, and determine what instance variables and methods are required. Although it is no panacea, object-oriented design leads to programs that are readable and reusable.

Further Readings

Many books on object-oriented programming and design have been published. Unfortunately, few of them are aimed at beginning programmers. The classic book on analysis and design is *Object-Oriented Analysis and Design, With Applications*, second

```
> (define cal (make-calendar 'jim))
> (cal 'add-event)
Starting time: Enter day, hour, and minute: monday 15 30
Ending time: Enter hour and minute:  16 30
Enter annotation, whom with, where:
  "office hours" cs128 new-building
> (cal 'add-event)
Starting time: Enter day, hour, and minute: 3 12 20
Ending time: Enter hour and minute:  13 30
Enter  annotation, whom with, where:
  "lunch" vincent Trekkers
> (cal 'print)
3 12:20  13:30    Appointment
monday 15:30  16:30    Weekly
> (cal 'whatsup)
Time period? Enter day, hour, and minute: 3 9 00
to Enter hour and minute:  18 00
3 12:20  13:30    Appointment

monday 15:30  16:30    Weekly
> (cal 'list-free)
Time period? Enter day, hour, and minute: 3 9 00
to Enter hour and minute:  19 00
9:00  to 12:20
13:30  to 19:00
> (cal 'add-event)
Starting time: Enter day, hour, and minute: 3 11 30
Ending time: Enter hour and minute:  13 00
Enter annotation, whom with, where:
  "class" cs100 old-building
Events conflict!
New: 3 11:30  13:00    Appointment
Existing: 3 12:20  13:30    Appointment
```

Figure 6-12   A calendar example

edition, by Grady Booch. This book is aimed at people with considerable programming experience, but is packed with insights.

One widely used language for object-oriented programming is C++. The best book for learning C++ is Stanley Lippman, *C++ Primer*. A good book that shows how data abstraction and object-oriented programming fit into C++ is Headington and Riley, *Data Abstraction and Structures Using C++*. Another widely used object-oriented language is Smalltalk. A good introduction to Smalltalk is *Practical Smalltalk* by Dan Shafer.

Key Words

Here are the *key words* introduced in this chapter. Make sure you understand what each one means.

behavior	GUI	object-oriented design
cardinality	identity	one-to-one
class	inheritance	one-to-many
class variable	instance	polymorphism
class method	instance variable	reusability
containment	instantiate	slot
delegation	legacy code	specialization
dispenser	message	state
external entity	narrative method	structured analysis
finding classes	object	user interface object
graphic user interface	object-based design	

Scheme Features Introduced in This Chapter

Special Forms

case   class

Cumulative List of Data Types

No new datatypes were introduced in this chapter.

Problems

1. Draw a snapshot after evaluating the following forms:

```
(define make-thing
  (lambda (sort)
    (lambda (in1 in2)
      (let ((memory '()))
        (if (eqv? in1 'insert)
          (set! memory (cons in2 memory))
          (if (eqv? in1 'show)
            memory))))))
(define odd-make-thing
  (lambda (x)
    (make-thing (if (odd? x) 'even 'odd))))
(define one-of-them (odd-make-thing 3))
```

2. Joel User has written some code that uses `list-ref`. The code is slow and Joel would like to count the number of times `list-ref` is called. To help Joel, write `list-ref%`, a version of `list-ref` that counts the number of times that it has been called. `list-ref%` returns the same value as `list-ref` when called with two arguments. It acts specially when called with one argument. If the argument is `#f`, it returns the number of times it has been called. If the argument is anything else, it resets its internal counter and returns `'reset`.

```
(list-ref% #t) ⇒ reset
(list-ref% #f) ⇒ 0
```

```
(define it (list 1 2 3 4 5))
(begin (list-ref% it 0) (list-ref% it 1) (list-ref% it 2))
(list-ref% #f) ⇒ 3
```

3. We are going to simulate a mailbox using object-oriented programming, using `define-class` to write a Scheme form that creates mailbox objects. A mailbox has the following information: an *address*, a number, given when the mailbox is created, that never changes; the *mails-in*, a Boolean flag that indicates whether something is in the mailbox (initially #f); and the *letters*, in a list. To create a mailbox we provide the address, as follows: (`define this-box (mailbox 'make 547)`).

   The mailbox object accepts the following messages:
   - `address` asks for the address.
   - `in?` returns true or false depending on the state of the flag.
   - `put` takes a letter (which we'll represent with any Scheme value) as its argument and adds that letter to the ones already in the box.
   - `get` empties the mailbox, returns the list of letters in it, and sets the flag to #f.

```
(this-box 'address) ⇒ 547
(this-box 'put 'hello)
(this-box 'in?) ⇒ #t
(this-box 'put '(another letter))
(this-box 'get) ⇒ ((another letter) hello)
(this-box 'in?) ⇒ #f
```

   Write the `define-class` form to implement mailboxes.

4. Within the context of the answer to Problem 3, use `define-class` to implement a movable-mailbox, which works just like a mailbox, except that there is an additional message `new-address` that takes a number as its argument and changes the address to that number, so that later `address` messages will get the new value. The movable-mailbox should respond to all other requests just like an ordinary mailbox. Use delegation to implement your solution. The new mailbox now works this way:

```
(define a-box (movable-mailbox 'make 2456))
(a-box 'address) ⇒ 2456
(a-box 'new-address 4321)
(a-box 'address) ⇒ 432
```

Self-Assessment

1. Devise an object that maintains a collections of user identification numbers and their associated passwords. Initially, there are no passwords.

```
> (define plist
    (check-passwords
      '( (jim . (ham . 0))
         (ed . (beef . 0)) (mary . (tuna . 0)))))
```

   This defines passwords for three users: `jim`, `ed` and `mary`. If the password is correct, `plist` responds "Ok"; if it is wrong, `plist` says, "Try again", but only three times. The fourth time `plist` sees an incorrect password, it responds "No way", and from then on it will not accept even a correct password. If a correct password arrives before the fourth time, `plist` resets the count to zero.

```
(plist 'jim 'ham) ⇒ "Ok"
(plist 'jim 'lettuce) ⇒ "Try again"
(plist 'jim 'chese) ⇒ "Try again"
(plist 'jim 'parsely) ⇒ "Try again"
(plist 'jim 'parsely) ⇒ "No way"
(plist 'ed 'boeuf) ⇒ "Try again"
(plist 'ed 'beef) ⇒ "Ok"
```

2. Draw the snapshot after evaluating the following forms:

```
> (define bar
    (lambda (kind)
      (lambda (message what)
        (case message
          (type kind)
          (mutate (set! x what))
          (value x)))))
> (define foo
    (lambda (x)
      (bar (if (< x 10) 'small 'large))))
> (define whatsit (foo 4))
```

3. You've been asked to devise an object `ballot-box` for use in the upcoming election. The `ballot-box` counts votes for the parties, and can tell you the current total for one party or all:

```
(define ballot-box
  (make-ballot-box
    (vote-list '(left right middle up down))))
(ballot-box 'vote 'left) ⇒ 1
(ballot-box 'vote 'left) ⇒ 2
(ballot-box 'vote 'right) ⇒ 1
(ballot-box 'tally 'left) ⇒ 2
(ballot-box 'tally 'all)
  ⇒ ((left . 2) (middle . 0) (right . 1) (up . 0) (down 0))
```

Procedure `vote-list` creates a list of tallies. Each tally is represented as a pair.

```
(vote-list '(a b c d)) ⇒ ((a . 0) (b . 0) (c . 0) (d . 0))
```

The input to `make-ballot-box` is a list of tallies. That gives us a representation for all the vote totals for the parties. To find a particular tally among the tallies, use `assv`, which searches a list of pairs to find the pair whose `car` matches the argument to `assv`:

```
(assv 'a (vote-list '(a b c d))) ⇒ (a . 0)
```

Thus, `assv` selects your individual tally. Write `make-ballot-box` to create the object that accepts the above messages. It's a simple object that takes two messages, `vote` and `tally`. You don't need to worry about error-checking or error messages.

4. Write `vote-list` from Question 4.

Programming Problems

1. At the beginning of this chapter we described how customers interact with tellers to access their accounts. Figure 6-1 shows some possible interactions with a teller. A teller is a user interface object whose state and behavior are concerned with interacting with the user.

    The customer walks into the bank, presents appropriate identification to the teller, and requests money from an account. The teller responds by deducting the amount from the account balance, and giving the money to the customer. It is not the *teller* who makes the decision to authorize the transaction, but the *account*. The teller's job is to transmit the customer's request to the account, and give the customer the money.

    Design and implement the teller class.

2. The calendar in the Case Study is a good start, but a great deal needs to be done to create a useful system. Here are two improvements.
    a. We've only given a partial implementation of **add-event**. Checking between weekly and daily events is not symmetric. How would you complete the implementation of **add-event** so that a weekly event can check all the appropriate days in the month to detect overlap?
    b. It might have been simpler to represent all days as lists of events and to treat weekly events as we do appointments. Setting up a weekly event, then, means to enter it in all the event lists for the days on which it occurs. The interface to the calendar remains the same. Design the internal representation for the day-oriented calendar, and the procedures for entering and removing events.

Chapter 7

Evaluators and Languages

Overview

What is a programming language? How do we *specify* valid programming languages? What do we mean by *syntax* and *semantics*? How do we *implement* a programming language? We look at the two basic methods of implementing a language: either *interpret* the program directly, or *compile* it into a simpler language. We'll see that Scheme's syntax is extensible: it can be customized by any programmer. Finally, we'll see how we can use the environment model and our understanding of programming languages to write an elegantly simple evaluator for Scheme.

Round and round the circle
Completing the charm
So the knot be unknotted
The crossed be uncrossed
The crooked be made straight
And the curse be ended.

— T. S. Eliot, *The Family Reunion*

We are now at a crucial point in our study of computer science. So far, we have been learning to *use* Scheme. We learned the fundamentals of programming in Scheme. We also looked at some programming techniques, algorithms, and design methods, and we applied those features and techniques to a number of problems. What we didn't do was to ask how Scheme evaluators work.

From one point of view, this is a pointless question. A computer user might say, "Why should we care *how* a Scheme system works, as long as we can use it when we need it?" After all, millions of people use computers without much insight about how they work.[1] But can a computer scientist argue the same way? If we want to understand how our program works, surely we need to know how the computer processes it.

As it happens, the principles behind the way that Scheme evaluators work are much the same as those behind evaluators for other programming languages. We therefore start by looking at some very simple languages to see how we can specify these languages and use those specifications to build implementations.

In Chapters 5 and 6, we built a sophisticated model of how a Scheme program is evaluated. Now we can put that model to use as the basis of a Scheme evaluator. Building that evaluator will give us an opportunity to study new data structures. When we're finished, we will have had an opportunity to study a program substantially larger than anything we've seen before.

We will also see throughout this chapter that programming languages aren't as different as they may appear. The same concepts and features recur in many languages.

---

[1] Books with titles like *DOS for the Brain-Dead* prove this claim!

7.1 Programming Languages

I am not like a lady at the court of Versailles, who said: 'What a dreadful pity that the bother at the tower of Babel got language all mixed up; but for that, everyone would always have spoken French.'
— Voltaire, Letter to Catherine the Great

Early programming languages were defined by listing a set of "features" that the language had to have. For example, the original version of FORTRAN (in 1956) was designed to be suitable for scientific computation. It was good for numerical operations, as one would expect in a *FOR*mula *TRAN*slator, but had very poor string processing.[2] People who wanted to process strings used *SNOBOL*. The 1961 version of the *CO*mmon *B*usiness-*O*riented *L*anguage (COBOL), on the other hand, was useless for both numerical computation and string processing, but had excellent file-processing features. Designers of software to control lathes and other pieces of factory equipment designed a language for *A*utomatically *P*rogrammed *T*ools (APT). People who wanted to write programs that simulated real-world processes, such as the loading of ships in a harbor, used *SIM*ulation *SCRIPT* (SIMSCRIPT). Artificial-intelligence researchers at MIT developed a language that was suitable for handling complex data structures, and called it *LIS*t *P*rocessor (LISP).

By the 1960s, it had become clear that as soon as one discovered a new type of computer application, one developed a language for that application. Each language had its own structure and rules, and no language looked much like another. One of the first systematic studies of languages, Jean Sammet's *Programming Languages: History and Implementation* (1969) organized the various languages into a computational Tower of Babel. The difficulty with this approach was that problems don't fit neatly into application areas. For example, a program that analyzes answers to a survey might require the numerical capabilities of FORTRAN, the file-processing features of COBOL, and string-processing features only found in another language.

One solution, popular in the 1960s, was the general-purpose language. Languages such as PL/I (developed by IBM) were attempts to provide all the features of earlier languages integrated into a systematic whole. Unfortunately, these languages became extremely complex in their attempts to integrate disparate features into a consistent whole. As a result, they were hard to learn and hard to implement on computers.[3] One surprising aspect of these complex languages was that they did *not* integrate all of the features that programmers wanted. The reason was simple: it was difficult to add new features to an already complex language. Rather than make the language easy to extend, the designers "froze" in those features they thought programmers wanted. Programmers soon wanted new features, however, that the designers had never thought of. As a result, as soon as one of these languages was developed, it became obsolete.

In 1965, the British computer scientist Peter Landin noted that some seven hundred programming languages had been developed. Some were very general-purpose (PL/I); some were aimed at a particular kind of application (FORTRAN and

---

[2] Modern versions of FORTRAN include quite good string-processing features.

[3] As of the early 1990s, PL/I is still used at some IBM installations, but is almost unused elsewhere.

COBOL); others were for specific purposes (ATLAS, which was designed for programming equipment that tested electronic devices). Landin noted that, even though each language had its own rules, the basic ideas, such as variables, conditionals, procedures, and looping, were the same. He suggested that it might make more sense to organize a language so that the basic rules were very simple, and put all of the special features into the set of primitive procedures. Different languages would follow the same rules for procedures, variables, and so on, but would have different sets of primitive procedures. Landin called his paper "The Next 700 Programming Languages". He invented a language called ISWIM ("If you See What I Mean") based on lambda-calculus, that was never implemented, but his work led directly to Scheme.

The environment model was a breakthrough. We now have a set of accurate rules for describing how Scheme forms are evaluated. The environment model is sufficient to evaluate *any* Scheme form, provided that we have defined the primitives that the evaluator is to place in the global environment. Scheme begins with a simple set of primitives to which we can add new primitives to extend Scheme in various directions, adding features such as graphics, databases, or text editing.[4]

Of course, this approach of adding primitives is not new to us. We have shown how to implement various Scheme primitives, using our *name%* notation, consistently in the preceding chapters. The approach is not unique to Scheme. Most other modern languages, such as Modula-2, C, and C++, follow the same approach of keeping the language rules simple, and then providing a good way to add libraries of "primitive" procedures. This makes the language easier to learn, and means that the only people who need to learn about a particular set of primitives are those who will use that set. Ease of learning isn't the only benefit of this approach. It also makes implementing the language simpler. We can concentrate on getting the basic evaluator structure correct, and then add the primitives we need.

There is no technical reason that there are still so many programming languages; rather, languages build cultures around them. People become comfortable with one language, and often resist changing to another, and with good reason. They don't want to rewrite all the code they've written, at a huge cost, and possibly introduce new bugs because they've switched to a new language. The only alternative is to learn several languages. After you have learned the first few, learning a new language is relatively easy.

7.1.1   Languages and Evaluators

We have talked about a Scheme *evaluator* that accepts Scheme forms and computes values. We have also discussed the Scheme *language*, which defines what Scheme forms are, and what each form means (i.e., what output should be produced for each form). But what is a language? And what is an evaluator?

Programming languages are closer to mathematics than to ordinary natural languages. But think for a moment of natural languages: What makes a sentence valid in everyday speech? The listener has a set of rules about what is and is not valid (syntax), and what valid sentences mean (semantics). Languages change over time.

---

[4] Doing this might require some systems knowledge; for example, you might have to write some of the code in a language such as C (most Scheme systems can use *foreign procedures*, procedures written in languages other than Scheme). Once the new primitives have been coded and tested, Scheme programmers can use them without knowing that they're any different from the built-in primitive procedures.

For example, Shakespeare would probably have trouble understanding a modern mystery novel. Sometimes the rules are inconsistent. Sometimes a sentence has several meanings, and the literal meaning isn't actually what's meant. Few people who answered "Would you mind passing the salt?" with "Yes, I would mind" would be invited back to dinner.

The best way to think about a programming language is to think about the programs (forms) we might write in that language. There are an infinite number of Scheme programs (although not all of them would be useful). Some of these programs produce the same result, for example, (+ 2 3) and (+ 3 2); even so, they are actually different programs.

The fact that a language consists of an infinite number of programs creates a problem. How do we know what the rules are? How do we know whether a program is valid? Early programming languages were defined by the implementation. If there was some doubt about syntax or semantics, programmers would write a small test program. The problem with this approach is that we might have two implementations, with different bugs. Which is the definitive implementation?

Instead of the "try it and see" approach, we can use a rulebook. People who invent programming languages often prepare a specification, a document that gives the precise rules for their language. For Scheme, the specification is a document called *The Revised^n Report on the Algorithmic Language Scheme* (called by Schemers R^nRS), written by a group of Schemers from various universities, companies, and research institutes. *Revised^n* is a shorthand for "Revised Revised ... Revised". On each revision, n is incremented by 1. As of this writing, $n = 4$; the fifth revision is currently in preparation.[5] Language specifications are not written to be easy to read or to teach the language, but to answer questions about the language rules.

A language by itself is useless unless there is a way to evaluate programs written in the language. For this, we need an evaluator: a device that accepts as input a valid program and produces the output of the program. Only when we have an evaluator can we actually talk about running a program.

An evaluator can be hardware, or software, or even a person. The only problem with having a person do this is that any real program involves millions of steps. People are simply too slow and error-prone, not to mention too easily bored, to run programs.[6] An evaluator is *universal*: it will do *anything* for which a program can be written. This fact distinguishes evaluators from other kinds of programs: whereas an "application" program does a specific task, an evaluator will do any task for which we can write a program.

It is possible to build a hardware Scheme evaluator, that is, a computer chip that responds directly to Scheme forms. However, with the wide availability of personal computers, it is much more appealing to write an evaluator as software.

The microprocessors in our computers are evaluators, although the language they understand is extremely primitive. The development of the microprocessor shows how useful the concept of evaluators is. In the 1960s, electronics designers built special-purpose circuits. The early microprocessors were designed not for

---

[5] To obtain a copy, see the Software Package.

[6] Prior to the wide availability of computers, mathematical calculations were done by a room full of mathematicians, each of whom was given a list of instructions for his or her part of the calculation. Calculations that would take several weeks when done by humans took only an hour or so on even the earliest computers. It is amusing to note that the term *computer* was originally used to refer to humans who did calculations.

personal computers but to replace these special-purpose circuits. Electrical engineers found that it was much easier and cheaper to buy a microprocessor and write a program for it than to build elaborate circuits. We will look at the structure of computers in more detail in Chapter 11.

7.1.2 Languages Are for People!

The design of programming languages is a human activity. A programming language is the input to a computer program, namely the evaluator for that language. We design languages that allow us to express algorithms effectively and efficiently. Computers do not care what their programming languages look like, but we have a long tradition of mathematics and natural language that we will not abandon.[7] Our programs and our evaluators should be user-friendly.

Computer scientists have evolved a set of principles about how to design languages. Almost all languages designed in the past fifteen years or so follow the principles listed below.[8]

- The language should be *expressive*, allowing the programmer to say exactly what the program is to do, at the right level of abstraction.
  One aspect of expressiveness is a complete set of data types. For example, early versions of FORTRAN had no character or string variables. In order to process non-numeric data, a FORTRAN programmer had to play tricks with numeric variables. This was so tedious that many programmers asked users to enter numeric codes rather than more easily understood commands.

- The language should be *readable*; programs are written once, but read many times. The language should encourage us to write programs that can be easily read by others familiar with the language. It should give us facilities for defining readable names, indenting programs in a readable way, and making comments.
  Early versions of BASIC limited variable names to at most two characters and did not allow procedures to have names, only line numbers. A program written in such a language requires many comments if it is to be readable later.

- The language should allow an evaluator to *detect mistakes*. Programmers can make mistakes, especially when the program is thousands of lines long. For example, to avoid errors, Scheme will not allow you to use an unbound name, and will not allow you to bind a name without initializing it.

- Languages should be *orthogonal*, that is, have a small set of concepts, and should allow any valid combination of these concepts that makes sense. Objects that are orthogonal are independent and cannot be described in terms of each other. Choosing features that are orthogonal should provide a language that is small, simple, and easy to learn and use. A good language is

---

[7] Not all programming languages are designed by English-speakers, of course. Where Scheme has the `newline` procedure, a French version might have `ligne`. Where Scheme uses the conventional Roman alphabet, a Russian version might use the Cyrillic alphabet.

[8] Not *all* languages follow these principles. A major software company's word-processing program comes with its own dialect of BASIC. This dialect is so peculiar and has so many strange rules and "undocumented features" (aka "bugs") that a book of over 800 pages was published just to explain the features that the software company "forgot" to document.

designed by listing the basic concepts the language is to have, and providing mechanisms for combining them effectively.[9]

Orthogonal languages treat most, if not all, data types as first-class citizens, whereas nonorthogonal languages have special rules about how various kinds of data may be used. One of the most astonishing examples of nonorthogonality was an implementation of PL/I for small IBM computers written around 1970. This compiler allowed Boolean expressions, but only in an `if` statement or a loop. The programmer could not have Boolean variables, Boolean arguments to procedures, or procedures that returned Boolean results.

- A language must be *efficiently implementable.* Language features that appear useful but prevent efficient implementation make the language unusable. Modern languages are designed by writing a sample evaluator in order to experiment with the ideas of the language and to ensure that there are no unforeseen problems in the structure of the evaluator.

☞ **Exercise 7–1**

We believe that Scheme exemplifies the above principles. Still, no language is perfect. Find an example in which Scheme violates each of these principles, except efficient implementation. (This is a hard exercise!) ❏

7.1.3   A Simple Programming Language

Our eventual goal is to develop an evaluator for Scheme with which we can enter Scheme programs (forms) and see their resulting output. Given that Scheme is a complicated language (as are all practical languages), let's start off with a **toy language**, one designed as a vehicle for studying one or more aspects of programming languages rather than for any useful programming purpose. A toy language is an experimenter's tool that lets us concentrate on the issues we're interested in without having to worry about irrelevant details.

Our first toy language is called Dream (rhymes with Scheme). Program 7–1 shows an example of a Dream program. As you can see, Dream programs are written in much the same way that Scheme programs are, though many details differ.

Stepping through Program 7–1, we notice the following:

- The `program` keyword must come first.
- The `variable` form names the variables in the program.
- The `assign` form is a mutation form, equivalent to `set!` in Scheme.
- Arithmetic is done in much the same way as in Scheme, but the primitives have different names.
- Conditionals are written using `test`, which takes *then* and *else* parts, as `if` does in Scheme.
- The `print` form writes out its argument, just as `display` does in Scheme.
- The `in-sequence` form specifies that its subforms must be evaluated in order, just as with `begin` in Scheme.

---

[9] The term *orthogonal* comes from linear algebra: the area marked out by two vectors is at a maximum when the vectors are at right angles, or orthogonal.

```
(program
  (variable a b c disc)
  (assign a 1)
  (assign b 4)
  (assign c 3)
  (assign disc (plus (times b b) (times 4 (times a c))))
  (test (less disc 0)
        (print "No solution")
        (in-sequence
            (print "Solution 1:")
            (print (divide
                    (plus (negative b) (sqrt disc))
                    (times 2 a)))
            (print "; solution 2: ")
            (print (divide
                    (difference (negative b) (sqrt disc))
                    (times 2 a))))))
```

Program 7-1   Example Dream program

Unlike Scheme, Dream is organized around assignment. The program begins by assigning values to the variables, and then printing expressions involving the variables. We can divide the components of Dream into two types: *operations* and *commands*. Operations return values; commands do not. Most commands are the equivalents of special forms in Scheme. Dream is a toy language, though, because there are no procedures and no looping.

☞ **Exercise 7-2**

From Program 7-1, identify the operations of Dream, and describe each. Do the same for the commands. ❑

☞ **Exercise 7-3**

Write a Dream program that determines whether an integer is divisible by 17. ❑

☞ **Exercise 7-4**

Dream programs are susceptible to a kind of bug that can never occur in Scheme programs. What is it? (Hint: look at `variable`). ❑

7.1.4   Formal Language Definitions

Now that we have defined Dream, we can determine if we're ready to design an evaluator for it. Early languages were designed as we designed Dream. The designers decided what features the language was to have, wrote a few programs in the language, wrote down a list of rules for the language, and then wrote an evaluator from the rules. If users had a question about the rules, they were asked to write a test program to see what the evaluator did.

The difficulties appeared when a language became so popular that other people decided to write their own evaluators. Today, evaluators are written in high-level

Language Profile: ALGOL 60

ALGOL 60 was originally developed as a language for writing readable algorithms, hence the name, which comes from "algorithmic language". Its designers expected that people, as well as computers, would read the programs. This was a new idea in 1960; most earlier languages used odd notations without a coherent design. ALGOL 60 was based on conventional mathematical notation; COBOL (Common Business-Oriented Language) was designed at about the same time to be an English-like programming language.

Here's an ALGOL 60 program to compute the geometric mean of two numbers:

```
begin
  procedure geometricmean(a, b)
  real a, b;
  begin
    geometricmean := sqrt(a*b);
  end;
  real x, y;
  readreal(x);
  readreal(y);
  writereal(geometricmean(x,y));
end
```

Some of the language concepts introduced in ALGOL 60 include static scoping, recursive procedures, and procedural arguments (the name *thunk* was invented by the ALGOL 60 committee). ALGOL 60 also included "structured" conditional (if) and looping statements that made programs much more readable than in earlier languages.

ALGOL 60 became very popular in Europe, but never caught on in North America. This was partly because of a fundamental mistake in the design of the language: the committee deliberately didn't include any input/output operations. As a result, each ALGOL 60 system had its own input/output primitives, and programs developed for one could not be run on another. In FORTRAN, on the other hand, input/output statements were defined in the language. (The readreal and writereal procedures in the above example aren't part of ALGOL 60, but might have been provided by a particular ALGOL 60 system.)

Language designers have always looked carefully at ALGOL 60. PL/I, published in 1964, was one of the first languages designed using ALGOL 60's framework. A few years later, the Swiss computer scientist Niklaus Wirth developed Pascal for teaching computer science. Pascal was inspired by ALGOL 60, but also included some sophisticated methods for structuring data (ALGOL 60 only allowed numbers, Booleans, and very limited use of strings).

In the 1960s, a group in Norway developed Simula-67, a language for writing simulation programs, again strongly based on ALGOL 60. Simula-67 was the first object-oriented language (the word *class* appears first in Simula-67). In the early 1980s, a scientist at Bell Laboratories, Bjarne Stroustrup, decided to add Simula's object-oriented features to C, another language indirectly based upon ALGOL 60. The resulting language, C++, has become very popular in North America. Many languages have much the same structure because they trace their descent from ALGOL 60. Almost all modern languages, including C, C++, Pascal, Modula-2, Ada, and Scheme, do.

languages such as C and Scheme. This makes it possible to *port* (transport) an evaluator from one computer to another. Even so, people want to write new evaluators. For example, students might want a Scheme evaluator that gives detailed error messages, whereas professional programmers might want one that runs programs quickly, even if the error messages are less helpful. Problems arise if different evaluators give different answers to the same test program.

The best way to write good programs is to start with a good *specification* of the problem. With a good specification, we can focus on making sure the program does what it is supposed to, rather than trying to guess what should be done in some unforeseen case. Thus, the answer to our problem is that the defining report for our language must be an accurate specification that says *exactly* which programs are legal and what the meaning of each language construct is.

The first language to do this was ALGOL 60, a language published by an international committee of computer scientists in 1960. Although it is no longer in use, ALGOL 60 is arguably the most important programming language ever developed, because its ideas formed the basis of so many languages, including Pascal, Modula-2, PL/I, Ada, and Scheme, among others.[10]

Because ALGOL 60 was intended to be implemented on different computers, by different organizations, its designers wanted to specify the language precisely. The specification had two parts: the syntax part said what programs were grammatically valid, and the semantics part said what each language feature meant.

To describe syntax, two members of the committee, John Backus and Peter Naur, developed a way of writing syntax rules. They studied the work of linguists who were attempting to develop rules for natural languages such as English.[11] Their system was adopted by the ALGOL 60 committee and used in the specification; it is now called **Backus-Naur Form** (BNF). When Niklaus Wirth was developing Pascal, he simplified Backus-Naur Form and called the result **Extended Backus-Naur Form** (EBNF). The purpose of EBNF is to *define the valid inputs to a program.* An EBNF specification tells you what inputs the program is prepared to process (provided, of course, that the program matches the specification).

The best way to see how an EBNF specification works is to use it for something practical. Many programs must process the addresses of people or companies. Each country has a code system for addresses. In the United States, the system is called the ZIP code system. The original ZIP code system was five digits, but was extended to nine digits in the late 1970s, for example, `95812` and `02138-0014`. In Canada, a postal code is a six-character value made up of alternating letters and digits, divided into two groups of three characters, for example, V6T 1Z4.[12]

We can write the EBNF shown in Program 7-2 to specify ZIP codes. What does this specification mean? A `code` is either a U.S. ZIP code or a Canadian postal code (the symbol |, pronounced "pipe", means "or" in EBNF). A U.S. ZIP code consists of a `main-zip` of five digits, followed optionally by the `plus-4` part (the square brackets `[...]` mean "optionally"). A `plus-4` consists of the character -, followed by four digits (the quotation marks `"..."` indicate something that is written literally).

---

[10] Although Scheme is a member of the Lisp family of languages, the ALGOL 60 influences on it were so strong that $R^n RS$ is written quite consciously as a parody of the original ALGOL 60 specification. For example, the ALGOL 60 report is dedicated to the memory of a committee member who died in an accident during the report's preparation; $R^n RS$ is dedicated to "the memory of ALGOL 60".

[11] Developing rules for natural languages is *much* harder than for programming languages.

[12] Canada Post accepts mail to Santa Claus, but requires the postal code H0H 0H0.

code:	US-ZIP-code | Can-postal-code
US-zip-code:	main-zip [plus-4]
main-zip:	digit digit digit digit digit
plus-4:	"-" digit digit digit digit
Can-postal-code:	letter digit letter digit letter digit
digit:	"0" | "1" | "2" | ... | "9"
letter:	"A" | "B" | "C" | ... | "Z"

Program 7-2   EBNF for ZIP codes

Because EBNF specifications are written for humans, rather than computers, to read, we can take shortcuts: for example, it isn't necessary to show all 26 capital letters.

☞ **Exercise 7-5**

The country of Ruritania uses a four-character postal code. Mail addressed to the Royal Palace has code A000, and all other addresses have a code consisting of one letter (which must not be A) followed by three digits. Modify the preceding rules to include Ruritanian postal codes. (Hint: You might want to change the definition of letter, but make sure that what you do still works correctly for U.S. and Canadian codes.) ❏

The expression main-zip shows how we say "is composed of exactly five digits", but what if any length at all is acceptable? To see what happens, let's write an EBNF specification for an integer. Our first try is slightly incorrect:

integer:	("+" | "-") {digit}
digit:	"0" | "1" | "2" | ... | "9"

In this example, we have used the braces {...} to say "any number of repetitions". We have also used parentheses for grouping. The first rule means "an integer is either a + or a -, followed by any number of digits". Unfortunately, this rule is incorrect for two reasons. First, it insists that all numbers start with a + or a - sign, whereas we don't usually write + signs (though it isn't wrong to do so). Second, we must be careful about what "any number of" means. It means "0 or more", so the rule allows +, for example. But it's easy to fix both of these mistakes:

integer:	["+" | "-"] digit {digit}
digit:	"0" | "1" | "2" | ... | "9"

The square brackets show that the sign is optional. We have also written a single digit outside the braces, which means that any integer must have at least one digit. Figure 7-1 summarizes the structure of EBNF rules.

☞ **Exercise 7-6**

Identify each of the following as valid or invalid, according to the corrected rules for integer. For the invalid cases, explain what is incorrect.
  a. +13
  b. +0
  c. +
  d. -0000 ❏

We can use EBNF to give some precise rules for Dream's syntax, but what about its semantics? Several methods for defining semantics in a formal way have been developed, but all of them are too complicated for our use. In fact, only specialists

A typical EBNF rule looks something like this:

```
category:        thing1 | ( [thing2] {thing3} ) | "whatever"
```

This defines a category of things called `category` in terms of other categories: `thing1`, `thing2`, and `thing3`.

- `|` means "or".
- `[...]` means "optionally".
- `{...}` means "0 or more repetitions".
- `"..."` is used to show text that is written as-is in the program.
- Parentheses are used to show grouping.

Figure 7-1   EBNF Summary

in programming languages bother to study methods for formal semantics. We will just explain the semantics in English (see Figure 7-2).

☞ **Exercise 7-7**

According to the EBNF specification for Dream, is (`divide` (`sqrt 4`) `3 1`) a valid `expr`? Why or why not? ❏

7.1.5   An Alternative Syntax for Dream

All languages have both syntax and semantics, and Dream is no exception. Suppose we like Dream's semantics, but not its syntax. Can we design a new language with the same semantics as Dream but with a different syntax? For example, some potential users of Dream might be accustomed to Pascal, and might object to all of the parentheses needed in a Dream program. We can indeed modify Dream, or, to be precise, we can make a new language with the same semantics as Dream but with a different syntax. Because it is somewhat like Pascal, we will call our language Nightmare. Program 7-3 shows a Nightmare translation of our quadratic equation program.

Nightmare programs look more compact than Dream programs, but a fair amount of the space saving is illusory: Nightmare uses operation characters rather than operation names. Note that the ampersands that end statements must be separated by spaces; this will vastly simplify our later implementation of Nightmare.[13] Semicolons are the traditional end-of-statement markers for languages like Dream, but their use is not compatible with the Scheme reader, which treats them as the beginning of comments. Program 7-4 shows an EBNF specification for Nightmare.

Is Nightmare a better programming language than Dream? Since every Nightmare program can be translated into a Dream program, there's nothing that can be done in Nightmare that can't be done in Dream, and vice versa. Some people might prefer Nightmare's syntax, while others might prefer Dream's. Programming languages aren't as different as their syntaxes might suggest. For example, there are compilers that translate Scheme into C.

---

[13] We're being sloppy about spaces in our EBNF specifications. This approach is typical of specifications for real languages, where the spacing rules are normally written separately from the EBNF syntax rules. There is no logical reason for this separation, except that including spacing rules throughout the EBNF would result in extremely messy rules.

- `dream-program:`   `"(" "program" {dream-command} ")"`
  Semantics: A program is evaluated by evaluating each `dream-command` in order. The value returned by a program is unspecified.
  Note: The `dream-program` (program) is valid.
- `dream-command:`   `declaration | assignment | test | block | print`
- `declaration:`   `"(" "variable" {name} ")"`
  Semantics: The scope of a variable extends from its declaration to the end of the program. It is an error to declare a variable more than once. It is an error to declare the `names program`, `variable`, `assign`, `test`, or `in-sequence`. It is an error to declare a variable with the same name as a built-in one.
  Note: It is perfectly legal to declare variables anywhere in a program.
- `assignment:`   `"(" "assign" name expr ")"`
  Semantics: The variable named `name` is assigned the value of the expression `expr`. It is an error to assign a value to an undeclared variable.
- `test:`   `"(" "test" expr command command ")"`
  Semantics: The first `expr` is evaluated. If it evaluates to #t, the first `command` is evaluated; otherwise the second `command` is evaluated.
  Note: Although `test` uses Boolean values, it is not possible to type one in!
- `print:`   `"(" "print" expr ")"`
  Semantics: The expression is evaluated and its result displayed on an output device.
  Note: This does not specificy where the result is printed, nor its format.
- `block:`   `"(" "in-sequence" {dream-command} ")"`
  Semantics: The `dream-commands` are evaluated in order.
- `expr:`   `"(" operation-name {expr} ")" | name | constant`
  Semantics: An `expr` surrounded by parentheses is evaluated by evaluating each of the exprs in turn, and then performing the operation specified by `operation-name`. The number of `exprs` must be correct for the operation.
- `operation-name:`   `"plus" | "minus" | "times" | "divide" | "less" | "equal" | "greater" | "negative" | "sqrt" | "floor"`
- `name:`   `letter {letter | digit | "-"}`
- `constant:`   `number | boolean | string`
- `number:`   `digit {digit}`
  Note: It is not possible to enter negative numbers or numbers with decimal places, even though such values can be computed during a Dream program.
- `boolean:`   `"#t" | "#f"`
- `string:`   `quote {any character} quote`
- `quote:`   `a single quote character, i.e., " " "`
- `letter:`   `"a" | "b" | "c" | ... | "z"`

Figure 7-2   Dream EBNF and semantics

```
(program
  declare a b c disc &
  a := 1 &
  b := 4 &
  c := 3 &
  disc := { { b * b } - { 4 * { a * c } } } &
  if { disc < 0 }
     write "No solution" &
  else
     write "Solution 1:" &
     write { { { negative b } + { sqrt disc } } / { 2 * a } } &
     write "; solution 2: " &
     write { { { negative b } - { sqrt disc } } / { 2 * a } } &
  endif & )
```

Program 7-3   Quadratic equations in Nightmare

- n-program: `"(" "program" {n-command} ")"`
- n-command: `n-decl | n-assign | n-test | n-write`
- n-decl: `"declare" {name} "&"`
- n-assign: `name ":=" n-expr "&"`
- n-test: `"if" n-expr {n-command} "else" {n-command} "endif" "&"`
- n-write: `"write" n-expr "&"`
- n-expr: `n-group | name | number`
- n-group: `"{" expr n-two-op expr "}" | "{" n-one-op expr "}"`
- n-two-op: `"+" | "-" | "*" | "/" | "<" | "=" | ">"`
- n-one-op: `"sqrt" | "negative" | "floor"`

Program 7-4   EBNF for Nightmare

7.2   Trees

I think that I shall never see
A poem lovely as a tree
. . .
Poems are made by fools like me
But only God can make a tree.

— Joyce Kilmer, "Trees"

Languages provide a notation for expressing algorithms for human consumption. There would be little interest in languages, however, if we could not *implement* them by designing evaluators for them, so that the resulting programs could perform useful computations. What does it mean to build an evaluator for a programming language, say Dream? We need a program that accepts Dream programs as input, and does whatever the Dream program says. This statement hides a shocking truth—we must learn to consider programs as data.

So far, we have talked about a program as if it were different from other things with which we were working. We made a distinction between lambda forms and procedures: one is part of the program, and one is a value inside the computer. But there is really no difference between programs and data. *Every* program you have written started off as data. A program is data that is read by the Scheme evaluator. The structure of Scheme programs is, by design, the same as its basic data structure, the list. The advantage is that Scheme programs are in a form that is sensible for evaluation. The structure of each form is a list with the important information, the lambda form, name of the procedure, or special form in its car.

In order to write any program, we must decide how to represent the data. In order to write an evaluator we must decide how to represent programs. What sort of data structure do we need to represent a Dream program? Program 7-5 shows a fragment of Dream code that is a list of statements, and each statement is a list. However, the lists are organized in a special way.

```
...
(assign foo 3)
(test (less bar 5)
      (in-sequence
         (print foo)
         (assign gum 22))
      (in-sequence
         (print "Invalid data")
         (assign bar 5)))
(print baz)
...
```

Program 7-5   Dream code fragment

This code segment consists of three Dream statements. Yet the second statement consists of an expression and two statements, each of which consists of additional statements. What we need is a data structure that can represent not only the data, but the grouping of that data. Trees are the answer.

7.2.1 Introduction to Trees

One of the most elegant and useful recursive data structures is the *tree*. Trees have been used for a long time to represent structures involving hierarchy.[14] For example, we could have an organization tree for Consolidated Software, Inc., as in Figure 7-3. This structure might go on for many levels until we reached individuals whose jobs were to sell or develop something, rather than to manage others. Consolidated's organization is called a **tree** because it looks like a tree. We call each element of the tree a **node**. The President is the **root node** (the President doesn't report to anybody), and people who don't manage anybody else are **leaf nodes**. The *depth* of the tree is the length of the longest path from the root node to a leaf.

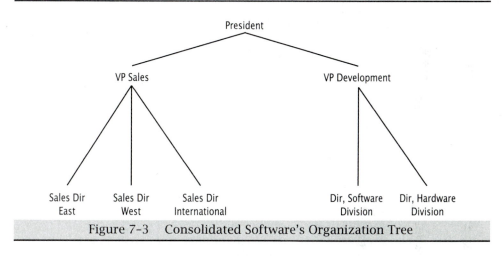

President

VP Sales   VP Development

Sales Dir   Sales Dir   Sales Dir   Dir, Software   Dir, Hardware
East   West   International   Division   Division

Figure 7-3   Consolidated Software's Organization Tree

Trees are inherently recursive structures. A tree whose root node is a node of another tree is a **subtree**. When Consolidated is bought by Galactic Enterprises, the President must report to Galactic, but the remaining structure can stay the same. At the other end of the tree, we might replace a leaf node by an entire subtree. For example, when Jane Bloggins has a new idea for a revolutionary spreadsheet program, she might be given authority to hire a group of programmers to implement it.

Note how the organization tree is more sophisticated than just a list of the employees for Sales and Development. The Vice President in each division manages the other directors, so that the tree structure shows relations among the employees as well as the divisions. If the tree showed more employees, it would also show more structure among them. A list of employees by division does not represent these relationships.

We can give a formal definition of a tree. A tree is either

- null, or
- a *node*, with zero or more subtrees.

---

[14] The word *hierarchy* comes from the Greek for "rule by priests". It was first used by Greek writers to describe the structure of Egyptian society. The priests were the only ones who could read and write. They therefore had all of the power.

The subtrees must be *distinct*, even if they look the same; that is, they share no nodes. For example, in Figure 7-4, structure (a) is a tree, but structure (b) is not.

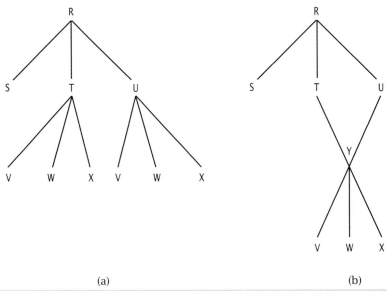

(a) (b)

Figure 7-4   Trees must have independent subtrees

Trees aren't just for organizations. For example, most computer operating systems organize the files on a disk into directories, each of which may have subdirectories. A typical computer disk may contain have several thousand files, and without some sort of organizing method, the user would get lost. By allowing users to group related files as they wish, the system helps them keep track of what files they're using. Such a directory structure is also a tree.

☞ **Exercise 7-8**

One use of the word *tree* with which most people are familiar occurs in the expression "family tree". Some thought should convince you that *tree* here is somewhat misused. Why? ❏

7.2.1.1   Representing and Traversing Trees   The most straightforward way to work with trees in Scheme is to follow the recursive definition: A tree may be null; if not, it consists of a node with an associated data item and zero or more subtrees. We can therefore represent a node as a list whose car is the item and whose cdr is the list of subtrees. For example, we could represent the tree in Figure 7-5 as the following list:

```
(A
    (B
        (E))
    (C)
    (D
```

```
(F)
(G)
(H)))
```
We've used indentation to show the level of nesting, but Scheme doesn't care.

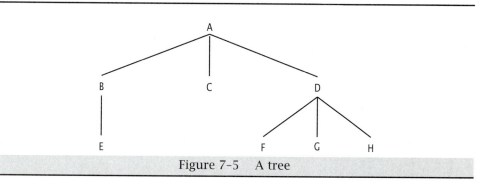

Figure 7–5   A tree

☞ **Exercise 7–9**

Using strings for the job titles, write a list representation of the Consolidated Software table of organization. ❑

☞ **Exercise 7–10**

Why isn't (a (b c) (d)) a list representation of a tree, by the definition we've used? ❑

We might want to visit all the nodes in, or **traverse**, a tree; the process of traversing a tree is called tree *traversal*.[15] We know how to traverse a list: the mapping procedures map and for-each do this; therefore, we should be able to write procedures for traversing trees. If we wanted to print out the names of all of the positions at Consolidated Software, for example, we could use the procedure in Program 7-6.

print-nodes uses a technique known as **tree recursion**. It follows the recursive definition of trees and has a terminal case corresponding to a null tree, and a nonterminal case that recurses on the subtrees. A tree-recursive procedure has the general framework shown in Program 7-7. (We first encountered tree recursion under the guise of *multiway recursion* in Chapter 2.)

When we run print-nodes, in Figure 7-6, we see that the grouping is lost in the output. It's not clear from the listing that the VP of Development reports to the President rather than to the Sales Director for International Markets.

Just as we can have generalized mapping procedures, we can write a generalized tree-traversal procedure, shown in Program 7-8. traverse-tree is applied for effect, not for its result. It does not combine the results of the application of proc to the elements of the tree. It directly generalizes print-nodes.

---

[15] *Traverse* means to go all the way across. We might speak of traversing North America, meaning traveling from one coast to the other. Some computer programmers use the term *walk*, as in, "Now we do a tree walk". However, most of us expect trees to stay rooted, and prefer to leave walking trees to writers such as Shakespeare (*Macbeth*) and J. R. R. Tolkien (*Lord of the Rings*).

```
(define print-nodes
  (lambda (tree)
    (letrec
      ((print-subtrees
         (lambda (list-of-subtrees)
           (if (null? list-of-subtrees)
               (void)
               (begin
                 (print-nodes (car list-of-subtrees))
                 (print-subtrees (cdr list-of-subtrees)))))))
      (if (null? tree)
          (void)
          (begin
            (display (car tree)) (newline)
            (print-subtrees (cdr tree)))))))
```

Program 7-6   Printing tree nodes

```
(define the-procedure
  (lambda (tree)
    (if (null? tree)
        the terminal case
        (handle the node and process the subtrees))))
```

Program 7-7   Framework for tree recursion

```
> (print-nodes consolidated)
President
VP Sales
Sales Dir East
Sales Dir West
Sales Dir International
VP Development
Dir, Software Division
Dir, Hardware Division
```

Figure 7-6   Printing tree nodes

The structure of print-nodes can be extended to other purposes, such as counting the number of nodes in a tree, as shown in Program 7-9. count-nodes doesn't just do recursive calls on the subtrees; it makes the calls and then combines the results, a common pattern in tree procedures.

☞ **Exercise 7-11**

Use traverse-tree to write a nonrecursive procedure, trav-print, that has the same effect as print-nodes. ❏

We might want to produce a result from a tree traversal. count-nodes counts the nodes in a tree by adding 1 for each node to the sum of the counts in the node's subtrees. The next exercise asks you to generalize count-nodes.

```
(define traverse-tree
  (lambda (proc tree)
    (letrec
      ((traverse-subtrees
         (lambda (node-list)
           (if (null? node-list)
             (void)
             (begin
               (traverse-tree proc (car node-list))
               (traverse-subtrees (cdr node-list)))))))
      (if (null? tree)
        (void)
        (begin
          (proc (car tree))
          (traverse-subtrees (cdr tree)))))))
```

Program 7-8   Generalized traversal

```
(define count-nodes
  (lambda (tree)
    (letrec
      ((count-subtrees
         (lambda (list-of-subtrees)
           (if (null? list-of-subtrees)
             0
             (+ (count-nodes (car list-of-subtrees))
                (count-subtrees (cdr list-of-subtrees)))))))
      (if (null? tree)
        0
        (add1 (count-subtrees (cdr tree)))))))
```

Program 7-9   Counting tree nodes

☞ **Exercise 7–12**

Write `traverse-tree-combine`, a version of `traverse-tree` that takes the following arguments: a binary procedure, the tree, a procedure to apply to each node, and the null value for the binary procedure. Then we can write (count-nodes atree) as (traverse-tree-combine + atree (lambda (x) 1) 0). ❏

7.3 Interpreters and Compilers

Interpretation is the revenge of intellect upon art.
— Susan Sontag, *Evergreen Review*, December 1964

BELINDA: Ay, but you know we must return good for evil.
LADY BRUTE: That may be a mistake in the translation.
— Sir John Vanbrugh, *The Provoked Wife*

We have studied the Dream and Nightmare languages. Now we want to implement these languages, to produce programs, written in Scheme, that allow us to enter programs in Dream and Nightmare and to run them.

There are two fundamental ways to implement a programming language:

- We can **interpret** the program, by analyzing and processing each command or expression in the program to produce the appropriate result.
- We can **translate** the program into a simpler language for which we already have an implementation.

Either technique gives us an evaluator; each technique has its own benefits.

7.3.1 A Dream Interpreter

Trees give us a way to write a Dream interpreter. The basic idea is to build a tree representation of a Dream program and traverse the tree. As we visit each node, we do whatever that node specifies. But haven't we just replaced one hard problem by another one? We know how to traverse trees, but how do we build a tree structure of a Dream program?

Fortunately, we have a Scheme primitive that does the job, namely read. Dream programs are written in list syntax. We don't have to use read explicitly; we can just provide the Dream program as a quoted list:

```
(define dream-program
  '(program
     (print 5))
)
```

The first and last line are Scheme code (as is the quote mark), but the middle lines are Dream code. We will write all of our Dream programs this way.

We must therefore write procedure dream-eval that accepts as an argument the Dream program to be evaluated. Then we can use dream-eval as follows:

```
> (dream-eval '(program (print (plus 2 2))))
4
> (define my-dream-program '(program (print "Hello, world!")))
> (dream-eval my-dream-program)
Hello, world!
```

The way is clear to build a Dream interpreter. Representing a Dream program as Scheme list structure gives us a program tree. To evaluate the corresponding program we only need to traverse that program tree. We'll start with expressions and then add the code for Dream statements.

7.3.2 Evaluating Dream Expressions

Dream expressions look like (plus (times 2 3) 5). We can produce the following recursive definition of a Dream expression:

- a constant (such as a number, Boolean, or string);
- a variable; or
- an expression in parentheses, consisting of

  — an operator name; and
  — zero or more operands.

The code in Program 7-10 defines the accessors and predicates of an expr type.

```
(define expr-constant?
  (lambda (e)
    (or (number? e) (boolean? e) (string? e))))
(define expr-variable?
  (lambda (x) (symbol? x)))
(define expr-op
  (lambda (x) (car x)))
(define expr-args
  (lambda (x) (cdr x)))
```

Program 7-10   Dream implementation: exprs

You might think that since exprs are program trees, we should be able to use traverse-tree to evaluate them. Dream trees are, in fact, not represented like the trees we first introduced. The Dream expression (A B C D) can be considered as a tree whose root node has three subtrees. We represented such a tree as (A (B) (C) (D)), originally. That representation simplified our first tree procedures, but seems clumsy for Dream expressions, so we didn't use it.

Instead of using traverse-tree, therefore, we must write a new procedure (shown in Program 7-11), though we can use traverse-tree as a model. Handling variables requires some work that we're not quite ready for, so Program 7-11 shows a stub version of variable-value.

dream-expr-eval uses a "table-driven" approach for handling expression operators such as plus and sqrt. Building a giant case into the procedure would make it very unmodular. Instead, we use a procedure named operator-procedure to obtain the Scheme procedure for a given operator. Program 7-12 shows how we implement operator-procedure as a giant alist. All operators, whether they have one or two arguments, take their arguments in a list.

☞ **Exercise 7-13**

Trace the evaluation of (dream-expr-eval '(times 2 (times 3 5))). ❏

☞ **Exercise 7-14**

All of the procedures in operator-name-table take the list operands apart and then call the corresponding Scheme primitives with the results. How can the apply primitive simplify this code? Revise dream-expr-eval and operator-name-table to use apply effectively. Does this use of apply cause any problems? ❏

```
(define dream-expr-eval
  (lambda (expr)
    (if (expr-constant? expr)
        expr
        (if (expr-variable? expr)
            (variable-value expr)
            (let
              ((op (operator-procedure (expr-op expr)))
               (operands (map dream-expr-eval (expr-args expr))))
              (op operands)))))))
(define variable-value
  (lambda (name)
    '*no-value*))
```

Program 7-11   Dream implementation: evaluating expressions

```
(define operator-name-list
  (list
    (cons 'plus
      (lambda (operands)
        (+ (car operands) (car (cdr operands)))))
    (cons 'difference
      (lambda (operands)
        (- (car operands) (car (cdr operands)))))
    ...
    (cons 'sqrt
      (lambda (operands)
        (sqrt (car operands))))
    (cons 'negative
      (lambda (operands)
        (- (car operands))))
    (cons 'floor
      (lambda (operands)
        (floor (car operands))))))
(define operator-procedure
  (lambda (op-symbol)
    (let ((x (assv op-symbol operator-name-list)))
      (if (not x)
          (error "Invalid operator!")
          (cdr x)))))
```

Program 7-12   Dream implementation: operators

7.3.3 Variables

Implementing variables is straightforward in Dream. There is no concept of scope in Dream, so all variables live in a common global environment. As in Scheme, variable bindings are created by declarations, and the values mutated by assignments. This fact suggests representing Dream's environment as a simple alist, since without scope we don't need to divide the environment into frames. We will need four variable operations:

- *clearing* the list of variables
- *declaring* a variable (placing it in the global environment, with no value)
- *assigning* a value to a variable (searching the global environment for the variable's name, and mutating its value if the variable is declared)
- *accessing* a variable's value (searching the global environment for the variable's name, and mutating its value if the variable is declared)

What if the variable hasn't been declared when we try to assign to it or access its value? What if it has been declared, but not assigned a value when we try to access its value? Both of these are errors, and a high-quality evaluator will most definitely give an error message. Our Dream interpreter, though, ignores errors on assignment, and gives the default value *no-value* on access. It might be better to do an (error ...) in this case, as in Program 7-13.

```
(define *variables* '())
(define variable-clear
  (lambda ()
    (set! *variables* '())))
(define variable-declare
  (lambda (name)
    (let ((x (assv name *variables*)))
      (if x
        (error 'variable-declare
          "Variable ~a already declared" name)
        (set! *variables*
          (cons
            (cons name '*no-value*)
            *variables*))))))
(define variable-assign
  (lambda (name value)
    (let ((x (assv name *variables*)))
      (if (not x)
        (error 'variable-assign "Variable ~a not declared" name)
        (set-cdr! x value)))))
(define variable-value
  (lambda (name)
    (let ((x (assv name *variables*)))
      (if (not x)
        '*no-value*
        (cdr x)))))
```

Program 7-13   Dream implementation: variables

7.3.3.1 The Dream Evaluator   The hardest part is behind us. All we have to do to evaluate Dream programs is to traverse the full program tree; the code is shown in Program 7-14. dream-eval itself does nothing, except to initialize the environment and then call dream-command-sequence for the actual commands. dream-command-sequence in turn calls dream-eval-command, whose job is to process a single

```
(define dream-eval
  (lambda (prog)
    (variable-clear)
    (dream-command-sequence (cdr prog))))
(define dream-command-sequence
  (lambda (command-list)
    (for-each dream-eval-command command-list)))
(define dream-eval-command
  (lambda (command)
    (case (car command)
      ((variable)
       (for-each variable-declare (cdr command)))
      ((assign)
       (variable-assign
         (list-ref command 1)
         (dream-expr-eval (list-ref command 2))))
      ((test)
       (dream-eval-command
         (list-ref
           command
           (if (dream-expr-eval (list-ref  command 1)) 2 3))))
      ((in-sequence)
       (dream-command-sequence (cdr command)))
      ((print)
       (format #t "~a~%" (dream-expr-eval (list-ref command 1))))
      (else
       #f))))
```

Program 7-14   Dream implementation: commands

command. This procedure is still recursive, because `tests` and `in-sequences` can themselves contain other commands.

☞ **Exercise 7-15**

The code in Program 7-14 won't catch errors involving the keyword `program`. How would you fix the code? Is it worth fixing? ❏

7.3.4   A Nightmare Compiler

It was straightforward to convert a Dream program into a list structure—we used Scheme's read procedure. From there, we were able to traverse the list structure during evaluation. We could do the same thing with Nightmare, but it's better to convert the Nightmare program into a Dream list structure and then use the Dream evaluator. This approach seems unlikely, until you realize two things: first, the semantics of Nightmare programs is exactly the same as that of Dream programs; and, second, it's not as easy to work out the list representation for a Nightmare program as it is for a Dream program.

When we designed these two languages, we deliberately gave them the same semantics. Since the semantics of programs in the two languages is identical, we can *translate* programs from Nightmare into Dream without any loss of information.[16] The difficulty of working out the list representation in Nightmare forces us to consider translation. The problem is that, unlike Dream, Nightmare forces us to work out the grouping *each time* we try to execute a line. Whereas Dream commands are parenthesized, Nightmare commands extend to the & statement terminator. There is no grouping for ifs: the *then* part extends to the keyword else, and the *else* part extends to endif. Working out the grouping is time-consuming for the computer. Translating the code allows us to determine the grouping *once*. The resulting Dream code can run at full speed.

Each time our Dream evaluator processes a command or expression, we must check to see whether the code is valid. If we do all of the checking during translation, the evaluator can dispense with all error checks because any errors would have been caught during translation. Many real imperative languages extend the notion of declaring variables. In these languages, a declaration includes not only the variable name, but also a specification of the type of values that it can bind. The semantics of these languages does not permit values of types other than the declared type to be bound to the variable. With this information, the compiler can perform **static type checking** to detect, at compile time, some errors involving types. In these languages, variables have types, but values do not contain information identifying their type.

In Scheme, as well as Dream and Nightmare, each value has a type, while variables do not. Scheme and languages like it detect misuse of types when the program is evaluated, while languages like Ada and C++ can detect only a limited set of errors at **run time**. If a program failure is catastrophic, then it is desirable to check such errors before run time. Associating types with variables increases safety but decreases flexibility. These approaches are not mutually exclusive, however. Research proceeds on performing static type analysis on Scheme programs, which can already be analyzed statically to determine some type uses. Likewise, with ever-increasing computer speeds, the overhead of some error-checking during evaluation becomes less and less significant.

Knowing the type of a value associated with a name also permits the compiler to generate efficient code that doesn't have to determine the type of a value before it uses the value. High-performance Scheme systems do a great deal during translation, and achieve most of the performance of more restrictive languages.

Programs that translate other programs from one language to another are called **compilers**.[17] A compiler processes a **source program** and produces an **object program**. Our Nightmare compiler accepts a source program written in Nightmare,

---

[16] The situation is not so easy with human languages. For example, the French for *mouse pad* translates as *mouse carpet*! Anyone who has translated poetry from one language to another is familiar with how difficult it is to achieve exactly the same shade of meaning in two different languages.

[17] The term *compiler* was coined by a group of programmers who were working with the EDSAC computer in Cambridge, England, about 1950. EDSAC programs were written as long sequences of detailed instructions; however, the programmers soon noticed that some sequences (e.g., for computing the square root of a number) were repeated. They developed a generic square-root procedure, and made it available to all of the programmers. But this wasn't enough. EDSAC programs were punched on paper tape, and soon somebody wrote a program that would read the program tape, along with a tape containing the mathematics procedures, and produce a new paper tape with all of the instructions needed for the program. They called this process "compiling the program tape", and the term was adopted for any programming language translation. If the EDSAC programmers had been terminologically consistent, we wouldn't have programs, but anthologies!

and outputs the corresponding Dream object program, as depicted in Figure 7-7. This Dream program can, in turn, be evaluated, using our regular Dream evaluator, as shown in Figure 7-8.

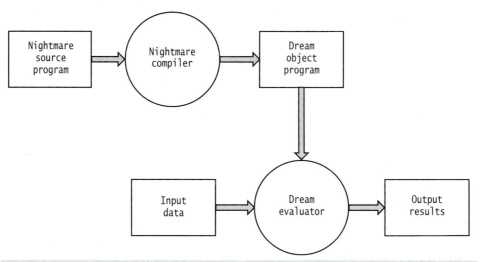

Figure 7-7   Translating a Nightmare program

```
> (define dream-quadratic-program '(program ...))
> (dream-eval dream-quadratic-program)
Solution 1:
-1
Solution 2:
-3
> (define nightmare-quadratic-program '(program ...))
> (dream-eval (nightmare-compile nightmare-quadratic-program))
Solution 1:
-1
Solution 2:
-3
```

Figure 7-8   Running a Dream program

Compilers have two jobs: they must *analyze* the input program, and *generate* output code based upon their analysis. Our Nightmare compiler does both analysis and generation tasks.

7.3.4.1   The Token Scanner

In general, programming languages are not designed to be as easy to read in as a Scheme list structure. The first job, therefore, is to break the input up into *tokens*, individual units of meaning. For example, in the Nightmare command write { 2 + 3 } &, the tokens are write, {, 2, +, 3, }, and &. We need a procedure that will give us the consecutive tokens of the program.

We can thereafter regard a Nightmare program as a long list of tokens. Various steps in analysis will "eat up" tokens. For example, if the compiler sees the token `write`, it must "eat up" enough tokens for an expression and then check that the next token is `&`. Fortunately, we don't actually have to divide the input into tokens; by requiring that Nightmare tokens be separated by spaces, we have ensured that typing a Nightmare program as a Scheme list will separate the tokens.[18]

The Nightmare compiler could divide the whole program into tokens, and then process it. However, since real programs can be extremely large, it doesn't make sense to do this. The token scanner must therefore get a new token each time we call it. However, sometimes we need to peek at a token before we get it. We can therefore arrange that our token scanner will accept a message argument saying whether to get the next token, or whether we just want to peek at it.

A good token scanner can simplify dealing with the end of the program. There are many places in the compiler where we must get the next token. We can arrange that the token scanner return a "fake" token (e.g., `***end-program***`) at the end of the program. Checking for the end of the program reduces to checking whether the next token is `***end-program***`.

We will implement our token scanner as an object. Procedure `make-scanner` will accept an argument consisting of the program we're going to scan, and will return a scanner procedure. `make-scanner` is `make-dispenser`, the procedure discussed in Section 6.2.1, that encapsulates a list and delivers one item at a time, so we won't show its code. It returns a different marker to indicate the end of data. The token scanner will output the next token each time it is called, removing it from the token list if its argument is `get`. Had we wanted to do elaborate character processing in our scanner (e.g., to allow for tokens not surrounded by spaces), the scanner routine would be the only part of the compiler that would be changed.

Often a translator knows what the next token should be. For example, after processing the expression in a `write` statement, the next token ought to be `&`. In an assignment command, the first token can be any name, but the second must be `:=`. Thus, the translator can check that the next token is correct by a `peek` into the scanner.

7.3.4.2 Of EBNF and Compilers   If you look back at our Dream interpreter and compare it to the EBNF specification for Dream, you will see a great deal of similarity. EBNF is a *specification* for Dream, and the interpreter is an *implementation*. The EBNF tells us how things group, which is exactly the question our compiler must answer as it analyzes a Nightmare program. The compiler should be based on the specification rules. We can, in essence, translate those rules directly into Scheme. The translation for most of Nightmare is so straightforward that we will not include the code, but it can be found in the Software Package.

Let's take a look at the EBNF for Nightmare and discuss the translation. Each EBNF statement is implemented as a procedure in the Nightmare compiler. When an EBNF statement is a set of alternatives, the procedure that implements it examines all the alternatives and calls the appropriate procedure.

- `n-program:     "(" "program" {n-command} ")"`
  Viewed just as a specification, this rule says, "A Nightmare program consists of an open parenthesis, the keyword `program`, zero or more `n-commands`,

---

[18] Real languages are not so forgiving to the compiler writer. After all, it's not very good human engineering to force the programmer to put in meaningless spaces.

and a close parenthesis. Viewed as a program for analyzing Nightmare programs, however, this rule says, "A Nightmare program is a list whose first element is the keyword `program`, and the rest of the list is zero or more `n-commands`".

`nightmare-compile` processes the Nightmare program, statement by statement, and conses the resulting Dream statements into a Dream program.

- `n-command:`   `n-decl | n-assign | n-test | n-write`
  Nightmare commands have been designed so that a program (or a human) can classify commands by looking only at the first token of the command. The keywords `declare`, `if`, and `write` signal the start of a variable declaration, conditional, or an output statement, respectively. Any other token signals the beginning of an assignment statement.[19]

- `n-decl:`   `"declare" {name} "&"`
  A variable declaration is handled by `n-declaration`, which loops through the names and builds up a Dream `variable` declaration. The command `declare <name>` translates to `(variable <name>)`.[20]

- `n-assign:`   `name ":=" n-expr "&"`
  The statement `n-assignment` is fairly straightforward. The first token of an assignment statement is the variable name. We pick that up, skip over the `:=`, and then produce the Dream code for the expression. The result is `(assign <name> <expr>)`.

- `n-test: "if" n-expr {n-command} "else" {n-command} "endif" "&"`
  An `if` statement consists of any number of statements for each of the `then` or `else` parts. We must translate these statements into Dream, and then organize them into a Dream `test` statement. Since Dream doesn't allow more than one statement as a `then` or `else` part, we must enclose them in an `in-sequence`. The result of `if <expr> <commands> else <commands> endif` is

  ```
  (test <condition>
    (in-sequence <d-commands>)
    (in-sequence <d-commands>))
  ```

- `n-write:`   `"write" n-expr "&"`
  This is a direct translation to `(print <expr>)`.

- `n-expr:`   `n-brack-expr | name | number | string`

- `n-brack-expr: "{" expr n-two-op expr "}" | "{" n-one-op expr "}"`

- `n-two-op:`   `"+" | "-" | "*" | "/" | "<" | "=" | ">"`

- `n-one-op:`   `"sqrt" | "negative"`
  We can tell what kind of an expression we have by examining the first token, which will either be a constant or a left bracket. In the latter case, we have a bracketed expression.

---

[19] The use of the first token to classify a command suggests that a language designer has to ensure that it is possible to classify commands and other language features easily. C is an example of a language in which, for reasons that seemed very good at the time, the designers did not follow this rule. As a result, it's a bit tricky to write a compiler for C. Not surprisingly, human readers often have trouble reading C.

[20] The order of the names reverses when going from Nightmare to Dream, but this doesn't matter.

Bracketed expressions are handled by checking for two different cases: either the expression starts with an n-one-op, or it consists of a left and right subexpression with an n-two-op in the middle. We identify the n-one-ops and n-two-ops via a pair of alists, in which the cdrs are the Dream translations.

```
(define n-two-ops
  '((+ . plus) (- . difference) (* . times) (/ . divide)
    (< . less) (> . greater) (= . equal)))
(define n-one-ops
  '((sqrt . sqrt) (negative . negative) (floor . floor)))
```

Nightmare demonstrates that the semantics for a programming language can be embodied in two different syntactic forms. The semantics of Dream and Nightmare are the same; thus, we translate Nightmare programs into Dream for evaluation. We could have written a Nightmare evaluator directly, but it's easier to translate into Dream.

7.4   Extending Scheme

> *"The Emperor has just appointed me General in Sejanus's place. Here's my commission. You are to go straight back to the Camp now, excused all guard duties. When you get there tell the other fellows that Macro's in charge now, and that there's thirty gold pieces coming to every man who knows how to obey orders."*
> — Robert Graves, *I, Claudius*

Before we specify the Scheme language, we will introduce *macros*, a way of adding special forms to Scheme. According to our understanding of Scheme, adding a new special form means specifying a special rule for each new special form. We have no mechanism now for adding special forms, but macros demonstrate how easy it is to extend a language with new special forms. Scheme makes macros easy because its syntax uses forms that transform into lists, its basic data structure. Transforming input forms becomes a matter of list processing. The resulting list structure is then interpreted as a form by the evaluator.

7.4.1   Macros

What we need is a way of adding our own rules to Scheme. We need to be able to say, "any form that begins with foo is to be handled in such-and-such a way". Procedures won't do the job; instead, we must introduce a new concept, the **macro**, a programmer-defined special form. The form define-macro is a special form whose purpose is to let a programmer introduce new special forms.[21] For example,

```
(define-macro increment!
    (lambda (form) (build-increment! form)))
(define build-increment!
```

---

[21] The form define-macro is not part of the specification of Scheme, but can be defined in most Scheme systems.

```
      (lambda (form)
        (let ((name (car (cdr form))))
          (list 'set! name (list 'add1 name)))))
(define i 5)
(increment! i)
i ⇒ 6
```

We define a macro by giving a procedure whose argument is the entire form
being evaluated. Thus, in the above example, the argument form would be bound
to (increment! i). The car of a macro's argument will always be the macro name
itself, and the nth element will be the nth form passed to the macro. We've written
the macro definition in two stages: the first calls the second procedure with the
form as argument; the second does the work. That way you can try out the effect
of build-increment! directly:

$$(build\text{-}increment! \ '(increment! \ j)) \Rightarrow (set! \ j \ (add1 \ j))$$

Macro names aren't bound or placed in the global environment. Instead, the
evaluator has a private table of all the macros defined, and uses that table to check,
each time a form is evaluated, whether the form invokes a macro.

A macro creates a list representing a form, which is then evaluated as form
by the Scheme evaluator, as if the form created by the macro had been typed in.
In the above example, the result of (increment! i) is (set! i (add1 i)). Scheme
then evaluates this list as a form, which in turn mutates i.

Defining a macro thus creates a new "special form rule". From then on, using
the macro name as the first argument in a form causes the procedure to be run with
the entire form as a list argument. The result is taken as a Scheme form to evaluate.

☞ **Exercise 7-16**

increment! is "unsafe" as shown; if the name argument is omitted, the macro will generate
a "cdr of null" error. Rewrite the macro so that it displays an error message if the number
of arguments isn't correct, for example,

```
> (increment!)
Error in build-increment!: incorrect number of arguments.
> (increment! foo bar)
Error in build-increment!: incorrect number of arguments.
> (increment! i)
> i
7
```

This problem is trickier than it looks. ❑

Macros allow us to take a coding pattern (incrementing a variable, for example), and making a new special form that does this job.[22] We write a macro when we
need a special form, because we don't want to evaluate some elements in a form.
In increment!, we want to treat the name as a name and not evaluate it. A macro
is not like an ordinary procedure: a procedure is a value, but a macro is a kind of

---

[22] The term *macro* was coined by M. D. McIlroy, a Bell Laboratories computer scientist, who in 1959
discovered this technique for assembly programs (see Chapter 11). He called the special instructions defined by the technique *macro-instructions*, meaning "large instructions". Soon the term was
shortened to *macro*.

special form. You can't apply a macro to anything or store it in a variable. A macro is something like a procedure, but it's used for one purpose only: to compute the actual form to be evaluated.[23]

☞ **Exercise 7-17**

Joel User likes `increment!` so much that he decides to write code like the following:

```
(let
  ((proc increment!)
   (i 45))
  (proc i)
  i)
```

Joel expects the result 46, and he is surprised at what happens when he evaluates this form. What happens, and why? ❏

☞ **Exercise 7-18**

Joel User decides to write `fact`, the factorial procedure, as a macro. If Joel wants to evaluate `(fact 10)`, then the following macro would suffice:

```
(define-macro fact
  (lambda (form) (build-fact form)))
(define build-fact
  (lambda (form)
    (letrec
      ((helper
         (lambda (x)
           (if (= x 0) 1 (* x (helper (sub1 x)))))))
      (helper (car (cdr form))))))
```

This macro would return a number as the result. What happens when Joel tries this macro on `(fact i)`? How would you write a `fact` macro to accept variables as input? ❏

7.4.2 Capturing Common Programming Patterns

Macros give us **syntactic abstraction**. Just as procedural abstraction lets us hide algorithms, and data abstraction lets us hide representations, syntactic abstraction lets us create new special forms representing common programming techniques, and hide the manner in which they're actually implemented. Thus, for example, a `letrec%` macro lets us forget about the `set!`s we need to use.

We can therefore define a `letrec%` macro in the same way we turn a `letrec` into a `let`. The `letrec` has the format (`letrec` *bindings body*), where *bindings* has the format (*(name value)*...). We must go through *bindings* twice, once to produce the list of names, and once to produce the `set!`s, as in Program 7-15.

☞ **Exercise 7-19**

By hand, work through the form

---

[23] Many sophisticated programs, such as Word for Windows and Ami Pro, come with "macro languages", but what they call *macro* we would call a procedure. However, words such as *procedure* frighten off nonprogrammers, whereas *macro* doesn't. (Nonprogrammers have been using "keyboard macros" for years.)

```
(letrec% ((foo (lambda (x) x))) (foo 3))
```

What values are bindings and body bound to? What is the result of each of the map calls? Evaluate (build-letrec '(letrec% ((foo (lambda (x) x))) (foo 3))). ❏

```
(define-macro letrec%
  (lambda (form) (build-letrec form)))
(define build-letrec
  (lambda (form)
    (let ((bindings (car (cdr form)))
          (body (cdr (cdr form))))
      (cons
       'let
       (cons
        (map
         (lambda (binding) (list (car binding) #f))
         bindings)
        (append
         (map
          (lambda (binding)
            (list 'set! (car binding) (car (cdr binding))))
          bindings)
         body))))))
```

Program 7-15   Macro for `letrec%`

We can use macros to mimic the programming structures of other languages. For example, Pascal (as well as Modula-2 and C) provide a number of loop statements, one of which has the Modula-2 syntax:

```
WHILE boolean-expression DO
    statements
END
```

We could build a similar special form in Scheme:

```
(while boolean-expression command...)
```

For example,

```
(let ((i 1))
  (while (<= i 10)
    (display i)
    (newline)
    (set! i (add1 i))))
```

This form displays the integers from 1 to 10, on separate lines.

We can write a macro for this purpose. Because many Scheme systems provide `while` forms already, we'll call ours `while%`. The idea is straightforward: if the Boolean expression is true, evaluate the statements and repeat. For example, we could write the above `while` form as follows:

```
(let ((i 1))
  (letrec
    ((helper (lambda ()
       (if (<= i 10)
         (begin
           (display i)
           (newline)
           (set! i (add1 i))
           (helper))))))
    (helper)))
```

We thus break the forms in the `while` form into the Boolean expression (the car of the cdr), and the command list (the cdr of the cdr). From there, it is fairly straightforward to construct a helper procedure as in Program 7-16. This is an ugly macro, but it correctly turns the `while%` form into a recursive helper procedure.

Unfortunately, `while%` has a very serious bug. Suppose we were to do

```
(define helper #t)
...
(while% (< i 10)
  (if (horrible-calculation i)
    (set! helper #f))
  (set! i (add1 i)))
```

The global binding of `helper` doesn't present a problem (unless we had tried to use `helper` inside the loop), but mutating `helper` will definitely cause a disaster when we try to do a recursive call. The problem is that the user of the `while%` macro must know not to use the name `helper` inside the loop.

One solution is to use an unlikely name, such as `arglebargle-while-helping-procedure`, but, still, this is a chancy technique. What if someone else uses this name, on the grounds it's unlikely to conflict with anyone else's names? That user would blame us for the problem!

We had a similar problem with global names, and we solved it by introducing local names and binding. A solution as clean as lambda binding isn't possible here, but we can solve the problem by using a **generated symbol**, or **gensym**, a symbol that is manufactured by Scheme. Such a symbol is defined not to be equal to any other symbol, even one that prints out the same. (Thus a user can never type in a generated symbol in.) Most Scheme systems provide a procedure `gensym` that delivers a new gensym each time it is called. (Most systems use symbols that look like g1, g2, and so on). Program 7-17 shows how we use gensyms to write `while%` reliably.

Practical Note

Scheme programmers have argued over whether to use macros, and, if so, how much. Macros are considerably more complex than we have made them appear. The pitfall we avoided with gensyms is just one of several similar problems that make macro programming complex and bug-prone. Extensive use of macros can make your program unreadable to anyone else, when the macros introduce odd or idiosyncratic syntax. If two programmers who are working on the same program use

```
(define-macro while%
  (lambda (form) (build-while form)))
(define build-while
  (lambda (form)
    (let ((bool-exp (car (cdr form)))
          (commands (cdr (cdr form))))
      (list
        'letrec
        (list
          (list
            'helper
            (list
              'lambda
              '()
              (list
                'if
                bool-exp
                (cons
                  'begin
                  (append
                    commands
                    '((helper))))))))
        '(helper)))))
```

Program 7-16   Macro for `while%`

different sets of macros, it's almost impossible to combine their code. Finally, many Scheme evaluators impose strict limitations on how macros can be used. Therefore, we will be conservative in our use of macros.

1. We will only use a macro when we want to create a special form that covers a new style of programming, like `define-class` and `while`. We will not use macros that are simply a matter of convenience, (for example, `increment!`). (You can, of course, use them in your programs if you like.)

2. We will define all macros in a program at the beginning only, so that the reader can clearly understand what the macros are and what they're for.

3. We will never write a macro definition anywhere other than at the top level. Many Scheme evaluators can't handle macros anywhere else; even if yours can, burying a macro deep inside some code is a recipe for disaster.

4. We will treat macro names as reserved words, and never use them for any other purpose, including as local variable names.

5. Any names we bind will be gensyms.

6. We will *never* write macros with side effects. We use macros to define classes and to increment variables, but the directly intended effect of the macro is the *only* effect of the macro.

```
(define-macro while%
  (lambda (form) (build-while form)))
(define build-while
  (lambda (form)
    (let ((bool-exp (car (cdr form)))
          (commands (cdr (cdr form)))
          (helper (gensym)))
      (list
        'letrec
        (list
          (list
            helper
            (list
              'lambda
              '()
              (list
                'if
                bool-exp
                (cons
                  'begin
                  (append
                    commands
                    (list (list helper)))))))))
        (list helper)))))
```

Program 7-17   Macro for `while%` using gensyms

☞ **Exercise 7-20**

Write a macro that gives Scheme the following special form

`(until` *boolean-expression   command...*`)`

An `until` form is evaluated by evaluating the *boolean-expression*. If it is `#f`, the *commands* are evaluated in turn, and the process is repeated; if the *boolean-expression* evaluates to `#t`, the `until` form returns an unspecified result. ❏

7.4.3   Scheme's Syntactic Sugar

We've already seen several special forms in Scheme that are not expressible in terms of other primitives. The basic special forms include `define`, `if`, `lambda`, `quote`, and `set!`. All of the other forms can be expressed in terms of these (using `define-macro`). We call any piece of syntax that isn't primitive **syntactic sugar**: it's provided to make the programmer's job sweeter, but doesn't really add power to the language. We've already seen the `let` family, `module`, the `case` form, and `define-class`; all of these forms are syntactic sugar. If Scheme didn't have them, we could still write any of the programs we've studied. However, programming would be so tedious that it would be difficult to write or read programs in a "sugarless" Scheme.

Some people have argued that languages should have a great deal of syntactic sugar. COBOL, for example, is designed to read like "business English". Others argue that too much syntactic sugar makes it harder to learn the language, because each special form might have its own syntax rules. The Scheme philosophy is to build a small simple language and then extend it with a minimal amount of syntactic sugar. `let` is a good example. It can be written as `lambda` application, but a `let` form is much more readable. Likewise, Scheme provides a useful special form for multiway conditional testing.

The `if` form allows us to do a one or two-way test, but sometimes we want to do a multiway test. `case` is one restricted form of multiway test, but it only works if we want to see whether a value is equal to one of a set of values.

Often, the conditions we want to test are more complex than this. We've seen how we can use `if` in such cases; for example, we might want to produce the letter grade corresponding to a student's final mark:

```
(if (>= mark 85)
  "A"
  (if (>= mark 72)
    "B"
    (if (>= mark 60)
      "C"
      (if (>= mark 50)
        "D"
        "F"))))
```

This code is unnecessarily hard to read. It's even hard to lay out on the page: as the cases get more deeply nested, they begin to march off the right side of the screen, and parentheses start to pile up on the right-hand side.

Lisp has always had a more general conditional form, known as `cond`. We haven't had much need for it so far, but as programs get more complicated, it becomes more useful. We could use `cond` to rewrite the above letter-grade code:

```
(cond
  ((>= mark 85) "A")
  ((>= mark 72) "B")
  ((>= mark 60) "C")
  ((>= mark 50) "D")
  (else         "F"))
```

This code is exactly equivalent to the above `if` form, but much more compact.

A `cond` has the following layout:

```
(cond
  (test  expression...)
  (test  expression...)
  ...
  (else expression...))
```

The *test*s are Boolean expressions, and the *expression*s can be any Scheme forms. A `cond` is evaluated by evaluating each of the tests in turn. As soon as one is found to be true, the *expression*s after it are evaluated, and the result is the value of the last one (i.e., the *expression*s form an implicit `begin`, just as with `lambda` and `let`). More than one *test* can be true; the first one that is true is the one whose *expression*s are evaluated.

Practical Note

The `else` part isn't required by Scheme; if none of the clauses is true, some unspecified value (null or void or something else) will be returned. However, a smart programmer will *always* include an `else` part; generating an error message saying `This can't happen!!!` is much better than computing with unspecified values.

The way we have implemented macros is a bit cumbersome. Our builder procedures construct the result form using `cons` and `list` and are, admittedly, difficult to read. Scheme has a construct, *quasiquote*, that simplifies writing builder procedures, but we will not burden you with an additional syntactic element. The point of this section is that a language can be extended by implementing procedures that rewrite input forms according to simple rules. We will soon extend the definition of Scheme to include macros in a way different from what we have discussed, using a high-level pattern language (see Chapter 10) and an implementation that avoids the problems of scope that we used `gensym` to circumvent.

☞ **Exercise 7-21**

In an exercise in Chapter 1, we studied the peculiar pricing policies of the Ruritanian post office. Rewrite your answer using `cond`. ❏

☞ **Exercise 7-22**

Write `case%`, a macro version of the Scheme special form `case`. ❏

7.5   A Scheme Evaluator

The code presented in this section can be found in file `selfeval.scm`.

> *Willy go round in circles, Willy fly high like a bird up in the sky*
> — Billy Preston

We have all the concepts needed to build a Scheme evaluator. We want to specify the behavior of an evaluator for Scheme and then implement the specification. The result will be a program that allows the user to enter Scheme forms, evaluate those forms, and display the results. In a sense, writing an evaluator for Scheme *in Scheme* seems like the ultimate in futility. In order to run our evaluator, we'll need a Scheme system, but if we already have a Scheme system, why would we want another one?

There are two answers to this question. First, our Scheme evaluator allows us to treat data as programs. For example, we can write a program that, during execution, reads a form from the user and evaluates it. One example is our plotting program from Chapter 3: it would be convenient to allow users to provide a procedure that transforms the data as required when they run the plotting program. Another example is sending Scheme programs over a computer network: in the Case Study for Chapter 8, we'll apply this technique to allow a workstation to formulate a database query as a Scheme program and send it to a remote mainframe that stores the data. Scheme already has a procedure named `eval` that lets us do this;[24] the evaluator we'll write here is in our tradition of duplicating interesting primitives.

A second answer is that we might *not* have a Scheme system at our disposal. Suppose we have a computer with no software—what do we do? As we'll see in the last two chapters, we can use what we'll learn as we build this evaluator to build an evaluator in the computer's machine language. Because this evaluator processes forms written in Scheme, and because it is written in Scheme, we'll call this evaluator the *self-evaluator*.

Our Dream and Nightmare implementations suggest two different ways of writing an evaluator. On the one hand, we can *interpret* forms directly (as we did with Dream); on the other, we can *compile* Scheme into some other language (as we did with Nightmare). Since we don't know any other practical language, we can't use the compilation approach.

In the interest of compactness, we're not going to write an evaluator for full Scheme. Much of that evaluator would be concerned with implementing the dozens of special forms and the hundred or so primitives that an $R^n RS$-compliant Scheme system must have. We're going to design a core language, a small subset that provides everything needed by the Scheme programmer. Our subset, Econo-Scheme, could be extended to support all of Scheme, either by adding additional primitives or by writing macros.

We will follow the strategy we used with Dream: first specify the language precisely, and then write an implementation that follows the specification. Our first task, therefore, is to write a specification for Econo-Scheme's syntax and semantics.

7.5.1   Specifying Scheme

Here's our specification in EBNF:

- `simple-form:`   `constant | symbol | special-form | application`
- `special-form:`   `definition | macro-definition | quote-form |`
    `lambda-form | set-form | if-form | begin-form | macro`
  Semantics: A special form is evaluated according to specific rules for each type of form. The names of special forms may not be used as variables or macros in the program.
  Note: Whether a parenthesized form is special can be determined by looking for a specific keyword at the beginning of the form.
- `definition:`   `"(" "define" name form ")"`
  Semantics: A definition is evaluated by binding the `name` to the value of the `form` in the environment (which will be the global frame, since a `definition` can only appear at the top level). The value of a `definition` is unspecified.
- `macro-definition:` `"(" "define-macro" name form ")"`
  Semantics: A macro-definition is evaluated by evaluating the `form`. The resulting value must be a procedure. The `name` is recorded as a macro, with the expander procedure given by the value of `form`. Because the environment in which the expander is evaluated is unspecified, the expander procedure may only access or mutate global variables. The value of a `macro-definition` is unspecified.

---

[24] This will appear in $R^5 RS$.

- `macro:`   `"(" name {form} ")"`
  Semantics: A `macro` is evaluated by evaluating the procedure recorded for macro `name`. (The environment the procedure is evaluated in is unspecified, which means that it must contain no free variables.) The result of the procedure must be a list or symbol representing a Scheme form, which is in turn evaluated. The result of this evaluation is the result of the `macro`.
- `quote-form:`   `"(" "quote" quotation ")"`
  Semantics: The value of a `quote-form` is `quotation`, unevaluated.
  Note: Scheme systems allow the user to type (quote a) as 'a. Internally, this form is stored as (quote a).
- `quotation:`   `constant | symbol | pair | list`
- `symbol:`   `name`
- `pair:`   `"(" quotation "." quotation ")"`
- `list:`   `"(" {quotation} ")"`
- `lambda-form:`   `"(" "lambda" lambda-params sequence ")"`
  Semantics: The value of a `lambda-form` is a procedure specifying the `lambda-params` and `sequence`, bound in the current environment.
- `set-form:`   `"(" "set!" name form ")"`
  Semantics: A `set-form` is evaluated by mutating the variable `name` to the value of the `form`. The `name` must be defined in the environment. The value of a `set-form` is unspecified.
- `if-form:`   `"(" "if" form form [form] ")"`
  Semantics: An `if-form` is evaluated by evaluating the first form. If its value is not false, the value is the value of the second form. If the value of the first form is false, the value is the value of the third form, if it was given. (Otherwise, the value of the entire form is unspecified.)
- `begin-form:`   `"(" "begin" sequence ")"`
  Semantics: The value of a `begin-form` is the value of the `sequence`.
- `sequence:`   `{form}`
  Semantics: A `sequence` is evaluated by evaluating each form in turn and throwing away the values of all forms except the last one. The value of the last form is the value of the `sequence`. If there are no forms, the value of the sequence is unspecified.
- `application:`   `"(" form {form} ")"`
  Semantics: An `application` is evaluated by evaluating the first form. The result must be a procedure (user-defined or primitive). All remaining forms are evaluated and passed as arguments to the procedure. The result is the value of the procedure.

We will not give rules for `constant`, which is intended to include such things as numbers, Booleans, characters, and strings, or for `name`. Doing this would result in a large number of rules with no real increase in clarity, although such rules are required in a formal language specification.

7.5.2   Self-Evaluator Strategy

We have already built an evaluator that can handle primitive expressions and a global environment with variables. We need to handle procedures, the fundamental building blocks of programs. A procedure abstracts the transformation between input and output that a sequence of expressions embodies. To provide that abstraction, a procedure presents an interface—its name and its parameters—and constructs a local frame in which its body is evaluated.

The only special forms provided in Econo-Scheme are `quote`, `define`, `begin`, `if`, `set!`, `lambda`, and `define-macro`. We can extend our evaluator to handle many of the Scheme elements we usually employ, such as `let` and `case`, by creating macros that, for example, transform the `let` form into an equivalent `lambda`.

The evaluator must create and manage frames, create and manage procedures, and evaluate the body of procedures in the environment that results from the concatenation of the frames. `Dream` used the data types of Scheme to handle its data, as will `self-eval`. However, we must control the environment ourselves in `self-eval`, so we must build data structures to handle frames and procedures explicitly.

7.5.3   Building the Self-Evaluator

The self-evaluator will be the biggest program we've produced. Before we start writing it, we should plan out a strategy. Often the first implementation of a programming language is written as the language is being developed. That implementation is usually buggy; it's difficult to write clean, modular code when new language features are being designed in the morning, implemented in the afternoon, and offered to eager users in the evening.

Once a language has stabilized and is better understood, we can develop a clean specification, using many of the design techniques we've studied, to build a production implementation. A finished product, on the other hand, has no little bits and pieces scattered around. Software engineers would like to build finished products, with no indication of the false starts and dead ends, rather than prototypes.[25] As computer scientists, however, we must sometimes wear a "prototyping" hat, and sometimes a "finished product" hat.

We can draw on many sources in designing a self-evaluator. In fact, the first book ever published on Lisp contained a self-evaluator.[26] Many people have written Scheme self-evaluators, so we don't have to figure out how to build one. We can concentrate instead on using specification and design techniques to make our code as understandable as possible.

Figure 7–9 shows the flow of forms and environments through the main components of the self-evaluator. The boxes represent the main procedures in the evaluator proper.

The evaluator is broken into the following modules:

- A *frame manager* lets us create frames, and access and mutate variable bindings.

- A *procedure manager* lets us create and access the components of a procedure.

---

[25] Occasionally, they succeed.

[26] *The LISP 1.5 Programming Language*, J. McCarthy et al., 1961.

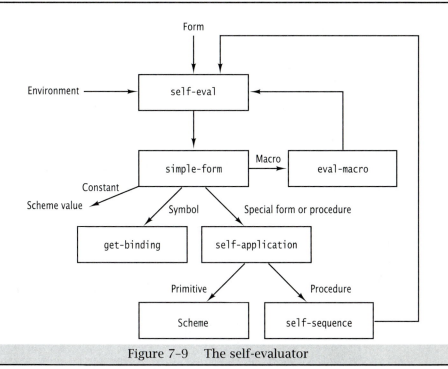

Figure 7-9   The self-evaluator

- A *primitive* module contains all of the primitive procedures.
- The *evaluator* proper examines the form being evaluated, and processes applications and special forms.
- A *user interface manager* handles all interaction with the user.
- An *output module* provides a version of display that handles procedures properly.

Throughout the code, we've sprinkled various elements of error-checking code. You should read the program carefully to see which errors are detected.

A complex program such as this is studied from the top down, so why are we doing it bottom up? You've already seen the recursive structure of an evaluator in dream-eval. What differs here is the complexity of the individual components (in particular the frame manager). Let's get acquainted with the components, with the exception of the output module, and then assemble them.

7.5.4   The Frame Manager

The frame manager module allows Scheme to create a new frame and connect it to an existing frame, and to access and mutate bindings. An environment is a collection of one or more linked frames. As we saw in Chapter 5, the primitive frame is a special frame that has no parent. It is the basis of the environment. Scheme adds the user frame each time the repl restarts. Together the primitive and user frames form the global environment.

When a procedure application occurs, the frame manager springs into action. When a procedure is applied, Scheme creates a new frame linked by the static link to the frame where the procedure was created. The new frame is the top frame of the environment in which the body of the procedure is evaluated. Scheme maintains the data structure connecting all procedures and the frames active when they were created. Any other objects are referred to by names in the global environment.

The environment in `self-eval` is a list of frames. Initially it is a list containing the primitive frame. The user frame is then consed onto the primitive frame. When `self-eval` creates a new frame, it is attached to an existing environment, that is, the new frame is consed onto an existing list of frames.

We have separate procedures for mutating a binding and defining a new binding. The ADT shown in Figure 7-10 defines a frame type.

Constructors

- (extend-environment *names values env*)
  Extend the environment by creating a new frame, with *names* bound to *values*, whose parent is *env*.

Accessors

- (get-binding *symb env*)
  Return the value of *symb* in *env*, or an evaluator error if no binding is found.

Mutators

- (set-binding! *symb val env*)
  Mutate the binding of *symb* to *val* in *env*. Signal an evaluator error if no binding is found.

- (def-binding! *symb env*)
  Mutate the binding of *symb* to *val* in the top frame of *env*. If no binding is found in the top frame, create a binding there.

Figure 7-10   **Abstract Data Type:** `frame`

We represent a frame as an association list in which the keys are the variable names, and the values are the associated variable values. The search for the binding of a variable starts in the current frame (the car of the list) and then continues in successive frames in the list. This process repeats until it arrives at the primitive frame. Programs 7-18 and 7-19 are the two pieces of the frame manager.

How does this rendition of frames compare with that in Chapter 5? Variable bindings are pretty much the same as in our snapshots, but what about the links and the resume point? If you look at the description of the search process, it should be clear that "searching previous frames on a list of frames" means exactly the same as "following the static links until we reach the global environment". The dynamic link and resume point are a bit more subtle: we'll explain those when we study the evaluator itself.

7.5.5   The Procedure Manager

To avoid confusion, we'll denote by *procedure record* the structure in `self-eval` that represents a procedure. The procedure manager contains procedures that make a procedure record, test to see whether something is a procedure record, and retrieve the arguments, body, and binding environment of the procedure record.

```
(module self-eval-frames
  (export extend-environment
          get-binding set-binding def-binding)
  (define extend-environment
    (lambda (names values env)
      (letrec
        ((new-frame
           (lambda (n v)
             (if (and (null? n) (null? v))
                 '()
                 (if (null? n)
                     (evaluator-error
                       "Too many arguments" (cons names values))
                     (if (null? v)
                         (evaluator-error
                           "Too few arguments" (cons names values))
                         (if (and (pair? n) (symbol? (car n)))
                             (cons
                               (cons (car n) (car v))
                               (new-frame (cdr n) (cdr v)))
                               (evaluator-error
                                 "Invalid parameter list" names)))))))))
        (cons (new-frame names values) env))))
  (define find-binding
    (lambda (symb env)
      (if (null? env)
          #f
          (let ((x (assv symb (car env))))
            (if (not x)
                (find-binding symb (cdr env))
                x))))))
```

Program 7-18   self-eval: frames and environments (1 of 2)

The ADT for a procedure record, shown in Figure 7-11, defines the format of a procedure record. A procedure record contains the code for a procedure, along with the frame that was current when the procedure was built. The representation used here is not particularly efficient. A procedure record is represented by a four-element list: (**procedure** params body env), where params is the parameter list of the procedure, body is the procedure's body, and env is the environment that was current at the time the procedure was created.

The output module contains a procedure, show, that recursively prints a list structure; when it sees a procedure record, it displays {procedure}, rather than attempting to print the list. This is essential because a procedure record contains an environment within it. If the procedure is the value of a binding, then the environment will contain a definition for that name. Hence, we get a circular structure, which will take a long time to print. show is an extension of the list display routine we studied in Chapter 4. Look in the Software Package if you want to see it.

Program 7-20 shows an implementation of the procedure ADT. It's straightforward, with the exception that the evaluator-error procedure is used to signal

```
     (define get-binding
       (lambda (symb env)
         (let ((x (find-binding symb env)))
           (if (not x)
               (evaluator-error "Unbound variable (get)" symb)
               (cdr x)))))
     (define set-binding
       (lambda (symb val env)
         (let ((x (find-binding symb env)))
           (if (not x)
               (evaluator-error "Unbound variable (set)" symb)
               (set-cdr! x val)))))
     (define def-binding
       (lambda (symb val env)
         (let ((x (assv symb (car env))))
           (if (not x)
               (set-car! env (cons (cons symb val) (car env)))
               (set-cdr! x val)))))
) ;;; end of module self-eval-frames
```

Program 7-19   `self-eval`: frames and environments (2 of 2)

Constructor

* `(make-procedure params body env)`
  Make a procedure containing *params* and *body*, connected to *env*.

Predicates

* `(is-procedure? x)`
  Return #t if x is a procedure, and #f if x is anything else.

Accessors

* `(procedure-params procedure)`
  Return the parameters of *procedure*.
* `(procedure-body procedure)`
  Return the body of *procedure*.
* `(procedure-env procedure)`
  Return the environment of *procedure*.

Figure 7-11   **Abstract Data Type:** `procedure`

program errors, where `self-eval` encounters something other than a procedure in the program it's evaluating.

When `self-eval` makes a procedure record, it doesn't check whether the elements of the procedure make sense. For example, it doesn't ensure that the parameters are names. If you look back to `extend-environment`, you'll see that it determines that the parameter list is ill-formed, and reports an evaluator error.

☞ **Exercise 7-23**

Wile E. Programmer decides to fool `self-eval` into accepting input that looks a legitimate procedure record, but isn't. How could we redesign the ADT to prevent this? ❑

```
(module self-eval-procedure
  (export make-procedure is-procedure? procedure-params
    procedure-body procedure-env)
  (define procedure-flag '**procedure**)
  (define make-procedure
    (lambda (args body env)
      (list procedure-flag args body env)))
  (define is-procedure?
    (lambda (proc)
      (and (pair? proc) (eqv? (car proc) procedure-flag))))
  (define procedure-params
    (lambda (proc)
      (if (is-procedure? proc)
        (list-ref proc 1)
        (evaluator-error "Procedure expected" proc))))
  (define procedure-body
    (lambda (proc)
      (if (is-procedure? proc)
        (list-ref proc 2)
        (evaluator-error "Procedure expected" proc))))
  (define procedure-env
    (lambda (proc)
      (if (is-procedure? proc)
        (list-ref proc 3)
        (evaluator-error "Procedure expected" proc))))
) ;;; end of module self-eval-procedure
```

Program 7-20   Procedure implementation

7.5.6   The Primitives

The primitives module appears in Program 7-21. It is separate only because, in a real Scheme system, there are many primitive procedures (as many as two or three hundred). The primitive procedures shown here are self-explanatory.

Part of the job we can assign to this module is building the primitive frame. You can insert whatever names you like, with whatever procedures or other values you choose. This module is intentionally kept small, with just enough primitives to show that things work.

This module exports the procedure `primitive-procedure`. Primitives are values; however, implementing `self-eval` in Scheme gives us the luxury of representing its primitives as plain Scheme procedures. Even so, in the interest of modularity, we'd like to hide this fact from the rest of the evaluator. We therefore create a trivial accessor to convert a primitive into a Scheme procedure. Each primitive takes its arguments in the form of a list.

```
(module self-eval-primitives
  (export is-primitive? primitive-procedure
          make-primitive-environment)
  (define is-primitive? procedure?)
  (define primitive-procedure (lambda (x) x))
  (define make-primitive-environment
    (lambda ()
    (let ((pf (extend-environment '() '() '())))
    (let
      ((def
        (lambda (name proc) (def-binding name proc pf))))
    (def '+ (lambda (x) (+ (car x) (car (cdr x)))))
    (def '- (lambda (x) (- (car x) (car (cdr x)))))
    (def '* (lambda (x) (* (car x) (car (cdr x)))))

    (def '/ (lambda (x) (/ (car x) (car (cdr x)))))
    (def '< (lambda (x) (< (car x) (car (cdr x)))))
    (def '= (lambda (x) (= (car x) (car (cdr x)))))
    (def '> (lambda (x) (> (car x) (car (cdr x)))))

    (def 'pi 3.1415926)

    (def 'car (lambda (x) (car (car x))))
    (def 'cdr (lambda (x) (cdr (car x))))
    (def 'cons (lambda (x) (cons (car x) (car (cdr x)))))
    (def 'null? (lambda (x) (null? (car x))))
    (def 'eqv? (lambda (x) (eqv? (car x) (car (cdr x)))))

    (def 'display (lambda (x) (show (car x))))
    (def 'newline (lambda (x) (newline)))

  pf))))
) ;;; end of module self-eval-primitives
```

Program 7-21   `self-eval`: primitive procedures

7.5.7   The Evaluator

The evaluator module's main procedure, `self-eval`, evaluates a form in an environment. Unlike `dream-eval`, `self-eval` is not two pieces, one that handles commands and another that handles expressions; all elements are handled uniformly. The form of `self-eval` is like the EBNF specification we gave earlier.

Essentially, each of the components in the EBNF can be paired with a procedure in `self-eval` that performs the corresponding transformation on the expression being evaluated. For example, `self-eval` has an association list, `*special-forms*`, each of whose elements contains as its car, the name of a special form, and as its cdr a procedure for handling that form. This approach makes it easier to extend the evaluator to handle additional special forms (e.g., `let`, `cond`, and `case`).

`self-eval` is shown in Program 7-22. It evaluates an expression in a given environment by calling `simple-form`, which in turn looks at the expression to determine whether it is a constant, a variable, or a pair (the only valid cases). Numbers and Booleans are self-evaluating; a symbol is evaluated by using the environment procedure `get-binding` to look it up. Any pair is evaluated by looking up its car on the special-forms list. If it is present, we apply the form's procedure; if not, we perform an application. Most of the special forms are self-explanatory. The `lambda` form is handled by making a procedure whose environment is the current environment.

```
(define self-eval
  (lambda (exp env)
    (simple-form exp env)))
(define constant?
  (lambda (exp)
    (or (number? exp) (boolean? exp) (string? exp))))
(define simple-form
  (lambda (exp env)
    (cond
      ((constant? exp)
       exp)
      ((symbol? exp)
       (get-binding exp env))
      ((pair? exp)
       (let ((b (assv (car exp) special-forms)))
         ((if b (cdr b) self-application) exp env)))
      (else (evaluator-error "Incorrect expression" exp)))))
```

Program 7-22   `self-eval`: the core

Another interesting aspect of the evaluator is revealed by the procedure `self-application`, which handles a procedure application. This procedure first evaluates all of the arguments recursively (in exactly the same way that `dream-eval` did), and then determines how to do the application:

- If the car is a primitive procedure, then it is a primitive, and is just applied (as in `dream-eval`).
- If it's a compound procedure, we must evaluate the body of the procedure in a new environment, made by binding the arguments of the application *in the procedure's environment*. (Make sure you understand why we're using the procedure's environment.)
- Anything else is an error.

The following shows the implementation of the core of the evaluator. Rather than show the whole module, we're going to look at the key pieces. Some auxiliary procedures are omitted for brevity, including those that select arguments from the list of arguments. `get-arg` gets the nth element of a list (counting from 0), and `get-rest` gets the nth tail of a list. These procedures are similar to `list-ref` and `list-tail`, but generate error messages if the element or tail isn't present (thus eliminating a great deal of clutter when we do error-checking).

For expressions that are pairs, we have two cases: either it's a special form or it's an application. The two cases are distinguished by the fact that the names of the special forms are predefined. We use an alist, `special-forms`, to keep these names; if the car of the form isn't on that alist, the form must be an application.

☞ **Exercise 7-24**

What about forms such as `((if foo bar baz) gum)`? How does `simple-form` know that this is an application, rather than a special form? ❏

Let's recall the specification and semantics of `application`:
application: "(" form {form} ")"
Semantics: An `application` is evaluated by evaluating the first form. The result must be a procedure (user-defined or primitive). All remaining forms are evaluated and passed as arguments to the procedure. The result is the value of the procedure. `self-application`, shown in Program 7-23, does this job.

```
(define self-application
  (lambda (exp env)
    (let*
      ((eval-arg (lambda (arg) (self-eval arg env)))
       (evaluated-args (map eval-arg exp))
       (operator (car evaluated-args))
       (operands (cdr evaluated-args)))
      (cond
        ((is-primitive? operator)
         ((primitive-procedure operator) operands))
        ((is-procedure? operator)
         (self-sequence
           (procedure-body operator)
           (extend-environment
             (procedure-params operator)
             operands
             (procedure-env operator))))
        (else
          (evaluator-error "Procedure required" exp))))))
```

Program 7-23   `self-eval`: evaluating applications

The basic idea is to look at the two cases. For primitives, all we have to do is to call the primitive's procedure. For compound procedures, we do a recursive call in an extended environment; the current environment is extended with the bindings for the arguments of the procedure.

Earlier, we mentioned that the static link is explicitly represented, in that an environment is a list of frames; to follow the static link, we just scan the list from left to right. We can see how application extends the environment: the call to `self-sequence` is done in an environment that has been extended with a single frame containing the argument bindings.

We also said that the dynamic link and resume point are represented implicitly. There is no data structure here saying what to do after the application is finished. We're going to call `self-sequence`, and *when we're finished*, we'll return from the call to `self-application`.

Nothing is being mutated here. We extend an environment by consing a new frame onto the front; when we return from the call, we return to the original binding of env. The only significant use of mutation in the self-evaluator is in mutating variable bindings.

What is self-sequence, and why do we call it? Many forms in Scheme support "implicit begin". We call a series of forms in an implicit begin a *sequence*.

Here's the specification for a sequence:

sequence: {form}

Semantics: A sequence is evaluated by evaluating each form in turn and throwing away the values of all forms except the last one. The value of the last form is the value of the sequence. If there are no forms, the value of the sequence is unspecified.

The code for sequences is shown in Program 7-24. The helper seq evaluates each expression in turn, and returns the value of the previous form when it runs off the end. Accordingly, we start seq off with an unspecified value. (We use the global variable unbound for this purpose.)

```
(define self-sequence
  (lambda (exp env)
    (letrec
      ((seq
        (lambda (val exp env)
          (if (null? exp)
              val
              (seq (self-eval (car exp) env) (cdr exp) env)))))
      (seq unbound exp env))))
```

Program 7-24 self-eval: sequences

Program 7-25 shows how we handle special forms. When simple-form discovers that the car of a form is on the special-forms list, it calls the associated "handler" procedure. The handler receives as arguments the form and the environment, and can do anything it wants. Sometimes it will want to evaluate some of its arguments; a recursive call to self-eval will do the job. The handler for set! shows how to implement a special form. set! wants its first argument (the variable name) unevaluated, but the second argument (the value) must be evaluated.

What about macros? The only code that self-eval needs for macros is the define-macro handler, and the procedure def-macro, shown in Program 7-26. def-macro creates a new special form whose name is the name of the macro, and whose body is a procedure that calls the expander procedure with the unevaluated arguments, parallel to self-application. Notice how the inner procedure captures an environment that binds expander. There's no other work we need to do in order to provide macros. The general special-form capability is all we need.

☞ **Exercise 7-25**

Write a special-form handler for let. ❏

```
(define special-forms '())
(define define-special
  (lambda (symb proc)
    (let ((x (assv symb special-forms)))
      (if x
          (set-cdr! x proc)
          (set! special-forms
            (cons (cons symb proc) special-forms))))))
(define define-special-forms
  (lambda ()
    (define-special 'quote
      (lambda (exp env) (get-arg exp 1)))
    (define-special 'lambda
      (lambda (exp env)
        (make-procedure
          (get-arg exp 1) (get-rest exp 2) env)))
    (define-special 'set!
      (lambda (exp env)
        (set-binding (get-arg exp 1)
          (self-eval (get-arg exp 2) env) env)
        (void)))
    (define-special 'if
      (lambda (exp env)
        (if (self-eval (get-arg exp 1) env)
            (self-eval (get-arg exp 2) env)
            (self-eval (get-arg exp 3) env))))
    (define-special 'begin
      (lambda (exp env)
        (self-sequence (get-rest exp 1) env)))
    (define-special 'define
      (lambda (exp env)
        (def-binding (get-arg exp 1)
          (self-eval (get-arg exp 2) env) env)
        (void)))
    (define-special 'define-macro
      (lambda (exp env)
        (def-macro (get-arg exp 1)
          (self-eval (get-arg exp 2) env))
        (void)))
))
```

Program 7-25   `self-eval`: special forms

7.5.8   The User Interface Manager

The user-interface manager, `self-eval-user`, contains two procedures: `top-level` interacts with the user, and `evaluator-error` reports errors. In Chapter 4, we discussed read-eval-print loops, or repls. A repl is a procedure that carries on a dialog with the user, evaluating each input and displaying the result. Production-quality Lisp and Scheme systems have elaborate repls that allow the user to do such things

```
(define def-macro
  (lambda (mac-name expander)
    (define-special mac-name
      (lambda (exp env)
        (self-eval
          (self-sequence
            (procedure-body expander)
            (extend-environment (procedure-params expander)
              (list exp) (procedure-env expander)))
          env)))))
```

Program 7-26   <code>self-eval</code>: macros

as recall and reevaluate previous inputs. Our repl, `top-level`, is quite simple; it displays a prompt (we use `se>`, to distinguish our top-level from the one built into Scheme), reads a form, evaluates it, and displays the result, as shown in Program 7-27.

top-level assumes that the primitive frame has already been built; however, the environment is extended with the user frame (by calling `extend-environment`) before entering the repl. It is convenient to keep user definitions out of the primitive frame, so as to ensure, while debugging, that if we call `top-level` several times, we are working with the same environment each time. A user can, nevertheless, mutate predefined variables.

Error-handling is rather complex in a real repl. An error message should be displayed, and then the user should have the choice of going to the next input form or entering a **debugger**, a procedure that lets a programmer examine the state of the program to locate bugs. Our repl simply displays an error message and then restarts `top-level`.[27]

7.5.9 What Have We Done?

We've implemented a series of evaluators, culminating in one that handles the essential elements of Scheme, including macros. Let's reexamine what we've really done. Are we cheating here?[28] What are we getting for free? The implementation of the evaluator shows how procedures are created and how their bodies are evaluated in the context they create. The implementation also shows how sequences are processed, and how expressions are broken down into their constituent parts. What have we left out? Well, all of the data types are handled by Scheme, and all of the list processing has been finessed by getting Scheme to do it. And the primitives do all the real work. Chapters 11 and 12 describe how the primitives are implemented on Gleam, a hypothetical computer that closely approximates a real machine.

An evaluator is called *tail-recursive* if it processes recursive procedures without requiring additional space for each call in the iteration. `self-eval` handles this

---

[27] Most Scheme systems allow the programmer to trap all errors, including errors detected by the hardware (e.g., division by 0). The techniques for doing this are system-dependent, and are beyond the scope of this book.

[28] It's traditional to cheat in implementing new languages. The first core evaluator is written in some base language, and then the rest of the evaluator is written in the target language. This practice is called *bootstrapping*, whereby one hauls oneself up by one's own bootstraps.

```
(module self-eval-user
  (export top-level evaluator-error)
  (define prompt        "se> ")
  (define answer-prefix " => ")
  (define terminator '(stop))
  (define top-level
    (lambda ()
      (define-special-forms)
      (let
        ((env (make-primitive-environment)))
        (letrec
          ((read-eval-print-loop
             (lambda ()
               (display prompt)
               (let
                 ((form (read)))
                 (if (equal? form terminator)
                   (begin
                     (format #t  "...and a pleasant day to you!~%")
                     (void))
                   (let ((answer (self-eval form env)))
                     (if (not (eqv? (void) answer))
                       (begin
                         (display answer-prefix)
                         (show answer)
                         (newline)))
                     (read-eval-print-loop)))))))
          (read-eval-print-loop)))))
  (define evaluator-error
    (lambda (what irritant)
      (format #t "~%Error in self-eval: ~a:" what)
      (if (not (eqv? (void) irritant))
        (display irritant))
      (format #t "~%...resetting to top level.~%")
      (top-level)))
) ;;; end of module self-eval-user
```

Program 7-27   self-eval: the top level

by processing the body of a procedure in `self-sequence` with the embedded procedure `seq`. If you examine `seq`, you'll see that it's tail-recursive! Thus, `self-eval` is tail-recursive, since Scheme itself handles the tail-recursive procedure `seq` tail-recursively.

These procedures that implement the self-evaluator should show you the mechanism that implements the environment model. Note how much simpler the code seems than the model! Program implementation is often simple once we understand what it is the program must do and to what sorts of objects. You may not have understood all the details of the environment model, but with `self-eval` to examine and experiment with, it should be much easier.

Case Study: Interpreting BASIC

In this Case Study, we will build an interpreter for a simple command language for an application program. Often an application provides facilities for data manipulation (e.g., signal processing). The basic data-manipulation operations in the application are the primitives of a language specific to the application. To make the application useful, we will add a simple language with variables, conditional statements, and constructs for looping, but no primitives specialized to the application.

We will base the language on BASIC, an imperative language that was one of the first interpreted languages to be widely used. Many programmers in the 1970s used BASIC or one of its derivatives for their own programming.[29] Our language will provide a minimum set of statement types. A programmer wishing to extend it for signal processing or laboratory data acquisition would modify the interpreter to add the desired statement types.

To understand our programming language, Beam (BASIC Evaluator for an Application Machine), let's take a Scheme program (shown in Program 7-28) and rewrite it in Beam. loop reads a number. If the number is nonnegative, it displays the product of the number and pi; otherwise, it stops. Program 7-29 shows the corresponding Beam program.

```
(define pi 3.14)
(define loop
  (lambda (d)
    (if (>= d 0)
      (begin
        (format #t "~a~%" (* pi d))
        (loop
          (begin
            (format #t "Enter~%")
            (read)))))))
(loop (begin (format #t "Enter~%") (read)))
```

Program 7-28   Scheme code implemented in Beam

This program has a more primitive aspect than one in any modern programming language. Each line starts with a line number that identifies the line. Line numbers arose because early programmers didn't have access to video terminals. On a typewriter (hard-copy) terminal, there is no way to move around in a program as on a video monitor. The only way to change a statement on these terminals was to specify its line number. As programs were entered, the language interpreter would increment the line number by some fixed increment, say 100. In Beam, the line numbers are part of the program, but the evaluator we will build does not assume that line numbers are in any order. (As video terminals and personal computers spread,

---

[29] BASIC has changed greatly since the version we show here. Modern versions of BASIC have structured programming features, elaborate procedure facilities, and so on. The language shown here is reminiscent of some of the early versions of BASIC. The limited and clumsy nature of the early versions is directly related to the limited machine resources of the time: a 64K machine might support four or five BASIC programmers.

```
(
100 let pi = 3.14 &
200 print "Enter: " &
300 input d &
400 if { d < 0 } goto 700 &
500 print { pi * d } &
600 goto 200 &
700 stop &
)
```

Program 7-29   Beam program

line numbers became less and less useful.) Each statement is terminated by a special symbol. In a real BASIC, this symbol was generally a newline character. We will use the same statement terminator as Nightmare, to make it visible.

Until the mid-1970s, many programmers used gotos to change the control in a program arbitrarily from one statement in the program to another. As programs grew larger, following the control flow became very difficult. Many programming languages have since downplayed the use of such constructs, and others eliminate them completely. Beam uses goto statements to implement repetition: one way to build a loop is to terminate the loop body by a goto statement, and to put in an if statement that jumps out of the loop within the body. We aren't advocating that you program with gotos, but many old programs still do useful things and are riddled with gotos. This legacy code could be rewritten, but we often don't have the time or resources to do so.

Beam has one feature that Scheme doesn't: it handles expressions as we do in algebra. Expressions are grouped according to the operators. For example, $1 + 2 * 3 \Rightarrow 7$, and $3 < 1 + 2 \Rightarrow$ #f. There are three groups of operators: relational operators (<, >, and =); addition operators (+ and -); and multiplications (* and /). We evaluate a Beam expression by first doing all the multiplications from left to right,[30] then all the additions from left to right, and finally all of the relations from left to right.[31]

We can implement Beam in a number of different ways. We could write an interpreter or a compiler. With a compiler, we could use Dream or Scheme for our object programs. We've chosen to write an interpreter.

The first step is to write an EBNF specification, as shown in Program 7-30. (name, number, string, and Boolean all have the same syntax as in Scheme.) There are only minor cosmetic differences between the EBNF for Beam and that for Nightmare, except for the introduction of goto. Beam only has a restricted form of conditional: there is no *else*-form, and the conditional only allows goto statements in the *then*-form. The restricted conditional is *universal*: any other type of conditional could be expressed with the restricted form.

One interesting aspect of the grammar is how it groups expressions. We have separated expressions into three rules: relations, additions, and multiplications. This separation causes the multiplications to group very tightly; to evaluate a relation, we must first do an entire multiplication. The structure of the grammar

---

[30] You might object to calling a / a multiplication. By *multiplication*, we mean "anything that groups in the same way as multiplication".

[31] Relations are restricted, in that $1 < 2 < 3$ is syntactically correct, but semantically it is nonsense: #t < 3 is invalid.

- program: "(" {statement} ")"
- statement: number command "&"
- command: goto | enter | assignment | test |
  write | goto | stop
- assignment: "let" name "=" expr
- test: "if" expr goto
- goto: "goto" number
- enter: "input" name
- write: "print" expr
- end: "stop"
- expr: relation
- relation: relation relop addition | addition
- relop: "<" | "=" | ">"
- addition: addition addop multiplication | multiplication
- addop: "+" | "-"
- multiplication: multiplication mulop factor | factor
- mulop: "*" | "/"
- factor: "{" expr "}" | name | constant
- constant: number | string | Boolean

Program 7-30   EBNF for Beam

expresses the **precedence**, (the order in which terms are grouped) among the binary operators: multiplications first, then additions, and finally relations.

A closer look at the expression rules shows that they're recursive. The recursion is on the left, so as to force grouping on the left. Thus, for example, to evaluate 5 - 3 + 1, we must group into an addition and a multiplication. The only way to do this is to have the addition be 5 - 3 and the multiplication be 1. The second addition groups into an addition of 5 and a multiplication of 3. The third addition must be multiplication (because it has no addop).

☞ **Exercise 7-26**

Express the following Scheme form in Beam:

```
(if (> d 5) (display d) (display (- d 3)))
```

❏

Being wise programmers, as we implement Beam, we'll steal as much as possible from Dream. Unlike Dream statements, Beam statements are not grouped by parentheses; as in Nightmare, however, there are statement terminators. There is, therefore, some extra complication in the procedures to find the next command. For simplicity, Beam lacks error-checking; later exercises will ask you to add some. The top-level procedure for Beam is shown in Program 7-31.

In Beam, unlike Dream, beam-interpret passes the entire program to beam-command-sequence. Neither Dream nor Nightmare has looping; in Beam the goto starts the evaluator at a different place in the program, not just the next statement. In Scheme, recursive procedures implement repetition. When a recursive procedure

```
(define beam-interpret
  (lambda (prog)
    (variable-clear)
    (interpret-command prog prog)))
```
Program 7-31   Beam: the top level

loops, the procedure is evaluated again. In Beam, control transfers to another location in the program, and the transfer point can be *anywhere*. The evaluator must therefore have access to the whole program.

Program 7-32 shows `interpret-command`, the main loop of the interpreter, which is called once for each command that is to be executed. The first argument to `interpret-command` refers to the beginning of a Beam command, starting with the line number. The main processing occurs in a `case` statement, which decides what kind of statement it's looking at, and then analyzes the statement.

Practical Note

`interpret-command` contains a good example of the use of a "this can't happen" `else` clause. The first version of `interpret-command` didn't have the `else`. Unfortunately, almost any bug causes `interpret-command` to be handed something that isn't the beginning of a command, which makes it go berserk. As soon as the `else` clause was added, it caught all of these bugs, generating a *useful* error message. This was a great help to the authors' debugging efforts.

Murphy's Law says "Whatever can go wrong will go wrong". Putting extra `else` clauses in your conditionals takes little time, and doesn't even cause much visual clutter, if you define a procedure `oops!` that writes out an error message or invokes a debugger, if you have one.

The `goto` and `if` statements pass control forward (or backward) in the text of the program to the right place. Program 7-33 shows a procedure that searches the program text to find the new command for the sequencer to evaluate after a `goto`.

`helper` skips to the end of each statement so that `beam-find` can be sure that it's examining a line number. Without the & terminating each statement, `helper` would have to distinguish between a number in an expression and a line number. How would it do that? Either expressions would have to be clearly marked in the program (by more delimiters like { and }, or `beam-find` would have to interpret each statement, and skip the appropriate elements. The easiest solution for the language *implementor* is to add statement terminators, but this isn't necessarily the easiest for the language *user*!

☞ **Exercise 7-27**

If a Beam program has *n* statements, how many statements would `beam-find`'s helper have to examine, in the worst case? Recall that the line numbers are in no particular order. ❏

Expressions are probably the trickiest part of the Beam evaluator; however, you can find your way through the expression code if you keep in mind the fact that EBNF is a programming language for analyzing programs. We can translate the

```scheme
(define interpret-command
  (lambda (commands prog)
    (let ((cmd (cdr commands)))
      (let
        ((rest ;; rest of the program after the current statement
          (case (car cmd)
            ((goto) ;; goto line-no &
             (beam-find
               (list-ref cmd 1) prog))
            ((input) ;; input name &
             (variable-assign (list-ref cmd 1) (read))
             (list-tail cmd 3))
            ((let) ;; let name = expr &
             (let ((val-rest (do-expression (list-tail cmd 3))))
               (variable-assign
                 (list-ref cmd 1) (car val-rest))
               (cdr (cdr val-rest))))
            ((if) ;; if expr goto xxx &
             (let ((val-rest (do-expression (list-tail cmd 1))))
               (if (car val-rest)
                 (beam-find (list-ref val-rest 2) prog)
                 (skip-to-end (cdr val-rest)))))
            ((print) ;; print expr &
             (let ((val-rest (do-expression (list-tail cmd 1))))
               (format #t "~a~%" (car val-rest))
               (cdr (cdr val-rest))))
            ((stop) 'done)
            (else
              (beam-error
                "Unknown statement type ~a" (car cmd))))))
        (if (eqv? rest 'done)
          (void)
          (interpret-command  rest prog)))))))
```

Program 7-32   Beam: commands

EBNF rules into Scheme, even if they contain recursive calls! Program 7-34 shows do-relation, which handles relations. This method of processing expressions is known as **recursive descent**.

do-relation calls do-addition for each of the additions. The recursion in the rules turns into the recursive helper, bin-helper, which is also used by do-addition and do-multiplication. bin-helper takes the result of the appropriate do-*xxx* procedure, a predicate, beam-relop?, to test whether an expression is a certain kind, and inner, the procedure to apply to the rest of the expression after the operator. These do-*xxx* procedures need to return two values: the value of the expression, and the rest of the command after the expression. This becomes clear when you examine expressions such as 2 + 3 and { 2 + 3 } * 4. Only analyzing the expression can tell us how many tokens an expression takes. We solve this problem by returning a pair, whose car contains the value, and whose cdr contains the rest of the command after the expression just evaluated.

```
(define skip-to-end
  (lambda (commands)
    (if (eqv? (car commands) end-of-statement)
        (cdr commands)
        (skip-to-end
          (cdr commands)))))
(define beam-find
  (lambda (line-number prog)
    (if (null? prog)
        (beam-error "No such line number ~a" line-number)
        (if (eqv? line-number (car prog))
            prog
            (beam-find line-number
              (skip-to-end (cdr prog)))))))
```

Program 7-33   Beam: finding the destination of a goto

The word *token* might cause you to remember the token scanner. Why didn't we use it here? There's no reason we couldn't; however, the token scanner would have been complicated by the need to adjust it when we did a goto. This isn't impossible, or even very hard. It just makes the scanner more complicated. On the other hand, our version can easily crash if the interpreter runs off the end of the program. A scanner-based interpreter wouldn't suffer from this problem.

We won't show do-addition and do-multiplication, because they're almost identical to do-relation. The only changes are that we must check for addition or multiplication operators instead of relational ones, and that, where do-relation calls do-addition, do-addition calls do-multiplication, and do-multiplication calls do-factor. do-factor (see Program 7-35) handles constants, variables, and bracketed expressions. The first two are straightforward; the third is done with a recursive call to do-expression.

Here's the output of beam-interpret, assuming prog is bound to the program shown in Program 7-29:

```
> (beam-interpret prog)
Enter: 4
12.56
Enter: 1
3.14
Enter: -1
```

☞ **Exercise 7-28**

Add error-checking to some part of Beam. ❏

☞ **Exercise 7-29**

We could also permit Beam to read several values in one input statement:

```
200 input d ! e ! f
```

Change interpret-command to add this feature. ❏

```
(define do-expression
  (lambda (commands) (do-relation commands)))
(define beam-relop?
  (lambda (op) (member op '(< > =))))
(define op-table
  (lambda (op)
    (cdr
      (assv op
        (list
          (cons '+ +) (cons '- -)
          (cons '* *) (cons '/ /)
          (cons '< <) (cons '> >)
          (cons '= =))))))
(define bin-helper
  (lambda (val-rest this? inner)
    (let*
      ((val1 (car val-rest))
       (op (car (cdr val-rest))))
      (if (this? op)
        (let
          ((val2 (inner (cdr (cdr val-rest)))))
          (bin-helper
            (cons ((op-table op) val1 (car val2)) (cdr val2))
            this? inner))
      val-rest))))
(define do-relation
  (lambda (commands)
    (bin-helper
      (do-addition commands)
      beam-relop? do-addition)))
```

Program 7-34   Beam: evaluating expressions

Programming Problems

1. Early versions of BASIC were interactive (it was one of the first interactive languages). Programmers could type lines in any order, and the system would reorder the numbered lines in ascending order. By contrast, our Beam interpreter simply executes the statements in the order of their appearance, even if they're not in line-number order.

   Write a top level for Beam that lets you enter statements in any order and that supports several useful commands:

   - list: Displays the statements in line-number order on the screen.
   - renumber: Changes the line numbers so that they start at 1000, and go up by 10 (this is useful after the programmer has made a number of changes to the program). The line numbers in if and goto statements are adjusted accordingly.
   - run: Executes the program.
   - quit: Terminates execution.

   A session with your top level might look something like this:

```
(define do-factor
  (lambda (commands)
    (if
      (eqv? start-expression (car commands))
      (let ((x (do-expression (cdr commands))))
        (if (eqv? (car (cdr x)) end-expression)
          (cons (car x) (cdr (cdr x)))
          (beam-error "Invalid expression" commands)))
      (if (expr-constant? (car commands))
        (cons (car commands) (cdr commands))
        (if (expr-variable? (car commands))
          (cons
            (variable-value (car commands))
            (cdr commands)))))))))
(define expr-constant?
  (lambda (e)
    (or (number? e) (boolean? e) (string? e))))
(define expr-variable? symbol?)
```

Program 7-35   Beam: factors

```
> (beam-top-level)
beam> 230 print "O frabjous day! Calloo! Callay!" &
beam> 220 print "Come to my arms, my beamish boy!" &
beam> 240 print "He chortled in his joy." &
beam> 210 print "And hast thou slain the Jabberwock?" &
beam> 250 stop
beam> run
And hast thou slain the Jabberwock?
Come to my arms, my beamish boy!
O frabjous day! Calloo! Callay!
He chortled in his joy.
beam> quit
```

A line beginning with a number is a program line (this might be a new line, a change to an existing line, or—if there's nothing else on the input line—a deletion). A line beginning with a symbol is a command.

Note: the easiest way to do renumber is to go through the program twice. On the first pass, change all of the line numbers, and build an alist whose keys are the old line numbers, and whose values are the new ones. On the second pass, use the alist to change the if and goto statements.

2. Add a rem ("remark") statement to add comments.

3. Classic BASIC had a gosub statement, which transferred control to a specified place, after saving the number of the next line to be executed. A return statement used the saved line number to go back to the original statement. Code that was in a gosub...return block could itself contain gosubs. For example,

```
100 gosub 300
110 print 1
120 gosub 300
```

```
130 print 2
140 stop
300 print 3
310 return
beam> run
1
3
2
3
```

Implement gosub/return. One way to handle the saved return points is to use a list. gosub puts at the front of this list the next statement to be executed after the return. return removes the first item from this list and uses it as the next command. (As we'll see in Chapter 9, this list is an example of a data structure known as a *stack*.)

4. Our implementation of goto requires searching through $O(n)$ statements in the program. A more reasonable way to handle gotos is to prescan the program before it is evaluated, and replace every goto by a reference to the destination statement. Don't try to print this prescanned program—this would create a circular list structure. The advantage of this preprocessing is that goto now takes $O(1)$ time. Implement this preprocessing.

Summary

We have studied languages and their evaluators. Beginning with Dream, we specified the syntax of the language with Extended Backus-Naur Form, and specified the semantics informally. The EBNF specification leads directly to an implemenation of an evaluator in Scheme. Nightmare provided an example of a language with the same semantics as Dream, but with a different syntax. We built a compiler for Nightmare that translates Nightmare code into Dream.

Before turning to Scheme evaluators, we showed how to extend Scheme's syntax by using macros, programmer-defined special forms. Finally, we saw how to use the environment model and our understanding of programming languages to write an elegantly simple evaluator for Scheme.

Further Readings

Programming languages are usually an advanced topic in computer science. An excellent text for a course in languages is *Essentials of Programming Languages*, by D. Friedman, M. Wand, and C. Haynes. *Crafting a Compiler*, by C. N. Fischer and R. J. LeBlanc, describes the workings of compilers. In particular, H. Abelson and G. Sussman's *Structure and Interpretation of Computer Programs* presents another Scheme evaluator in Scheme. ML is a computer language that is very similar to Scheme, but has a more elaborate syntax that pays more attention to data types. It has achieved considerable popularity. A good book on ML is *ML for the Working Programmer*, by L. C. Paulson.

Key Words

Here are the *key words* introduced in this chapter. Make sure you understand what each one means.

Backus-Naur Form (BNF)
debugger
Extended Backus-Naur Form (EBNF)
generated symbol (gensym)
interpret
leaf node
macro

node
object program
orthogonal
precedence
root node
run time
source program
static type checking
syntactic abstraction

syntactic sugar
toy language
translate
traverse
tree
tree recursion
tail recursion

Problems

1. You are given the following EBNF that describes the rules for valid telephone numbers in North America prior to the early 1990s. (Recall that [...] means something is optional and {...} means 0 or more times.)

   ```
   blank: Any normal white space consisting of tabs or spaces.
   digit:  ''6'' | ''5'' | ''4'' | ''3'' | ''2''| ''1'' | ''0''
   tel_num : [area_code] exchange#  local#
   area_code : ''('' digit (''0''|''1'') digit '')'' {blank}
   exchange#: digit digit digit
   local#: ''-'' digit {digit}
   ```

   Based on these rules, decide whether the following numbers are valid `tel_nums`. Justify your answers.
   a. (684)   000-00000000
   b. (604)22-0
   c. (604) 822-5729

2. Extend the EBNF in Question 1 so that a telephone number may have an optional extension number at the end. If the extension is present, it obeys the following rules. There is exactly one space between the last digit of the local # and the start of the extension part. The extension part consists of the character sequence EXT, followed by 1 or more spaces followed by 0 or more digits. Also, if an extension is given, an area code must be present. The only changes you are allowed to make to the EBNF in Question 1 are changes to the definition of `tel_num` and the addition of a new rule to describe what an extension is.

3. Internal nodes are tree nodes that have at least one non-null subtree. Write a recursive procedure, `count-internal`, to count the number of internal nodes of a tree.

   ```
   > (count-internal  '(A (B (E)) (C) (D (F)(G)(H)))) ⇒ 3
   > (count-internal  '(1 (5 (2) (3)) (4))) ⇒ 2
   ```

4. The following Dream program has a subtle error.

   ```
   (program
     (variable x y z)
     (assign x 23)
     (print "x is ") (print x)
     (assign y 71)
     (test (less x y)
   ```

```
        (in-sequence
          (assign z (divide x y))
          (print "less "))
      (print "greater or equal"))
    (divide x (+ 3 z)))
```

What is the error and when does it occur?

5. Write cond%, a macro version of the cond special form.

6. Translate the following case form into a cond:

```
(case test-val
  ((slow fast) (change-speed test-val))
  ((stop) (halt))
  ((reverse) (change-direction))
  (else (format #t "Unknown command ~a~%" test-val)))
```

7. Modify the self-evaluator so that it always evaluates the arguments in a procedure call from left to right, regardless of the order of evaluation in the underlying Scheme.

Self-Assessment

1. Extra Bright Nuclear Furnaces, Inc., ("We give your food that festive party glow") has developed a new microwave oven that is controlled not by the familiar touch panel, but by an ASCII keyboard. Commands are provided to set the power level (P followed by a single digit), and the cooking time (T followed by a sequence of digits representing the cooking time in seconds). Either command may be repeated any number of times; only the last occurrence of a given command takes effect. (This allows the user to correct an entry error.) The power level is optional: if it isn't given, 9 is assumed. However, at least one time specification is required. A third command, S, tells the oven to start cooking. The T and P commands may be given in any order, but the S command always comes last.

   The company wants to include a formal specification of the oven's command language in their manual. Write an EBNF specification for the language.

2. Suppose we have a tree that represents the structure of files and directories (folders) on disk. The leaves represent files, and the nonleaves represent directories. A leaf node contains the name of a file and the number of bytes that file takes; a nonleaf contains the name of a directory and the files or directories stored within that directory. For example, we might have the tree in Figure 7-12, in which the numbers are the file sizes:

   Write a procedure that displays the full names (e.g., \joe\scheme\tree.scm if you're a DOS user) of all files taking more than *n* bytes. (Hint: Use a helper that takes the full name of the current directory as an argument.)

3. Write a form using traverse-tree-combine that collects all the names of the people in the company, and then write a form whose value is a string representing all the titles of people in Consolidated Software, that is:

   ```
   "President, VP Sales, Sales Dir East, Sales Dir West,
   Sales Dir International, VP Development, Dir Software Division,
   Dir Hardware Division"
   ```

   (The line breaks divide the string for printing; your code needn't insert them.) ❏

4. Some people don't like Scheme because they don't like function notation. Such people pre-

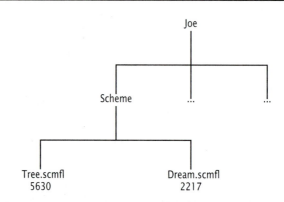

Figure 7-12   A file tree

fer an "infix notation", in which the procedure appears between the operands, for example, [2+3] rather than (+ 2 3). Write a procedure that accepts a list representing a Scheme form, and displays it in infix notation. Assume that all of the subforms have exactly two operands, and that each form on output is to be surrounded by square brackets.

5. Give complexity estimates, using $O(\dots)$ notation, of the following:
   a. accessing a variable in the self-evaluator
   b. defining a variable in the self-evaluator

6. Joel User is modifying the evaluator and decides to implement display as a special form, rather than a primitive. Is this possible? Is it a good idea?

7. Suppose you are writing a version of Scheme that lacks the and form. Write an and% macro that behaves the same way. (Hint: (and) ⇒ #t). ❏

Programming Problems

All of the problems in this section relate to LOGO, a language designed in the 1960s and still widely used by children and other noncomputer experts. LOGO was a variation on the Lisp systems of the time. In this problem set, you will implement a simple LOGO-like language. Because our language isn't exactly the same as LOGO, we will call our version POGO.

POGO is like BASIC (in the Case Study), in that the unit of execution is the line. (Early versions of LOGO used line numbers; more modern versions omit them.) A simple POGO command might be

```
print { sum { product 3 4 } 7 } &
```

A POGO command consists of one or more operands, each of which is either a number, a variable, or a command in braces. POGO commands may be grouped into procedures, bracketed by to and end:

```
to foo n &
print "foo!" &
output { sum n 1 } &
end &
```

The output command gives the value that is to be returned by the procedure, and stops execution. Thus (assuming > is a prompt),

```
> print { foo { product 4 5 } } &
foo!
21
```

Procedures can't be nested (unlike Scheme) and use *dynamic scoping*. Unlike static scoping, dynamic scoping means that variables are found by following the dynamic link of a procedure, not its static link (which isn't needed in a dynamically scoped language). The rules for calling a procedure are different from Scheme's. When a procedure is called, the evaluator creates a new frame containing

- the variable bindings for the arguments
- a resume point immediately after the call
- a dynamic link to the current frame

When a variable is evaluated, the evaluator looks in the current frame and then follows dynamic links to the global environment. When a procedure returns a value, the evaluator follows the dynamic link to the parent frame.

Finally, every call to a procedure has a *truth flag*, which can be used via the primitive procedures `test` (which stores its argument in the truth flag), and `iftrue`/`iffalse` (which execute a command if the truth flag has the appropriate setting. Here's a POGO version of factorial:

```
to fact n &
test { equal? n 0 } &
iftrue output 1 &
iffalse output { product n { fact { difference n 1 } } } &
end &
```

(`to`, `iftrue`, and `iffalse` are special forms, rather than primitive procedures. The primitives in `fact` are `test`, `output`, `product`, and `difference`.)

1. Write an EBNF for POGO.

2. Write a procedure that evaluates a single POGO command line, having only calls to primitive procedures, and excluding the special forms, `output` and `test`, as well as variables.

3. Design a data structure for environments. Each frame will need the variable bindings for that procedure call, along with a box (or maybe just an extra pair) for the truth flag. You can adapt most of the code you need from the self-evaluator.

4. Write a procedure that converts a POGO procedure to some sort of internal form. This will not be a procedure, but merely some sort of list structure.

5. Modify your command-execution procedure so that it will handle calls to user-defined procedures. This will require you to hook in the environment-handling code.

6. Add `output` and `test`/`iftrue`/`iffalse`.

Chapter 8

Databases

Overview

This chapter introduces database management systems, computer systems for handling large collections of data. Modern database systems are based on tables, collections of data organized into rows and columns. A few extremely powerful "relational operators" allow us to extract data from tables and to combine tables to produce new tables. Although many database systems have their own languages, it is relatively easy to interface them to languages like Scheme. We will build DBScheme, a relational-language extension of Scheme, to explore using tables and relational operators in Scheme. As before, we're not content just to use an application; we go on to study the code that implements the interface. Once we have a clear idea of how the system works, we'll study issues related to database design.

Now go, write it before them in a table, and note it in a book.

— The Book of Isaiah

A large library might have a million books, each of which must be cataloged. A telephone company might have millions of customer accounts. The design of an airplane involves millions of parts, from rivets to carpets to fuel tanks. A large collection of data accessed via a general interface is a **database**. Almost any area of human activity can benefit from organizing data into a database.

Databases have brought an increase in the size and complexity of the programs that work with the data. Each program is not so complex on its own, but a large organization wants to do a great deal with the data it has. Consider the needs of a financial institution:

- Monthly statements must be sent to each customer.
- Customers with irregularities in their accounts (e.g., overdrafts) must be notified.
- Regulators require statements showing the amount of money currently on deposit.
- Reports must be sent to the government and to customers for tax purposes.

If the institution opens a new branch in Riverdale, it will want to notify each of its customers who live in the area about this new branch.

With increasing competition among banks, the way they do business must be much more flexible. Many tasks, such as responding to changes in rates by competitors, must be accomplished quickly, without waiting for enormous amounts of programming to be done.

In the early days of computing, programmers worked on individual programs that processed files of data. Each program would do a specific task. One program would read in a day's deposits and withdrawals, and update the customers' balances accordingly; another would compute interest on the balances; another would handle loan payments. Before there were interactive terminals, transactions were recorded on pieces of paper, and at the end of the day, clerks prepared punch cards with the day's information. The program was run overnight, and balances were updated the next day, provided that the computer didn't crash in the meantime. Sometimes balances were days out of date. Daily interest was so difficult that the banks wouldn't compute it. Running the interest program was an all-night proposition, and was done once a month, or perhaps once every six months.

Since all of these programs were working with the same data, programmers quickly agreed upon standard ways of organizing it. Standardizing the data formats allowed different programs to work on the same data; it also allowed the output from one program to be used as the input to another. Programmers soon recognized that programs themselves might come and go, but the data formats were permanent. Data abstraction, if the programmers had known about it, would have helped immensely, by providing a common interface for all the programs, and freeing the programmers from bondage to the file data formats.

Early programmers were constantly "reinventing the wheel". Each program required basically the same logic: read a customer record, do something to it, write out the updated customer record. Not only was writing the same code over and over again dreary (especially since much of it was written in machine language!), but also there were many possibilities for errors.

In the early 1960s, some programmers at IBM noticed the structural similarity of these programs and wrote a "generator" program, which in turn wrote data-processing programs. Programmers only had to specify what was unique about a particular program, and the generator did the rest. Of course, if the program was very different from the standard data-processing problem, the generator wasn't much help, but for many commercial applications, it saved a tremendous amount of work. IBM's Report Program Generator (RPG) is still in use in various versions. The successors to the early generators, Fourth Generation Languages, or 4GLs, are widely used in data-processing installations.

The problems of this approach are

- There is a lot of data.
- The organization of the data is complicated.
- Every program must know about the organization of the data.

Generators only support procedural abstraction. The program specification that the programmer writes is similar to the arguments of a procedure. Just as it's infeasible to have a procedure that can do anything, the range of applications for which a generator is useful is extremely limited.

This problem became much worse as programs that worked with large data sets moved beyond purely business applications. Scientists collect large data sets. Engineers, architects, and other designers must prepare design documents that rely upon huge collections of data. Even in business applications, the range of tasks has vastly increased: banks require handwriting analysis to verify signatures; brokerages require sophisticated financial models to predict stock performance; and senior managers need to analyze data in new and unique ways in order to make major long-term decisions.

All applications must store, update, and retrieve portions of the data. For large data sets, the programming effort (much of which is repeated, with only minor changes, in each program) is a substantial problem. The remedy for these problems is data abstraction. We design a **database layer**, a collection of procedures that manages the data. Programs that want to use the data can then call procedures in the database layer to retrieve and modify it. The database layer hides the **physical structure** of the data, (i.e., the way it is stored). Programmers who use the database procedures need only be concerned with the **logical structure** of the data.

Separating the physical organization of the data from its use in any particular program yields several benefits:

- Programmers can ignore aspects of the data that do not concern them: they just ask for the data they need, and get it.
- Those responsible for organizing the data can do so in the most efficient way, without concern that changes in the data structure will affect programs.
- The logical view of the data serves as an interface that both the programmers and the custodians of the database can agree upon.

All of these benefits come from any successful use of data abstraction. The complex data used in real applications makes the payoff that much greater.

We can go one step further: instead of designing a set of database procedures for a single application, we can build a **database management system**, or **DBMS**, a set of general procedures that facilitates the construction of *any* database. Programmers using a DBMS do two things:

- They prepare a **database description** that defines what information must be stored, and how it is organized.
- They write code that calls the DBMS to access or modify the data.

Given the database description, which is only a *logical* description of the data, the DBMS can physically organize the data so that the programmer can work with it at a logical level. All access to the data is through the DBMS, which alone can modify the data.

Many database management systems have been developed, including Microsoft Access, Borland's Paradox, Oracle Corporation's Oracle, and IBM's DB2. The Microsoft and Borland products run on desktop computers; DB2 and Oracle run on desktop and mainframe computers. If you look at a packaged DBMS, you will see a bewildering array of programming tools, including software to help design screens and reports, and to help write programs for querying the database. Most DBMSs come with a programming language and are intended to be a complete solution for the programmer. These systems are complex to learn, but extremely powerful.

We are interested in discovering how a DBMS helps define the logical and physical structure of the data. Accordingly, we're going to build a simplified DBMS in Scheme. Our system will have only the features that let us study the structure of the data. It won't have features for elaborate reports and data-entry screens, but it will let us look at a number of interesting and useful problems.

8.1 Tables and the Relational Model

Few have heard of Fra Luca Pacioli, the inventor of double-entry book-keeping; but he has probably had much more influence on human life than has Dante or Michelangelo. — H. J. Muller, *The Uses of the Past*

To build a DBMS, we must start by finding a good general way to look at data. Whatever we come up with has to work across a wide range of applications. At the same time, programmers are going to use our DBMS for real-world applications, so it must be efficient. As an example, let's look at a department store's credit-card billing. In the early days of computing, a customer's account was represented by a punch card containing the customer's information, for example:

```
127171Lee, W.R.      729 Oak Crescent              147.55
127185Jones, T.F.X. #329-4455 Maple Drive           73.11
```

Generally, the information had a fixed format, with specific pieces of information in specific columns. (In the above example, the customer account number is in columns 1 through 6, the name is in columns 7 through 20, and so on.)[1]

Each time a customer made a purchase or payment, a punch card was prepared for the transaction, for example,

```
127171 P    9.95
127171 Y  147.55
127171 P   23.50
127185 Y   73.11
127185 P   49.95
```

In this example, the code P means "purchase", and the code Y means "payment".

Each month, we must prepare customer statements. Early **batch-processing** programs required the operator to arrange the customer cards in order by account number (to **sort** them), and then to insert the transaction cards in the appropriate order (to **merge** them):

```
127171Lee, W.R.      729 Oak Crescent              147.55
127171 P    9.95
127171 Y  147.55
127171 P   23.50
127185Jones, T.F.X. #329-4455 Maple Drive           73.11
127185 Y   73.11
127185 P   49.95
```

The program would then read in the cards and do two things: punch out a new card for each customer with the customer's new balance, and print out bills to be mailed.

---

[1] Most keypunches were incapable of easily producing lowercase letters, though. The punch card's size was chosen because its inventor, Herman Hollerith, was attempting to find a way to organize the data for the U.S. 1890 census. He was given an old banknote press; hence the most common card size, right up to the death of punch cards in the mid 1980s, was the size of the 19th-century U.S. dollar. Most types of punch card had 80 columns, a legacy that lives on today in the fact that character-mode terminals often have 80-character lines.

This all seems hopelessly clumsy compared to the way things are done now, but there are things to be learned from it:

- We can represent complex information by a **record structure**, a collection of simpler pieces of information.[2]
- All records about a particular thing have the same format, so we can write loops that process customer (or payment, or whatever) data easily.
- Much of the work consists of rearranging information so that it can be easily processed. In this case, we have the operator interleaving the customer account and transaction cards.

Our plan requires us to find a set of primitive operations that we can combine in order to access the database in whatever way we need. We should have as few primitives as possible, but they should provide everything we need. Fortunately, relational databases provide a way to look at data and a set of primitive operations that do the job.

8.1.1 Tables

We can now forget about punch cards, and just view the data as a collection of tables. In our customer-account system, we might have one table for the customers, and one for the transactions each customer makes, as shown in Figure 8-1.

customer-number	name	address	balance
127171	Lee, W.R.	729 Oak Crescent	147.55
127185	Jones, T.F.X.	329-4455 Maple Drive	73.11

customer-number	type	amount
127171	P	9.95
127171	Y	147.55
127171	P	23.50
127185	Y	73.11
127185	P	49.95

Figure 8-1   Customers

A **table** consists of a number of rows, each representing information about one individual (a customer or transaction). A **row** is what we have been calling a *record*. Alternatively, you can consider a table to be a number of **columns**, each with one type of information; thus the columns in this example are the sets of names, addresses, and phone numbers, respectively. We use the word **field** to describe the intersection of a given row and column. We would say that customer 127185's `balance` field contains `73.11`.

---

[2] In Scheme, we use lists for this purpose. Most Scheme implementations also include a macro, `define-record`, which allows the programmer to define all of the accessors, mutators, and predicates for a record structure, and which sometimes uses vectors, which we'll study in Chapter 9. We've built our record structures manually.

We can build tables of other kinds of data. A phone book can be thought of as a table, as in Figure 8-2.

name	address	phone
Smith, G.	123 Elm St	555-2131
Jones, M.	345 Larch St	555-6781
Chan, B.	234 Maple St	555-2365
Singh, R.	432 Alder St	555-2311

Figure 8-2   Phones

In the Case Study in Chapter 5, we built a simplified airline reservation system. Figure 8-3 (a) shows a table of flights in an airline reservation system, and Figure 8-3 (b) shows a table of passenger manifests. In the flight table, the rows represent particular flights, and the columns are the various attributes of each flight.[3] In the passenger manifest table, each row represents a single reservation, and each column represents a specific kind of information gathered about reservations.

flt-no	from	to	time
136	Vancouver	Toronto	0900
149	Toronto	Vancouver	1700
801	Toronto	Boston	0700
802	Boston	Toronto	1200
107	Vancouver	Calgary	2200
105	Vancouver	Brandon	1200

(a) Airline flight schedule

flt-no	date	name	phone
136	Jan23	Wilson, R.	555-2384
136	Jan24	Cohen, P.	555-6783
136	Jan24	Gianelli, C.	555-6183
801	Jan24	Wilson, R.	555-2384

(b) Passenger manifest

Figure 8-3   Airline tables

These two tables are created in different ways. The schedule table is created by airline management, after deciding where and when to fly and obtaining regulatory approval. The passenger manifest, on the other hand, is ultimately created by the

---

[3] Lest you object that planes will pile up in Calgary and Brandon, please be assured that this is only part of the full timetable.

passengers themselves as they make and cancel reservations.[4]

With these two tables, we can answer more complicated questions. For example, we can ask "Where is passenger Wilson ticketed to on January 24?" The passenger manifest tells us that Wilson is flying on January 23 and 24. Choosing the row for January 24, we note that Wilson is on flight 801. Now we refer to the schedule, which tells us that Flight 801 ends at Boston.

☞ **Exercise 8–1**

Another question we could answer is "Which passengers are departing from Boston?" How would we use these tables to answer this question? ❏

A real airline reservation system would include different passenger lists; there might be a separate one for each day. (Obviously, the clerk at the gate gets a list for today's flight, but a master list must still be stored.) There would also be tables for planes, airports, special food requests, and so on. One often thinks of a database as a large object that contains all the data, each table being just a particular subset of the data. However, we will construct a completely separate table for each kind of data and for the results of each question.

In our flight example, all of the passenger lists will have the same **layout**, or list of column names, even though the rows in each table will be different.[5] The important point is that all passenger lists have the same layout, just as all instances of a class have the same structure.

The use of such tables has become standard in industry. Within a table, we often have information that can be cross-referenced with information in other tables. We can thus construct new tables that contain information extracted and rearranged from existing tables.

☞ **Exercise 8–2**

For each of the following questions, show one table that could be used to represent information relevant to the question. To show a table, just list the column names. (You don't need to make up any data to go in the table.)
   a. your shopping list
   b. your academic transcript
   c. your collection of audio tapes or CDs: (Don't worry about composer, only the performers.) ❏

---

[4] This discussion is open to the charge that it is so grossly oversimplified as to be useless. For example, in order to confirm a reservation, we must check that there are available seats on that flight. We must also check with crew schedules, equipment-maintenance records, and the like, in order to ensure that we can have a fully crewed plane at the departure gate at the appropriate time. In a real airline reservation system, there would be hundreds of tables. As for our gross oversimplifications, what do you expect in an introductory textbook, anyway?

[5] Where we use the word *layout*, database specialists use words such as *structure*, *format*, or even *schema*, which is the most commonly used term. We decided to introduce a new term, since *schema* is too close to Scheme.

8.1.2   The Relational Operators

Tables embody a simple but powerful abstraction for organizing data: relations. A **relation** is a way of describing information in tabular form: an element in the table at the intersection of a row and a column holds the information relating the row and column. Relations provide an abstract view of how to manipulate information in rows and columns without considering the way the data is represented, which frees the database user from issues of implementation.

What's interesting about tables is that we can extract data from them. We can also combine them according to specific rules, called **relational operations** to build new tables. What's even more interesting is that we need only a small number of relational operations in order to allow any access we like to the data in a collection of tables.[6]

Almost any processing of tables can be done in terms of three basic operations:

- We certainly want to be able to choose rows that satisfy certain criteria. For example, we might want to find all students with grade-point averages (GPAs) greater than 3.5, or all employees with salaries greater than $50,000, or all items in stock whose quantity on hand is less than a minimum and must thus be reordered. (The minimum value will differ for each item; we can generally afford to keep more boxes of disks in a warehouse than grand pianos.)

- We want to be able to build a new table with only certain columns of an original table. For example, we might have a table containing student name, student number, and final grade. A printout to be posted should not include the name so we want to extract only student number and final grade.

- We want to be able to derive a new table by combining existing tables according to a specific column. If the airline has a route table and a passenger manifest, we can answer the question about where a particular passenger is going by creating a new table that includes the from and to fields of the flight table and the name field of the passenger table.

The first two operations take a table and produce a new table that is a subset of the input table; the first produces a subset of the rows, and the second produces a subset of the columns. The third operation combines two tables. Each of these operations produces a table, so we can use them in combination. It turns out that these operations are (almost) enough to do anything we might want, and will be enough for our purposes.

You might object that we might want to do many things with data that these operations don't handle. With these operations, we can't, for example, say how we want to sort or format our data. Any real DBMS must provide options for sorting and formatting output data. No matter how you arrange data, however, it's still the same data. We're mainly interested in operations for accessing or updating data.

In relational language, we speak of the operations of *selection*, *projection*, and *join*. We can study each of these operations by using them to process information about students at a college.

---

[6] Needless to say, real relational DBMSs complicate things by providing an army of features and options. These extras are extremely useful in practice, but don't actually add any computational power. (Macros in Scheme are an example of a similar phenomenon.)

Figure 8-4 (a) shows how we can **select** rows from a table according to one or more criteria. To find the students with GPAs greater than 3.5, we might do a selection that asks for all rows in which the GPA field is greater than 3.5. This selection operation gives us a new table, shown in Figure 8-4 (b).

st-no	name	gpa
123	Adams, J.	3.2
417	Baker, R.	3.7
603	Cox, P.	3.1
618	Dunn, A.	3.4
801	Edgar, G.	3.9

(a) The students table

st-no	name	gpa
417	Baker, R.	3.7
801	Edgar, G.	3.9

(b) Select gpa > 3.5 from students

st-no	gpa
123	3.2
417	3.7
603	3.1
108	3.4
801	3.9

(c) Project students on st-no and gpa

Figure 8-4 The students table

☞ **Exercise 8-3**

Show the result of the following selections from grades:
  a. student number equal to 417
  b. GPA greater than 4.0 ❏

Sometimes we want a kind of name or ID for each row. That is, we want a column in which no two values are equal, so that we can uniquely select a particular row by choosing its ID. We call the values in such a column keys; they identify particular rows, just as a key value identifies a particular item in an alist. For example, we would normally expect the student number to be a key, because we would require each student to have a different number. On the other hand, we would not expect the student's names to be unique. We wouldn't want Joe Dumont's grades to be mistakenly recorded as Jane Dumont's.

Our next relational operation is called **projection**. We project a table by extracting one or more columns from it. Returning to our students example, we can prepare a list of grades suitable for posting by projecting the table onto the student

Privacy, Security, and Cross-matching

It is common to wonder about the social implications of technology. Databases are collections of vast amounts of information about the world. If knowledge is power, then a database represents a tremendous amount of power. Mailing lists, credit records, university/college/school records, all contain information about people that those people might not want others to have. For example, many people with HIV do not want their status to become a matter of public record. A potential employer or landlord who had unauthorized access to medical records might use this information to discriminate against the employee or tenant, even though such discrimination might be illegal.

Even worse would be unauthorized modification of the data. Putting damaging false information about a person into a database should surely be prevented. In fact, any modification to a database should be logged, so that it is possible to determine who made that change and why.

These two issues, access and modification, are central. We need access control to guarantee **privacy**. We need modification control in order to guarantee **security**. Much research in both databases and operating systems focuses on ways to assure both privacy and security. Techniques such as passwords and access control help ensure that information in a database is protected against unauthorized use or modification. Other techniques, such as encryption, help ensure that information being transmitted through a network is protected against unauthorized use or modification.

We want our databases to be safe from unauthorized modification, but should the government have access to private databases? On one hand, we would certainly appreciate it if the government could extract information that could help track criminals. On the other hand, most people feel uncomfortable with the knowledge that the government can rummage through databases and extract information about someone's personal life. Even if the government only uses its power against people who are obvious criminals, what is to prevent an unscrupulous government employee from profiting from this information? There is serious argument as to where the access/privacy line should be drawn.

One could argue that any government use in a free and democratic society would require a search warrant, with the same burden of proof in a court that any other warrant requires. However, information is transmitted via networks. You might think that encrypted information (see Chapter 3) would be safe. As we write this, however, the United States government has proposed an encryption standard named Clipper, in which the encryption keys would be deposited with the government, in order to allow criminal activities to be monitored. Both supporters and opponents of the Clipper plan agree that it places a great deal of responsibility on the government to use this power wisely. Opponents believe that the potential dangers outweigh the potential benefits.

Suppose we have a file of welfare records; we could join this with income tax records to catch welfare cheats. But when one files an income tax return in many countries, the government promises that it will only use this information for specific tax purposes, which presumably don't include searching for welfare fraud. If the government can do this, perhaps it could join motor vehicle records with tax records and catch people who are driving cars too expensive for them to afford. What about joining public-service employee records with political contribution records, to catch people who support the "wrong" political party? For these reasons joining tables that are not related, or **cross-matching**, is a serious public concern.

number and GPA columns, as shown in Figure 8-4 (c). Obviously some information is lost, but only in the dimension (the columns) you left out in the projection.

One motivation for projection and selection is security. If you can't see the data, you can't misuse it. Consider the employees table in Figure 8-5.

name	office	dept	salary
P. Cohen	202	Engineering	50,000
G. Moran	212	Engineering	58,000
R. Singh	182	Accounting	62,000
S. Savard	187	Accounting	42,000

Figure 8-5   Employee data

The receptionist only needs to see the columns name, office, and dept to direct visitors to the employees. The secretary for the department can justify seeing all of the columns, but only for the rows representing employees in the department. A **hot view** is a dynamically constructed table that represents some subset of the data in a table. These tables are called *hot* because they continually reflect the changing data in the database; they are not just static snapshots.

We can use combinations of selection and projection to extract any information we want from the table. For example, suppose we want to know the names of all the students with GPA greater than 3.3. First, we select the rows with GPA greater than 3.3, obtaining Figure 8-6 (a). Next we project on the name column, obtaining Figure 8-6 (b).

st-no	name	gpa
417	Baker, R.	3.7
618	Dunn, A.	3.4
801	Edgar, G.	3.9

(a) Step 1: select students with GPA greater than 3.3

name
Baker, R.
Dunn, A.
Edgar, G.

(b) Step 2: project the result on column name

Figure 8-6   Finding the names of students with good grades

Selection and projection allow us to extract any information we want from a single table, but we often want to obtain information from different tables. For example, suppose that we want to mail out transcripts for our students. We will need a second table named addresses, shown in Figure 8-7 (a).

st-no	name	address	city
123	Adams, J.	123 Elm St.	Richmond
417	Baker, R.	47A Computron Cr.	Bellevue
603	Cox, P.	78014 Larch St.	Langley
618	Dunn, A.	8086 River Rd.	Victoria
801	Edgar, G.	1885 Hemlock St.	New Ork

(a) The addresses table

st-no	name	address	city	gpa
123	Adams, J.	123 Elm St.	Richmond	3.2
417	Baker, R.	47A Computron Cr.	Bellevue	3.7
603	Cox, P.	78014 Larch St.	Langley	3.1
618	Dunn, A.	8086 River Rd.	Victoria	3.4
801	Edgar, G.	1885 Hemlock St.	New Ork	3.9

(b) students and addresses joined on st-no

Figure 8-7   Joining students with addresses

We can construct the transcripts by **joining** students and addresses together. We can think of a join operation as being a way of "zipping" these tables together. We identify a column that appears in both tables, and create a new table in which each row contains information from both of the original tables, as in Figure 8-7 (b).

It's not necessary to have the same number of rows in the two tables. Furthermore, a column might contain keys in one table, and nonkeys in another. Figure 8-8 (a) shows a final-grades table that contains the final grades for this semester.

If we join final-grades and addresses on the student number field, we get the table shown in Figure 8-8 (b). Since no course grades were reported for some students, this table doesn't have any rows for them. On the other hand, there are several rows for other students. We might want to know about rows that don't contribute to a join; for example, they might be students taking no courses, or customers who have made no purchases. Each row in the new table results from matching the student-number fields in the two tables. For example, student 123 has two marks in the grades table, so there are two rows in the new table, collecting columns from both tables.

☞ **Exercise 8-4**

Using the tables final-grades and addresses, give a series of relational operations that will produce a one-column table of the home cities of students who got As. ❏

st-no	course	gr
123	CS124	A
123	MA120	B+
618	EN100	A–
618	CS124	B–
618	CS124	B+
801	MA221	A+

(a) The `final-grades` table

st-no	name	address	city	course	gr
123	Adams, J.	123 Elm St.	Richmond	CS124	A
123	Adams, J.	123 Elm St.	Richmond	MA120	B+
618	Dunn, A.	8086 River Rd.	Victoria	EN100	A–
618	Dunn, A.	8086 River Rd.	Victoria	CS124	B–
618	Dunn, A.	8086 River Rd.	Victoria	CS124	B+
801	Edgar, G.	1885 Hemlock St.	New Ork	MA221	A+

(b) Joining addresses with `final-grades`

Figure 8-8   Producing grade reports

8.2   A Database Language for Scheme

Knowledge is of two kinds. We know a subject ourselves, or we know where we can find information upon it.   — Samuel Johnson, in Boswell's *Life*

Relational DBMSs are designed to work in one of two ways: either the system has its own programming language, or the DBMS can be accessed from standard programming languages. Each approach has its advantage. A language designed for DBMS use can be organized to make database access particularly easy; on the other hand, such languages are often inflexible. A DBMS organized as a set of procedures that can be called from the programmer's favorite language is perhaps less easy to use than the alternative, but often gives the programmer more power. We're going to adopt the latter approach. Our system, called DBScheme, will allow us to create and manipulate tables while staying in a Scheme framework.

The best way to study DBScheme is through an example. Turing College wants to build a system to manage its student records. The college's Information Systems Department has asked us to develop such a system. The first step is to analyze the problem. Accordingly, we interview the college's registrar and learn the following:

When a student is admitted to the college, information about that student must be entered into the system. This information would include the student's address, phone number, previous academic history (grades from high school or other colleges), and so on. At the end of each semester,

Validity Checking

If you spend millions of dollars building a database with unchecked data, nobody will trust your database, and you'll have billions of useless bits. Databases often contain invalid data that is only discovered after it is too late to find the correct data.

The best time to get rid of invalid data is when it's entered. Real database systems have elaborate checking facilities that allow any data entered to be examined both for validity and plausibility. **Validity** is straightforward enough: clearly the "name" B4231 is invalid (unless our system allows aliens or robots, of course). **Plausibility** is a bit more complicated: we must ask whether the proposed data item makes sense. For example, in 1972 the town of Framingham, Massachusetts, found its budget completely in error. The cause was traced to a punch card containing a property-tax assessment for a beat-up old car. A stray hole in the card had made the car worth not $950 but $7,000,950. As a result, there was a $290,000 shortfall in property-tax revenues. Surely any assessment this large ought to have been flagged for human attention!

A program that reads data should insist on a specific format for each field. This can be done by associating a "picture" with the field, indicating what's allowed. For example, we might have the picture 9999 associated with a four-character numeric field, aaaaaa with a six-character field containing lowercase letters, and 9999/99/99 with a date entered in the order *year*, *month*, *day*. Languages such as COBOL allow the programmer to associate a picture with a field, and to check whether the data in that field matches the picture. Pictures aren't enough, however. Consider the "date" 1995/23/10, in which (according to our picture) the month and day were interchanged. No picture will help, though we can write a small procedure to check for the data.

Since an incorrect key could identify the wrong row, key checking is essential. Most keys incorporate a "check digit": one of the digits is calculated by a formula from the other digits. For example, suppose we add all the digits together and then take the low-order digit of the sum. Then the check digit will be the low digit of $1 + 2 + 4 + 6 + 1 = 14$, or 4. Now, the customer sees the account number as 124614. If that is later typed in as 124514, then when we do the check calculation, we will find that the check digit ought to have been the low digit of $1 + 2 + 4 + 5 + 1 = 13$, or 3. Since the check digit we gave was 4, we know this number is invalid. This particular check-digit algorithm is easy to explain, but a poor choice, because it doesn't detect many kinds of mistakes. For example, the incorrect key 214614 will pass the check-digit test. One of the most common kinds of mistakes that fast typists make is a "transposition" error, in which they type characters in the wrong order.

Check digits are a form of validity checking. There are other appropriate forms. Particular fields might be constrained to be dollar amounts or dates.

Some validity checking requires looking at more than just one field. For example, a withdrawal from a bank account requires that we check the customer's balance. We can think of this as "semantic" validity checking, as opposed to the "syntactic" validity checking given by pictures. A "check this field to make sure it's valid" procedure won't help here; we must check the interactions of a number of fields.

Regardless of what precautions we take, some errors will creep in. Humans aren't perfect, and computer hardware and software certainly crash. We therefore need some way to recover from errors. A real database system also keeps an **audit trail**, a record of each change that was made. The audit trail makes it much easier to track down errors and fix them.

instructors submit final marks (as percentages) for each student in their classes; the student records system must prepare transcripts to be mailed to the student, showing the grades the student has achieved, and the student's average.

☞ **Exercise 8-5**

This description is incomplete. Find at least one step in the above process that was missed during the interview (and that might be financially embarrassing to the college). ❏

The first step is to make a table to contain the student data. We will resist the temptation to include a large number of columns, and will just record the student's name, student number, and telephone.

```
> (define students
    (make-table (cons 'student-no number?) 'name 'phone))
```

We will represent a table as a Scheme value. `make-table` is a variadic procedure (a procedure that takes any number of arguments); its arguments are descriptions of the columns of the table being constructed. A column description may be just a symbol (e.g., `name`), or a pair whose car is a symbol, and whose cdr is a procedure. The symbol will be a column name. The procedure is a validity checking procedure, which takes as its argument a field value, and which returns true if the value is value for this column, and false otherwise.

☞ **Exercise 8-6**

Write a `make-table` form for a bank account, including appropriate validity checking. ❏

We can use `table-add-rows!`, which puts new rows in a table, to add new students.

```
> (table-add-rows! students
    '(((student-no . 123)
       (name . "Smith, W.") (phone . "555-1024"))
      ((student-no . 284)
       (name . "Schmidt, S.") (phone . "555-4830"))
      ((student-no . 457)
       (name . "Lee, R.") (phone . "555-5205"))
      ((student-no . 651)
       (name . "Levy, T.") (phone . "555-2012"))
      ((student-no . 912)
       (name . "Gomez, D.") (phone . "555-6144"))))
```

The first argument is the table, and its second is a list of row descriptions, each of which is an association list of the field names and corresponding values. We use an association list, not just a list of the values, because we don't know in what order the columns of the table are stored; therefore, we need some way to associate a particular value with its column. While the internal representation of rows certainly has an order, the interface makes no commitment about the order imposed internally. `table-add-rows!` mutates an existing table, rather than returning a new one.

Adding a row to a table activates the validity-checking procedures for columns. In the `students` table, only the `student-no` column has a validity-checking procedure. By using `number?`, we can make sure that student numbers are actual numbers. An attempt to add a row with a non-numeric student number field results in an error message.

```
> (table-add-rows! students
    '(((student-no . foo)
       (name . "Fake, I.M.A.") (phone "555-5555"))))
Error: Invalid value for field  student-no    foo
```

☞ **Exercise 8-7**

Suggest validation procedures for the name and phone columns. ❏

By this point, we might want to take a look at our table.

```
> (table-print students 'student-no compare-numbers)
student-no  name         phone
----------  ----------   ----------
123         Smith, W.    555-1024
284         Schmidt, S.  555-4830
457         Lee, R.      555-5205
651         Levy, T.     555-2012
912         Gomez, D.    555-6144
```

It's unlikely that we would want to print out the whole student list of a real college, but the table shown here only has a few rows. Any print-out of a table should be in some sorted order. Listing several thousand students in random order is useless. Here, we've sorted the data by student number in ascending order.

How do we define the sort order we want? We could insist that the column we sort on be numeric, but that would limit us too much. The obvious solution is to pass a procedure that can be used to compare elements. A Boolean isn't sufficient, however; we need a three-way choice, reflecting *less than*, *equal to*, and *greater than* conditions. Comparison, therefore, is done with a procedure, called a **comparator**, that returns one of the symbols less-than, equal-to, and greater-than. Program 8-1 shows two useful comparators.

```
(define compare-numbers
  (lambda (a b)
    (if (< a b) 'less-than
      (if (= a b) 'equal-to
        'greater-than))))
(define compare-strings
  (lambda (a b)
    (if (string<? a b) 'less-than
      (if (string=? a b) 'equal-to
        'greater-than))))
```

Program 8-1   Comparison procedures for sorting

table-print accepts three arguments: the table, the name of a column on which to sort the table, and a comparison procedure. In this case, we have asked table-print to do a numerical sort on the student-number field. We can also sort on other columns, as shown in Figure 8-9.

```
> (table-print students 'name compare-strings)
  student-no  name        phone
  ----------  ----------  ----------
  912         Gomez, D.   555-6144
  457         Lee, R.     555-5205
  651         Levy, T.    555-2012
  284         Schmidt, S. 555-4830
  123         Smith, W.   555-1024
```

Figure 8-9   Printing a table, sorted on a second column

It's now time to record the final marks. Each instructor must send in a list of the final marks for her class. We enter them into a table:

```
> (define final-marks
    (make-table 'student-no 'course 'mark))
```

First, the Computer Science marks:

```
> (table-add-rows! final-marks
    '(((student-no . 123) (course . "cs124") (mark . 85))
      ((student-no . 284) (course . "cs124") (mark . 75))
      ((student-no . 457) (course . "cs124") (mark . 91))
      ((student-no . 912) (course . "cs124") (mark . 72))))
```

Next, some Math marks:

```
> (table-add-rows! final-marks
    '(((student-no . 284) (course . "ma120") (mark . 78))
      ((student-no . 912) (course . "ma120") (mark . 71))))
```

Finally, we get the English marks:

```
> (table-add-rows! final-marks
    '(((student-no . 123) (course . "en110") (mark . 90))
      ((student-no . 284) (course . "en110") (mark . 81))))
```

☞ **Exercise 8-8**

How do we know we have all of the marks? Some instructors do not get their marks in on time, so we need to know the courses for which we haven't yet received marks. Suggest a table structure that would help us. ❑

Once we have all the marks, we can print them out.

```
> (table-print final-marks 'student-no compare-numbers)
  student-no  course      mark
  ----------  ----------  ----------
  123         cs124       85
  123         en110       90
  284         cs124       75
  284         ma120       78
  284         en110       81
  457         cs124       91
```

```
912            ma120        71
912            cs124        72
```

To find Susan Schmidt's marks, we can do a selection on `final-marks`.

```
> (table-print
     (table-select final-marks 'student-no = 284)
     'student-no compare-numbers)
student-no  course       mark
----------  ----------   ----------
284         en110        81
284         ma120        78
284         cs124        75
```

`table-select` takes four arguments: the table, a column on which we are selecting, a binary predicate, and a value to compare with. It returns a new table in which each row satisfies our selection criteria. We can only select on one field at a time.

`table-select` does not use a comparison procedure, but instead a binary predicate. It does not need to order the elements, but it must decide whether the value of a field satisfies some test that depends on its last argument, the comparison value. Numerical equality is a simple case of a much more general situation.

☞ **Exercise 8–9**

Write a selection form to find all marks greater than 85%. ❏

Let's put the marks aside for a moment. We've been asked to prepare a campus phone directory. We can use the student records as the basis for the directory; all we have to do is to project `students` on name and phone.

```
> (table-print
     (table-project students '(name phone))
     'name compare-strings)
name        phone
----------  ----------
Gomez, D.   555-6144
Lee, R.     555-5205
Levy, T.    555-2012
Schmidt, S. 555-4830
Smith, W.   555-1024
```

`table-project` takes two arguments: the table and a list of the fields to appear in the resulting table. Sorting the projected table is a good way of getting the phone book in order.

Just after the phone book is printed, Bill Smith discovers that his phone number was recorded incorrectly. We must update `students`, and regenerate the phone directory.

```
> (table-update!
     students 'name string=? "Smith, W."
     'phone "555-1204")
> (table-print
     (table-project students '(name phone))
     'name compare-strings)
```

name	phone
Gomez, D.	555-6144
Lee, R.	555-5205
Levy, T.	555-2012
Schmidt, S.	555-4830
Smith, W.	555-1204

To produce transcripts, we need to join two tables: `students` has general information about the students, and `final-marks` has the specific grade information.

```
> (table-print
    (table-join students final-marks 'student-no compare-numbers)
    'student-no compare-numbers)
```

mark	course	student-no	name	phone
90	en110	123	Smith, W.	555-1204
85	cs124	123	Smith, W.	555-1204
81	en110	284	Schmidt, S.	555-4830
78	ma120	284	Schmidt, S.	555-4830
75	cs124	284	Schmidt, S.	555-4830
91	cs124	457	Lee, R.	555-5205
71	ma120	912	Gomez, D.	555-6144
72	cs124	912	Gomez, D.	555-6144

`table-join` is given the two tables, the name of the column on which they are to be joined, and a comparison procedure. The comparison procedure is used not only to test equality, but also to order the rows in the tables, so that the join can be implemented efficiently. We can use our `compare-numbers` procedure. There are no rows for Tom Levy. No marks were reported for him, so there are no matches between the two tables on key 651, and hence no output rows were produced.[7]

Suppose we want a list of students and their marks. We can do this by projecting the result of the previous join onto the desired columns.

```
> (table-print
    (table-project
      (table-join students final-marks 'student-no compare-numbers)
      '(student-no name course mark))
    'student-no compare-numbers)
```

student-no	name	course	mark
123	Smith, W.	en110	90
123	Smith, W.	cs124	85
284	Schmidt, S.	en110	81
284	Schmidt, S.	ma120	78
284	Schmidt, S.	cs124	75
457	Lee, R.	cs124	91
912	Levy, T.	ma120	71

---

[7] Relational DBMSs support another form of join, known as "outer join", that produces at least one row per individual. We can use outer join if we want to ensure that even students who took no courses receive a transcript.

```
912           Gomez, D.    cs124      72
```

Finally, we need to produce a table of student averages. This requires us to *summarize* the data, i.e., to collapse a number of related rows in the input table into one output table. What we want is a table of student numbers and averages. (We'll use percentages, for simplicity.) Unfortunately, our DBScheme procedures aren't powerful enough to do this job. This statement may confuse you, since earlier we claimed that selection, projection, and join were almost universal. However, DBScheme is a simplified database language; both selection and projection as we've seen them are somewhat less powerful than their full relational equivalents. In any case, there will always be some operations that are better performed on a row-by-row basis.

We'll build the `student-averages` table by scanning the `final-marks` table. For each row in that table, we add the corresponding mark to a total for the student, and increment the number of courses. (In a real student system, we'd probably count credits, not courses.) Then we can scan `student-averages` itself, computing an average mark.

We start by making an empty table:

```
> (define student-averages
    (make-table 'student-no 'total-grade 'num-courses 'average))
```

Now we use a DBScheme procedure named `table-for-each-row` to do the scan. `table-for-each-row` is an analog of `for-each`. It goes through a table and applies a specified procedure to selected fields of the row. In this case, we want to go through `students` in order to initialize `student-averages` with just the student numbers. We pass a procedure that returns no value, but mutates table `student-averages`, using `table-add-rows!`.

```
> (table-for-each-row students '(student-no)
    (lambda (s-no)
      (table-add-rows! student-averages
        (list
          (list (cons 'student-no s-no)
            '(total-grade . 0) '(num-courses . 0)
            '(average . 0))))))
> (table-print student-averages 'student-no compare-numbers)
student-no  total-grade num-courses average
----------  ----------  ----------  ----------
123         0           0           0
284         0           0           0
457         0           0           0
651         0           0           0
912         0           0           0
```

Roughly stated, the code says, "Go through `students`. For each row, apply the procedure to the `student-no` field. The procedure itself builds the specification of a row in which the `student-no` field is as given, and the other fields are zero."

Our next step is to scan `final-marks` and count the total marks and number of courses for each student. For this, we need to be able to get data from a table. `table-select` certainly does that, but we need a way to get data in a form that we can work with directly. For this, we need `table-find`, a DBScheme procedure that gives us a list of the values found in a particular field. For example, (table-find final-marks 'student-no = 123 course) ⇒ ("cs124" "en110"). As before, table-for-each-row returns no value, so it produces its effect by mutating table student-averages, this time using table-update!.

```
> (table-for-each-row final-marks '(student-no mark)
    (lambda (s-no mark)
      (let
        ((tot
           (table-find student-averages
             'student-no = s-no
             'total-grade))
         (num
           (table-find student-averages
             'student-no = s-no
             'num-courses)))
        (table-update! student-averages
          'student-no = s-no
          'total-grade (+ (car tot) mark))
        (table-update! student-averages
          'student-no = s-no
          'num-courses (+ (car num) 1)))))
```

☞ **Exercise 8-10**

table-find returns a list, which might be null or might have more than one element. In the above code, we just take the car of tot or num, without checking the length of the list. What reason do we have for believing that the list will have exactly one element? Is it good programming style to make this assumption? ❏

The final step is to go through student-averages and compute the final averages. This is fairly straightforward. The data is in the fields specified as column names and passed as arguments to the procedure mapped over the rows. Each step mutates table student-averages.

```
> (table-for-each-row student-averages
    '(student-no total-grade num-courses)
    (lambda (s-no tot num)
      (if (> num 0)
        (table-update! student-averages
          'student-no = s-no
          'average (/ tot (* 1.0 num))))))
> (table-print student-averages 'student-no compare-numbers)
```

student-no	total-grade	num-courses	average
123	175	2	87.5
284	234	3	78
457	91	1	91
651	0	0	0
912	143	2	71.5

A table is a collection of data organized into rows and columns. The data in each column is of the same type; the data in each row corresponds to an individual item.

Constructor

- (make-table *column-descriptor*...)
  Build a table according to the specified *column-descriptor*s, each of which is either a symbol or a pair whose car is a symbol, and whose cdr is a validation procedure. The symbol is taken as the name of the column. The validation procedure is a Boolean procedure of one argument, which returns true if a given value is valid for that column. For column descriptors that are symbols, rather than pairs, the validation procedure is taken as (lambda (x) #t).
  It is an error if two *column-descriptor*s specify the same column name.

Database operations

- (table-select *table column proc value*)
  Create a new table from *table*, containing all rows of the original table in which the column named *column* has a value *x* for which (proc *x value*) returns #t.
  It is an error if
  1. *table* doesn't have a column named *column*.
  2. *x* or *value* is an invalid argument to *proc*.
  3. *proc* doesn't return a Boolean value.
  The newly created table does not share storage with the original one, that is, a new, separate table is created; any changes to this new table will not affect the original one, and vice versa.

- (table-project *table columns*)
  Create a new table from the specified *table*, containing all columns of the original table that are specified in the list *columns*, which must be a list of symbols.
  It is an error if one of the *columns* is not the name of a column in the original table.
  The newly created table does not share storage with the original ones.

- (table-join *table1 table2 column proc*)
  Create a new table from *table1* and *table2*, containing one row for each pair of rows in the original tables for which the comparison procedure proc returns equal-to on the fields named column.
  It is an error if column does not appear in both tables.
  The newly created table does not share storage with the original ones.

Figure 8-10   **Abstract Data Type:** table: part 1

We have now seen all of DBScheme's features. Since DBScheme is nothing more than a set of procedures that manage tables, the ADT for the type table *is* DBScheme. A specification is shown in Figures 8-10 and 8-11.

You might think of the table ADT as a specification of the whole DBMS. Given that, it makes sense to start with a precise specification of the DBScheme operations. For each operation, we'll list some of the error conditions that could occur. We don't

Mutators

- (table-add-rows! *table rowlist*)
  Mutate the specified table by adding rows specified by *rowlist*, which must be a list. Each item of *rowlist* must be a specification for a single row, an association list whose cars are the names of columns, and whose cdrs are the corresponding values.
  It is an error if

  1. an element of *rowlist* specifies a column name that is not part of *table*.
  2. an element of *rowlist* omits a column of *table*.
  3. the value for a field does not satisfy the validation procedure for the column.

- (table-update! *table column1 proc value1 column2 value2*)
  Find all rows in table by identifying all rows in which column *column1* contains a value x such that (*proc x value1*) returns #t (this is the set of rows that would be identified for a selection), and mutating each so that the field for column *column2* contains *value2*.
  It is an error if

  1. table does not contain columns named column1 and column2.
  2. x or *value1* is an invalid argument to *proc*.

Mapping procedures

- (table-for-each-row *table columns proc*)
  Apply *proc* to the specified fields of each row of *table*; *columns* is a list of symbols that are column names in *table*. table-for-each-row scans *table*; for each row, it extracts the specified fields, and applies *proc* to the fields. *proc* should have one argument for each field. The arguments to *proc* are presented in the order in which the column names appear in *columns*.
  Return an unspecified value.

Output procedure

- (table-print *table column proc*)
  Display *table*, with the columns in the order given in the original call to make-table. (The relational model explicitly says that the order of the columns doesn't matter. Using the original column order is a feature of table-print.) Rows will be sorted according to the column named *column*; one row will be before another if *proc* indicates that the *column* field of the first row is less than that of the second.

Figure 8-11   **Abstract Data Type:** table: part 2

check for all of them (it's impossible to check for some of them), but it's worthwhile to know what errors could occur.

☞ **Exercise 8-11**

List three errors that could occur in the table ADT that we have not included in our collection of errors. ❏

8.3   Implementing DBScheme

*While there's no difference between theory and practice in theory, there's a
huge gulf between theory and practice in practice.*   — Author unknown

The code presented in this section can be found in file `dbscheme.scm`.

Now that we've seen DBScheme from a user viewpoint, it's time to build an implementation. The previous section presented the interface to the DBMS, the external
view of the system. This section examines one possible internal organization. In
keeping with our "schematic" approach, we're mostly going to concentrate on getting something that works, ignoring such things as error-handling and efficiency.
However, a usable DBMS must be designed to be reliable and efficient.

Figure 8-12 shows the connections among the modules.

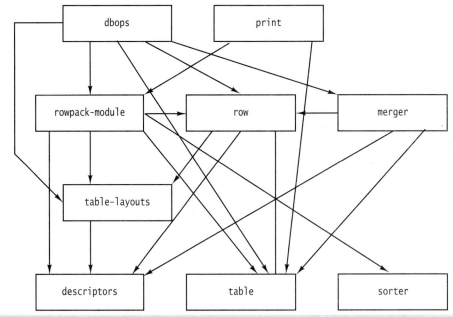

Figure 8-12   Connections among modules

An arrow connects two modules when the module at the head calls the module to
which the arrow points. We might want to build a system of modules where the
structure looks more regular, for simplicity, but real systems often are much more
complicated.[8] The modules at the top of the figure, with no incoming arrows, are

---

[8] DBScheme is only a schematic of a real DBMS! Real database systems are generally huge programs,
with many features and options.

only called by the user. The modules at the bottom, such as `table`, contain utility procedures used by the other modules.

8.3.1   Implementing Tables

The first step in building a table should be fairly straightforward. There are two parts of a table: the column descriptor information, which we call the *layout*, and the actual data stored in the rows, which we call a *rowpack* (row package). Programs 8-2 and 8-3 show the module that implements all the procedures in the interface to DBScheme.

```
(module dbops
  (export make-table table-add-rows! table-select table-find
    table-update! table-project table-join table-for-each-row)
  (define make-table
    (lambda column-specifications
      (construct-table
        (make-table-layout column-specifications) '())))
  (define table-add-rows!
    (lambda (table data)
      (for-each
        (lambda (item)
          (table-add-single-row! table (make-row table item)))
        data)))
  (define table-select
    (lambda (table name predicate value)
      (construct-table (table-layout table)
        (select-rowpack
          (table-layout table) (table-rowpack table)
          name predicate value))))
  (define table-find
    (lambda (table name1 predicate value name2)
      (let
        ((answer
          (table-project
            (table-select table name1 predicate value)
            (list name2))))
        (map car (table-rowpack answer)))))
```

Program 8-2   Operations module (part 1 of 2)

Program 8-4 shows how we can treat a table as a pair, with low-level procedures for extracting or updating the layout or rowpack information. The column descriptors are simply pairs, but to make the code more readable, we've implemented an interface to them, also shown in Program 8-4.

A layout is a list of column descriptors, just as the DBScheme user specifies them; columns for which no validation procedure was specified are given a default validation procedure. The code is shown in Program 8-5. The code for handling validation procedures is used by several of the other modules, but is implemented here because it accesses directly the structures within the layout.

```
(define table-update!
  (lambda (table name1 predicate value1 name2 value2)
    (let
      ((layout (table-layout table)))
      (type-check layout name2 value2)
      (let
        ((update-row
           (lambda (row)
             (if (predicate (row-get row layout name1) value1)
                 (row-set! row layout name2 value2)))))
        (for-each update-row (table-rowpack table))))))
(define table-project
  (lambda (table col-names)
    (build-projected-table
      (table-layout table)
      (table-rowpack table)
      col-names)))
(define table-sort
  (lambda (table sort-proc name)
    (construct-table
      (table-layout table)
      (sort-rowpack table sort-proc name))))
(define table-join
  (lambda (table1 table2 join-column sort-proc)
    (let
      ((t1 (table-sort table1 sort-proc join-column))
       (t2 (table-sort table2 sort-proc join-column)))
      (merge-tables t1 t2 join-column sort-proc))))
(define table-for-each-row
  (lambda (table columns proc)
    (let
      ((layout (table-layout table))
       (rows (table-rowpack table)))
      (for-each
        (lambda (row)
          (apply proc
            (map
              (lambda (colname)
                (row-get row layout colname))
              columns)))
        rows))))
)
```

Program 8-3   Operations module (part 2 of 2)

We can't describe layouts by themselves, because there's an intimate relationship between layouts and rows. We must therefore introduce a row ADT, shown in Figure 8-13.

The implementation of these procedures is fairly straightforward. make-row uses the layout to construct the row by using the layout as an association list. For

```
(module table
  (export table-layout table-rowpack
    table-add-single-row! construct-table)
  (define construct-table cons)
  (define table-layout car)
  (define table-rowpack cdr)
  (define table-add-single-row!
    (lambda (table row)
      (set-cdr! table (cons row (cdr table))))))
(module descriptors
  (export make-column-desc column-desc-name column-desc-checker)
  (define make-column-desc cons)
  (define column-desc-name car)
  (define column-desc-checker cdr))
```

| Program 8-4 | Table and descriptor modules |

each column descriptor of the layout, it attempts to get the corresponding field from `field-specs`, and then **type checks** it, by calling the validation procedure. The implementation of rows is in Program 8-6.

`row-get` and `row-set!` use a helper procedure named `row-scan` to search for the item. They illustrate an interesting style of program design. We don't know whether we're going to find the affected row until we actually find it. Good program design dictates that we check for the error case. The method we've chosen is to pass a procedure to `row-scan`. If `row-scan` finds the row, it calls the procedure. Otherwise, an error is generated. Validity checking is handled by a procedure named `type-check`, shown in Program 8-5.

A row is a list of fields, stored in the same order as the column names of the layout.

Constructor

- (make-row *table fields*)
  Create a new row, using the layout of `table`. `fields` is an association list, in the same format as a row of `table-add-rows!`.

Accessor

- (row-get *row layout name*)
  Return the field of *row* specified by *name* in the *layout*.

Mutator

- (row-set! *layout name value*)
  Mutate the field of *row* specified by *name* in the *layout* to *value*. This does not create a new row, but mutates an existing row.

| Figure 8-13 | **Abstract Data Type:** row |

```
(module table-layouts
  (export
    table-layout-column-names table-layout-type-checker
    make-table-layout type-check)
  (define make-table-layout
    (lambda (column-info)
      (let
        ((column-descriptor
           (lambda (x)
             (cond
               ((symbol? x) (make-column-desc x (lambda (val) #t)))
               ((and (pair? x) (symbol? (car x))(procedure? (cdr x)))
                (make-column-desc (car x) (cdr x)))
               (else
                 (error 'make-table-layout
                   "Invalid column specification ~a" x))))))
        (map column-descriptor column-info))))
  (define table-layout-column-names
    (lambda (layout)
      (map column-desc-name layout)))
  (define table-layout-type-checker
    (lambda (layout name)
      (column-desc-checker (table-layout-helper layout name))))
  (define type-check
    (lambda (layout name value)
      (if (not ((table-layout-type-checker layout name) value))
        (error 'type-check
          "Invalid value for field ~a ~a" name value))))
  (define table-layout-helper
    (lambda (layout name)
      (let ((x (assv name layout)))
        (if (not x)
          (error 'table-layout-helper
            "Invalid column name ~a" name)
          x))))
  (define table-layout-for-each
    (lambda (layout proc)
      (for-each
        (lambda (col-desc) (proc (car col-desc) (cdr col-desc)))
        layout)))
)
```

Program 8-5   Layout module

```
(module row
  (export make-row row-get row-set!)
  (define make-row
    (lambda (table field-specs)
      (let ((layout (table-layout table))
            (get-field
              (lambda (name)
                (let ((x (assv name field-specs)))
                  (if (null? x)
                      (error 'make-row "Invalid field spec ~a" name)
                      (cdr x))))))
        (map (lambda (column-spec)
               (let* ((col-name (car column-spec))
                      (val (get-field col-name)))
                 (type-check layout col-name val)
                 val))
          layout)))))
  (define row-get
    (lambda (row layout name)
      (row-scan row layout name (lambda (item) (car item)))))
  (define row-set!
    (lambda (row layout name val)
      (row-scan row layout name (lambda (x) (set-car! x val)))))
  (define row-scan
    (lambda (row layout name proc)
      (if (null? layout)
          (error 'row-scan "Invalid field name ~a" name)
          (if (eqv? name (column-desc-name (car layout)))
              (proc row)
              (row-scan (cdr row) (cdr layout) name proc))))))
```

Program 8-6   Row module

8.3.2   Rowpacks and Persistence

We now come to one of the most difficult problems in databases: How do we represent a rowpack? Our solution has probably already occurred to you, namely, to use a list of the rows. This representation is sufficient for our purposes; we'll consider ways to improve it later. For real applications, however, we must consider another aspect of data. Our database is created anew whenever we want to use tables, but a real database must exist even between uses—it must be persistent.

A **persistent** value is one that lasts after the program has terminated. We can't store persistent values in the computer's main memory, because almost all computers use semiconductor memory chips that lose their data when the power is switched off.[9] Even if there were no danger of losing data, memory is too expensive to be dedicated to one program. When the program finishes, the memory is used to store data for other programs.

As a result, we need some external storage device other than main memory where we can save our database between applications. In fact, a database usually resides primarily on an external storage device; only the active portion of the data is brought into main memory. Almost all computers have external storage devices, such as floppy and hard disks, optical drives, WORM ("write once, read many times") drives, CD-ROM, and so on. All of these devices can store much more than main memory (as of 1994, a computer with 8 megabytes of main memory often has a hard disk capable of storing several hundred megabytes of data), but there is a substantial performance difference between these devices and main memory.

Whereas main memory is entirely electronic, external storage devices have moving parts. A computer can access a main memory location in about 70 nanoseconds (= 70×10^{-9} seconds), but even a fast hard disk drive takes an average of perhaps 10 milliseconds (= 10×10^{-3} seconds) to access data, a factor of over ten thousand. Main memory is organized into millions of **cells**, each of which can contain a single value. External storage devices organize data into **blocks**, each of which contains as much data as perhaps a thousand cells. On an external storage device, an entire block can be read or written in the same amount of time as a single cell. It makes sense, therefore, to put several pieces of information into one block. We will return to external storage devices in Chapter 11.

In our programs, we have assumed that we can access a value just by mentioning it. For example, if we write (+ a b), the computer must access the contents of the cells named a and b. Our analysis of algorithms has implicitly followed this principle, right from Chapter 2. But if accessing a block on an external storage device is very much more expensive in time than accessing a single value in main memory, it makes sense to design algorithms that obtain an entire block at a time and process the elements afterwards.

Program 8-7 shows a procedure that returns a single data item at a time, even though it actually gets the data in larger chunks. The list is a **buffer**, a temporary holding place for data as it passes between external storage and internal program space. Initially the buffer is empty, but then access-data reads a block of data (a list of items, presumably at least of length 1). Thereafter, access-data returns the first

---

[9] Most personal computers have a small amount of CMOS (complementary metal-oxide semiconductor) memory, which does not lose information when the power is off. CMOS memory is used to store information needed while the computer is booting; however, it is not practical to use CMOS for the machine's main memory.

```
(define access-data
  (let
    ((buffer '()))
    (lambda ()
      (if (null? buffer)
        (begin
          (set! buffer (read-block))
          (let
            ((val (car buffer)))
            (set! buffer (cdr buffer))
            val))
        (let
          ((val (car buffer)))
          (set! buffer (cdr buffer))
          val)))))
```

Program 8-7   Buffering

item in the list until it runs out of data, when it reads another block. `access-data` *buffers* the data from the external device.

In our DBScheme implementation, we'll represent a rowpack as a list of rows. Be warned, though, that this is unrealistic. To be somewhat realistic, we can think of all the rows as being stored on disk while they're not being used, and read in from disk when they're needed.

Let's return to our implementation of rowpacks. The code to add rows to a table, `table-add-rows!` is in Program 8-2. It uses another procedure, `table-add-single-row!`, shown in Program 8-4. The mapping procedure `table-for-each-row`, shown in Program 8-3, is no more complicated.

8.3.3   Selection and Projection

Now that we know how rowpacks work, we can do selection and projection, as in Program 8-8. Updating can be done in the same way as selection, except we don't have to build a new table; the code for `table-update!` appears in Program 8-2. Note the use of the type checker.

Projection, too, is quite straightforward. All we need to do is to build a new table by pairing the new layout with the specified columns with the rowpack created by choosing the specified columns from each row in the rowpack, as in Program 8-8.

Selection and projection are the basis of `table-find`. We can select on the specified *column*, and then project on *column2*, as in Program 8-2.

8.3.4   Sorting

Our two remaining DBScheme procedures, `table-join` and `table-print`, both require that we be able to sort data. Sorting (arranging data in a specified order) is a common task in many different programs. Computer scientists have studied various algorithms for sorting, right from the dawn of computers. We will examine a method known as **insertion sort**, based on the method that card players use to keep their hands in order. Even though insertion sort won't be fast enough for practical

```
(module rowpack-module
  (export select-rowpack build-projected-table sort-rowpack)
  (define select-rowpack
    (lambda (layout rowpack name predicate value)
      (letrec
        ((helper
          (lambda (rp)
            (if (null? rp) '()
              (if
                (predicate
                  (row-get (car rp) layout name)
                  value)
                (cons (car rp) (helper (cdr rp)))
                (helper (cdr rp)))))))
        (helper rowpack))))
  (define build-projected-table
    (lambda (layout rowpack col-names)
      (let
        ((new-layout
          (map
            (lambda (x)
              (make-column-desc x
                (table-layout-type-checker layout x)))
            col-names))
         (new-rowpack
          (map
            (lambda (row)
              (map
                (lambda (name) (row-get row layout name))
                col-names))
            rowpack)))
        (construct-table new-layout new-rowpack))))
  (define sort-rowpack
    (lambda (table compare name)
      (let
        ((layout (table-layout table))
         (rowpack (table-rowpack table)))
        (insertion-sort rowpack
          (lambda (a b)
            (compare
              (row-get a layout name)
              (row-get b layout name)))))))
)
```

Program 8-8   Implementing selection and projection

applications, a slow method is better than nothing at all. (In Chapter 9, we'll look at Quicksort, which is extremely efficient.)

Suppose that we want to sort a list of integers. We will build a new list, with the integers in order; each time we take an integer from the list, we'll put it into the appropriate place in the list we're building, as shown in Figure 8-14.

Original list	New list
(33 14 87 14 22 16 18 46 81)	()
(14 87 14 22 16 18 46 81)	(33)
(87 14 22 16 18 46 81)	(14 33)
(14 22 16 18 46 81)	(14 33 87)
(22 16 18 46 81)	(14 14 33 87)
(16 18 46 81)	(14 14 22 33 87)
(18 46 81)	(14 14 16 22 33 87)
(46 81)	(14 14 16 18 22 33 87)
(81)	(14 14 16 18 22 33 46 87)
()	(14 14 16 18 22 33 46 81 87)

Figure 8-14   Insertion sort at work

insertion-sort (Program 8-9) takes two arguments, the list to be sorted, and a comparator procedure (see page 426). insertion-sort takes the first item from the original list and calls insert-in-order to insert this item, in the correct order, in the new list obtained by applying insertion-sort to the rest of the original list.

```
(module sorter
  (export insertion-sort)
  (define insertion-sort
    (lambda (lst compare)
      (if (null? lst)
        '()
        (insert-in-order
          (car lst)
          (insertion-sort (cdr lst) compare)
          compare))))
  (define insert-in-order
    (lambda (item lst compare)
      (if (null? lst)
        (cons item '())
        (if (eqv? (compare item (car lst)) 'greater-than)
          (cons (car lst)
            (insert-in-order item (cdr lst) compare))
          (cons item lst)))))
)
```

Program 8-9   Sorter module

insertion-sort only checks for greater-than, so we might still be able to get away with using Boolean procedures such as <. However, some of the sorting algorithms we'll study in the next chapter require a three-way comparison; we use comparators so we can keep the interface the same for all of our sorting procedures.

☞ **Exercise 8-12**

Why is the name insertion-sort a poor choice for this procedure? Hint: What information about the procedure should be given in its name? ❏

The best way to determine the computational cost of insertion-sort is to count the number of times the compare procedure is called. If we have a list of n items, a single call to insert-in-order will require between 1 and n comparisons. Since we must call insert-in-order once for each item in the list, we must do $O(n^2)$ comparison operations. On average, we would expect to do something like $n^2/4$ comparisons, since insert-in-order should probably find the place for the item to be inserted about halfway through the list, and the average length of the list is $n/2$. (It starts out with zero length and grows to n items.)

Program 8-3 shows that table-sort uses insertion-sort to sort an entire table. sort-rowpack just calls insertion-sort, providing it with a suitable comparison procedure, which in turn calls the compare argument (see Program 8-8).

8.3.5   Join

The join operation takes two tables and a column common to both, and produces a new table by matching rows from the two tables. We can imagine that the join first produces a huge table, in which every row in the first table is paired with every row in the second; then, join keeps only those rows where column entries match. This requires creating, from tables of size m and n, an intermediate table of size $m \times n$.

A better way to perform a join is to take the first value of the join column in the first table, and look through the entire second table for values that match it. Then take the second one in the first table, and look through the entire second table again. Thus, for each of m rows we look through n rows in the second. This takes the same amount of time as the first method, but less space, since we don't have to create the large intermediate table.

However, there's an even better way. If both tables are in order with respect to the join column, then we can just merge the two tables. That was the way the customer-billing example at the beginning of this chapter worked. The customer cards were sorted, then the transaction cards were sorted by customer number, and finally the two sorted collections were merged.

What do we mean by merge? The simplest form of merge is to take two ordered sets of items and create a new ordered set. Program 8-10 shows merge-lists, which merges two lists whose items are in order; that is, the lists are sorted. The procedure given as the compare argument decides the ordering among two items, as it did when input lists were originally sorted.

The other two arguments to merge-lists are the two lists. At each step, merge-lists puts either the left or right input into the output, depending on which is less. It takes only $O(n)$ comparisons (calls to compare) to merge two sorted lists, each of length n, because at each step, an item either from left or right is moved to the output. After at most $2n$ steps, all the input has been copied to the output. A join operation, like merging, is fast when both inputs are ordered. If the left and right don't match, the list with the lesser item advances until the cars of the lists match.

```
(define merge-lists
  (lambda (left right compare)
    (cond
      ((null? left) right)
      ((null? right) left)
      (else
        (let ((res (compare (car left) (car right))))
          (case res
            ((less-than equal-to)
             (cons (car left)
               (merge-lists (cdr left) right compare)))
            ((greater-than)
             (cons (car right)
               (merge-lists  left (cdr right) compare)))))))))
```

Program 8-10   Merging lists

Program 8-11 shows code to join lists. copy-and-join does the work. When the two lists are lined up, it steps down the right list outputting pairs (joined rows) until the rows don't match. Then it begins again with the next item in the left list, and the right list again where the first match occurred.

```
(define join-lists
  (lambda (left right compare)
    (if (or (null? left) (null? right))
      '()
      (let ((res (compare (car left) (car right))))
        (case res
          ((less-than)
           (join-lists (cdr left) right compare))
          ((equal-to)
           (copy-and-join left right compare (car left) right))
          ((greater-than)
           (join-lists  left (cdr right) compare)))))))
(define copy-and-join
  (lambda (left right compare item orig)
    (if (null? right)
      '()
      (if (eqv? (compare item (car right)) 'less-than)
        (join-lists (cdr left) orig compare)
        (cons (cons item (car right))
          (copy-and-join
            left (cdr right)
            compare item orig))))))
```

Program 8-11   Joining lists

In join, the output isn't one-for-one: if we have three final-marks rows for one student, we output three items. In fact, if we have *i* items in the first table with a given key value, and *j* items in the second table with the same key value, we must output ij rows. Here's the output of join-lists:

```
> (join-lists '(1 2 2 3) '(2 2 3 3 3 5) compare-numbers)
((2 . 2) (2 . 2) (2 . 2) (2 . 2) (3 . 3) (3 . 3) (3 . 3))
```

The best way to implement join, then, is to put the two tables into some order, and then merge the result, as in join-lists. The last statement is phrased carefully; many databases have indexes, data structures that let the database access items rapidly, that are usually based on some ordering. (We'll look at indexing techniques in Chapter 9.) If the database has an index on the join column, merging can use the index. If not, we can sort the database on the join column, and then merge.

In the join operation, the merge operation is a bit complicated, because we must decide how to organize the fields in the result. (It must have all fields from the first table, along with all fields from the second table, with no duplicates.) The best approach is to decide ahead of time how we want the resulting table to look, and then do the actual merge, as in the following sketch.

```
(define table-join
  (lambda (table1 table2 join-column sort-proc)
    (let
      ((t1 (table-sort table1 sort-proc join-column))
       (t2 (table-sort table2 sort-proc join-column)))
      (merge-tables t1 t2 join-column sort-proc))))
```

We need to know what fields from the original tables are to be used to build each row in the resulting table. Accordingly, merge-tables creates a *merge strategy*, a grandiose name for a list of the fields in the resulting table, each accompanied by an indication of which table a given field comes from. The merge strategy is used as an input to the actual merging procedure.[10]

For example, if we want to join students with final-marks, we will get the following merge strategy:

```
> (merge-strategy students final-marks)
(((mark . #{procedure}) . 2)
 ((course . #{procedure}) . 2)
 ((student-no . #{number?}) . 1)
 ((name . #{procedure}) . 1)
 ((phone . #{procedure}) . 1))
```

The car of each pair is the column descriptor, while the 1 or 2 value in the cdr of each item indicates whether we are to take this column from the first or the second column.

merge-strategy operates by creating a strategy from the first layout, with each column flagged with a code value of 1. Then, each column from the second layout is checked. If it is already present, nothing is done; otherwise, it is added to the strategy, with a code of 2.

---

[10] We need not have used a merge strategy. We could, instead, have just built a list of resulting fields, and decided during the actual merging where to get the results from. This approach would result in doing a certain amount of meaningless work for each row we're merging. By precomputing the strategy, we save considerable time. Any real DBMS must handle huge tables: any precomputation can save vast amounts of time during the processing.

☞ **Exercise 8-13**

What assumption is made here about columns that appear in both tables? ❏

    `merge-tables` looks rather complicated, but fortunately it is broken down into a set of cooperating procedures. Of these, `helper` is the most significant: it is given a pair of rowpacks, and scans down each. It uses `compare-rows` to find out whether the first row in the first rowpack has the same join column value as the first row in the second. If the two rows don't match, it calls itself recursively (remember that since the rowpacks have been sorted, if one or the other row is less, it has no match anywhere in the other rowpack).

    If `helper` encounters two matching rows, it calls `equal-rows` to output the merged rows. This process is somewhat complicated, since, as we saw above, there might be *ij* rows in the output. `equal-rows`, therefore, outputs a new row for each row in the second rowpack that matches the first.

    Compare the code shown in Programs 8-12 and 8-13 with `join-lists` in Program 8-11.

```
(module merger
  (export merge-tables)
  (define not-already-there?
    (lambda (col-name strategy)
      (if (null? strategy) #t
        (if (eqv? col-name
          (column-desc-name (car (car strategy))))
            #f
            (not-already-there? col-name (cdr strategy))))))
  (define merge-strategy
    (lambda (t1 t2)
      (let*
        ((lo1 (table-layout t1))
         (lo2 (table-layout t2))
         (strat
           (map
             (lambda (col-spec) (cons col-spec 1)) lo1)))
        (for-each
          (lambda (col-spec)
            (if (not-already-there?
                  (column-desc-name col-spec) strat)
              (set! strat (cons (cons col-spec 2) strat))))
          lo2)
        strat)))
```

Program 8-12   Merge module (part 1 of 2)

☞ **Exercise 8-14**

A telephone company has a subscriber database with about 3 million rows, containing name, address, and other information. Each time a long-distance call is made, a row containing the calling and called phone numbers, as well as the number of minutes taken, is produced. Each customer makes an average of five long-distance calls per month. At the

```
(define merge-tables
  (lambda (t1 t2 merge-column sort-proc)
    (let
      ((strategy (merge-strategy t1 t2)))
      (letrec
        ((lo1 (table-layout t1))
         (lo2 (table-layout t2))
         (compare-rows
           (lambda (r1 r2)
             (sort-proc
               (row-get r1 lo1 merge-column)
               (row-get r2 lo2 merge-column))))
         (merge-row
           (lambda (r1 r2)
             (map
               (lambda (strate1)
                 (if (= (cdr strate1) 1)
                     (row-get r1 lo1 (car (car strate1)))
                     (row-get r2 lo2 (car (car strate1)))))
               strategy)))
         (equal-rows
           (lambda (r rp)
             (if (or (null? rp))
                 '()
                 (if (eqv? (compare-rows r (car rp)) 'equal-to)
                     (cons (merge-row r (car rp))
                           (equal-rows r (cdr rp)))
                     '()))))
         (helper
           (lambda (rp1 rp2)
             (if (or (null? rp1) (null? rp2))
                 '()
                 (let
                   ((r1 (car rp1))
                    (r2 (car rp2)))
                   (case (compare-rows r1 r2)
                     ((less-than) (helper (cdr rp1) rp2))
                     ((equal-to)
                      (append
                        (equal-rows r1 rp2)
                        (helper (cdr rp1) rp2)))
                     ((greater-than)
                      (helper rp1 (cdr rp2)))))))))
        (construct-table
          (map car strategy)
          (helper (table-rowpack t1) (table-rowpack t2)))))))
)
```

Program 8-13   Merge module (part 2 of 2)

end of each month, the two tables are joined on the phone number field to produce the customer statements. Let's make the unrealistic assumption that the telephone company doesn't keep its records sorted. Assuming that our implementation of `insertion-sort` can make a million comparisons per second, how many years will it take to do the sorting needed to prepare for the join? ❏

8.3.6   Printing

We have now virtually completed our DBScheme system. All that's left is to write the code to print a table. This is a straightforward task, and we leave it as an exercise for you. (Our DBScheme implementation includes a `table-print` procedure.)

☞ **Exercise 8-15**

In an important special case, insertion sort takes far fewer than $O(n^2)$ comparisons. What is that special case, and why is it significant in relation to `table-print`? (If you haven't written your own, look at our solution in the Software Package.) ❏

☞ **Exercise 8-16**

Referring to the version of `table-print` in the Software Package, how would you modify the format of layouts and the printing code, so that you can specify the format for a column when it is printed? ❏

8.3.7   In Retrospect

Our DBScheme system is now complete. We have seen a number of interesting algorithms and a lot of code. How good a database system have we built? From one point of view, we have done everything we needed to. This system works, and produces the correct results, although the error-checking is insufficient. Even ignoring the issue of persistence, however, our system is too slow to be usable, because we use poor algorithms. We'll learn how to improve them in the next chapter.

We need ways to tell the DBMS more about our data, and ways for a DBMS to take advantage of this information. We call such techniques **query optimization**; they are critical to the success of any real DBMS. Query optimization is an advanced topic; we discuss it briefly in Chapter 9. Refer to one of the advanced database books listed at the end of the chapter for more information on query optimization.

8.4   Designing a Database

You may abuse a tragedy, though you cannot write one. You may scold a carpenter who has made you a bad table, though you cannot make a table. It is not your trade to make tables.   — Samuel Johnson, in Boswell's *Life*

Just as writing Scheme code requires preliminary design work, so we must design our databases. The design of a database commits us for the long term. We can change or replace programs at will, but it is much harder to modify or replace a database that affects hundreds of programs.

What do we mean by database design? Any database consists of a collection of tables, which together represent whatever view of data we think is reasonable. The designer of a database must develop a set of tables that lets the program access the data we want and that also minimizes the chance of error and maximizes efficient use of storage.

In Chapter 6, we saw how object-oriented design can help in building programs. Database design is a different process. We're only interested in discovering how to organize the data we have into tables that allow the programs that use them to be efficient and reliable. Programmers can use object-oriented design to plan the program, and then use database design to decide how to represent information in the resulting program.[11]

We can identify two design strategies. The first, which we can call the *shoebox* method, puts all of the data into one giant table, much as some people keep all of their financial records in a shoebox. There are some advantages to the shoebox method; for example, we never have to do any joins! Unfortunately, the shoebox method creates a number of serious problems. For one thing, any program that does anything at all must have access to the table. In our student records example, we created final-marks tables for individual classes. We would not be able to do so in the shoebox method; each instructor would have to run a program that worked directly on the main table. The possibilities for error and confusion here are simply too great.

Another design method might be called the *little scraps of paper* method. Each time we have some data, we put it into a table. For example, we might have two documents for each student: an application for admission form, and an application for a particular program. We might also have the student's registration information for each semester. In the "little scraps of paper" approach, we create a single table for each document. The problem with this approach is that much information is duplicated on these documents (e.g., the student's name or home address). This wastes a great deal of storage and, more important, introduces a chance of serious error if, for example, there is inconsistent information across the various documents. What happens if a student changes his or her name during the semester? We must locate each table that contains this information, and change it in each one. We'll almost certainly miss one.

The conclusion is clear. We must develop a method of analyzing the data we need to store, and organizing it in modular tables. We need to use a number of criteria for our design:

- It should reflect the way we view our data.
- It should reflect the way data enters the system.
- It should ensure that each piece of information is stored exactly once.
- It should minimize the number of joins required for normal processing.

---

[11] There are genuine object-oriented database systems, which can be thought of as using the interface of `define-class` to manage persistent objects. Relational database systems are slowly acquiring objectlike features. Even a purely relational DBMS can be used effectively with object-oriented design.

8.4.1   Normalization

Normalizing a database organizes the data effectively; it means that the tables satisfy a set of rules that make sure that only necessary information is stored and that each piece of information is stored in only one place. Database researchers have identified a number of **normal forms**, each of which puts a specific restriction upon the table. We will study the most important normal forms and see how to transform our tables so that they satisfy the rules for each form. Don't confuse the term *form* used here with the term used to refer to expressions in Scheme. A normal form is a format, a way of structuring a set of tables; we will examine three different normal forms of tables.

One caution: you can't normalize a table without knowing a good deal about the data. You must therefore identify keys and determine where data comes from before you attempt to do any normalization. We'll use as our example a variation on the student records system, in which the columns will have fairly obvious significance. In a real problem, though, you would have to get much more information about the data than we will provide here.

We'll start with an example that appears to have been designed by the shoebox method, shown in Figure 8-15. This table might be created, for example, by throwing together the "Report of Grades" forms that instructors fill out at the end of the semester.

course	instructor	info
CS124	Cohen	1234, Smith, 91, A ; 1572, Jones, 81, B+
MA120	Gutierrez	1234, Smith, 79, B

Figure 8-15   Shoebox

The first thing to notice about this table is that it's very difficult to find useful information. For example, we can't compute Smith's grade-point average with a selection, because selection is based upon rows. The first row contains information from course CS124, both on Smith and Jones—selecting that row gives us too much information. In fact, this table is useless with our procedures.

We can put the table into **First Normal Form**, or **1NF**, by following the rule that *each field must be a simple piece of data, not a collection.*[12] That way, at the very least, we can use selection, projection, and join usefully. The resulting table is shown in Figure 8-16.

☞ **Exercise 8-17**

You have decided to catalog your music collection. For each album, you have identified the album name and label. For each piece, you have identified the title, composer, and performer. Here is a very brief extract of the information you have gathered.

• The album *A Surfeit of Music*, on the ABC label, contains two pieces, "The Unbegun" and "Pervertimento for Bagpipe and Balloon", both composed by P. D. Q. Bach, as well as "Go For Baroque", composed by Box Bodobeek. All pieces are performed by the University of Western East Virginia Concert Orchestra.

---

[12] Most real DBMSs restrict fields to contain fundamental values, such as strings or numbers. This requirement is too strong. All that is necessary is that we *treat* the field as atomic.

• The album *Intense Tepidity*, on the Super-Cool label, contains "Notes", by Klix Davis, performed by Irving Chan; "More Notes", also by Klix Davis, performed by Parlee Charker, and "The Hour of Scampering", composed and performed by Box Bodobeek.

Show this database as a single table in 1NF. ❏

st-no	name	course	instructor	mark	grade
1234	Smith	CS124	Cohen	91	A
1234	Smith	MA120	Gutierrez	79	B
1572	Jones	CS124	Cohen	81	B+

Figure 8-16   First Normal Form

Our 1NF table has data that is repeated from row to row. The possibilities for error and the waste of space inherent in repeating data suggest that we find another organization for the data.

Studying the table, we realize that the key is actually a pair of columns, st-no and course; when we know the values of these two fields, exactly one row is specified. (A table often has a key that is actually a combination of fields.) We say that another column is **functionally dependent** upon another if the first column's values are determined by the second's values. For example, we say that name is functionally dependent upon st-no. Once we know a given st-no, we can use the table to find the corresponding name. On the other hand, name isn't functionally dependent upon instructor.

In **Second Normal Form**, or **2NF**, we require that *no column be functionally dependent upon just one part of the key*. For example, name is just dependent upon st-no, and instructor is just dependent upon course. (We assume that each course is taught by exactly one instructor.) How do we convert our table to 2NF? We must split it into several tables, as shown in Figure 8-17. This version has three tables, with no repeated information; that is, there's no place where several rows in a table repeat the same data. Each row contains information dependent on only one key. The student table has a key of st-no; the key of the courses table is course, and the key of the final marks table is the pair (st-no, course). This form of the data may actually occupy more bytes in memory, but it is more logically concise.

2NF is actually closer to the way we actually obtain and use the data. The student information comes from the student's original application form, the course data is normally chosen by a department chair, and the final marks information comes from the Report of Grades form at the end of the semester. From that point of view, we might have been lucky and gone directly to 2NF if we had done our analysis properly. It often happens that a 2NF table more closely represents the actual situation than does a shoebox table.

☞ **Exercise 8-18**

Assuming that the titles of all albums and of all pieces are distinct, and that a single piece might be on several albums (perhaps with different performers) show the database of Exercise 8-17 in 2NF. ❏

There is still some degree of functional dependency in the above tables, though. The problem is the field grade. This can be computed directly from mark, generally

st-no	name
1234	Smith
1572	Jones

st-no	course	mark	grade
1234	CS124	91	A
1234	MA120	79	B
1572	CS124	81	B+

st-no	course	mark	grade
1234	CS124	91	A
1234	MA120	79	B
1572	CS124	81	B+

Figure 8-17   Second Normal Form

by a formula. Even if no formula existed, we could create another table that related grades to marks (mark would be the key). We can again avoid some degree of error (for example, the instructor may enter the letter grade incorrectly on the Report of Grades) if we exclude it from the final-marks table. The result is shown in Figure 8-18.

st-no	name	course	instructor
1234	Smith	CS124	Smith
1572	Jones	MA120	Gutierrez

st-no	course	mark	mark	grade
1234	CS124	91	91	A
1234	MA120	79	79	B
1572	CS124	81	81	B+

Figure 8-18   Third Normal Form

We say that a table is in **Third Normal Form**, or **3NF**, if *no nonkey field depends upon a field other than the key.* In this case, grade depended upon the key (st-no, course), but also, more directly, upon mark. We therefore excluded it. The students table included here is only partial, clearly, and could easily be implemented by a function for computing grades from marks.

Converting our tables into 3NF gives us a database in which each item is recorded just once,[13] so there is no redundancy. 3NF form creates many tables and the key appears in each one, but we don't consider its multiple appearance as redundancy. In fact, the keys act as glue to bind the tables together.

You might object to 3NF on the grounds that it requires unnecessary joins. (A table in 1NF could tell us "What grades did Cohen give?" without requiring a join.) Fortunately, we are most likely to join 3NF tables on the key. DBMSs go to great lengths to optimize joins on keys, and therefore this is not a serious problem.

---

[13] 3NF isn't strong enough to eliminate redundant records completely. An additional normal form, called Boyce-Codd, imposes some other restrictions that are needed in some cases. Look in any book on databases for a description of Boyce-Codd Normal Form.

Once we have built a multitable database, we may become confused as to which fields are in which tables. Accordingly, a database designer creates a **data dictionary**, which is a list of all of the columns in any tables in the database, along with a specification of each one (including such things as format, validation requirements, etc.) In most DBMSs, the data dictionary itself is stored as a table.

☞ **Exercise 8-19**

Again assuming that the titles of all albums and of all pieces are distinct, and that a single piece might be on several albums (perhaps with different performers), modify your answer to Exercise 8-18 so that the tables are in 3NF. ❏

8.4.2   Internal Consistency

Suppose that a student graduates from the college. We might delete that student's row from the table of students, but fail to delete the corresponding rows from the final-marks table. As a result, we will have some useless rows in the latter table. They will never show up in a join, and, therefore we are likely to be unaware of their existence.

Such a state of affairs is an error on the programmer's part. We clearly must require that every row in the final-marks table correspond to a row in both the students and courses tables. The attempt to delete a row from the students table is an error, and the DBMS should have reported this fact.

We therefore require that a DBMS preserve **referential integrity**, the condition that rows in one table that are referenced by another must actually exist. Many early DBMSs had no automatic support for this; most modern ones do. The programmer, in planning the database organization, states which tables refer to which other ones. (This information can often be deduced from the data dictionary, but generally requires some assistance from the programmer.)

☞ **Exercise 8-20**

In Exercises 8-17, 8-18, and 8-19, you designed some tables for representing your music collection. Examine the three tables from Exercise 8-19. Would the database be consistent if you deleted a row from the table of pieces? Would it be consistent if you deleted a row from the table of composers? The table of albums? ❏

8.4.3   Access Authorization

Any real database has many different users who fall into various groups. Each group has its own set of privileges. For example, students, instructors, and student-records staff might all be able to access data; however, students should only be able to view their own data; instructors should be able to view or enter data for students in their classes; and student-records staff should be able to access anything.

One possibility is to give people different programs. Students might run only a viewer, while instructors run a program that lets them work with class lists, and student-records staff can access or update anything. The problem with this is obvious: What happens if somebody obtains a program they aren't supposed to use?

We must therefore decide *who* gets to see *what* data, and *how* the data can be seen, and then we must include that information in the database. The "what" is a set of rows and columns. The "how" is a choice of *read* (to use as input to another

Language Profile: SQL

Early databases each had their own language. As database users became more sophisticated, they wanted a database language that was powerful, but also standard. With a standard database language, a programmer can move a program from one DBMS to another with minimal reprogramming.

One of the first relational DBMSs was built at IBM, and used a language called Sequel. This language was gradually refined and improved, and eventually became known as SQL (pronounced "sequel"), the Structured Query Language. SQL has become popular enough that virtually all sophisticated DBMSs allow its use, even if they support another (native) language such as dBASE.

SQL isn't a general-purpose language; it includes only the facilities needed to support database operations. The intention is that SQL statements are to be mixed in with regular statements in the programmer's choice of conventional language. The compiler for that language must know about SQL, and be able to handle its statements. Alternatively, most SQL DBMSs allow "dynamic SQL", in which a SQL statement is represented as a string. Some Scheme systems have been extended with interfaces that allow Scheme programmers to access a database using dynamic SQL.

The most common SQL statement is the `select` statement, which supports all of the relational operators. For example, to find out what marks student 123 obtained, we can write

```
select
    student_no, course, mark
from final_marks
where student_no = 123
```

`select` in SQL begins by describing projection! The columns named after `select` form the subset of columns that we want to appear in the final table. The selection occurs in the last line of the query: `where student_no = 123` specifies the rows that are selected.

SQL also supports join. If we want to build a table of final grades, we can write

```
select
    student_no, name, course, mark
from students, final_marks
where students.student_no = final_marks.student_no
```

SQL provides facilities to manage tables, to grant or revoke privileges, and to ensure the consistency of the tables. When used with a programming language, it supports all the operations needed to access or update information in one or more tables.

Because SQL is intended to work with languages like COBOL, in which procedures aren't first-class, it has no direct counterpart to `table-for-each-row`. Instead, the programmer can create a "cursor" that identifies a specific row of a table, and advance this cursor to scan through the table.

Most DBMSs support SQL, either built-in, or as an extra-cost option. Unfortunately, the standard for SQL omits several important features. DBMS vendors have therefore extended it in various incompatible ways, ruining the chance of writing portable code that uses SQL. However, a new standard, at present under development, will make DBMSs more compatible.

table), *write*, or *view*. Sometimes, we might give access to summary information but not to the detailed rows; in a census application, for example, users might be able to see average income for a census tract (a region of a city) but not for individual households.

What about the "who"? We must give each user an account, and require that users prove their right to use that account. The most common way is with a **password** known only to the user, who can provide it to prove her identity to the system. More complicated systems, such as access cards for Automated Teller Machines, can also be used.

Hot views (tables that are constructed dynamically by evaluating a DBScheme form) are an excellent way of controlling access. For example, users may be given no direct access to a table of employees, but may be given read-only access to a hot view that provides name and office location. Authorized users (e.g., management and payroll) may have access to the table itself.

Case Study: Client-Server Computing

The code presented in this section can be found in file `dbscmcli.scm`.

One of the most convenient ways to use a database is to store the data on a central computer, and allow programs access the database over a network. For example, if Turing College puts a satellite campus in another city, it can connect the satellite with the main campus via a leased line. Student-records clerks at the satellite can use desktop computers to access the database.

Such a design requires that we do as much work as we can on the desktop computer, and as little as possible on the central computer. Otherwise, we are likely to overload the central computer. We want to let it manage the database, and run all the applications on the desktop machines. When a program needs access to the database, it formulates a request to the database software on the central computer. Many large computers, especially mainframes, are optimized to run database software. For example, IBM mainframes use various clever tricks to get data from a disk drive to the computer as quickly as possible. The approach we are suggesting lets us use the mainframe to manage databases, while running the actual application on a desktop machine.

This approach is called *client/server computing*. We run the database software as a **server** that listens to the network, waits for a command, carries it out, and sends a reply back to the requestor. The software on the desktop machine is called a client; it makes network requests to obtain data. The server can support many clients since most of the time the clients are not accessing the database.

We will build a basic user interface package for our student records system. Our package will let us enter a command; it then formulates a request to the server and the result is a table that the client can print out. We leave it to you to replace our user interface with a GUI.

```
student->(find-student 123)
student-no  name        phone
----------  ----------  ----------
123         Smith, W.   555-1204
```

```
student->(find-student 100)
student-no  name        phone
----------  ----------  ----------
```

How should the client and server communicate? One possibility is SQL, but there is a better solution—BScheme forms. We can build a DBScheme form and send it over the network. The server will process the form and send back a table as a result. The client can do what it wants with the result, including, of course, printing it. Our client program, therefore, can concentrate on the needs of the user.

Our DBMS, running on the central computer, must therefore allow us to send it DBScheme forms, and must contain an evaluator. We could use self-eval to model this system, but that is too cumbersome to be practical. Fortunately, most Scheme systems provide a primitive procedure named eval,[14] which behaves similarly to self-eval, but much more efficiently.

Our client code is thus quite straightforward. The top level prompts for a command and then executes it, as shown in Program 8-14.

```
(define command-loop
  (lambda ()
    (display "student->")
    (let
      ((cmd (read)))
      (if (eqv? cmd 'stop)
        "Bye"
        (begin
          (let
            ((result (do-command cmd)))
            (if (not (eqv? result 'failure))
              (table-print result 'student-no compare-numbers)))
          (command-loop))))))
```

Program 8-14   Top-level of records system

do-command is a case on the type of command, as shown in Program 8-15.

Finally, the two procedures that carry out commands must build a DBScheme query and send it out over the network; they are shown in Program 8-16.

The final stage is send-to-network. Our version will just use stub procedures. It wouldn't require too many lines of code to use a network in the process, and many Scheme systems support the network primitives needed to do this. For our purposes, though, we'll just evaluate the form. Before doing so, we'll display the DBScheme form, so we can see what the program is doing.

```
(define send-to-network
  (lambda (command)
    (format #t "sending ~a~%" command)
    (eval command)))
```

---

[14] The current Scheme standard, defined in R^4RS, does not include eval, but most implementations do. It computes the value of the form that is its argument, in the global context. R^5RS will include eval.

```
(define do-command
  (lambda (cmd)
    (if (or (null? cmd) (not (pair? cmd)))
      (begin
        (display "Invalid command: ")
        (display cmd)
        (newline)
        'failure)
      (case (car cmd)
        ((find-student)
         (search-for-student (car (cdr cmd))))
        ((add-mark)
         (add-mark (cdr cmd)))
        (else
         (display "Invalid command: ")
         (display cmd)
         (newline)
         'failure)))))
```

Program 8-15   Command handling in records system

We can now try out our program.

```
> (command-loop)
student->(find-student 123)
sending:(table-select students (quote student-no) = (quote 123))
student-no  name        phone
----------  ----------  ----------
123         Smith, W.   555-1204
student->(find-student 100)
sending:(table-select students (quote student-no) = (quote 100))
student-no  name        phone
----------  ----------  ----------
student->stop
```

```
(define search-for-student
  (lambda (s-no)
    (send-to-network
      (list
        'table-select
        'students
        ''student-no
        '=
        (list 'quote s-no)))))
(define add-mark
  (lambda (mark-info)
    (let
      ((s-no (car mark-info))
       (course (car (cdr mark-info)))
       (mark (car (cdr (cdr mark-info)))))
      (send-to-network
        (list
          'table-add-rows!
          'final-marks
          (list
            'list
            (list
              'list
              (list 'cons ''student-no (list 'quote s-no))
              (list 'cons ''course (list 'quote course))
              (list 'cons ''mark (list 'quote mark))))))
      (send-to-network
        (list
          'table-select
          'final-marks
          ''student-no
          '=
          (list 'quote s-no))))))
```

Program 8-16   Query creation in records system

Summary

This chapter has introduced the relational model for databases, including the three relational operators: select, project, and join. Several types of queries were answered on a range of tables, using the relational operators. Then the chapter described DB-Scheme, a relational database language embedded in Scheme. After showing the use of the relational operators in DBScheme, the chapter implemented DBScheme and tables in Scheme, showing the full implementation of the three relational operators. Finally, we returned to database design with several goals in mind, primarily that of reducing the chance of errors in the data.

Further Readings

A good general introduction to databases is C. J. Date, *Database: A Primer*.

You may wish to experiment with a commercial database system. Two powerful DBMSs in wide use at present are Microsoft's Access and Borland's Paradox. Because of the rapid rate of change of these systems, we are unable to recommend books on these systems: a book may be published and go out of print within a year. Check with your local bookstore.

The following books on databases are fairly advanced: C. J. Date, *An Introduction to Database Systems*, Volume 1, Fifth Ed.; H. F. Korth and A. Silberschatz, *Database System Concepts*; and J. D. Ullman, *Principles of Database Systems*.

The following books on systems analysis show methods for designing database applications in a business environment: A. L. Eliason, *Systems Development: Application, Design, and Implementation*; M. J. Powers, D. R. Adams, and H. D. Mills, *Computer Information Systems Development: Analysis and Design*; and J. L. Whitten, L. D. Bentley, and T. I. Ho., *Systems Analysis and Design Methods*. 1986).

The Social Impact of Computers by R. S. Rosenberg provides a perspective on the use and abuse of information technology.

Key Words

Here are the *key words* introduced in this chapter. Make sure you understand what each one means.

audit trail	First Normal Form	query optimization
block	functionally dependent	record structure
buffer	hot view	referential integrity
cell	insertion sort	relational operations
client	join	row
column	layout	Second Normal Form
comparator	logical structure	security
cross-matching	merge	selection
database	normal forms	server
database description	normalizing	sort
database layer	password	table
database management	persistent data	Third Normal Form
system (DBMS)	physical structure	type check
data dictionary	plausibility	validation
data editing	privacy	validity
field	projection	

Problems

1. Write down, informally, a portion (just this chapter) of the table that describes the contents of the chapters of this book.

2. A database has been constructed from information from the central room-booking agency on campus. The following two tables, Courses and Rooms, are being used. (H is used for Thursday.)

room	time	course-name
13	MWF 8:30	Prin CS
85	TH 9:30	Prin CS II
90	TH 16:30	Intr to Phys
25	TH 16:30	Intro Psych
13	MWF 8:30	English Lit

Room	Seats	Building
13	200	CSCI
25	35	HENN
85	100	KENN
90	26	BUCH

Rumor has it that there are several courses with more than 150 students in them that have booked into the same room at the same time. A clerk in the booking office wants to determine if any of these conflicts occur in the MWF 8:30 time slot.

Write a DBScheme form that displays the course-names, building code, and room number for all courses with more than 150 students that take place during the MWF 8:30 time slot. The output of the query should be sorted so that anyone can easily determine which courses are in conflict. You may assume the existence of any compare functions you need, but write down a brief (one sentence) English description of any such function indicating what it compares.

3. Write a DBScheme form to create the table in problem 1.

4. Refer back to the `flights` and `passengers` tables from Section 8.1. We asked, "Where is passenger Wilson ticketed to on January 24?" Write DBScheme forms to answer that query, given that the tables are named `flights` and `passengers`.

5. Write DBScheme forms to answer the query, "Which passengers are departing from Boston?"

6. You are writing a library circulation system. Show two tables that we could join to produce a list of borrowers who have taken books out.

7. Our `merge-strategy` code is less than beautiful. The section where layouts are being combined uses

   ```
   (for-each ... (set! ...) ... lo2)
   ```

   Rewrite that code to use a more functional style of programming.

8. Are the tables in the previous question in 3NF? Why or why not?

Self-Assessment

1. Suppose we are building a database of information about courses and departments, using information from the University Calendar. We might have two tables, as follows:

dept	courses	course-name
CPSC	124	Prin CS I
CPSC	126	Prin CS II
PHYS	120	Intr to Phys
PSYC	100	Intro Psych
ENGL	100	English Lit

dept	dept-name	bldg
CPSC	Computer Science	CSCI
PHYS	Physics	HENN
PSYC	Psychology	KENN
ENGL	English	BUCH

Write a DBScheme form that displays the name of the department that offers the course named `Prin CS II`.

2. Suppose we have a database of information about cars. We might have two tables:

make	model	fuel-economy
Firb	Rolo	7.1
Zip	Dood	18.3
Zip	Hog	22.1
Wow	Dog	14.1
Fud	Ding100	91.

make	name	sales
Firb	Fir Bunyan	4
Zip	Zaphod	1
Wow	Wo Waon	2
Fud	Frod	3

Write a DBScheme form that displays the name of the company that sells the car with the model name `Hog`.

3. Suppose that Cyclone Taylor, Inc. (CTI) wants to keep track of its hockey stick inventory. The store buys sticks from various suppliers; each stick has a type that depends on the player who endorses the stick. CTI wants to be able to record information like the following: "We have 17 sticks of type "Mario Lemieux", whose handedness is left; the supplier is CCM".

     a. Show a layout that would be appropriate for a database table recording this information.

     b. Which field or fields appear(s) to be a key?

     c. Explain why it would not be sensible to index on the "number of sticks in stock" attribute.

4. Suppose you are building a table to contain data about countries, including the name of the capital city, and the total population. Write a `make-table` form, including validity checkers, to create this table. Is it possible to create a validator that prevents a row for an incorrect country, for example, the Untied Kingdome of Grate Britayn and Northurn Iceland, being added? If so, show how.

5. Suppose we have a table with *n* rows and *c* columns. How many rows and columns will be in the result if we
     a. select from it?
     b. project it?

6. We are joining two tables, of size *m* and *n* rows, respectively, on a column that is a key in both of the tables. What is the maximum number of possible rows in the resulting table?

7. You are building a library circulation system that tracks books that have been borrowed. For our purposes, each book has an *accession number*, which uniquely identifies a particular book. (If the library has several copies of the same book, they will have different accession numbers.) Show a set of tables in 3NF that would be useful in this problem.

Programming Problems

1. We talked about producing a table of student averages, to collapse a number of related rows in the input table into one output table. How could we build a new DBScheme procedure to perform the operations that we implemented with `table-add-rows!`?

2. Nested selection operations have the effect of `and`ing together the selection criteria. The way `table-select` has been implemented, only one selection criterion is specified per call. To avoid having to nest selections, implement `table-select` so that it accepts one or more criteria. Noting the similarity between selection and filtering, return to Chapter 4 for ideas on how to combine the results of Boolean operations. Each criterion can be interpreted as a Boolean operation, where `equal-to` is interpreted as `true`, and anything else is `false`.

Chapter 9

Data Structures and Algorithms

Overview

This chapter explores more deeply the topic of data structures, the data representations that implement abstract data types. It concentrates on analysis of the data structures, both in the average and worst cases, and on choosing efficient implementations. We reexamine list structures to understand the complexity of adding and removing items at both the head and tail of lists. We have used searching and sorting in many applications, from dictionaries to environments to databases, but without great concern for efficiency. Here we learn how to implement binary search trees to speed up search. Search trees let us see how to build sorting procedures, but we develop a more practical sorting procedure: Quicksort. Quicksort is explained in terms of list processing, but a new Scheme data type, *vectors*, leads to a more efficient implementation. We extend our range of data structures to include stacks and queues, and see how both are used in a graphics language and an inventory system.

Good order is the foundation of all good things.
> — Edmund Burke, "The Reflections on the Revolution in France"

In a sense, any computing problem can be solved in a few pages of code. We built a Scheme evaluator and a database system each in a few hundred lines of code, for example, yet real Scheme systems consist of perhaps twenty to fifty thousand lines of code, and a production database system might include as much as a million lines.

In part, our systems suffer from not handling user errors and exceptional cases. We have either ignored the question of error-handling, or we have done something rather too drastic. The major portion of many real programs is concerned with handling exceptional cases; only a small fraction of the code is related to the actual problem.

In part, though, our systems are based upon extremely primitive data structures. To be useful, a database system must manage complex collections of data on disk, and must retrieve information promptly. Our system, with its $O(n)$ searching algorithm and $O(n^2)$ sorting algorithm, is useless for any practical application. Even if we could achieve a thousandfold improvement in the rate of comparisons, sorting a million-element table would still be too slow to be of any use.

It is often said that the hardest part of designing many programs is finding the right data structure. We already know how procedural and data abstraction allow us to design a program independently of the data structure, but we must still implement that data structure.

Algorithms and data structures are intimately related. Many data structures can be used to implement a given abstraction, but different data structures have different speed and memory requirements. The choice of data structure to implement an algorithm can have striking effects upon the performance of a program.

Thus far, we've designed data structures to solve particular problems. Periodically, we specified an ADT such as dictionary, or introduced a class of data structures such as trees. What remains is to examine some of the data structures that are useful in a wide range of problems. The principles we will discover will stand you in good stead when you design your own data structures.

9.1   Complexity Revisited

Some of the most useful algorithms we've seen are the list-processing procedures such as `reverse` and `append`. We've used these procedures as basic building blocks in our programs. We can analyze the costs of using them.

`reverse` is central to many programs we've written. Program 9-1 (a) shows a tail-recursive implementation of `reverse`. To reverse a list of length n, it calls its helper n times, doing n conses. Thus, the total time and space requirements are $O(n)$.

```
(define reverse%
  (lambda (1)
    (letrec
      ((helper
         (lambda (in out)
           (if (null? in)
               out
               (helper (cdr in) (cons (car in) out)))))))
      (helper 1 '()))))
                        (a) Tail-recursive version
(define a-reverse
  (lambda (1)
    (if (null? 1)
        '()
        (append (a-reverse (cdr 1)) (list (car 1)))))))
                        (b) reverse using append
```

Program 9-1   Implementing reverse

Instead of using a tail-recursive approach, we might be tempted to use `append` to take elements from the beginning of the list and put them at the end of the recursive result. The more obvious recursive version is shown in Program 9-1 (b). Even though this code is much simpler, it is fatally flawed. As we saw in Chapter 4, `append` takes $O(n)$ time. Because `a-reverse` calls itself n times, the total time for `a-reverse` is $O(n^2)$. Using `append` here produces simple, but very expensive code. Even more problematic is the fact that `append` copies its first argument, so there will be $O(n^2)$ useless pairs created during `a-reverse`. Mutation wouldn't help speed up `a-reverse`, either. `append!` doesn't create any new pairs, but it still steps down the input list, so `a-reverse` using `append!` would still have time complexity $O(n^2)$.

How can we insert items at the end of a list without cdring down the list in $O(n)$ time? If we remember the last pair in the list, then we have a handle on the end of the list. An easy way to remember the last pair of the list is to maintain an extra pair whose car identifies the front of the list, and whose cdr identifies the back. Either both the car and cdr of the extra pair are null, in which case the list is empty, or both are non-null, in which case the list is not empty. A list together with an additional pair used to hold the first and last pair of the list is sometimes called a **tlist**, in honor of Warren Teitelman, a legendary Lisp hacker, who added a set of procedures to a Lisp system he maintained to support this feature. Figure 9-1 shows the box-and-arrow diagram of a tlist representing (1 2 3).

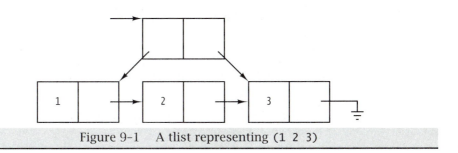

Figure 9-1   A tlist representing (1 2 3)

The code that implements tlists is shown in Program 9-2.

The time required for a tlist to add items on the left or right end of the list is independent of the length of the list. Tlists are used as follows:

```
(define t (make-tlist))
(tlist-add-left! t 'a)
(tlist->list t)⇒ (a)
(tlist-add-right! t 'b)
(tlist-add-right! t 'c)
(tlist->list t)⇒ (a b c)
(tlist-remove-right! t)⇒ c
(tlist->list t)⇒ (a b)
(tlist-remove-left! t)⇒ a
(tlist->list t)⇒ (b)
(list->tlist (list 'hello 'world))⇒ ((hello world) world)
```

Programs that use tlists begin with an empty structure and mutate the structure whenever an item is added. What have we gained by using tlists? tl-reverse reverses a list, as in a-reverse, but using tlists.

```
(define tl-reverse
  (lambda (l)
    (tlist->list (tl-reverse-help (list->tlist l)))))
(define tl-reverse-help
  (lambda (t)
    (if (tlist-empty? t)
        t
        (let ((left (tlist-remove-left! t)))
          (tlist-add-right! (tl-reverse-help t) left)
          t))))
```

This procedure has the same time and space complexity as reverse%, the tail-recursive implementation of reverse. At each step, we take the first item from the front of list t, and place it at the end of the result of reversing the rest of the list.

☞ **Exercise 9-1**

The form (tlist-append! t1 t2) is like (append! a1 a2): it mutates t1 so that the cdr

```
(module tlist-module
  (export make-tlist tlist-right tlist-left tlist-empty?
    tlist-add-left! tlist-add-right! tlist-remove-left!
    tlist-remove-right! tlist->list list->tlist)
  ;; tlist-remove-right! is left as an exercise.
  (define make-tlist
    (lambda () (cons '() '())))
  (define tlist-right (lambda (x) (car (cdr x))))
  (define tlist-left (lambda (x) (car (car x))))
  (define tlist-empty?
    (lambda (tlist)
      ;; could check either the car or the cdr.
      (null? (car tlist))))
  (define tlist->list car)
  (define list->tlist
    (lambda (x)
      (cons x (list-tail x (max 0 (sub1 (list-length x)))))))
  (define tlist-add-right!
    (lambda (tlist item)
      (let ((x (cons item '())))
        (if (tlist-empty? tlist)
          (set-car! tlist x)
          (set-cdr! (cdr tlist) x))
        (set-cdr! tlist x))))
  (define tlist-add-left!
    (lambda (tlist item)
      (let ((x (cons item (car tlist))))
        (if (tlist-empty? tlist)
          (set-cdr! tlist x))
        (set-car! tlist x))))
  (define tlist-remove-left!
    (lambda (tlist)
      (if (tlist-empty? tlist)
        (error 'tlist "Attempt to remove from empty tlist left")
        (let ((x (car tlist)))
          (set-car! tlist (cdr (car tlist)))
          (car x))))))
```

Program 9-2   Tlists

of the last pair in t1 is the first pair in t2, unless t1 is empty, when it returns t2. Write tlist-append!. ❏

What is the cost of using tlists? Each tlist requires one extra pair, compared to a list; moreover, the code for handling tlists leads to slightly more complex programs than that for using simple lists. Tlists don't *always* produce more efficient programs, as Exercise 9-2 shows.

☞ **Exercise 9-2**

Are there any tlist operations that don't take constant time? Adding to the left and right takes constant time, as does removing an element from the left. Removing an element from the right, however, requires scanning the list from the left until the pair just before the last pair is encountered. Write `tlist-remove-right!`, which removes the rightmost element from a tlist. ❏

Tlists use lists, which are biased toward cdring operations. We'd need more structure to make moving leftwards take constant time.

In a sense, tlists don't provide anything more than lists do. All of the tlist operations have list counterparts; hence it would be straightforward to write a module that provides the same interface as `tlist-module` does, but whose implementation just uses lists. The difference between the two modules is not what they do, but how quickly they do it. Thus, we can append two lists of size n in $O(n)$ time using lists or $O(1)$ time using tlists.

We have used this concept of replacing a slow algorithm with a faster one since Chapter 2. In this case, rather than look directly for a better algorithm, we found a better data structure, which in turn determined the algorithms to use. Many programs execute quickly enough that we have no incentive to hunt for better algorithms. If a program is sluggish, improving its algorithms is more likely to improve its performance than is the use of clever programming tricks or rewriting the program in a more "efficient" language.

In DBScheme, it was obvious that the sorting algorithm was a bottleneck. In order to understand what's taking time, a programmer must have a good understanding of the whole program. With a program of even a few hundred lines, it is easy to lose track of which procedures are being called frequently and why. Most programmers, therefore, rely upon software packages known as **profilers**, which keep track of the time spent in each procedure.[1] For most programs, a profiler will report that the majority of the execution time is spent in a small fraction of the code. It is useless to pick a procedure at random and attempt to optimize it. Instead, we should use the profiler output to identify time-consuming procedures that deserve optimization.

☞ **Exercise 9-3**

Suppose you profile a program and find that two procedures, a and b, account for 25% and 3% of the execution time, respectively. Discuss the effects on the total execution time of doubling the speed of a versus those of multiplying the speed of b by 10. ❏

Profilers often reveal that one of the best ways to speed up programs is to improve searching and sorting techniques. These are general problems. For example, our Scheme evaluator must search for variable names in the environment. DBScheme must search for rows to be selected, and sort data prior to a join. Computer scientists have studied these problems extensively, and have developed efficient algorithms. In the next section, we'll examine how to build data structures and algorithms that speed up searching.

---

[1] A simple profiler could be built in Scheme by tracing every procedure and writing the trace output to a file. A separate program would read the trace output file and count the number of times each procedure would be called, giving percentages. A better approximation is produced by periodically interrupting the program (say once per millisecond), and keeping track of which procedure was running each time the program was interrupted.

9.2 Searching

If we do not find anything pleasant, at least we shall find something new.
— Voltaire, *Candide*

The Scheme self-evaluator and DBScheme both search for a certain value in a list of possible values. Profiling the self-evaluator will demonstrate that it spends a great deal of its time finding the values of variables in environments. In DBScheme, `table-select` searches for rows that satisfy our requirements.

Thus far we have taken the naive approach to searching, looking at each list element in turn until we find the one we want. Program 9-3 summarizes this naive approach by showing a generalized `search` procedure that finds the first element of a list, x, satisfying a specific requirement. `search` takes four arguments:

1. a list to search
2. a predicate that tells us whether an item is the one we were looking for
3. a procedure to be executed when the search succeeds
4. a procedure to be evaluated when the search fails

```
(define search
  (lambda (choices pred? succeed fail)
    (if (null? choices)
        (fail)
        (if (pred? (car choices))
            (succeed (car choices))
            (search (cdr choices) pred? succeed fail)))))
```

Program 9-3   Procedure search

`search` is a generalization of `assv`. If the predicate handed to `search` only compared the car of each item to a given value, then `search` would really be `assv`. Since we can use any method we like to select an item, depending upon the choice of predicate procedure, `search` is more general than `assv`.

What if more than one item in the list satisfies the predicate? As soon as the `pred?` procedure returns #t for some item, it terminates with that item, so `search` returns the first item satisfying the predicate. When `search` encounters a list item that satisfies `pred?`, it returns the result of applying `succeed` to that list item. Often we just want to return the item that satisfies `pred?`, but we might also want to alter the item. Consider using an alist to implement a variable dictionary with `search`. When looking up a variable, `succeed` would just return the cdr of the successful pair; when altering a variable binding, `succeed` could mutate the cdr of the pair.

The `fail` procedure is evaluated when no item in the list satisfies the predicate. Instead of using a `fail` procedure, `search` could, upon failure, return #f like `assv` or terminate with an error. Using a `fail` procedure is much more flexible. The caller of `search` decides what should be done: return a default value, generate an error, or query the user for a value. The following code shows uses of `search`:

```
(define slist '((the . 1) (cat . 2) (in . 99) (the) (hat . rack)))
(search slist
  (lambda (w) (eqv? (car w) 'cat))
  (lambda (x) x)
  (lambda () 'not-found!))
 ⇒ (cat . 2)
(search slist
  (lambda (w) (eqv? w 'blorg))
  (lambda (x) x)
  (lambda () 'not-found!))
 ⇒ not-found!
(search slist
  (lambda (w) (eqv? (cdr w) 99))
  (lambda (x) x)
  (lambda () 'not-found!))
 ⇒ (in . 99)
```

By using eqv? on the cars of the pairs in the alist, search can implement assv.

```
(define assv%
  (lambda (symb alist)
    (search
      alist
      (lambda (w) (eqv? symb (car w)))
      (lambda (x) x)
      (lambda () #f))))
```

☞ **Exercise 9-4**

Consider the list data, defined by

```
(define data '((1 . 4) (93 . 7)
               (42 . 81) (17 . 89)))
```

  a. Write a call to search that finds the first item in data whose car and cdr add up to a number greater than 100, and returns no-luck if no such item exists.
  b. Write a call to search that finds the first item whose cdr is evenly divisible by 3 (use remainder), and generates an error if no such item exists. ❑

9.2.1 Efficiency of Searching

search is unacceptably slow for a large collection of data. Suppose you asked the telephone company for your account balance. If the company's billing software used search, the program would have to check each account record to see if it was yours. Assuming 3,000,000 accounts and a computer that can process 1,000 accounts per second, it would take 3,000 seconds (50 minutes), to check all the accounts.

How long will search take? The number of calls depends on the position of the item in the list. Thus, if the item is close to the beginning, search will be very fast; if it is toward the end, it will be very slow. To analyze the general case, we assume that the item we're looking for is equally likely to be anywhere in the list. Thus, in a list of n elements, search must examine, on average, $n/2$ elements; the number of calls will thus be $O(n)$. Why $n/2$? The element we're looking for could be at the beginning, the middle, or the end. If we average the number of calls needed to search for each value, we will get $(1 + 2 + \cdots + n)/n$, or approximately $n/2$ (so, it would only take 1500 seconds, on average, to find your account). We're assuming that we search for each element with equal probability. If we don't make that assumption, we can speed up the search process by putting the most frequently occurring elements at the front of the list. Because the number of calls in search is a linear function of n, we call this method *linear search.*

If you wanted to look up Ethelred Nordleplatt in the telephone book, you'd open it in the middle. Seeing that the top name on the page was Ferdinand Lollop, you'd turn a few pages forward, reaching Ethelred's listing after checking perhaps two or three more pages. We can search rapidly in the phone book because the information is ordered. By comparing "Nordleplatt" with the names on the middle page, we can decide whether to look in the pages in the front of the book or the back of the book. One comparison lets us eliminate half of the book.

9.2.2   Binary Search Trees

search   did the job, but it wasn't efficient. We need a method of organizing a collection of data so that we can search it efficiently.

In Chapter 7 we used trees to represent hierarchies, family trees, expressions in algebra, and computer languages. We developed procedures to traverse trees, applying a procedure to each node and recursing on the subtrees. There we allowed trees to have any number of subtrees. We defined a tree as either

- null, or
- a node, with zero or more subtrees.

Figure 9-2 shows a special kind of tree called a *binary search tree,* in which the keys are ordered to facilitate rapid searching. Each node has at most two subtrees. The keys in the nodes in the left subtree are less than the key of the root node, and the keys in the nodes in the right subtree are greater than the root node. This makes it easy to find a given key value: start at the root, and compare the key you're looking for with the root key. If they're equal, stop; if the root is greater, go to the left subtree; and if the root is less, go to the right subtree. If you do this consistently, you will either reach the key you're looking for, or you will reach a leaf, at which point you must conclude that the key isn't in the tree.[2]

More formally, a **binary search tree** or **BST** is either

1. empty, or
2. a root node containing a key, k, together with
   a. a left subtree, a BST containing only nodes with keys less than k, and
   b. a right subtree, a BST containing only nodes with keys greater than k.

This is a recursive definition, because the subtrees of a BST are themselves BSTs. The ordering of the subtrees is important: the keys in the left subtree are less than the keys in the right subtree.

---

[2] What happens if the tree isn't organized with the lesser nodes on the left and the greater ones on the right? In that case, you will not find some keys, even though they're in the tree. Suppose that Wombat had been where Bat is. In this case, a search for Wombat would have gone through Hyena, Okapi, Porpoise, Zebra, and Quahog before concluding that Wombat wasn't found.

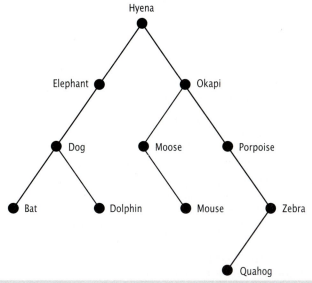

Figure 9-2   Binary search tree (BST)

You will note that this definition doesn't completely agree with what we said about nodes having at most two subtrees. According to the definition, though, a node has *exactly* two subtrees; however, a tree can be null. There is really no conflict between these two views, unless you like arguing about the difference between two kinds of nothing! Our diagrams don't show null left and right subtrees.

☞ **Exercise 9–5**

Why isn't

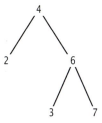

a BST? Does it contain any BST? ❏

Figure 9-3 shows an abstract data type for BSTs. We have followed the model of dictionaries in planning the interface.

9.2.3   Binary Search Tree Lookup

We will want to use a BST to get the value associated with a given key. Our strategy is to use the recursive definition. If we try to search for a key in an empty BST, we

Constructor

- (make-bst)
  Return a new BST, with no entries.

Accessors

- (bst-search *bst key*)
  Return the value *value* associated with key *key* in BST *bst*. If *key* is not present, return #f.

Mutators

- (bst-insert! *bst key value*)
  Insert the key *key* with value *value* in BST *bst*. If *key* is already present, just mutate the associated value to *value*.

Mapping procedure

- (bst-traverse *bst proc*)
  Apply *proc* to each of the nodes of *bst*. Return an undefined value (i.e., bst-traverse is like for-each, rather than map).

Predicate

- (bst-empty? *bst*)
  Return #f if *bst* has at least one entry, and #t if it is empty.

Figure 9-3   **Abstract Data Type:** binary search tree

do not find it; otherwise, we must compare the key of the node with the key we're looking for, called the *search key*. There are three cases:

1. If the two keys are equal, we can return the value.

2. If the search key is less, we must try the left subtree.

3. If the search key is greater, we must try the right subtree.

It is instructive to compare this search technique with the recursive definition of binary trees given previously. The code for bst-search appears in Program 9-4.

```
(define bst-search
  (lambda (t k)
    (if (bst-empty? t)
      #f
      (let ((k1 (bst-node-key t)))
        (if (< k k1)
          (bst-search (bst-node-left t) k)
          (if (> k k1)
            (bst-search (bst-node-right t) k)
            (bst-node-value t)))))))
```

Program 9-4   Searching a BST

Figure 9-4 shows an ADT specification for the nodes of a BST. This is the first time we've introduced an ADT that is only used internally to another ADT, but we should become accustomed to this practice. We can implement the bst-node ADT as a simple list of its elements. Accessing and setting elements is then list access and mutation.

Constructor

- (make-bst-node *key value left right*)
  Return a new BST node with key *key*, value *value*, and subtrees *left* and *right*.

Accessors

- (bst-node-key *node*)
  Return the key *key* in node *node*.
- (bst-node-value *node*)
  Return the value *value* in node *node*.
- (bst-node-left *node*)
  Return the left subtree in node *node*.
- (bst-node-right *node*)
  Return the right subtree in node *node*.

Mutators

Each of the elements x that can be accessed can be mutated by a mutator of the form set-bst-node-x!.

Figure 9-4   **Abstract Data Type:** bst-node

9.2.4   Entering an Item in a BST

Clearly, if we want to search within a BST, we must have a BST to start with. One possibility would be to build the BST beforehand as a list structure. More commonly, though, we must add an item to an already existing BST. This is, of course, an act of mutation; we must locate where the key ought to be and insert it. For example, suppose that we want to add Fox to the tree shown in Figure 9-2. We will start at Hyena, and then proceed to Elephant, and then proceed to an empty tree (stored in the element at position 3 in the list, since it's a right subtree). This empty tree must be mutated into a new BST with key Fox and empty left and right subtrees.

The mutation here is complicated by the fact that we want to start off with an empty BST, which we implement as a null list. The first node added requires us to mutate not some position in the list, but whatever variable has the empty BST as its value. This requires us to do a set! each time we enter a key:

```
(define mytree (make-bst))
(set! mytree (bst-insert! mytree 3 'three))
(set! mytree (bst-insert! mytree 5 'five))
```

and so on. This way, we don't have to treat the first node specially. Because the initial empty BST is implemented as a null list, we can't mutate that, and so must return the new node as the value of bst-insert!.

Writing bst-insert! is straightforward. We start with the same framework as bst-search, but when we reach a null node, we don't just return #f. Instead, we create a new node. The tree is mutated to contain that new node, by relying on whoever called us (probably a recursive call) to do the mutation. We can't do it ourselves, because all we have is the empty tree. We don't know where that tree belongs. The code appears in Program 9-5. The mutation is done by set-bst-node-left! and -right!.

We could have avoided the mutation at each step by implementing an empty BST as a box with special contents. Then, when we implement bst-insert!, we

```
(define bst-insert!
  (lambda (t k v)
    (if (bst-empty? t)
      (make-bst-node k v '() '())
      (let ((k1 (bst-node-key t)))
        (if (< k k1)
          (set-bst-node-left! t
            (bst-insert! (bst-node-left t) k v))
          (if (> k k1)
            (set-bst-node-right! t
              (bst-insert! (bst-node-right t) k v))
            (bst-node-value t)))
        t)))))
```

Program 9-5   Inserting a new key-value pair in a BST

need to extract the contents of the box before we handle the node, as shown in Program 9-6.

```
(define make-bst
  (lambda () (make-box '()))))
(define box-bst-insert!
  (lambda (t k v)
    (if (bst-empty? t)
      (bst-set-node! t (make-bst-node k v (make-bst) (make-bst)))
      (let*
        ((node (box-ref t))
         (k1 (bst-node-key node)))
        (if (< k k1)
          (box-bst-insert! (bst-node-left node) k v)
          (if (> k k1)
            (box-bst-insert! (bst-node-right node) k v)
            (bst-node-value node)))))))
```

Program 9-6   Procedure `bst-insert!` using boxes

Now you needn't treat the top node specially:

```
(define mytree (make-bst))
(box-bst-insert! mytree 3 'three)
```

We are faced with another trade-off. To avoid mutation, we must add another level of data structure, the boxes to hold the nodes, and the code becomes slightly more complicated. We chose our original implementation because it's simpler, at the cost of handling the mutation at the root node.

☞ **Exercise 9-6**

Show the binary search tree built by inserting the keys 13, 22, 16, 10, and 12, in that order, into an initially empty binary search tree.

a. Draw it as a graph. b. Display it as a list. ❏

☞ **Exercise 9–7**

Implement a dictionary using BSTs, recalling that we originally implemented dictionaries using boxes in Chapter 5. ❏

☞ **Exercise 9–8**

Give a sequence of 11 keys, which if inserted in the order given, into an initially empty binary search tree, will produce a perfectly balanced tree; that is, each node has two subtrees except for the leaves. ❏

☞ **Exercise 9–9**

Give a sequence of 11 keys, which if inserted in the order given, into an initially empty binary search tree, will produce a tree with a perfect upside-down **V** shape. That is, if you start at the root and visit only the left nodes on the left subtree of the root, and then visit only the right nodes on the right subtree of the root, you will have visited every node. ❏

9.2.5 Efficiency

The whole point of BSTs was to make it possible to search efficiently. Has that goal been met? Consider a BST with 24 levels. Each time, we split into two subtrees. If we do that 24 times, our tree will have $2^{24} - 1 = 16777215$ nodes, yet 24 comparisons/recursive calls will take only a small fraction of a second.

To understand the efficiency of BSTs, we need to describe how many comparisons we use in finding a node in the BST. In a well-structured BST with n nodes, the number of nodes on the path between the root and the farthest leaf is $\lg n$. That's why we only need 24 comparisons to reach the farthest leaf in a (good) BST with $2^{24} - 1 = 16777215$ nodes. The expression $\lg n$ is the worst-case number of comparisons, because that's the maximum number necessary to reach a leaf, where we either encounter the key we're looking for or determine that it is not in the BST. To analyze the time or space complexity of an algorithm whose performance depends not just on the number of items, but also on the particular values of the items, we look at the performance in the worst case.

We measure the time required for searching and sorting by the number of comparisons. Many other operations are involved in our searching programs, but we use comparisons because their number depends on the order in which the data appears, the fundamental variant in searching and sorting. Because our data is ordered, each comparison narrows the area of search and makes progress toward the solution. Each cycle involves other operations, but the fundamental step is the comparison, justifying our identification of comparisons with time. However, when we compare two algorithms that make comparisons in the same order for the same data, the algorithm with simpler steps will have better time complexity (e.g., $2n$ as opposed to $5n$). Both are asymptotically the same; that is, they are both $O(n)$, but the algorithm with the smaller constant multiplier is clearly better.

The fact that the tree splits in half each time is fundamental to achieving logarithmic performance. Unfortunately, the order in which we insert keys makes a huge difference. Suppose we were building a tree with keys 1, 2, 3, . . . , 100. If we inserted 50 first, then 25 and 75, and so on, we would have a tree with about 7 levels. If, on the other hand, we inserted the keys in order (1, 2, and so on), our tree would have 100 levels.

There are techniques, beyond the scope of this book, for ensuring that the number of levels remains approximately logarithmic in the number of nodes. These techniques (AVL trees, 2-3 trees) rearrange the nodes of the tree during its construction, so that the length of the path from the root to the farthest leaf doesn't grow too quickly. From now on, when we talk about the performance of BSTs, we will assume that we are using one of these balancing techniques to ensure that the worst-case performance remains $O(\lg n)$.

9.2.6   Traversing a Binary Search Tree

Binary search trees have one more great virtue: it is possible to go through a BST in order by key. `bst-traverse` steps through the nodes in a BST (Program 9-7).

```
(define bst-traverse
  (lambda (tree proc)
    (if (not (bst-empty? tree))
      (begin
        (bst-traverse (bst-node-left tree) proc)
        (proc (bst-node-key tree) (bst-node-value tree))
        (bst-traverse (bst-node-right tree) proc)))))
```

Program 9-7   BST traversal

`bst-traverse` takes a tree and a procedure as arguments. If the tree is null, `bst-traverse` does nothing at all. If the tree is non-null, however, then `bst-traverse` recurses on the left and right subtrees, applying the procedure to the key and value of the current node in between. For example, suppose we evaluate

```
(bst-traverse mytree
  (lambda (k v) (format #t "My key and value are ~a and ~a~%" k v)))
```

where `mytree` is bound to the tree

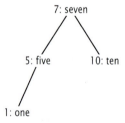

The key and value fields are separated by a colon. The output will be

```
My key and value are 1 and one
My key and value are 5 and five
My key and value are 7 and seven
My key and value are 10 and ten
```

Why does `bst-traverse` work? First, let's convince ourselves that it visits all the nodes in the tree. Recall our definition of a BST: either it is null, or it contains a root node and a left and a right sub-BST. A null tree has no nodes, and therefore produces no output. bst-traverse does nothing when the tree is null. For a tree that is not null, we must traverse both subtrees to visit their nodes, and also call the procedure given by the proc parameter for the root node. bst-traverse in fact recurses on both subtrees.

You may be puzzled about how bst-traverse "gets back" to the root node after traversing the left subtree. By the time we get to the node with key 1, we have three nested frames, each with a different binding of tree.[3] The recursive call to bst-traverse for the left subtree of that node causes a fourth frame to be created, in which tree is bound to the null list. The snapshot at this point appears in Figure 9–5. The fourth frame is immediately thrown away, since a null tree causes bst-traverse to return immediately. When it returns, control passes to the previous frame. But which frame is the previous frame? The dynamic link in the frame indicates the new active frame. Figure 9–5 shows the dynamic links connecting the frames that Scheme generates as it steps down the left branches of the tree. The dynamic links mirror the left branches of the tree.

You may be prepared to accept that bst-traverse actually does visit all the nodes. But why does it visit them in order? Consider any node in the tree: bst-traverse processes all nodes in its left subtree before it, so all nodes with keys less than its key are processed before bst-traverse applies proc to its key and value. Likewise, bst-traverse processes all nodes in its right subtree after it, so all nodes with keys greater than its key are processed after it. Hence all nodes are processed in increasing order of their keys. bst-traverse performs an **in-order** traversal of the nodes in the BST.

Standard practice defines two kinds of tree traversal: pre-order traversal, where the node is processed before the left and right subtrees, and post-order traversal, where the left and right trees are processed before the node. The exercises and problems ask you to write procedures to traverse trees in these ways.

There is little or no value in pre-order or post-order traversals of BSTs, but other kinds of trees can usefully be processed in pre-order or post-order. For example, a Scheme evaluator can be regarded as doing a post-order traversal of the tree that represents the form to be evaluated.

☞ **Exercise 9–10**

Write pre-order, a binary tree-traversal procedure. Describe the output produced by

```
> (pre-order mytree
     (lambda (k v) (format #t "My key and value are ~a and ~a~%" k v)))
```

❏

---

[3] Each of these frames also has a binding for proc, but all these bindings have the same value.

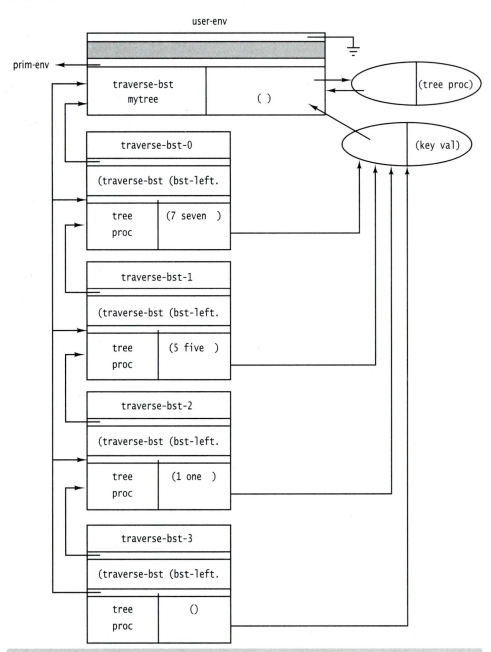

Figure 9-5   Snapshot of `bst-traverse`: at end of left branch

9.2.7 Indexing in DBScheme

One of the problems in designing efficient DBMSs is rapid access to the rows of the DBMS. Many databases have indexes, data structures that let the database access items rapidly, usually based on an ordering. The basic idea is straightforward: along with the table, we store a BST that gets us to particular rows quickly. Assume that we have the table shown in Figure 9-6, and suppose we decide that `number` should be a key. In this case, we can build a BST in which the numbers are keys and the corresponding rows are the values. Using the BST, we can access selected rows in logarithmic time.

number	name
5	funf
7	sieben
12	zwolf
20	zwanzig

Figure 9-6   A table that can be indexed

It is important to understand that when we make a row a value, we're not making a copy of the row. Instead, the same row pairs are found both in the table and in the BST. This means that if we mutate a row field (e.g., with `update`), accessing the row via the index will give us the new field value. Why? Because the same pairs are used regardless of whether we started off from the table or from the tree.

A box-and-arrow diagram is helpful in understanding complex structures such as this. We've shown part of the structure in Figure 9-7. It uses two main kinds of lists: the four-element lists are the tree nodes, and the two-element lists are the table rows (because this table has two columns). In addition, the `rowpack` data structure from Chapter 8 is built with a list of rows. To access a row, we can follow the list of rows, which is known as **sequential retrieval**. Alternatively, we can search for a key in the tree, and then use the `value` element of the node to reach the row.

We can modify `table-select` so that it checks whether it's selecting on the key field. If so, it uses the index. Otherwise, it works as before, checking every row. We can access any row in a table, via the index, in $O(\lg n)$ calls, assuming that there are n rows. In a table with 1,000,000 rows, using the index, we can find any row in about 20 calls. We can still do "sequential" processing on the table. This will take $O(n)$ calls, but that's necessary, when we want to process every row.

One common application would be to use the index field as the inquiry field. For example, in a customer-account application, we would index on the account-number field. A customer who wanted to find his balance would give the account number and get a speedy reply. On the other hand, each month the store would want to produce bills. Listing each call, obviously, means that each row must be processed. We actually have a choice about the order for processing the rows. We could scan the table, the way `table-print` does, or we could traverse the index. Since the table might be in a pretty random order, but the index can be traversed in key order, it seems reasonable to choose index traversal.

A table can have more than one index. For example, note that the `name` fields in Figure 9-6 are also unique. We can therefore add a second BST that indexes the `name` field, which allows us to retrieve quickly on either `name` or `number` values.

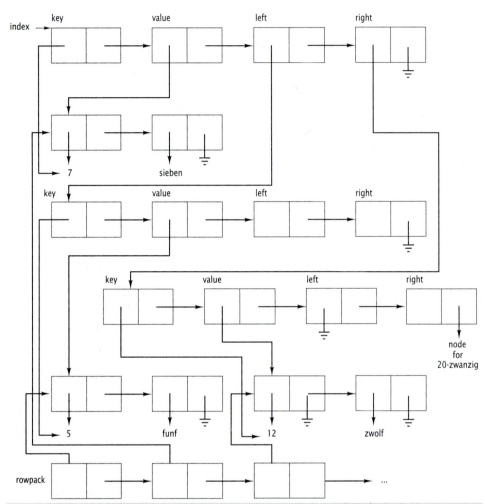

Figure 9-7   Part of the BST index for the number-German table

We can even index fields that are not key fields. For example, suppose that a store wants to build an index of its account table on the customer's name. Names aren't unique; in a large city, there might be dozens of people named Septimius Glorpwangel. We index on a nonunique field by having the value be not the row in question, but a list of all the applicable rows instead. When a customer appears at the store, either account number or name may be used. If the customer provides her name, the clerk will see a collection of rows, and can ask for additional information (e.g., home address) in order to narrow down the inquiry.

Indexing improves retrieval so much that some people are tempted to index every field in a table, but this approach wastes time and space. Additional space must be set aside for the indexes. Also, each time a row is inserted or deleted all of the indexes must be updated. In most databases, programmers index the frequently occurring fields, and leave the others unindexed. Rarely occurring queries will therefore require a sequential search, but we assume that such queries are so infrequent that we don't care.

In Chapter 8, we mentioned query optimization, a set of techniques that allow a DBMS to plan how to answer a complex query. Such a query examines more than one column in a table; for example, "Find all customers whose last name is Smith and whose balance is greater than $100." We might index a customer table on last name, but we would not index on balance. There are two ways to answer this query. We could search the entire table, or use the last-name index to find Smiths, and then search this much smaller table for customers with a large balance. Alternatively, we could search the entire table for customers with large balances, and then search this much smaller table for Smiths. In this example, the first solution is obviously much more efficient than the second, but often the choice isn't as clear. Much of the complexity of real DBMSs is due to the sophistication of their query optimizers.

The implementation of indexes need not be visible to the user of `select-table`. We add the indexes to the layout of the table; `select-table` then checks whether it's working on an indexed field. If so, it uses the index; otherwise, it uses a sequential search.

You might be worried about the disaster that would occur if we didn't keep the index tree balanced. In fact, with the BST algorithms we've studied, an unbalanced tree is quite likely. If the table was originally in sorted order, `bst-insert!` will produce a "pessimal" tree (one that is as bad as possible). Balancing techniques are used in real indexes to prevent this problem. Because of this and the issue of memory management, the indexing algorithms needed for large tables are beyond the scope of this book.

9.3   Sorting

> *'It's a poor sort of memory that only works backwards,' the Queen remarked.*
> — Lewis Carroll, "Alice Through the Looking Glass"

Probably the most important task in computing is that of arranging data in some order. Sorting is critical for one of the fundamental relational database operators, `table-join`. A naive implementation of the join operation would simply search the entire second table for every row in the first table. This means that if the first table has m rows and the second has n, the naive implementation must examine $m \times n$ combinations of rows. We could have built a special $O(mn)$ join routine, but we already needed to be able to sort tables, in the DBMS, for printing. After sorting the two tables, we only needed an efficient merge procedure. However, the $O(n^2)$ sorting method we used in Chapter 8 is too time-consuming to be practical. We therefore need to find some better sorting algorithms.

9.3.1   Treesort

We already have one data structure that organizes data by key values: the BST. Why not insert the list elements into a binary search tree, and then traverse the tree to get the keys? Using a BST in this way gives us the algorithm Treesort, which builds a BST with the keys. (The values are unused.) Treesort then traverses the BST, putting the keys in a list. Program 9-8 shows `treesort`, a sorting procedure that uses a BST to sort a list. Evaluating

    (treesort '(12 10 15 11 17 13 18 14 10 19))

builds the BST shown in Figure 9-8.

```
(define treesort
  (lambda (x)
    (let
      ((tree '())
       (newlist '()))
      (for-each
        (lambda (y) (set! tree (bst-insert! tree y '())))
        x)
      (bst-traverse tree
        (lambda (k v) (set! newlist (cons k newlist))))
      (reverse newlist))))
```

Program 9-8   Treesort

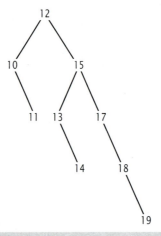

Figure 9-8   The BST made by (treesort '(12 10 15 11 17 13 18 14 10 19))

Unfortunately, there are two serious problems with Treesort:

1. Duplicate keys are quietly deleted from the tree. This could be fixed by having the value be the number of times a given key occurs, or (even better, since we may be doing the sorting on only part of a key), a list of the actual items.

2. Making a BST uses space that isn't needed in the resulting sorted list, so it is both costly and unnecessary.

On the other hand, Treesort is very fast.

- Each insertion into the tree takes $O(\lg n)$ time (provided a balancing technique is used).

- Inserting n items into the tree takes $O(n \lg n)$.[4]
- Tree traversal takes $O(n)$ operations, as does reversal.

Putting this all together, we see that the total time will be $O(n \lg n)$.

How much faster is Treesort than insertion sort? Consider a list with 10,000 elements. Insertion sort will take on the order of 100 million operations, whereas Treesort will take about $10000 \times \lg 10000$, or about $135,000$ operations. Assuming one operation per microsecond, Treesort will take about 0.135 seconds, whereas insertion sort will take about 100 seconds (nearly 2 minutes). Ideally, it should be possible to sort a large list without making any additional pairs (i.e., that we sort the list by mutation).

☞ **Exercise 9-11**

`treesort` conses the keys during in-order traversal onto the front of a list, and then returns the reverse of the list. We could also write `treesort` by appending new cells onto the end of the list during traversal, and avoid reversing the result list. Compare the number of conses for each of these two implementations. ❏

9.3.2 Quicksort

Quicksort is an algorithm developed by the British computer scientist C. A. R. Hoare, and published in 1960. Quicksort enjoys a number of distinctions:

1. On average, it is one of the fastest known general sorting algorithms.
2. It was the first widely published recursive algorithm.
3. It was one of the first algorithms to be proven correct, using a method developed by Hoare.

Hoare, then a programmer with English Electric, Ltd., was assigned the task of writing a sort subroutine for a new computer system. He produced a program that neither he nor anyone else could really understand, but which sorted data incredibly quickly. Then a colleague suggested he rewrite the program in a new language, ALGOL 60, for publication. Merely by applying principles of recursion, he was able to simplify the program so that it was understandable and clear.

A simplified version of Quicksort is shown in Program 9-9.

```
(define quicksort
  (lambda (x)
    (let ((smaller '())
          (larger '()))
      (put-items-into-either-smaller-or-larger)
      (append (quicksort smaller) (quicksort larger)))))
```

Program 9-9 Pseudocode for Quicksort

Quicksort separates small and large elements into two separate lists, `smaller` and `larger`. This operation, called **partitioning**, divides the original list of n elements

---

[4] Each insertion makes the tree bigger, so in fact the earlier insertions don't take as long as the later ones do. This fact doesn't alter our results, thanks to the magic of big-oh notation.

into two sublists, each with about $n/2$ elements. Quicksort then recursively sorts the two lists and joins the returned sorted lists.

Whether `quicksort` is an efficient sorting procedure depends upon the partitioning method (the procedure `put-items-into-either-smaller-or-larger`). If we can partition input of size n in $O(n)$ time, and if the lists `smaller` and `larger` each have approximately $n/2$ elements, then we will need about $\lg n$ "layers" of recursive calls for Quicksort to sort the list.

The following example demonstrates what is meant by *layer*.

```
          (2 1 101 100 11 10 201 200)
      (2 1 11 10)                 (101 100 201 200)
   (2 1)     (11 10)       (101 100)        (201 200)
 (1)   (2)   (10)   (11)  (100)   (101)   (200)   (201)
```

Each layer is a reading of this tree of lists along one level. If the total time to partition a list is $O(m)$, where m is the number of elements in the list, then the total time for partitioning all of the lists on a given layer is $O(n)$ (i.e., the total number of items on any layer remains the same over all layers). Since there are $\lg n$ layers, the total time for the entire Quicksort is $O(n \lg n)$. Can you spot the unspoken assumption?

You might object that the `append` calls will change things. `append` is an expensive operation ($O(n)$ time), but it doesn't change the total $O(n \lg n)$ running time. We could get by without doing the `append`, but that would clutter up the code to the point that it became unreadable. Our explanation of Quicksort ignores the fact that we are creating a new list structure at each step.

We can sort in $O(n \lg n)$ time, but only if we can find an $O(n)$ partitioning method, and if this method produces two halves that are roughly the same size. The effectiveness of any partitioning method depends upon what we mean by *small* and *large*. Obviously, the definition of these terms depends upon the data at hand. For example, 97 is an extremely large value for a student's mark, but an extremely small value for a car's odometer reading.

Hoare's key idea was to choose one of the items to be partitioned as a **pivot**.[5] Anything less than the pivot is considered small, and anything larger than the pivot is considered large. For example, if Quicksort is partitioning the list (20 17 35 12 21 19) using the first element, 20, as a pivot, then the small elements would be (17 12 19), and the large ones would be (35 21). The pivot itself must be in neither of the resulting partitions. If we put it with the larger elements, then what happens if the pivot is the smallest item in the list? Figure 9-9 shows the results with input (1 2 3 4 5 6) and pivot 1. All of the original list items then go into the large list, and Quicksort handles the original list recursively. This is an infinite loop. A similar objection can be raised to putting the pivot into the smaller list.

Accordingly, we will have *three* lists:

1. those items smaller than the pivot
2. those items larger than the pivot
3. those items equal to the pivot. (This list will contain only one item, unless the pivot value is repeated in the original list.)

Quicksort is shown in Program 9-10. It uses a comparator procedure such as `compare-numbers`, from Chapter 8. A comparator returns one of three symbols, `less-than`, `equal-to`, or `greater-than`, depending upon the values of its arguments.

---

[5] We are not using Hoare's original pivoting technique, but an easier-to-understand method developed by Jon Bentley. (See the Further Readings for this chapter for a reference.)

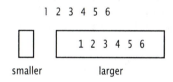

Figure 9-9   An incorrect partitioning into two groups

```
(define quicksort
  (lambda (x compare)
    (if (null? x)
        x
        (let*
          ((pivot (car x))
           (smaller '()) (equal '()) (larger '())
           (classify
             (lambda (item)
               (case (compare item pivot)
                 ((less-than)
                  (set! smaller (cons item smaller)))
                 ((equal-to)
                  (set! equal (cons item equal)))
                 ((greater-than)
                  (set! larger (cons item larger)))))))
          (for-each classify x)
          (format #t "smaller: ~a equal: ~a larger: ~%"
            smaller equal larger)
          (append (quicksort smaller compare)
            equal (quicksort larger compare)))))))
```

Program 9-10   Quicksort

The following output shows how `quicksort` works.

```
> (quicksort '(20 10 30 25 19 17 23 42 16 29) compare-numbers)
smaller: (16 17 19 10) equal: (20) larger: (29 42 23 25 30)
smaller: (25 23) equal: (29) larger: (30 42)
smaller: () equal: (30) larger: (42)
smaller: () equal: (42) larger: ()
smaller: (23) equal: (25) larger: ()
smaller: () equal: (23) larger: ()
smaller: (10) equal: (16) larger: (19 17)
smaller: (17) equal: (19) larger: ()
smaller: () equal: (17) larger: ()
smaller: () equal: (10) larger: ()
(10 16 17 19 20 23 25 29 30 42)
```

The full value of Quicksort is only realized in sorting large lists. In the above
example, the partitions soon get small enough that one or more of them are null.

9.3.3   The Dark Side of Quicksort

Quicksort has a particularly bad trap for the unwary. Anyone who presorts the data "to make it easier for the computer" will trigger Quicksort's worst-case behavior. Suppose that Quicksort inadvertently chose the smallest value as the pivot. In that case, the `smaller` list will be empty, and the `larger` list will contain every element except the pivot. Quicksort then recurses. Suppose that Quicksort again hit the smallest element as the pivot: again we have an empty `smaller` list, and now the `larger` list has $n - 2$ elements. Picking the smallest element as the pivot each time forces Quicksort to make n recursive calls. Since Quicksort partitions the entire list each time, the total time using the smallest element as the pivot is $O(n^2)$.

Presorted data results in the worst-case behavior of Quicksort if the pivot is always the car of the input list. Because of the way the partitions are built, we will alternately pick the smallest and largest items as pivots, but the effect is the same. We can fix the worst-case behavior by choosing a random element from the list as the pivot, instead of the car of the list. Then no particular input list will cause the worst-case behavior of Quicksort. We expect the split of the input to be reasonably well balanced on average. In fact, the probability of hitting a worst case decreases as the list gets larger. To select a random element from the input, we'll need to keep track of the size of the lists, but that only adds a small cost to the algorithm.

Why use Quicksort, then, if it has a worst-case behavior that is $O(n^2)$? For special cases, it is always possible to construct faster procedures than Quicksort, but it is very efficient on average. A full analysis of the randomized algorithm (i.e., using a random pivot), is beyond the scope of our discussion, but the analysis shows that, on average, the time required by Quicksort is approximately $n \lg n$. You might object that Treesort (with balanced trees) is already $O(n \lg n)$ in the *worst* case. The constants hidden by big-oh notation for most algorithms are large enough that Quicksort comes out ahead.

It is interesting to compare insertion sort with Quicksort. On the average, as we showed in Chapter 8, insertion sort should perform approximately $n^2/4$ comparisons when the list items are random. The worst case for insertion sort occurs with presorted data; then $n^2/2$ comparisons are necessary. Both its average case and worst case require $O(n^2)$ comparisons. Quicksort, however, has $O(n^2)$ worst-case time complexity, but only $O(n \lg n)$ average-case time complexity.

9.3.4   Testing Quicksort

The best way to test Quicksort is to build some procedures that manufacture lists, as shown in Program 9–11. The two cases that we might want to test are a sorted list (which should cause worst-case behavior) and a list of random values (which should cause average behavior). The Scheme primitive (`random` n) returns an integer between 0 and $n - 1$.

9.3.5   Mutant Quicksort

Quicksort is simple and efficient, but our implementation of it doesn't actually give better performance than other sorting algorithms. For small lists, Quicksort saves

```
(define make-sorted-list
  (lambda (n)
    (letrec
      ((helper (lambda (i)
         (if (> i n)
           '()
           (cons i (make-sorted-list (add1 i)))))))
    (helper 1))))
(define make-random-list
  (lambda (n w)
    (if (= n 0)
      '()
      (cons (random w)
            (make-random-list (sub1 n) w)))))
```

Program 9-11   Procedures for generating sorted and random lists

you little time, but it is much more complicated than insertion sort.[6] Only when the lists get large is Quicksort worthwhile.

Practical Note

Often the relative advantage of one algorithm over another is not apparent when the input size is small. For two algorithms A and B, where A is $O(n^2)$ and B is $O(n \lg n)$, the time requirements for $n = 16$ would be 256 and 64, respectively. However, we've ignored the constants in this comparison. Generally, algorithms with better complexity gain their speed by using clever data structures and making better decisions at each step, but each step is more costly. The constants involved are usually larger than the simpler but less efficient algorithms. Let's assume that the complexity of A is n^2 (the constant is 1), while the complexity of B is $4n \lg n$. Then the times required for input size $n = 16$ are both 256. There is no reason to choose one or the other. For $n = 1024$, however, A's time is $1,048,576 = 2^{20}$, while B needs only $40960 = 2^{15.3}$. Now B is approximately 32 times faster!

One more important factor is startup costs, which we express as additive constants in the time computation for an algorithm. Again, clever algorithms usually have more elaborate startup procedures, so their startup costs are usually large. Therefore, including this cost, A might be better even for n up to, say, 100. Thus, we often use simple (but not the most efficient) algorithms when we know that the input size will remain small under almost all circumstances.

Our version of Quicksort wastes an enormous amount of time. Not only do we make a new sorted list, but each of the partitions is made anew, using cons. Even sorting a medium-sized list (e.g., 100 items), will waste a large amount of space.[7]

---

[6] If you're on a computer on which the time to sort a 10-element list, using any sorting method, is noticeable, you will probably get little useful work done!

[7] One run of Quicksort to sort 100 randomly chosen numbers called cons 579 times.

It's important to realize that consing is a somewhat expensive proposition, because each pair takes up a certain amount of memory. Even though memory is cheap, if we do enough consing, we will eventually fill up memory with useless pairs. Scheme systems have a procedure known as a *garbage collector*, whose purpose is to scan memory for useless pairs. The space occupied by these useless pairs can be recovered, but running the garbage collector slows down execution.

Program 9-12 shows Mutant Quicksort, a mutating version of Quicksort that does no consing at all.

```
(define quicksort!
  (lambda (x compare)
    (if (null? x)
        x
        (letrec
          ((pivot (car x))
           (smaller '()) (equal '()) (larger '())
           (partition
             (lambda (info)
               (if (not (null? info))
                   (let
                     ((item (car info))
                      (next (cdr info)))
                     (case (compare item pivot)
                       ((less-than) (set-cdr! info smaller)
                        (set! smaller info))
                       ((equal-to) (set-cdr! info equal)
                        (set! equal info))
                       ((greater-than) (set-cdr! info larger)
                        (set! larger info)))
                     (partition next)))))))
          (partition x)
          (format #t "smaller: ~a~% equal: ~a~% larger: ~a~%"
            smaller equal larger)
          (append!
            (quicksort! smaller compare)
            equal
            (quicksort! larger compare)))))))
```
Program 9-12   Procedure `quicksort!`

Notice that it is very much like the original Quicksort procedure. Instead of taking each item and consing it onto one of the partitions, however, this version works with the pairs themselves. The helper `partition` determines which partition contains an element and then physically mutates the pair containing the item, so that its cdr is the appropriate partition (see Figure 9-10).

`quicksort!` does no extra consing. It changes the structure of the input list at each step, so that the partitions contain the appropriate elements. We didn't present `quicksort!` first because `quicksort` is much simpler. You need to understand the process of partitioning before you understand the additional complications introduced by mutation.

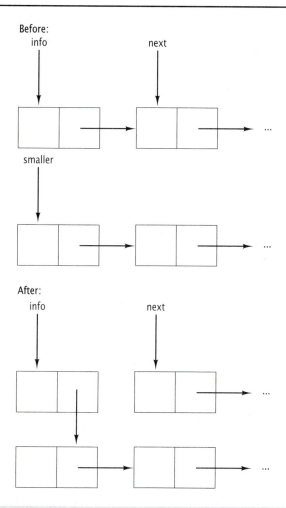

Figure 9-10   Mutating list structure in `quicksort!`

9.3.6 Vector Quicksort

Quicksort is one of the fastest known sorting algorithms, but our implementations, even Mutant Quicksort, must rearrange lists. We can produce an even faster version provided we store the input as a **vector**, a collection of items, like a list, but stored in such a way that we can access any item in the vector in constant time. Vectors are often called **arrays** in other computer languages, and are extended to store items with more than one reference position, called the index of the item.

We can make a vector in Scheme with the primitive procedure `make-vector`. Thus, the value of (`make-vector 4 8`) is a four-element vector (index numbers 0 through 3), with each element initialized to 8. We can work on the individual elements of the vector with the operations `vector-ref` and `vector-set!`, which access and mutate vector elements. `vector-length` returns the number of elements in the vector. An easy way to create a vector with specific contents is `list->vector`. Figure 9-11 shows the result of (`list->vector` '(1 9 2 11 12)); the numbers below the boxes are the indices of the vector elements. Each box can be accessed or mutated independently by `vector-ref` and `vector-set!`, respectively, referenced by position. Figure 9-12 lists the elements of the primitive data type `vector`. In addition, we can specify a constant vector; for example, a three-element vector is written '#(1 4 9).

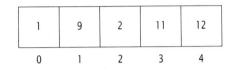

Figure 9-11   The vector (`list->vector` '(1 9 2 11 12))

Constructors

- (`make-vector` *k fill*)
  Return a new vector of *k* elements; *fill* is optional. If given, each element of the vector is initialized to its value. Otherwise, they have unspecified values.
- (`list->vector` *item1 item2 ... itemn*)
  Make a list containing the evaluated arguments in the given order.
- (`vector` *obj1 ...*)
  Returns a vector whose elements contain the arguments. Similar to `list`.

Accessors

- (`vector-ref` *any-list*)
  Get the *k*th element of *vector*.
- (`vector-length` *vector*)
  Return the number of items in *vector*.
- (`vector->list` *vector*)
  Convert the vector into a list.

Mutators

- (`vector-set!` *vector k obj*)
  Set the *k*th element of *vector*.

Predicates

- (`vector?` *x*)
  Return #t if *x* is a vector, and #f otherwise.

Figure 9-12   **Primitive Data Type:** `vector`

☞ **Exercise 9-12**

Write a procedure that counts the number of times that #f occurs in a vector. ❑

☞ **Exercise 9-13**

A *rotation* of an ordered collection of items $a_0, a_1, \ldots, a_n$ is a new collection of items in the same order, but with the first moved to the last position or vice versa. A *left rotation* produces $a_1, a_2, \ldots, a_n, a_0$ while a *right rotation* produces $a_n, a_0, a_1, \ldots, a_{n-1}$. Write a vector procedure (vleft! vec) that rotates a vector to the left. ❏

☞ **Exercise 9-14**

We can use vectors to contain collections, much as we've used lists. Write a procedure that deletes from such a collection the element at position p, and moves all the remaining elements above p (whose index is greater than p) down. (You can't actually delete an item from a vector; the number of elements is permanently fixed when a vector is created. This question asks you to delete an item from the collection, not from the vector.) ❏

qsort is a vector implementation of Quicksort; its basic structure follows:

```
(define qsort
  (lambda (x lower upper)
    (if (< lower upper)
      (begin
        ;;; partition vector around a value, the pivot,
        ;;; that ends up in the correct position, middle
        (qsort x lower (sub1 middle))
        (qsort x (add1 middle) upper))))))
```

The partitioning step of qsort is based on the swap operation: two elements in the vector exchange places. The importance of swapping becomes clear when we implement the partition step of Quicksort. The partition step iterates i from lower+1 to upper, and maintains the vector so that the following invariant is always true:

- Position 0 contains the pivot.
- For positions up to and including middle, the values are less than the pivot value.
- For positions above middle+1 and below i, the values are greater than or equal to the pivot value.
- Positions from i on are unknown.

Figure 9-13 show the three stages of partitioning. The pivot value is shown as T, M denotes the position of middle, and I shows the position of the iteration variable i. We start with a vector of data, as in Figure 9-14.

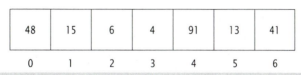

48	15	6	4	91	13	41
0	1	2	3	4	5	6

Figure 9-14   Initial vector for partition in qsort

As in string recursion, we process vectors recursively by stepping through the positions in the vector from first to last (referred to as upper). In partition, the pivot is at lower (we will use 0 as lower for convenience); T is bound to the pivot value,

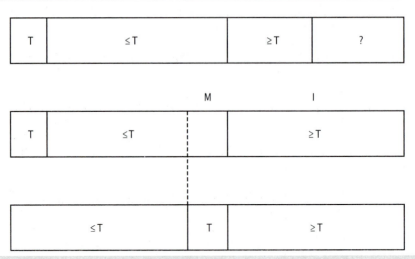

Figure 9-13   Partitioning in qsort

48. At each step, the vector item at position I is compared with T. If the item is less than the pivot value T, then M is incremented, and the items at M and I are swapped. The code appears in Program 9-13.

Initially, I is 1, and M is 0. At each step, the Ith element is compared with pivot. If it is greater than or equal to pivot, then the invariant is true; otherwise, we increment M (M now locates a value greater than pivot) and swap the value at M with the value at I. The invariant is thus satisfied again.

The iterations, with I,M at the beginning of the iteration, are shown in Figure 9-15. The first iteration shown uses I=2. At each iteration, M and I advance together, until the fourth, where 91 exceeds the pivot, and I advances, but M does not. At the next step, the value at I, 13, is below the pivot, so it swaps positions with the first element past M, since that element is the first one known to be greater than the pivot. Iterations continue until I passes upper (or the end of the vector, in our example). To complete partitioning, the final step is to swap the first element of the vector with the item at M, giving

        41 15   6   4 13 48 91

☞ **Exercise 9-15**

The following keys are to be sorted using qsort. Show the vector after the first partition pass, assuming that the pivot is 17. Be sure to make it clear where the partitions are.
17 23 19 12 18 11 21 3 14 ❑

qsort is more efficient than quicksort, but at some expense. Partitioning is very clear in quicksort, but it requires some effort to understand how partition in qsort achieves its results through swapping. We are often presented with similar trade-offs between simplicity and efficiency. A data structure that is not only simple but also efficient is a great pleasure to find.

```
(define qsort
  (lambda (x lower upper)
    (letrec
      ((middle lower)
       (pivot #f)
       (partition
         (lambda (i)
           (if (<= i upper)
             (begin
               (if (< (vector-ref x i) pivot)
                 (begin
                   (set! middle (add1 middle))
                   (swap x middle i)))
               (partition (add1 i)))))))
      (if (< lower upper)
        (begin
          (swap x lower
            (+ lower (random (- upper lower))))
          (set! pivot (vector-ref x lower))
          (partition (add1 lower))
          (swap x lower middle)
          (qsort x lower (sub1 middle))
          (qsort x (add1 middle) upper))))))
(define swap
  (lambda (x i j)
    (let ((temp (vector-ref x i)))
      (vector-set! x i (vector-ref x j))
      (vector-set! x j temp))))
```

Program 9-13   Procedure qsort

 Practical Note

What savings do we get from using vectors in Quicksort? On random lists up to size 10,000, quicksort! competes very well with qsort. Neither is a clear winner in tests under the version of Scheme that we use. In all these tests, however, quicksort actually uses the least computing time, if we don't count the time spent recovering the storage of those useless pairs that quicksort creates. quicksort!, by eliminating consing, wins the total cost competition. The list-structure mutation operations in quicksort! are no more expensive than vector operations, since they create no new pairs and only modify existing pairs.

9.3.7   Searching with Vectors

If we want to access a fixed collection of items rapidly, we can store them in a vector. Given that we have a way of ordering the items (i.e., a way of deciding which of two items is "less than" the other), we can put the ordered items in a vector. We have

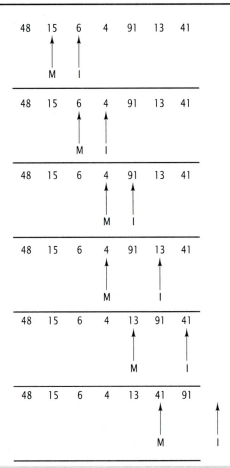

Figure 9-15 Iterations of partition

already seen a method for locating a specific item in Chapter 2, although you may not recall it: bisection. With our items stored in a vector, in order, we can write a simple search procedure—shown in Program 9-14—to locate an item by dividing the range (the number of elements in the vector) in half at each step.

binary-search merely reports success or failure; we'd usually want to do more with the items when search is successful. What's interesting here is the behavior of binary-search. Regardless of the actual values in the vector, at each step one-half of the remaining range is eliminated. To observe its performance, we can trace it. (pvec prints a vector, ten elements per line.)

```
> (define vec (list->vector (make-random-list 15 100)))
> (qsort vec 0 14)
> (pvec vec)
7 19 21 29 34 36 38 41 42 61
70 76 85 89 89
> (trace binary-search)
```

```
(define binary-search
  (lambda (v low up item compare)
    (if (> (- up low) 1)
      (let ((half (ceiling (/ (+ low up) 2))))
        (case (compare (vector-ref v half) item)
          ((less-than) (binary-search v half up item compare))
          ((equal-to) 'success)
          ((greater-than) (binary-search v low half item compare))))
      (if (or (eqv? (compare (vector-ref v low) item) 'same)
              (eqv? (compare (vector-ref v (sub1 low)) item) 'same))
        'success
        'failure)))))
```

Program 9-14   Procedure binary-search

```
> (binary-search vec 0 14 70 compare-numbers)
call binary-search: #15(vec) 0 14 70 #<proc compare-numbers>
| call binary-search: #15(vec) 7 14 70 #<proc compare-numbers>
| | call binary-search: #15(vec) 7 11 70 #<proc compare-numbers>
| | | call binary-search: #15(vec) 9 11 70 #<proc compare-numbers>
| | | return from binary-search: success
| | return from binary-search: success
| return from binary-search: success
return from binary-search: success
```

The range of search decreases from 15 to 7 to 4 to 2, at which point the item is found in the midpoint of that region. Vectors permit rapid searching. Binary search has logarithmic performance, and each step uses simple calculation of vector positions. Inserting a new element into a sorted vector takes $O(n)$ operations, so using a sorted vector is good when insertions occur rarely and lookup is the most frequent operation. We can use either lists or vectors to implement search structures, with proper interfaces to the client code.

 Practical Note

We've seen that vectors are efficient for searching existing collections of elements. To insert a new element, however, is costly. BSTs are efficient for both operations, although each step may be more complex in searching a BST. We have not yet considered *deletion* from a search structure, that is, removal of an element from an existing search structure. Both vectors and BSTs can implement deletion, although with some complication for BSTs. (The code is quite complicated, but still only requires $O(\lg n)$ time.) In choosing a search structure, we must be aware of the mix of operations, insertions, deletions, and searches that it must handle.

9.3.8   Looking Back at Quicksort

By introducing random choices, we ensure that no commonly occurring pattern, such as presorted data, causes Quicksort's worst case. We also used mutation to construct an efficient Quicksort, still using list structures. Finally, we introduced *vectors*, structures that permit constant-time access, which are used to implement the fast versions of Quicksort used in practice. Because the individual steps in `qsort` are so simple, its running time is very fast in practice, which justifies preferring it over other algorithms, such as Treesort, with better worst-case behavior.

☞ **Exercise 9–16**

Write `vector-append`, a procedure that takes two vectors and produces a new vector whose length is the sum of their lengths and that contains all elements from the two vectors. ❑

9.4   Time-Ordered Structures

> *An Englishman, even if he is alone, forms an orderly queue of one.*
> — George Mikes, *How To Be An Alien*

The code presented in this section can be found in file `inventry.scm`.

Sometimes we want to use a data structure to store items so that we can retrieve them in a particular order. If we want to order the items by a key, we can use a BST or just keep the items in a list and sort them periodically. If arrival (insertion) time is our criterion, however, we must build data structures to hold the data for further processing. We call such data structures **time-ordered structures**, since their behavior depends on the order of arrival of their contents. We could use BSTs to store such data; we merely need to use the arrival time as the key. But there are simpler structures, with better performance, that are specially tailored to hold data arranged by arrival time, and deliver either the most recently arrived data item or the item stored for the longest time.

One of the oldest applications of arrival-time ordering is inventory management in a warehouse. The warehouse periodically *receives* items into stock; from time to time, orders are received, and the warehouse staff must *ship* items. An inventory-management software package must decide which items to ship in response to an order. It must also decide which items must be reordered from a supplier. We won't look at the reorder problem here;[8] however, the problem of deciding which inventory items to ship bears further study.

There are two basic policies that we could follow: in a **first-in-first-out (FIFO)** policy, we ship the items that have been in the inventory the longest, whereas in a **last-in-first-out (LIFO)** policy, we ship the items that we have most recently received. Each policy has its merits. If our items are large boxes of nails, we are probably going to take the boxes at the front of the warehouse (i.e., those which were most recently received). On the other hand, if our items are perishable groceries such

---

[8] It's not completely trivial; our supplies of sun-tan lotion might fall quite low at the end of the summer, but we don't simply want to reissue the order we placed a month before!

as vegetables, we will want to get the oldest item first. We can summarize the differences between the two approaches by saying that the FIFO policy emphasizes *fairness*, attempting to ensure that items stay in the warehouse for roughly equal amounts of time, whereas LIFO emphasizes *convenience of access*.

Our inventory-management system will require two ADTs to manage the inventory: one for individual items, and the other for the whole warehouse. Our `item` ADT, shown in Figure 9-16, assumes that each item has a *product number* that is the same for all items of the same product, and a *lot number* that identifies a given item, as well as a description. We'll only show the operations we actually need for the inventory system; you can write additional procedures to flesh this ADT out. The implementation of the `item` type appears in the Software Package.

---

constructor

- (make-item *product-number lot-number description*)
  Create an item using the given information.

accessor

- (item-product *item*)
  Return the product number for the item.

output procedure

- (item-display *item*)
  Display *item* in a readable format.

Figure 9-16   **Abstract Data Type:** `item`

The `warehouse` ADT, shown in Figure 9-17, manages items. Client code can ask it to receive items, or can request that a given number of items be shipped in response to a request.[9]

Constructor

- (make-warehouse *policy*)
  Create a new warehouse with no inventory. *policy* is one of the symbols `FIFO` or `LIFO`, with the obvious meanings.

Mutators

- (warehouse-receive! *warehouse item*)
  Receive a specified *item* into the inventory for *warehouse*.

- (warehouse-ship! *warehouse product-no n*)
  Attempt to ship *n* items of product *product-no* from *warehouse*, following the warehouse's shipping policy. If fewer than *n* items are on hand, only the number on hand are shipped; the remainder are back-ordered.

Figure 9-17   **Abstract Data Type:** `warehouse`

---

[9] The shipping policy is arguably a poor policy. It might be better to back-order this entire shipment; perhaps another order could be filled with the quantity on hand. Inventory management is a complex subject; we refer you to texts on management science for more detail.

Program 9-15 shows a test program to demonstrate the use of the warehouse ADT. The helper procedures r and s allow us to write our tests more compactly.

```
(define test-warehouse
  (lambda (policy)
    (let*
      ((w (make-warehouse policy))
       (r (lambda (p i d) (warehouse-receive! w (make-item p i d))))
       (s (lambda (p n) (warehouse-ship! w p n))))
      (r 123 1047 "Asparagus")
      (r 123 1073 "Asparagus")
      (r 227 1081 "Broccoli")
      (r 231 1102 "Bok Choy")
      (r 231 1238 "Bok Choy")
      (s 123 1)
      (r 231 1471 "Bok Choy")
      (s 231 4)
      (r 123 1686 "Asparagus")
      (s 123 2))))
```

Program 9-15   Testing code for warehouse

Figure 9-18 shows a run of test-warehouse using the FIFO policy.

```
> (test-warehouse 'FIFO)
Receiving:    Item 123, lot 1047: Asparagus
Receiving:    Item 123, lot 1073: Asparagus
Receiving:    Item 227, lot 1081: Broccoli
Receiving:    Item 231, lot 1102: Bok Choy
Receiving:    Item 231, lot 1238: Bok Choy
Shipping product 123, quantity 1
  Item 123, lot 1047: Asparagus
End of shipment.
Receiving:    Item 231, lot 1471: Bok Choy
Shipping product 231, quantity 4
  Item 231, lot 1102: Bok Choy
  Item 231, lot 1238: Bok Choy
  Item 231, lot 1471: Bok Choy
Not enough stock on hand.  We'll back-order 1 items more.
Receiving:    Item 123, lot 1686: Asparagus
Shipping product 123, quantity 2
  Item 123, lot 1073: Asparagus
  Item 123, lot 1686: Asparagus
End of shipment.
```

Figure 9-18   Output with FIFO policy

Figure 9-19 shows the same run using a LIFO policy.

```
> (test-warehouse 'LIFO)
Receiving:    Item 123, lot 1047: Asparagus
Receiving:    Item 123, lot 1073: Asparagus
Receiving:    Item 227, lot 1081: Broccoli
Receiving:    Item 231, lot 1102: Bok Choy
Receiving:    Item 231, lot 1238: Bok Choy
Shipping product 123, quantity 1
  Item 123, lot 1073: Asparagus
End of shipment.
Receiving:    Item 231, lot 1471: Bok Choy
Shipping product 231, quantity 4
  Item 231, lot 1471: Bok Choy
  Item 231, lot 1238: Bok Choy
  Item 231, lot 1102: Bok Choy
Not enough stock on hand.  We'll back-order 1 items more.
Receiving:    Item 123, lot 1686: Asparagus
Shipping product 123, quantity 2
  Item 123, lot 1686: Asparagus
  Item 123, lot 1047: Asparagus
End of shipment.
```

Figure 9-19   Output with LIFO policy

To implement the warehouse ADT, we need time-ordered structures that follow the LIFO and FIFO policies. These structures should allow values to be inserted and retrieved. Retrieval should follow the structure's policy; the programmer should not be asked to say which item is to be retrieved next. The structures should allow both insertion and removal to be done in $O(1)$ time. (Anything much worse would approach the $O(\lg n)$ time we can get with a balanced BST.)

A time-ordered structure that follows a LIFO policy is called a **stack** or **push-down stack**. Each time we insert a value into the stack, all of the values already in the stack are moved one position down. Each time we retrieve a value, the top value is removed from the stack and returned.[10] Common terminology is that an insertion onto a stack is called a **push**, and a retrieval is called a **pop**. The ADT specification for stacks is shown in Figure 9-20.

---

[10] An often-used analogy is to a stack of cafeteria trays. Each time a tray is put on the top, the other trays move down one position (thanks to a spring-loaded plate underneath the trays). People take trays from the top, thus following a LIFO policy.

Constructor

- (make-stack)
  Return a new stack, with no entries.

Mutators

- (stack-push! *stack item*)
  Mutate *stack* by pushing *item* onto the front. Return value undefined.

- (stack-pop! *stack*)
  Return (and remove) the most recently pushed item from *stack*. Generate an error if the stack is empty.

Predicate

- (stack-empty? *stack*)
  Return #f if *stack* has at least one entry, and #t if it is empty.

Figure 9-20   **Abstract Data Type:** stack

We can implement stacks in several ways, but a simple list implementation is quite satisfactory. We represent a stack as a box that contains a list, and mutate the box as we push and pop values, as shown in Program 9-16.

```
(define make-stack
  (lambda () (make-box '())))
(define stack-push!
  (lambda (stack it) (box-set! stack (cons it (box-ref stack)))))
(define stack-pop!
  (lambda (stack)
    (if (stack-empty? stack)
        (error 'stack "Attempt to pop from an empty stack")
        (let ((item (car (box-ref stack))))
          (box-set! stack (cdr (box-ref stack)))
          item))))
(define stack-empty?
  (lambda (stack) (null? (box-ref stack))))
```

Program 9-16   Stack code

☞ **Exercise 9-17**

Show the output produced by the following code:

```
(define s (make-stack))
(stack-push! s 23)
(stack-push! s 24)
(stack-push! s 47)
(display (stack-pop! s))
(stack-push! s 66)
(display (stack-pop! s))
(display (stack-pop! s))
```

❏

☞ **Exercise 9-18**

Implement a stack by using vectors. Assume that the stack has a fixed size limit of 100 (but make this limit easy to change). In a real implementation, with vectors, we would need to be careful not to exceed the stack limit determined by the vector length. Using lists, we have limitless conses (up to the amount of memory) provided by Scheme. ❏

☞ **Exercise 9-19**

Implement `reverse-s`, a list-reversal procedure, using stacks. ❏

The standard name for a FIFO structure is a queue. Queues provide the same operations as stacks, but use different terminology. Instead of *pushing* and *popping* values, we *insert* and *remove* them. The ADT specification is shown in Figure 9-21.

Constructor

- (make-queue)
  Create an empty queue, and return it.

Mutators

- (queue-insert! *queue item*)
  Mutate *queue* by inserting *value* at the end. Return value undefined.
- (queue-remove! *queue*)
  Remove the oldest value from *queue*, and return it, after mutating *queue* so as to delete the retrieved value. Generate an error if the queue is empty.

Predicate

- (queue-empty? *queue*)
  Return #f if *queue* has at least one entry, and #t if it is empty.

Figure 9-21   **Abstract Data Type:** queue

☞ **Exercise 9-20**

Suppose we execute the following code:

```
(define s (make-queue))
(queue-insert! s 23)
(queue-insert! s 24)
(queue-insert! s 47)
(display (queue-remove! s))
(queue-insert! s 66)
(display (queue-remove! s))
(display (queue-remove! s))
```

What output will be produced? ❏

The external interface of the queue ADT is remarkably similar to that of stack, but we have a slight implementation problem. We have to keep track of the oldest element, so our technique in the stack implementation, whereby we do the insertions and retrievals at the front of the list, won't work. Instead, we must do insertions at one end and retrievals at the other. We will arbitrarily choose to retrieve from the front and insert at the back, so the values will actually be sorted from oldest to newest. We already have a data structure that we can use: tlists. Implementing queues is easy then, as shown in Program 9-17.

```
(define make-queue make-tlist)
(define queue-insert! tlist-add-right!)
(define queue-remove! tlist-remove-left!)
(define queue-empty? tlist-empty?)
```

Program 9-17   Definition of queues

Now we can build our `warehouse` implementation. We want to design our inventory-management package so that it can use either LIFO or FIFO. Since our stack and queue interfaces are designed to be compatible, we can build into each warehouse the insertion and deletion procedures it uses. For example, we can call `warehouse-obtain!` without having to know whether the stack or the queue package is being used. All we have to do is to define the appropriate procedures in the warehouse when it's created.

We'll represent the inventory of the warehouse as an alist in which the keys are the product codes and the corresponding values are the storage structures for each product. Each warehouse will be represented as a list: the car of the list will be the time-ordered data structure storing the warehouse items, and the remaining elements are the procedures that implement the time-ordered data structure. Program 9-18 shows the code for making a new warehouse. The accessor procedures are stored with the warehouse.

```
(define make-warehouse
  (lambda (policy)
    (case policy
      ((LIFO)
       (list '() make-stack stack-pop! stack-push! stack-empty?))
      ((FIFO)
       (list '()
             make-queue queue-remove! queue-insert! queue-empty?))
      (else
       (error 'warehouse "Unknown inventory policy")))))
(define warehouse-new-product (lambda (x) (list-ref x 1)))
(define warehouse-obtain! (lambda (x) (list-ref x 2)))
(define warehouse-record! (lambda (x) (list-ref x 3)))
(define warehouse-none-available? (lambda (x) (list-ref x 4)))
```

Program 9-18   Creating a warehouse

When receiving an item, we look it up in the warehouse's alist and enter it into inventory for the appropriate product. We call `warehouse-record!` for this purpose. It returns the appropriate procedure, `stack-push!` or `queue-insert!`, to mutate the structure. The code is shown in Program 9-19.

```
(define warehouse-receive!
  (lambda (warehouse item)
    (let ((prod (item-product item)))
      (let ((x (assv prod (car warehouse))))
        (if x
          ((warehouse-record! warehouse) (cdr x) item)
          (let ((new-entry ((warehouse-new-product warehouse))))
            (set-car! warehouse
              (cons (cons prod new-entry) (car warehouse)))
            ((warehouse-record! warehouse) new-entry item)))
        (format #t "Receiving: ")
        (item-display item)))))
```
Program 9-19   Receiving items

Shipping is somewhat complicated because we must keep removing items
from the inventory for the specific product until the order is complete. A helper
procedure is useful here. The code for shipping is shown in Program 9-20.

```
(define warehouse-ship!
  (lambda (warehouse product-no n)
    (format #t "Shipping product ~a, quantity ~a~%" product-no n)
    (let ((x (assv product-no (car warehouse))))
      (if x
        (warehouse-ship-items! warehouse (cdr x) n)
        (format #t "Sorry, product not known.~%")))))
(define warehouse-ship-items!
  (lambda (warehouse product n)
    (if (= n 0)
      (format #t "End of shipment.~%")
      (let ((x (warehouse-extract! warehouse product)))
        (if x
          (begin
            (item-display x)
            (warehouse-ship-items! warehouse product (sub1 n)))
          (begin
            (format #t "Not enough stock on hand. ")
            (format #t "We'll back-order ~a items more~%" n)))))))
(define warehouse-extract!
  (lambda (warehouse product)
    (if ((warehouse-none-available? warehouse) product)
      #f
      ((warehouse-obtain! warehouse) product))))
```
Program 9-20   Warehouse code

Our inventory program allows us to keep track of various items without ever
including any specific code to manage the retrieval policy, other than setting it
up when we create a warehouse. This separation of **policy**, the general rules by

which the program operates, from **mechanism**, the specific techniques by which the program achieves its end, is an important program design tool. Although it's nothing more than a special form of abstraction, it helps us design programs that are more modifiable. Here we showed how we can choose between LIFO and FIFO policies without modifying the warehouse code.

Stacks and queues are generally applicable in wide areas of computer science. Stacks, though, have a particularly interesting property, in that they mirror the last-in-first-out property of procedure calls. (The last procedure called is the first procedure exited, in the normal sequence of procedure application, so that the sequence of frames in the environment acts like a stack.) As part of the implementation of procedure application, a stack becomes an essential ingredient in any serious language implementation. Our detailed Scheme implementations in Chapter 12 depend on the use of stacks.

9.5 A Graphics Language

Thou seest the world, Volumnius, how it goes;
Our enemies have beat us to the pit:
It is more worthy to leap in ourselves,
Than tarry till they push us.
— William Shakespeare, *Julius Caesar*

 The code presented in this section can be found in file `subscrip.scm`.

We've been using graphics procedures such as `draw-line` without thinking too much about how they work. That approach is satisfactory if all we want to do is to show a picture on the screen while our program is running; however, sometimes we want to send a drawing to a friend over a computer network, or to print it out. We therefore need a way to treat a drawing as a data file. In this section we will see how a common graphics language relies on the use of the stack data structure.

The simplest approach is based on the fact that the majority of graphics devices, both video displays and printers, are **raster devices**. A **raster** is nothing more than a two-dimensional grid of picture elements, or **pixels**, each of which is a small dot. A picture to be sent to a raster device is a **raster image** that is displayed by coloring each pixel in order from the top left corner, along each horizontal row. Television monitors are raster devices that usually scan the raster in interleaved fashion, displaying all the odd rows first, then the even rows. On a monochrome device such as a laser printer, each pixel can be either black or white; on color displays and printers, a pixel can be one of perhaps 256, or even as many as 16,777,216 (2^{24}) colors. Printing an image, then, is nothing more than sending the numerical pixel values in order to a printing device. If we write the pixel values as numbers to a file, we can give the file to a friend, who can use a simple program that sets each pixel on the screen to the appropriate value from the file. Such programs are often called *graphics viewers*.

We'd need many pixels to send the image on our screen to a laser printer. A standard 300-dot-per-inch laser printer has almost 8 million black-and-white pixels on the page. Printing the same page at 1270 dots per inch (the resolution of many typesetting machines) would require 135 million pixels, or nearly 17 megabytes.

If we want to print an image that is complex or has many different colors, the best we can do is to **compress** the data, that is, reduce its volume by noticing regularities in the distribution of colors or shapes in the image. But often we're printing the same shapes over and over again. In a **computer-assisted design**, or **CAD**, program such as AutoCAD, we might use the symbol for a window dozens of times in the same drawing of a house. Even plain text consists of the same letters over and over again.[11] No matter how many times we send the letter *e* to the printer (assuming that the same font and size are used), the same pixels are sent each time.

In the early 1980s, two computer scientists, John Warnock and Chuck Geschke, studied this problem. Their solution was simple and elegant: they proposed building a special programming language into the printer, and sending, as data, programs in this language. Their language, PostScript, has become a standard typesetting, graphics, and desktop publishing tool.

PostScript is quite a different language from anything we've studied before, because its goals are different. Most languages are meant for human use in writing and reading programs. PostScript is designed solely to represent graphic data compactly. Human programmers may write some PostScript code, but most PostScript code is generated by other programs, for consumption by printers and other devices running PostScript evaluators.

Why not use Scheme or some other similar language for this purpose? We want to build this language into printers, so it must be quite simple. But evaluators for Scheme and similar languages are rather complicated.[12] What we need is a simple language for which we can write a simple evaluator. Rather than PostScript, we will work with a similar language of our own design, called SubScript. Although SubScript isn't quite the same as PostScript, it involves many of the same ideas.

Suppose that we want to write a program to draw squares. A Scheme procedure that draws a square is shown in Program 9–21 (a). We've used a hypothetical drawing primitive (draw-rel dx dy) that draws a line from the current position (x, y) to $(x + dx, y + dy)$ and sets the new position to $(x + dx, y + dy)$. Instead of using our drawing primitives, we decide to use SubScript, so we could rewrite this procedure as shown in Program 9–21 (b).

This procedure doesn't actually draw anything at all. It writes out some SubScript code that, if processed by a SubScript evaluator, will do the actual drawing. For example, the call

```
(draw-square 100 200 300)
```

will write out

```
100 200 move 300 square
```

We would normally write it out to a file, and then send the contents of the file to a SubScript printer.

Whereas move is an operation defined in SubScript, square is not; it is defined by the programmer. There are two kinds of SubScript programmers:

---

[11] Almost everything in this book, other than the figures, consists of letters and other characters in a small number of fonts, as well as some lines and other simple shapes.

[12] Nonetheless, PostScript was strongly influenced by Lisp. An experienced Scheme programmer will recognize many familiar ideas in PostScript.

```
(define draw-square
  (lambda (x y size)
    (draw-move x y)
    (draw-rel 0 size)
    (draw-rel size 0)
    (draw-rel 0 (- size))
    (draw-rel (- size) 0)))
```
            (a) A Scheme procedure that draws directly
```
(define draw-square
  (lambda (x y size)
    (for-each (lambda (x) (format #t "~a " x))
      (list x y 'move size 'square))
    (newline)))
```
            (b) A Scheme procedure that writes SubScript code

> Program 9-21   Drawing a square in Scheme and SubScript

1. Most SubScript programs are written by other programs. There's nothing special about SubScript that ties it to Scheme. Programs in any language that can write text to a file can produce a SubScript program.

2. Human programmers prepare definitions of procedures to use in SubScript programs. The procedure `square` is not a SubScript primitive, but will have been defined by a human programmer.

A SubScript programmer should use short procedure names, since they're not intended for humans to read.

Our Subscript program consists of two parts: a prolog that includes the definitions of any procedures being used, followed by the actual picture. A program that draws a set of squares might look something like Program 9-22.

```
;; Beginning of prolog.
  (square)
  ((size) swap define
   0 size draw-rel
   size 0 draw-rel
   0 size negate draw-rel
   size negate 0 draw-rel)
define
;; End of prolog.
clear
0 0 move 100 square
100 100 move 100 square
200 200 move 100 square
0 0 move 400 square
```

> Program 9-22   Subscript code

The program contains a prolog where `square` is defined, followed by a series of SubScript commands that clear the picture, and then draw squares at $(0,0)$, $(100, 100)$ and $(200, 200)$. The output of this SubScript code is in Figure 9-22.

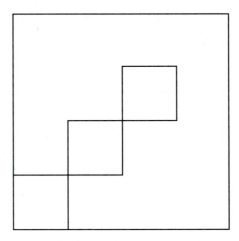

Figure 9-22   Squares by SubScript

SubScript is a stack-based language. The SubScript evaluator maintains two stacks (*operand* and *execution*) and updates them during the evaluation of an expression. We evaluate an expression such as 100 200 move as follows:

1. 100 is a number; push it onto the operand stack.
2. 200 is a number; push it onto the operand stack.
3. move is a name; look it up. Since it is found to be bound to a primitive, execute that primitive procedure. move's primitive procedure pops *x* and *y* values from the stack, and uses them to move to the appropriate place on the page.

The operand stack contains the values that have been pushed by the programmer, or that are the results of other operations. For example, the SubScript code 5 7 add 2 multiply does the following:

1. Push 5 onto the operand stack.
2. Push 7 onto the operand stack.
3. Execute the SubScript primitive add, which pushes the top two values from the operand stack, adds them, and pushes the result.
4. Push 2 onto the operand stack.
5. Execute the SubScript primitive multiply, which pushes the top two values from the operand stack, multiplies them, and pushes the result.

At the end, the stack contains 24.

Why use a stack to hold operands? Stacks allow us to embed the above code fragment in a more complicated expression, for example, 100 5 7 add 2 multiply move, which moves to (100, 24) on the printer page.

☞ **Exercise 9-21**

Evaluate the SubScript expression 4 2 7 add multiply 11 add 2 multiply. ❑

Procedures in SubScript are sequences of simpler SubScript expressions, enclosed in parentheses. Our Scheme implementation of SubScript, however, will treat them as lists. We can define procedures using the `define` primitive, which expects two operands on the operand stack: the first is the name of the procedure (in parentheses), and the second is the procedure itself.

When a name is used, it is looked up in a variable dictionary, which in SubScript is global (i.e., there is no equivalent to Scheme's `lambda` variables.).[13] If the name is bound to a primitive procedure, that procedure is executed. If the name is bound to a programmer-defined procedure, that procedure is pushed onto the second stack, the *execution stack*. If the name is bound to anything else, the value is pushed onto the operand stack.[14]

We can now explain the `square` procedure shown in Program 9–22. It is given one argument, the size of the square. The first step is to define a temporary variable, `size`, as the argument (so that we can easily use it to draw each of the sides of the square). Next, we draw the four sides of the square. (The SubScript primitive `draw-rel` is a "relative draw": it draws a line from the current position (x_0, y_0) to $(x_0 + x, y_0 + y)$, where x and y are its arguments. By contrast, Scheme's draw-line is an "absolute draw": it simply draws a line to (x, y) from (x_0, y_0). Relative draws are more useful than absolute ones in a SubScript procedure; SubScript provides both forms.) The third and fourth sides are drawn with negative lengths: the primitive `negate` pops the top element from the stack and pushes its negative.

The SubScript evaluator can now be described in full. First, get the first item from the top element of the execution stack; if the execution stack is empty, get the first item from the input. Second, examine this item:

1. If it is a number or a list, it is self-evaluating; push it onto the operand stack.
2. If it is a name, look it up in the variable dictionary. There are three cases. If its value is a primitive, just execute it. If its value is a user-defined procedure, push the value onto the execution stack. If its value is anything else, push it onto the operand stack.

For example, to evaluate

```
(foo) 4 3 add define
```

SubScript first pushes the list (foo), then the numbers 4 and 3 (in that order, so the top element will be 3), onto the operand stack. (foo) is a list, not just the name foo, so that Subscript won't try to look up foo in the variable dictionary. The name add is bound to a primitive procedure. Accordingly, the evaluator executes that procedure, after which the stack contains 7 and (foo), with 7 at the top of the stack. The evaluator now finds the name define, which again is bound to a primitive procedure. The evaluator executes the primitive procedure, with the result that foo is bound to 7 in the variable dictionary.

We can describe SubScript's primitive operations by showing what is on the stack before the primitive procedure is executed, and what is left on the stack afterwards. The drawing procedures are executed with respect to a *current point* (x_0, y_0). (That's how Scheme's drawing procedures work.)

---

[13] In PostScript, a third stack, the *dictionary stack*, is used to allow for a form of local bindings. In the interests of compactness, we have not included a similar feature in SubScript.

[14] In SubScript, therefore, procedures aren't first-class citizens. PostScript has a number of elaborate mechanisms to allow procedures to be pushed onto the operand stack, and thus used as general values.

- *x y* draw draws a line from the current point to (x, y).
- *x y* move moves to (x, y), without drawing a line.
- *x y* draw-rel draws a line from the current point to $(x_0 + x, y_0 + y)$.
- *x y* move-rel moves to $(x_0 + x, y_0 + y)$.
- *(name) value* define places a binding in the variable dictionary in which *name* is bound to *value*. In order to prevent a name from being evaluated, we put it into a list.
- *a b* add evaluates *a+b*.
- *a b* multiply evaluates *ab*.
- *a* negate evaluates *-a*.
- *a b* swap puts *b a* on the operand stack.

The simplicity of a SubScript evaluator comes from the simplicity of the Sub-Script language; but of course we will use the data structures we've studied in this and previous chapters. The main loop is just a translation of our English-language description of the evaluation process (Program 9–23). evaluate-subscript needs to get items from the execution stack or the input, as appropriate. The procedure get-item gets the items.

get-item usually gets new items from the input; however, when the evaluator encounters a user-defined procedure, it pushes the body of that procedure onto the execution stack. Then the SubScript evaluator takes its input, item by item, from the execution stack. Each item on the execution stack is the body of a user-defined procedure, which is a list of SubScript code. If a user-defined procedure happens to call another user-defined procedure, the body of the second procedure is pushed onto the execution stack. When the second procedure has been evaluated, top is null, and get-item is called recursively and finds the list of remaining code in the original procedure as the top item of the execution stack. When that code is done, the evaluator returns to the input list for new SubScript code.

There's a substantial inefficiency in get-item: to get an item from the execution stack, we must pop the top procedure and then push the cdr back. If we could look behind the abstraction barrier that hides the implementation of stacks, we could write much more efficient (and hardly less clear) code. A real PostScript evaluator accesses the items of procedures directly, without going through stack interface code.

get-item reads the input program one token at a time. set-input! and get-input implement a simple token scanner that stores the program as a list and returns successive elements on each call.

There's no need to show the procedures that manipulate the variable dictionary. We just use an alist here.[15] Program 9–24 shows part of the initial variable dictionary giving the primitive procedures. These are the initial bindings for the draw and add primitive procedures. The values are Scheme procedures. Note how the arguments of the procedures are popped off the operand stack, and the result is pushed back onto the stack.

---

[15] You might expect a PostScript evaluator to represent a dictionary as a binary search tree, but even faster performance can be achieved by using a technique known as *hashing*, which is beyond the scope of this book. Some Scheme implementations use hashing to represent environments.

```
(define execution-stack #f)
(define operand-stack #f)
(define subscript
  (lambda (prog)
    (set-input! prog)
    (set! execution-stack (make-stack))
    (set! operand-stack (make-stack))
    (evaluate-subscript)))
(define evaluate-subscript
  (lambda ()
    (let ((x (get-item)))
      (cond
        ((eqv? x 'stop))
        ((or (number? x) (list? x))
         (stack-push! operand-stack x)
         (evaluate-subscript))
        ((symbol? x)
         (let ((val (get-variable x)))
           (if (procedure? val)
               (val)
               (stack-push!
                 (if (list? val) execution-stack operand-stack)
                 val)))
         (evaluate-subscript))))))
(define get-item
  (lambda ()
    (if (stack-empty? execution-stack)
        (get-input)
        (let ((top (stack-pop! execution-stack)))
          (if (null? top)
              (get-item)
              (let ((first (car top)))
                (stack-push! execution-stack (cdr top))
                first))))))
```

Program 9-23   Subscript main loop

Case Study: Simulating a Box Office

The code presented in this section can be found in file `tixsim.scm`.

Simulation is a powerful technique for solving many kinds of problems. In a sense, all programs simulate the world, but some problems are best studied by developing a model and then running it to see what happens. The predator/prey model in Chapter 2 was an example of a simulation program; here, we will study a different technique known as a **discrete event simulation**.

In a discrete event simulation, the program maintains a *clock* representing simulated time, which occurs in discrete steps called *ticks*. Each time the clock ticks, some events occur. Events can cause other events to occur at a future time. Discrete event simulations are particularly useful for simulating systems in which

```
(define vardict
  (list
    (cons 'draw
      (lambda ()
        (let*
          ((y (stack-pop! operand-stack))
           (x (stack-pop! operand-stack)))
          (set! current-x x)
          (set! current-y y)
          (draw-move current-x current-y))))
    ...
    (cons 'add
      (lambda ()
        (let*
          ((y (stack-pop! operand-stack))
           (x (stack-pop! operand-stack)))
          (stack-push! operand-stack (+ x y)))))
    ...))
```

Program 9-24   Variable dictionary

people or things arrive, go through several activities, and then leave. For example, an airport may need to decide whether to build another runway. It can gather data on plane arrivals and write a program to simulate the airport with an additional runway. The program would generate simulated plane arrivals at random times; each arrival would trigger a landing at a future point, and a subsequent taxi to the terminal. By measuring how frequently a runway is available for landing, the program can determine whether an additional runway would help.

In this Case Study, the management of a box office has received some complaints about the amount of time it takes to buy tickets. They decide to build a simulation program to find out how to improve the situation, perhaps by hiring additional clerks. First, they station someone in the box office to measure arrival times of customers. After a few days, they get enough data to compute the average number of customers who arrive in 1 time unit (say 5 minutes).

Now they can write a program that allows them to try various arrangements of clerks, and see what the average waiting time is. There isn't enough space to show the code for multiple clerks, but we can show a simpler program that simulates one clerk, to see what happens. The results will show whether one clerk is sufficient, but they don't tell us how many clerks are needed.

How do we write the simulation program? For each time unit, we generate a random number of customers and put them into the queue. Customer arrivals take no time. We assume that each customer takes 1 time unit to serve. We serve the customer, if there is one present. Otherwise we record the fact that the clerk is idle. We keep doing this until the close of business, at which point we print out statistics.

Program 9-25 shows the top-level procedure in the simulator. end is the number of the time unit at the end of the day, when we close the doors; average-arrival is the average number of customers who arrive in 1 time unit.

To write start-simulation (shown in Program 9-26), we need to decide what information it must keep track of. We'll need some global variables to keep track of the simulated time, as well as the amount of time customers spend waiting, the

```
(define ticket-simulation
  (lambda (end average-arrival)
    (start-simulation)
    (run-simulation end average-arrival)
    (display-statistics)))
```

Program 9-25   Ticket simulator top level

```
(define *clock* #f)
(define *customer-queue* #f)
(define *idle-time* #f)
(define *num-customers* #f)
(define *total-wait* #f)
(define start-simulation
  (lambda ()
    (set! *clock* 0)
    (set! *customer-queue* (make-queue))
    (set! *idle-time* 0)
    (set! *num-customers* 0)
    (set! *total-wait* 0)))
```

Program 9-26   Starting the simulation

number of customers, and other statistics. We'll also need a queue of the customers currently waiting for service. The simulation code is shown in Program 9-27 (a). The helper is run once for each time unit. On each time unit, `generate-customers` puts a random number of customers into the queue. The simulator then calls `look-for-customer` to see whether there is a customer in the queue; if so, that customer is served, and the clock is incremented to go on to the next time unit. `message` is a procedure that writes out its arguments.

Unfortunately, `run-simulation-WRONG` has a bug. At the end of the simulation, some customers may still be in line. The corrected procedure, shown in Program 9-27 (b), `run-simulation`, serves them before terminating.

`generate-customers` computes a random number for the number of customers who arrive in that time unit, and then adds that number of customers to the queue, as shown in Program 9-28 (a). `random-number-of-customers` returns an integer representing the number of customers who arrive in this time unit; `average-arrival` is the average number of customers who arrive per time unit. You might want to use `random` to implement `random-number-of-customers`, but that would be wrong, because `random` returns any integer with equal probability. Here, we assume that the most likely returned value is close to `average-arrival`, but any number of customers could arrive in 1 time unit. We need a random number generator that chooses numbers from a Poisson distribution. The Poisson distribution ensures that the average time between customer arrivals is fixed, although the arrival times themselves are random. See the simulation code for a procedure that generates the number of customers arriving per time period. Details such as proper distribution of arrivals are critical in producing reliable simulations. Determining the correct distribution requires an understanding both of the nature of the problem and the nature of distributions.

```
(define run-simulation-WRONG
  (lambda (end average-arrival)
    (letrec
      ((helper
        (lambda ()
          (if (<= *clock* end)
            (begin
              (message "*** Time " *clock*)
              (generate-customers average-arrival)
              (look-for-customer)
              (set! *clock* (add1 *clock*))
              (helper))))))
      (helper))))
```

(a) Wrong version

```
(define run-simulation
  (lambda (end average-arrival)
    (letrec
      ((doors-open-helper
        (lambda ()
          (if (<= *clock* end)
            (begin
              (message "*** Time " *clock*)
              (generate-customers average-arrival)
              (look-for-customer)
              (set! *clock* (add1 *clock*))
              (doors-open-helper)))))
      (doors-closed-helper
        (lambda ()
          (if (not (queue-empty? *customer-queue*))
            (begin
              (message "*** Time " *clock*)
              (look-for-customer)
              (set! *clock* (add1 *clock*))
              (doors-closed-helper))))))
      (doors-open-helper)
      (message "***Doors closed***")
      (doors-closed-helper))))
```

(b) Corrected version

Program 9-27   Running the simulation: right and wrong

```
(define generate-customers
  (lambda (average-arrival)
    (letrec
      ((helper
         (lambda (n)
           (if (> n 0)
             (begin
               (new-customer)
               (helper (sub1 n)))))))
      (helper (random-number-of-customers average-arrival)))))
```
(a) Generating a random number of customers

```
(define new-customer
  (lambda ()
    (set! *num-customers* (add1 *num-customers*))
    (queue-insert! *customer-queue* (cons *num-customers* *clock*))
    (message
      "Customer " *num-customers* " arrives at time " *clock*)))
```
(b) Adding a customer to the queue

Program 9-28   Generating arrivals

Practical Note

It is easy to write a simulation program that produces impressive but wrong results. Designing a useful simulation requires techniques from computer science, applied mathematics and statistics, and business administration. These techniques together form the basis of management science. Make sure you understand the underlying statistical model before you try to write an elegant simulation program!

Program 9-28 (b) shows customer arrivals. We insert a new customer into the queue and write out a message indicating that a customer has arrived. The queue item for each customer consists of the customer's serial number (so that we can make sense of output telling us when a particular customer was served), along with the time the customer arrived.

After calling generate-customers, run-simulation needs to check whether there are any customers waiting. There are two possibilities: either there is a customer, in which case we serve that customer, or there isn't, in which case we record the fact that the clerk is idle. Program 9-29 shows the code for customers. Finally, the simulation prints out statistics at the end. Figure 9-23 shows a run of this program.

The program produced the following results when run for 200 time units.

```
> (ticket-simulation 200 0.9)

...
End of simulation.
Total number of customers:  184
Average wait time:  2.7119565217391
Clerk was idle:  26  units
```

```
(define look-for-customer
  (lambda ()
    (if (queue-empty? *customer-queue*)
        (clerk-is-idle)
        (service-customer))))
(define clerk-is-idle
  (lambda ()
    (set! *idle-time* (add1 *idle-time*))
    (message "Clerk is idle")))
(define service-customer
  (lambda ()
    (let*
      ((cust (queue-remove! *customer-queue*))
       (cust-id (car cust))
       (cust-arrival-time (cdr cust))
       (wait-time (- *clock* cust-arrival-time)))
      (set! *total-wait* (+ *total-wait* wait-time))
      (message "Serving customer " cust-id
        " arrived at " cust-arrival-time
        " waited " wait-time))))
```

Program 9-29   Simulation of customers

We were surprised that the average customer had to wait, even though the clerk was idle about 12% of the time. The box office management can modify this simulation program to see what happens if more than one clerk is serving customers. That might or might not justify adding a clerk. We leave the modifications as a programming project for you.

We shouldn't necessarily believe the output of this or any other simulation program. More than most programs, a simulation involves a host of unstated assumptions. Here, for example, we are assuming that all customers take the same amount of time. In a real box office, we might have two kinds of events: those with unreserved ("festival") seating, and those with reserved seats. Customers purchasing reserved seats might take longer, because the clerk has to show them a chart of the seating, and to allow them to select seats. If the box office is moving towards more events with reserved seating, the average customer-service time might increase and outweigh any improvement we can get by adding a clerk. Provided that the simulation model is accurate, and that we have written the program correctly, the program can give us a great deal of useful information about customer behavior and waiting time— information that we could not obtain in any other way, except by trying each setup in the ticket office. Given the expense and inconvenience of trying each setup, a simulation program is an attractive alternative.

We chose to base our Case Study on something outside the normal range of computer applications, but many of you will recognize the issues of queuing and time-ordered data structures from computer operating systems. When more than one process is active in a computer, the tasks must be scheduled, that is, given access to the processor on the basis of some priority. Queues are central to ordering tasks. When you used a network printer to print out your labs for computer science classes, the spooling process queued your printer requests.

```
> (ticket-simulation 5 0.9)
Time:  0
Customer  1  arrives at time  0
Serving customer  1  arrived at  0  waited  0
Time:  1
Clerk is idle
Time:  2
Customer  2  arrives at time  2
Serving customer  2  arrived at  2  waited  0
Time:  3
Customer  3  arrives at time  3
Customer  4  arrives at time  3
Serving customer  3  arrived at  3  waited  0
Time:  4
Customer  5  arrives at time  4
Customer  6  arrives at time  4
Serving customer  4  arrived at  3  waited  1
Time:  5
Customer  7  arrives at time  5
Customer  8  arrives at time  5
Serving customer  5  arrived at  4  waited  1
***Doors closed***
*** Time  6
Serving customer  6  arrived at  4  waited  2
*** Time  7
Serving customer  7  arrived at  5  waited  2
*** Time  8
Serving customer  8  arrived at  5  waited  3

End of simulation.
Total number of customers:  8
Average wait time:  +1.125
Clerk was idle:  1  units
```

Figure 9-23   Simulation output

Summary

We began this chapter by reviewing the data structures we've used in many list-processing programs. We developed *tlists*, data structures that let us perform certain list operations, such as append, rapidly, with little added cost. We next studied searching, developing binary search trees (BSTs) to let us search n items in $O(\lg n)$ time. This led us to improve the $O(n^2)$ time complexity of insertion sort to $O(n \lg n)$ in treesort. Quicksort is another sorting algorithm that acheives the same average-case behavior but also can be implemented very efficiently. We used *vectors*, a new Scheme construct, to implement Quicksort, and then used vectors to build a data structure for fast binary search. Next we studied time-ordered structure, where the order of insertion of the data, not the actual data, matters. We looked at stacks, which behave according to last-in, first-out (LIFO), and queues, which behave according to first-in, first-out (FIFO). We used these two structures extensively in programs for picture description and warehouse simulation, respectively. Through these studies, we learned several new data structures, how to analyze their use, and how data structures influence algorithms.

Further Readings

The discussion of the vector implementation of Quicksort was taken from *Programming Pearls* by J. Bentley. *Programming Pearls* contains insights on many levels, including design and implementation of algorithms and data structures, especially with regard to correctness as well as efficiency of implementations. Bentley's other book, *More Programming Pearls* is also very useful.

There are many excellent texts on data structures, including *Introduction to Data Structures using C++* by R. Kruse, *Algorithms in C++* by R. Sedgwick, *Data Abstraction and Structures Using C++*, by M.R. Headington and D.D. Riley, and *Introduction to Algorithms* by T.H. Cormen, C.E. Leiserson, and R.L. Rivest.

The following books by D. E. Knuth are important reference texts: *Fundamental Algorithms*, *Seminumerical Algorithms*, and *Sorting and Searching*. They form the three volumes of *The Art of Computer Programming*.

Key Words

Here are the *key words* introduced in this chapter. Make sure you understand what each one means.

array	last-in-first-out (LIFO)	push
binary search tree (BST)	mechanism	raster device
computer-assisted design (CAD)	partition	raster image
	pivot	root
compress	pixel	sequential retrieval
discrete event simulation	policy	simulation
first-in-first-out (FIFO)	pop	stack (push-down stack)
image	pivot	swap
index	post-order	time-ordered structures
in-order	pre-order	tlist
insert	profiler	vector

Scheme Features Introduced in This Chapter

Primitive Procedures

list->vector   make-vector   vector   vector-ref

vector-set!   vector-length   vector->list   vector?

Cumulative List of Data Types

Name	Constructor	Accessors	Predicate
Boolean	—	—	boolean?
character	integer->char	char->integer	char?
list	list	car, cdr	list?
number	—	—	number?
pair	cons	car, cdr	pair?
procedure	lambda	—	procedure?
string	string	string-ref	string?
symbol	string->symbol	—	symbol?
vector	make-vector	vector-ref	vector
void	void	—	void?

Problems

1. Write `post-order`, a binary tree traversal procedure. Show the output produced by

   ```
   > (post-order mytree
       (lambda (key val)
       (format #t "My key is ~a  and my value is ~a~%" key val)))
   ```

   when `mytree` has the value used in Section 9.2.6.

2. Modify Quicksort to pivot on the median of the first, middle, and last elements of the current set of data. You can compare its behavior with the basic Quicksort (pivot on the first element) and the random-pivot Quicksort. Then compare its behavior with the original version on sorted lists. (You should observe little or no difference on random lists.)

3. A fast-talking CS student from another university attempts to sell you a sorting algorithm that sorts arbitrary input on a single computer in $O(\lg n)$ time. Since you've studied this chapter, you know this person is wrong. Explain. Are there any cases where the usual worst-case complexity can be bettered?

4. Write `insertion-sort-v`, a procedure that uses vectors to implement insertion sort. `lst` is a list and `compare` is a comparison procedure.

5. Our insertion sort performs worst when the data are already sorted. Fix `insertion-sort-v` so that the best performance occurs with already sorted data.

Self-Assessment

1. Devise a sequence of seven numbers that creates a well-balanced tree when used as input to create a BST, and show the tree the sequence creates.

2. Implement a queue using vectors. You can assume, as you did with the stack, that the queue has a fixed size limit, say 100. Since you add items at one end of the queue and remove from the other, the size restriction does not solve all your problems.

3. We want to handle a collection of procedures that will be accessed by the name of the procedure. Moreover, we want to keep track of how many times each procedure is accessed. Each data item is a triple: name, procedure, and a count. The interaction looks like this:

```
> (define procedure-list ...)
> (define foo (lambda (x) 1))
> (set! procedure-list (enter-procedure 'foo foo procedure-list))
> (find-procedure 'foo procedure-list)
#<procedure foo>
```

   a. Devise a way to represent the triples, and then write `enter-procedure` and `find-procedure`. If the procedure is not in the list, `find-procedure` should return #f. Each time `find-procedure` references a procedure, it should increment its count. (Note: the fact that these are procedures stored in this data structure is irrelevant!)
      Hint: There is a well-known Scheme procedure and data structure that we have used frequently to represent data like this!

   b. We want to keep this list of procedure data sorted by the number of times a procedure is accessed. Write a compare procedure for `quicksort` (it returns `less-than`, `equal-to`, or `greater-than`) to sort our list of procedures.

   c. If we don't sort the list of procedures every time one is entered, how many operations (use big-oh notation) will it take to find the procedure we want in a list of n procedures? Assume that all procedures are equally likely to be accessed.

   d. If we manage the list of procedures in a balanced binary search tree, how many operations do we expect to use to find the procedure?

4. Draw the binary search tree that would result from inserting the following keys, *in the order given*, into an empty tree: 15 3 17 1 20 30 22 25 35

5. Provide a list of keys (numbers will do) that, when inserted into a binary search tree in the order given, will yield search times that are no better than those of a linear list.

6. Write a procedure `(vright! vec)` that rotates a vector to the right.

Programming Problems

1. Design a list structure that lets you move equally easily both forward and backward.

2. Insertion sort is quite efficient when the input is almost in sorted order; in its best case, in fact, the input is sorted. One clever extension to Quicksort is to terminate recursion in Quicksort when the input is small, say less than eight elements, and then run insertion sort on the resulting almost-sorted vector. Why is this method efficient? Partitioning creates blocks of elements that, while not sorted, are no farther than the block size b from their correct destination. Then each step in insertion sort can at most have b comparisons and, on average, only $b/2$ comparisons.

   Write a version of `qsort` that terminates when the block size is small, and passes the result to insertion sort to finish sorting. Compare the time it takes with standard `qsort` over a range of inputs: sorted, reverse-sorted, and random order, all with large inputs.

3. Modify the ticket-simulation program so that it allows any number of clerks to be serving customers. Using the resulting program, find the optimum number of clerks that minimizes waiting time without having a significant number of idle clerks.

Chapter 10

Facts and Rules

Overview

Many complicated problems are best solved not by developing elaborate algorithms, but by writing a set of rules that define what the program is to do. These rules can then be used in conjunction with a general program; changes in the problem can be easily accommodated by changing the rules. In this chapter, we look at a number of problems in which a rule-based approach works well. Because each of our rules uses a *pattern* to determine whether it applies to the current situation, we must examine patterns and matching. After looking at some applications of rules and patterns, we study mathematical logic, which gives us a very general way to write rule-based programs.

The three fundamental Laws of Robotics . . . One, a robot may not injure a human being, or, through inaction, allow a human being to come to harm . . . Two, a robot must obey the orders given to it by a human being except where such orders would conflict with the First Law . . . Three, a robot must protect its own existence as long as such protection does not conflict with the First or Second Laws. — Isaac Asimov, *I, Robot*

Early computer programmers thought that the way to solve problems was to examine each case and write code that handled that case. This is an excellent approach if there are a small number of cases, but the real world isn't so simple. In many programs, the vast majority of the code is designed to handle special cases, many of which happen only rarely. These programs are often intimidating nests of conditionals, and are tedious to write, difficult to debug, and impossible to read.

Object-oriented programming gives us one way to reduce complexity. We can write specific class definitions, with specific methods for handling special cases. For example, we can have five different kinds of bank accounts, each of which responds in a slightly different way to a `withdraw` request. Delegation lets us build "customized" versions of our classes to adapt to special cases (e.g., a bank-account class for young children).

However, when the problem focuses on navigating an extremely complicated web of conditions and special cases, object-oriented programming doesn't help. We can create thousands of classes, all related by delegation, but each class will have only one or two instances.

For example, suppose we want to write a program to check that a student has the prerequisites needed to take a course. A quick look at a typical college course description will show the complications involved:

Computer Science 128: *Principles of Computer Science.* Basic concepts of computation: recursion, data structures, state, object-oriented programming, evaluators, databases, logic programming, machines. Prerequisites: Computer Science 100, or prior computing experience; Mathematics 100 or 110 (may be taken concurrently).

An on-line registration system might accept a student's request to take this course, subject to eligibility, but how does the system determine eligibility? It can look at the student's transcript to see what courses have been taken. For students who have not already taken a mathematics course, the system must also look at the other courses the student is planning to take this semester. Students can take CS100, which is a new course, or they may have taken an older course, CS108, which is no longer offered. The program must allow students with CS108 or CS100 into CS128. Thus, there will be more combinations of valid prerequisites for some courses than the course description shows. "Prior computing experience" is best assessed by a faculty advisor, who can override a negative decision by the system.

We *could* write a program that checked all of the combinations of prerequisites for each course, but it would be very complicated. If the college offers 500 courses and each averages three different combinations of prerequisites, the program would have to include 1500 different cases. Most programmers cannot make sense of a cond with 1500 cases.

A better approach is to take the information given in the course description and build a representative data structure. When a student registers for a course, the program consults the data structure, using information about the student's past and present courses to check the prerequisites. This data structure consists of a set of rules in an "**IF**...**THEN**..." format. For example, "**IF** the student has taken CS100, **THEN** the student may take CS128". A **rule** consists of a set of conditions that must be true in order to draw a specific conclusion. Rules are useful in many problems beside prerequisite checking; whenever we design a program that makes decisions, using rules can lead to a more structured program.

We would also have a set of facts, each of which provides a specific piece of information; for example, "Diane Muller has taken CS100". A **fact** is a specific statement about the world and corresponds to data.

The rules for the CS128 description would look like this:

- **IF** the student has CS prerequisites **AND** the student has calculus prerequisites, **THEN** the student can take CS128.
- **IF** the student has taken CS108, **THEN** the student has CS prerequisites.
- **IF** the student has taken CS100, **THEN** the student has CS prerequisites.
- **IF** the student has permission from an advisor, **THEN** the student has CS prerequisites.
- **IF** the student has taken MATH 100, **THEN** the student has calculus prerequisites.
- **IF** the student is taking MATH 100, **THEN** the student has calculus prerequisites.
- **IF** the student has taken MATH 110, **THEN** the student has calculus prerequisites.
- **IF** the student is taking MATH 110, **THEN** the student has calculus prerequisites.

☞ **Exercise 10–1**

Suppose the college decides that all students taking CS128 must already have taken Grade 12 physics. How would we modify the rules to indicate this? ❏

We can represent facts with lists or tables and write `if`s or DBScheme forms to answer questions about our facts. What's new here is that we can represent the rules as data, and then build a general program that uses this data structure to answer questions. Any changes to the problem will only require changes to the rules, not changes to the program.

Everyday life involves facts and rules. We use complicated rules to make sense of what we see, and when a person makes a request, we use the rules of English grammar to decode the request. Researchers in the field of **artificial intelligence** (AI) use a rule-based approach, among other techniques, to write programs that exhibit human behavior.

Some programs act as "consultants", systems that interpret data to assist a human. For example, we might want a program that can diagnose problems in automotive electronic systems. Such a program must look at all sorts of data, including failure codes from the car's microprocessors, engine performance, and fuel-mixture characteristics. Various combinations of data will cause the program to diagnose the various problems. The best way to structure a diagnostic program is as a set of rules: "**IF** the fuel mixture is low on oxygen **AND** the microprocessor has reported failure code 0172, **THEN** perform diagnostic procedure 301".

Other rule-based programs have been built to monitor the effectiveness of human learning. For example, a flight simulator used to train pilots gathers data on altitude, airspeed, direction, and attitude to diagnose problems in flight maneuvers. The rules allow extremely precise diagnosis of pilot errors.

Many of the most sophisticated electronic mail (email) systems use rules. As the use of email becomes more common, users get more messages, and have to spend their time reading junk mail. Some email systems allow users to create a set of rules to handle messages automatically; for example:

- **IF** the message is from my boss, **THEN** show it to me right away.
- **IF** the message is from anyone at Acme University, **THEN** forward it to Barb Levy.
- **IF** the message's subject says `You may already have won $1,000,000`, **THEN** discard it.

Rule-based approaches work well for a variety of problems ranging from our prerequisite problem to answering questions about the rules of the road. Gradually, we'll work our way from rule languages for specific applications to a general rule language. We must start by looking at patterns that allow us to classify list structures. We will build a pattern language within Scheme, and examine the algorithms needed to match patterns with lists. We'll use this pattern language first as a way to implement tables, and then as part of a rule language for a consultant that can answer questions about the rules of the road. We will ask whether we need a special rule language for each problem, and we will find that mathematical logic gives us a powerful way to specify problems. Finally, we will build a logic-based language within Scheme, and study evaluators for it.

10.1   Patterns and Rules

> *Matchmaker, matchmaker, make me a match*
> *Find me a find, catch me a catch.*
> — Jerry Bock and Sheldon Harneck, *Fiddler on the Roof*

A rule-based program identifies and then uses an applicable rule. In some cases, the action triggers additional actions; in others, such as the course-prerequisite problem, determining whether the rule is applicable requires additional rules.

Rules in a program will be list structures. Each rule consists of two parts:

- a **pattern**, a list that is used to determine whether, based upon the input data, the rule is applicable
- an **action**, a list that tells us what to do

One meaning of the word *pattern* is "a regular form or order". For example, we speak of a person's behavior following a pattern. For us, a pattern is a data structure that can be used to determine whether a list is a member of a set of lists with similar structure. This means that we will represent the pattern and action as lists. For example, one of our course prerequisite rules might look like

```
(   (has-calculus ?x)        (has-taken ?x MA100)    )
```

This is an almost direct translation of the following rule:

- **IF** the student has taken MA100, **THEN** the student has the calculus prerequisite.

We represent a simple fact as a list, for example, (has-taken Linda CS100). We must therefore determine whether or not this rule is applicable.

A list such as (has-taken ?x CS100) is called a *pattern*, and we speak of **matching** it to a specific fact. You should be familiar with the concept of patterns and matching. For example, in MS-DOS, the command

```
copy a*.txt c:\backup
```

copies all of the files matching the pattern a*.txt. The * character is called a **wild card** and indicates a part of the filename where anything will match.[1] Suppose the current directory contains the files alpha.txt, beta.scm, aardvark.txt, and wombat.txt. The copy command above will copy alpha.txt and aardvark.txt into the backup directory.[2]

The expression a*.txt is a pattern because it specifies not a single value, but a group of values that match the pattern. The DOS copy command scans the current file directory, matching the pattern to each filename, and copying any name that matches the pattern to the backup directory.

This section is about patterns—how they work, how pattern-matchers are built, and how predicates tell us whether a pattern matches a specific list. We will

---

[1] In many card games, a wild card can have any face value the player chooses.

[2] MS-DOS patterns use ? to match a single character, and * to match any number of characters. Other operating systems, such as UNIX, provide very elaborate filename-matching features. In UNIX you can, for example, copy all files whose names have a vowel as the third character! On the other hand, in the famously easy-to-use Macintosh system, you have to select the files you want one by one, with no pattern-matching ability at all.

build a pattern language that allows us to match Scheme lists and gradually add features to it so that it can handle more complex patterns.

10.1.1 A Simple Pattern-Matcher

We'll start by exploring a simple list pattern-matcher that tells us whether a **target** list matches a pattern. Patterns can include "constant" symbols, which are symbols that must appear, as is, in the list, as well as **pattern variables**, which act as wild cards.

The simplest pattern-matcher is equal?, which doesn't support wild cards. We can use the basic structure of equal? to build a more sophisticated pattern language, in which ? is used as a pattern variable that matches any single value in the target.

A few examples will demonstrate our matcher:

```
(simple-match? '(i like ?) '(i like yogurt))    ⇒  #t
(simple-match? '(i like ?) '(i like mango juice))  ⇒  #f
(simple-match? '(i like ? ?) '(i like mango juice))  ⇒  #t
(simple-match? '(? likes ?) '(fred likes apples))  ⇒  #t
(simple-match? '(? likes ? ?) '(fred likes apples))  ⇒  #f
```

The code for simple-match? is shown in Program 10-1; it accepts a pattern and a target, and compares the items of the pattern list with those of the target. Each time it encounters a ? in the pattern, it accepts anything in the corresponding position of the target. If all of the items match, it returns #t. It returns #f if any items don't match, or the lists have different lengths.

```
(define simple-match?
  (lambda (pattern target)
    (cond
      ((null? pattern) (null? target))
      ((null? target) #f)
      ((eqv? (car pattern) '?)
       (simple-match? (cdr pattern) (cdr target)))
      ((equal? (car pattern) (car target))
       (simple-match? (cdr pattern) (cdr target)))
      (else #f)))))
```

Program 10-1   Procedure simple-match?

☞ **Exercise 10-2**

Evaluate
  a. (simple-match? '(? ?) '(walla walla))
  b. (simple-match? '(? ?) '(pouce coupe))
  c. (simple-match? '(?) 'peoria) ❏

simple-match? doesn't support recursive patterns. Pattern variables are only recognized as top-level items in the pattern and not as elements in pattern items that are themselves lists.

```
(simple-match? '(my name is (joe ?)) '(my name is (joe lee)))  ⇒  #f
```

☞ **Exercise 10-3**

Modify `simple-match?` to support recursive patterns. ❏

In `simple-match?` we match a target against a pattern, getting either a "success" (the result is #t) or a "failure" (the result is #f). In our example of the MS-DOS copy command, a file in the current directory either matches or it doesn't. In general, matching just for success or failure is not enough; we also need to know exactly what matched.

Our next matcher, `var-match?`, has a much more general concept of a pattern variable. In `var-match?` we can have as many *different* pattern variables as we want. We will choose to consider any symbol starting with ? as a pattern variable. In particular, ? by itself is a pattern variable.

`var-match?` accepts the same arguments as `simple-match?`: a pattern and a target. However, `var-match?` not only tells us whether the pattern matches, but also what part of the candidate list matches each place in the pattern. We speak of the *binding* of a pattern variable as the element in the target that it matches. `var-match?` returns one of three values:

1. #f, if the pattern doesn't match
2. #t, if the pattern does match, but contains no pattern variables
3. an alist, if the pattern does match and contains pattern variables; the alist will contain the bindings of the pattern variables.[3]

Here are some examples of `var-match?` at work:

```
(var-match? '(2 1) '(2 1))    ⇒  #t
(var-match? '(?x 1) '(2 1))   ⇒  ((?x . 2))
(var-match? '(?x 1 ?y) '(2 1 3))  ⇒  ((?y . 3) (?x . 2))
(var-match? '(?x 1 ?x) '(2 1 3))  ⇒  #f
(var-match? '(?x 1 ?x) '(2 1 2))   ⇒  ((?x . 2))
```

The last two examples demonstrate one of `var-match?`'s subtleties. Once a pattern variable matches somewhere, it must match the same value everywhere else.

Each time `var-match?` encounters a pattern variable in the pattern, it checks to see if this particular pattern variable has been found before. If so, the corresponding target item must match the pattern variable. If not, the pattern variable and the corresponding target item are recorded for future reference. We say that a pattern variable "agrees with" a target item if

1. the pattern variable hasn't been seen before, or
2. the pattern variable has been seen before, and matched the same target item.

`var-match?` is shown in Program 10-2. The core, `match-helper`, takes three arguments: the pattern, the target, and an alist of the values found so far. `match-helper` is based on `simple-match?`; the only major difference is in the code for pattern variables. When a pattern variable is found, a check is made (by `agrees-with?`) to see whether its match agrees with the value bound to the pattern variable in the alist. `agrees-with?` returns #f only if the pattern variable is bound to a value

---

[3] It would be much cleaner to return an empty alist, rather than #t, if the pattern matches but contains no pattern variables. Unfortunately, some older versions of Scheme treat the empty list as equivalent to #f. Since we'd like our code to run on these older Scheme systems—even though we don't agree with their treatment of null lists—we've chosen to use #t instead.

```
(module var-pattern-matcher
  (export var-match?)
  (define var-match?
    (lambda (pattern target) (match-helper pattern target '())))
  (define match-helper
    (lambda (pat targ answers)
      (cond
        ((null? pat)
         (if (null? targ)
             (if (null? answers) #t answers)
             #f))
        ((null? targ) #f)
        ((pattern-variable? (car pat))
         (if (agrees-with? (car pat) (car targ) answers)
             (match-helper
               (cdr pat) (cdr targ)
               (add-answer (car pat) (car targ) answers))
             #f))
        ((equal? (car pat) (car targ))
         (match-helper (cdr pat) (cdr targ) answers))
        (else #f))))
  (define add-answer
    (lambda (patvar value answers)
      (if (assv patvar answers)
          answers
          (cons (cons patvar value) answers))))
  (define agrees-with?
    (lambda (patvar targvar answers)
      (let ((x (assv patvar answers)))
        (if x
            (equal? targvar (cdr x))
            #t))))
)
```

Program 10-2   Procedure `var-match?`

different from the current match; if it is, the whole match fails. If `agrees-with?`
returns #t, match-helper can proceed to the next item of the pattern and target.
add-answer produces the alist that `match-helper` uses; it returns the original alist
if the match is old, or a new alist containing the new binding as well as all previous
bindings.

Practical Note

var-match? does two assv calls when it finds a pattern variable: one in `agrees-with?`
and one in add-answer. You might be tempted to combine these two operations in
order to speed things up. This isn't unreasonable, but it would complicate the code.
For example, we might have a combined procedure that returns an alist if the pattern
variable agrees with the target item, and #f otherwise. Such a procedure violates

our rule that each procedure should do exactly one thing. On the other hand, in many programs the execution time of the matcher can easily dominate everything else. Make the program understandable and correct before you make it fast.

The procedure pattern-variable? is not included in the var-pattern-matcher module, but is defined separately, because we'll need to use it in some other programs that use our matcher. Since we'll be producing an improved version of var-match? later, it makes sense to define pattern-variable separately. Program 10-3 shows the definition of pattern-variable?.

```
(define pattern-variable?
  (lambda (x)
    (and
      (symbol? x)
      (char=? (string-ref (symbol->string x) 0) #\?))))
```

Program 10-3   Procedure pattern-variable?

10.1.2   DBScheme with Patterns

Our first real use of patterns and var-match? is to provide an alternate implementation of the DBScheme operations. We do this not because it is more efficient, but because it shows how we can use patterns to manipulate a data structure.

Instead of using DBScheme with the table in Figure 10-1 in DBScheme, we can represent it as a list and use the matcher.

student-no	name	faculty	phone
123	Smith, W.	arts	555-1010
185	Jones, F.	science	555-7878
923	Lee, J.	arts	555-2325
752	Singh, R.	arts	555-6812
999	Laze, E.	science	555-0000
703	Okura, G.	science	555-2264
892	Wilson, B.	engineering	555-9876

Figure 10-1   A simple student table

This makes sense because the DBScheme procedures operate on columns. In DBScheme we specify those columns by means of field names, but there are other ways. If we consider each row to be a list, as in DBScheme, we can access the fields of a row by means of their positions. Since matching works on a positional basis, it can be used for this purpose. We can therefore represent a table as a list of rows, and use var-match? to process the rows.

```
(define student-list
  '((123 "Smith, W."   arts          555-1010)
```

```
        (185 "Jones, F."  science     555-7878)
        (923 "Lee, J."    arts        555-2325)
        (752 "Singh, R."  arts        555-6812)
        (999 "Laze, E."   science     555-0000)
        (703 "Okura, G."  science     555-2264)
        (892 "Wilson, B." engineering 555-9876)))
```

Thus,

```
(var-match? '(?x ?y arts ?z) (car student-list))
  ⇒  ((?z . 555-1010) (?y . "Smith, W.") (?x . 123))
```

☞ **Exercise 10-4**

Using `var-match?`, write a procedure that finds all of the arts students. ❏

We can now implement the selection, projection, and join operators using pattern matching. For ease of implementation, we chose a different interface from that in DBScheme.

In addition, some DBScheme features (e.g., finding rows in which a specified field contains a value greater than a minimum value) can't be done with pattern matching.

To implement `table-select` using the matcher, we just need to loop over all elements in the list and check whether the matcher succeeds on each element. Program 10-4 shows the code. Here's our procedure in action:

```
> (m-select-table student-list '(?x ?y arts ?z))
((123 "Smith, W." arts 555-1010)
 (923 "Lee, J." arts 555-2325)
 (752 "Singh, R." arts 555-6812))
```

Projection is a bit more complicated. We need a way to identify the columns that must appear in the result. We can use patterns in two different ways to accomplish this. First, we use a pattern that gives pattern variables for each of the columns (the "input pattern"); a second pattern shows how to construct the result.

```
(m-project-table student-list '(?a ?b ?c ?d) '(?b ?d)) ⇒
  (("Smith, W." 555-1010)
   ("Jones, F." 555-7878)
   ("Lee, J." 555-2325)
   ("Singh, R." 555-6812)
   ("Laze, E." 555-0000)
   ("Okura, G." 555-2264)
   ("Wilson, B." 555-9876))
```

`m-project-table` steps down the table, a list of rows, and matches the input pattern `patin` against the row. All rows match, since they have the same structure as the pattern, which consists only of pattern variables. The result of the matcher is an alist that binds the pattern variables to the columns in the row:

```
(var-match? '(?a ?b ?c ?d) (car student-list))
  ⇒  ((?d . 555-1010) (?c . arts) (?b . "Smith, W.") (?a . 123))
```

```
(define m-select-table
  (lambda (lst pat)
    (if (null? lst)
        '()
        (if (var-match? pat (car lst))
            (cons (car lst) (m-select-table (cdr lst) pat))
            (m-select-table (cdr lst) pat)))))
(define m-project-table
  (lambda (in patin patout)
    (letrec
      ((project
         (lambda (lst)
           (if (null? lst)
               '()
               (let ((m (var-match? patin (car lst))))
                 (if m
                     (cons
                       (substitute-alist patout m)
                       (project (cdr lst)))
                     (project (cdr lst))))))))
      (project in))))
(define substitute-alist
  (lambda (pat alist)
    (let
      ((replace-var
         (lambda (item)
           (if (pattern-variable? item)
               (let ((res (assv item alist)))
                 (if res (cdr res) item))
               item))))
      (map replace-var pat))))
```

Program 10-4   Selection and projection using patterns

The output of `m-project-table` is produced by `substitute-alist`, which replaces the pattern variables in `patout` by the values to which they are bound in the alist returned by the matcher:

```
(substitute-alist '(?b ?d)
  (var-match? '(?a ?b ?c ?d) (car student-list)))
⇒  ("Smith, W." 555-1010)
```

☞ **Exercise 10-5**

Show how you can use `m-project-table` to do a selection. ❏

We can write `m-join-table`, a procedure that takes the following:
- two tables, represented as lists of rows
- two patterns, one for each of the input tables
- an output pattern

and joins the two tables according to the two patterns for the input tables, to produce rows in the form of the output pattern. Where a pattern variable occurs in the two input patterns, the joining process checks that the matcher has bound the variables to the same values. Because m-join-table uses pattern-matching, it is actually more general that the standard implementation of join. Several columns can be forced to be the same, by using more than one common pattern variable in the input patterns. The output pattern, moreover, can be any subset of the input pattern variables. The simplest implementation compares each row in the first table with all rows in the other table. Its time complexity is $O(n^2)$ for tables of size n.

Suppose we have the following grades table:

```
(define grades-list
  '((123 CS100 A)
    (123 CS120 B+)
    (999 MA110 B+)))
```

We can join the student and grades tables on the student number field:

```
(m-join-table student-list grades-list
    '(?a ?b ?c ?d) '(?a ?e ?f)
    '(?a ?b ?c ?d ?e ?f)) ⇒
  ((123 "Smith, W." arts 555-1010 cs100 a)
   (123 "Smith, W." arts 555-1010 cs120 b+)
   (999 "Laze, E." science 555-0000 ma110 b+))
```

The pattern for students is (?a ?b ?c ?d). The student field occurs in the first position in both tables, so the matching pattern in the grades table is (?a ?e ?f). The result combines the elements from both tables.

☞ **Exercise 10-6**

Write m-join-table. ❏

A pattern-matching database system has one main advantage over DBScheme: our operations can be more free-form than in DBScheme. Patterns can be combined so that we can do any database reorganization in one step. Further, we can apply the principles above to structures that are not strictly tables.

However, there are a significant number of weaknesses. First, the pattern-matching approach doesn't allow for indexing. Therefore all operations must be $O(n)$, or $O(n^2)$, in the case of join. Second, the pattern language that var-match? understands only supports equality. This isn't a fatal objection, since we could build a much more flexible pattern language; however, that would require an extremely complex matcher. Because of these weaknesses, we don't recommend pattern matching for real databases, but it's a useful way to navigate through complicated data structures.

10.2   A Driving Consultant

I don't want to talk grammar, I want to talk like a lady.
— George Bernard Shaw, *Pygmalion*

The code presented in this section can be found in file `driver.scm`.

In the movies, computers often carry on conversations with their human users. In *WarGames* (1983), a young genius nearly manages to trigger World War III by causing a computer to run a simulation of a game called Global Thermonuclear War.[4] The hero interacts with the computer not with some arcane command language, but in plain English. At one point, he asks the computer, "Is this a game, or is it real"? The computer replies, "What's the difference"?

Researchers have worked on the problem of natural-language understanding for the past 40 years or so, but have not been able to build a system that can have an intelligent conversation with a user. If we have much more modest goals, however, we can have modest successes. Suppose we abandon the attempt to build a general system and create instead a program that lets the user work in a language that *looks like* English, but is much more restricted. One way to do this is to restrict the problem domain. To understand the sentence, "The goal-keeper slipped in the mud and lost the game", you need to know that "goal-keeper" is a soccer position, soccer is played outdoors, the ground gets muddy when it rains, mud is slippery, and a misplay by a goal-keeper can allow the opposing team to score. A system that answers questions about stock prices need know none of these facts. Another technique is to simplify the accepted syntax. A program that converses with the user on one subject only needs to understand the sentences a user would use to converse about that subject.

At one extreme, we have an extremely tedious program that has a list of input sentences, and responds to these sentences in predefined ways. At the other extreme, we have a program that can answer any question. In the middle, we have patterns.

☞ **Exercise 10–7**

In many languages the form of a question bears a simple relation to the declarative sentence, for example:

```
The ball is red.  Is the ball red?
```

Write a procedure, `question`, that acts like this:

```
(question '(the ball is red))  ⇒  (is the ball red)
```

The input will be a declarative sentence such as, "The computer is slow", "The student is clever", or "The street is long", with just the same structure as the original. Hint: You can use the `var-match?` and `substitute-alist` in your answer. ❑

---

[4] This story is far-fetched, but there was a real incident on which it was based: in 1979, there was a brief war scare when a simulation tape was mistakenly loaded onto a Strategic Air Command computer system.

To show how patterns are useful in natural-language processing, we built a small program that lets a user ask questions about the rules of the road, perhaps when studying for a driver's license.

```
> (driver-system)
Driver consultant . . . how can I help you?
driver> (how do I make a left turn)
Move into the left lane first.
driver> (can I make a right turn on red)
Yes, but you must come to a full stop first.
driver> (is it ok to make a right turn when the light is red)
Yes, but you must come to a full stop first.
driver> (please tell me if I can pass on a hill)
You can pass when going up a hill, but not near the top.
driver> (what do I have to do when I turn)
You must signal before you turn.
driver> (can a driver with a class 5 license drive a truck)
See the booklet GETTING A CLASS 5 LICENSE.
driver> (what should I do when a pedestrian steps into the road)
Yield. The pedestrian has the right of way.
driver> (do I have to yield to flying saucers)
Sorry, I don't understand your question.
driver> bye
Bye, and good luck on the test!
```

As you can see, the system seems to know what the user is talking about, and can make appropriate responses. The limited ability of the program is demonstrated by the question about flying saucers. The program has no way of telling that this is a silly question, and can only generate a polite "try again" response.

This program looks impressive; it appears to "understand" a great deal, not only about driving, but also about English: two different ways of asking the same question got the same (correct) response. However, the true nature of the program can be demonstrated by a few more inputs.

```
driver> (what should I do if I run over a pedestrian)
Yield. The pedestrian has the right of way.
driver> (can you turn lead into gold)
You must signal before you turn.
```

Clearly, the program doesn't really understand what the user is typing; it's just looking for patterns and giving the corresponding answer.

Program 10-5 shows the rules the program uses; each rule consists of a pattern and a response. The patterns use an additional pattern element, ??, to signify "0 or more items that I don't care about". For example, the first pattern, (?? right turn ?? red) matches

```
(right turn red)
(chipmunk right turn squirrel red)
(I want to make a right turn on a red light)
```

but not (x right y turn z red) since there is no ?? between right and turn.

```
(define driving-rules
  '(
    ((?? right turn ?? red ??)
     ("Yes, but you must come to a full stop first."))
    ((?? right turn ??)
     ("Move into the right lane first."))
    ((?? left turn ??)
     ("Move into the left lane first."))
    ((?? turn ??)
     ("You must signal before you turn."))
    ((?? pass ?? hill ??)
     ("You can pass when going up a hill, but not near the top."))
    ((?? pass ??)
     ("Always pass in the left lane."))
    ((?? pedestrian ??)
     ("Yield. The pedestrian has the right of way."))
    ((?? class ?a ??)
     ("See the booklet GETTING A CLASS" ?a "LICENSE."))
    ((??)
     ("Sorry, I don't understand your question."))
  ))
(define rule-pattern
  (lambda (rule)
    (car rule)))
(define rule-answer
  (lambda (rule)
    (car (cdr rule)))))
```

Program 10-5   Driving consultant: rules

We have defined an ADT for rules, shown in Figure 10-2. This ADT is very rudimentary, and only exists because of our reluctance to use car and cdr as accessors (as opposed to using them for list manipulation).

Accessor

- (rule-pattern *rule*)
  Return the pattern in the rule.

- (rule-answer *rule*)
  Return the answer in the rule.

Figure 10-2   **Abstract Data Type:** rule

var-match? doesn't support ??, so we must modify our matcher again. Program 10-6 shows our new matcher, match?. It is very much like var-match?: the helper must be modified to check for ??, and a new procedure, match-arbitrary, has been added that attempts to match the remainder of the pattern against the target. If this match succeeds, match-arbitrary returns success; if not, match-arbitrary calls itself on the cdr of the target.

In Program 10-5 more than one pattern might match the same target. For

```
(define match?
  (lambda (pattern goal)
    (match-helper pattern goal '())))
(define match-helper
  (lambda (pat targ answers)
    (cond
      ((null? pat)
       (make-answer (null? targ) answers))
      ((equal? (car pat) '??)
       (match-arbitrary (cdr pat) targ answers))
      ((null? targ)
       (make-answer #f answers))
      ((pattern-variable? (car pat))
       (if (agrees-with? (car pat) (car targ) answers)
           (match-helper (cdr pat) (cdr targ)
             (add-answer (car pat) (car targ) answers))
           (make-answer #f answers)))
      ((equal? (car pat) (car targ))
       (match-helper (cdr pat) (cdr targ) answers))
      (else
       (make-answer #f answers)))))
(define match-arbitrary
  (lambda (pat targ answers)
    (if (null? targ)
        (make-answer (null? pat) answers)
        (let ((new-ans (match-helper pat targ answers)))
          (if new-ans
              new-ans
              (match-arbitrary  pat (cdr targ) answers))))))
(define make-answer
    (lambda (matched? answers)
      (if matched?
          (cons #t answers)
          #f)))
```

Program 10-6   Procedure match?

example, (can I make a right turn on red) matches both (?? right turn ??)
and (?? right turn ?? red). The ordering of the rules is therefore significant and
we will use the *first* rule that matches. This allows us to have specific and general
rules that use the same keywords (e.g., left turn red and left turn).

We can now build the program itself, as shown in Program 10-7. The key is
the procedure answer-question, which scans through the rules from top to bottom
in order to identify the applicable rule, and then calls produce-answer to display
the result.

```
(define driver-system
  (lambda ()
    (letrec
      ((helper
        (lambda ()
          (display "driver> ")
          (let ((x (read)))
            (if (pair? x)
              (begin
                (answer-question x driving-rules)
                (helper)))))))
      (format #t "Driver consultant . . . how can I help you?~%")
      (helper)
      (format #t "Bye, and good luck on the test!~%"))))
(define answer-question
  (lambda (question rules)
    (if (null? rules)
      (error 'driver-consultant "Internal error: no rules match.")
      (let ((x (match? (rule-pattern (car rules)) question)))
        (if x
          (produce-answer x (rule-answer (car rules)))
          (answer-question question (cdr rules)))))))
(define produce-answer
  (lambda (bindings answer)
    (if (null? answer)
      (newline)
      (begin
        (display
          (if (pattern-variable? (car answer))
            (lookup (car answer) bindings)
            (car answer)))
        (display #\space)
        (produce-answer bindings (cdr answer))))))
(define lookup
  (lambda (patvar bindings)
    (if (pair? bindings)
      (let ((x (assv patvar bindings)))
        (if x
          (cdr x)
          (error 'driver-consultant
            "Internal error: unknown pattern variable")))
      (error 'driver-consultant
        "Internal error: unknown pattern variable"))))
```

Program 10-7   The driving consultant

☞ **Exercise 10–8**

For each set of examples and counterexamples, write a pattern that matches the examples but not the counterexamples. For example, (? blue ?) matches (a blue a) and (red blue red) but not (a blue dog).

  a. Examples:

    (bill is here)
    (melinda is here)

    Counterexamples:

    (bill was here)
    (melinda ate here)

  b. Examples:

    (bill is here now)
    (tom is not here)

    Counterexamples:

    (bill was here then)
    (tom eats here often)

  c. Examples:

    (Do not eat this now)
    (jane is not here this morning)
    (not for this)

    Counterexamples:

    (not ready at this time)
    (i will not go there this time)

10.3 Logic and Logic Programming

> *It is more important that a proposition be interesting than that it be true. This statement is almost a tautology. For the energy of operation of a proposition in an occasion of experience is its interest, and is its importance. But of course a true proposition is more apt to be interesting than a false one.*
> — A. N. Whitehead, *Adventures of Ideas*

Our use of patterns allowed us to write a compact program to express complicated information-processing requirements. The driving consultant could be extended to include just about any reasonable question a driver might ask, though we would probably want a more powerful pattern-matcher. We are now ready to apply pattern matching to rule-based programming.

10.3.1 Tables and Their Limitations

At the beginning of the chapter, we asked how we could write a program that would automate the process of checking whether a student had the prerequisites to reg-

The Thinking Computer

One of the earliest books on computers, published in 1949, was called *Giant Brains, or Machines That Think*, by Edmund Berkeley. Early computing machines, with perhaps 4K of memory, were too primitive to do anything but extremely simple calculations; nonetheless, the fact that they could do the calculations on their own, without a human pushing buttons at each step, caught the public's imagination.

Most of the early computer designers saw their machines as nothing more than automatic calculators. The exception was Alan Turing, who designed an automatic code-breaking machine during World War II. After the war, Turing began to design general-purpose computers. His machine, the Pilot ACE, was no more powerful than the other early machines, but it served as a basis for Turing's speculations about truly intelligent machines.

In a paper published in 1950, Turing asked how we could tell whether a machine was actually capable of thought. He proposed an elegant experiment: put a human experimenter in a room with a computer terminal. In another room, there is either a computer or a human imposter at a second computer terminal, connected to the experimenter's terminal; the experimenter does not know whether the other party is human or computer. The experimenter may type anything she wants to; the imposter replies to the experimenter's comments in whatever way she wants to; the computer has been programmed to respond exactly as a human would. The conversation might look like this. (The experimenter's comments begin with e>; the other party's begin with m> for "mystery".)

```
e> I was kind of grumpy the other day when my car died.
m> Yeah, I know what you mean. I can't live without wheels.
e> So I took it into the shop.
m> What was wrong?
e> Electrical fault.
m> Oh, that's pretty easy to fix. So, who do you pick in the
   Boston--Toronto game?
```

Turing defined a machine as intelligent if it could fool an experimenter who was given as much time, and could ask whatever questions, as she wanted. Turing's definition focused not on the internal structure of the computer or its program, but on its behavior. All it needs to do is to be able to respond in the same way a human does.

The computer scientist Joseph Weizenbaum, who expressed doubts about the validity of the Turing test, wrote a program called Eliza to demonstrate his doubts. Eliza has a "script" that consists of patterns and responses. Weizenbaum's script made Eliza respond like a (Rogerian) psychologist. The resulting program might respond like this:

```
>I worry about computers.
You have your mind on computers, it seems.
>Yes, I certainly do!
Why do you say yes you certainly do?
>Because I think computers might take over the world.
Is it because you think computers might take over the
world that you came to me?
```

```
>Yes.
I see . . .  Well, what makes you believe this is so?
>My mother told me to watch out for sneaky computers.
You think too much about computers.
>My mother says a lot of things about them.
Tell me something about your family.
```

Even though this looks like a conversation between two beings, a little additional dialog will demonstrate that it's a fraud:

```
>I would like to frabistulate you.
Perhaps we frabistulate each other in your dreams.
```

Eliza is nothing more than a giant pattern matcher; it "knows" nothing about what any of the inputs mean. ("Eliza" comes from Eliza Doolittle, a character in Shaw's play *Pygmalion*, who learns to speak very upper-class British English without necessarily understanding much about what she is saying.) Even though Eliza (the program) could fool people for a few minutes, almost everyone quickly saw through the fraud.

Since the 1960s, computer programs have been written to perform many tasks that were thought to require human intelligence. Programs have been written to diagnose diseases, to configure complex computer systems, and to make sense of complex visual images. In 1994, a program beat the world chess champion, Gary Kasparov, at speed chess.

These programs contain no mystical elements, only clever algorithms. Sometimes, these programs rely upon brute force, considering millions of alternatives before choosing an answer. Artificial intelligence programs can often avoid brute force by employing "heuristics", methods that provide efficient approximate solutions most of the time. (Such a program will generally check to see whether it has any appropriate heuristics, and resort to brute force only if not.) Are algorithms, fast computation, and heuristics all there is to thought?

Answering this question requires us to define "thought". AI programs duplicate *cognitive* processes, which involve purposeful problem-solving activities. Human thought also involves intuition and emotion. Nobody has ever built a genuinely intuitive or emotional program (though it's trivial to write a program that *appears* to be emotional—(display "I'm so happy!") will do the job).

The jury is out on whether we can build a robot that can understand English, let alone build one that will sulk if you insult it.

Some people, such as Marvin Minsky, a well-known artificial intelligence researcher, have argued that there are processes that enable people to think, and there is no reason why we can't build devices that duplicate those processes. Others argue that consciousness is unique and that it is impossible for humans to duplicate in a machine the processes we use for thinking. To these people, any machine would inevitably fail the Turing test; it might be able to fool people for a very long time, but it would inevitably make a mistake.

Many artificial intelligence researchers prefer to sidestep the issue. One wit once defined artificial intelligence as "the set of problems we haven't yet figured out how to solve". Even if it were impossible to build a thinking computer, solving problems in natural language, computer vision, and robotics can still have immensely practical benefits.

ister in a given course. Why isn't DBScheme sufficient to solve this problem? Can rules help us write a modular, understandable program?

Let's carefully characterize the prerequisite problem. At the beginning of each semester, students register for courses, using an on-line registration system. Necessarily, the order in which students access the system is an important aspect of the system. As of the early 1990s, most on-line registration systems do the check for space in the section immediately; checking prerequisites is often an overnight batch process. For each course, we would like the system to give an immediate response as to whether there is room in the desired section, and whether the students have the necessary prerequisites.[5]

The on-line registration system would have access to five tables:

- `students`, a table of basic student information, including name and student number
- `grades`, a table of the grades students have achieved in prior semesters
- `prerequisites`, a table with one row for each valid combination of prerequisites for a course
- `courses`, a table of the courses students are currently taking, along with their status in each
- `overrides`, a table of all permissions that have been granted by faculty to register in a section

Figure 10-3 shows an example of `courses`, which is just a collection of the courses and sections students have registered for. This table can be used in many ways throughout the semester, including the production of a list of students for each section, and a report of final grades at the end.[6] Each time a faculty member allows a student to register in a section without the required prerequisites, a row is written to `overrides`.

student-no	course	section
123	CS128	002
123	MA110	004
456	EN105	008
123	PS101	002

Figure 10-3   A sample `courses` table

☞ **Exercise 10-9**

Suppose we also wanted to check for time conflicts, so as to warn a student when two courses are scheduled for the same time. How should we change our table structure? How would we do the time check? ❏

---

[5] Different institutions have different philosophies about prerequisites. Some insist that all students have the necessary prerequisites, while others leave it up to the students to ensure that they have the necessary background. In such an institution, our system would still be useful: denying a student admission to a class would force that student to get permission from a faculty advisor, at which point appropriate warning could be given.

[6] Of course a real student-records system would have a vastly more complicated structure; however, these tables will be sufficient for our checker.

One way to do the prerequisite checking in DBScheme is to join `courses` and `prerequisites` to produce a table of the required prerequisites for each student. In this and all the following joins, we use the course number as the join field. We can then join this table with `grades` to produce a table showing the grades students have achieved in prerequisite courses. We now join this table with `overrides`. Each row of the resulting table has the student name and number, a course, one of its prerequisites, the grade achieved in the prerequisite, and any override information. Finally, we can scan the resulting table to confirm that each student has either passed each prerequisite or received a faculty override.

Because different arrangements of prerequisites require different kinds of joins, there are generally limited numbers of allowed prerequisites. Often, allowable prerequisites include courses not presently offered: a course might have been replaced with a different one, but the college still wants to let students use the older course as a prerequisite. Somehow the prerequisite-checker must incorporate all of these factors. It's no wonder that automated prerequisite checking is complicated.

There's nothing impossible about using a table-based approach, but it's not very flexible. If we need other sources of information (e.g., scores on a diagnostic placement test), the prerequisite-checking code must be modified accordingly.

The best approach is to build a set of rules that describe the exact prerequisite arrangements. These rules can then be used in combination with the existing tables of data to answer immediately the question of whether a given student has the prerequisites to take a given course. A rule-based approach offers a much cleaner way of doing things. Rules can be added as needed to allow for changes in course prerequisites, as well as new courses. As obsolete courses recede into history, the college can remove rules that refer to them. The flexibility of rules makes them an attractive approach for the designers of most prerequisite-checking programs.

10.3.2 Logic

Our prerequisite-checker has the job of answering questions such as, "Is Winona Smith qualified to take CS216"? We could proceed directly to write a rule-based program for this job, but it's profitable to think about the problem more deeply. Often in computer science people have a choice: they can either attempt to build a program by starting their analysis from scratch, or they can base the program on an applicable theory that might help. Some of our Case Studies have used different areas of theory: the lunar lander was based on physics, the predator/prey model on population dynamics (a branch of ecology), and the ticket-simulator on statistics and queueing theory. In recent years, several areas of computer science theory have borne fruitful results. Notable theoretically based products include the Rivest-Shamir-Adelman (RSA) encryption system, the Lempel-Ziv-Welch data compression method (LZW), and Ethernet. Even Scheme is based on an area of mathematics (lambda calculus) that initially was thought to have no practical application.[7]

☞ **Exercise 10–10**

Find out what area of computer science theory each of the above products (RSA, LZW, and Ethernet) is based upon. A trip to the library might be in order. ❏

---

[7] To begin the study of lambda calculus, you might read *Essentials of Programming Languages*, cited in the Bibliography.

What kind of theory might be useful in organizing the rules for the prerequisite-checker? To answer this question, we need to think carefully about the checker's job, which is to use the available information to show why a student is or is not qualified to take a course. The rules state things like "If A, B, and C are true, then D is true". Usually A will be something like "The student can take CS124". To show that a student is qualified, the checker must argue the truth of a statement (e.g., "Fred can take CS124") from the truth of other statements (e.g., "Fred has taken Math 100"), using the rules. If a human were doing this job, we would call it *reasoning*. The branch of knowledge that deals with the structure of arguments is **logic**.

People have thought about reasoning for thousands of years. In mathematics, we want to be able to answer questions about the truth of a proposition. The Greek mathematician Euclid (ca. 300 B.C.) was the first to demonstrate how to do this effectively. He identified a number of **axioms**, or statements that were taken as given, and then demonstrated a method of proving further **theorems** from them. His *Elements* was such an effective geometry textbook that it was used in some countries into the twentieth century.

Just as computer programmers try to produce as clean and simple a program as possible, so mathematicians try to use as few axioms as possible. The aim is to be able to prove the largest number of theorems from the smallest set of axioms, that is, to take the fewest number of things for granted, and to use the smallest number of rules for the proof.

At about the same time as Euclid, Aristotle asked how we can tell whether or not a chain of reasoning is valid. He was not as interested in mathematics as Euclid; rather, he was concerned with the arguments spun by politicians and philosophers. Aristotle developed a system of rules for determining whether or not an argument was valid.

Aristotle's method was quite simple in concept. He organized the argument into a series of statements, and showed how it was possible to prove each statement in the light of those that were already known to be true. Aristotle saw a number of patterns in the way that arguments can be made; he called them **syllogisms**.

For example, consider the following syllogism:

1. All humans are mortal.
2. Socrates is a human.
3. Therefore, Socrates is mortal.

This particular syllogism begins with a rule ("All x are y"), and then gives a statement of fact ("z is an x"). Aristotle asserted that one can draw the conclusion "z is a y" from this argument. Aristotle and his successors in both classical and medieval times elaborated this system into a list of a hundred or so different syllogisms. A complicated chain of reasoning could then be checked by seeing whether each part matched one of the syllogisms.

A syllogism consists of premises and conclusions. A **premise** is an assertion that we are expected to believe; a **conclusion** is a statement that can be **proved** true using the premises and a set of **proof rules**. The Aristotelian classification of syllogisms was an early set of proof rules.

A chain of reasoning is **valid** if each step, except the assumptions, can be proved from the previous ones.

1. All insects have six legs.
2. My dog is an insect.
3. Therefore, my dog has six legs.

This is a syllogism; however the conclusion isn't true, because one of the premises is false. On the other hand, considering the following:

1. All houses have doorways.
2. Charles de Gaulle was the President of France.
3. Therefore, Scheme is a programming language.

This argument is not a syllogism, because the various steps have nothing to do with each other. Nonetheless, we do agree with the conclusion!

For a syllogism to produce an untrue conclusion, one of the assumptions must be incorrect. A valid argument from false premises, on the other hand, can lead to a true conclusion:

1. Anything that has four legs is a programming language.
2. Scheme has four legs.
3. Therefore, Scheme is a programming language.

The important fact is this: If the premises are true, a valid argument produces a true conclusion.

☞ **Exercise 10–11**

The syllogism based on false premises is beloved by certain politicans: if they can get an audience to accept the incorrect assumptions, then they must accept the conclusions. You have just been listening to some politicians speak. Identify each of their arguments as valid or invalid, and their conclusions as true or false.

    a. "People with brown eyes are a threat to our morality and indeed our national security. We cannot stand by and watch our nation destroyed by its enemies. We can only protect ourselves by restricting the freedom of brown-eyed people. Therefore, we must deny brown-eyed people equal rights."

    b. "We need to begin a new era of economic cooperation. In the new economy, change is a constant. A new economy demands new ideas. It is time for us to shed our traditional ideas, and enter the global economy, with world-class solutions to world-class problems. Therefore, we must increase educational opportunities, and ensure that everyone has access to the education needed for a worthwhile and satisfying career." ❏

10.3.3 Propositional Logic

The method of syllogisms is useful to humans, but almost impossible to use as the basis of a computer program. For one thing, the computer would have to be able to understand the natural language in which arguments are expressed.[8] This does not bode well for our prerequisite-checker. We need, instead, a notation that is amenable to computation.

The nineteenth-century mathematician George Boole was the first person to develop an algebraic formalism for logical arguments. There had been earlier attempts, but they were based on syllogisms, and didn't seem to lead anywhere. One result of Boole's work has become quite familiar. The Boolean operators and values of all programming languages were developed by Boole, even though he had no concept of computers or programming.

Boole's work developed into a simple system known as **propositional logic**, in which individual symbols stand for **propositions**, statements to which one can

---

[8] This is ironic in light of the fact that researchers in computer understanding of natural language now use logic as the basis of their programs!

attribute truth or falsity. For example, "Orson Welles directed the movie *Citizen Kane*", "Water boils when its temperature reaches 0 degrees Celsius", and "Scheme is a programming language" are propositions that have a clearly defined **truth value**.[9]

Propositional logic uses operators—the logical connectives and, or, and not—with which we are already familiar. We can define these operators by listing all possible combinations of truth values and showing the result for each one in what we call a **truth table**. Truth tables for the familiar Boolean operators are shown in Figure 10-4.

a	*b*	*a* and *b*	*a* or *b*	not *a*
false	false	false	false	true
false	true	false	true	true
true	false	false	true	false
true	true	true	true	false

Figure 10-4   Truth tables for and, or, and not

One of the most important of the Boolean connectives is called **implication**, the connective that expresses "*a implies b*"; its truth table is shown in Figure 10-5.

a	*b*	*a* implies *b*
false	false	true
false	true	true
true	false	false
true	true	true

Figure 10-5   The truth table for implication

We say that proposition *a implies* proposition *b* if either *a* and *b* are both true, or if *a* is false; *a* implies *b* has the same truth table as (not *a*) or *b*. Implication is important because it corresponds to the "if . . . then . . ." of English. If we know that *a* is true, the implication *a* implies *b* allows us to conclude that *b* is true.[10]

Our Socrates syllogism can thus be written as follows:

---

[9] In our logic, propositions are either true or false. There are multi-valued logics, with additional values such as don't care or maybe. Fuzzy logic, in which truth values are numbers between 0 and 1, has become very popular in recent years. In fuzzy logic, a proposition might be "John is tall": a value of 0 would mean that John is short, a value of 0.75 that John is reasonably tall, and a value of 1.0 that John is definitely tall. Fuzzy logic has been found to be very useful for building certain sorts of computer programs, in particular those that control devices. For example, a computer-controlled elevator can adjust its behavior to meet differing demands during the day.

[10] Implication has one *very* important difference from the usual meaning of "if . . . then . . .". The truth of (not *a*) lets us conclude (not *a*) or *b*, which is the same as *a* implies *b*. However, in English, we would find it odd to say "It's not raining, so if it's raining, then I'm a giraffe", but that follows from a literal use of logic.

1. Socrates-is-human implies Socrates-is-mortal
2. Socrates-is-human
3. Therefore, Socrates-is-mortal

We call a proposition that is always true a **tautology**; p or (not p) is a tautology, for any proposition p. Either it is raining outside or it is not raining outside is an example. We call a proposition that is never true a **contradiction**. p and (not p) is a contradiction, for any proposition p. For example, It is raining outside, and it is not raining outside can never be true.

We must make sure that none of our premises are either tautologies or contradictions. Tautologies are useful in developing proofs; after all, mathematics is composed entirely of tautologies. However, a tautological premise doesn't help our program. When we're trying to show whether Rachel can take CS315, it is useless to remark that either she can or she can't. A contradiction is much worse. Once we have both p and (not p) as premises, sound logical reasoning will lead us to nonsense, as well as sense!

What good is propositional logic? It's a first step at a notation for expressing chains of reasoning. Also, it provides a means of calculating the truth value of any propositional formula. If we have the truth values of all the propositional variables (e.g., p, q), in a formula, the truth tables let us evaluate the whole formula. That turns out to be good enough for the Boolean variables of programming languages, but not good enough for general rules.

Propositional logic has another, perhaps surprising, application. Digital electronics is based upon combining electrical (or other) signals that represent bits; much of a computer, or any other digital device, consists of components that compute Boolean functions on these signals. In fact, to a digital electronic engineer, the word "logic" means not what we have been studying, but hardware for doing Boolean computations.[11]

10.3.4 Predicate Logic

Propositional logic deals quite well with individuals. Syllogisms, however, include rules of the sort "All x are y". In our discussion of propositional logic, we handled such a rule as a special case, Socrates-is-human implies Socrates-is-mortal. This isn't good enough; we need a way to write a general rule that says, "Any human being is mortal". To represent these rules, we must extend our notation.

A look at a sentence such as "Socrates is mortal" or "All humans are mortal" is instructive. In English grammar, we refer to "Socrates" as the *subject* of the first sentence, and "is mortal" as the *predicate*. The two sentences both have the same predicate, but they have different subjects. In **predicate logic**, our propositions refer not only to individuals, but to predicates. We can write, for example, mortal(Socrates) to say that Socrates is mortal. Similarly, we can write mortal(Plato) or mortal(Elvis).

When we say mortal(Socrates), we are assuming a predicate mortal, which applies to **individuals** such as Socrates. We can also write mortal(x); of course, in this case the truth value of the proposition isn't known unless we know what x refers

---

[11] Actually, there are two types of circuits that a digital designer uses: *combinational logic* computes Boolean functions, and *sequential logic* stores bit values for further use.

to. Predicate notation looks very much like mathematical function notation, and indeed there are similarities. We can think of a predicate as a mathematical function whose arguments are individuals and whose values are the Boolean values.

We can use predicate notation with the propositional operators. In fact, when a predicate is applied to an individual, such as mortal(Descartes), it can be treated as a proposition. For example, we can say

- mortal(Descartes) and philosopher(Descartes)
- foo(x) and not foo(x) (a contradiction, regardless of the meaning of foo).

This brings up an interesting question: What exactly does mortal(x) mean? Does it mean "Every individual is mortal", or does it mean "There is at least one individual who is mortal"? The real issue here is that of variable binding. We solved this problem in Scheme by using forms such as lambda and let to allow us to introduce variables. Variables in logic don't have values, but we still have to bind them. In logic, binding is known as **quantification** and there are two forms:

- forall x, mortal(x)
  The **universal quantification** forall x, ... introduces a new variable and asserts that the proposition is true for *any* individual. Thus, we are saying "Every individual is mortal". This means that mortal(Socrates) is true, and mortal(Descartes) is true and . . . , for each and every individual.
- exists x, mortal(x)
  The **existential quantification** exists x, ... introduces a new variable, and asserts that the proposition is true for *at least one* individual. This means that mortal(Socrates) is true, or mortal(Spinoza) is true or . . . , for each and every individual.

We can now write our Socrates syllogism as follows:

1. forall x, human(x) implies mortal(x)
2. human(Socrates)
3. Therefore, mortal(Socrates)

A statement such as "All humans are mortal" turns into a universally quantified implication.

☞ **Exercise 10–12**

Write each of the following statements in predicate logic.
  a. Bill is a student.
  b. All computers run DOS. (Hint: Use the predicate runs(x, y) to say that computer x runs program y.)
  c. Some computers run DOS.
  d. Any computer that runs DOS can run MegaCalc. ❏

More complex statements that use more than one variable follow the same static scoping rules as Scheme uses. For example, we can say that every student takes at least one course:

forall x, student(x) implies (exists y, takes(x, y))

Stated literally, this statement says, "For each student, there is at least one course that this student takes". On the other hand,

exists y, (forall x, student(x) implies takes(x, y))

says, "There is at least one course that every student takes".

☞ **Exercise 10–13**

Write each of the following statements in predicate logic.

    a. Every computer can run every program.
    b. Some programs can be run on any computer.
    c. Any computer can run programs.
    d. There is at least one program that can't be run on any computer. ❏

☞ **Exercise 10–14**

Write the English equivalents of the following predicate logic statements.
    a. exists *y*, food(*y*) and forall *x*, person(*x*) implies not likes(*x, y*)
    b. forall *x*, food(*x*) implies exists *y*, person(*y*) and likes(*y, x*)
    c. exists *y*, person(*y*) and forall *x*, food(*x*) implies likes(*x, y*) ❏

    Predicates by themselves aren't particularly useful. Writing mortal(Socrates) isn't much more useful than writing mortal-socrates in propositional logic. To be useful, predicate calculus must include a way to represent rules.

    We could allow our rules to include any statement in predicate calculus, but there are good objections to doing so, from both logicians and computer scientists. We will therefore require that our rules be in a very simple format. Each rule is either

- a fact, such as mortal(Socrates), or can-take(*x*, CS100). Facts can include variables, as in the second example ("everyone can take CS100").

- a compound rule, such as
  can-take(*x*, CS216) if has-taken(*x*, CS128) and has-taken(*x*, MA100)
  A compound rule is an implication; it is conventional to write the conclusion (the then part) on the left and the premises (the if part) on the right. The only connective permitted is and; not is not allowed at all (we can't say anything is not something[12]), and or can be accomplished by using more than one rule.

What does a fact such as can-take(*x*, CS100) mean? What we're saying is that anyone can take CS100, that is, all facts that include variables are implicitly universally quantified.

    Our rules can only express and. How do we handle or? Suppose, for example, we want to have the prerequisites for CS293, Computer Hardware, as either Physics 125, Electricity and Magnetism, or Electrical Engineering 105, Linear Circuits. We must use two rules:

    can-take(x, CS293) if has-taken(x, PH125)
    can-take(x, CS293) if has-taken(x, EE105)

    There are excellent technical reasons for the restrictions we impose. It turns out to be convenient to write the premises of a rule on the right and the conclusion on the left. For example, we can say that all Greek philosophers read Plato:
    reads(x, Plato) if Greek(x) and philosopher(x)
    As a second example, we can say that something is mortal if it's a computer or it's a human.[13]

---

[12] This is really an upbeat language!

[13] Another way of saying this is "computers and humans are both mortal". This example should serve to convince you that logic is much more precise about the meaning of words such as "and" and "or" than everyday English is.

mortal(x) if computer(x)
mortal(x) if human(x)

Note how we've used two rules to express or.

We are now ready to write a set of logic rules for the prerequisite problem. Figure 10-6 shows the course prerequisites. The notation "(concurr.)" indicates that a prerequisite can be taken at the same time, or may already have been taken.

Course	Title	Prerequisites
MA100	Calculus I	none
MA101	Calculus II	MA100
MA110	Calculus I/II	none
CS100	Intro to CS	none
CS108	Intro to Pascal	MA100
CS124	Principles CS I	MA100 or MA110 (concurr.)
CS126	Principles CS II	CS124
CS128	Principles CS	CS100 or 108; MA100 or MA110 (concurr.)
CS216	Data structures	CS124 or CS126
CS218	Computer arch	CS124 or CS126
CS220	Theory of CS	CS124 or CS126; MA101
CS315	Operating systems	CS216 and CS218

Figure 10-6   Prerequisites at Lambda University

To translate Figure 10-6 into rules, we can assume that we know whether a given person has taken a given course. The predicate has-taken(x,y) is true if student x has taken course y, and is-taking(x,y) is true if student x is currently registered in course y. Program 10-8 provides some initial data that we would expect to get from tables, but to keep things simple for now, we'll provide the data directly.

has-taken(Jared, CS100)
has-taken(Jared, MA100)
is-taking(Dana, MA100)
is-taking(Dana, PS101)
has-taken(Linda, CS124)
has-taken(Diane, CS216)
has-taken(Diane, CS218)

Program 10-8   Initial data for prerequisite-checker

Program 10-9 is a set of logic rules for the prerequisite-checker. We've used additional predicates to make the code modular. For example, introducing the predicate has-intro-CS(x) makes our code clearer, because some courses have two alternative entrance requirements (CS126 or CS128). If we didn't use has-intro-CS, CS216, CS218, and CS220 would each require an additional rule.

Proving Programs Correct

Computer scientists and engineers have long dreamed of being able to prove that a program is correct, that is, that it does what its specifications demand. Some programs have actually been proven correct; we mentioned the proof of Quicksort in the previous chapter.

Central to proving any program is a detailed and accurate *specification* of the program. Specifying the valid arguments to a procedure, and a condition on the return value, is a first step. Recently, logic-based **specification languages** have been built. These languages aren't yet (and may never be) practical for large programs; however, it is possible to prove complicated algorithms correct, which is a lot better than nothing. One interesting aspect of program proof is that it can often show us how to write the program. Given an algorithm and its input/output specifications, deriving a proof of an as-yet unwritten program can be extremely useful in building the program.

The basic idea behind program proof is known as **mathematical induction**. As the name suggests, this technique is not specific to computer science; it was developed by mathematicians. To see how mathematical induction works, let's consider the problem of computing n^2 without using multiplication. Looking at the values of n and n^2 for $n = 1 \ldots 10$, you might see a pattern. It looks as though $n^2 = 1 + 3 + 5 + \cdots + 2n - 1$ (i.e., the sum of the first n odd integers). You *could* write a program based on this, but you would be more confident if you were certain that this formula was correct. All sorts of mathematical patterns work for a while, and then stop working (if you look at the integers 3, 5, and 7, you might conclude that all odd integers greater than 1 are prime!). Can we prove our formula?

In mathematical induction, we assume that our formula is true for some integer i, and then prove that it's true for $i + 1$. By itself, this isn't a proof; however, if we can prove that the formula works for a base case such as $i = 1$, then we have proved the formula for all other values. Can we do this in this case?

Base part It is certainly true that $1^2 = 1$, the sum of the first 1 odd integers.

Induction part Suppose we know that i^2 does equal the sum of the first i odd integers. Also, by algebra, we know that $(i + 1)^2 = i^2 + 2i + 1 = i^2 + 2(i + 1) - 1$ (note that $2i - 1$ is the ith odd number). Therefore, if i^2 is the sum of the first i odd integers, $(i + 1)^2$ is the sum of the first $i + 1$ odd integers.

What's particularly nice about this proof is that it leads in a straightforward way to a Scheme procedure:

```
(define square
  (lambda (n)
    (if (= n 1)
      1
      (+ n n -1 (square (sub1 n)))))))
```

Likewise, induction applies to structures defined recursively, such as trees and lists. We can therefore use inductive methods to prove properties of data structures and programs that are defined recursively.

It is possible that nobody will ever prove a payroll program correct. It *is* possible to prove complicated algorithms (e.g., for database management) on which the payroll program depends. Even this is a significant achievement.

```
can-take(x, MA100)
can-take(x, MA101) if has-taken(x, MA100)
can-take(x, CS100)
can-take(x, CS124) if has-calculus(x)
has-calculus(x) if has-taken(x, MA100)
has-calculus(x) if has-taken(x, MA110)
has-calculus(x) if is-taking(x, MA100)
has-calculus(x) if is-taking(x, MA110)
can-take(x, CS126) if has-taken(x, CS124)
can-take(x, CS128) if has-taken(x, CS100) and has-calculus(x)
can-take(x, CS128) if has-taken(x, CS108) and has-calculus(x)
can-take(x, CS216) if has-intro-CS(x)
has-intro-CS(x) if has-taken(x, CS126)
has-intro-CS(x) if has-taken(x, CS128)
can-take(x, CS218) if has-intro-CS(x)
can-take(x, CS220) if has-intro-CS(x) and has-taken(x, MA101)
can-take(x, CS315) if has-taken(x, CS216) and has-taken(x, 218)
```

Program 10-9   Logic rules for CS prerequisites

10.3.5   The Nature of Proof

To prove something, we want to demonstrate that the conclusion follows from the original facts and rules; that is, if one accepts the original facts, the conclusion must be true. In our prerequisite system, we want to be able to prove from our facts and rules that a given student may take a specific course.

In **logic programming**, we use proof as the framework for computing. A logic program consists of a set of rules; the input data consists of facts and a desired conclusion. An evaluator for a logic programming language must use this information to show that the conclusion actually follows from the available information. Therefore, it's reasonable to assume that a logic programming evaluator must work differently from a human being. A person might work on a complicated chain of reasoning in an apparently random manner until a whole proof had been constructed, but we prefer a computer program to use a systematic method of proof. Therefore, while a talented person might use intuition, a logic evaluator must use a specific **proof method**.

Logicians have developed a number of proof methods. Two methods that were in common use long before logicians studied them are of most interest to us. In **forward chaining**, we start with the original information and work our way to the conclusion. In **backward chaining**, we start with the conclusion and work backwards. The two methods are shown in Figure 10-7. We can read the arrows going downward as "implies" and the arrows going upward as "is implied by".

Let's use forward chaining to show can-take(Jared, CS128). We must start with our original premises and work forward to the conclusion:

1. We know has-taken(Jared, CS100) and has-taken(Jared, MA100)

2. We are therefore allowed to conclude that has-calculus(Jared).

3. This result lets us conclude can-take(Jared, CS128).

Backward chaining starts with the answer we're trying to show, and attempts to prove that we can produce this answer from our original facts and rules:

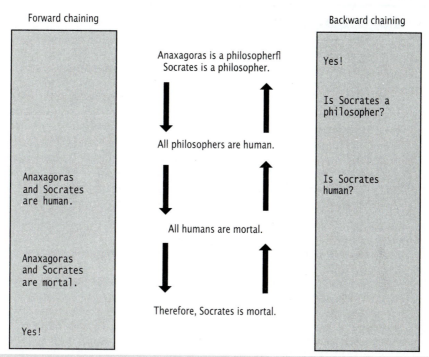

Forward chaining

Backward chaining

Anaxagoras is a philosopherfl
Socrates is a philosopher.

All philosophers are human.

All humans are mortal.

Therefore, Socrates is mortal.

Anaxagoras
and Socrates
are human.

Anaxagoras
and Socrates
are mortal.

Yes!

Yes!

Is Socrates a
philosopher?

Is Socrates
human?

Figure 10-7   Forward and backward chaining

1. Is it true that can-take(Jared, CS128)? We don't have a fact that tells us this, but we do have a rule can-take(x, CS128) if has-taken(x, CS100) and has-calculus(x). We must therefore ask whether has-taken(Jared, CS100) and has-calculus(Jared).

2. We know has-taken(Jared, CS100).

3. We do not know has-calculus(Jared). We do have a number of rules about has–calculus. Three of these rules lead nowhere, but the rule has-calculus(x) if has-taken(x, MA100) is useful.

4. We know has-taken(Jared, MA100).

5. We can therefore conclude that has-calculus(Jared), and this lets us conclude that can-take(Jared, CS128).

10.4   Logic Languages and Evaluators

For nothing worthy proving can be proven
Nor yet disproven; wherefore thou be wise
Cleave ever to the sunnier side of doubt.
— Alfred, Lord Tennyson, "The Ancient Sage"

We have seen how we can represent facts and rules in logic. By itself, this is interesting only to logicians. To build a prerequisite-checker, we must develop a way to represent rules, and build a program that uses them. Since we can use both forward and backward chaining in such a program, we will look at both. Forward chaining is considerably easier to implement and understand than backward chaining, but much less useful.

10.4.1   QScheme

The code presented in this section can be found in file `qsrules.scm`.

Our first step is to define a logic-programming language. We call ours QScheme, because it can be used to answer queries. QScheme consists of two Scheme procedures: `rules` for defining a set of rules and facts, and `query`, which uses a set of rules to answer a specific query. Program 10–10 shows the use of the `rules` and `query` procedures. `rules` takes as its argument a quoted list of rules, each of which is a more-or-less direct translation of the predicate logic rules we studied earlier.

```
(define mortality
  (rules
    '(((mortal ?x)    (human ?x))
      ((human socrates)))))
(query '(mortal socrates) mortality)
```
Program 10-10   Socrates in QScheme

For example, `((mortal ?x) (human ?x))` is a translation of mortal(x) if human(x). The first list in a rule is the conclusion; the remaining lists (zero or more) are the conditions that must be true in order for the conclusion to be true. `rules` returns an internal data structure known as a **ruleset**.

`query` takes as arguments a quoted list representing a query and a ruleset. It returns a list of all answers to the query that can be drawn from the ruleset. In this example, `query` will return `((mortal socrates))`.

☞ **Exercise 10–15**

Write QScheme rules for each of the following (no claims are made that they are true!).
  a. All computers run DOS.
  b. All computers that run DOS can run MegaCalc.
  c. All computers that run DOS or UNIX can run MegaCalc. ❏

QScheme programming consists primarily of producing rules. We can convert our prerequisite information into QScheme, as shown in Program 10-11.

```
(define prerequisites
  (rules
    '(
       ((can-take ?x MA100))
       ((can-take ?x MA101)   (has-taken ?x MA100))
       ((can-take ?x CS100))
       ((can-take ?x CS124)   (has-calculus ?x))
       ((has-calculus ?x)     (has-taken ?x MA100))
       ((has-calculus ?x)     (has-taken ?x MA110))
       ((has-calculus ?x)     (is-taking ?x MA100))
       ((has-calculus ?x)     (is-taking ?x MA110))
       ((can-take ?x CS126)   (has-taken ?x CS124))
       ((can-take ?x CS128)   (has-taken ?x CS100) (has-calculus ?x))
       ((can-take ?x CS128)   (has-taken ?x CS108) (has-calculus ?x))
       ((can-take ?x CS216)   (has-intro-CS ?x))
       ((has-intro-CS ?x)     (has-taken ?x CS126))
       ((has-intro-CS ?x)     (has-taken ?x CS128))
       ((can-take ?x CS218)   (has-intro-CS ?x))
       ((can-take ?x CS220)   (has-intro-CS ?x) (has-taken ?x MA101))
       ((can-take ?x CS315)   (has-taken ?x CS216)
                              (has-taken ?x CS218))

       ;; Now the specific information about the students.
       ((has-taken Jared CS100))
       ((has-taken Jared MA100))
       ((is-taking Dana MA100))
       ((is-taking Dana PS101))
       ((has-taken Linda CS124))
       ((has-taken Diane CS216))
       ((has-taken Diane CS218))
     )
))
```

Program 10-11   Prerequisites in QScheme

We can use QScheme to answer various questions. First, can Jared take CS124?

```
(query '(can-take jared cs124) prerequisites)
  ⇒  ((can-take jared cs124))
```

The answer is not a simple Boolean value, but a list of all the applicable facts. Can Jared take CS128 or CS216?

```
(query '(can-take jared cs128) prerequisites)
  ⇒  ((can-take jared cs128))
(query '(can-take jared cs216) prerequisites)  ⇒   ()
```

Who can take CS124 and CS128?

```
(query '(can-take ?x cs124) prerequisites)
  ⇒ ((can-take dana cs124) (can-take jared cs124))
(query '(can-take ?x cs128) prerequisites)
  ⇒ ((can-take jared cs128))
```

Who can take any course?

```
(query '(can-take ?x ?y) prerequisites) ⇒
  ((can-take dana cs124) (can-take jared cs124)
   (can-take jared cs128) (can-take jared ma101)
   (can-take linda cs126) (can-take diane cs315)
   (can-take ?x cs100) (can-take ?x ma100))
```

Can Bill (about whom we know nothing) take CS100?

```
(query '(can-take bill cs100) prerequisites)
  ⇒ ((can-take ?x cs100))
```

This answer is a bit peculiar. What we're getting back is a fact: anyone can take CS100. Could we not replace ?x with bill in the result? It so happens that our forward-chaining system doesn't do that. Nonetheless, the list isn't null, so we know Bill can in fact take CS100.

We can also use QScheme for other things. Program 10–12 shows who works for whom at Foo Corporation.

```
(define foo-corp
  (rules
    '(
      ((indirectly-supervises ?x ?y)
       (indirectly-supervises ?x ?z) (supervises ?z ?y))
      ((indirectly-supervises ?x ?y) (supervises ?x ?y))
      ((supervises edna bill))
      ((supervises edna eric))
      ((supervises bill joe))
      ((supervises joe mary))
      ((supervises mary tom))
      ((supervises kevin jeff))
      ((supervises doris glenda))
    )))
```

Program 10-12   Foo Corp's management structure

For example, (supervises ?a ?b) indicates that ?b directly works for ?a. To find whether ?a is ?b's boss, or boss's boss, or boss's boss's boss, we can use the rules for indirectly-supervises. The first rule says that ?x indirectly supervises ?y if ?x indirectly supervises ?y's supervisor. This is a recursive rule, so we need a base case: ?x indirectly supervises ?y if ?x directly supervises ?y.

The indirectly-supervises rules show something else about QScheme: we can introduce additional variables on the right-hand side. A new variable is considered to match anything the first time it appears in the right-hand side of a rule; after the first occurrence in a rule, the variable must match whatever it matched the first time. In the first rule for indirectly-supervises, for example,

```
((indirectly-supervises ?x ?y)
 (indirectly-supervises ?x ?z) (supervises ?z ?y))
```

The variable ?z in (indirectly-supervises ?x ?z) can match any individual. Once a particular value has been chosen for ?z, however, that value must be used for checking whether (supervises ?z ?y).

Writing this rule in logic shows how the variables are interpreted:

```
forall x,
  forall y,
    indirectly-supervises(x, y) if
      exists z,
        indirectly-supervises(x, z) and
        supervises(z, y)
```

Variables that appear on the left-hand side are considered to be universally quantified, whereas variables on the right-hand side are existentially quantified. QScheme needs no other techniques for quantification.

We can see our rules at work as follows:

```
(query '(supervises edna ?x) foo-corp)
  ⇒  ((supervises edna bill) (supervises edna eric))
(query '(indirectly-supervises edna tom) foo-corp)
  ⇒  ((indirectly-supervises edna tom))
(query '(indirectly-supervises eric tom) foo-corp) ⇒  ()
(query '(indirectly-supervises bill tom) foo-corp)
  ⇒  ((indirectly-supervises bill tom))
(query '(indirectly-supervises edna ?x) foo-corp) ⇒
  ((indirectly-supervises edna tom)
   (indirectly-supervises edna mary)
   (indirectly-supervises edna joe)
   (indirectly-supervises edna bill)
   (indirectly-supervises edna eric))
```

Our first query asks whom Edna directly supervises. We get a list of the two relevant facts. Edna indirectly supervises Tom; we have to use several levels of recursion on indirectly-supervises to show this. Edna supervises Bill, who supervises Joe, who supervises Mary, who supervises Tom. Eric doesn't supervise Tom: the null result shows this.

☞ **Exercise 10–16**

We can say that two employees are in the same division if the same person indirectly supervises them, or if one indirectly supervises the other. Write rules for this predicate. ❏

It's worth looking at what QScheme *can't* do. The language is obviously based upon pattern matching. We can't say, for example, that a student has passed a course if the final grade was greater than 50 percent. Real logic-programming languages have much more flexible patterns (including numeric or string comparison, and input/output), than does QScheme. QScheme is not a general-purpose language, but it is powerful enough to let us see how logic-programming languages work. In any case, nobody says we have to write our whole program in QScheme. It's just a tool: we can use it where it's useful, and use other techniques (databases, objects, or just plain raw Scheme) in other parts of the program.

10.4.2   A Forward-Chaining Inference Engine

The code presented in this section can be found in file `fqscheme.scm`.

We speak of `query` as an **inference engine**, a procedure whose job is to answer a query by producing a list of the facts that are either provided in the original rules or that can be proved by using the rules. An inference engine takes the rules and a query as arguments, and produces a list of all the answers. There are many different ways to design an inference engine. The simplest is to use the technique of forward chaining: start with the facts that are known, and use the rules to produce new facts. We repeat this recursively until we either have the desired answer, or reach a dead end.

This seems like a naive way to solve the problem. Why not restrict the search to facts and rules that are directly relevant? Such a brute-force approach wastes a great deal of time. Still, we have no alternative, because we don't know that rules are going to be relevant until we try them. Accordingly, our forward-chaining inference engine works in the simplest possible way: it makes a list of *all* facts that can be proved from the ruleset, and then extracts those that are answers to the original query.

Program 10-13 shows the top level. `forward` is what we've been calling `query` in the discussion of QScheme. In our backward-chaining inference engine, we'll have a procedure named `backward` that is also top-level. Using different names for the two query procedures allows you to have both engines loaded at the same time. To allow the code in the QScheme discussion to work, just do (`define query forward`).

```
(define forward
  (lambda (qry ruleset)
    (extract qry
      (forward-everything ruleset))))
(define extract
    (lambda (qry answers)
      (cond
       ((null? answers) '())
       ((match? qry (car answers))
        (cons (car answers)
          (extract qry (cdr answers))))
       ((match? (car answers) qry)
        (cons qry
          (extract qry (cdr answers))))
       (else (extract qry (cdr answers)))))))
```

Program 10-13   Forward chaining: the top level

All `forward` does is to call `forward-everything` to produce a list of all the facts that can be proved from the rules, and then call `extract` to find those facts that are answers to the query. The two calls to `match?` are necessary because both the original query and facts in the ruleset might have pattern variables in them. Consider the query (`can-take ?x cs128`), which includes a pattern variable. On the other hand, (`can-take bill cs100`) has no pattern variable in the query, but the corresponding fact in the ruleset is (`can-take ?x cs100`). Some queries, therefore, might have pattern variables in them, but might match facts with no pattern variables. Other queries might have no pattern variables, but might match facts with pattern variables.

Forward chaining starts with a rule or fact, and finds what can be proven from that rule or fact. Facts are taken as is; rules generate new facts. To see how forward-everything works, we must first look at how rules are represented. We treat rules and facts differently in forward chaining. Accordingly, rules builds a pair whose car is a list of the rules and whose cdr is the list of the facts in the ruleset. Program 10-14 shows this preprocessing. The heart of the forward-chainer is forward-everything and its helper forward1, shown in Program 10-15. forward1 is passed two arguments: the list of rules and the list of facts. It builds, in new, a list of all the facts that can be proved from these rules and facts.

```
(define rules
  (lambda (ruleset)
    (separate-facts-and-rules ruleset '() '())))
(define separate-facts-and-rules
  (lambda (rules-facts rules facts)
    (if (null? rules-facts)
      (cons rules facts)
      (let ((current (car rules-facts)))
        (if (null? (cdr current))
            (separate-facts-and-rules (cdr rules-facts)
              rules
              (cons (car current) facts))
            (separate-facts-and-rules (cdr rules-facts)
              (cons current rules)
              facts))))))
(define rule-lhs
  (lambda (rule) (car rule)))
(define rule-rhs
  (lambda (rule) (cdr rule)))
```

Program 10-14   Forward chaining: building the rules

forward1 adds to new all of the facts that can be found by using the existing rules; the double for-each (one in forward1 itself and one in use-rule) has the effect of taking each fact and each rule and adding to new all of the facts that can be proved by this combination. Each call to forward1 expands the set of facts. When the set of facts does not change after a call to forward1, the process stops. This process is reminiscent of the airline route-finder in Chapter 4, which starts from a city and creates the set of cities reachable in one step from the starting point, then the set for two steps, and so on. Here we generate the facts that can be found from the initial facts by one rule application, then two rule applications, and so on.

For example, suppose that we have the following rules and facts:

```
((mortal ?x) (human ?x))         ; Rule 1.
((human ?x) (philosopher ?x))    ; Rule 2.
((philosopher Socrates))         ; Fact 1.
((philosopher Hegel))            ; Fact 2.
```

```
(define forward-everything
  (lambda (rules-facts)
    (forward1 (car rules-facts) (cdr rules-facts))))
(define forward1
  (lambda (rules old)
    (let ((new '()))
      (letrec
        ((add-fact
           (lambda (lhs bindings)
             (let ((new-fact (substitute-alist lhs bindings)))
               (if (not (or (member new-fact old)
                            (member new-fact new)))
                 (set! new (cons new-fact new))))))
         (ground
           (lambda (fact head rhs lhs bindings)
             (let ((result (match? head fact)))
               (if result
                 (ground2 result rhs lhs bindings)
                 #f))))
         (ground2
           (lambda (result rhs lhs bindings)
             (let ((newbindings (merge-bindings result bindings)))
               (if (null? rhs)
                   (add-fact lhs newbindings)
                   (let ((newhead
                           (substitute-alist (car rhs)
                                             newbindings)))
                     (for-each
                       (lambda (item)
                         (ground item newhead
                           (cdr rhs) lhs newbindings))
                       old))))))
         (use-rule
           (lambda (single-rule)
             (for-each
               (lambda (fact)
                 (ground fact (car (cdr single-rule))
                   (cdr (cdr single-rule)) (car single-rule) '()))
               old))))
        (for-each use-rule rules)
        (if (null? new)
            old
            (forward1 rules (append new old)))))))
```

Program 10-15   Forward chaining

We start with Rule 1 and Fact 1. No new fact can be proved. Now we try Rule 1 and Fact 2. Again, no new fact. Now Rule 2 and Fact 1. Success! We can add the fact (human Socrates) to new. Rule 2 and Fact 2 together allow us to conclude that (human Hegel).

This iteration added two facts to new. Because we might be able to prove more with these new facts, we combine the new facts with the old ones and see what we can now prove. The recursive call to forward1 is given the following information:

```
((mortal ?x) (human ?x))          ; Rule 1.
((human ?x) (philosopher ?x))     ; Rule 2.
((philosopher Socrates))          ; Fact 1.
((philosopher Hegel))             ; Fact 2.
((human Socrates))                ; Fact 3.
((human Hegel))                   ; Fact 4.
```

Again we try Rule 1 and Fact 1, and then Rule 1 and Fact 2. No luck with either of these. Rule 1 and Fact 3 allow us to conclude (mortal Socrates); Rule 1 and Fact 4 give us (mortal Hegel). Now on to Rule 2. Since we have the same facts as on the previous run, we again conclude that Socrates and Hegel are human. To avoid duplicating facts, add-fact refuses to record any new fact if it is already known (i.e., if it appears in either new or old). Again, we make a recursive call to forward1, with old bound to the list of the six facts. This time, no new facts are proved, and we return old, the list of the six facts.

All we need to study now is ground and its helper ground2, which find all facts given by a given fact and rule combination. ground takes five arguments:

1. the fact
2. the first item of the right-hand side of the rule (the "head" of the rule)
3. the remaining items of the right-hand rule
4. the left-hand side of the rule
5. the pattern-variable bindings for the rule

The procedure's strategy is simple: look at the first item of the right-hand side to see whether the fact will support this item; if so, then (via ground2) recursively scan the rest of the rule. This scanning operation builds a new rule head by taking the current item and replacing any pattern variables with their bindings, and then using this new head in a recursive call to ground. If ground2 reaches the end of the rule, then the fact in question (represented by the left-hand side combined with the bindings) can be added.

If every rule had only one item on the right-hand side, ground would be very straightforward. However, there can be more than one item, and some items might introduce new variables. We must therefore match each item on the right-hand side of each rule; whatever bindings are obtained from the match are replaced in the succeeding items. If a particular set of bindings makes it all the way through the right-hand side, then the left-hand side is indeed a fact.

For example, consider

```
((can-take ?x cs128) (has-taken ?x cs100) (has-calculus ?x))
```

If ground is called with the fact (has-taken jared cs100), it will create the binding list ((?x . jared)). ground calls ground2 with this binding, the remainder of the right-hand side, now (has-calculus ?x), the left-hand side and the original bindings. ground2 merges the new binding ((?x . jared)) with the original bindings, and substitutes these bindings into (has-calculus ?x) to give (has-calculus jared). ground2, in a for-each over old, will match every known fact against (has-calculus jared). This match might succeed or fail, depending upon whether we already have that fact. If it does fail, some future iteration of the outer for-eaches will produce (has-calculus jared), at which point this rule can be used to produce (can-take jared cs128).

Program 10-16 shows the utility procedures needed by the forward-chainer, which manage bindings and substitution back into patterns. substitute-alist differs from the earlier versions only in that it doesn't treat an unknown pattern variable as an error.

```
(define merge-bindings
  (lambda (result bindings)
    (if (list? result)
      (merge-alist result bindings)
      bindings)))
(define merge-alist
  (lambda (alist1 alist2)
    (if (null? alist1)
      alist2
      (if (assv (car (car alist1)) alist2)
        (merge-alist (cdr alist1) alist2)
        (cons (car alist1) (merge-alist (cdr alist1) alist2))))))
(define substitute-alist
  (lambda (lhs bindings)
    (map
      (lambda (x)
        (if (pattern-variable? x)
          (let ((bdg (assv x bindings)))
            (if bdg (cdr bdg) x))
          x))
      lhs)))
```

Program 10-16   Forward chaining: utility procedures

☞ **Exercise 10-17**

Find a query that would not work if substitute-alist generated an error on an unknown pattern variable. (Hint: Look carefully at what forward gets back from forward-everything.) ❏

Forward chaining certainly gives us the answers. So long as we have a finite set of facts, forward chaining will always terminate with all of the answers. Because forward-everything keeps iterating until it finds no new facts, eventually every provable fact will appear in the result. The answers might include pattern variables, but those wild cards will match *any* individual; thus, (forward '(can-take ?s cs100) prerequisites) will return ((can-take ?x cs100)).

Forward chaining does not answer some queries we might expect it to answer. It can tell us that "Anyone can take cs100", and it can say that "Fred can take cs100", but it can't find what courses Fred can take; (forward '(can-take fred ?y) pre-requisites) returns (). The problem is that forward chaining starts from facts. Our initial facts include (can-take ?x cs100), so extract can determine direct queries about cs100. However, our rules don't represent anything about Fred, so nothing explicit about Fred will end up in the final set of facts; for example, (can-take fred ?y) doesn't match anything in the final facts.

Forward chaining is not a practical way to answer questions for even a small collection of facts and rules. The basic problem is that we have no way to guide the inference engine. If we have a large amount of data that is irrelevant to the query at hand, the inference engine will blindly grind through it, producing hundreds, thousands, or millions of completely irrelevant conclusions. In fact, our forward-chainer takes $O(k^n)$ time, where k is the average number of facts and rules per iteration, and n is the number of facts and rules. As with other exponential algorithms, such as the airline route-finder in Chapter 4, the program is too slow to be practical for any problem with real data. In fact, forward chaining on even a simple set of rules on a 66MHz 486/DX2 takes an appreciable amount of time (about 10 seconds for the foo-corp ruleset). We can speed up the query process by checking to see whether the answer to our query appears in the new facts added in each iteration of forward1. Still, the worst-case behavior will not change.

This exponential behavior is fundamental to forward chaining. We have no way of knowing, when we add a fact to our rule base, whether it will be useful in answering some query. We could augment QScheme with features that let us guide the inference engine; indeed, usable forward-chaining engines have been built this way. In such an engine, the programmer must provide hints about how rules interact, or say which rules might be useful in answering certain queries. But by the time one adds all of this information, it's not a rule-based system any more! Backward chaining provides a better solution, without requiring extra information.

10.4.3 Backward Chaining

The code presented in this section can be found in file bqscheme.scm.

Recall from Figure 10-7 that backward chaining starts at the conclusion we're trying to draw and works backward to see whether that conclusion can be proven given the available facts and rules. This seems to be a promising line of attack. For one thing, it seems more similar to the way that human problem-solvers work than does forward chaining. Backward chaining should also eliminate the exponential explosion of forward chaining, because we only pursue a line of reasoning if we believe it is useful in answering a query. Forward chaining pursues all lines of reasoning from the initial facts; backward chaining only pursues lines that could lead to the conclusion. Nevertheless, there's no guarantee that backward chaining won't run into dead ends.

The backward-chaining inference engine has the same interface as forward: it processes QScheme rules and a query, and returns a list of answers.

```
(backward '(supervises edna ?x) foo-corp)
   ⇒   ((supervises edna bill) (supervises edna eric))
```

The idea of backward chaining is simple enough. We start with the query, and see if we can find a matching fact or rule in the knowledge base. If a fact is found, the query is answered. If a rule is found, we recursively attempt to check all of the items on the right-hand side. The query succeeds if we reach a fact, which requires no further proof. It fails if we find ourselves blocked, unable to prove one of the items on the right-hand side of a rule.

Whereas forward chaining uses the right-hand side of a rule to create a fact from the left-hand side and the bindings, backward chaining is exactly the reverse. A backward-chaining inference engine will identify an applicable rule by matching the query against the left hand side; if the rule is applicable, then the inference engine will attempt to see whether the items on the right-hand side apply. It does so by "filtering" the bindings through each of the items; variables are added to or deleted from the binding list as they occur in items on the right-hand side of the rule. The process is illustrated in Figure 10–8.

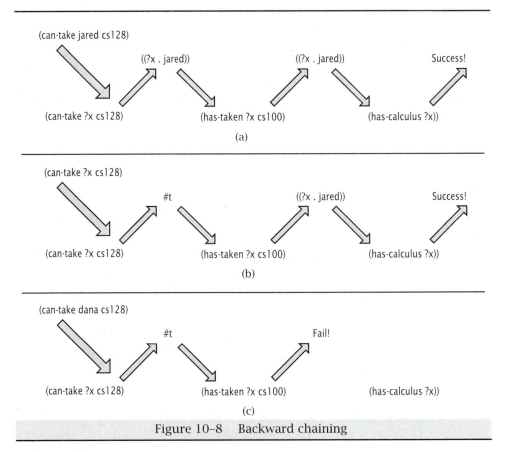

Figure 10–8   Backward chaining

For example, suppose we again use our philosopher rules to answer the query `(mortal socrates)`:

```
((mortal ?x) (human ?x))           ; Rule 1.
((human ?x) (philosopher ?x))      ; Rule 2.
((philosopher Socrates))           ; Rule 3.
((philosopher Hegel))              ; Rule 4.
```

Unlike forward chaining, backward chaining doesn't require us to separate facts and rules. The scan starts with Rule 1, which does in fact match, with ?x bound to socrates. As we start a scan of the right-hand side, the first item causes us to try to match (human socrates). A scan of the rules yields Rule 2, with ?x bound to socrates. Now we hunt for (philosopher socrates), which is found on another recursive scan.

The filtering process often leads to dead ends. For example, suppose we extend our ruleset as follows:

```
((mortal ?x) (human ?x))
((human ?x) (philosopher ?x))
((educated ?x)
 (philosopher ?y) (reads ?x ?y))
((philosopher Socrates))
((philosopher Hegel))
((reads johnny hegel))
((reads mary russell))
```

If we attempt to answer (educated johnny), we will find ourselves attempting to answer the query (philosopher ?y), which succeeds twice. We therefore attempt to answer the queries (reads johnny socrates), which fails,[14] and (reads johnny hegel), which succeeds.[15]

An interesting aspect of backward chaining is that our pattern matching must change. Sometimes we find pattern variables in the query, and sometimes we find them in rules. This was an interesting curiosity in forward chaining, but becomes a burning issue in backward chaining. Consider, for example, the rules

```
((can-take ?x cs236) (has-taken ?x cs135))
((has-taken brenda cs135))
```

and the query (can-take brenda ?y). Clearly the answer should be ((can-take brenda cs236)). Yet that fact appears nowhere. To produce this answer, the match of (can-take ?x cs236) with (can-take brenda ?y) must succeed, producing the bindings ((?x . brenda) (?y . cs236)). match?, as we've seen it, cannot do that, because it makes a distinction between the pattern and the target.

What we need is a generalization of matching that treats the pattern and target symmetrically, matching pattern variables in one against items or even other pattern variables in the other, and producing a result that contains bindings for each variable in either the pattern or the target. We call this generalization of matching **unification**. The process is similar to the way in which we solve an equation such as $3x - 2 = 4x + 7$. We look for a value of x that can be substituted on both sides to make the equation true. Just as there are mechanical ways to solve such equations, so there are mechanical ways of doing this symmetrical pattern matching.

In the 1960s, the earliest attempts to do logic programming failed because the only algorithms that could do this symmetrical matching were themselves exponential. For a while, researchers contented themselves with shaving the constants.

---

[14] Socrates' writings, if any, have been lost; all we know of Socrates is what Plato wrote about him.

[15] This rule might be more efficient if we asked whom Johnny is reading first. The efficient answer depends upon whether we have more information about whom Johnny reads, or who is a philosopher. The rule as shown would be more efficient if we had more information on Johnny's reading habits than on philosophers.

Language Profile: Prolog

Our inference engines have been written as packages that can be loaded into Scheme, which allows us to do logic programming and still write the other parts of the program in plain Scheme. But can we build a general-purpose logic-programming language?

The best known logic-programming language is Prolog ("Programming in Logic"), developed by Alain Colmerauer and his colleagues at the Université de Marseille in 1974. Prolog has become popular, not only for research in logic programming, but also as a practical programming language.

A Prolog program is a collection of rules, just as in QScheme (which is modeled on Prolog). Here's a Prolog program for the Foo Corporation example:

```
indirectly-supervises(X, Y) :-
 indirectly-supervises(X, Z), supervises(Z, Y).
indirectly-supervises(X, Y) :- supervises(X, Y).
supervises(edna, bill).
. . .
supervises(doris, glenda).
```

Prolog was also influenced by Lisp, and therefore has facilities equivalent to car, append, and so on. We can use these facilities to write append in Prolog:

```
append(nil, X, X).
append(cons(A, B), X, cons(A, C)) :- append(B, X, C).
```

This says that appending any list, X, onto nil (Prolog's equivalent of ()) produces X (the base case), while appending (A . B) and X produces the list (A . C) if, and only if, appending B and X produces C. cons is not built into Prolog (though all systems provide it); something like cons(*a*, *b*) is known as a *term*, and constitutes Prolog's equivalent of a pair structure. You can tell the difference between terms and predicates: the former are nested inside the latter.

This definition for append works in two directions. We can use it to append two lists as well as to find out what lists can be appended together to form a known result list. All Prolog programs share this ambiguity: the same code can be used to put data together or to take it apart. (QScheme is similar; recall how we could answer both "Who can take CS124?" and "What courses can Jared take?").

We can write member in Prolog, using the built-in equal predicate.

```
member(X, cons(X, _)).
member(X, cons(Y, _)) :- equal(X, Y).
member(X, cons(_, Y)) :- member(X, Y).
```

As a general-purpose language, Prolog has arithmetic and input/output features. Input and output raise a specific problem. As we saw in Chapters 3 and 5, effects are incompatible with an applicative framework; they are also incompatible with a logic framework. Prolog programmers find themselves worrying about the order of evaluation, just as Scheme programmers do.

Nonetheless, for problems involving a fair amount of inference, Prolog has proven itself to be powerful and effective. If you found QScheme interesting, you owe it to yourself to study Prolog.

Eventually, a general unification algorithm that works in linear time was discovered that made logic programming practical.

Now that we have a better matcher, we can revisit forward chaining. If we rewrite `extract` to use the generalized match procedure, as shown in Program 10-17.

```
(define extract
    (lambda (qry answers)
      (if
       (null? answers)
       '()
       (let ((b (match qry (car answers))))
  (if (car b)
      (substitute-alist qry (cdr b))
      (extract qry (cdr answers)))))))
```

Program 10-17   Procedure extract

`(match '(can-take fred ?y) '(can-take ?x cs100))` will return the bindings `((?y . cs100) (?x . fred))`, which `substitute-alist` can insert in the query to get `(can-take fred cs100)`.

The backward-chaining inference engine is an exception to our practice in this book. Instead of showing carefully annotated and explained code, we refer you to the code in the Software Package. Study that code and its accompanying comments carefully, to become familiar with the many small technical points in the code.

☞ **Exercise 10-18**

Backward chaining does have pitfalls: We can write rules that lead to infinite loops. The following rules are causing us some problems:

```
(define flights
  (rules
    '(((flt vancouver seattle))
      ((flt chicago toronto))
      ((flt boston new-york))
      ((flt seattle chicago))
      ((flt toronto boston))
      ((connect ?x ?y) (flt ?x ?y))
      ((connect ?x ?y) (connect ?z ?y) (flt ?x ?z)))))
```

Every time we try `(backward '(connect vancouver new-york) flights)`, backward runs into an infinite loop. Explain. ❏

Case Study: Connecting a Query Language to a Database

Our forward-chaining inference engine separates the rules from the facts. In Chapter 8, we looked at database management systems. Most of the real information in the world is stored in databases, yet our discussion of facts in this chapter has ignored databases and their indexing capabilities. We must remedy this omission. In many real problems, such as our prerequisite-checker, we need to combine information in a central database with logic rules. We must therefore see how to build a hybrid system that uses both.

We can use the technology of databases together with an inference engine to make a powerful information manager. This way, we can use rules to express relationships, and still access factual data from a database management system. Hybrid systems are frequently used in a client/server environment (see Case Study 8). We can build a rule-based system to do complex inferences and also access a central database system.

Database management systems use high-performance technologies with sophisticated indexing techniques, such as search trees. Production database systems use a mixture of advanced algorithms, special-case optimization, and machine- or network-dependent tuning. There is no way for a casual programming team to duplicate the performance that a database management system provides, so it makes sense to use a specialized product like a database management system to manage the facts.

Our student example from Chapter 8 involved two tables: a table of student numbers, names, and phone numbers, and a table of final marks, including student numbers, course taken, and final marks. The `final-marks` and `students` tables print as follows.

```
> (table-print final-marks compare-numbers 'student-no)
student-no   course        mark
----------   ----------    ----------
123          cs124         85
123          en110         90
284          cs124         75
284          ma120         78
284          en110         81
457          cs124         91
912          cs124         72
912          ma120         71
> (table-print students compare-numbers 'student-no)
student-no   name          phone
----------   ----------    ----------
123          Smith, W.     555-1024
284          Schmidt, S.   555-4830
457          Lee, R.       555-5205
651          Levy, T.      555-2012
912          Gomez, D.     555-6144
```

A database is organized as a set of large tables, so constructing facts from the records means selecting rows and columns from appropriate tables in order to answer a query. Let's construct a means for the query system to get a phone number from the `students` database. To get the phone number for student 123, we just say (phone 123 ?x). DBScheme's `table-find` procedure gives us a list of the values found in a particular field. `table-find` selects rows and then projects one column out of the resulting table, returning that column as a list. For example, (table-find students 'student-no = 123 'phone) ⇒ (555-1024).

There's no advantage to storing phone numbers as facts, because the College's records system probably has a table with this information. We need to enable the query system and the database manager to work together. If the query system can't answer the query (has-taken joe ma12), for example, it can look in the database for a table named has-taken. The easiest way to do this is to keep a dictionary of known tables, in which the cars are the predicate names. If the database is small (i.e., there are only a few tables), an alist will suffice.

```
( (has-taken . <has-taken table>) . . . )
```

We could store this dictionary in a global variable, or we could encapsulate the dictionary in an object.

When the inference engine looks for a match, it can also look at the available tables; instead of proceeding to match with rules, it will search the tables. When should this happen? Should we look in the database first, or try to answer the query first? It might appear that we should look in the database; however, looking for a fact provides more flexibility, by letting us override information in the database.

In the forward-chaining engine, we can start the process by scanning the alist to find any tables that might have relevant information, (i.e., names that match the predicate at hand). After calling forward-everything, we fetch the relevant rows and add them to the set of facts for this query. Of course, this approach is completely impractical, in keeping with the general inefficiency of forward chaining.

In backward chaining, the database can just kick in when the engine fails to prove a query. The engine can then look in the alist for a table that answers the query; if it's there, the engine can construct the appropriate operation on the database and get the answers. The table needs to know how to plug the parameters of the query into the database formula. In this study we outline how to translate a few typical queries into accesses in the database system. The results of the database access will be data that can be used as bindings in the query response.

To answer a (phone 123 ?x) query, backward just needs to plug the first argument into the table-find form:

```
(table-find students 'student-no = 123 'phone) ⇒ ("555-1024")
```

What do we need to handle (phone ?x "555-1024")? Unfortunately, while the QScheme query format is symmetric, the database form must be altered somewhat to use a different equality predicate:

```
(table-find students 'phone string-equal? "555-1024" 'student-no)
  ⇒ (123)
```

To get all the students and their phone numbers, (phone ?x ?y), we need two columns. There are two ways to do this. First, we could project the entire table onto the phone and student number columns, and then pull the rows out of the table, using the table procedure table-rowpack:

```
(table-rowpack (table-project students '(student-no phone)))
```

Second, we could pull this, more indirectly, by performing two finds and putting them together:

```
(let
  ((one
    (table-find students 'phone (lambda (x y) #t) #t 'student-no))
   (two
      (table-find students 'phone (lambda (x y) #t) #t 'phone)))
  (map (lambda (x y) (list x y)) one two))
```

We've used two tricks here. First, we used `table-find` to get all of a column by giving it a test procedure that always returns #t, so that it selects all rows. Second, since the order of elements in the table has not changed between the two `table-finds`, the order of the results is the same. The inference engine can then use the two column lists as bindings for its answer, confident that corresponding elements refer to the same object. Both of the above methods return

```
((912 "555-6144")
 (651 "555-2012")
 (457 "555-5205")
 (284 "555-4830")
 (123 "555-1024"))
```

Consider a property (completed ?x ?y) that says whether a student ?x has completed course ?y. The `final-marks` table contains this information; a student who has a final mark has completed the course. This query is quite simple: to find (completed 123 ?x), use

```
(table-find final-marks 'student-no = 123 'course)
   ⇒  (en110 cs124)
```

It's even easier to identify (completed 123 cs124): just check to see that (member 'cs124 (table-find final-marks 'student-no = 123 'course)) is not #f! We might even construct a predicate. What if we don't have has-taken, but have to construct a query to the DB? The query (has-taken 123 cs124) succeeds if student 123 has a final mark in course `cs124` that is greater than or equal to 55. We need to perform two selections to get this information: one to select rows for student 123, and one to select the row from that set that contains the mark for cs124. The query succeeds if

```
(>= (car (table-find (table-select  final-marks 'student-no = 123)
   'course eqv? 'cs124 'mark)) 55)
```

returns #t. The table procedures return a list containing the mark for student 123

```
(table-find (table-select  final-marks 'student-no = 123)
   'course eqv? 'cs124 'mark)
   ⇒  (85)
```

and we say that a student can use the course as a prerequisite if the mark is greater than or equal to 55.

There is one final issue: when two tables participate in the query, we must join them before using `table-find`. Suppose we have a query (name-of-taker cs124 ?x) that asks for the name of the person who took `cs124`. The database puts student names in the table `students`, while the course information is in `final-marks`. Thus, we have

```
(table-find
   (table-join  students final-marks 'student-no compare-numbers)
      'course eqv? 'cs124 'name)
   ⇒  ("Smith, W." "Schmidt, S." "Lee, R." "Gomez, D.")
```

An interesting question is how to encode the procedures that access a database for a query system. We've gone through several cases:

- A single column or several columns contains the relevant data.
- The query is definite (it has all arguments supplied and just needs a yes/no), or it has one or more variables.
- More than one table is involved.

Each of these cases required a slightly different use of the `table` procedures, but a pattern was emerging. The important thing to see is how we can connect the reasoning power of a query system with the storage and retrieval capacity of a database system, using only the procedures that manage the data and our understanding of the query system.

☞ **Exercise 10-19**

Write a procedure, `phone-of-student`, that calls `table-find` with the appropriate table, column name, and so on, to reply to queries like (`phone 123 ?x`), which would translate to (`phone-of-student 123`). ❏

☞ **Exercise 10-20**

Write a procedure `student-of-phone` that calls `table-find` with the appropriate table, column name, and so on, to reply to queries like (`phone ?x "555-1024"`), which would translate to (`student-of-phone "555-1024"`). ❏

Summary

This chapter shows that programs need not consist of sequences of expressions or actions, but can instead consist of a set of rules. We saw how to represent information symbolically and then use patterns to drive a rule-based program. Logic provides a general way to write rules; we saw that "answering a question" is the same as "proving a result using logic". QScheme is a programming language that allows us to write logic programs. Apart from minor syntax issues, a QScheme rule is identical to a logic rule (provided we restrict logic rules to implications that only use and). Finally, we studied an impractical but simple inference engine, `forward`, and looked at backward chaining, an efficient method for answering queries.

Further Readings

Steven Tanimoto's *The Elements of Artificial Intelligence* is a good general introduction to artificial intelligence. Patrick H. Winston's *Artificial Intelligence* is a comprehensive introduction that is widely used. Turing's original paper, which is still worth reading, was reprinted in *Computers and Thought*, edited by Edward Feigenbaum and Julian Feldman. Two strongly expressed positions on whether computers can think are found in Marvin Minsky's *The Society of Mind*, and Hubert Dreyfuss's *What Computers Still Can't Do*.

There are many excellent textbooks on introductory logic, including *Introduction to Logic*, 7th Ed., by Irving M. Copi; *Elements of Formal Logic*, by Norman Kretzmann; and *An Introduction to Symbolic Logic*, 3rd Ed., by Suzanne K. Langer.

Programming in Prolog, 3rd Ed., by W. Clocksin and C. Mellish provides an introduction to Prolog. *Computing with Logic* by D. Maier and D. Warren is an excellent introduction to logic programming in general.

Key Words

Here are the *key words* introduced in this chapter. Make sure you understand what each one means.

action	match	ruleset
artificial intelligence (AI)	mathematical induction	specification language
axiom	pattern	subject
backward chaining	pattern variable	syllogism
conclusion	predicate	target
contradiction	predicate logic	tautology
existential quantification	premise	theorem
fact	proof method	truth table
forward chaining	proof rule	truth value
implication	proposition	unification
individual	propositional logic	universal quantification
inference engine	quantification	valid
logic programming	rule	wild card

Problems

1. Write a table-driven procedure `phones` that determines the correct arguments to `table-find` and calls it with them, based on the structure of the query about phones. `phones` generalizes the two procedures in the previous exercises. You can use `pattern-variable?`. ❏

2. Write a procedure `evaluate` that determines the value of a logical expression given the expression and an alist describing the variables and their values, for example:

   ```
   (evaluate
     '(and a (or (not b) (not a)))
     '((a . #t) (b . #f)))
   ⇒  #t
   ```

   The logical expression may contain `and`, `or` or `not`. ❏

3. Write a procedure, `evaluate-logical`, that is given a logical expression and an alist of variables and Boolean values and returns the value of the logical expression when the values are substituted.

   ```
   (evaluate-logical '(and (not a) (or b (not c)))
     '((a . #f) (b . #f) (c . #f)))
   ⇒  #t
   ```

   ❏

4. Write a procedure, `truth-table`, that is given a list of variables and a logical expression and produces a truth table. It must list all possible combinations of the values of the input variables and the value of the expression. You can use `evaluate` from the previous question to determine the value of the logical expression. The problem then becomes generating the combinations of the values of the variables. ❏

5. We could specify a pattern simply by the number of occurrences of items without regard to the order of appearance of the items in the target. The pattern could just be an alist in which the data is the number of occurrences. The matcher would only need to count the occurrences of the elements:

```
(any-order
  '((not . 2) (red . 1))
  '(she did not say that red is not her favorite))
  ⇒  #t
(any-order
  '((not . 2) (red . 1))
  '(red not not))
  ⇒  #t
```

Write any-order. ❑

6. The rules in Exercise 10–18 cause an infinite loop in backward. Rewrite them to avoid the loop. Hint: Consider the two connect rules as elements in a recursive procedure; make sure that the procedure (backward) makes some progress toward its goal before it calls itself recursively. ❑

Self-Assessment

1. Evaluate each of the following forms.

```
(match?
  '(I like ?x)
  '(I like sardines))
(match?
  '(joe lives in ?x ?x)
  '(joe lives in st louis))
(match?
  '(scheme prolog cobol)
  '(prolog scheme cobol))
(match?
  '(I ?? ?x ?y)
  '(I like to program computers))
```

❑

2. Write each of the following in predicate logic:
   a. Everybody who takes Computer Science 124 knows Scheme.
   b. None of my friends know Scheme.
   c. Everyone who knows Scheme also knows another language. ❑

3. Using forward chaining, answer the query computer-scientist(Don) using these rules:

```
computer-scientist(x) if likes-to-program(x) and publishes(x).
publishes(x) if published(x,y,z) and refereed(z).
published(Don, Scheme-is-Fun, Computers-for-Idiots).
published(Don, The-Complexity-of-Megasort, Bitty-Bytes).
refereed(Bitty-Bytes).
likes-to-program(Don).
```

❑

4. Answer the query of the Question 4, using backward chaining. ❏

5. Show a truth table for the formula not a and b. ❏

Programming Problems

1. We introduced pattern matching by reminding you that many operating systems allow us to use patterns to refer to groups of files. We can go in the reverse direction by writing a procedure, map-files, that takes three arguments: a procedure, a list of filenames, and a pattern. The filenames and patterns are strings. File patterns use the character * to mean "0 or more characters", and ? to mean "exactly one character".

   For example,

   ```
   > (map-files
       (lambda (filename)
         (format #t "~a contains Scheme code.~%" filename))
       "*.scm"
       '("foo.scm" "bar.doc" "bar.scm"))
   foo.scm contains Scheme code.
   bar.scm contains Scheme code.
   ```

   Your procedure should turn the filename pattern into a pattern in our language, and then use match? to do the matching. The Scheme primitive procedure string->list will be useful.

   When you have this procedure working, investigate your Scheme system documentation to see if you can get a list containing the names of the files in a directory. If so, write a procedure, map-files-in-directory, that takes a procedure and a file-name pattern as arguments, and applies the procedure to all of the files whose names match the pattern in the directory.

2. QScheme is limited because the only patterns it can match involve testing symbols for equality. This means that we can't write even extremely simple queries in QScheme. For example, suppose that we want to add a rule to our prerequisite-checker to say that a minimum grade of 60% is needed. In logic, this is straightforward:

   forall x, exists y, exists z,
     has-prerequisite(x, y) if
       grade(x, y, z) and z >= 60

   that is, "x has prerequisite credit for course y if the x's grade in y is z, and z is at least 60". But how do we express "greater than" in QScheme?

   One way is to add special patterns for arithmetic. A more elegant method is to allow pattern items to be QScheme procedures. The pattern matches if the procedure returns true when applied to the corresponding target value,

   We might write the has-prerequisite rule in QScheme as follows:

   ```
   ((has-prerequisite ?x ?y)
    (grade ?x ?y ?z)
    (?! ?z (lambda (a) (>= a 60))))
   ```

   A QScheme item may now be a three-element list beginning with ?!; the other two items of this list are the QScheme pattern variable to be used, and a Scheme predicate (of one argument) that says whether the item matches or not.

   Modify the forward-chaining inference engine to support these new items by building a

Scheme procedure call and evaluating it with the recursive evaluator.

You will have to restrict the way these new kinds of items can be used. What will you choose?

Chapter 11

Gleam, the Ghost in the Machine

Overview

In this chapter we will look at a machine that closely resembles modern computers. Before we examine how this machine works, we will discuss how data is represented in a computer. Numbers and characters are the bulk of the data we have used, so we will study these types of data in depth and see how a computer transforms internal representations of numbers into external representations that we can read (sequences of characters).

Then we will explore the machinery of our abstract machine, its component parts, and the operations they perform. Control and computation are the two prominent components. Programs are composed of instructions that direct the operation of the machine's components: the movement of values among the computing elements, the memory and the outside world, and transformations of values. We will see how to write programs both in the internal language of the machine and our external representation.

Next we will see how to express familiar program elements in the language of our abstract machine: arithmetic expressions, conditional operations, loops, vectors, list processing, and finally procedures. We will study a simulator for this machine and see how to express the operation of the component elements as Scheme procedures.

Finally, we will examine some algorithms for graphics, and see how we can use them to implement Scheme's drawing primitives.

Sirs, I have tested your machine. It adds a new terror to life, and makes death a long-felt want. — Sir Herbert Beerbohm Tree (1852–1917)[1]

We must now shift our focus in our studies of Scheme and its implementation. We studied the self-evaluator, which is useful as a tool in learning how Scheme works. We saw how environments are created, how names are looked up, and how procedures connect with environments. Then we stepped up a level of abstraction to evaluators that act as embedded languages in Scheme. First we looked at DBScheme to see how a relational data model is embedded in Scheme. Then we moved our abstraction level higher and studied QScheme, a reasoning system implemented with pattern matching between rules and facts. QScheme illustrates another more complex abstraction of computation built on top of Scheme.

Now we will see how a real computer can do the same computations a Scheme system can, from simple arithmetic expressions to recursive procedures. To understand these issues, we'll study a machine that closely resembles many common computers. We'll examine its design and learn the language in which it is programmed. We'll write some programs in the language and show how to translate Scheme programs into the language of this machine. We'll explore how vectors are implemented on the machine and demonstrate their use in graphics. The next chapter completes the mapping on the abstract machine by implementing a Scheme evaluator in this machine's language.

---

[1] When asked for an endorsement by a gramophone company.

11.1   Representing Data

Where is the Life we have lost in living?
Where is the wisdom we have lost in knowledge?
Where is the knowledge we have lost in information?

— T. S. Eliot, *The Rock*

Every data value in the computer represents an object or property of an object in the world. We use a few standard representations in most of our programs: characters, Booleans, numbers, lists, pairs, symbols, null, and vectors. Before exploring the internals of computers, we will look at how computers represent characters, Booleans, and numbers and see how to write code to translate between the external and internal representations of numbers. We must understand the relationship between the machine's internal structures and the external world before we can understand how the machine manipulates those internal structures. Later in this chapter we'll see how to represent vectors. In Chapter 12, we will study representations of Scheme's other data types.

11.1.1   Analog and Digital Data

Computers fall into two main groups, analog and digital. In an **analog** computer, information is represented by some continuous quantity, such as a voltage or current, or the speed of water in a pipe ("fluidic computers" have been designed for some specialized purposes). Analog computers are useful for solving certain scientific and engineering problems, but they do not store programs. If they did, they would lose much of their advantage in power and compactness.[2] There has been considerable interest recently in *neural networks*, computing devices composed of collections of simple analog elements interconnected in a network with multiple layers. Part of the interest arises from the hope that neural networks can explain the behavior of the human brain. In addition, they can be "trained" to perform computations, instead of being programmed.

The alternative to analog computation is **digital** computation. In a digital computer, information is represented in symbolic form. The term *digital* refers to the digits of a number, although computers can process many things other than numbers. Digital computers are vastly more flexible than analog computers.

Each memory element of a computer can contain one of a fixed number of values. We call the elementary values a digital computer manipulates **glyphs**, from the Greek word for "carving".[3] Glyphs don't have any meaning as far as the computer is concerned; they're just distinguishable values. It's up to programmers to give them meaning.

We can represent a finite set of glyphs in an analog computer by dividing up the range that the continuous value can assume into ranges, assigning, say, the

---

[2] Today there is a resurgence of interest in analog computers for sensors (e.g., silicon retinas and auditory sensors). They are fast, compact and low-power; moreover, the computational elements in the sensor can be integrated into the sensing elements, as in "smart cameras".

[3] Compare the word *hieroglyph*, meaning, originally, "carvings by [Egyptian] priests".

glyph 0 to the range from 0.0 to 0.5 and 1 to values in the range greater than 0.5 to 1. All we care about is that they are different glyphs. In fact, every digital computer works also this way, since all digital computers represent information by an analog value such as voltage. Thus, the digital computer is an abstraction. We can ignore the analog values that the machine actually uses, and only pay attention to how the machine uses glyphs to represent information.

We can think of a computer's memory as containing a large collection of memory elements (perhaps 64 million, for a typical 1994 personal computer), each containing a specific glyph. We speak of the contents of a memory element as being its state; memory elements are mutable. If there are k glyphs in a computer's glyph set, then each memory element is in one of k states at any time. If there are n memory elements, we can speak of the entire memory being in any one of k^n states. For a typical 1994 personal computer, $k = 2$ glyphs, and $n = 64,000,000$, which means that the total number of different states the memory can be in is $2^{64,000,000}$, or about $10^{20,000,000}$. Therefore, we don't generally think of the state of the entire memory at any given time, but only of a specific small number of memory elements.

11.1.2 Bits and Characters

The way a computer represents a glyph is specific to the hardware. The hardware designer's job is to build a device that records, operates, and transmits glyphs correctly. A glyph is discrete: in a binary computer, we have 0 and 1, and nothing in between. If the physical computer is electronic, the underlying hardware sets all voltages to one of two values.

How many different glyphs should a computer be able to understand? It would be convenient to represent each character by a different glyph. In practice, though, the glyph set for a computer must be sharply restricted. With 256 different characters, a voltage range from 0 to 5 volts would have to be divided into intervals of less than 0.02 volts each. Because of noise, designing a circuit that can treat a voltage of 0.01 volts differently from one of 0.03 volts, and so on up to 4.999 volts, and do so reliably, millions of times per second, is not easy. Such circuits can be built, but they would be too expensive to use in an ordinary computer system.

Practical considerations dictate that we use the smallest set of glyphs, two, which we arbitrarily call 0 and 1, although these representations have nothing whatsoever to do with the numbers 0 and 1. We refer to the glyphs 0 and 1 as **binary digits**, or **bits**. Use of a two-glyph set has become universal on present-day computers, which are therefore known as *binary computers*. To represent a set of larger than two elements, we need to group bits into larger values. With n bits, there are 2^n different bit patterns of size n; for 256 characters, we need $256 = 2^8$ patterns, or 8 bits. We can encode the characters in any way, but of course a systematic approach is better. (Refer to our discussion of character representations in Chapter 3.) In the same way, any more complex value can be represented by a sequence of bits.

11.1.3 Numbers

If we were to use ten different glyphs, it would be easy to represent a number. For example, if we wanted to represent numbers with up to six digits, we could use six memory elements. Thus, for example, the number 1234 would be represented as 001234. However, we have only two different glyphs. We can still use the same method, but now we must use base two. In base two, we store numbers using powers

Computer systems

Computer users often classify machines into various groups. For example, there are PCs, Macintoshes, UNIX workstations, network-server computers, and mainframes. Many computers are hidden. Vending machines, microwave ovens, and VCRs contain computers, and such use of computers is growing rapidly. Some of the more unusual devices include intelligent caps on medicine bottles that record the times and frequencies of use. Radical applications—so-called intelligent buildings, appliances, and other machines—will soon become commonplace.

Although there are many different types of computers, we only need to distinguish between **embedded** computers and **general-purpose** computers. Embedded controllers or microcontrollers run a limited set of programs, and are built into products such as VCRs, automobiles, and microwave ovens. The programs for embedded computers only accept small changes in their control; they cannot run general programs. Embedded computers may even be implemented on general-purpose computers; it is actually cheaper to use a general-purpose computer (a microprocessor) than to design and test a new machine specifically for an application. Embedded machines also play an important role in controlling machinery, such as milling equipment—even up to the scale of controlling an entire process, such as that of a chemical refinery.

General-purpose machines have a wide range of capabilities, from personal workstations to supercomputers, but the range of computing power in these machines has recently been compressed. There are differences, especially in I/O capacity, but today most software runs on almost all machines except specialized parallel computers.

Today, the trend is *not* to distinguish between embedded and general-purpose computers. Instead, we connect them all into networks, for example, in factories, where intelligent devices communicate status information to a central mainframe. The mainframe responds with commands to the devices. Computation *everywhere*!

We can measure the performance of computer systems in several ways. The amount of random access memory (RAM) in megabytes is one parameter, and the speed in millions of instructions per second (MIPS) is another. Each instruction is a basic operation of the computer, such as an adding two numbers or comparing two items. MIPS has been called Meaningless Indicator of Processor Speed, since machine instructions vary widely in complexity. Another measure is how many floating-point operations per second (FLOPS) a machine performs. Comparing machine performance is tricky, since some machines may have fast computation, while others have sophisticated I/O.

Price has strongly influenced the spread of computers. In the early 1950s, a computer with 8K of memory was a multimillion dollar machine. A famous U.S. National Bureau of Standards report of the time predicted that the United States could use as many as four such computers. By the mid-1960s, a minicomputer with 4K words of memory cost less than $10,000. The earliest microcomputers (circa 1976) cost a few thousand dollars; as of 1994, a 486 computer system can cost as little as $1,500. These figures do not take inflation into account. That 1965 minicomputer cost a year's salary for a professional person; the 1994 microcomputer costs less than two weeks' salary for a person doing a comparable job.

These figures reflect enormous changes in technology and in the use of computers. The following ironic comment on computer progress rings true: "If the car industry progressed as rapidly as the computer industry has over the past 20 years, a Rolls Royce would cost 5 dollars, cruise all day at 1000 miles per hour on a thimble of gas, and blow up killing all passengers, once a month." The increase in computer power has not been accompanied by a corresponding increase in reliability.

There is a dark side to the phenomenon of increased computer power. Programmers have been delighted to have faster machines with more memory. They have taken advantage of these features, giving rise to what we have already called *software bloat*— programs expand to use all of the resources available. For example, an early version of UNIX allowed two or three users to share a 56KB computer with 5MB of disk space. In 1994, UNIX requires at least 8MB of memory and 200MB of disk space. A single user on such a system often complains that it's slow and doesn't have enough disk space. Of course, there has been a corresponding increase in our expectations of the services that computers can provide; early versions of UNIX had very simple editors, simple language compilers, no spreadsheets, and no network file systems! Even more taxing on computer system resources are graphical user interfaces and multimedia, which require windows (each with approximately 1 million pixels) and images (same size) that can be animated, with accompanying sound data. Small wonder that many new computers come with CD ROM devices that can hold gigabytes (billions of bytes) of data!

of 2. Thus, for example, 1234 in base two is 0000010011010010; reading the bits from right to left, we interpret each 1 as a power of 2, as shown in Figure 11-1.

2^{15}	2^{14}	2^{13}	2^{12}	2^{11}	2^{10}	2^9	2^8	2^7	2^6	2^5	2^4	2^3	2^2	2^1	2^0
0	0	0	0	0	1	0	0	1	1	0	1	0	0	1	0

Figure 11-1   Bits and powers of 2 in a binary number

$$1234 = 1 * 2^{10} + 1 * 2^7 + 1 * 2^6 + 1 * 2^4 + 1 * 2^1 = 1024 + 128 + 64 + 16 + 2$$

This example assumes that 16 bits represent a number. The number of bits used to store a number is an important parameter in computer design, known as the **wordsize**.[4] A wordsize of 16 was typical on personal computers of the 1980s; on most modern computers, 32 or 64 are common word sizes. Scheme lets you have numbers of almost any magnitude, although it must do much more work when working with numbers that are too large to be stored in 32 bits. If, on the other hand, you are working at the machine level or in many other languages, you may become painfully aware of the maximum numeric value for your computer.

---

[4] This term is a hangover from some early computers, on which 6 bits were used for a character, and the word size was 36; on such a computer, a word could store six characters. Since typing teachers have from the dawn of time taught that a typical word in a business letter consisted of five characters plus a space, it was only to be expected that the term would be used when talking of computers.

11.1.3.1 Characters and Booleans   We can use binary values to represent other kinds of values. A character can be represented as a sequence of 8 bits, corresponding to the ASCII value for the character, although 16-bit character representations are becoming more common because of international language concerns. The Unicode character set allows 2^{16} different characters, including characters from Cyrillic (Slavic), Chinese, Japanese, Korean, and South Asian alphabets.

Suppose we are looking at the bit sequence 01000010; is this the character #\B in ASCII, or the number 66? The answer may be surprising—you can't tell. All there is inside a computer is just bits; what those bits mean is up to us. Recall that in Chapter 3 we learned about characters and their internal representation. Scheme provides conversion procedures between integers and characters, but never confuses the two on its own. Scheme marks each value it handles with an indication of what type of value it is. This indication is what is queried by procedures such as number? and pair?. As Scheme programmers, we don't have to worry about this information. At the machine level, though, we must program carefully, in order not to make errors in how we use data. For example, it makes sense to add two numbers; it makes no sense to add two characters. Scheme would catch an attempt to add two characters when it evaluated the offending expression, but without the extra information that Scheme keeps, a machine would happily add the two characters without complaint. Remember, they're both only strings of bits.

Boolean values are also easy to represent. We pick one value for false, and one value for true. By convention, programmers generally pick 0 for false, and nonzero for true.

11.1.3.2 Hexadecimal Notation   Because binary notation is quite cumbersome, programmers prefer to use shorthand. The easiest way to abbreviate a long binary number is to use a base that is itself a power of two. In the early days of computing, base 8 (**octal** notation) was often used. In more recent years, base 16 (**hexadecimal** notation) has become almost universal. In base 16, we use the digit glyphs 0, 1, . . . , 9, A, B, C, D, E, and F, as shown in Figure 11-2.

Hex	Binary	Decimal	Hex	Binary	Decimal
0	0000	0	8	1000	8
1	0001	1	9	1001	9
2	0010	2	A	1010	10
3	0011	3	B	1011	11
4	0100	4	C	1100	12
5	0101	5	D	1101	13
6	0110	6	E	1110	14
7	0111	7	F	1111	15

Figure 11-2   Hexadecimal notation

Thus, for example, the base-16 number 2F5 is $2 * 16^2 + 15 * 16^1 + 5 * 16^0 = 512 + 240 + 5 = 757$. Base 16 has a direct correspondence to base 2, in that each hexadecimal digit corresponds to a set of 4 binary digits. Scheme allows us to write a hexadecimal number, but we must use the #x prefix. Remember that the hexadecimal digit A has nothing to do with the character A. The hex digit A is shorthand for the 4 binary digits 1010; the ASCII code for the character A is 01000001, or #x41. Scheme also lets you enter binary numbers, so you can write #xA as #b01000001. If you are puzzled about the relationship between binary and hexadecimal notation, remember that almost all computers use binary notation; hexadecimal is nothing more than programmers' shorthand.

☞ **Exercise 11–1**

Write the values #b1001011000010010 and #b10111010110110101011001110 in hexadecimal. ❏

☞ **Exercise 11–2**

In octal notation (base 8), the digits range from 0 to 7. Write 9, 65 and 128 in octal. ❏

11.1.3.3 Floating-Point Numbers

All general-purpose computers also support a representation for floating-point numbers. The fundamental idea is to represent a number as two components: a fraction, called the *mantissa*, and a multiplier, called the *exponent*. Thus the number 0.75 can be represented as 0.75×10^0, where the mantissa is 0.75 and the exponent is 0. The number 197326.82 can be represented as 0.19732682×10^6.

Since computers normally use binary, the base of exponents in a computer representation of a floating-point number is normally a power of 2, and the mantissa is a binary fraction. This can lead to somewhat surprising results. For example, 0.1 in decimal is a repeating fraction ($0.0\overline{0011}$) in binary. Because the number of bits in the mantissa is fixed, we can only get an approximate representation of 0.1 in most computers. This means that in many Scheme systems (= (* 0.1 10.0) 1.0) ⇒ #f!

The ability to represent real numbers is important for many numerical applications, but we will not treat real numbers in the rest of our discussion of machines. We can also represent fractions directly, by keeping a pair of the numerator and denominator. When we talk about numbers, however, we mean integers.

11.1.4 Input and Output of Numbers

We distinguish between a *numeral*, a string of characters that represents a number, and the number itself. In order to explore this distinction, we can write Scheme procedures to read and write numerals. These procedures are unnecessary in Scheme; we can use read and display. Writing them, however, will help us see how to convert between internal and external quantities. We will write our procedures in this section using only Scheme's character input/output primitives.

It is important to see that, inside the computer, a number *always* consists of a collection of bits. Outside the computer, though, we don't have numbers; we only have characters. Therefore, converting from external to internal form consists of finding internal values that correspond to the external ones. Suppose we want to read the characters 1234 as a numeral. The way to do this becomes apparent when we look at this sequence as a number in base 10:

$$1234 = 1 * 10^3 + 2 * 10^2 + 3 * 10^1 + 4 * 10^0$$

Input Devices

The earliest input devices were switches that could be turned on or off, but Teletype communications equipment was soon adopted. These devices had keyboards through which the user could interact with the computer directly, but early computers were too expensive to be used interactively. Communications equipment also allowed users to prepare data on a paper tape and then feed the tape into the computer with little human intervention.

Paper tape was suitable for scientific data, but was not very useful for data processing; although it was inexpensive, it was fragile and difficult to handle. Companies had been storing data on punched cards since the early part of this century. The punch card was invented by Hermann Hollerith of the U.S. Census Bureau for processing the data from the 1880 census. It was the major input medium from the early days of business computers until the early 1980s. Both paper tapes and punch cards allowed off-line data preparation; the user entered the information onto the medium without any assistance from the computer. Then, in a high-speed operation, the computer read the cards or tape into memory for use either at that time or later. Computer time was a scarce resource, not to be squandered on editors for data or programs.

Modern computer systems use keyboards as a primary input device, and the computer is extensively involved in on-line program and data entry. Software systems have evolved from single-user systems to multiple users entering whole "jobs" to be processed when time is available, and then to multiple users simultaneously interacting with the system ("time-sharing", where each user sees the machine as if it were a single-user machine). Now the user is back on a single machine, a workstation connected in a local-area network to other workstations.

There are many input devices besides keyboards, including mice, trackballs, hand and head-trackers, and foot-pedals. Recently, pen input has become available, which is convenient for small amounts of data. Users can enter data with a pen, as well as navigate menus. Pen devices accept a limited range of script, mostly block letters. Recognition of handwritten text is still an unsolved problem.

As more and more people use computer equipment, it has been discovered that extensive use of keyboards, mice, and other input devices can bring on Repetitive Stress Injuries (RSI), of which the best known is Carpal Tunnel Syndrome. Experienced computer users pay attention to such issues as posture, and take a break every hour or so.

Simple voice recognition is possible, when a machine is "trained" to a particular voice, or for limited tasks. For example, a phone system may ask, "Will you accept a collect call?" The answer is yes/no, and the voice system can reasonably determine whether you've said yes or no, but this is a limited range of possible speech. Many privacy issues arise when systems can recognize speech, because it would be easy to monitor conversations.

We shouldn't ignore cameras; image input is becoming standard, and recent machines can easily handle the stream of data (10 megabytes of data per second) from a video camera. Data compression chips can compress color video signals at real-time rates for storage and transmission by computer systems. The rapid move to multimedia computing and communication means that applications will become more capable of accepting a wide range of data.

A bit of algebra tells us that this is the same as

$$(((0 * 10 + 1)*10 + 2)*10 + 3)*10 + 4$$

In other words, if we already have a number x, then we can glue the next digit d on the right by computing $x * 10 + d$. This leads us to the procedure for reading a number that is shown in Program 11-1.

```
(define read-digit
  (lambda ()
    (let ((ch (read-char)))
      (if (char-numeric? ch)
          -1
          (- (char->integer ch) (char->integer #\0))))))
(define read-number
  (lambda ()
    (letrec
      ((rdn
         (lambda (x)
           (let ((d (read-digit)))
             (if (< d 0)
                 x
                 (rdn (+ (* 10 x) d)))))))
      (rdn 0))))
```

Program 11-1   Procedure `read-number`

`read-digit` should read a single digit and return it as a number; if the character is not a number, it should return -1. We could write `read-digit` as a large case statement, one case for each character (see our discussion in Chapter 3). However, in ASCII, and in every other coding system in use, the characters for the numeric digits have binary code values that are in order. In ASCII, for example, #\0 corresponds to 00110000, #\1 to 00110001, and so on. `char-numeric?` determines whether the character is numeric. The primitive procedure `char->integer` returns the numeric code for a character. Subtracting the numeric code for #\0 from a digit's numeric code gives the numeric value of the digit.

A procedure for writing a number is shown in Program 11-2. We will use `write-char` to write out a digit. Just as we read a number digit by digit, writing a number is done as a recursive operation over digits. For example, we can write the number 12345 out in two steps:

1. Write out (recursively) the left portion, `(quotient 12345 10)`.
2. Write out the rightmost digit, `(remainder 12345 10)`, which is 5.

We have called the procedure for writing a number `write-positive-number` because it only works correctly on numbers strictly greater than zero. We could modify the termination condition and recursion step to handle negative and zero cases, but the result would be complicated. Instead, `write-number` tests whether the number is positive (in which case it calls `write-positive-number`), negative (it

```
(define write-digit
  (lambda (d)
    (write-char (integer->char (+ (char->integer #\0) d)))))
(define write-positive-number
  (lambda (x)
    (if (> x 0)
      (begin
        (write-positive-number (quotient x 10))
        (write-digit (remainder x 10))))))
(define write-number
  (lambda (x)
    (cond
      ((> x 0) (write-positive-number x))
      ((< x 0) (write-char #\-) (write-positive-number (- x)))
      (else (write-char #\0)))))
```

Program 11-2   A procedure to print a positive number

writes out a minus sign, and calls `write-positive-number` on the absolute value), or zero (it just writes out 0).

☞ **Exercise 11-3**

Write `read-hex-number`, a procedure that reads a sequence of characters representing a number in hexadecimal form:

```
> (read-hex-number)10
16
> (read-hex-number)1A
26
```

The characters are input right after the form because `read-char` in our version of Scheme begins reading new input as soon as it encounters the right parenthesis completing the form it's reading. Other Scheme systems have slightly different behavior, which is a source of irritation to those who try to write portable programs that use `read-char`. Some versions wait until the end of the input line. ❏

☞ **Exercise 11-4**

It is sometimes convenient to write out a number preceded by leading zeros. On a check, for example, we want to make it harder for someone to alter the amount. Write a procedure that writes out a nonnegative number in *n* columns, with leading zeros. ❏

11.1.5   Negative Numbers

You may have wondered how a computer represents negative numbers. We will study two different representations of negative numbers. To understand the first one, consider a crooked car dealer who wants to reduce the odometer reading on a car. He has discovered that, just as driving forward causes the odometer reading to increase, driving backwards causes it to decrease. Next time the dealer goes on a holiday, he drives the car backwards across the continent. This reduces the odometer reading by several thousand kilometres, and thus raises the selling price of the car. Suppose the dealer drives the car backwards further than it was driven forwards. The odometer might end up reading 99997, which we would interpret as -3 kilometres. Drive the car forward 3 kilometres, and you will end up with a reading of 0. $(-3)+(+3)=0$.

Even if the reverse gear on the car doesn't work, it's still possible to lower the odometer reading. For example, to lower the reading by 1 kilometre, just drive forward 99,999 kilometres (because 99,999, on this odometer, corresponds to -1). Subtracting 1 from the odometer is the same as adding 99999. Similarly, subtracting 500 kilometres is the same as adding 99,500 kilometres. Subtracting k kilometres is the same as adding $100,000 - k$ kilometres.

We go to an antique shop to encounter our second representation, where we might find a 1950s adding machine. Numbers were added on this machine by pushing keys on a keyboard, and then turning a large handle. This caused various gears inside to rotate according to the digit value of the key pressed. Doing this twice produced the sum.

If you look closely at one of these adding machines, you might notice a second set of numbers, in red, on the keys. Whereas the first numbers increased from 0 to 9, the second, smaller set decreased from 9 to 0 (thus a key might be labeled 4, with a red number of 5). The numbers are red to indicate they're negative, as customary in accounting. If you pressed the keys whose red labels corresponded to the digits of a number and then turned the crank, the machine would show the result of *subtracting* the red value.

Again, we have converted a subtraction problem into an addition problem (we still turn the crank the same way). This time, instead of subtracting 50, we add 99949 (as you can see by looking at the red/black diagram in Figure 11-3). Thus $75 - 50 = 75 + 99949 = 00024 + 1 = 00025$. Note that the adding machine had to give us some help; when the total went over 99999, the machine added 1 more (this is known as *end-around carry*).

Both the car odometer and the adding machine converted subtraction problems into additions, but the precise techniques were a bit different. To subtract on the odometer requires subtracting the value from 100,000; the red/black system on the adding machine subtracts from 99,999. These two systems are known, respectively, as **ten's-complement** and **nine's-complement** systems. The ten's complement of x is computed as $10^k - x$, where k is the number of digits. The nine's complement is computed by subtracting each digit from 9.

In ten's-complement there is no particular digit value that always matches a particular digit value in the complement. In nine's-complement, the red value and the black value always add up to 9. Ten's complement is easier to work with (no end-around carry), but nine's complement is easier for the human user to convert.

A similar system can be used in binary. Suppose we are storing 8 bits per word, and we want to compute $45 - 22$. We perform this subtraction by adding the **two's-complement** of 22, which is 00010110 (the sum of the two values $22 = 00010110$ and $-22 = 11101010$ is 00000000). In binary, 45 is 00101101. Now we add:

```
00101101
11101010
--------
00010111
```

(Binary addition is just like decimal addition, except the table is much smaller: $0+0 = 0, 0+1 = 1$, and $1 + 1 = 0$, with a carry of 1.) The result is $2^4 + 2^2 + 2^1 + 2^0 = 16 + 4 + 2 + 1 = 23$, which is indeed correct.

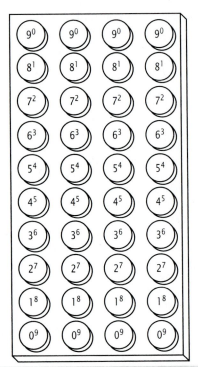

Figure 11-3   An adding machine keyboard

We computed the complement by subtracting from 2^k, but there's an easier way: subtract the number from a number consisting only of the 1 digits, and then add 1. Since subtracting a binary value from 1 is the same as flipping the bit ($1 - 0 = 1$, $1 - 1 = 0$), and since we already know how to add, subtracting a number using the two's-complement system is straightforward. This method is shown in Figure 11-4 (a).

The **one's-complement** of a binary number is computed by subtracting the binary representation of the number from a number consisting of all 1's.

☞ **Exercise 11-5**

What is the relationship between the two's and one's complement of a number? ❏

Almost all computers use two's-complement for representing negative numbers; one's-complement is rarely used directly, but it is essential in computing the two's complement.[5] Why isn't one's-complement used? Certainly it's easier to negate a number in one's-complement arithmetic. But each time we add a negative number (in one's-complement), we have to carry around from the top digit to the 0 bit, as shown in Figure 11-4 (b). Moving the carry bit from the top digit to the 0 bit complicates the adder circuitry; we add much more often than we negate numbers.

---

[5] If you assign 0 and 1 the meanings *false* and *true*, then one's-complement and negation (not) are the same thing.

```
Compute: 18 - 11
                        18 =  00010010
                        11 =  00001011

                       -11 =  11110100 + 1 = 11110101

                  18+-11 =  00010010
                               11110101
                               --------
                               00000111 = 7
```
            (a) : Two's complement

```
            3+-1 = 011
                     110
                     ---
                     001
         + carry  1
             = 010 = 2
```
            (b) : One's complement

Figure 11-4   Subtraction examples

☞ **Exercise 11-6**

In one's-complement arithmetic there is one number that has two different representations. Which is it? ❑

☞ **Exercise 11-7**

In two's-complement arithmetic, no number has two different representations, but this number system represents one number and not its complement. Why? ❑

11.2   The Gleam **Computer**

> *Launch your vessel*
> *And crowd your canvas*
> *And, ere it vanishes*
> *Over the margin*
> *After it, follow it*
> *Follow The Gleam.*
>
>   — Alfred, Lord Tennyson, *Merlin and the Gleam*

In this section we'll survey a range of computer architectures and then introduce our own abstract machine, Gleam. We will detail the components of the machine, especially the central processor, and describe its instructions. Then we'll see how to write simple parts of programs. Finally, we'll look at a simulator that implements in Scheme the fundamental elements of Gleam.

Output Devices

In the earliest days, computer output was in flashing lights, or dials. An early memory device, the Williams tube, was related to the cathode-ray tube found in many modern video display devices, which made it possible to look at output in the form of oscilloscope traces. Teletypes soon proved to be useful devices for output, as well as input. It was possible to write to both the printing element (for human-readable output) and the paper-tape punch (for preparing output that might be read in a subsequent run).

Teletypes were too slow for the volume of printing needed in commercial data processing. Card punches were also used for output, along with high-speed line printers. These could produce much greater amounts of output, but they cost so much that only a centralized data center could afford them. When minicomputers became available in the 1960s, the Teletype came into its own as an inexpensive (if slow) device that allowed users to interact with the computer without requiring the resources of a data center.

The earliest printers had hammers that struck keys corresponding to the various characters, much like a typewriter. These *line printers* were the standard output device in commercial data processing. They were slow, noisy, and quite expensive. Graphics were difficult on line printers: each pixel was printed by a combination of characters struck at one position to create the desired darkness. The result was crude and hard to read. Variations of these printers persisted into the early 1970s, when *dot-matrix* printers became common as inexpensive but low-performance printers. These printers have a row of tiny hammers, arranged vertically. As the hammers move horizontally, they sweep out a matrix of points. Initially, dot-matrix printers only responded to particular character codes, but manufacturers soon provided a "graphics mode," in which the programmer could control each hammer to put a mark at any point in the matrix. Dot-matrix printers have very few moving parts, so inexpensive versions can be reliable, and they have become a consumer item. However, they have not replaced line printers for high-volume applications. Line printers are still used for printing on preprinted forms that must be carefully controlled (e.g., checks).

By the mid-1970s, printers based upon the principles of xerography were developed. Like a copier, these printers have a photosensitive, electrostatically charged drum. Laser light discharges most of the drum; charged carbon toner sticks to the unexposed part, and is then transferred to the paper. The paper is then "fused," a process in which heat melts the carbon that remains on the paper. By the mid-1980s, a number of inexpensive laser printer engines had been developed, and now there are many low-cost laser printers.

11.2.1   Gleam's Basic Architecture

What we want to understand is the **architecture**, or programmer's view, of a typical computer. The architecture of a computer is a description of the values the machine manipulates and what operations it can perform on these values; thus, it is an abstraction of the functions of the machine. It is up to a hardware designer to determine the best way to build a machine that operates according to the architecture.

Unfortunately, real computer architectures have many peculiarities that make them useful, but perhaps harder to study than they ought to be. Therefore we will describe a new hypothetical computer, named Gleam, which stands for "General

Lambda Evaluation and Application Machine." The Gleam architecture is typical of real computers.

Gleam has five major components:

1. an *input device*, probably a keyboard, that generates characters and sends them to the computer
2. an *output device*, probably a video screen, that accepts characters from the computer and displays them
3. a *memory* that stores the values on which the user is operating
4. a *central processing unit*, or CPU, that oversees the operation, in effect carrying out the steps of the program
5. a *front panel* that lets the user enter data into memory, examine memory, and start/halt the computer

Figure 11–5 shows the organization of the components of the Gleam computer. The computer itself is represented by the shaded area. Input and output devices are connected to the computer at the CPU.

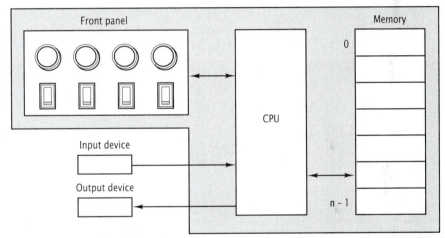

Figure 11–5   The Gleam computer

Gleam has only one input and one output device. You can think of the input device as a keyboard, and the output device as a printer or video display, although other devices might be used instead. Gleam has no disk. Therefore, each Gleam program must be loaded into the computer from the outside before it is executed, and Gleam cannot store the results of a program's execution in a file for use by another program.

Gleam's memory holds 65,536 (2^{16}) locations, or cells, each of which can contain one value, represented as 32 bits. In this chapter, we will only be concerned with integers and characters. In Chapter 12, we'll see how to represent any Scheme value in a cell. The memory locations are numbered between 0 and 65,535.

In the previous paragraph, the word *bits* has two different senses. On the one hand, a bit is a *value*, 0 or 1. On the other hand, a Gleam storage cell contains 32 *bit positions*, or storage elements. Programmers use *bits* in both senses, and are rarely

Computer Architectures

The oldest architecture still in wide use was developed by IBM for their System/360 family in 1964. IBM still builds computers that understand the same instructions and data formats as their original System/360 computers did. The majority of mainframes use the System/360 architecture.

Digital Equipment Corporation built the world's most popular minicomputer in the 1970's, the PDP-11 minicomputer. Its descendant is the VAX computer architecture, which is widely used.

Intel Corp. developed the Intel 8086 in the late 1970s. IBM adopted this architecture for its original Personal Computer. (IBM actually used the 8088 chip, which appears the same to the programmer as the 8086, but is less powerful, and less expensive.) Subsequent PCs and compatibles have used the successors to the 8086, notably the 80486 and, more recently, the Pentium. (Intel was driven to introduce a non-numerical name by the success of compatible machines from other companies that could legally use the numerical designation.) This architecture is probably the most widely used in the world.

Motorola developed the 68000 at about the same time that Intel was developing the 8086. Difficulties in delivery caused IBM not to use it in the Personal Computer, but Amiga, Apple, Atari, Hewlett-Packard, NeXT Computer, and Sun Microsystems, among others, have built computers based upon the 68000 and its successors, notably the 68040.

All of the above architectures are based upon the principle of the computer having a large set of very powerful instructions. A number of researchers argued that powerful instructions were actually a hindrance in making fast computers: the instructions were so complicated that even though one could express a very complicated operation in a few instructions, each instruction took a long time to execute. So-called RISCs ("reduced instruction-set computers") emerged from this study. In a RISC, the instructions are very simple, but the machine is designed to execute them very quickly. As a result, RISCs have considerably better performance than traditional CISCs ("complex instruction-set computers") for a comparable price. We will examine the RISC philosophy in more detail in Chapter 12.

As of 1994, the leading-edge architectures are Intel's Pentium and the PowerPC (Apple/IBM/Motorola). Some other players include SPARC (Sun Microsystems), HP-PA (Hewlett-Packard microprocessor) and Alpha (Digital Equipment Corporation).

Computer processors have become larger; that is, they have many more transistor elements. In the late 1970s the Intel 8086 chip contained about 29,000 transistors; in the late 1980s its successor, the 486, had about 1.2 million transistors, and current processors contain over 3 million transistors.

confused. The best way to think of memory is as a street in a subdivision where all of the houses look the same. Each house (cell) has a street address (location number) and each house has somebody living in it (a value). We call the number that identifies the location of a memory cell an **address**.

We now turn to the central processing unit (CPU). Memory is the passive storage element in the computer and the CPU is the active element that transforms the data in memory from its original state to the final state specified by the program. A program specifies a computation as a series of instructions. The **stored program** is a major element of the modern digital computer. The idea of the stored program was originated by the inventors of the modern computer, Eckert and Mauchly, von Neumann, Turing, Zuse, and others (see page 11). The program, the description of the computation, is stored in a digital computer in the same way as the data that it transforms. This was a revolutionary idea; before its advent, a program was either stored in a different medium or entered by setting switches that controlled connections among the arithmetic and logical units in the computer. Once the program is treated as data, it becomes an object that the computer can manipulate. The powerful editors, compilers, debuggers and other tools that programmers use would not be possible if we could not treat a program as data.

The job of the CPU is to execute the instructions that specify its program and transform the initial data to produce the result intended by the program. Gleam's CPU is divided into five units:

1. the Memory-Access Unit (MAU) manages the transfer of data between memory and the CPU.

2. the Input/Output Unit (IOU) manages the transfer of data between the input/output devices and the CPU.

3. the CPU Register Unit (RU) contains a small collection of cells that are used as a scratch pad.

4. the Arithmetic/Logic Unit (ALU) contains circuitry for doing the basic operations specified by the program.

5. the Control Unit (CU) is the overall "boss" of the CPU. Its circuitry causes the other units to carry out their tasks in the sequence specified by the program.

Figure 11–6 shows the organization of the components of the Gleam CPU. Each unit contains circuitry for carrying out its task, along with some registers, which are scratch-pad cells that the unit uses in doing its work. For example, suppose we want a program that adds the codes for two characters and displays the code for the character corresponding to the sum:

1. The CU commands the IOU to read the first character and to transfer the data from the IOU to a cell in the RU.

2. The CU commands the IOU to read the second character and to transfer the data from the IOU to a cell in the RU.

3. The CU commands the ALU to add the contents of the two cells in the RU, storing the result in another cell in the RU.

4. The CU commands the IOU to write the contents of the RU result cell to the output device.

5. The CU stops the computer.

Each step of the program is carried out because the CU has demanded that it occur. Just as the CPU is the active part of a computer (the memory passively responds to requests to store and retrieve values), the CU is the active part of the CPU (other units passively do their jobs upon request by the CU).

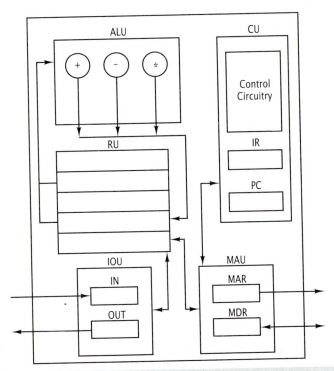

Figure 11-6   The CPU of the Gleam computer

11.2.2   The Structure of the CPU

Now we will examine each of the components of the Gleam CPU in detail. We'll look at the flow of information and control, see how Gleam stores information in the CPU and examine how Gleam processes instructions. The various components of Gleam's CPU are quite independent, and have well-defined interfaces with each other. Therefore, we can examine each component separately.

11.2.2.1   The MAU   Much of what the CPU has to do involves transferring data to and from memory. The terms *reading* and *writing* are used for these activities, but they are too strongly associated with input/output to be satisfactory. We will use the terms memread and memwrite. When the CPU requires a data value from memory, it performs a memread, specifying the cell number in memory. When the CPU is to mutate a cell in memory, it performs a memwrite, specifying the cell number and the new value to be inserted.

A memread is analogous to the self-evaluator's get-binding procedure, and a memwrite is analogous to set-binding!. Unlike get-binding and set-binding!, memread and memwrite don't have to search for the cell to be used, since every reference is phrased in terms of the numeric location of the cell, not a symbolic name. Each location in memory is equally accessible; thus, such a memory is termed **random access**. We use the term **RAM (random access memory)** to refer to memory devices in computers that can also perform read/write operations. **ROM (read only memory)** is also random access, but it can't be written to.

The MAU performs memory operations. It has two registers, the **Memory Address Register** (MAR), which holds the number of the memory cell to be used, and the **Memory Data Register** (MDR), which holds the value to be transferred to or from memory. To do a memread, the MAU sends the contents of the MAR to memory, as the number of the memory cell to be used, and then awaits an answer. It loads that answer into the MDR. A memwrite is the opposite: again the MAR holds the cell number, but this time the MDR holds the value to be stored in that cell.

11.2.2.2 The IOU   Gleam's IOU manages data transfer as a sequence of characters, between the CPU and input/output devices. It contains two registers, the OUT and IN registers, for storing data to be sent to/received from the IO device. When a Gleam program performs an input operation, the contents of the IN register are transferred to the CPU. The input device places values into the IN register. If no value has been read from the device into the IOU, Gleam stops until the user enters an input value. Output operations are similar. The program transfers a value to the OUT register and then continues. The IOU transfers the value to the output device.

Gleam's input and output capabilities are limited to characters and integers. Any other value must be converted to its internal representation from a character representation on input, and converted to a character representation on output. The IOU doesn't do everything that Scheme's display does; it only reads and writes characters. Library routines and conversion primitives must do the rest.

11.2.2.3 The Register Unit   All computers need **general registers** that hold data for computation. In Gleam, all computation occurs on data in the registers. For example, if we wanted to compute a+b, we first must memread a, and then memread b. A memread brings data into the MDR, and then into a cell (a register) in the RU. The second memread brings more data into the MDR, and then into another register. Then the CPU can add a to b.

For this reason, Gleam's CPU contains a collection of 16 registers, known as the register unit (RU), numbered from 0 through 15. Each register can contain any value, except for register number 0, which always contains the value 0. The value 0 is needed frequently, so it is convenient to keep it in a register. For indexing, discussed below, we also want a register that always contains 0.

11.2.2.4 The Arithmetic/Logic Unit   The engine that performs the arithmetic and logical operations within the CPU is the Arithmetic/Logic Unit, the ALU. Gleam's ALU performs the numerical operations and compares items to produce numeric values that it can treat as Boolean values. An ALU performs a specific set of functions (e.g., we showed add, subtract, and multiply in Figure 11-6).

11.2.2.5 The Control Unit   The Control Unit (CU) is designed to execute the following loop until it encounters a halt instruction:

1. Get the next instruction from memory.
2. Analyze it to determine what task is needed.
3. Command the appropriate CPU units to do what is needed to carry out the task.
4. Go on to the next instruction.

Mass Storage Devices

In the early days, punch cards and paper tape were used as storage media, as well as input and output. A customer-billing program would read one set of cards containing customer balances, and another recording purchases and returns. The program would produce another set of cards containing updated balances. Needless to say, punch-card manufacturers liked this arrangement.

However, magnetic tape devices were used by the more powerful computers for input and output. Magnetic tapes are faster than cards, more compact, and reusable. Magnetic tape is still the preferred medium for storing enormous amounts of data that is not frequently accessed, but disk storage has supplanted it in most cases.

A disk consists of a platter, coated with magnetic material, that spins at high speed (see the diagram below). A read-write head, like that in a magnetic tape device, is positioned over the platter. As the platter rotates about the spindle, the head traces out a circular path (known as a track) on the platter. The *actuator* moves the head towards or away from the spindle to access a large number of tracks. A typical personal computer disk might store 345 megabytes of data, with an average access time of 10 milliseconds. Technology has changed rapidly. In 1965, a 7.5 MB drive was the size of a washing machine. A 1994 250 MB disk drive is the size of a paperback book. The disks in file-server computers typically hold more than a gigabyte (1 billion bytes).

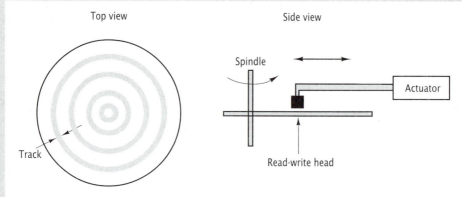

The term *hard disk* arose to differentiate disk drives from removable diskette drives, which use so-called floppy disks. A CD-ROM (compact disk read only memory) drive reads disks that are very similar to audio CDs and contain over 500 MB of digital data. CD-ROMs are useful for distributing massive databases. For example, some workstation manufacturers supply the entire UNIX software distribution (the operating system, compilers, utility programs, and documentation) on a CD.

Mass storage devices play two roles: first, they store large quantities of data (either the input or output of programs), while a program is not running. In this role they act as *persistent* memory elements, in contrast with the *transient* memory of the computer that exists while a program is running. The second role of mass storage devices is to augment the main memory (usually RAM) of a computer while a program is running. In this role, storage devices (almost always disks) act as *virtual* memory. Portions of a running program that are not being used can be copied, or *paged*, to a disk until needed.

The CU evaluates the program stored in memory, which is why the terms *evaluator* and *general-purpose computer* are synonymous. The self-evaluator doesn't contain any code to compute (fact 10), but can compute it if you evaluate the appropriate forms. Likewise, a computer contains no circuitry for evaluating the factorial of 10, but it can evaluate it if you enter a program that computes factorials. A special-purpose computer performs a specific, limited, function. For economic reasons, engineers often use a general-purpose computer with a program in read-only memory.

The CU loop is a critical component of the idea behind a stored-program computer. Rather than wiring the CU to do a particular task, we wire it to accept a sequence of instructions saying what is to be done. Then we can do different tasks merely by providing various instruction sequences.

To control the order in which instructions are evaluated, the CU also has two registers: the **program counter** (PC) and the **instruction register** (IR). The PC holds the number of the cell in memory that contains the next instruction. The CPU does a memread on this cell, and loads the MDR into the IR; this is the **fetch** cycle of the CU. The contents of the IR are taken as an instruction; this is the **decode** cycle. Then the specified operation is performed; this is the **execute** cycle. The CU performs these three steps repeatedly in the **fetch/decode/execute loop**. After each decode cycle, the CU increments the PC.

11.2.3   Instructions

The **instruction set** of a computer is the collection of fundamental operations it implements. What operations should Gleam provide? Obviously, we can have (within limits) as many different kinds of operations as we want. However, each kind of operation requires the ALU circuitry that can handle it. After a while, the law of diminishing returns kicks in, and we find ourselves paying for operations we will never use. In the sidebar on computer architecture in Section 11.2.1, we mentioned RISC computers. We also discuss RISC machines in a sidebar in Chapter 12. Gleam's design follows the RISC philosophy, though for technical reasons computer designers would probably not call Gleam a RISC.

The **operations** in a computer are the functions that it implements. The **instructions** of the computer are the patterns of bits stored in its memory that the CPU will interpret as commands to perform certain operations. Machine language is the language of bit patterns that the machine interprets. Computer scientists often use the term *instruction* for both the operations that the machine implements and the particular bit pattern that the machine interprets as a command to perform that operation. We will continue that abuse of terminology; the meaning we intend should be clear from the context.

Gleam's instructions fall into the following general classes:

- data transfer (load, store, copy): instructions that move data between memory and the CPU, or within the CPU
- arithmetic (add, sub, mpy, quo, rem): instructions that perform simple arithmetic operations
- arithmetic predicates (lss?, gtr?, eql?): instructions that place *true* or *false* into a CPU register depending upon the result of a comparison
- bitwise operations (and, or, not): instructions that perform Boolean operation on values considered as collections of bits

- jumps (`jtrue`, `jfalse`, `jump`): instructions that change the PC value. At any given time, the CPU is executing the instruction whose address is in the program counter; therefore, changing the program counter value has the effect of transferring control to a different location. This allows us to create Gleam's equivalent of `if` forms and loops. Jumps can be conditional (depending upon the contents of a register) or unconditional.
- procedure call (`call`): like `jump`, except that it stores the value of the PC plus 1 into a register, so that control can return to the point after the call.
- input/output (`inchar`, `outchar`, `innum`, `outnum`): instructions that transfer information (either single characters or numbers) between the CPU and the outside world.
- the system-control operation `halt`.

The lists following each class name identify the instructions by their mnemonic names, which we use in our programs.

Gleam's instructions fall into one of two categories. The first comprises instructions that access a memory location; hence, we call these **memory-reference instructions**. The second comprises instructions that only need to access data in the registers; hence, we call these **register instructions**.

For example, `load` is a memory-reference instruction; it specifies a memory address from which a value will be loaded, and a CPU register into which the value is to be placed. On the other hand, `add` is a register instruction; it specifies two **source registers** that contain the values to be added, and a third **destination register** into which the result is to be placed.

A table of Gleam's memory-reference instructions appears in Figure 11-7 (a). The register instructions appear in Figure 11-7 (b). Appendix C provides a complete description of the Gleam instructions. For each instruction, we show the mnemonic code, its **opcode** (i.e., the numeric code representing the instruction in the machine), and a brief description of what the instruction does.

11.2.3.1 Representing Instructions   It is important to realize that an instruction is a kind of value. An instruction is placed into a memory location and executed when the PC contains the address of this memory location. Following the structure of every real computer, we represent Gleam instructions as sequences of bits. The representation is shown in Figure 11-8.

The numbers above the box in Figure 11-8 show the bit numbers. Gleam cells are made up of 32 bits. Following a convention used by many computer scientists, we number the bits from the right, with the rightmost bit numbered 0.

Figure 11-8 shows the layouts of the two Gleam instruction types. Both types have four fields. In Gleam memory-reference instructions, the first 8 bits (from the left) are used to store the operation code; the next 4 are used for the destination register; the next 4 are used for the **index register**, and the final 16 are used for the memory address. Indexing, discussed later, uses the contents of the index register to modify the memory address. In Gleam register instructions, the first 8 bits (from the left) are used to store the operation code; the next 4 are used for the destination register; the next 12 are ignored; the next 4 are used for the first source register, and the final four are used for the second source register. For example, the instruction (`add 4 5 6`) adds the contents of register 5 to the contents of register 6 and leaves the result in register 4. We can describe the effect of the instruction more abstractly as (`set! r4 (+ r5 r6)`). This instruction is represented by the bit values in Figure 11-9, shown in groups of 4 for legibility.

Mnemonic code	Opcode	Operation performed
load	#x00	Transfer a memory value to the CPU.
store	#x01	Transfer a CPU value to memory.
jtrue	#x02	If register holds true, jump to given location.
jfalse	#x03	If register holds false, jump to given location.
jump	#x04	Unconditionally jump to given location.
call	#x05	Call a procedure.

(a) : Memory Reference

Mnemonic code	Opcode	Operation performed
copy	#x86	Transfer a value from one register to another.
add	#x87	Compute the sum of two values.
sub	#x88	Compute the difference of two values.
mpy	#x89	Compute the product of two values.
quo	#x8A	Compute the quotient of two values.
rem	#x8B	Compute the remainder of two values.
lss?	#x8C	Test value1 less than value2.
gtr?	#x8D	Test value1 greater than value2.
eql?	#x8E	Test value1 equal to value2.
and	#x90	Set each destination bit to "and" of sources.
or	#x91	Set each destination bit to "or" of sources.
not	#x92	Set each destination bit to inverse of source bit.
inchar	#x9c	Read a single character.
outchar	#x9d	Write a single character.
innum	#x9e	Read a decimal integer.
outnum	#x9f	Write a decimal integer.
halt	#xa0	Stop the computer.

(b) : Register Instructions

Figure 11-7   Gleam Instructions

☞ **Exercise 11-8**

Show the internal representation of the following:
   a. an instruction that stores the contents of register 6 into memory location 43AC.
   b. an instruction that computes the product of registers 7 and 9, and places the result into register 2. ❏

11.2.4   The Gleam Assembler: gap

Gleam itself operates on instructions represented as sequences of bits. This is essential, since bits are the only objects that the machine directly understands. Programmers, however, cannot write programs of any size in that notation; it is

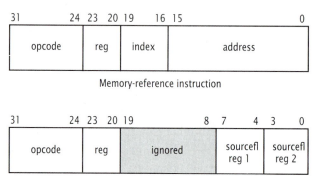

Figure 11-8   Gleam instruction representations

1000 0111	0100	0000 0000 0000	0101	0110
opcode	reg	ignored	source reg 1	source reg 2

Figure 11-9   The bit representation of (add 4 5 6)

too cumbersome. *Assembly language* is an intermediate language that can be easily translated into the machine language of Gleam. An **assembler** is a program that converts assembly language to the machine language of a particular machine. We have given the name gap to both the assembly language for Gleam and its assembler.

The first function of gap is to translate a gap program into machine language. Each list identifies the contents of a location; when the list specifies an instruction, gap constructs a 32-bit number from the components of the instruction and deposits it in the location. Let's go through the program shown in Program 11-3 step-by-step.

```
;;;    gap code          Gleam equivalent
(      (load 4 5)        ; 0: 00400005
       (outchar 4)       ; 1: 9D400000
       (load 4 6)        ; 2: 00400006
       (outchar 4)       ; 3: 9D400000
       (halt)            ; 4: A0000000
       (dataword 72)     ; 5: 00000048
       (dataword 105) )  ; 6: 00000069
```

Program 11-3   A gap program with corresponding machine language

- The first item is a load instruction. Gleam will load the contents of memory location 5 into CPU register 4.
- The second instruction is an outchar instruction, which outputs the character found in a register. We have chosen register 4 for this purpose.

- The third and fourth instructions load the contents of memory location 6 into CPU register 4, and then output it.
- The fifth instruction stops the computer. In a halt instruction, the source and destination register numbers aren't used.
- Finally, the last two items set two memory locations to the values 72 and 105 respectively. (These happen to be the ASCII codes for H and i.) dataword isn't a Gleam instruction; it's just a simple code to tell gap to set a memory word to a particular value. If you count from the top, starting at 0, you will find that the first dataword is at location 5, and the second is at location 6. Now look at the instructions loaded into locations 0 and 2.

The machine language corresponding to our program also appears in Program 11-3; each instruction corresponds to a 32-bit number shown in hexadecimal. Program 11-4 shows a listing of the machine language with the interpretation in terms of instruction components. The program that lists the instructions cannot tell that the items at locations 5 and 6 are simply data.

```
0: 00400005 opcode:  0 reg 4 index 0 address 5
1: 9D400000 opcode: 9D dest-reg 4 source-reg1 0 source-reg2 0
2: 00400006 opcode:  0 reg 4 index 0 address 6
3: 9D400000 opcode: 9D dest-reg 4 source-reg1 0 source-reg2 0
4: A0000000 opcode: A0 dest-reg 0 source-reg1 0 source-reg2 0
5: 00000048 opcode:  0 reg 0 index 0 address 48
6: 00000069 opcode:  0 reg 0 index 0 address 69
```

Program 11-4   Interpreting Gleam instructions

This program is not only difficult to read, but also unmodifiable. Changing the program by adding or deleting instructions would mean that all the addresses would be renumbered, so the program would have to be rewritten from scratch. Computer programmers soon solved this problem, by adding to their assembler the ability to define symbolic names. The programmer can use these symbolic names instead of the actual addresses. At *assembly* time, the assembler records the correspondence between the locations and the symbolic names, later replacing the symbolic names with the addresses of the locations. Written in gap with symbolic address names, the program we just examined appears as Program 11-5.

```
( start       (load 4 letter-h)
              (outchar 4)
              (load 4 letter-i)
              (outchar 4)
              (halt)
  letter-h    (dataword 72)
  letter-i    (dataword 105) )
```

Program 11-5   A gap program with symbolic addresses

Here, we've defined three symbolic names: start, letter-h, and letter-i. Any item that is a symbol is taken as a name, which is defined as the number of the current instruction. Now we can use a symbolic name in an address, and leave it to the assembler to replace that by the actual number. If, for example, we were to interchange the two datawords along with their names and then reassemble the program, the assembler would then define letter-h as 6 and letter-i as 5. Even though different locations were being used, in any one version of the program the assembler would ensure that things were consistent.

We will use many registers for special purposes in our programs. Naming the registers by numbers can lead to confusion; it's hard to figure out code such as

```
(add 5 2 3)
(store 5 foo)
```

The assembler allows registers to be symbols so that we can write

```
(add res tmp1 tmp2)
(store res foo)
```

which is a bit more readable.

The mechanism for defining names is the define-symbols directive in the assembly language. To define the names res, tmp1, and tmp2, we write

```
(define-symbols (res . 5) (tmp1 . 2) (tmp2 . 3))
```

at the beginning of the program. The names are added to the collection of symbols the assembler knows about. Each symbol definition is a pair whose car is a name to be defined, and whose cdr is a value. Defined names can be used as register numbers, as addresses, or as dataword values.

The gap language is a human-readable format for specifying Gleam programs. The assembler translates the assembly-language programs into machine language. The rules for translating gap code into machine instructions follow:

- If an item is a symbol, it is defined as a location name.
- If an item is a list whose car is the symbolic name for an instruction, a word is output with the binary representation for that instruction.
- If an item is a list whose car is an assembler directive, then that assembler directive is performed.

We represent an assembly-language program as a list whose elements are one of the above three items. For example, consider assembling the following list:

```
(foo     (load 5 twelve)
         (halt)
 twelve (dataword 12)))
```

The only complication is that a symbol might be used before being defined. Therefore, the assembler reads the entire program twice, first building up a table of symbols and their values, and then replacing the symbols with appropriate values.

In this example, the first item is a symbol, so the assembler adds the pair (foo . 0) to its table of known symbols. The cdr of this pair is the location at which foo occurred. On the first pass the assembler collects the table of symbols. On the second pass the assembler replaces any occurrences of symbols in instructions with the actual address referenced by the symbol. The second item in the program list, (load 5 twelve), is a list whose car is the name of an instruction, so the assembler outputs the binary code for the load instruction, #x0000000, with the register field set to 5 and the address field to the address specified by twelve: it puts #x00500002 in location 0. The third item is a halt instruction, so the assembler puts #xA0000000 in location 1. The fourth item is a symbol. The fifth item, (dataword 12), is list whose car is an assembler directive. In the second pass the assembler places the data value 12 (#x0000000C) in location 2.

There are two assembler directives in gap:

- (dataword *x*) specifies that *x* is loaded into the current program location.
- (define-symbols (*sym1* . *val1*) (*sym2* . *val2*) ... (*symn* . *valn*)) specifies that sym*i* is to be replaced by val*i* when it appears in the register, address, or index position in an instruction.

The Gleam register instructions need varying numbers of registers. Most require that the source and both destination registers appear in the gap code. copy needs only the destination and one source register. inchar, outchar, innum, and outnum only need the destination register. gap ignores the other registers if they are specified, for these instructions.

☞ **Exercise 11-9**

Assemble the following code by hand. What output is produced?

```
start  (load 4 xx)
       (load 5 yy)
       (eql? 6 4 5)
       (jtrue 6 next)
       (load 4 diff)
       (jump 0 done)
next   (load 4 same)
done   (outnum 4)
       (halt)
diff   (dataword 46)
same   (dataword 77)
xx     (dataword 10)
yy     (dataword 12)
```

❏

11.3 Programming in gap

> *If you gave Ruth a rose, she'd peel all the petals off to make sure there weren't any greenfly. And when she'd done that, she'd turn round and say, do you call that a rose? Look at it, it's all in bits.*
> — Alan Ayckbourn, *Table Manners*

This section shows how to write procedures in gap to perform some of the familiar processes that we've written before in Scheme. We'll begin with simple arithmetic and conditional forms, and then see how tail-recursive procedures can be written for Gleam. Finally we'll discover how to implement recursive procedures that are not tail-recursive.

At one time all programs were written in assembly language. As recently as the 1960s, programs for payroll or scientific computation were routinely written in assembly language. In part, people used assembly language because the available high-level languages of the time were very limited. In addition, programs written in assembly language often ran much more quickly than their high-level counterparts.

The first nail in the coffin of assembly language was the UNIX operating system, which was completely rewritten in the high-level language C in 1973. The designers of UNIX discovered that the choice of a high-level language added little to the memory or time requirements, but allowed them to choose better algorithms and data structures than they would otherwise have used. High-level languages also can produce portable programs that run with little or no change on many different kinds of computers. Within a few years, UNIX was running on virtually every kind of computer, from desktop computers to mainframes.

Compilers, too, have become much better than they used to be. Modern "optimizing" compilers can sometimes produce machine-language programs that are *better* than those a human programmer can write. As a result, programmers rarely write programs of any size in assembly language; in fact, many programmers don't even bother to learn the machine language of many of the computers they use.

Still, there is a point to writing assembly language, even today. Sometimes, for example, we must gain access to some specialized machine feature that is not available in the programming language we're using. On a personal computer, for example, we might need to interact with special-purpose hardware, or use esoteric features of the operating system. There's another reason for being able to program in assembly language. In many large programs, most of the procedures are only occasionally used; a few procedures account for the majority of the execution time. Even though a good compiler can do a better job than a human expert on a large program, a human can still sometimes beat the compiler in choosing the best instructions for one frequently executed procedure, as indicated by a profiler.

11.3.1   Arithmetic Expressions

High-level languages like Scheme let us write complex forms such as (+ (* x y) (- (* a b) c)) without worrying about registers and sequences of operations. Even as simple a form as this takes several instructions; Program 11–6 shows the translation into gap. Each variable must be loaded into a register. Intermediate results, such as (* a b), are stored in registers and used in subsequent computations.

☞ **Exercise 11–10**

Briefly explain the difference, in gap, between

        (load 5 1)

and

        (load 5 one)
        ...
one   (dataword 1)

❏

☞ **Exercise 11–11**

Write a segment of gap code that computes the sum of the quotient of a and b and the remainder of a and b, where a is in register 2 and b is in register 9. ❏

```
(load 4 x)    ; load x into r4
(load 5 y)    ; load y into r5
(mpy 4 4 5)   ; r4 assigned r4*r5
(load 5 a)    ; load a into r5
(load 6 b)    ; load b into r6
(mpy 5 5 6)   ; r5 assigned r5*r6
(load 6 c)    ; load c into r6
(sub 5 5 6)   ; r5 assigned r5-r6
(add 4 4 5)   ; r4 assigned r4+r5
```

Program 11-6   The form (+ (* x y) (- (* a b) c)) in gap

☞ **Exercise 11-12**

Gleam has no instruction that computes the complement of a number y: $x = -y$. Write a sequence of instructions that puts the complement of register 4 into register 5. ❑

11.3.2   Conditional Operations

In Scheme, if is the fundamental decision-maker (both case and cond forms can be written using just if). Gleam has two operations, jtrue and jfalse for this purpose. Each of these operations looks at a register. With jtrue, if the register contains *true* (which is anything but 0—*false* is 0), we will jump to the address given in the instruction. Thus, for example,

```
(load 3 x)
(load 4 y)
(eql? 2 3 4)
(jtrue 2 lab)
```

loads the value stored in location x into register 3, loads the value stored in location y into register 4, and then compares the contents of register 3 with the contents of register 4. If the two values are equal, then register 2 will contain *true*; otherwise it will contain *false*. The jtrue instruction will set the program counter to the address of location lab if register 2 contains *true*, and to the address of the next program location if register 2 contains *false.*

Gleam also provides an instruction for jumping unconditionally. The jump instruction ignores the contents of the register (which nevertheless must be specified, by convention register 0) and jumps to the effective address. Program 11-7 shows a gap program that displays the smaller of the characters at locations foo and bar.

☞ **Exercise 11-13**

Rewrite Program 11-7 using jtrue. ❑

11.3.3   Loops

The jump instructions are also useful for making loops. Consider the Scheme procedure in Program 11-8 and its translation into gap. Loops in Scheme are done with recursion. The last operation just says, "Go back and do it again", which can be done in Gleam by setting the PC to the address of the first instruction of the loop. We can

```
                    (display (if (< foo bar) foo bar))
```

(a) Scheme code

```
start    (load 8 foo)         ; Get foo.
         (load 9 bar)         ; Get bar
         (lss? 7 8 9)         ; Compare with bar.
         (jfalse 7 show)      ; Jump to show if foo>=bar.
         (copy 9 8)           ; We will display foo.
show     (outchar 9)          ; Display it.
         (halt)               ; Stop execution.
foo      (dataword 65)        ; #\A.
bar      (dataword 67)        ; #\C.
```

(b) gap code

Program 11-7   A display form in Scheme and gap

```
(define echo
  (lambda ()
    (let ((ch (read-char)))
      (if (eqv? ch #\.)
        (display ch)
        (begin
          (display ch)
          (echo))))))
```

(a) Scheme version

```
         (load 4 endchar)    ; put endchar in r4
start    (inchar 5)          ; Get a character.
         (eql? 3 4 5)        ; Put #t in r3 if = endchar.
         (jtrue 3 done)      ; Jump to done if r3 = #t.
         (outchar 5)         ; Display character.
         (jump 0 start)      ; Go back for more.
done     (outchar 4)         ; Display it.
         (halt)              ;
;; Data.
endchar(dataword 46)         ; (code for period).
```

(b) gap version

Program 11-8   Procedure echo in Scheme and gap

translate echo into gap code as shown in Program 11-8. Note that only tail-recursive procedures can be translated so easily. In general, recursive procedures require a more complex translation (as we will see in Section 11.3.7).

In the early days of computing, people did not distinguish between conditionals, loops, and other less savory kinds of jumps. The resulting programs had many jumps, and it was difficult to figure out what a program was doing without hand-simulating it instruction by instruction. This "spaghetti code" (sometimes called "write-only code") could sometimes be understood by drawing a flowchart, a diagram of each program step, with arrows showing the jumps. On these flowcharts, a loop appeared as a closed cycle of arrows and a complex set of them looked like a plate of spaghetti, that's where the name came from.

As programmers became more concerned to make their programs readable, they began to remove the spaghetti from their code. Early languages had statements equivalent to jumps, but most modern languages provide conditional and looping structures that make jumps unnecessary.

11.3.4   Vectors and Indexing

Why are vectors so efficient in Scheme? Access to the ith element of a vector takes constant time because elements of a vector can be stored in adjacent memory locations. So, for example, if we have a vector stored in locations #x1000 through #x1110, we can select the third element of the vector by merely adding 2 to the starting address of the vector, so that the cell at location 105 will be used. There's no searching involved! The reason computer scientists prefer to use 0 as the index of the first element in a vector should be obvious now: adding i to the address of the first element gives you the address of the ith element in the vector.

One way to access a vector element on Gleam is by means of **self-modifying code** which causes the program to create new instructions and execute them as it runs. Program 11-9 shows how we would write out element number 2 of our vector, using self-modifying code.

```
              . . .
              (load 8 index)
              (load 9 loadinstr)
              (add 8 8 9)
              (store 8 next)
    next      (dataword 0)      ; Set by store instruction.
              (outnum 6)
              . . .
    index     (dataword 2)
    loadinst  (load 6 #x1000)
```

Program 11-9   Using self-modifying code to access a vector element

☞ **Exercise 11-14**

In Program 11-9, what will be the contents of memory location next when the outnum instruction is executed? ❏

Practical Note

In most places, we use decimal notation to represent addresses. Here, we're using hexadecimal, so that we can see what the addresses are in instructions. Either system is reasonable, but make sure you're very clear about which system you're using. We always prefix our hexadecimal numbers with #x.

The use of self-modifying code makes programs extremely difficult to read. To make vectors easier to use, all computers have special indexing facilities to make this process efficient. Gleam is no different; the fourth field of the Gleam memory access instruction is the index register field. Program 11-10 shows how we would write the preceding vector access in gap.

```
            (load 8 index)
            (load 6 1000 8)
            (outnum 6)
            . . .
index       (dataword 2)
```

Program 11-10   Vector access in gap

The first instruction loads the number 2 into register 8. While decoding the next instruction, Gleam adds the contents of the index register to the address field in the instruction to form the **effective address** used to access memory. Thus, the second instruction loads into register 6 the contents of location 1000+2. The contents of the registers before and after the load are

```
before       r6: ---   r8: 2        Memory     1000: 444
                                                1001: 555
after        r6: 666   r8: 2                    1002: 666
```

This version is simpler and shorter than the self-modifying one; it needs only two load instructions, rather than three. This version also doesn't require an extra register (register 9 in the self-modifying version) to hold a temporary load instruction.

Gleam computes the effective address for every memory-reference instruction, but if an index register is not given, then the assembler assumes that register 0 is used. Since register 0 always contains 0, when register 0 is the index register, the effective address is just the address specified in the instruction.

A simple procedure to sum the elements of a vector appears in Program 11-11, both in Scheme and gap. The vector is stored in a consecutive set of memory locations beginning at vec. Procedure sum is a loop on an index variable. It is interesting to compare sum with echo (Program 11-8). Note that the last step in sum-helper is to increment i in register 5 by adding the contents of register 1. By convention, register 1 always contains 1.

sum includes a line for returning to its caller. When Gleam transfers control to the beginning of sum, information on how to get back to the calling routine must be stored somewhere. The Gleam call instruction takes care of storing the information. The call is written as (call pcr sum). By convention we have defined the symbol pcr to refer to a register that we will use in every procedure. Gleam puts the address of the next location after the call instruction into register pcr. When sum finishes, control should return to this **return address**.

We return by replacing the ..procedure return.. with (jump 0 0 pcr). When Gleam calculates the effective address for the jump instruction, it retrieves the return address for sum, which has been stored in register pcr by the call (provided that we haven't altered register pcr, and we don't). Thus the jump takes Gleam back right to the address after the call. Using an index register to contain an address

```
(define sum
  (lambda (n)
    (letrec
      ((sum-help
         (lambda (i tot)
           (if (>= i n)
               total
               (sum-help (add1 i) (+ tot (vector-ref vec i)))))))
        (sum-help 0 0))))
```
                        (a) Scheme version

```
;;; r3 contains n.  r4 gets result.
sum        (copy 4 0)           ; Initialize sum.
           (copy 5 0)           ; Initialize counter.
sum-help   (lss? 6 5 3)
           (jfalse 6 sum-done)  ; if so.
           (load 6 vec 5)
           (add 4 4 6)          ; add this element to sum.
           (add 5 5 1)
           (jump 0 sum-help)
sum-done   ..procedure return..
```
                        (b) gap version

```
sum        (copy 4 0)           ; Initialize sum.
           (copy 5 0)           ; Initialize counter.
sum-help   (lss? 6 5 3)
           (jfalse 6 sum-done)  ; if so.
           (load 6 vec 5)
           (add 4 4 6)          ; add this element to sum.
           (add 5 5 1)
           (jump 0 sum-helper)
sum-done   (jump 0 0 pcr)       ; pcr has return address
```
                 (c) gap version with procedure return

Program 11-11   Procedure sum in Scheme and gap

into a region of memory is called using it as a **base register**. Because address calculation adds the address portion of the instruction to the contents of the index register, the machine needn't treat a base register specially.

Calling a procedure, in this simple case, is therefore straightforward. The call instruction is designed both to transfer control to the beginning of the procedure and to store the return address in a register. The called procedure makes sure not to destroy the contents of the register and then executes a jump, using the register as an index. sum now looks like Program 11-11 (c).

☞ **Exercise 11-15**

Assume that the (call pcr sum) instruction is loaded at address 50 and that procedure sum begins at location 100. Show how the PC is loaded into pcr at the call and how the saved value is loaded back into the PC from the PCR at the jump. ❏

☞ **Exercise 11-16**

Write a gap procedure that implements the following code:

```
(define diff
  (lambda (n)
    (letrec ((help
               (lambda (i)
                 (if (< i n)
                   (begin
                     (vector-set! vecc (vector-ref veca i)
                     (vector-ref vecb i))
                   (help (add1 i)))))))
      (help 0))))
```

Assume that veca starts at memory location #x1000, and vecb at #x1400. ❑

11.3.5   The Stack

Calling and returning from a procedure like sum is especially simple, because sum doesn't call any other procedure. If it executed a (call pcr foo), however, the contents of register pcr would be lost! Many procedures do call other procedures, so how do we ensure that we can get back the right contents of register pcr? One way to handle this is to use a stack.

Many computers use a stack to save return addresses: each time a procedure is called, the machine executes a **prolog** to the procedure, which pushes the return address onto the stack. In gap, this translates to

```
(store pcr 0 sr)
(add sr sr 1)
```

Our programs will reserve a register, sr, to contain the address of the top cell in the stack; we'll arbitrarily use register 15 for sr. At the beginning of the program, the code must load the address of the stack into register sr:

```
(load sr stack-origin)
....
stack-origin (dataword 3000)
```

This states that 3000 is the beginning of the stack.

When the procedure returns, the machine pops the return address and places it in the program counter:

```
(sub sr sr 1)
(load pcr 0 sr)
(jump 0 0 pcr)
```

Gleam's stack is typical: register sr contains the address of the current element on the stack; pushing and popping are done by adding 1 to or subtracting 1 from register sr. Register sr must therefore have a defined value before any procedure call. We've arbitrarily used the locations starting at 3000 to hold our stack.

Program 11-12 (a) shows the Scheme code for foo and bar. The gap code for foo is shown in Program 11-12 (b). Not only must foo save the return address on the stack, it must save the value of x. After bar returns, foo pops x back into register

```
(define foo
  (lambda (x)
    (+ x (bar (+ x 2)))))
(define bar
  (lambda (y)
    (* y 3)))
```

(b) Scheme

```
foo     (store pcr 0 sr);; x in r4
        (add sr sr 1)
        (store 4 0 sr)   ;; push x
        (add sr sr 1)
        (load 6 two)
        (add 4 4 6)
        (call pcr bar)   ;; result in reg4
        (sub sr sr 1)
        (load 4 0 sr)    ;; pop x
        (add 4 4 5)
        (sub sr sr 1)
        (load pcr 0 sr)
        (jump 0 0 pcr)   ;; result in reg4
two     (dataword 2)
...
bar     (load 6 three)   ;; y in reg4
        (mpy 5 4 6)
        (jump 0 0 pcr)   ;; result in reg5
three   (dataword 3)
```

(b) gap version

Program 11-12   Procedures foo and bar

4 and computes the sum of it and the result of bar. The procedure bar doesn't have to push and pop pcr because it calls no other procedure.

Once you have initialized the stack register containing the stack origin, then everything is automatic. Of course, there must be enough room in memory to hold all the return addresses generated by calls in the program. In any program containing recursive procedures, the number of recursive procedure calls generated is called the depth of the recursion. The amount of space required by the program depends directly on the depth of the recursion, since each call pushes a return address on the stack, unless, of course, the procedure is tail-recursive. The next section shows how tail recursion eliminates the need for stacking return addresses.

11.3.6   Tail Recursion

We have used jump to implement tail-recursive procedures without procedure calls. We implemented a tail-recursive helper procedure in sum that way. Other procedures can benefit from this technique as well. Consider xfoo, a slight change to foo, shown in Program 11-13 (a).

xfoo is not tail-recursive, but there is no remaining computation to be done after xfoo calls bar. A procedure call as the last operation of a procedure is a **tail**

```
(define xfoo
  (lambda (x)
    (bar (+ x 2))))
(define bar
  (lambda (y)
    (* y 3)))
```

(a) Scheme version

```
xfoo   (store pcr 0 sr) ;; x in r4
       (add sr sr 1)
       (load 6 two)
       (add 4 4 6)
       (call pcr bar)
       (sub sr sr 1)
       (load pcr 0 sr)
       (jump 0 0 pcr)
two    (dataword 2)
```

(b) xfoo in gap

```
;;; assume argument arrives in reg4
xfoo   (load 5 two)
       (add 4 4 5)
       (jump 0 bar)
two    (dataword 2)
```

(c) xfoo in gap with tail-calling eliminated

Program 11-13   Procedures xfoo and bar

---

call. The gap code for the tail-calling version of xfoo appears in Program 11-13 (b). However, it uses the standard sequence of pushing and popping the return address on the stack. x isn't pushed on the stack, because it's not needed after bar has returned. Why should we return from bar to xfoo, only to return immediately to xfoo's caller? Program 11-13 (c) shows a simple solution. Now when bar returns, it returns to xfoo's caller, not to xfoo. Short-circuiting the return process in this way is just a more general application of the observation that leads to efficient implementation of tail-recursive procedures. This way of chaining procedures not only saves an extra return operation, it skips pushing the return address on the stack. Procedures linked in this way do not need new space to contain their return addresses.

Consider the factorial procedure shown in Program 11-14(a). The procedure fact2 is tail-recursive: the recursive call is the last thing done on each call. The corresponding gap code for fact2 is shown in Program 11-14(b). The argument, n, is passed in register 2. The code at label fact2 loads 1 into register 3.

The gap program works by reusing the *same* memory location for each iteration of the loop. This is exactly what tail recursion does. Hence tail recursion can be implemented by jumps at the machine level.

```
(define fact2
  (lambda (n)
    (letrec
      ((helper
          (lambda (n acc)
            (if (= n 0)
                acc
                (fact2 (sub1 n) (* n acc))))))
      (fact2 n 1))))
```

(a) Scheme version

```
fact2        (copy 3 1)            ; r1 has 1, r2 has n, r3 has acc
fact2-loop   (eql? 4 2 0)          ; if n = 0 then...
             (jtrue 4 fact2-done)  ; ... jump to fact2-done.
             (mpy 3 3 2)           ; ... n*acc ...
             (sub 2 2 1)           ; Set n to...
             (jump 0 fact2-loop)   ; Repeat the process.
fact2-done   (jump 0 0 pcr)
```

(b) gap version

Program 11-14   Tail-recursive factorial

11.3.7   General Recursive Procedures and the Stack

We've seen that tail recursion can be done in Gleam with jumps. We should also be able to write simple recursive procedures that are not tail-recursive in Gleam. Recall the stack that we used earlier to record the address to which control returns when a procedure returns. The procedure prolog and return code that we put in each procedure manage a stack of return addresses, using register sr to store the address of the top of the stack.

How do we use the stack? Consider fact1, shown in Program 11–15(a). When we implemented tail-recursive procedures in gap, we reused the binding of the parameters, putting the argument for the recursive call in the same register as when it arrived. This technique destroys the old binding. When we implement fact1, which isn't tail-recursive, we can't reuse the binding for n because the old value must be there when we finish computing the recursive call to fact1. To save the old value until after the recursive call is complete, we can put it on the stack, use just one binding during computation of the recursive call, and pop the old value off the stack to restore it when fact1 returns from the recursive call.

Just as we used the stack to store return addresses, we can also push and pop data values, such as n in fact1, onto the stack. The code for fact1, using a stack for recursion, appears in Program 11–15(b). fact1 is, arbitrarily, loaded at location 100. Addresses for instructions are shown at the left.

What happens when evaluating fact1 with 3 as the argument? When fact1 first calls itself recursively, at 107: (call pcr fact1) (see Figure 11–10 (a)), the stack (shown on the right) contains the return address, 50. (We assume fact1's caller is at 50 to be concrete.) The second entry in the stack is the pushed value of n. The braces in the figure delimit the values pushed on the stack by each call of fact1: the return address and n. The registers appear on the left. Register 0 contains 0, as always. Register 1 contains 1, by convention. Register 2 contains the new value of n.

```
(define fact1
   (lambda (n)
      (if (= n 0) 1 (* n (fact1 (sub1 n)))))))
```
                           (a) Scheme version

```
100: fact1        (store pcr 0 sr)    ; r2 has n, result in r3
101:              (add sr sr 1)
102:              (eql? 4 2 0)         ; if n = 0 then...
103:              (jtrue 4 fact1-done) ; ... jump to fact1-done.
104:              (store 2 0 sr)       ; push reg2 onto the stack
105:              (add sr sr 1)        ; increment stack register
106:              (sub 2 2 1)
107:              (call pcr fact1)     ; result in reg3
108:              (sub sr sr 1)        ; pop n off stack
109:              (load 2 0 sr)        ; now in reg2
110:              (mpy 3 3 2)          ; result in reg3
111:              (sub sr sr 1)
112:              (load pcr 0 sr)
113:              (jump 0 0 pcr)
114: fact1-done   (copy 3 1)          ; the result is 1
115:              (sub sr sr 1)
116:              (load pcr 0 sr)
117:              (jump 0 0 pcr)
```
                           (b) gap version

Program 11-15   Non-tail-recursive factorial

On the second recursive call to fact1 (Figure 11–10 (b)), the return address of fact1 (1008) appears at 1002, then n, pushed again. Register sr has been incremented to 1004.

The stack grows as more recursive calls are made. When fact1 returns after getting 0 as its argument (at line 117), the stack and registers appear as in Figure 11–11 (a). fact1 then pops the value 1 into register 2, multiplies it by the value in 3, and returns. The next time, it pops 2, multiplies into register 3, and returns (see Figure 11–11 (b)). The next time, it pops 3 off the stack and multiplies that by register 3. Finally it returns to its original caller, and register 3 contains the factorial of 3.

Practical Note

We are using one stack to contain both return addresses and data items, which means that you can get into serious trouble if you write a procedure that doesn't do an equal number of pushes and pops (a common error in using stacks). Whenever you're programming in assembly language, check each procedure to make sure that all pushes and pops are matched.

Writing this code out by hand should make it clear to you why it's much easier to rely on an evaluator that hides all this detail, such as Scheme.

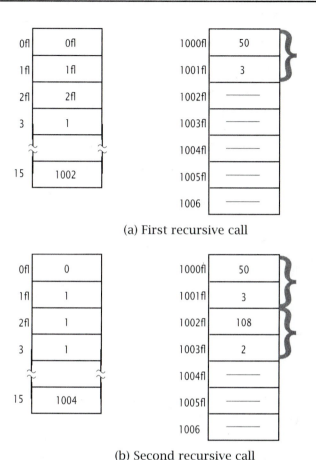

(a) First recursive call

(b) Second recursive call

Figure 11-10   Registers and stack in `fact1`

☞ **Exercise 11–17**

The Fibonacci numbers, F_i, are defined by the following recursive relation:

$$F_i = F_{i-1} + F_{i-2}, F_0 = F_1 = 1$$

Write a gap program to compute the nth Fibonacci number, using this relation. ❏

☞ **Exercise 11–18**

Translate `write-positive-number` from Program 11-2 into gap. ❏

☞ **Exercise 11–19**

When we described the environment model, we said that every procedure extends the environment with a frame to store its arguments. When a recursive procedure like `fact1` calls itself many times, it creates many frames. In droid diagrams, these frames are represented as droids waiting for results. Where do we see these frames in gap procedures? ❏

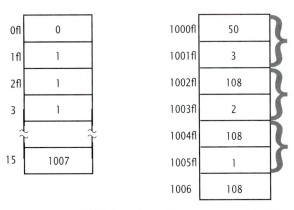

(a) Returning when argument is 0

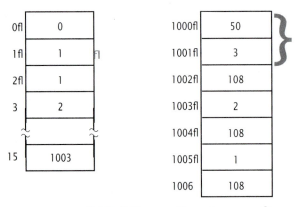

(b) Building up the return result

Figure 11-11   Registers and stack in `fact1`: continued

11.4 Implementing Gleam

 The code presented in this section can be found in file `gleam.scm`.

Ah! THEN, if mine had been the Painter's hand,
To express what then I saw; and add the gleam,
The light that never was, on sea or land,
The consecration, and the Poet's dream.
— William Wordsworth, "Elegiac Stanzas"

In this section, we will use Scheme to simulate a Gleam machine. This exercise involves a reversal of the usual abstraction levels. Ordinarily we think of a Scheme program as a high-level abstraction, that (beyond our view) is implemented by being translated into the native language of whatever computer we're running on. So it would be natural to see a Scheme program and a machine-language program and assume that the machine-language one implements the Scheme one. In this section, however, when you see a Scheme program, you must imagine that you're looking at an electronic circuit diagram—something at an even lower level than the machine-language program. The machine language is implemented by the electronics in a real computer. Our simulated computer implements machine language by a Scheme program that understands and carries out the machine-language instructions.

The Scheme program specifies the computations that occur during each stage of carrying out a machine instruction. Current hardware design often begins by specifying the design in a high-level language that can be interpreted by a simulator, so that the designers can understand the implications of their design by observing the behavior of the simulation. Hardware design is not the same as software design. For example, hardware designers are generally limited by such factors as the number of logic elements they can get on a chip. Still, many of the basic principles of hardware and software design have begun to converge, and it is becoming increasingly difficult to tell these two areas apart.

The simulator we will build describes the computations that occur in each of the components of the Gleam machine. This simulator runs the machine-language programs output by the gap assembler. Our Gleam simulator has five major groups of procedures, corresponding to the five units of the Gleam CPU.

11.4.1   The Memory-Access Unit

The MAU is responsible for managing the flow of information between the CPU and memory. It must carry out memread and memwrite operations on behalf of the rest of the CPU. Less obvious is the fact that in the Gleam simulator it must also hide the data structure corresponding to memory. We implement the MAU as a vector.

```
(define memory (make-vector memory-size garbage))
(define memread
  (lambda (mar) (vector-ref memory mar)))
(define memwrite!
  (lambda (mar mdr) (vector-set! memory mar mdr) garbage))
```

The value garbage is a nonsense value (similar to Scheme's void value) that Gleam returns as the value of memwrite! and as the value of memread when the location has not previously been assigned a value.

11.4.2   The I/O Unit

The I/O unit transfers data from the CPU to output devices and into the CPU from input devices. There are four procedures: io-in and io-out, which get/put single characters, and io-read and io-display, which get/put entire data structures.

Real computers don't have innum and outnum, but these can easily be simulated using inchar and outchar to write gap equivalents of read-number and write-number.

In real computers, the inchar and outchar instructions are nontrivial, because I/O devices are generally rather tricky to program. Since the computer is much faster than even the fastest typist, some degree of synchronization is needed to make sure that data has been loaded into the IN register before we try to access it.

Chapter 12 discusses machine-level input/output in further detail.

11.4.3   The Register Unit

The register unit works as the MAU does, except that in a real hardware implementation, register access will be much faster than memory access. We have no way to show this in our Scheme implementation, though, since we implement both the memory and the registers as vectors.

11.4.4   The Arithmetic/Logic Unit

This component of the CPU is not implemented separately. Each instruction in this ALU is directly evaluated in Scheme by the CU program.

11.4.5   The Control Unit

The control unit is responsible for processing instructions. Its job is fairly straight-forward: it uses the program counter to locate the next instruction to be executed, and then executes it.

How do you design a control unit? The best abstraction that computer designers have found is our now-familiar concept of state. The processing of instructions happens in a number of stages. All instructions will go through all the stages (a `jump` instruction will set the program counter itself), so we can think of instruction processing as going from one state to the next.

Gleam's control unit has four states:

- In `fetch` state, it gets the next instruction.
- In `decode` state, it decodes the instruction and increments the program counter by 1.
- In `execute` state, it executes the most recently decoded instruction.
- In `stop` state, the machine is not executing instructions at all.

One way to handle control unit state is to pass the current state (as a symbol) as an argument to the control loop, which is implemented as a `case` form using that symbol (e.g., see Program 11-16). Each state performs the necessary operations, then continues by calling `cu-loop` recursively with the name of the next state. This doesn't consume stack space on each iteration, since `cu-loop` is tail-recursive.

The CU accounts for the largest chunk of code in the simulator; however, much of it is highly repetitive, consisting of "For this instruction, do these particular operations". We'll omit the bulk of the code and just show you the skeleton of the simulator (see Program 11-16). The states of the simulator have become elements in the `case` form: each calls `cu-loop` as its final steps. For a typical instruction such as `load`, the state after `execute` is `fetch`, but for a `halt`, the next state is `stop`.

11.5   Implementing Graphics on Gleam

Drawing is the true test of art.   — J. A. D. Ingres (1780–1867)

Graphics is a complex but fascinating area of computer science. The results can often be spectacular, such as a computer-generated movie of an ultrafast plane flying through an intricate mountain range, or a trip through a human body from

```
(define control-unit
 (lambda (program-counter)
  (let (...
   (letrec
    ((cu-loop
      (lambda (cu-state)
       (case cu-state
         ((fetch)
          ...
          (cu-loop 'decode))
         ((decode)
          ...
          (cu-loop 'execute))
         ((execute)
          ...
          (case opcode
           ((#x00)    ; LOAD -- load register from memory.
             (if (> reg 0)
               (set-register! reg (memread address)))
             (cu-loop 'fetch))
           ...
           ((#x04)    ; JUMP -- goto address.
             (if (or (< address 0) (>= address memory-size))
               (error 'jump "address out of bounds"))
             (set! program-counter address)
             (cu-loop 'fetch))
           ((#xa0)     ; HALT -- terminate execution.
             (cu-loop 'stop))
           ...
           ))
         ((stop)
          (format #t "Execution terminated~%"))))))
     (cu-loop 'fetch))))))
```

Program 11-16   Skeleton of the simulator

a blood-cell's viewpoint. High-quality graphics requires algorithms and advanced hardware. Even implementing our simple graphics package on a computer requires us to understand the computer's graphics hardware, and to use complex algorithms.

In this section, we'll see how to write our own versions of the Scheme graphics procedures we've used, using two implementations.

1. Our first implementation will be written in Scheme, and will use "character graphics", in which we use a character (space or asterisk) to represent a pixel. Character graphics is low-resolution (an entire printed page might only have 60 rows and 80 columns), but has the advantage of requiring no special hardware. We'll use character graphics to study the algorithms needed for drawing lines and text.

2. Once we understand our graphics algorithms, we'll look at Gleam's video graphics hardware. Using this hardware, we'll write gap implementations of the graphics algorithms.

Let's get some of the details out of the way. draw-line% and draw-move% rely upon the concept of the current point. draw-move% sets the current point, and draw-line% draws from the current point to another point. We can implement these procedures using global variables to hold the coordinates of the current point, as shown in Program 11-17. The procedure basic-draw-line draws a line from $(x1, y1)$ to $(x2, y2)$; we'll study it in Section 11.5.2.

```
(define current-x 0)
(define current-y 0)
(define draw-move%
  (lambda (x y)
    (set! current-x x)
    (set! current-y y)))
(define draw-line%
  (lambda (x y)
    (basic-draw-line current-x current-y x y)
    (set! current-col x)
    (set! current-row y)))
```

Program 11-17   Procedures draw-line% and draw-move%

Practical Note

Why didn't we use object-oriented techniques in these procedures? By creating a pen object, we could have encapsulated the current point (and, in a more sophisticated package, other attributes such as color and line width). We could have had as many pens as we wanted.

We didn't use an object-oriented approach because we're trying to duplicate some non-object-oriented procedures. draw-move% and draw-line% allow only one pen, and don't have options for color or line width. We studied them long before we learned about objects. Implementing these procedures according to their specifications, with no extra features, doesn't benefit from object-oriented programming.

☞ **Exercise 11–20**

There is an inconsistency between the use of (x, y) coordinates and row/column coordinates. People often work with images using rows and columns, with the origin in the upper left-hand corner. However, our Scheme procedures place the origin at the lower left corner. Modify draw-line% and/or draw-move% so that they use a lower-left origin. You will need one additional piece of information. What is it? ❑

11.5.1   Bitmaps

An artist uses paint and canvas to produce a picture. Each time the artist applies paint to part of the canvas, whatever was there before is covered up. Our "canvas" might be a video screen or a printed page. It can be represented as a grid of pixels,

Graphics Output Devices

Video display terminals have been in use since the early 1950s, both as graphics devices and standard terminals. By the middle 1960s, **vector graphics** display systems were large,expensive devices that operated by drawing lines on the screen. Vector graphics is not directly related to Scheme vectors, but refers to the fact that these devices drew lines on a cathode ray tube (CRT) display. A CRT consists of an electron gun that fires a beam of electrons at the screen; phosphors on the screen light up when hit by the beam. The positioning is effected by two magnets, which provide horizontal and vertical deflection. A typical display system of the time was capable of showing images with up to about 6,000 vectors, and cost about $150,000. Because the phosphor glow decays with time, it is necessary to redraw the image on a CRT several times per second. The disadvantage of vector graphics is that the more vectors in a display on a vector screen, the longer it takes to redraw the image, which results in a great deal of flicker in complex images.

The cost of video displays started to drop with the invention of **raster graphics** displays, which operate in the same way that a television does: the beam traces out a series of horizontal lines on the screen, and is rapidly turned on and off, giving the effect of dots, or pixels (picture elements), on the screen. Again, the redrawing happens many times per second. Raster technology has the advantage of allowing us to display extremely complex images on the screen, and to move beyond lines to filled shapes and even photographic images. Raster graphics hardware has become quite inexpensive, and is included with all modern desktop computer systems.

Raster graphics has a downside, though. A vector image with just a few lines requires very little data. On the other hand, any raster graphics image requires a large number of pixels, even if it only contains a few lines. Therefore, raster images take a considerable amount of memory and disk space, and can take a relatively long time to transmit over a network. Video, involving perhaps thirty graphics images per second, requires even more resources. Sophisticated data compression methods have been developed specifically for raster graphics and video images. (Most of the popular graphics formats for images, including GIF and TIFF, are raster graphics formats that use data compression to decrease the file size.) A typical video display system on a personal computer is capable of 1024 horizontal lines, with 768 dots on each line, in 256 different colors. The cost for the system (interface and monitor) is under $1,000.

As with input devices, graphics devices can create considerable human-factors problems. For some time, there has been suspicion that the radiation emissions from cathode ray tubes are harmful. Although the case against radiation emissions is not proven, many CRT monitors are designed to follow emission standards devised in Sweden, known as MPR-II. (Liquid-crystal or LCD displays, which do not use high magnetic fields, are used in small personal computers and may eventually supplant CRTs.) What *is* clear is that staring at a display for long periods of time can do substantial damage, including problems in the eyes and in the neck and back.

each of which represents the color of a single spot. Drawing on our canvas means setting the values of specific pixels to the desired colors.

We will therefore represent an image as a **bitmap**, a data structure that represents a raster graphics image. A bitmap is a grid of pixels, each of which can be set to a specific color. The ADT specification for bitmaps is shown in Figure 11-12.

Constants

- `pixel-white`
  An integer value that specifies a white pixel.
- `pixel-black`
  An integer value that specifies a black pixel.

Constructor

- (`make-bitmap` *rows columns*)
  Create a bitmap with the specified number of rows and columns, with each pixel initialized to the color `pixel-white`.

Accessors

- (`bitmap-pixels` *bitmap*)
  Return a vector of the pixels in the bitmap.
- (`bitmap-rows` *bitmap*)
  Return the number of rows in *bitmap*.
- (`bitmap-cols` *bitmap*)
  Return the number of columns in *bitmap*.

Pixel manipulation

- (`bitmap-set-pixel!` *bitmap row col color*)
  Set the pixel at row *row* and column *col* to color *color*.
- (`bitmap-get-pixel` *bitmap row col*)
  Return the color of the pixel at row *row* and column *col*.

Figure 11-12   Abstract Data Type: `bitmap`

To implement a bitmap, we need a **two-dimensional array**, a data structure that can be indexed by row and column. Scheme does not provide two-dimensional arrays, but we can easily use a Scheme vector as an implementation. The basic idea is to store the bitmap data in a vector row by row. The vector must have one element for each pixel, which means that we must create it with *rows* × *cols* elements. Figure 11-13 shows a 4×4 bitmap and its vector representation. We can now access a specific element of the bitmap by using a **storage-mapping function**, a mathematical function that computes the position in the vector, given the row and column number in the bitmap.

The storage-mapping function we need is based on the principle that to access element (r, c) of the bitmap, we must skip over r rows and then over c elements to reach the corresponding vector element. If i is the index of that element, $i = nc \times r + c$ where nc is the number of columns in the bitmap. In our graphics package, we will use one bitmap as the **frame buffer**, and we will find uses for additional bitmaps. Program 11-18 shows the Scheme implementation of bitmaps.

11.5.2   Drawing Lines

The first task we'll tackle is drawing lines. Our implementation of `draw-line%` used a procedure called `basic-draw-line`:

```
(define basic-draw-line
  (lambda (x1 y1 x2 y2)
    (line-drawing-procedure frame-buffer x1 y1 x2 y2)))
```

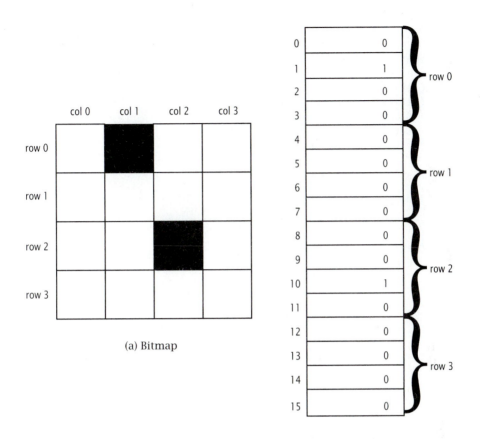

(a) Bitmap

(b) Vector representation

Figure 11-13   Vector representation of a bitmap

We may want to draw many kinds of lines. A line to be drawn might be horizontal, or vertical, or might have any slope. Each of these lines requires us to move through the bitmap, setting pixels in a different pattern. How do we design a procedure to handle all of these cases?

The best way to start is to look at one case. Program 11-19 shows a procedure that draws a horizontal line, which has the same interface as `line-drawing-procedure`. Therefore, its two *y* coordinates must be equal. The helper is given two arguments: the left and right *x* coordinates of the line.

One way to build a general line-drawing procedure is to generalize the behavior of `draw-horizontal-line`. Instead of moving right one pixel on each iteration, let's calculate an *x* and a *y* amount to move by, and set one pixel on each iteration. This algorithm is called the Digital Differential Analyzer, or DDA (see Program 11-20). The number of steps is computed by taking the maximum difference between coordinates. The procedure `line` is then told to start moving from (x1, y1) with increments (xincr, yincr). The result is shown in Figure 11-14.

```
(define make-bitmap
  (lambda (nr nc)
    (cons (make-vector (* nr nc) pixel-white)
      (cons nr nc))))
(define bitmap-pixels car)
(define bitmap-rows (lambda (bm) (car (cdr bm))))
(define bitmap-cols (lambda (bm) (cdr (cdr bm))))
(define bitmap-set-pixel!
  (lambda (bm r c val)
    (bitmap-check bm r c)
    (vector-set! (bitmap-pixels bm)
      (+ (* r (bitmap-cols bm)) c) val)))
(define bitmap-get-pixel
  (lambda (bm r c)
    (bitmap-check bm r c)
    (vector-ref (bitmap-pixels bm)
      (+ (* r (bitmap-cols bm)) c))))
(define bitmap-check
  (lambda (bm r c)
    (if (or (< r 0) (< c 0)
          (>= r (bitmap-rows bm)) (>= c (bitmap-cols bm)))
      (error 'bitmap "Invalid row or column value" r c))))
```

Program 11-18   Implementation of `bitmap`

```
(define draw-horizontal-line
  (lambda (fb x1 y1 x2 y2)
    (letrec
      ((help
        (lambda (i n)
          (if (<= i n)
            (begin
              (bitmap-set-pixel! fb y1 i pixel-black)
              (help (add1 i) n))))))
      (if (= y1 y2)
        (if (< x1 x2)
          (help x1 x2)
          (help x2 x1))
        (error 'draw-horizontal-line
          "y coordinates don't match" x1 y1 x2 y2)))))
```

Program 11-19   Procedure `draw-horizontal-line`

The procedure `round-to-integer` handles a minor Scheme annoyance. The values passed to `set-pixel!` are floating-point numbers. The Scheme primitive `round` yields the nearest integer to its argument. Thus, for example, (round 2.7) ⇒ 3.0. Even though the result of `round` is a whole number, it isn't an exact integer; think of the result as 3.0, rather than 3. We must therefore use `inexact->exact` to obtain an exact integer, as required by the vector operations.

The DDA algorithm is straightforward, but it has two serious limitations:

```
(define round-to-integer
  (lambda (x) (inexact->exact (round x))))
(define dda
  (lambda (bitmap x1 y1 x2 y2)
    (letrec
      ((set-pixel!
        (lambda (x y)
          (bitmap-set-pixel! bitmap
            (round-to-integer y) (round-to-integer x)
            pixel-black))))
      (let
        ((n-steps
          (max (abs (- x2 x1)) (abs (- y2 y1)))))
        (if (> n-steps 0)
          (let
            ((x-incr (/ (- x2 x1) n-steps))
             (y-incr (/ (- y2 y1) n-steps)))
            (letrec
              ((line
                (lambda (x y x-incr y-incr n)
                  (if (> n 0)
                    (begin
                      (set-pixel! x y)
                      (line (+ x x-incr) (+ y y-incr) (sub1 n)))))))
              (line x1 y1 n-steps)
              (set-pixel! x1 y1)))))))))
```

Program 11-20   The Digital Differential Analyzer

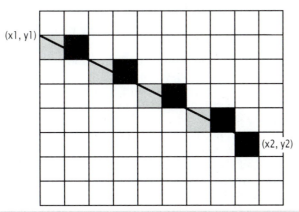

Figure 11-14   Lines drawn by a DDA

1. It uses floating-point arithmetic, which complicates it and slows it down. Remember that a complex drawing may have hundreds or thousands of lines.
2. It doesn't do the best job of line drawing. Lines drawn by a DDA often have "jaggies", small bends caused by less-than-optimal pixel placement.

More sophisticated line-drawing algorithms solve these problems, as described in the graphics texts listed in the "Further Readings".

11.5.3   Text

There are two ways of drawing characters. We can create a bitmap for each character, or we can write a program for each character that draws that character. The latter approach is far more powerful, and is the basis for scalable type technologies such as TrueType and Adobe Type I PostScript. Characters produced by these technologies can be shown at any size, without any loss of quality. In contrast, bitmap characters cannot be magnified without producing jaggies.

If this is so, why would we consider bitmap characters? We do so because they allow us to use a very powerful technique known as **bitblting** (pronounced "bit-blitting") to draw characters conveniently. This operation has many applications beyond character drawing. `bitblt` is an operation that takes two bitmaps, a source and a destination, and copies some or all of the bits of the source bitmap into corresponding bits of the destination.[6] Our version of `bitblt` takes eight arguments.

- `src` is the source bitmap.
- `src-row` and `src-col` are the coordinates of the upper left corner of a rectangle in the source bitmap.
- `dst` is the destination bitmap.
- `dst-row` and `dst-col` are the coordinates of the upper left corner of a rectangle in the destination bitmap.
- `n-rows` and `n-cols` are the size of the rectangle to be copied.

An example `bitblt`, in which we copy the gray area of the source bitmap to the gray area of the destination rectangle, is shown in Figure 11-15. `bitmap-bitblt` itself is shown in Program 11-21 (a).

A more sophisticated version of `bitmap-bitblt` would allow us to perform a Boolean operation between the source and destination. Our version allows you to move a block of bits into a bitmap. With Boolean operations, it is possible to combine the source pixels with destination pixels in useful ways. For example, a cursor on the screen is moved by using the exclusive-or operation.

We will need a bitmap named `char-bitmap` with all of the characters, part of which is shown in Figure 11-16. Each character is six columns wide (the last column is always blank, for spacing), and five rows high. With such a low resolution, it is almost impossible to render lowercase characters readably. `char-bitmap` can be said to be a **font**, or collection of characters. Nothing in our graphics package restricts

---

[6] The term comes from the BLT (block transfer) instruction of the Digital Equipment PDP-10 computer, which in the late 1960s and early 1970s was heavily used for graphics research. Researchers noted that many common graphics operations could be implemented with this instruction. The term has outlived the PDP-10, and many modern assembly languages use BLT for "branch if less than".

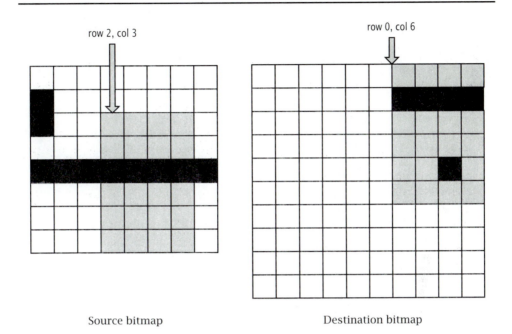

row 2, col 3

row 0, col 6

Source bitmap   Destination bitmap

(bitmap-bitblt src 2 2 dst 0 6 5 4)

Figure 11-15   Bitblt example

us to using the font we've supplied—if you want Cyrillic (Slavic), Hebrew, Arabic, or Klingon, you need only change the contents of `char-bitmap`.[7]

Procedure `draw-text%` is shown in Program 11-21 (b). It takes each character of `str` and bitblts the character's bitmap into the appropriate place in the frame buffer. `char-bitmap-index` (not shown) takes a character and returns an integer index of the five-by-six region of `char-bitmap` corresponding to the character. For example, `(char-bitmap-index #\A)` ⇒ 0, and `(char-bitmap-index #\C)` ⇒ 2. We use `n-cols` and `n-rows` to represent the size of the bitmap of a single character.[8]

11.5.4   A Graphics Package for Gleam

We are now ready to translate our graphics package into gap. To do this, we will have to look at Gleam's video hardware and learn to use it. Gleam's video hardware consists of an electronic interface that converts pixel values into "scan lines", and an attached monitor that displays the scan lines. The video display is extremely

---

[7] Font design requires a deep understanding of typography and aesthetics. Amateurs (such as the authors) must content themselves with designing fonts that can be used to typeset ransom notes, or depict the writings of unartistic aliens.

[8] We have used *monospacing* for our characters: each character has the same width. A better quality, which would make sense if we had substantially higher resolution, is *proportional spacing*, in which each character has its own width. To implement proportional spacing, we would need a table of *font metrics*, giving the width of each character.

```
(define bitmap-bitblt
  (lambda (src src-row src-col
               dst dst-row dst-col
               n-rows n-cols)
    (letrec
      ((helper
        (lambda (i)
          (if (< i n-rows)
              (begin
                (do-row i 0)
                (helper (add1 i))))))
       (do-row
        (lambda (i j)
          (if (< j n-cols)
              (begin
                (bitmap-set-pixel!
                  dst (+ i dst-row) (+ j dst-col)
                  (bitmap-get-pixel
                    src (+ i src-row) (+ j src-col)))
                (do-row i (add1 j)))))))
      (helper 0))))
```

(a) Definition of `bitmap-bitblt`

```
(define n-rows 5)
(define n-cols 6)
(define draw-text%
  (lambda (str)
    (letrec
      ((helper
        (lambda (i n pos)
          (if (< i n)
              (begin
                (bitmap-bitblt char-bitmap
                  0 (* n-cols (char-bitmap-index (string-ref str i)))
                  frame-buffer current-y pos
                  n-rows n-cols)
                (helper (add1 i) n (+ pos n-cols)))))))
      (helper 0 (string-length str) current-x))))
```

(b) Using `bitmap-bitblt` in draw-text

Program 11-21   Procedure `bitmap-bitblt` and its use

---

limited, and provides two colors, black and white, with a resolution of 320 columns by 200 rows. Even such a limited resolution results in a large number of pixels—64,000, to be precise. It is not feasible to store each pixel in its own word. If we store 32 pixels per word, we will only need 2000 words.

As far as the programmer is concerned, the video adapter is represented by a frame buffer at locations #xE000 through #xE7CF. Each word contains 32 pixels, arranged from right to left. The pixel values placed into the frame buffer are used

Figure 11-16   Character bitmaps

by the video adapter to generate the image, without any programmer intervention.

We can represent a bitmap as a sequence of three words containing the address of the first word of pixels, the number of rows, and the number of columns. Given that representation, it is easy to write a procedure for setting pixel values, as shown in Program 11-22.

```
;   r2: bitmap address, r3: row number
;   r4: column number,  r5: pixel value
bitmap-set-pixel
        (load 5 5 2)              ; # of columns
        (mpy 3 3 5)              ; multiply by row number
        (load 6 bits-per-word)
        (quo 7 4 6)             ; compute word number
        (load 8 0 2)            ; get address of first word
        (add 8 1 7)            ; compute address of desired word
        (load 9 0 8)           ; load desired word
        (rem 10 4 6)          ; compute bit number
        (copy 11 1)          ; initial mask
pixloop
        (eql? 12 10 0)         ; loop count = 0?
        (jtrue 12 pixdone)
        (add 11 11 11)        ; double pixel value
        (add 5 5 5)          ; double mask
        (sub 10 10 1)        ; decrement loop count
        (jump 0 pixloop)
pixdone
        (not 11 11)          ; mask is 0 for desired position
        (and 9 9 11)         ; drop old pixel value
        (or 9 9 5)          ; set new pixel value
        (store 9 0 8)       ; update word
        (jump 0 0 pcr)
bits-per-word
        (dataword 32)
```

Program 11-22   Get and set pixels in gap

This procedure uses several programming techniques. Prior to `pixloop`, the code computes the address of the word to be changed. However, that word contains 32 pixel values, one in each bit position. We must select the desired bit of the word and insert the new pixel value in that position. Real computers have "shift" instructions to do this. Gleam doesn't have shift instructions, but we can achieve the same effect by doubling the pixel value once for each bit position between the desired position and the right-hand end of the word. This technique is called **masking**. As we shift the pixel bit left, we shift a 1 bit left the same number of positions. We use Gleam's not instruction to flip all the bits of this "mask" value. Then we use an and to switch off the old pixel value, and an or to set in the new pixel value. Figure 11-17 shows an example (limited to 8 bits).

```
Original word                01110101
New pixel                           1
Bit number                          2
Pixel                        00000100
Mask value                   00000100
Negated mask value           11111011
Original and negated mask    01110001
Result or pixel bit          01110101
```

Figure 11-17   Masking example

We won't show the Gleam translations of dda or bitmap-bitblt, because of their length. Because we've centralized all of the pixel setting in the procedures in Program 11-22, the rest of our Scheme code can be translated in a straightforward manner.

Practical Note

Gleam's video hardware is fairly easy to use. The video hardware on modern computers is much more complex. Sometimes programmers write programs that access the hardware directly, for efficiency. Such programs are not only hard to read, but won't work if the video hardware is changed even slightly. Don't access the video hardware directly in your programs. Find and use a good package of graphics procedures.

We've seen how raster graphics can be done with bitmaps and a few procedures to draw shapes. Whether you're using character graphics or high-resolution color graphics, the algorithms are the same. Although there is considerable room for improvement in the algorithms we've studied, both our line-drawing and our bitblt algorithms show the principles involved in graphics programming.

Gleam's capabilities determine the quality of the graphics we can achieve. We must know the number of rows and columns of the display before we can write any graphics programs. At the lowest level, we—or the procedures we call—must access the video adapter's frame buffer. Graphic programming therefore involves knowledge of both algorithms and hardware.

Case Study: Analyzing Scientific Data

The code presented in this section can be found in file `glexp.scm`.

In this Case Study, we will develop a system in Scheme for handling scientific data. Once the system is complete, we will implement it in gap. Suppose that we have a piece of scientific apparatus that is collecting data. One thousand times a second, the device measures a value, such as a temperature, and sends the collected data (1000 values) to a computer for further processing. We might want to compute and display the average temperature value per second, for example. Our goal is to design the system that collects and analyzes the data.

The system has two components: one collects the data and the second analyzes the collected data. A list of 1000 elements seems like a plausible way to represent the data. Unfortunately, such a list is an unwieldy data structure, and suffers from efficiency problems. Suppose that the scientist wants to access individual elements? Accessing the ith element of an n-element list is an $O(n)$ task, which will reduce our program's overall speed. Program 11-23 (a) shows how we can use a vector to store the data. Lacking a million-dollar piece of scientific equipment, we had to fake `obtain-observation`. (If you happen to have access to a cyclotron nobody else is using, you might want to modify `obtain-observation` accordingly.)

Now the procedure for finding the sum is the same as shown in Program 11-11, except that the vector summed is given the name `observations`. Our computer only operates on integers, so to produce the printed value of the mean to two decimal digits, for example, we need to write a special procedure (see Program 11-23 (b)).

During the analysis, we'll often want to get a particular observation by its number, which we'll do simply by using `vector-ref` (see Program 11-23 (c)).

Finally, we want to write an analysis procedure that lets a scientist work with the data. In this case, we would like to display the mean and the value of observation number 378 (which will occupy position 377 in the vector, since we start counting in vectors from 0). A more sophisticated analysis procedure might let the scientist graph the values and their derivatives, or find the maximum and minimum values. Our analysis procedure is shown in Program 11-23 (d). This code uses `display`, a machine instruction from the extended Gleam machine that we describe in Section 12.1.

How do we translate this all into gap? Program 11-24 (a) shows the most basic procedure, `obtain-observations`. At the beginning of the program we have defined the symbols `obs-vec` to be 1000; `sr`, the stack register, to be 15; and `pcr`, the register containing the return address, to be 14. We're using a simple strategy for managing registers. Each procedure uses a different pair for its argument and its returned value, so they don't interfere with each other.

Now on to `fill-observations`. Before showing the code for this procedure, we must deal with how a vector is going to be represented in Gleam. In our solution, shown in Program 11-24 (b), we've arbitrarily chosen to store our observation vector in locations 1000 to 1999. This procedure uses indexing: the `store` instruction specifies both an address and an index register, which means that the location stored into will be computed when the instruction is executed, as the sum of 1000 and the contents of register 3. If register 3 contains 57, then the location stored into will be $1000 + 57 = 1057$. The next time around the loop, register 3 will contain 58 (because we're adding 1 each time), and therefore we will store into location 1058.

```
(define observations (make-vector 1000))
(define obtain-observation
  (lambda (i) (* i 0.1)))
(define fill-observations
  (lambda (i n)
    (if (< i n)
      (begin
        (vector-set! observations i (obtain-observation i))
        (fill-observations (add1 i) n)))))
```
(a) The observations procedures

```
(define display-ratio
  (lambda (dividend divisor)
    (format #t "~d.~d" (quotient dividend divisor)
      (quotient (* 100 (remainder dividend divisor)) divisor))))
```
(b) printing a ration as a real number

```
(define get-observation
  (lambda (i) (vector-ref observations i)))
```
(c) The observations procedures

```
(define analyze
  (lambda ()
    (fill-observations 0 1000)
    (display "The mean value is: ")
    (display-ratio (sum 1000) 1000)
    (display "Element 378 is:     ")
    (display (get-observation 377))
    (newline)))
```
(d) The analysis main program

Program 11-23   The analysis program

Unlike the other procedures in this program, `fill-observations` calls another procedure, `obtain-observation`. Thus, `fill-observations` must store the return address on the stack and pop it off the stack when it returns. All other procedures keep the return address in register `pcr`, without storing it on the stack. The longest chain of procedure calls is from `main-program` to `fill-observations` to `obtain-observation`. None of these uses many registers, so we don't run out of registers. Larger programs must pay careful attention to managing the registers, including saving the contents of registers on the stack. We'll return to this issue in Chapter 12.

The procedure for finding the sum is straightforward because our Scheme version of `sum` was tail-recursive (see Program 11-11). Here `vec` should be replaced by `obs-vec`. `get-observation` appears in Program 11-24 (c).

Finally, the main program, which fills the vector, does the analysis and outputs the result and a sample vector element, is shown in Program 11-25.

In this Case Study, we've developed an application for analyzing scientific data. Our justification for writing this application in assembly language was the rapid rate of observations. If observation were taken once each minute, there would

```
obtain-observation   (load 6 fake-factor)
                     (mpy 6 3 6)     ; obs number in 3
                     (jump 0 0 pcr) ; result in 6
fake-factor          (dataword 3)
```

(a) Obtaining observations

```
fill-observations
   (store pcr 0 sr)                  ;; r3 has start no.
   (add sr sr 1)                     ;; r4 has no. of observations
fillobs-loop
   (lss? 2 3 4)                      ;; finished?
   (jfalse 2 fillobs-done)           ;; done.
   (call pcr obtain-observation)     ;; no, get one.
   (store 6 obs-vec 3)               ;; result in 6
   (add 3 3 1)                       ;; increment
   (jump 0 fillobs-loop)             ;; loop
fillobs-done
   (sub sr sr 1)                     ;; return
   (load pcr 0 sr)
   (jump 0 0 pcr)
```

(b) Filling the observations vector

```
get-observation         ;; observation no. in r2
   (load 3 obs-vec 2) ;; result in r3
   (jump 0 0 pcr)
```

(c) Accessing an observation

Program 11-24   Analysis procedures in gap

be no justification for assembly language: a Scheme program would be fast enough to process the data adequately.

On the other hand, the gap code is much less readable than the corresponding Scheme code. Further, a Scheme program can be moved from machine to machine relatively easily. Our program must be completely rewritten if we want to move it to another machine.

Faced with problems like this, most programmers adopt a mixed-language approach. They write the majority of the code in their favorite high-level language. The part that is time-dependent is prototyped in the high-level language; a production version is written in assembly language and linked to the Scheme code as a set of foreign procedures. These procedures can be carefully commented and documented (the Scheme prototype serves as very valuable documentation), and thus the overall program is still extremely readable, even to those who don't know assembly language.

☞ **Exercise 11-21**

Write display-ratio in gap. ❏

```
(
(define-symbols (obs-vec . 1000) (sr . 15) (pcr . 14))
main-program
  (load sr stack-origin)
  (load 1 one)
  (load 3 starting-obs)
  (load 4 ending-obs)
  (call pcr fill-observations)
  (load 3 message-1)
  (display 3)
  (load 3 ending-obs)
  (call pcr sum)                ;; compute sum
  (load 13 message-1)
  (display 13)
  (call pcr display-ratio)      ;; sum in r4, n in r3
  (load 3 newline)
  (outchar 3)
  (load 3 message-2)
  (display 3)
  (load 2 obs-no)
  (call pcr get-observation)    ;; Now display element 378.
  (outnum 3)
  (load 3 newline)
  (outchar 3)
  (halt)
stack-origin  (dataword 2000)
starting-obs  (dataword 0)
ending-obs  (dataword 1000)
message-1  (dataword "The mean value is:  ")
message-2  (dataword "Element 378 is:     ")
obs-no  (dataword 377)
newline  (dataword 10) ;#\newline
one  (dataword 1)
...other procedures appear here...
)
```

Program 11-25   Main program in gap

This Case Study has shown the value of prototyping your code in Scheme and then translating it into assembly language. Translate each of the procedures in Exercise 11–22 through Exercise 11–24 into gap. Assume that the arguments to each procedure are passed in registers 2, 3, . . . , and that the result of the procedure will be returned in register 8.

☞ **Exercise 11–22**

```
(define add3
  (lambda (n)
    (+ n 3)))
```

❏

☞ **Exercise 11–23**

```
(define a-plus-b-plus-1
  (lambda (a b)
    (+ a b 1)))
```

❏

☞ **Exercise 11–24**

```
(define fact
  (lambda (n a)
    (if (= n 1)
        a
        (fact (sub1 n) (* n a)))))
```

❏

Summary

In this chapter we've examined the architecture of an abstract machine, the Gleam machine, that closely resembles real computers. We've studied its design and examined the units that compose it: the memory, the input/output system, and the central processing unit. We've seen how the instructions of the machine are expressed in gap, an assembly language for Gleam. We've written some procedures as well as some full programs in the assembly language. We mapped some Scheme constructs onto this machine, and saw how both simple recursive and tail-recursive procedures are implemented. Finally we implemented vectors and demonstrated their use on graphics examples.

Further Readings

Some useful texts include *Computer Organization and Architecture: Principles of Structure and Function* by William Stallings, *Computation Structures* by Stephen A. Ward and Robert J. Halstead, and *Machine Organization: Basic Principles* by John L. Hennesy and David A. Patterson.

Two good texts on graphics are *Computer Graphics* by Francis S. Hill Jr. and *Computer Graphics Principles and Practice* by J. D. Foley, A. van Dam, S. K. Feiner, and J. F. Hughes.

Key Words

Here are the *key words* introduced in this chapter. Make sure you understand what each one means.

address	frame buffer	opcode
ALU: Arithmetic/logic unit (of CPU)	general-purpose computer	operation prolog
analog	index register	PC: Program counter (in CU)
architecture	IOU: Input/output unit (of CPU)	random access
assembler	instruction	random access
base register	IR: Instruction register (in CU)	memory (RAM)
binary digits (bits)	instruction set	raster graphics
bitblt	MAR: Memory-address register (in MAU)	read only memory
bitmap	masking	register instruction
CPU: Central processing unit	MAU: Memory-access unit (of CPU)	RU: Register Unit (of CPU)
CU: Control unit (of CPU)	MDR: Memory data register (in MAU)	return address
decode cycle	memory-reference instruction	self-modifying code
destination register		source register
digital		stored program
effective address		storage-mapping
embedded computer		

execute cycle	memread	function
fetch cycle	memwrite	tail call
fetch/decode/execute	nine's/ten's complement	two-dimensional array
loop	octal	vector graphics
font	one's/two's complement	wordsize

Problems

1. ZYX Corporation is making an embedded computer based on Gleam, and it wants to hold down costs by making a very simple machine. Which of the memory-reference instructions could ZYX's designers eliminate without crippling the resulting machine? ❏

2. Write a gap program to read a set of integers. The program computes the total of the numbers input, until a negative number is input, when the program displays the current total, zeros the total, and continues reading input. ❏

3. Many painting programs have a small "paint-can" icon. Clicking on this icon allows you to fill a region with a color. Assume that you are given the row and column number of a white pixel. Your job is to color all of the pixels black until you reach a black boundary.

   Recursion allows us to solve this problem effectively. If we're outside the bitmap, or the pixel we're looking at is black, we can terminate. Otherwise, color the pixel black, and recursively visit the four neighbors (north, south, east, and west) of the current pixel. ❏

4. We wrote a procedure diff in gap to take the difference of two vectors, element by element, and store the result in a third vector. The vectors were fixed (i.e., defined in the code). Here's another Scheme version:

```
(define diff2
  (lambda (vec1 vec2 vec3 n)
    (letrec
      ((help
         (lambda (i)
           (if (< i n)
             (begin
               (vector-set! vec3
                 (vector-ref vec1 i)
                 (vector-ref vec2 i))
               (help (add1 i)))))))
      (help 0))))
```

   Translate this version into gap. ❏

5. Write a procedure, vector-reverse, in gap, that reverses the items of a vector; in a vector of n items, the items at positions i and $n - i$ exchange places. ❏

Self-Assessment

1. Write a procedure, write-positive-hex-number, to print out a positive number in hexadecimal. Assume that some other procedure has printed the #x prefix. ❏

2. Translate the following Scheme form into gap. Assume that each of the variables has been assigned a memory location using the dataword directive.

```
(if p (+ c 1) (+ d 2))
```

❏

3. Suppose that Scheme had a `while` form that evaluates its body as long as its condition evaluates to anything but `#f`. Translate the following code into gap. Assume that each variable has been assigned a memory location. Initially i has a positive value.

```
(while (> i 0)
  (set! j (+ i 2))
  (set! i (- i 1)))
```

❏

4. Write a gap procedure to sum the first n cubes, that is, $\sum_{i=1}^{n} i^3$. Assume that n is passed in register 4, and the result is returned in register 5. ❏

5. Consider the following piece of gap code:

```
start (copy 5 0)
lab1  (load 9 nine)
      (lss? 8  9 5)
      (jtrue 8 lab2)
      (load 6 temp)
      (add 5 5 6)
      (store 5 temp)
      (jump 0 lab1)
lab2  (load 6 temp)
stop  (halt)
nine  (dataword 9)
temp  (dataword 5)
```

a. What value is in register 6 when the program halts?
b. Suppose that instead of writing (jtrue 8 lab2) we had written (jtrue 8 stop). What would be in register 6?
c. Modern computers seldom have a halt instruction. One of the effects of the halt instruction is to prevent the PC from being advanced to the next instruction. Provide one line of gap code that accomplishes this function.

❏

6. Which variables must be pushed on the stack during evaluation of (foo 3 5 4)? Which procedures must push their return addresses on the stack?

```
(define foo
  (lambda (x y z)
    (+ (bar x y) z)))
(define bar
  (lambda (a b)
    (let ((c (bar (* 2 b) a)))
      (baz (* c (/ a 3))))))
(define baz
  (lambda (m)
    (* 3 (sqrt m))))
```

❏

Programming Problems

1. Dollar amounts are conventionally written out with a leading dollar sign immediately before the first digit, and with commas separating thousands, millions, and so on. Negative numbers are often written with a trailing CR (for "credit"). Write a procedure that accepts an integer representing an amount in pennies, and the number of columns, and that writes out the amount according to the above rules. (The trailing CR, if negative, or two spaces, if positive, would be counted in the number of columns.) For example, if your procedure were asked to print -123456 in 11 columns, it would write $1,234.56CR. ❏

2. The vector-based Quicksort algorithm described in Chapter 9, qsort, translates very easily to gap. One reason that Quicksort is very efficient for most problems is that the number of instructions per comparison is quite small. Implement qsort in gap. ❏

3. We've built a complex simulator for Gleam, but the principles behind its implementation also apply to simulators for less complex machines. For example, take your favorite programmable calculator. Usually such a calculator lets you enter a sequence of instructions, and then re-evaluate those instructions either with the existing data in the memory of the machine or with data entered according to input instructions in the program. Design and implement a simulator for your calculator. ❏

Chapter 12

Virtual Machines

How does a machine like **Gleam** provide facilities like pairs and lists, a Scheme evaluator, and an operating system? To answer this question, we must look at another form of abstraction: machine abstraction. **Gleam** can be extended to support pairs and lists, using the same programming model we developed in Chapter 11. **Gleam**/2 adds new instructions to **Gleam** that allow us to write recursive list-processing programs in gap.

We will see how to extend **Gleam** and **Gleam**/2 by including libraries of procedures, including one that explains **Gleam**/2 instructions in terms of **Gleam** instructions. To do so, however, we need to explore the storage-management and tagged-data facilities that are used in Scheme. Scheme manages pairs for the programmer, controlling allocation and deallocation of pairs, and recovering deallocated pairs using its *garbage collector*. Then we will see how to extend **Gleam**'s input and output.

We will then specify a Scheme evaluator in gap, using **Gleam**/2 operations. The *imperative evaluator* is a large gap program that is a translation of the self-evaluator using **Gleam**/2 instructions. To do this efficiently, we write the imperative evaluator as a collection of routines that connect to each other by jumping to the next routine. This section shows how tail-recursion in Scheme is implemented at the gap level.

Finally we will extend the machine abstraction by examining the facilities an operating system provides. including processes, files, devices, memory, and network communication.

12.1   Gleam/2

12.2   The Gleam **Virtual Machine**

12.3   The Imperative Evaluator

12.4   Operating Systems

Summary, Further Readings, Key Words

Problems, Self-Assessment, Programming Problems

So naturalists observe, a flea
Hath smaller fleas that on him prey;
And these have smaller fleas to bite 'em,
And so proceed ad infinitum.
Thus every poet, in his kind,
Is bit by him that comes behind.

— Jonathan Swift, *On Poetry*

Although we can rewrite any Scheme program in gap, Gleam's world is starkly different from Scheme's. A Scheme programmer sees a friendly system with a rich set of primitives; although some Scheme evaluators only read, evaluate, and print the values of forms, others provide an elaborate multiwindowed programming environment, with interactive debugging systems. Gleam provides a specific set of instructions for processing registers, and nothing more. Many errors in Scheme result in error messages. A gap program might actually erase itself as the result of a bug. gap programmers must therefore think at the machine's level. Although there are elaborate debugging systems for assembly language, a programmer is often reduced to picking through the remains of a buggy program, desperately seeking any clue to the program's failure.

We can and should use abstraction, both procedural and data, in designing programs. A well-written gap program will be divided into modular, well-commented procedures, just as Scheme, C++, or COBOL programs are. The most modular, well-commented, assembly-language program can still crash in a spectacular way from an error as trivial as loading an argument into the wrong register. Scheme programs can crash as well, but they can't crash because of errors in machine addresses, prematurely deallocated storage, doing floating-point arithmetic on fixed-point numbers, or trying to put two things in the same register at once, because the Scheme evaluator handles all those things automatically.

We need a way to bridge the gap between our real machines and our Scheme environment. We can solve the same problems in Scheme and gap; the difference is in the level of detail we must think about. Whereas a gap programmer must worry about each and every detail of the machine, a Scheme programmer can think about much higher concepts, such as objects, procedures, and environments. This makes the Scheme programmer much more productive than his gap counterpart.

A difference in level of detail is a difference in abstraction level. Here, we speak not of the abstractions designed by the programmer, but those provided by the machine. There is a fourth kind of abstraction, along with procedural, data, and syntactic abstraction: **machine abstraction**, in which the machine designer provides appropriate abstractions for the machine's user.

Banks provide a common example of machine abstraction. A customer who uses an automated teller can consider it to be a special-purpose computer with `Withdraw` and `Deposit` command buttons. A teller must master a fairly sophisticated command language in order to perform all the transactions a customer might want. The bank's programmers probably use database and networking software, as well as application code written in a language such as Scheme. The database and networking software are also written in a high-level language. In turn, the high-level language is processed by an evaluator that operates at the Gleam level. Gleam computers are built out of integrated circuits by computer designers; these circuits move electrons around, and are therefore governed by the laws of physics.

A given machine abstraction can be provided by either hardware or software. At the lowest level, we have to provide a physical machine. Above that level, we can either build a special-purpose hardware machine, or we can program a lower-level machine to behave in the way specified by our abstraction. There is therefore a hierarchy of machines; the hierarchy in the banking example is shown in Figure 12–1. All of these machines are engaged in the same task; pressing the buttons on an automated teller machine results in the customer's balance being decremented and money appearing in the output tray. The difference in these machines is the level of detail.

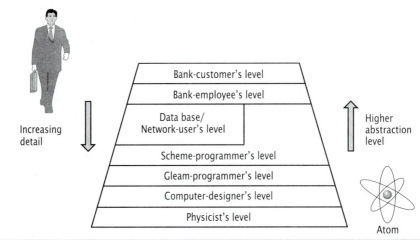

Figure 12–1   The tower of machine abstractions

The machine the programmer sees might itself not be a piece of hardware, but rather a software simulator. The programmer follows the rules given by the architecture of the machine, whether it is implemented as a physical machine, or as a software simulator. The use of a software simulator has a number of benefits. For example, a rich variety of software currently exists for PC-compatible (which use Intel 80x86 CPUs) and Macintosh (which use Motorola 680x0 CPUs). Newer CPU chips, such as the PowerPC, MIPS R4000, and DEC Alpha, have totally different structures from those of their predecessors. However, simulation allows the earlier programs to run on these newer CPUs without the user having to do anything special, and without appreciable slowdown.

Simulators for older CPUs are fine as far as they go. But what stops us from building software machines that could never feasibly be implemented in hardware? Such a machine might have much more flexibility than a hardware machine. It could run many different programs concurrently. It could be programmed in a high-level language. We call such a computer, programmed in software and running on a physical machine, a **virtual machine**. This chapter explores virtual machines. We'll see how to extend Gleam's power. We'll also see where Gleam doesn't match real computers, and how we can build a Gleam virtual machine that *does* run on real computers. We'll see how we can build a Scheme evaluator that converts Gleam into a Scheme virtual machine. Finally, we'll look at operating systems, programs that manage the activities of a computer system, by creating virtual machines for application programs to run on.

12.1   Gleam/2

> *Who will change old lamps for new ones? ... new lamps for old ones?*
> — *The Thousand and One Nights*, "The History of Aladdin"

In the last chapter we learned how to program the Gleam machine in gap. We computed with numbers, characters, and vectors, but we haven't yet used Scheme data structures such as pairs. We'd like a machine that handles lists as easily as Scheme. Gleam/2 is a new machine whose instructions include operations for processing pairs. It has all of Gleam's instructions, as well as the instructions shown in Figure 12–2. When we write a program for Gleam/2, we use the same control structures as for Gleam, but we can assume that a register can hold a pair. The next section shows how to implement pairs on Gleam so that a pair can fit into Gleam's 32-bit cells. Later, we will implement Scheme on the Gleam architecture. Gleam/2 is a step on the way toward that goal.

There are two types of register instructions introduced in Gleam/2: list operations and type-checking predicates. These new list operations (cons, car, cdr, symbol?, setcar, setcdr) are the exact counterparts of the corresponding Scheme operations. Similarly, the type-checking predicates (boolean?, symbol?, number?, char?, string?, pair?, null?) are the exact counterparts of the corresponding Scheme operations. eqv? implements the Scheme predicate, and read and display read and write Scheme values.

Mnemonic code	Op	Operation performed
cons	#xc0	Make a new pair.
car	#xc1	Take the car of a register.
cdr	#xc2	Take the cdr of a register.
setcar	#xc3	Mutate the car of a pair.
setcdr	#xc4	Mutate the cdr of a pair.
boolean?	#xc5	Set dest-reg to true if from-reg1 contains a boolean.
symbol?	#xc6	Set dest-reg true if from-reg1 contains a symbol.
number?	#xc7	Set dest-reg to true if from-reg1 contains a number.
char?	#xc8	Set dest-reg to true if from-reg1 contains a char.
string?	#xc9	Set dest-reg to true if from-reg1 contains a string.
pair?	#xca	Set dest-reg to true if from-reg1 contains a pair.
null?	#xcb	Set dest-reg to true if from-reg1 contains null.
eqv?	#xcc	Set dest-reg to true if from-reg1 is eqv to from-reg2.
read	#xcd	The same as (read) in Scheme.
display	#xce	The same as (display ...) in Scheme.

Figure 12-2   Gleam/2 Register Instructions

12.1.1   List Processing

We can use Gleam/2's pair instructions to write a list-processing procedure. Program 12-1 (a) shows our starting point, a tail-recursive version of reverse in Scheme. The key idea to grasp here is how we can turn the tail-recursive call to helper into a jump instruction. In other words, suppose that we have x in register 5, and a in register 6. We can then check to see if register 5 is null. If so, we return the value of a. If not, we set register 5 to its cdr, and set register 6 to be (cons (car x) a). We would then jump back to the beginning of the procedure. This gives us the program in Program 12-1 (b).

Note how the gap code reflects the use of a helper: the main procedure simply sets a to null, and then "drops through" into the helper, which begins at revloop. The first step in the helper is to see whether x is null; if it is, the machine jumps to the label revdone. The null test puts true (nonzero) or false (zero) in register 7.

Once we've decided that x isn't null, the next step is to compute (cdr x), and (cons (car x) a), the values for the next iteration. It's important to set register 7 to (car x) first, unlike the Scheme code, since (cdr 5 5) destroys the value in register 5.

A trace through this code is instructive; suppose that initially register 5 contains (b c) and register 6 contains (a).

```
(car 7 5)      r5: (b c)   r6: (a)     r7: b
(cons 6 7 6)   r5: (b c)   r6: (b a)   r7: b
(cdr 5 5)      r5: (c)     r6: (b a)   r7: b
```

As you can see, this code has done one step on the way to reversing the list.

We have shown how augmenting Gleam with list-processing instructions and type predicates is straightforward. Each instruction performs one operation on a

```
(define reverse%
  (lambda (w)
    (letrec ((helper
      (lambda (x a)
        (if (null? x)
          a
          (helper (cdr x) (cons (car x) a))))))
      (helper w '()))))
```
(a) Scheme version

```
;;; x is in register 5, a is in register 6.
reverse%    (load 6 null)     ; set up a
revloop     (null? 7 5)       ; is x null?
            (jtrue 7 revdone) ; Exit procedure if so.
            (car 7 5)         ; reg7 <- car x
            (cons 6 7 6)      ; (cons (car x) res)
            (cdr 5 5)         ; Set reg 5 to (cdr <reg 5>).
            (jump 0 revloop)
revdone     (copy 5 6)        ; move result into reg 5
            (jump 0 0 pcr)
null        (dataword '())
```
(b) gap version

Program 12-1   Two versions of reverse

value or a pair. We can then write gap programs to implement the list processing primitives in Scheme as well as all other procedures that use list structure. The next section shows how to handle the pair data abstraction on the Gleam machine.

☞ **Exercise 12-1**

Write append% in gap:

```
(define append%
  (lambda (x y)
    (if (null? x)
        y
        (cons (car x) (append% (cdr x) y)))))
```

❏

12.2   The Gleam **Virtual Machine**

> *The truth is rarely pure, and never simple.*
> — Oscar Wilde, *The Importance of Being Earnest*

Gleam's basic operations are limited; the only way to write a complicated program is as a long sequence of machine instructions. The longer the program, the more likely we are to make mistakes. On the other hand, Gleam/2's instructions are not typical of modern computers; these include the pair instructions, type-checking instructions such as `number?`, and the input/output instructions.

Gleam/2 occupies just one point on a spectrum. Gleam lacks its more complex instructions. An even more powerful version of Gleam/2 could be built with additional instructions for standard Scheme operations such as `reverse`, `append`, and `assv`. In this section, we look at "what makes Gleam Gleam". We'll start off by raising the abstraction level, by designing a library of procedures that give the `gap` programmer the same primitives as those enjoyed by the Scheme programmer. We'll then go in the other direction, to see how Gleam/2's instructions can be defined in terms of simpler ones. Finally, we'll look at RISC (reduced instruction set computer) architectures, which trade powerful instructions for speed.

12.2.1   Designing a Library

One way to raise the abstraction level is to define a library of procedures, an organized set of procedures that implement a collection of related abstractions. A library gives the programmer the ability to work at a higher abstraction level, that of the language *plus* the library. In this section, we'll look at the design of a library for Gleam.

Libraries came early in the history of computing. The first libraries provided routines for elementary mathematical functions such as sine, cosine, and so on. When graphical output devices such as plotters and graphics screens were developed, a simple library of procedures for operations such as drawing lines was provided.

Libraries were also developed early to provide procedures for floating-point addition, subtraction, and so on. Early machines often did not have floating-point instructions, although hardware floating-point instructions on mainframes date from the 1960s. Gleam is typical of inexpensive CPUs up to about 1990: it has no hardware instructions for doing floating-point operations. Microprocessor floating-point was not feasible until it was possible to put hundreds of thousands or millions of components onto one circuit. Before that, many CPU designers used a hybrid approach, in which an optional "coprocessor" chip provided the floating-point features.

We would like to run our programs on computers without the floating-point features, but to take advantage of hardware floating-point if it is available. An **unimplemented instruction exception** is one way to do this. When the CPU attempts to execute a floating-point operation, one of two things happens: either this CPU has hardware floating-point, in which case the operation proceeds normally, or it doesn't, in which case the machine calls a procedure at a specific location in memory. This procedure is an **emulator**: it analyzes the instruction that caused the machine to jump to it, and calls a corresponding procedure. From the programmer's point of view, there is no difference between the CPUs with floating point and those with an emulator. Both execute floating-point instructions, although the emulator is much slower.

Graphics provides another example of how a capability can be provided either by hardware or software. Gleam's video hardware (discussed in Chapter 11) allows us to set pixels, but little else. We used this hardware to write procedures for drawing lines and doing bitblts. Programs that do a great deal of graphics using these procedures will be slow. However, it is possible to produce a special-purpose chip, a **graphics accelerator**, that does line drawing and bitblts very quickly. The only change that must be made to programs is to replace the software line-drawing and bitblting procedures with procedures that use the graphics accelerator.

In more recent years, **class libraries** have become common. A class library is nothing more than an integrated set of classes, in an object-oriented language, that provide a unified set of abstractions. One common variety of class library provides for graphical user interface elements such as windows, dialog boxes, and menus. The programmer uses these classes, and never has to worry about the display hardware or the underlying low-level software (in theory, anyway).

What should the Gleam library contain? Floating-point would be desirable, but implementing floating-point requires a bit more math than we'd like to go into here. One thing is certain: Gleam would be much more convenient to program if it had Scheme's comprehensive set of list-processing primitives such as equal?, assv, member, and so on.

We aren't going to explore the implementation here; it will be sufficient to design our procedures so that they can be called in a standard way. To do this effectively, we must design a set of **register conventions** that determine how the arguments and return values are used. We adopt the following conventions:

- Registers 0 and 1 always contain the values 0 and 1, respectively, because these values are so frequently used. (The use of register 0 is actually a machine feature; see Chapter 11.)
- Registers 2 through 6 are known as tmp0, tmp1, tmp2, tmp3, and tmp4. These can be used for any purposes within a procedure. Normally, arguments and return values are passed in these registers.
- Register 14 is known as pcr (the "program counter register"). When we call a procedure, the return address is placed in this register.
- Register 15 is known as sr (the "stack register"). This must be initialized with the address of the bottom of the stack at the beginning of execution.

Our implementation of memv, using the register conventions, appears in Program 12-2.

```
;;; args in tmp0: item, tmp1:any-list, result in tmp0
memv        (null? tmp2 tmp1)
            (jtrue tmp2 memv-done)
            (car tmp2 tmp1)
            (eqv? tmp2 tmp2 tmp0)
            (jfalse tmp2 memv-more)
            (copy tmp0 tmp1)
            (jump 0 0 pcr)
memv-more   (cdr tmp1 tmp1)
            (jump 0 memv)
memv-done   (load tmp0 false)
            (jump 0 0 pcr)
false       (dataword #f)
```
Program 12-2   The primitive memv using Gleam/2 operations

☞ **Exercise 12-2**

Write list-ref, following our conventions. ❏

☞ **Exercise 12–3**

Write `assv`, following our conventions. ❏

12.2.2   Gleam/2's Instructions

We've seen how to raise Gleam's abstraction level. Gleam/2 already operates at a higher level than many real machines do. A number of Gleam/2's instructions don't have counterparts on other computers, including

- pair operations: `cons`, `car`, `cdr`, `setcar`, `setcdr`
- predicates: `number?`, `boolean?`, `pair?`, `symbol?`, `char?`, `null?`, `string?`, `eqv?`
- input/output operations: `inchar`, `outchar`, `read`, `display`

We equipped Gleam/2 with these instructions in order to make the machine easier to program. Now we will see that these instructions can be written as procedures that use only regular Gleam instructions. (Counterparts of these regular instructions exist on *every* computer.)

We will now show how a procedure for accomplishing the same task as each of Gleam/2's instructions can be written using only regular instructions. Even though a procedure call does not look the same as a single instruction, translating a program so that it uses only regular instructions and calls to these special procedures is a mechanical task.

12.2.2.1   Representing Pairs and Symbols   Scheme requires that any variable be able to hold any kind of value, even a vector or string. Gleam also stores all values inside a single memory cell, including pairs. In Chapter 11, we saw that Gleam represents a vector as a block of consecutive memory cells. The address of the first cell appears in the `load` instructions, and the index register carries the value of the index into the vector. The only necessary information about the vector is its address. To implement the pair instructions, we must design a representation for pairs that also uses a compact representation that can be stored in a single cell.

Pairs contain two values. Following our vector idea, we'll store a pair as two consecutive memory cells, one for the car and one for the cdr. To represent the pair as a value, we'll use the *address* of the first cell. For example, we might represent the pair (1 . 2) by storing the numeric value 1 in memory location 500, and 2 in location 501. The pair value itself would be the address 500.

Using addresses as representations for data is a central idea in computing. The combination of the address, plus a plan for organizing information in memory, provides a mechanism for storing data structures. Vectors use a contiguous block of memory, represented by an address and the length of the block. Pairs use two consecutive cells, represented by the address of the first.

An example of this representation is shown in Figure 12–3. The list structure (foo (1 . foo) #f) is shown first in a conventional box-and-arrow diagram, and then as a collection of storage cells. In this example, we have placed the pairs at consecutive memory locations starting at 1000. We have labeled the corresponding pairs in the box-and-arrow and memory-cell pictures with the same Greek letters. Note how the arrows are represented by the use of memory addresses. For example, the cdr of pair α is pair β; accordingly, memory cell 1001 contains 1002.

We have represented the symbol foo as a sequence of four storage locations, starting at location 2000: the first contains the number of characters, and the remaining locations contain the characters of the symbol's name: 102 is the ASCII

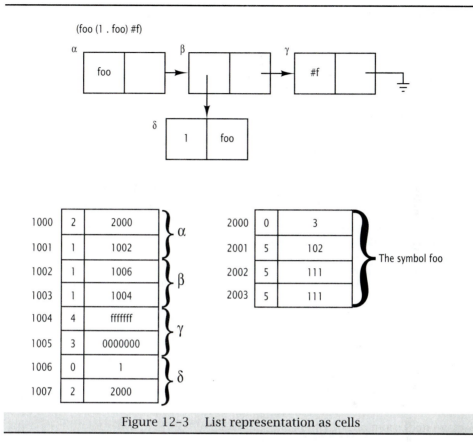

Figure 12-3   List representation as cells

code for #\f, and 111 is the ASCII code for #\o. In the list, the symbol is represented by the address of its first storage location. Both uses of the symbol foo in the list lead to the same storage location. To ensure that there is only one symbol foo, there is a dictionary of all of the symbols: whenever a given symbol is used, the same address will be used. This technique guarantees that symbol equality can be tested in a single instruction by comparing addresses.[1]

We have used two other conventions, in pair *y*: we represent the Boolean value #f as hexadecimal ffffff, and null as 0000000.

The above values are only seven hexadecimal digits, and the car and cdr of each pair have an additional hexadecimal digit at the left. We need this extra hexadecimal digit to identify the kind of values in the cells. In Scheme, values are "self-identifying": we can ask a value to tell us, for example, whether it is a number, a string, or whatever. In Gleam, on the other hand, memory cells just contain 32 bits, whose meaning is up to the programmer. Our solution to this problem is to

---

[1] You might think to use a binary search tree to store the symbols. However, a data structure known as a *hash table* allows for more efficient searching, at the cost of not being able to retrieve symbols in order. This is not a significant loss, and Scheme systems universally use hash tables for storing symbols. Further, our representation wastes considerable amounts of space; real Scheme systems might pack characters two or four to a cell.

reserve the leftmost 4 bits of each value for a **tag** that identifies the type of the value in the cell. We have adopted the following tag values:

- #x0: The value is a positive integer.
- #x1: The value is the address of a pair.
- #x2: The value is the address of a symbol.
- #x3: The value must be 000000, which represents null.
- #x4: The value is a Boolean.
- #x5: The value is a character.
- #x6: The value is a string.
- #xf: The value is a negative integer.

Scheme systems typically have more data types, and therefore use most or all of the possible tags. We've used a trick to make arithmetic on tagged integers a bit easier. We use #x0 as the tag for positive and #xf as the tag for negative integers. That way the hardware doesn't even notice that there's a tag during arithmetic operations.

12.2.2.2 Gleam/2's Instructions   We said that all of Gleam/2's instructions are equivalent to sequences of simple instructions. With our representation, we can simulate many of these instructions in one or two simple instructions. First, let's do the predicates. The trick for the type-checking predicates is to extract the tag. Suppose we want to put the tag of the value in register 5 into register 6, as an integer between 0 and 15. This can be done with the following code:

```
        (copy 6 5)
        (load 7 tagdivide)
        (quotient 6 6 7)
        ...
tagdivide
        (dataword #x10000000)
```

Dividing by the value in `tagdivide` has the effect of throwing away the value part of the contents of register 6.[2]

If we now want to see whether the value in register 5 is a pair, all we must do is to check whether the tag value is 1:

```
        (load 7 tagpair)
        (eql? 6 6 7)
        ...
tagpair
        (dataword 1)
```

We can simulate all of the other type-checking predicates in the same way.

The predicate eqv? is easy to implement. According to the rules of Scheme, two values are equivalent if they have the same type and the same value. This test can be done merely by comparing the two words with Gleam's eql? instruction, in the case of symbols, Booleans, the empty list, pairs, and nonempty strings and

---

[2] In most real machines, we would use a "right-shift" instruction instead. The shift instructions move the bits a specified number of positions to the left or right; thus right-shifting the value #x12345678 by 4 positions gives the result #x01234567. Gleam doesn't have shift instructions, but division will suffice.

vectors.[3] In Scheme, eqv? provides an equality predicate that handles these cases as well as numbers and characters. Scheme implementors can choose how to implement numbers. For example, there is no reason why there can't be multiple copies of a particular number. Simply testing equality of addresses might give the right answer on one Scheme implementation and the wrong answer on another. Scheme includes eqv? so that we can test numbers and characters as we test other data types. Thus, to implement eqv? completely, we must also test numbers and characters correctly.

The car and cdr primitives are trivial, using indexing and offsets. Suppose we have a pair in register 5, and we want to load its car into register 6 and its cdr into register 7:

```
(load 6 0 5)
(load 7 1 5)
```

If register 5 contains 1000, the first load will load the contents of location 1000, and the second will load those of 1001.

☞ **Exercise 12–4**

The gap code for loading the car and cdr is incomplete. What must we do first, before taking the car or cdr? Show the code. ❑

If the accessors are done with loads, the mutators can be done with stores. Suppose that we have the address of a pair in register 5, and we want to set the car and cdr of the pair to the values in registers 6 and 7, respectively. This is straightforward:

```
(store 6 0 5)
(store 7 1 5)
```

12.2.2.3 cons and the Free List   The pair constructor, cons, requires that we **allocate** memory. When we write the instruction

```
(cons 5 6 7)
```

we expect register 5 to be assigned the address of a new pair that does not share memory with any existing pair. Thus, we need a region of memory that contains all of the pairs; we call this region the **heap**.

The heap initially contains only **free pairs**, pairs not in use. Gradually, conses will allocate some of the heap to contain pairs. Later, the heap will contain both free pairs and pairs in use. Each cons finds a free pair in the heap. One possibility for identifying a free pair is to put a "funny" tag value into the car of the pair, and scan the heap for a pair with this tag value. Since our heap may have millions of pairs, however, a scan is undesirable. The alternative is to link all of the free pairs into the **free list**. The free list is a Scheme system data structure that contains no data used by the program. Its purpose is to record the free pairs efficiently. The cdr of each pair contains the address of the next free pair. During initialization, a procedure must be called to go through the heap and build a free list.

---

[3] This discussion ignores "bignums", numbers that are too large to fit in a machine location. Neither eq1? nor eqv? can handle these. A loop is needed to go through all the digits of such a number. As a result, comparing very large numbers can't be done in constant time.

In the snapshot of the heap shown in Figure 12–4, one of the four pairs has been used to represent the pair (123 . 456). This pair has been placed at locations 1004 and 1005. The other three pairs are free. When we call cons, we want it to scan the heap and return the address of a free pair, at which point the pair is no longer free. cons is therefore like a seater in a restaurant: when a party enters the restaurant, they are allocated a free table.

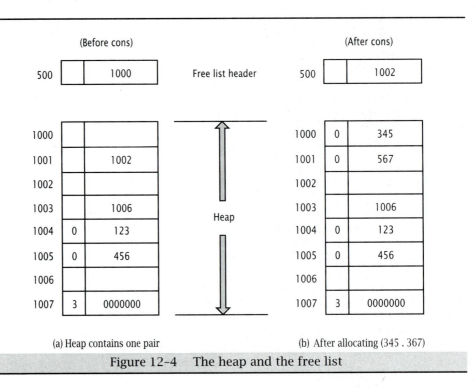

Figure 12–4   The heap and the free list

In Figure 12–4, we are doing (cons 345 567). After the call to the cons procedure, the first pair on the free list has been allocated, and the free list address has been updated. The 1002 at location 1001 is the address of the next free pair. One of the four pairs (the one at locations 1004 and 1005) was already allocated; thus the contents of location 1003 causes the free list to skip this pair.

In the following code, we want to allocate a new pair. We start by checking that the free list isn't null; if it is, we branch to an error-handler. Otherwise, we update the free list address to the next pair in the list, and now register 1 contains the address of the newly allocated pair.

```
(load 1 freelist)
(null? 2 1)
(jtrue 2 consfail)
(cdr 2 1)
(store 2 freelist)
```

12.2.2.4 Garbage Collection   Imagine a restaurant that employed nobody to clear the tables. Each group that enters would be shown to a clean table. When the group left, the table would be left uncleared. Soon, there would be no clean tables. All of the food would be thrown out, the restaurant would be closed, and the building demolished. This is essentially what our cons code does. Even after a pair is no longer in use, it is just left there, unavailable for reuse. Even the most trivial computation that doesn't ever call cons would die for lack of storage, since each procedure call creates a new frame, which requires pairs to be created. Thus, we may have created many millions of pairs during the execution of a program. However, many of those pairs are no longer of interest to us. Therefore, *we only need to store those pairs that we can still access.*

The heap has three kinds of pairs. Some are available for use; others are in use, and a third kind were formerly in use but are now available for reuse. For example, when we return from a procedure, the pairs in its frame (provided it's not captured), are no longer needed; their storage space can be reused for other pairs.

Programming language designers have taken two approaches to this problem. In some languages, such as C and Pascal, it is up to the programmer to notice that an object is no longer needed, so that its storage may therefore be reused. A programmer's mistakes, however, can make such a program difficult to debug. Two common errors occur. First, the programmer can release storage that is still in use. In our restaurant, this corresponds to clearing off a table while the diners are still eating. The second error is a subtle variation of the first. The programmer allocates storage, and then creates some structure that shares storage with the original. Then the programmer deallocates the original storage, forgetting that the memory is shared by another structure. That's like putting two sets of diners at one table and clearing out both sets of dishes when the first group finishes. Both errors are fatal; the second is particularly subtle and hard to debug.

Many languages, including Scheme, use another technique, known as **garbage collection**. In this approach, the programmer never explicitly releases storage. Instead, when cons is unable to allocate a pair, it calls a subroutine that scans the heap for unused storage. Only if no unused storage is found does cons give up. The key to garbage collection lies in the free list. During initialization, as we saw in the previous section, all of the cells in the heap are put onto the free list, and cons takes the front pair off the free list. In the code we saw above, if there are no more pairs left, control passes to the label consfail.

The simplest thing to do at consfail is to write out an error message, Error: out of memory, and halt. As we've seen, however, a nonrecycling approach to the heap will rapidly cause this failure. Instead, the code at consfail must invoke a procedure known as the **garbage collector** to scan for pairs that can be reused and put them back on the free list.

The garbage collector must be able to identify all the pairs that are currently in use and leave them alone. All other pairs return to the free list for further allocation. Once the garbage collector has been run, it should be possible to allocate the requested pair; if not, then we have a genuine "Out of memory" error.

Our garbage collector is what is known as a *mark-and-sweep* collector.[4] In the first (mark) phase, we identify all of the pairs that are still in use. In the second (sweep) phase, we add the unused pairs to the free list. But how can we identify all

---

[4] Modern garbage collectors use a different technique that works much better when the heap is large.

of the used pairs? This requires careful planning: we must be able to identify all variables that contain the addresses of valid pairs. We write a *mark* procedure that is called for each variable containing a pair. It marks the current pair, perhaps by setting an unused bit of the tag to 1, and then calls itself recursively on the car and cdr of the pair. Whenever it reaches a marked pair, or a nonpair, it terminates.

As an example, suppose that the only variables in our program that contain the addresses of pairs are locations 407 and 408, as shown in Figure 12–5 (a). We start by marking the pair at location 1000 (we show marked pairs in gray), which in turn leads us to location 1004. If the car of this pair had been the address of another pair, we would have followed it too. We mark the pair at 1004, and find ourselves reaching null. Now we mark the pair whose address is in location 408, at location 1006. Again, this leads to 1004, which is already marked. This configuration is shown in Figure 12–5 (b).

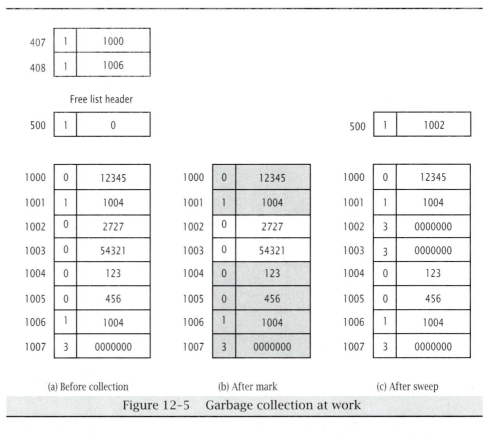

(a) Before collection   (b) After mark   (c) After sweep

Figure 12–5   Garbage collection at work

The sweep phase is a linear scan of the entire heap. Any marked node is unmarked; unmarked nodes are added to the free list, resulting in Figure 12–5 (c). The free list address variable at location 500 has been updated by the garbage collection process.

Pseudocode for a primitive mark/sweep garbage collector is shown in Program 12–3. `collect` assumes that three global variables, `var1`, `var2`, and `var3`, are the only variables that contain the addresses of pairs. The mark process is recursive, and stops when it reaches a value that is either not a pair or already marked. The sweep process adds unused pairs to the free list.

```
(define collect
  (lambda ()
      (mark var1)
      (mark var2)
      (mark var3)
      (sweep)))
(define mark
  (lambda (val)
    (if (and (pair? val) (not (marked? val)))
      (begin
        (set-mark! val #t)
        (mark (car val))
        (mark (cdr val))))))
(define sweep
  (lambda ()
    (letrec
      ((help (pos)
        (let ((val (the pair at addr pos)))
          (if (< pos high)
            (begin
              (if (marked? val)
                (set-mark! val #f)
                (begin
                  (set-cdr! val free)
                  (set! free val)))
              (help (+ pos 2)))))))
      (help low))))
```

Program 12–3   Mark/sweep garbage collector

You might object to this code because it does a linear scan of the heap, and we already said that, for performance reasons, cons must not require a linear scan. However, collect is only invoked when cons runs out of pairs, perhaps once every hundred thousand conses. The few seconds of CPU time needed for this scan are, in general, not significant. However, this fact creates a problem for **real-time** programs, which must be able to respond to an event within a fixed amount of time. If garbage collection occurs at the wrong time, the response might be delayed. People using Scheme for real-time applications (e.g., robotics) must be careful about garbage collection. In fact, Schemers who do robotics often don't do garbage collection at all.

There are more direct worries about our mark/sweep algorithm. First, the assumption that we can identify all variables that hold the addresses of pairs is not, in general, valid. In a gap program, *any* variable might hold the address of a pair; the program doesn't maintain any data structure that records the location of data, which is interspersed among the instructions. Finding the data is a significant problem! Several interesting solutions to this problem exist, but we will take the easy way out and design our Scheme evaluator for gap so that we can identify all of the pair variables.

Another problem is the recursive nature of mark. Since a list can have, in general, any length or depth, we don't know how many levels of recursion to allow for, and hence how big the stack space should be. Furthermore, if we have a big enough heap to worry about this problem, the size of the stack needed to run the garbage collector will be significant. Potentially, we'll need one word of stack space for each pair in the heap. This is one place where elegance does not win out over implementation concerns. We must use a nonrecursive marking algorithm. Such algorithms have been developed, but they are too complicated to cover here. The best garbage collection algorithms pay considerable attention to organizing the heap for efficient access, and only add a few percent to the execution time of large programs.

12.2.3   Input and Output

In Chapter 4 we saw how to write procedures that read or write a list. In Chapter 11 we saw how to write procedures that read and write integers. All of these procedures, fundamentally, call Scheme's low-level read-char and write-char procedures. These low-level procedures correspond to Gleam's inchar and outchar instructions, respectively. We must therefore   concentrate on these instructions, with the assumption that once we understand how these instructions work, we can write a comprehensive package that simulates the complex read and display instructions.

Real machines don't have inchar or outchar instructions for two reasons. First, we will generally have more than one device, so we need a way to specify the device to be accessed. Second, real devices are far more complicated to operate than our hypothetical keyboard.

Computer designers have chosen between two methods of implementing input and output. Some computers (notably Intel's 80x86 series) use special instructions to do input/output. Others (notably the Motorola 68x00 series and the PowerPC, developed by IBM and Motorola) reserve some of the memory addresses for this purpose. We follow the second approach and add **memory-mapped input/output** to Gleam.

In Chapter 11, we saw that Gleam's memread and memwrite operations work by providing an address to the memory system. But what if an address doesn't correspond to memory? Suppose we built a circuit that responded to addresses in the same way that memory does, but that did something other than just store the data. Figure 12-6 shows a Gleam system configured in this way. The address and data information from the MAU is sent now to two devices: the memory and a keyboard interface. The memory responds to addresses in the range from #x0000 to #xEFFF. The keyboard subsystem responds to addresses #xF000 and #xF001. Other addresses greater than #xF001 might be assigned to other interfaces (e.g., video, network, or disk). An address that isn't assigned to memory or a device is invalid; we won't say what happens when such an address is used. The address and data connections don't go directly to the keyboard, but to a keyboard subsystem, or **device interface**. This interface, in turn, is responsible for getting the information from the physical keyboard.

As far as the programmer is concerned, an interface consists of a number of **device registers**, each one concerned with some aspect of the device's state. The

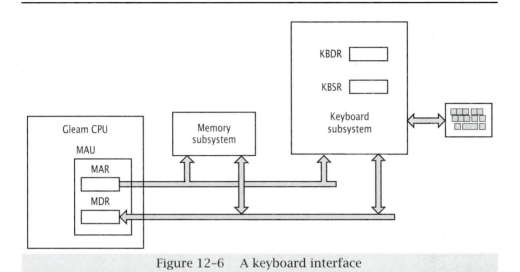

Figure 12-6   A keyboard interface

term *device registers* might confuse you: these are not CPU registers, but are physically and logically part of the device subsystem. We address them with memory addresses. Our keyboard interface has two such registers: the keyboard data register (KBDR) contains the character most recently typed by the user. It can be read by loading its value into a CPU register: the code

```
(load 5 #xF001)
```

loads the contents of the KBDR into register 5.

Unfortunately, this isn't enough. We must also know *when* a character was typed. Maybe the user wasn't fast enough, and hasn't typed a character in yet! For this reason, we also have the keyboard status register (KBSR), which is zero when no character has been typed, and nonzero if a character has been typed. If we want to read a character, we must wait until the KBSR is nonzero:

```
loop    (load 5 #xF000)    ; Get KBSR.
        (eql? 5 0)         ; Zero?
        (jtrue 5 loop)     ; Repeat if so.
        (load 5 #xF001)    ; Get KBDR.
```

When the program reads the data register, the device automatically zeroes the ready bit. If the program were responsible for zeroing the bit, the user could type a character in between the data being read and the zeroing of the bit, which would be erroneous.

This code makes use of a peculiar programming construct known as a *spin wait*, in which we repeatedly test whether a variable is ready to assume a value, without doing anything to make it assume that value. A spin wait only makes sense if something else (in this case, the keyboard interface) is going to set the variable. Spin wait is impractical in a real multiprocessing system, but is simple to describe. Such machines are organized so that the input device can notify, or **interrupt**, the program to say that data is available. Then the program can get data using the device registers, as we've described.

Real device interfaces, however, are sometimes extremely complex. Writing a procedure that reads a block from a disk is not for the fainthearted. Normally, programmers don't access the interface directly, but call a procedure known as a **driver**, written by the device interface designers, to do so for them.

12.3   The Imperative Evaluator

'But the Emperor has nothing on at all!' cried a little child.
— Hans Christian Anderson, "The Emperor's New Clothes"

The code presented in this section can be found in file `impeval.scm`.

In the previous section, we looked at more and less powerful versions of Gleam. The original Gleam does not even have list-processing instructions, unlike Gleam/2, and we could augment both with an elaborate procedure library. However, all three were recognizably Gleam, and required us to work at the assembler/machine-language level. It is now time to use Gleam as machines of the 1990s are actually used: as the basis for building a virtual machine that processes programs in a high-level language, namely Scheme. What we want is to insulate the programmer from all of the details of the machine, so that it is as if the machine itself ran Scheme programs.[5]

As a first step, we need to think about the various methods of implementing programming languages. In Chapter 7, we saw that we can implement a programming language with an interpreter, which works on the original program text, or with a compiler, which translates the program into another language for which we already have an interpreter. The self-evaluator was an example of an interpreter. An alternative to the self-evaluator might be to build a compiler that translates Scheme programs into Gleam code.

Why shouldn't we just build machines that can directly execute Scheme programs? One reason is that not everyone in the world wants to program in Scheme. The authors, on the other hand, would have little use for a machine that directly executed COBOL programs! We want to be able to use any language we like on our machines, rather than having to buy a separate computer for each language.

Still, if we could get a tremendous increase in program speed, it might be worth it. Scheme CPUs have been designed and implemented as prototypes, and Lisp machines have been marketed as commercial products. The Lisp machine doesn't have Lisp as its machine language. Instead, like Gleam/2, its machine language includes list-processing primitives to make Lisp easier to run. Initially, the Lisp machines were much more powerful than their non-Lisp counterparts. Eventually, though, these machines became *less* powerful than their general-purpose counterparts. The specialized Lisp machines had a much smaller market than unspecialized machines. Consequently, the hardware designers of the unspecialized machines had more

---

[5] Good Scheme systems generally give the programmer access to low-level features of the machine. With these features, for example, it is possible to write graphics and networking software. Often, Scheme systems provide a "foreign procedure" interface, in which a procedure written in assembly language or C can be called from Scheme. Foreign procedures represent a blurring of the boundary between Scheme and the machine itself. A programmer who doesn't use them operates at the Scheme level, and need not worry about the machine.

The RISC Debate

Early computers had whatever instruction types their designers felt were appropriate and could afford to build. Often these early machines had peculiar properties that just "happened", or that were created for efficiency. For example, the IBM 7040/7090 series of the early 1960s allowed multiple index registers, but if an instruction specified more than one index register, the contents of the registers were combined by oring the bits.

As hardware designers grew more confident, they built machines with more systematic instruction sets. The IBM System/360 (1964) was the first machine designed this way. It supported many different data types, including integers, floating-point, binary-coded decimal numbers, and character strings. The Digital Equipment PDP-10 (1965) was an assembly-language programmer's dream. Every reasonable combination of operands was supported, and the powerful instruction set could be summarized in one page of normal-size type.

Machines soon began to sport larger instruction sets. In 1978, Digital's VAX included instructions for computing polynomials and checking the validity of blocks of data sent over communications lines. The goal was to make programs short and to make the job of the assembly-language programmer simpler. In about 1980, some people began to question this approach. Would it not make more sense to make the instruction set simple and regular? Such a machine could be built to process more instructions per second than a "complex instruction set computer" (CISC), as they called the conventional machines. Their "reduced instruction set computer" (RISC) designs were not pleasant to program in assembly language, but this had become less of an issue, because programmers had overwhelmingly switched to high-level languages. The focus switched to simplicity of implementation rather than supporting features of high-level languages. The result is that the compiler is expected to handle the translation from the high-level to the lower-level, simple instruction set.

RISC advocates claimed that by eliminating rarely used instructions, they could concentrate on making the CPU run more quickly. One early RISC machine did not even have integer multiplication or division: these were accomplished by procedure calls. Yet the cost/performance ratio of these computers was very good. Relative to adding or subtracting, integer multiplication and division are rarely performed; thus, speeding up additions and subtractions at the cost of multiplications and divisions gives an overall improvement in performance. A set of simple instructions can each be made to execute in a fixed time. This lets the machine **pipeline** the instructions, overlapping the fetch, decode, and execution cycles of a series of instructions, leading to impressive speedups.

Designers have been able to improve performance on some machines by giving instructions peculiar quirks, for example, making jump instructions not take effect until the instruction after the jump has been executed. As long as compilers know about these quirks, most programmers need not care about them.

A number of RISC CPUs have achieved considerable commercial success, but, the most widely sold CPU, the Intel 80x86 series, is not a RISC architecture. Proponents and opponents of RISC have argued for several years about whether it is really beneficial. However, in one sense, the argument has become moot: RISC and CISC are converging. For example, the designers of Intel's 486 and Pentium (both CISC) use a number of RISC techniques, while some RISC designs (e.g., the IBM/Motorola/Apple PowerPC) have well over 100 different instruction types.

resources to improve their machines. Eventually, their greater speed on basic instructions outweighed the advantages of the specialized machines, even for the particular language for which they were designed.

The alternative to constructing a hardware Scheme system is to build, in ɢᴀᴘ, an evaluator for Scheme. Once we have loaded this evaluator into the machine, it will take over. As far as the programmer is concerned, the evaluator *is* the machine. Yet we still preserve the flexibility of being able to switch languages: another person can use the same computer to run BASIC programs.

You may flinch at the idea of writing a large program in ɢᴀᴘ, and there is an alternative. If we have a language that can be automatically translated into Gleam code, we can write our program in that language. To do this, we would need a translator, or compiler, to translate that language into Gleam code. One language that satisfies this requirement is C. Compilers for C have been written for most computers, and therefore people often write Scheme evaluators in C.

It is possible to write a Scheme evaluator in Scheme, provided we write it as a compiler itself, and provided we have another Scheme system to run it on first. For example, suppose we have a Scheme system running on a PC. We could write, in Scheme, a compiler from Scheme into Gleam code, and run this compiler on the PC. We can use this compiler to **cross-compile** programs: the compiler runs on the PC, and the compiler's output is transferred to Gleam to be run. This is a common method of programming small computer systems. Once we have cross-compilation working, we can then compile the compiler on the PC. What we get is a compiler that can be run on Gleam.

Many good Scheme systems do take the compiler approach. However, a Scheme compiler is harder to write than a Scheme interpreter; therefore, we'll take the latter approach. We already have a Scheme interpreter, namely the self-evaluator of Chapter 7. We need to translate the self-evaluator into ɢᴀᴘ. Our translation won't quite be line-by-line, because there are clever machine tricks that can help us improve its speed substantially.

Nonetheless, we can still write a significant part of the system in Scheme. Many of the primitive procedures can be written in Scheme conveniently. Further, we can write many of the special forms as macros. We will only implement Econo-Scheme, the core of Scheme, as we did in the self-evaluator. Therefore we will only write a "kernel" of the evaluator in ɢᴀᴘ: the remainder can be written in Scheme. We call our kernel the **imperative evaluator**. This section discusses the problems we must address in the design of the imperative evaluator, and gives an overview of the design. The imperative evaluator is too long to reprint here. After you have read this section carefully, you should study the source code in the Software Package.

12.3.1   The Strategy

Our imperative evaluator implementation is modeled on the self-evaluator. As with the self-evaluator, we only need to implement a small number of primitives, just enough to see what's going on. Much of the rest of the self-evaluator consists of the code for managing environments and frames.

☞ **Exercise 12–5**

Translate the code that handles the `procedure` ADT in the self-evaluator into ɢᴀᴘ. ❏

We will assume that we've already translated the code for managing procedures and environments into ɢᴀᴘ. The hard part is the core of the evaluator, which operates as a nest of recursive calls. We could do a translation, but this would not be the most effective way to proceed.

The whole structure of Gleam is uncongenial to writing recursive procedures; a naive translation of Scheme code is quite inefficient. A procedure call, as we've seen it, requires extensive pushing and popping of registers. Unnecessary pushing and popping is inefficient. In an application program, we wouldn't try to squeeze out the last bit of efficiency, but we're going to use the evaluator to run all of our programs. Even a small amount of inefficiency in its core will result in a substantial slowdown in running Scheme programs.

The stack must be used only when necessary. This means two things. First, the evaluator will use a set of procedures that continue, one into the next, without increasing the stack size; that is, the evaluator will be tail-recursive. Moreover, when evaluating tail-recursive Scheme procedures, the evaluator will not increase the stack. The resulting program will be divided into clean procedures—and they will more or less match the procedures of the self-evaluator—but procedures will in general not take explicit arguments. Instead, we will adopt a convention in which the registers hold certain values. If we were programming in Scheme, our style would correspond to using no arguments, but only global variables. In general, this is a bad way to structure a Scheme program, but quite suitable for our purposes. The number of values kept in registers is small, so we will not become confused in managing them.

Our imperative evaluator is written in gap. We will present pseudocode for the program, since it is too long to present here. The pseudocode in this section is written to be trivially translatable to gap. This means that no procedures have arguments; all variables in the code are understood to be registers. Once you have understood the pseudocode, you will have no trouble understanding the gap version, or, for that matter, building your own, in gap or any other language.

12.3.2 General Structure of the Evaluator

The self-evaluator receives a form to evaluate; when the evaluator needs the value of a subform, it calls itself recursively. A philosophy that better suits Gleam is to place the form in a register, and repeatedly process it until the value has been obtained. We will designate one of the registers as exp; it will contain the form to be evaluated. Another register will be known as val, and it will contain the value of the form. The imperative evaluator analyzes the contents of exp, and places the value in val.

The core of the imperative evaluator is shown, in pseudocode, in Program 12-4. This code handles constants and variables, and calls process-compound to process all other forms, which must be lists. impeval is given a form in exp, and produces the corresponding value in val. get-binding is part of the environment package, which we have assumed has already been translated into gap. This version is different from the original Scheme version; it accepts its argument—and returns its value—in registers.

The call to process-compound in Program 12-4 is in the tail position of the procedure. The discussion of tail recursion in Chapter 11 demonstrates that such a procedure call will not return; accordingly, the gap translation of the tail call will be just a jump instruction. General procedure calls are translated into call instructions.

Procedure process-compound is responsible for evaluating any form that is a list. It must check for special forms; any other form is an application. In pseudocode, process-compound appears as shown in Program 12-5.

```
(define exp #f)    ; These correspond to registers.
(define val #f)
(define impeval
  (lambda ()
    (if (or (number? exp) (boolean? exp) (string? exp))
      (set! val exp)
      (if (symbol? exp)
        (get-binding)
        (process-compound)))))
```

Program 12-4   Processing simple forms

```
(define spec-table
  (list (list 'define definition-proc)
        (list 'quote quote-proc)
        ...
        (list 'lambda lambda-proc)))
(define process-compound
  (lambda ()
      (set! tmp3 (assv (car exp)))
      (if (null? tmp3)
        (application)    ; Procedure application.
        ((cdr tmp3)))))) ; Special form.
```

(a) Pseudocode for applications and special forms

```
spec-table
      (dataword 'define) (dataword definition-proc)
      (dataword 'quote)  (dataword quote-proc)
      (dataword 'set!)   (dataword assignment-proc)
      (dataword 'if)     (dataword if-proc)
      (dataword 'lambda) (dataword lambda-proc)
      (dataword '())
```

(b) The dispatch table in gap

Program 12-5   Compound forms

Our translation into gap is a bit unexpected. Rather than using a list and assv, the gap version uses a vector in which alternating elements are the symbols to be checked for and the addresses of the corresponding procedures. We can search this table by a simple linear scan. The scan terminates when it encounters the sentinel value (null) after the last word. This is a bit faster than assv; since process-compound is part of the core of the evaluator, any increase in speed, even a tiny one, is worthwhile.

12.3.3   Managing Control in the Handlers

All we have left to do is create the "handler" procedures for the special forms, along with procedure applications. In this section, we'll look at some of the most basic handlers; Section 12.3.4 looks at procedure applications.

Program 12-6 shows the special form handler for `quote` Unfortunately, the method used for `quote` fails when we attempt to write the handler for `define`. What's the difference between `quote` and `define`? Definitions include nested forms, which means that they must call `impeval`. We have already said that a general recursive call to handle a nested form is unacceptable. To implement `define` we need to develop some conventions about how to handle nested forms.

```
(define quote-proc
  (lambda ()
    (set! val (car (cdr exp)))))
```
Program 12-6   Procedure quote, without placemarkers

In Chapter 11 we saw that we must use an explicit push-down stack to implement recursion. If we separate register pushing and popping from procedure calls, and push and pop registers only when necessary, we will save both time and stack space.

Applying the placemarker technique to the handler for `define` gives us the code in Program 12-7. `push-reg` pushes the contents of the register onto the stack, and `pop-reg` pops the top of the stack into the specified register. These operations are implemented with stores and loads respectively.

```
(define define-proc
  (lambda ()
    (set! rest (car (cdr exp)))
    (set! exp (car (cdr (cdr exp))))
    (push-reg rest)
    (push-reg env)
    (push-reg mark)
    (set! mark finish-definition)
    (impeval)))
(define finish-definition
  (lambda ()
    (set! mark (pop-reg))
    (set! env (pop-reg))
    (set! rest (pop-reg))
    (def-binding)
    (set! val void)
    (mark)))
```
Program 12-7   A handler for define

It is not obvious how the actual recursion is accomplished. We could use `call` instructions, but there aren't any nontail calls in this code. Instead, we use **placemarkers**, values that tell us what to do *after* we have processed the current code.

The imperative evaluator implements placemarkers by using a register, mark, to hold the address of the instruction to perform after evaluating the next instruction. We will revise impeval so that after evaluating any form, it jumps to the address found in mark. The procedure mark in our pseudocode means the same as (jump 0 0 mark).

We need placemarkers because impeval is called from so many places, and these calls need to be done efficiently, without causing the stack to grow unnecessarily. Placemarkers let us take control of what is done next. We could use call instructions, but each call pushes the return address on the stack. In many locations, instead of a call, we change the placemarker to the next place, and jump to the appropriate code. When impeval jumps to the address specified by the placemarker, it's as if it were returning.

Suppose we evaluate (define a 1).

1. impeval is called with exp equal to (define a 1). It determines that this is a compound form, and eventually jumps to define-proc.

2. The code at define-proc places the name a into rest and the form 1 into exp. It also places the address of finish-definition into mark, and then jumps to impeval.

3. impeval sees that exp contains a constant. It places the value of this constant, 1, into val, and then jumps to the address found in mark. This leads back to finish-definition. Now rest contains the name of the variable to be defined, and val the value. We can call def-binding to install that binding into the environment.

4. The final step in processing a definition is to jump to the placemarker that was restored at the beginning of finish-definition, which was the original placemarker when define-proc was entered.

The pushes and pops executed by define-proc are those that relate to registers that this procedure is actually using.

- Register rest contains the name.
- Register env might be changed if the nested form introduces any stack frames (e.g., if it is a procedure call).
- Register mark originally contains a placemarker for the whole definition; we need to create a placemarker for the nested form.

The rules that the definition-handler (and all handlers) must follow are simple enough.

- Anything that is pushed in the handler must be popped in the handler.
- Any register that is needed after the nested form has been evaluated must be pushed before and popped afterwards.

We mentioned that impeval must be altered to support placemarkers. Program 12-8 shows the revised code. impeval-init sets mark to the placemarker for the whole form, namely the address of impeval-exit; when control reaches impeval-exit, the imperative evaluator returns; val contains the form's value.

Any code that evaluates a form must therefore end by jumping to the placemarker for that form. Even lowly quote must do this, as Program 12-9 shows.

If you examine Gleam's program counter while the imperative evaluator is running, you will see an interesting pattern. The code at impeval runs, and then transfers control to one of the special form handlers or to application, which uses placemarkers in the same way. The handler does whatever it is supposed to,

```
(define impeval-init
  (lambda ()
    (set! mark impeval-exit)
    (impeval)))
(define impeval
  (lambda ()
    (if (or (number? exp) (boolean? exp) (string? exp))
      (begin
        (set! val exp)
        (mark))
      (if (symbol? exp)
        (begin
          (get-binding)
          (mark))
        (process-compound)))))
(define impeval-exit
  (lambda ()
    (return-from-the-evaluator)))
```

Program 12-8   Procedure `impeval` with placemarkers

```
(define quote-proc
  (lambda ()
    (set! val (car (cdr exp)))
    (mark)))
```

Program 12-9   Procedure `quote` with placemarkers

and then jumps back to `impeval` to evaluate the next form. The parallel with the fetch/decode/execute cycle of Gleam is striking: `impeval` analyzes the form in the `exp` register, and then calls a handler to execute it. Once the handler is complete, control passes back to `impeval` to process the next form. There is a significant difference, though. Gleam normally executes instructions one after another, unless a jump is performed. The imperative evaluator evaluates nested forms. Therefore, instead of being able to use a single program-counter register, the imperative evaluator needs a stack of placemarkers to allow it to step through the various forms it's currently processing.

12.3.4   Applying Procedures

In the self-evaluator, applying procedures is quite straightforward: map `self-eval` onto all of the elements of the application, and then invoke the procedure, the first element of the list. Things are not as straightforward in the imperative evaluator. On the one hand, we want to execute procedure calls efficiently; on the other, we must be concerned about tail recursion. R^nRS requires that any implementation of Scheme must turn tail-recursive calls into jumps. In fact, *any* call at the end of a procedure should be turned into a jump, whether or not it is a recursive call.

It is important to distinguish between procedures with arguments and procedures without. There is a significant amount of setup code involved with evaluating arguments, and therefore the evaluator considers these cases separately. Program 12-10 shows the code for procedures with no arguments.

```
(define application
  (lambda ()
    (set! rest (cdr exp))
    (set! exp (car exp))
    (if (null? rest)
      (begin
        (push-reg mark)
        (set! mark noarg-apply)
        (impeval))
      (app-args))))
(define noarg-apply
  (lambda ()
    (set! proc val)
    (set! args '())
    (apply-procedure)))
```

Program 12-10   Applying procedures with no arguments

The first step is to separate the application into the procedure part (stored in exp) and the argument part (stored in rest). If there are no arguments, we go back to impeval to evaluate the procedure form. As with any nested form, the value is left in val. For a no-argument call, all that is necessary now is to call the procedure, which we do by jumping to apply-procedure. This code expects the procedure to be in register proc, and the list of arguments in register args.

The code for applying a procedure with arguments, shown in Program 12-11, is quite intricate. The major complication arises because we want to handle the last argument specially, which saves us from having to save env and rest.

Program 12-12 contains the code for applying a procedure. There are two cases. First, we can call a primitive procedure merely by a call instruction, after we obtain its address. Second, Scheme procedures can be processed in the same way as in the self-evaluator: create a new frame with bindings, and then process a sequence of code.

One interesting point here is that we must reverse the argument list first. We have processed arguments from left to right; consing the results together produces a list in reverse order. Given this approach, it might be more efficient to process the arguments from right to left.[6] In Chapter 3, we saw that the arguments of a procedure are evaluated in an unspecified order. For the imperative evaluator, it might be better to do evaluation from right to left; for other systems, it might be better to do evaluation from left to right. It is far better to allow the implementer to evaluate arguments in whatever order is best; all we lose is the ability to write code that depends upon the order of evaluation, and such code is generally hard to understand anyway. We have always said that Scheme doesn't depend on argument order evaluation, just because the implementor might need to evaluate arguments, for efficiency, in some order other than left to right. Now we see why.

---

[6] This would require a certain amount of preprocessing of the program to put the original forms into the correct order.

```
(define app-args
  (lambda ()
    (push-reg mark)  (push-reg env)  (push-reg rest)
    (set! mark args)
    (impeval)))
(define args
  (lambda ()
    (set! rest (pop-reg)) (set! env (pop-reg))
    (set! proc val) (set! args '())
    (push-reg proc)
    (arg-loop)))
(define arg-loop
  (lambda ()
    (push-reg args)
    (set! exp (car rest))
    (if (null? (cdr rest))
      (last-arg)
      (begin
        (push-reg env) (push-reg rest)
        (set! mark next-arg)
        (impeval)))))
(define next-arg
  (lambda ()
    (set! rest (cdr (pop-reg)))
    (set! env (pop-reg))
    (set! args (cons val (pop-reg)))
    (arg-loop)))
(define last-arg
  (lambda ()
    (set! mark got-last-arg)
    (impeval)))
(define got-last-arg
  (lambda ()
    (set! args (cons val (pop-reg)))
    (set! proc (pop-reg))
    (apply-procedure)))
```

Program 12-11   Applications with arguments

Program 12-13 shows the final step in processing applications is the procedure sequence, which processes a sequence of forms, as is found in lambda, begin, case, cond, and so on. These procedures are fairly straightforward, except for one complication: we must handle tail recursion here.

Procedure sequence-last plays an important role. Each element of the sequence but the last causes sequence to push the rest of the form and the environment on the stack. The last element is treated specially; there is no pushing, so the frame of the environment is not preserved after the last form has been evaluated. The placemarker describing what is done after the application is popped off the stack. The mark was originally pushed at the beginning of the application process, in application. Because the frame is not kept, this implements tail calling, that is,

```
(define apply-procedure
  (lambda ()
    (set! args (reverse args))
    (if (is-primitive? proc)
      (begin
        (set! proc (the address of the procedure))
        (proc)
        (set! pcr (pop-reg))
        (pcr))
      (begin
        (set! env (proc-environ))
        (set! val (proc-params))
        (set! env (make-frame-in-env))
        (set! rest (proc-body))
        (sequence)))))
```

Program 12-12   Applying a procedure

```
(define sequence
  (lambda ()
    (set! exp (car rest))
    (if (null? (cdr rest))
      (sequence-last)
      (begin
        (push-reg rest)
        (push-reg env)
        (set! mark sequence-next)
        (impeval)))))
(define sequence-next
  (lambda ()
    (set! env (pop-reg))
    (set! rest (cdr (pop-reg)))
    (sequence)))
(define sequence-last
  (lambda ()
    (load mark (pop-reg))
    (impeval)))
```

Program 12-13   Sequences

implementing the return from procedure call at the end of a sequence by a jump
to the address after the sequence.

12.3.5   An Assessment

We have now designed the main parts of the imperative evaluator. At this time,
you should study the pseudocode carefully, to convince yourself that it really does
work, and to see how the various extra parts (e.g., the primitives) are handled.

Each model we have studied has been more and more precise. Our imperative
evaluator is less useful than the environment model for *understanding* Scheme,

but it can be run on a computer. It is still a model, though, and computational archaeologists from the future would have no difficulty reconstructing Scheme's syntax and semantics from a listing of the evaluator.

Substantial improvement is possible in several areas of the imperative evaluator. Apart from the error-checking, which in our implementation is almost nonexistent, one of the most important areas to improve is the amount of consing going on. As we evaluate arguments, we prepare a list of the values. We then prepare another list that is the reverse of this list. When we call a procedure, we create a new frame, which is later garbage-collected.

Researchers at MIT designed a CPU chip to execute Scheme programs directly, that operated much as our evaluator does.[7] Measurements showed that the vast majority of the execution time was spent in cons and the garbage collector.

Much of this overhead can be eliminated by various programming tricks. One possibility is to push everything onto the stack; this is the basis for the implementations of most other languages. However, a returned procedure requires that environment frames not disappear when we return from the procedure, as the code in Program 12-14 shows. This means that frames must be allocated on the heap and therefore garbage-collected.

```
> (define foo
    (lambda (x)
      (lambda (y)
        (format #t "x: ~a and y: ~a~%" x y))))
> (define bar (foo 3))
> (bar 5)
x: 3 and y: 5
> (bar 10)
x: 3 and y: 10
```

Program 12-14   Why frames need to be kept for a returned procedure

An area in which substantial improvement is possible is in accessing variables. All of our variable access is through the environment procedures get-binding, put-binding, and def-binding. Each of these searches the environment for the variable in question. It should be possible to access a variable without having to call a procedure, since the results are going to be the same anywhere a given variable is accessed in a procedure. In fact, wherever a variable appears in a program, it is possible to calculate the variable's address, in the form "Go up f frames, and pick the nth variable in that frame." This is a consequence of lexical scoping. A smarter evaluator would do this calculation first, before running the program at all.

An even smarter technique is to convert the original Scheme form into a sequence of Gleam instructions first. Evaluating the form then consists of jumping to the first instruction of the sequence. This approach requires no overhead for deciding what kind of form is being evaluated; all analysis and error checking can be done during the conversion phase. A program that does this conversion is a compiler, but rather than processing the whole program at once, as a compiler for C or

---

[7] Not surprising, since both the chip and our evaluator were based upon an "explicit control" evaluator described in Abelson and Sussman's *Structure and Interpretation of Computer Programs.*

Pascal does, a Scheme compiler can operate on a form-by-form basis. As a result, a Scheme compiler can be as interactive and friendly as an interpreter, but can run programs much more quickly.

12.4   Operating Systems

The code presented in this section can be found in file os.scm.

> *One Ring to rule them all, One Ring to find them/One Ring to bring them all and in the darkness bind them.*   — J. R. R. Tolkien, *The Fellowship of the Ring*

Virtual machines allow us to create a computing environment that matches the abstractions we want to use in programming. The success of this concept is apparent, since virtually nobody writes entire application programs at the machine level. Even people who work in assembly language get help from procedure libraries.

The abstractions we have dealt with so far are language-based. However, a computing system must deal with other abstractions. DBScheme is not useful in practice, because it works with data structures that disappear when the program ends. In real problems, we need to be able to manage data structures that endure indefinitely, whether or not a program is running. The solution is obvious: Store such databases in disk files. But where do the disk files come from and who manages them?

Handling disk files can't be the exclusive task of just one programming language; otherwise, users of other languages would be unable to read our files or write files for our use. We need a layer of software that provides *any* program with abstractions such as disk files. This software must be independent of any language on the system. If it fails to work with any of them, the users of that language will have to bypass it, which results in a tremendous waste of effort—programming disk drives and network cards is a complicated task. Because bypassing such a layer would lead to a compromise in security, all modern machines provide such an abstraction.

Modern computer systems are capable of running many different programs at the same time. For example, a desktop PC user may be working on a Scheme program while using a communications program to download a file in the background; meanwhile, a third program displays a small clock in a corner of the screen. Each of these programs must somehow be given the illusion that it alone has control of the computer; otherwise, each program must be written to know about the others, which is impractical.

Running more than one program on the same computer requires us to think about security. We must isolate each program, so that any malfunction affects only that program. Further, many of our resources are shared. For example, someone might write a game program that others want to play. The author places the software on a network, so that everyone else can access it. No author would feel comfortable about doing this without being certain that other people couldn't modify the program and cheat. Our software layer must centralize all access to the game file to ensure respect for the author's wishes.[8]

---

[8] If the game program wants to keep a file of current scores, another security problem arises. We

Such a software layer is called an **operating system**. We can think of an operating system as a manager. Following the user's commands, it loads programs such as a Scheme evaluator or communications program into memory, presents a virtual machine that allows the programmer to get her job done (including abstractions such as files and network connections), and ensures that different programs can't interfere with each other, either accidentally or on purpose.

The term *operating system* is often used more broadly than this. For example, Microsoft Windows is an operating system.[9] Windows includes a number of applications, as well as game programs, fonts, screen savers, and other bric-a-brac. This material is all very useful, but the operating system proper is the smaller set of programs that provides the services discussed above. For our purposes, an operating system is a software layer that does the following:

- manages system activities, loading and running programs according to the user's wishes
- provides a virtual machine with appropriate abstractions for things such as input and output
- controls access to the system's resources

12.4.1   A Simple Operating System

Scheme's read-eval-print loop is an example of an operating system. It repeatedly reads in a program and runs it. Of course, the read-eval-print loop is a part of a Scheme evaluator, but how does that evaluator get started? To answer this question, we will design a simple operating system that allows a user to enter the name of a program from the keyboard. The operating system (OS) will load this program into memory. During execution, the program can call OS procedures to read or write data to/from either the keyboard and display or files on disk.

One important part of an operating system is the **shell**, the program that reads commands and executes them. Here is a simple shell session:

```
command> (scheme)
> (+ 2 2)
4
> (quit)
command> (copy-file myfile.data backup.data)
command> (fortune)
It was a brave person who ate the first raw oyster.
```

Our shell reads a command, and then executes it. For simplicity, we represent commands as lists, though in practice they are delimited by newlines or semicolons. Each command can be thought of as a set of strings; the first represents the program name, and the remaining strings represent arguments to the program. In the above shell session, the user first invoked a Scheme system, and then a program named copy-file, which duplicates a file under a new name. Finally, the user runs a program named fortune, which displays a "saying of the day".

---

don't want the game players to be able to alter this file, except by playing the game. We must therefore have security mechanisms that not only control *who* may access a file, but also allow programmers to control *how* a file may be accessed.

[9] As of 1994, Windows requires DOS; Windows 95 will run without any other operating system.

We can store the binary version of a program (essentially, the output of gap) as a file. To process a command, the shell finds an **executable file**, using a name based upon the car of the command. Many operating systems encode the type of the file in its name; in DOS, for example, the names of executable files end with .exe.[10]

Program 12-15 shows the shell. It reads a command and then calls load-executable-program to load the program. The command itself is stored in location 0. (A list will take several locations; we're doing it this way for simplicity.) The program can then access its arguments by referencing location 0. The first instruction in the program is assumed to be location 1.

```
(define shell
  (lambda ()
    (display "command> ")
    (let*
      ((command (read))
       (loaded? (load-executable-file (car command))))
      (set-memory-word 0 command)
      (go 1))
    (shell)))
(define load-executable-file
  (lambda (filename)
    (with-input-from-file filename
      (letrec
        ((loadvals
           (lambda ()
             (let*
               ((address (read))
                (data (read)))
               (if (eqv? address 'end)
                 #t
                 (begin
                   (set-memory-word address data)
                   (loadvals)))))))
        (loadvals)))))
```

Program 12-15   A simple operating system shell

The helper load-executable-file is used to read the contents of an executable file into memory. Our executable file format is extremely simple: it consists of alternating *address* and *data* values. load-executable-file reads each pair in, and stores each data value at the specified address. An example of an executable file is shown in Figure 12-7.

We can modify gap so that it produces executable files instead of placing the program directly into memory. Most compilers can create executable files. The compiler can itself be compiled, resulting in an executable file that can be loaded into memory in order to compile a program. (This is why compiler writers often want

---

[10] Most modern operating systems allow commands to be stored in various directories, and provide a *search path* to specify which directories are to be searched. Our system only has one directory, so no search path is necessary.

```
Program                          Executable file

(                             |
commands: (dataword 0)        |  #x0000  #x00000000
begin:                        |
   (inchar 0)                 |  #x0001  #x9c000000
   (outchar 0)                |  #x0002  #x9d00000
   (halt 0)                   |  #x0003  #xA0000000
)                             |  end      end
```

Figure 12-7   A gap program and its executable file

to write the compiler in its own language.) The compilation process is shown in Figure 12-8.

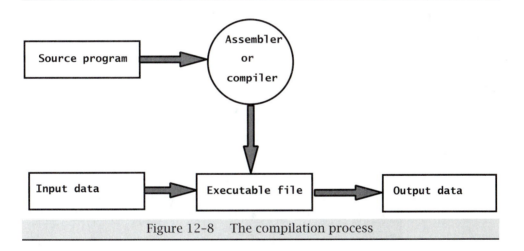

Figure 12-8   The compilation process

12.4.2   Disks and Files

One of the most basic abstractions that any OS must present is that of a *file*. We would like our programs to work correctly with any reasonable device. For example, on one run of a graphics program we might want to type data in directly from the keyboard; on the next run, we may want to use data that was produced by another program.

When disk drives became widespread in the 1960s, many programs would not work with them. Each disk drive had its own peculiarities: each had its own block size, and some required the programmer to use a complicated addressing system to select a particular block. In addition to these problems of **device dependence**, disks created other problems. Because so few applications used the full capacity of a machine's disk drive, it seemed reasonable to place several sets of data onto the same disk.   But how do we keep track of which blocks contain which information? A reasonable solution is to store that information on the disk. Furthermore, we can let the programmers forget about the actual block numbering, and consider each data set to be a collection of blocks, numbered from 0 on up. Programmers will then see not a physical disk, but a collection of **files**, each of which contains one data set.

Our simple OS will keep a **directory** of files. An application program can then call an OS procedure to search for a specified file in the directory. We call this process **opening** the file. There are two cases: either the file is being read, or it is being written. In the former case, the file must already be present; in the latter, the file might be new, in which case it must be created if it is not there. At the very minimum, a directory must record the name of the file along with the blocks that have been allocated to it. An application program never uses an absolute block number, so the operating system is free to move a file from one place on the disk to another without the application program ever being aware of it.

We have mentioned the problem of device dependence—but we would like to be able to use the computer's keyboard or display where it makes sense. The solution is straightforward enough. We permit a program to open a "pseudo-file", which the system connects to the keyboard. Our OS uses the name <con> (for "console") for this purpose; a program that opens <con> will read from the keyboard and write to the display.[11]

12.4.2.1 The `channel` Abstraction

Opening a file should create some value that represents the file; read, write, and close operations can then use this value to indicate which file to process. Various names have been used for such values: Scheme calls them *ports*; C++ uses the name *stream*. Many languages call these values *files*, which is confusing. We use the name `channel`: Like a TV channel, a `channel` does not originate any data, but merely carries it between the originator and the receiver.

Technically, we should distinguish between channels and high-level language values such as ports. A channel represents a connection between the program and a disk file or other device. Ports and I/O streams generally have additional features, such as being able to read a sequence of characters representing a number and convert it to a binary numeric value. Figure 12–9 shows the ADT for channels.

Constructors are usually named `make-`*xxx*. The name `channel-open` is more in keeping with the tradition in operating systems. At any moment, an open channel corresponds to a particular file or device, in the case of <con>. When a file is opened, its index is set to zero. Reads or writes will therefore start in the first byte of the file. To keep track of the program's progress through the data set, a disk channel keeps track of the file's *size* as well as an *index* to the current position in the file.

12.4.2.2 Using channels

We can start with a simple procedure that writes a string to a channel, as shown in Program 12–16 (a). The device independence that channels afford can be demonstrated by some simple procedures. Program 12–16 (b) shows a procedure that copies a file. This procedure is deceptively simple; it can also be used to create a file from the keyboard or display an existing file, merely by using <con> as one of the arguments.[12]

---

[11] MS-DOS uses the name CON, and UNIX uses /dev/tty.

[12] It was the designers of UNIX who noticed how powerful "pseudo-files" such as <con> are.

Constructor

- (channel-open *filename write? create?*)
  Open the file *filename* on disk (or the keyboard and display if *filename* is
  <con>), and create a channel for it; *write?* describes whether writing will
  occur; *create?* says what to do if a disk file doesn't already exist. If it is *true*,
  a new file is created on disk; if it is *false*, an error is generated.

Channel operators

- (channel-read *channel*)
  Read the next character from the file or console connected via the channel,
  and return it. If there is no more data, return the symbol eof.
- (channel-write *channel ch*)
  Write ch, which must be a character, to *channel*.
- (channel-close *channel*)
  Close the channel; update the directory if necessary.

Figure 12-9   **Abstract Data Type:** channel

☞ **Exercise 12-6**

In the example of a shell session, an executable file called copy-file was invented. Write
copy-file in Scheme using file-copy. Assume that the procedure program-arguments
returns a list of the program's arguments that looks exactly like the input command. ❏

☞ **Exercise 12-7**

Modify file-copy so that it will accept a list of filenames as a source argument, as well
as just a string, as before. The destination file will contain the contents of the first file,
followed immediately by those of the second file, and so on. ❏

Program 12-17 is a procedure that counts the number of characters in a file.
What good are channels are to Scheme programmers? Scheme has powerful
input/output capabilities, using ports. Where Scheme's facilities are satisfactory,
there is no point in using channels; the port provides a higher level of abstraction by providing more services, such as interpreting characters as Scheme forms.
However, most operating systems' channel counterparts provide features such as
random access and networking that are not available to the Scheme programmer.
Therefore, many Scheme systems allow programmers to work with channels as well
as the easier-to-use ports. Some Scheme systems allow programmers to create their
own new kinds of ports, using channels. This allows sophisticated networking programs, for example, to do input/output using standard Scheme primitives, along
with custom ports. Of course the authors of the Scheme evaluator need channels,
as well, in order to implement ports.

12.4.2.3 Implementing Channels   We begin with the implementation of the
procedures that support the channel ADT, as shown in Program 12-18. In our
object-oriented approach, a channel is represented as a procedure, to which the
other procedures send messages such as read, write, and close. Our channel implementation doesn't really do anything, but serves as a "dispatcher". Based upon the

```
(define channel-write-string
  (lambda (chan str)
    (let ((len (string-length str)))
      (letrec
        ((help
          (lambda (i)
            (if (< i len)
              (begin
                (channel-write chan (string-ref str i))
                (help (+ i 1)))))))
        (help 0)))))
```

(a) Writing a string to a channel

```
(define file-copy
  (lambda (source destination)
    (let ((f1 (channel-open source #f #f))
          (f2 (channel-open destination #f #t)))
      (letrec
        ((copy (lambda ()
                 (let ((ch (channel-read f1)))
                   (if (eqv? ch 'eof)
                     #f
                     (begin
                       (channel-write f2 ch)
                       (copy)))))))
        (copy)
        (channel-close f1)
        (channel-close f2)))))
```

(b) Copying a file

Program 12-16   Examples of using channels

```
(define count-chars
  (lambda (filename)
    (let ((chan (channel-open filename #f #f)))
      (letrec
        ((help
          (lambda (count)
            (let ((ch (channel-read chan)))
              (if (eqv? ch 'eof)
                count
                (help (+ count 1)))))))
        (let ((x (help 0)))
          (channel-close chan)
          (channel-write-string (number->string x)))))))
```

Program 12-17   Counting characters in a file

filename given, channel-open calls one of two procedures: if the filename is <con>, the channel is created by console-driver; otherwise it is created by file-driver.

We therefore structure the system by centralizing the code for a given type of file or pseudofile into a driver, an object-oriented procedure that provides procedures for performing read, write, and close operations.

```
(module channels
  (export channel-open channel-read channel-write channel-close)
  (define channel-open
    (lambda (filename write? create?)
      (if (string=? filename "<con>")
        (console-driver)
        (file-driver filename write? create?))))
  (define channel-read
    (lambda (channel)
      (channel 'read)))
  (define channel-write
    (lambda (channel ch)
      (channel 'write ch)))
  (define channel-close
    (lambda (channel)
      (channel 'close)))
)
```

Program 12-18   channel implementation

console-driver and file-driver are drivers: interface procedures that hide the details of a physical device. Actually, file-driver hides more than just the details of the physical disk drive; it also hides the data structures and algorithms needed to represent files on a disk. We should therefore think of two levels of drivers: at a high level, a driver is a module that supports channels on a particular kind of device, but at a low level, a driver is designed to move data between that device and the computer. For our purposes, it's not worth making that distinction.

The first, and simplest, driver we will look at is the console driver, shown in Program 12-19. We assume hypothetical procedures read-char-from-keyboard and write-char-to-screen for transferring characters to and from the console. These procedures essentially do Gleam's inchar and outchar operations. We have assumed that read-char-from-keyboard returns Scheme's "eof object" when a specific combination of keys is pressed (e.g., [Control-D] or [Control-Z]).

This console driver is rather primitive. A better version would provide for either "raw" mode, in which characters are read directly from the keyboard, or "cooked" mode, in which characters are read into a vector, and only sent back (one per read call) after the [Enter] key has been pressed. In cooked mode, characters such as [Backspace], for deleting the last character, and [Control-U] or [Esc], for deleting the entire line and starting again, can be honored.

12.4.2.4 Disk Files   The disk file driver is a long program. This section describes it briefly, but you should refer to the Software Package to study the complete driver.

When a file is opened, we must search the directory to find the block or blocks that contain the file's data. Once we have done this, any read or write operation can

```
(module console
  (export console-driver)
  (define console-driver
    (lambda ()
      (lambda (message . args)
        (case message
          ((read)
           (let ((ch (read-char-from-keyboard)))
             (if (eof-object? ch) 'eof ch)))
          ((write)
           (write-char-to-screen (car args)))
          ((close)
           #f)))))
)
```

Program 12-19   The console driver

be done in terms of the block numbers for the file. Write operations might add new blocks to the file; accordingly, when we close the file, we must update the directory entry.

The first issue we must resolve is the layout of the disk. Our layout is rather inflexible, but it serves our purposes well. Our disk has n blocks and we have decided to lay them out as follows:

- Block 0 will hold the **bootstrap** program, loaded into memory when the computer is switched on.
- Block 1 holds a "map" of the blocks, whose purpose is explained later.
- Block 2 holds the directory.
- Blocks 3 through $n - 1$ are used as file blocks.

We assume that our disk has blocks of size 256, which is smaller than on a real disk, but sufficient for our purposes. In both our disk-file driver and a real one, a single block isn't sufficient for the bootstrap, map, or directory; accordingly, operating systems tend to use more than one block for these purposes. Showing this in our driver, however, is a needless complication.

We can consider the directory as a table, as in Figure 12-10. This directory contains two filenames, scheme.exe and foo. The first entry specifies a file size of 11124 (a bit small for a Scheme evaluator), and four blocks. The second entry, for foo, specifies 180 bytes, and only one block (number 63). Our driver restricts a file to four blocks, because of the directory-entry format. One way to increase a file's maximum size, not implemented here, is to allow one of the file's four blocks to contain block numbers, instead of data.

File name	File size	Block 1	Block 2	Block 3	Block 4
scheme.exe	11124	27	43	22	38
foo	180	63	0	0	0

Figure 12-10   Directory structure

☞ **Exercise 12–8**

Given that we have the block numbers, why do we need the file size? ❑

When the driver is asked to open a file, it scans the directory and builds a channel from the directory entry. The channel encapsulates the information from the entry, as well as a "file index" that tells us the byte number of the next byte to be read or written. The file index is incremented each time. A `read` is performed by calculating the number of the disk block on which the desired character appears, reading this block, and then extracting this character.

There is an efficiency problem here. Given that a disk operation might take 10 milliseconds, reading each character by fetching the disk block wastes a great deal of time. The solution is to buffer the disk by holding an entire block in memory and only reading from the disk when a different block is needed. Even after the file has been closed, the operating system may not write the data until the buffer (the memory storage area) is needed, or the disk is not busy. People who switch their computers off without doing a "sync" (a special command) to flush the buffers often complain that their disks have been scrambled.

Writes are similar to reads: to write a character, we read in the affected block, modify the appropriate character position, and write the block back to the disk. Again, a `write` causes two disk operations, which is an even stronger reason for using buffering.

There is another problem with writes: What if no block has been allocated? In this case, we must find a free block and allocate it to this file. To solve this problem, we keep a *disk map*, a block containing only characters that indicate whether a block is free. To allocate a block, we read this block, scan for a free block, and mark the block as allocated. When a file is deleted, the blocks it used are marked as free again.

Our block-allocation strategy is simple, but, again, it leads to efficiency problems. After a large number of files have been created and deleted, the block map is likely to have large numbers of small groups of free blocks. Thus, when a new file is created, the blocks are scattered over the disk. This *disk fragmentation* again results in an efficiency problem, because it takes a disk longer to access a block that is far away from the block it just accessed.

The file system we've presented suffers from many limitations, but one stands out. It is not conceptually difficult to make the block map or directory cover many blocks, thus allowing a large disk to store many files, but the larger the directory, the longer it takes to scan it. As the disk holds more files, opening a file becomes more and more time-consuming. With a large disk and many files, it is also difficult to find the files for a specific project.

The solution is to allow more than one directory. But how does the system know which directory to use? One possibility is to keep track of the directory that is currently in use, and have a command that allows us to change the directory. Thus, we could have a directory for each user or project on the disk. A useful variation is to keep directories in the disk's data blocks as well, and to allow a directory entry to appear in another directory. We would need a flag in each entry to tell us whether it was for a directory or a plain file.

We might attempt to open the file `/user/lau/scheme/logic.scm`. The system starts by scanning a *root directory* for an entry `user`. This entry leads to a directory that contains an entry `lau`, and then to a directory named `scheme`. In that directory, there is an entry for `logic.scm`, which can be opened. As the term *root directory* suggests, this leads to a tree structure. Most modern operating systems provide this capability.

☞ **Exercise 12-9**

What restriction would we have to place on directories and files in order to have a tree structure? ❏

12.4.3   Networks and Distributed Operating Systems

It is now common for computer systems to be interconnected via a network that allows machines to communicate with each other and to share resources. For example, a network can have just one good printer, connected to one of the machines. When a program on another machine wants to print, it sends the data to be printed to the machine that has the printer.

12.4.3.1   Networks and Protocols   Machines that are connected must all follow the same rules about how to communicate information. These rules, or **protocols**, specify how to select the destination for a message, the format of the message, and many other details. A group of protocols intended to work together to specify all of these details is known as a **protocol family**; examples include TCP/IP (designed under the auspices of the U.S. government, and widely used by both public and private-sector networks), the NetWare protocols (designed by Novell Corporation), and SNA (designed by IBM and used in mainframe networks). People write software to allow machines to communicate using these protocol families.

Regardless of the protocol, the principle behind networks is very simple. Each machine is assigned an address, which is a public piece of information. Any other machine that wants to send it a message prefixes the machine's address to the message. Other machines may (depending upon the details of the network) see this message, but will ignore it, because the address isn't theirs. This poses an obvious security problem, which can be resolved by encrypting the data in the message.

The messages sent by networks tend to be of a fixed size. One of the protocols in any protocol family defines how to break up a longer message into pieces of the fixed size, and how to reassemble the pieces at the receiving end. Any of the pieces might be lost because of a problem in the network, and might have to be retransmitted. The protocol provides specific rules for doing this, too. Thus, programs don't have to worry about the details; they can just assume that their messages will be received reliably. Of course, the recipient still might not process the message correctly—it could experience a power failure, for example. The design of *fault tolerant* software that recovers effectively from such problems is still an active research area.

There are many useful ways of sending a message to a remote computer, but one of the best is to have a program known as a *server*, which listens for messages, processes them, and sends the result back to the *client*, the program that initiated the request. Our printing example might therefore be structured with a client program that sends blocks of data to the server, which prints each block. After the last block, the server sends back a status message indicating that the file has been successfully processed.

One interesting kind of server is known as a **file server**. A file server contains a directory with a large number of files that users might want to access. Centralizing the files on one machine allows users to access their files from any machine on the network. Further, it is much easier to back up everyone's files, without their having to worry about it.

A file server waits for messages such as, "Please send me block number 2 of file foo.scm". It responds with the block in question. Of course, there are security concerns: we must associate each file with an account, so that two users don't accidentally create a file with the same name. Further, some users may wish their files to be private. Therefore, these messages to the file server may include information such as a user account or password.

The client can be almost trivially written as a new driver. We modify channel-open so that any filename that starts with <net> (e.g., <net>foo.scm), is treated as a remote file. Instead of creating a channel with our regular disk-file driver, we use a remote driver, which passes the read and write messages it receives over the network to the file server, and waits for the file server's reply. Two very well-known systems that work this way are Novell's NetWare system, and Sun's Network File System, which is commonly used in UNIX environments. Programs that access files on remote file-server machines need not be aware of the fact that they are using the network. Even users may not be aware that their files aren't on the local disk drive in their machine.

Of course, things aren't quite so trivial as we've suggested; security and reliability create all sorts of problems that must be resolved. Moreover, a centralized service like a file server can strand every client by failing, and is subject to access bottlenecks when all clients try to use it. Nonetheless, file servers are a vivid demonstration of the benefits of structuring an operating system in an object-oriented, modular, manner.

12.4.4   Concurrency

Any computer network provides concurrency, the ability to run more than one program at the same time. In the file-server example, many clients may make requests of the file server at the same time; the server takes the requests, one at a time, and processes them. In a network, we don't have to do anything special to provide concurrency. However, this form of concurrency isn't enough. We might want to run more than one program at the same time on a single computer. Earlier, we gave the example of running a Scheme session while using a communications program to transfer data in the background. Even the assumption in the previous paragraph that the file server would process requests one at a time is dubious. It might be possible to handle several requests at the same time, if each request is for a block on a different disk drive.

All of these examples rely upon one basic premise: the speed of the CPU and memory is very much faster than that of devices or humans in the outside world. Therefore, the Scheme evaluator spends most of its time waiting for the user to press keys; the file server spends most of its time waiting for a disk. A typical machine instruction might take 50 nanoseconds (50×10^{-9} seconds); reading a disk block might take 10 milliseconds; getting a block of data from a modem might take 50 milliseconds; and a very fast typist might be able to enter characters at a rate of one every 100 milliseconds. If we dedicate a computer to just one of these activities, it will spend almost all of its time waiting.

Users *want* to have more than one thing going on at the same time on their computer. Their uses of concurrency range from the sensible examples above all the way down to having an icon whose eyes follow the mouse cursor around the screen. Also, a machine that is running a file server can bog a network down if it processes requests in a strict sequential order, adding a substantial delay each time the disk is accessed.

We must therefore be able to do more than one thing on a single CPU.[13] This seems impossible, until we start thinking about the time scale. We don't have to be running programs at the same time, so long as *the user thinks that we're doing so*. The solution is simple. Each time a program starts an input/output operation (e.g., requests a character from the keyboard), the operating system takes control away from the program, and starts up another program. When the operation is complete, the system takes control away from the second program, and restarts the first. Thus, each program is running while the machine would otherwise be idle.

To transfer from one program to another, we simply save the first program's registers and the program counter, and load the registers and program counter for the second program. We call this operation a **context switch**. It consists (in the case of Gleam) of 17 stores followed by 17 loads, and is therefore extremely fast. Each program occupies its own memory area and should not access data outside its area; the only shared program resource is the registers, which the operating system manages. A snapshot of the memory layout is shown in Figure 12-11.

```
┌─────────────────────────┐
│ Operating system        │
├─────────────────────────┤
│ Regs for proc 1         │
├─────────────────────────┤
│ Regs for proc 2         │
├─────────────────────────┤
│ Memory for              │
│ process 1               │
│                         │
│                         │
│                         │
├─────────────────────────┤
│ Memory for              │
│ process 2               │
│                         │
└─────────────────────────┘
```

Figure 12-11   Memory layout: two concurrent processes

There's nothing to stop us from running one program twice. For example, we might be running two Scheme evaluators, each in its own window on the screen. We therefore talk of running **processes**: a process is the execution of a program. How

---

[13] In fact, there are multiple CPU desktop—and even more commonly, server—machines. Even in a multi-CPU machine, therefore, we want to be able to have concurrent activities on each CPU.

does the OS switch between processes? It is, somewhat surprisingly, the driver's responsibility to trigger the context switch. For example, suppose we call `channel-read` to read a character from the console keyboard. The version of `channel-read` we have shown calls `read-char-from-keyboard`; a real version sets the keyboard's device register and then calls the OS to switch contexts to another process. At some future point, the user will press a key, at which point the keyboard will send a hardware signal called an interrupt back to the CPU to indicate this fact. In turn, the CPU will activate a part of the console driver, the *completion routine*, which does a context switch back to the original process. To the process, it appears that `channel-read` was called and returned with a character; the context switch is invisible to the process. The flow of control is shown in Figure 12-12.

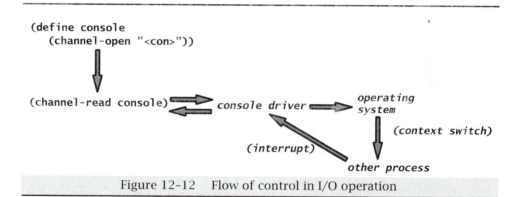

Figure 12-12   Flow of control in I/O operation

What about programs that don't do any input/output? We don't want such a program to hog the CPU. Accordingly, we can take advantage of a device that is found in every CPU, the *timer*. Periodically (the exact frequency depends upon the computer, but ranges from 18 to 100 times per second), the timer sends an interrupt signal to the CPU, which is used to force a context switch to another process. As a result, even a process that does no input or output will periodically lose control of the CPU. Again, this loss of control is invisible to the program.

Summary

This chapter has covered a broad spectrum of computing areas. The unifying idea is the virtual machine: every machine is composed of layers of abstraction, each of which present a new abstract machine.

We saw first how Gleam is not so much a machine as a family of machines by introducing Gleam/2, a version of Gleam with pair primitives. We then showed how to build a library that extends its powers, and how Gleam is quite capable of doing anything that Gleam/2 can do. Our study of the imperative evaluator showed us how to implement Scheme even on a conventional computer. In the interests of efficiency, the evaluator's control structure was changed to use placemarkers.

Each of these extensions to Gleam presents a new virtual machine: one has pairs, another has an extensive library of procedures, another a Scheme evaluator. An operating system exemplifies how a collection of abstractions—files (for data), virtual memory (for memory pages), channels (for devices), and processes (for computations)—as a group present a new virtual machine.

Finally, we saw that operating systems create virtual machines that allow programmers to use resources such as files and memory without having to know how data are stored physically; these resources can even be spread across a network.

Further Readings

This chapter presents some issues that are dealt with in some of the classics of computer science. The best introductions to computer architecture are Andrew Tanenbaum, *Structured Computer Organization*, 3rd ed., and John L. Hennesy and David A. Patterson., *Machine Organization: Basic Principles*

Because Scheme is so easy to implement, people often want further pointers on how to build their own system. The imperative evaluator discussed here is based upon one described in Hal Abelson and Gerald Sussman's *Structure and Interpretation of Computer Programs*, which discusses some of the more obscure topics in further depth. The best comprehensive survey of garbage-collection techniques is still found in Volume 1 of Donald Knuth's *Art of Computer Programming*, though it was written before virtual memory became common. (Volume 2 presents algorithms for floating-point computation.) Also see Jacques Cohen's survey paper on the subject in the journal *Computing Surveys*, circa 1979. A very elegant garbage collection method is discussed in C. J. Cheney, "A Non-Recursive List Compacting Algorithm". The classic book on compilers is A. Aho, R. Sethi, and J. Ullman, *Principles of Compiler Design*, 2nd ed., which approaches the subject from a Pascal/C viewpoint, but discusses the subject thoroughly. Unfortunately, no introductory book on compiling Scheme has been written (though there are many research papers on the subject).

Two excellent books on operating systems and networking are also by Andrew Tanenbaum: *Modern Operating Systems*, and *Computer Networks*, 2nd ed.

Key Words

Here are the *key words* introduced in this chapter. Make sure you understand what each one means.

allocate	heap	real-time
class libraries	imperative evaluator	register allocation
cross-compile	interrupt	register conventions
device interface	machine abstraction	root directory
device registers	mark	scheduling
emulator	memory-mapped	tag
free pair	input and output	unimplemented
free list	open	instruction exception
garbage collection	parse	virtual machine
garbage collector	pipeline	
graphics accelerator	placemarker	

Problems

1. Write `equal?%` for Gleam/2, as described in Chapter 5, following the register conventions given in this chapter. ❏

Self-Assessment

1. Write `subst` for Gleam/2; it should replace all occurrences of an item with another item:

   ```
   (subst 'one 1 '(1 2 3 4 1)) ⇒ (one 2 3 4 one)
   (subst 'one 1 '(1 2 (1 2) 3 4) ) ⇒ (one 2 (one 2) 3 4)
   ```

   ❏

2. We used placemarkers in the imperative evaluator because we couldn't tolerate the efficiency problems caused by a direct translation of the self-evaluator into gap. Under what circumstances would a sloppy translation of the self-evaluator cause an overflow of the memory allocated for the stack? ❏

3. The imperative evaluator uses registers to hold its global variables and its procedures don't take explicit arguments. What are the advantages and disadvantages of this approach? ❏

4. Explain the difference between a channel and a file. ❏

Programming Problems

The software we've studied in this chapter is more open-ended than in any other chapter. The imperative evaluator and the file system, can be extended and elaborated in many different ways. Here are a few suggestions.

1. Modify the imperative evaluator so that it does a thorough job of error-checking. Malformed forms (e.g., (if a b c d e)) should be detected, and an appropriate error message should be produced. ❏

2. Modify the imperative evaluator to support macros. This is a fairly trivial task, if you do it right. (Look at the self-evaluator carefully.) ❏

3. Modify the file system to support standard file operations, including the ability to delete and rename files. Modify the file system so that channels can be used in "random-access" mode. This would involve a new operation, `channel-seek`, which would set the file index to a value given as an argument. (For this problem, it is an error if the new value for the file index is greater than the length of the file.) ❏

5. Recursion step: Using your favorite programming language other than Scheme, write a Scheme interpreter. Test it on the programs in this book. ❏

Coda

My English text is chaste, and all licentious passages are left in the obscurity of a learned language.   — Edward Gibbon, *Memoirs of My Life*

We have reached the end of a rather long path. We started with nothing more than basic mathematics—a few functions and the ability to define new ones. We added a few data types, and even fewer special forms. With these tools, we built two Scheme evaluators, a database system, a logic system, and an operating system. None of these applications includes the error-checking and user interfaces of a real software product, but each system contains what is needed to solve the basic problem. The basic principles used in developing each application—specification and abstraction, in particular—were similar.

We hope that you were able to follow along while we built these systems. There is a great deal of pleasure in designing useful programs, and seeing them work. There is even more pleasure in applying the techniques we have learned to solve new problems.

We have just scratched the surface of computer science. Each area we studied can be pursued in much more depth. Surprisingly, the connection between theory and practice has narrowed. As you study additional computer science, you will find many connections among areas of research and the way you design and implement programs.

There is much more to discover and many unsolved problems in computer science. Algorithmic complexity, artificial intelligence and robotics, and distributed computer systems all have hosts of unsolved problems. Some of these problems, if solved, could allow us to develop new computer applications. In many cases, we can't predict which problems have practical applications, any more than 19th century scientists could look at bread molds and foresee penicillin, or 1950s scientists could imagine the need for more than a few computers in the entire world.

Is there an end to it? Perhaps one day all of computer science will be completely understood. But we suspect that the range of computer applications spans all of human endeavor. Even if, one day, the computer science discipline is no more relevant than long division today, people will probably still want to develop new computer applications.

In this world of conflict and upheaval, some people argue that computers and software are an irrelevant waste of time, when half the world's population has never used a telephone.

We disagree. Computer science and software engineering have the potential to help the human race manage scarce resources more effectively, and develop new techniques that will revolutionize science, business, education, medicine, and the arts. It is up to each of us to make sure that computer applications are humane.

In this book, we have taught you the basic concepts and techniques of computation. We have not been able to teach you how and where to apply them. That is a skill for you to acquire, whether or not you become an information systems professional.

Appendix A

Answers

Answers to Chapter 1 Exercises

Exercise 1-1 Don't put them in your programs in the first place!

This facetious answer serves to underline the source of errors—those who specify problems and those who write the programs.

Exercise 1-2 Data: `income` is our name for the taxpayer's income; `donations` is the name for charitable donations; `net-income` is our name for the income after the $6,000 deduction; `taxable-income` is the income subject to taxation after all deductions.

1. Let `net-income` be the result of subtracting 6000 from `income`.
2. If `donations` is more than $1000, then `taxable-income` is the result of subtracting 1000 from `net-income`.
3. If `donations` is not more than $1000, then `taxable-income` is the result of subtracting `donations` from `net-income`.
4. If `taxable-income` is negative, then the income tax is 0.
5. If `taxable-income` is not negative, then the income tax is the result of multiplying `taxable-income` by 0.17.

It doesn't matter whether you do the charitable donations before or after the $6000 deduction; you'll get the same answer either way.

Exercise 1-3 Data: as in previous exercise.

1. Let `net-income` be the result of subtracting 6000 from `income`.
2. If `donations` is more than $2000, then `taxable-income` is the result of subtracting 1500 from `net-income`.
3. If `donations` is more than $1000 and not more than $2000, then `taxable-income` is the result of subtracting $\frac{donations-1000}{2}+1000$ from `net-income`.
4. If `donations` is not more than $1000, then `taxable-income` is the result of subtracting `donations` from `net-income`.
5. If `taxable-income` is negative, then the income tax is 0.
6. If `taxable-income` is not negative, then the income tax is the result of multiplying `taxable-income` by 0.17.

Exercise 1-4 The bulleted step—"If this student's `mark` is larger than `top-mark`,"—causes us to skip ties. If we rephrased this step as— "If this student's `mark` is not smaller than `top-mark`,"—then we would pick the last student in case of ties.

Exercise 1-5 A course with no students has no top student. Either the course was canceled, or it was so unpopular that everybody dropped it!

Exercise 1-6 Our "bug" was assuming that only one student has the top mark. A reasonable fix is to maintain a list of the students with the top mark:

If this student's `mark` is larger than `top-mark`,
1. Put this student's name as the only entry of the list of names, `top-names`.
2. Let `top-mark` be this student's mark.

else if this student's mark equals `top-mark`, add this student's name to the end of the list of names, `top-names`.

When the process is complete, the answer is the list called `top-names`.

Exercise 1-7 The algorithm is as follows:
1. If d is less than 200, let $d_1 = 200$.
2. If d is not less than 200, let $d_1 = d$.
3. Let $p = d_1 * 0.75 + 25.00$.

Exercise 1-8 The algorithm is as follows:
1. On a piece of paper, write down the names A and B, and write a 0 next to each one.
2. For each ballot:
   a. If the voter chose A, cross out the number written next to A, and write in a number 1 larger.
   b. Otherwise, the voter has chosen B, so cross out the number written next to B, and write in a number 1 larger.
3. If the number next to A is larger than the number next to B, then A has won; otherwise B has won.

Unfortunately, real life is seldom so simple. In a real election, there may be many candidates, rather than just two. Some ballots may be "spoiled". It is possible that two candidates could get the same number of votes, meaning that we can't pick a winner. An algorithm that takes all these factors into account will be much more complicated than ours.

Exercise 1-9 We said "An author once gave Abraham Lincoln a copy of his very dull book." It's not clear from this who wrote the book: the author or Lincoln. You probably had no trouble understanding the story, but to do so, you had to know that if Lincoln had written the book, he wouldn't have been likely to write a thank-you note to the author. This example might convince you of the difficulty of writing a computer program that understands human languages.

Exercise 1-10 a. Syntactically valid, but semantic nonsense; hot and cold, in normal English, are opposites.   b. Semantic nonsense, unless you happen to know that *fungible* means "interchangeable"; the sentence is therefore quite valid.   c. Syntactically invalid, but semantically quite valid: you know that John is a baseball player. d. Syntactically and semantically valid; the prohibition against *ain't* is basically one of elegance, rather than validity.   e. Syntactically and semantically valid. The statement just happens to be false, though.

Exercise 1-11 The giveaway in the second and third cases is the font.
a. form   b. form   c. value

Exercise 1-12 `(- (* 3.1415926 (* 2 12)) (* 3.1415926 (* 2 10)))`

Exercise 1-13 a. **7** b. **14** c. **3** d. Error: division by 0 is undefined. The answer you will get if you try this on a computer will depend upon the Scheme system. Some will give a nonsensical answer: **0** and **5** are possible wrong answers. Other Scheme systems will refuse to give an answer, but will just report an error message, such as `Division by zero error`.   e. Error: (3) isn't a valid form.

Exercise 1-14 a. `(+ 2 (* 3 4))` b. `(+ (* 2 3) 4)`
c. `(- (* (+ 1 5) 6) (/ 12 3))`

Exercise 1-15 `(* (- (+ 24718 14284) 6000) 0.17)`

We're fortunate that John earned more than $6000; otherwise, he would be owed income tax.

Exercise 1-16 In each of these, we've followed our left-to-right convention. You can get the correct answer in many other ways, but this is our standard method.

a.

```
(+ 7 13)                          Application
  (+ 7 13)                        Number
  (+ 7 13)                        Number
(+ 7 13)                          Primitive
20
```

b.

```
(- (* 2 14) 8)                    Application
  (- (* 2 14) 8)                  Application
    (- (* 2 14) 8)                Number,Number
  (- (* 2 14) 8)                  Primitive
  (- 28 8)                        Number
(- 28 8)                          Primitive
20
```

Exercise 1-17   a. Substituting *5* for x gives us the form (+ *5* 2), which in turn has the value *7*.   b. Substituting *7* for x and *4* for y gives us (+ *7* (* *4* 3)), which has the value *19*.   c. This one is a bit more complicated. The form is an application of a `lambda` form whose body is itself an application of a `lambda` form. That means we substitute *4* for x, giving ((lambda (y) (* y 2)) (+ *4* 3)). Now repeat the process, substituting *7* for y. This gives (* *7* 2), or *14*.

Exercise 1-18   a. (lambda (x) (* (/ 5 9) (- x 32)))
b. (lambda (x y) (* (+ x (* 3 y)) (- x y))) or
(lambda (x) (lambda (y) (* (+ x (* 3 y)) (- x y))))
The first is preferable, because it's easier to read.

Exercise 1-19

```
(lambda (length width cost)
  (+ (* (* length width) cost) 50))
```

Exercise 1-20   There are several assumptions. For our procedure, the weighting of the exams is midterms count 25% each and the final counts 50%; the maximum for each exam is 100%; the result will be a percentage.
```
(define final-mark
  (lambda (mid1 mid2 final)
    (+ (* 0.25 (+ mid1 mid2)) (* 0.50 final))))
```
Much was left out of this problem, and many different assumptions can be put in. For example, any weights that add up to 1.0 make sense. You cannot be sure that the procedure is correct until you have checked these assumptions.

Exercise 1-21   (discr 7 2 0) ⇒ *49*, which looks correct. On the other hand, (discr 7 2 1) ⇒ *57*, which is wrong; the correct answer is *41*. This example demonstrates that a single test case might happen to "luck out". Therefore, you should always test a procedure with more than one set of data.

Exercise 1-22   The environment is as follows:

```
u        35
v        17
w        595
x        612
f        (lambda (a b) (+ a (* b 2)))
```

Exercise 1-23   a. *35* b. *612* c. *(lambda (a b) (+ a (* b 2)))* d. *52*
e. *(f 595 35)* ⇒ 665 f. 6

Exercise 1-24   (define add2 (lambda (x) (+ x 2)))

Exercise 1-25   (define fraction (lambda (n) (sqrt (/ (sub1 n) (add1 n)))))

Exercise 1-26

```
(define times2
  (lambda (x) (* 2 x)))
(define times64
  (lambda (x)
    (times2
      (times2
        (times2 (times2 (times2 (times2 x)))))))))
```

Exercise 1-27

```
(define triangle-area
  (lambda (x y z)
    (triangle-area-helper (semiperimeter x y z) x y z)))
(define semiperimeter
  (lambda (x y z) (/ (+ x (+ y z)) 2)))
(define triangle-area-helper
  (lambda (s x y z)
    (sqrt (* s (* (- s x) (* (- s y) (- s z)))))))
```

We could have eliminated `semiperimeter`, but only at the cost of making the body of the procedure `triangle-area` much more complicated.

Exercise 1-28   a. "Socrates is a Greek and Socrates is a philosopher"   b. "Mary is taking computer science and Mary is not taking geometry" (This is as close as we can come; the notion of *instead of* can't be easily expressed with the Boolean operations we have studied.)   c. "John has not taken computer science, and John has not taken mathematics"

Exercise 1-29   `(define one? (lambda (x) (= x 1)))`

Exercise 1-30   The result of (< 5 6) is the Boolean value #t. The predicate `zero?`, on the other hand, expects a number as its input. Boolean values are not numbers.

Exercise 1-31   `(define between? (lambda (a x y) (and (<= x a) (<= a y))))`

Exercise 1-32   `(define not=? (lambda (x y) (not (= x y))))`
or
`(define not=? (lambda (x y) (or (< x y) (> x y))))`

Exercise 1-33   `(define <? <)`

Exercise 1-34

```
(define postage
  (lambda (weight)
    (if (< weight 30) 15
      (if (and (>= weight 30) (< weight 49)) 17
        (if (and (>= weight 50) (< weight 99)) 22
          (/ weight 4))))))
```

Unfortunately, this solution contains a bug. A letter weighing 49.5 grams will be charged 12.375 cents, rather than (presumably) 15 cents. Closer examination shows that the bug isn't really in the procedure, but in the original problem statement. Rather than just writing the procedure, you should check with the Post Office to clarify their intentions.

Exercise 1-35   The sequence of evaluations is:

```
(my-procedure 2)                          Application
  (my-procedure 2)                          Name
  ((lambda (x) (+ what x)) 2)             Number
((lambda (x) (+ what x)) 2)              Procedure
(+ what 2)                                Application
  (+ what 2)                               Name,Name
(#{plus} 33 2)                          Primitive
35
```

Exercise 1-36   Most modern clocks are digital, and have no hands.

Answers to Chapter 1 Self-Assessment Questions

Question 1   a. We need the name and address of the person who has checked the book out, the date it was due, and today's date.
b. The algorithm is:
1. Let t be today's date.
2. For each book:
   a. Let d be the due date.
   b. If $t - d > 7$, then send a reminder letter.

Question 2   The information needed on the questionnaires is the ID number and the set of 25 answers.

The main algorithm is:
1. For each questionnaire,
   a. If this person is an activist, display the person's ID number.

How to find out whether somebody is an activist:
1. Let n initially be 0.
2. For each question:
   a. If the person is interested in this question, add 1 to n.
3. The person is an activist if $n \geq 10$.

How to find out whether somebody is interested in a particular question:
1. The person is interested in a question if the answer is 4 or 5.

You probably didn't use two subalgorithms. However, the way we've done it makes it easy to see what must be changed, either the number of questions or the interest level. (Remember, one procedure should do exactly one thing.)

Question 3   (/ (+ 0.86 (+ 0.78 0.91)) 3)

Question 4

```
(define cylinder-surface-area
  (lambda (height radius)
    (* height (* pi (* 2 radius)))))
```

In this question, the formula is given in terms of the diameter, but the procedure is supposed to accept the radius as an argument.

Question 5   The sequence of evaluations is:

```
((lambda (x) (* 2 x))
  ((lambda (y) (+ y 1)) 3))   Application, Lambda
((lambda (x) (* 2 x))
  ((lambda (y) (+ y 1)) 3))   Application, Lambda, Number
((lambda (x) (* 2 x))
  ((lambda (y) (+ y 1)) 3))   Procedure, Application, Name, Number
((lambda (x) (* 2 x))
  (#{plus} 3 1))              Primitive
((lambda (x) (* 2 x))  4)     Procedure
(* 2 4)                       Application, Name, Number
(#{times} 2 4)                Primitive
8
```

Question 6

Question 7

```
(define cube (lambda (x) (* x (* x x))))

(define c 299800000)
(define lorentz
  (lambda (v) (sqrt (- 1 (/ (* v v) (* c c))))))
```

Question 8

```
(define in-range?
  (lambda (x)
    (or (and (> x -5) (< x -3)) (and (> x 2) (<= x 4)))))
```

Answers to Chapter 2 Exercises

Exercise 2-1　The essential difference is that the droid diagram, Figure A-1, only shows the points in the evaluation where `factorial` is applied (the Application rule), and where it finishes the application (the Procedure rule). All other steps are not displayed.

Exercise 2-2　The answer is shown in Figure A-2

Exercise 2-3　Each call to `power` creates a new droid. The droid evaluating (`power 7 3`) calls a droid to evaluate (`power 7 2`), which in turn calls a droid to evaluate (`power 7 1`), which calls a droid to do (`power 7 1`). At this point, there are four droids; three are waiting for the results of the droids they have called. As each gets the value it awaits, it multiplies the value by 7, and returns the result to its caller.

Exercise 2-4

```
(define mult%
  (lambda (a b)
    (if (= b 0)
        0
        (+ a (mult% a (sub1 b))))))
```

Exercise 2-5　The Rules prints every rule and all intermediate values of the computation. The trace shows only the selected procedure applications, the procedure and the arguments, and then the returned value of the procedure. The Rules does show the sequence of applications and procedure returns in the same order as the trace. The trace output is very close to what you get with the Droid Model.

Exercise 2-6　(`add% 1 2.5`) ⇒ (`add% 2 1.5`) ⇒ (`add% 3 0.5`) ⇒ (`add% 4 -0.5`) ⇒ (`add% 5 -1.5`) ... As soon as b is negative, we're in trouble.

Exercise 2-7

```
(define add-negative
  (lambda (a b)
    (if (= b 0)
```

```
(factorial 3)                              Application, Name, Number
((lambda (n) (if (= n 0) ...)) 3)          Procedure
(if (= 3 0) 1 (* 3 (factorial (- 3 1))))   If, Application, Name,
                                           Number
(if (#{equal} 3 0) 1
    (* 3 (factorial (- 3 1))))             Primitive
(* 3 (factorial (- 3 1)))                  Application, Name
(#{times} 3 (factorial (- 3 1)))          Application, Name
(#{times} 3
    ((lambda (n) (if (= n 0) ...))
     (- 3 1)))                             Application, Name, Number
(#{times} 3
    ((lambda (n) (if (= n 0) ...))
       (#{minus} 3 1)))                    Primitive
(#{times} 3
    ((lambda (n) (if (= n 0) ...)) 2)      Procedure
(#{times} 3
    (if (= 2 0) 1
       (* 2 (factorial (- 2 1)))))         If
                   ....
(#{times} 3 (#{times} 2 (#{times} 1
    (if (= 0 0) 1
        (* 0 (factorial (- 0 1)))))))      If, Application, Name,
                                           Number
(#{times} 3 (#{times} 2 (#{times} 1
    (if (#{equal} 0 0) 1
        (* 0 (factorial (- 0 1)))))))      Primitive
(#{times} 3 (#{times} 2 (#{times} 1 1)))   Number
(#{times} 3 (#{times} 2 (#{times} 1 1)))   Primitive
(#{times} 3 (#{times} 2 1))                Primitive
                   ...
6
```

Figure A-1

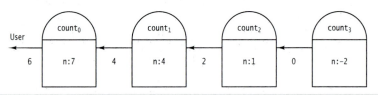

Figure A-2

```
         a
         (add-negative (sub1 a) (add1 b)))))
(define add-integer
  (lambda (a b)
    (if (>= b 0)
      (add% a b)
      (add-negative a b)))))
```

Exercise 2-8

```
(define count-even
  (lambda (number)
    (if (= number 0)
```

```
    0
    (if (even? (remainder number 10))
        (+ 1 (count-even (quotient number 10)))
        (count-even (quotient number 10))))))
```

Exercise 2-9   The cube-root procedure loops infinitely, when (/ (+ x0 x1) 2.0) is equal to either x0 or x1, and their difference is no less than $1e - 4$.

Exercise 2-10   The problem is that we compute the initial estimate as $a/2$, but for numbers between 0 and 1, the initial estimate should be *larger* than a. Here's a solution:

```
(define cube-root
  (lambda (a)
    (if (>= a 1.0)
        (cube-root-solve a 1.0 a)
        (cube-root-solve a a 1.0))))
```

The initial estimate for $\sqrt[3]{a}$ is halfway between a and 1 for $a < 1$.

Can you rewrite this procedure without using an if?

Exercise 2-11   cube-root-solve assumes that x0 is less than x1. Its arguments should obey this assumption. Our procedure should be

```
(define cube-root
  (lambda (a)
    (if (< a 0.0)
        (- (cube-root (abs a)))
        (if (>= a 1.0)
            (cube-root-solve a 1.0 a)
            (cube-root-solve a a 1.0)))))
```

cube-root is recursive in a trivial way. It will never do more than one level of recursion.

Exercise 2-12

```
(define sum-digits
  (lambda (x)
    (if (= x 0)
        (+ (remainder x 10)
           (sum-digits (quotient x 10))))))
```

Exercise 2-13

```
(define collect-evens
  (lambda (n)
    (if (= n 0)
        0
        (if (even? (remainder n 10))
            (+ (* 10 (collect-evens (quotient n 10)))
               (remainder n 10))
            (collect-evens (quotient n 10))))))
```

Exercise 2-14   `(define compute-straights`
`(lambda (size n) (add1 (- n size))))`

Exercise 2-15   A procedure that runs in $O(n!)$ time would have to loop n times, each time calling itself. Such a loop structure is tricky to build. Joel is therefore almost certainly mistaken. Even if he were correct, his procedure would probably not be very useful. $n!$ grows very quickly. Even 10! is over 3 million. A procedure with time $O(n!)$ would probably have no practical use for reasonable values of n.

Exercise 2-16   If the argument is n, then we will do $\lfloor n/3 \rfloor + 1$ recursive calls. (The notation $\lfloor \ldots \rfloor$ means "the largest integer less than".) The term 1 may be thrown away; if we throw away the $\lfloor \ldots \rfloor$, we will never be more than 1 call out. Finally, we can get rid of the coefficient. The answer is therefore $O(n)$.

Exercise 2-17 (define foo (lambda (n) 5)) does the same thing as the procedure in Exercise 2-16, but in one step.

Exercise 2-18 The big-oh notation ignores constant multipliers in the expression for the running time of the program. Since p2 is $O(1)$, its running time is independent of n, its input, for all n greater than some n_0. p2's running time could be an enormous constant, however, and for all but very large n, p1 could be faster.

Exercise 2-19 If called with an argument n, bar2 will call itself with $n/3$. By the same analysis as for mult%2, we can conclude that bar2 has running time $O(\log_3 n) = O(\log n)$. We can convert logarithms from one base to another by multiplying by a constant; therefore, from a big-oh standpoint, all logarithm functions have the same complexity. We do quite often write that a procedure has running time $O(\lg n)$, but that's mostly because most useful logarithmic-time procedures involve division by 2.

Procedure bar1 follows the same model as add, and therefore has running time $O(n)$. On each repetition of bar1, Scheme evaluates (bar2 b) (b starts out as n, and never changes). Accordingly, we can compute the running time of the whole thing by multiplying the two factors, giving a final answer of $O(n \log n)$.

Exercise 2-20 You're extremely skeptical. We say that a computer can multiply numbers of a certain small number of digits (less than 30) in $O(1)$ time, but clearly it would take some time just to read in numbers with thousands of digits! Any multiplication algorithm must recurse until it reaches a base case. The larger the number, the more recursions. Don't buy the procedure.

Exercise 2-21 add is tail-recursive. The other two are not.

Exercise 2-22

```
(define sum1
  (lambda (n)
    (if (= n 1)
        1
        (+ n (sum1 (sub1 n)))))))
```

Exercise 2-23

```
(define sum2-helper
  (lambda (start end answer)
    (if (> start end)
        answer
        (sum2-helper (add1 start) end (+ start answer))))))
(define sum2
  (lambda (n)
    (sum2-helper 1 n 0)))
```

Exercise 2-24 To compute $a + (a+1) + \cdots + (b-1) + b$, consider that $(a+1) + (b-1) = a+b$. This means that, for example, $1 + 2 + \cdots + 99 + 100$ (the problem Gauss was given) can be computed as

$$(1 + 100) + (2 + 99) + \cdots + (50 + 50) =$$

$$\overbrace{101 + 101 + \cdots + 101}^{50\ times}$$

, or 5050. To compute $1 + 2 + \cdots + n$, the answer is $\frac{n}{2}(n+1)$. (Convince yourself that this formula works when n is odd.)

Exercise 2-25 The answer is shown in figure Figure A–3. It doesn't matter what value we use for a, so we can pick a couple of reasonable ones. We'd need to hit each of the three basic cases for b in the code, which means an even number, an odd number,

a b expected result

```
7  7       49
7  4       28
7  1        7
12 9      108
12 6       72
12 1       12
12 0        0
4  -5    undefined
5 2.3    undefined
```

Figure A-3

and 1. The numbers 0 and 1 are special for multiplication. We should also try a couple of invalid values for b, just so we can say what happens.

Answers to Chapter 2 Self-Assessment Questions

Question 1   13

Question 2   4

Question 3

```
(define product-of-even
  (lambda (n)
    (if (= n 1)
      2
      (* (* 2 n) (product-of-even (sub1 n)))))))
```

Question 4

```
(define product-of-even
  (lambda (n) (product-helper n 2)))
(define product-helper
  (lambda (n acc)
    (if (= n 1)
      acc
      (product-helper (sub1 n) (* 2 n acc))))))
```

Question 5

```
(define kth-digit
  (lambda (k n)
    (if (= k 0)
      (remainder n 10)
      (kth-digit (sub1 k) (quotient n 10))))))
```

Question 6   (power-close-to 2 32) $\Rightarrow$ 6
The time complexity of power-close-to is $O(\log_b n)$.

Question 7

```
(define 0-digit (lambda (x) (help-0-digit x 0)))
(define help-0-digit
  (lambda (x n)
    (if (= (remainder x 10) 0)
      n
      (help-0-digit (quotient x 10) (add1 n))))))
```

Answers to Chapter 3 Exercises

Exercise 3-1   a. character   b. Boolean   c. depends upon the value of the variable t.

Exercise 3-2

```
(define color-name?
  (lambda (ch)
    (or
      (char-ci=? ch #\R)
      (char-ci=? ch #\O)
      (char-ci=? ch #\Y)
      (char-ci=? ch #\G)
      (char-ci=? ch #\B)
      (char-ci=? ch #\I)
      (char-ci=? ch #\V))))
```

Exercise 3-3

```
(define char-ci=?%
  (lambda (char1 char2)
    (char=? (char-downcase char1) (char-downcase char2))))
```

Exercise 3-4

```
(define letter->number
  (lambda (ch)
    (if (and (char>=? ch #\A) (char<=? ch #\Z))
        (- (char->integer ch) (char->integer #\A))
        (if (and (char>=? ch #\a) (char<=? ch #\z))
            (- (char->integer ch) (char->integer #\a))
            -1))))
```

Note the use of forms such as (char->integer #\A). We may know that this form evaluates to 65, but it's foolish to put that information into the program. What if we wanted to make this procedure work on another coding system? Smart programmers would use forms such as the one we've used, rather than hard-wiring "magic numbers" into the program.

Exercise 3-5

```
(define number->letter
  (lambda (num)
    (if (and (>= num 0) (<= num 25))
        (integer->char (+ num (char->integer #\a)))
        #\+)))
```

Exercise 3-6   "bric-a-brac"

Exercise 3-7

```
(define string-upcase
  (lambda (str)
    (if (string=? str "")
        ""
        (string-append
          (string (char-upcase (string-ref str 0)))
          (string-upcase
            (substring str 1 (string-length str)))))))
```

Exercise 3-8   number-length assumes its argument is positive.

```
(define palindrome-n?
  (lambda (num)
    (palindrome-n-help num 0 (sub1 (number-length num)))))
(define number-length
  (lambda (n) (number-length-helper (/ (log n) (log 10)))))
(define number-length-helper
```

```scheme
      (lambda (log10)
        (if (= log10 (floor log10))
          (add1 log10)
          (ceiling log10)))))
    (define number-ref
      (lambda (n pos)
        (floor (/ (mod n (expt 10 (+ 1 pos))) (expt 10 pos)))))
    (define palindrome-n-help
      (lambda (num pos1 pos2)
        (if (>= pos1 pos2)
          #t
          (if (= (number-ref num pos1) (number-ref num pos2))
            (palindrome-n-help num (add1 pos1) (sub1 pos2))
            #f)))))
```

Exercise 3-9

```scheme
    (define string-rotate
      (lambda (str k)
        (string-rotate-helper str 0 (string-length str) k)))
    (define string-rotate-helper
      (lambda (str pos len k)
        (if (>= pos len)
          ""
          (string-append
            (string (string-ref str (remainder (+ pos k) len)))
            (string-rotate-helper str (add1 pos) len k)))))
```

Exercise 3-10
Exercise 3-11

```scheme
    (define newline% (lambda () (display #\newline)))
```

```scheme
    (define arithmetic
      (lambda (a b)
        (begin
          (display (+ a b)) (newline)
          (display (* a b)) (newline)
          (max a b) (newline))))
```

Exercise 3-12

```scheme
    > (quadratic 1 -2 -8)
    x^2 + -2x + -8 = 0 has two real roots, -2 and 4.
    (define discr
      (lambda (pa pb pc)
        (- (* pb pb) (* 4 (* pa pc)))))
    (define quadratic
      (lambda (ina inb inc)
        (format
          #t
          "~ax^2 + ~ax + ~a = 0  has two ~a roots, ~a and ~a.~%"
            ina inb inc
            (if (>= (discr ina inb inc) 0.0) "real" "complex")
            (/ (- (- inb) (sqrt (discr ina inb inc)))
               (* 2 ina))
            (/ (+ (- inb) (sqrt (discr ina inb inc)))
               (* 2 ina)))))
```

Exercise 3-13

(atx,aty) specifies the lower left-hand corner of the rectangle.

```scheme
    (define draw-rect
      (lambda (atx aty dx dy)
        (draw-move atx aty)
```

```
        (draw-line (+ atx dx) aty)
        (draw-line (+ atx dx) (+ aty dy))
        (draw-line atx (+ aty dy))
        (draw-line atx aty)))
(define draw-tri
  (lambda (atx aty size)
    (draw-move atx aty)
    (draw-line (+ atx size) aty)
    (draw-line (+ atx (/ size 2.0))
      (+ aty (* size (/ (sqrt 3.0) 2.0)))))
    (draw-line atx aty)))
(define house
  (lambda (atx aty dx dy)
    (draw-rect atx aty dx dy)
    (draw-tri atx (+ aty dy) dx)))
```

Exercise 3-14   The solution below uses `letter->number` and `number->letter`. The latter is defined in Exercise 3-5. You can get more clever if you want to keep upper- and lowercase separate.

```
(define rot13
  (lambda (ch)
    (string
      (if (char-alphabetic? ch)
        (number->letter
          (remainder (+ (letter->number ch) 13) 26))
        ch))))
```

This indeed works:

```
> (encrypt-string rot13 "How many earth people does it take
to change a light bulb?")
"ubj znal rnegu crbcyr qbrf vg gnxr
gb punatr n yvtug ohyo?"
```

(The answer is 5: one to hold the bulb and four to turn the planet.)

Exercise 3-15

```
(define process-temperatures
  (lambda (in-name out-name)
    (with-input-from-file in-name
      (lambda ()
        (with-output-to-file out-name
          (lambda () (process-helper (read)))))))))
(define process-helper
  (lambda (x) (if x (process-helper2 x (read)))))
(define process-helper2
  (lambda (x y)
    (display (- x y)) (newline) (process-helper (read))))
```

Exercise 3-16   6

Exercise 3-17   33

Exercise 3-18   It's best to do this in two steps. First, do the inner one. That gives us
`(let ((w 3)) ((lambda (x) (/ w x)) 4))`. Now the second:
`((lambda (w) ((lambda (x) (/ w x)) 4)) 3)`. Yecch!

Exercise 3-19

```
(let ((x 5))
  (let ((y (+ x 3)))
    (+ (* 2 y) x)))
```

Exercise 3-20   No. The scopes of two procedures that have been separately defined are completely separate. There's no confusion between the two uses of the name pos, so you can trust that the program will work correctly.

Exercise 3-21   13: the x in (+ x y) is bound to 3, while the x in (* 2 x) is bound to 5.

Exercise 3-22   9: x in (+ x y) *and* in (* 2 x) is bound to 3.

Exercise 3-23

```
(define discr
   (lambda (pa pb pc)
     (let*
        ((b2 (* pb pb))
         (4ac (* 4 (* pa pc)))
         (val (- b2 4ac)))
      (sqrt val))))
```

Exercise 3-24   (distance (make-location 147 223) (make-location 308 14))

Exercise 3-25   Negative values and values greater than 1000 create problems. For example, (make-location -1 100) ⇒ -900, which is the same value as (make-location -2 1100).

Similar behavior occurs when we pick nonintegral values; for example, (make-location 0.5 0) ⇒ 500, which appears to correspond to (0, 500)!

Exercise 3-26   *char-height* is the system text size in the y dimension and *char-width* is the text size in x.

```
(define popsk-demo
  (lambda (draw-phase)
    (draw-clear)
    (draw-axes 100 50 "years" "numbers")
    (popsk 1.1 .01 0.9 0.02 10 10 0 0 100 100 draw-phase)))
(define draw-axes
  (lambda (xlen ylen xstring ystring)
    (draw-move 0 0)
    (draw-line xlen 0)
    (let ((width (* *char-width* (string-length xstring))))
      (draw-move (* 0.5 (- xlen width)) (- *char-height*))
      (draw-text xstring))
    (let ((ht (* *char-height* (string-length ystring))))
      (draw-move (- *char-width*)
        (- ylen (* 0.5 (- ylen ht))))
      (draw-text-vertical ystring))))
(define draw-text-vertical
  (lambda (str)
    (letrec
      ((len (string-length str))
       (help
         (lambda (pos)
           (if (< pos len)
             (begin
               (draw-text (substring str pos (add1 pos)))
               (help (add1 pos)))))))
      (help 0))))
```

Answers to Chapter 3 Self-Assessment Questions

Question 1

```
(define count-spaces
  (lambda (str)
    (count-space-helper str 0 (string-length str))))
```

```
(define count-space-helper
  (lambda (str pos len)
    (if (>= pos len)
        0
        (+
          (if (char=? (string-ref str pos) #\space) 1 0)
          (count-space-helper str (add1 pos) len)))))
```

A tail-recursive solution to this problem is also fine.

Question 2

```
(define zip
  (lambda (str-a str-b)
    (zip-helper str-a str-b 0 (string-length str-a))))
(define zip-helper
  (lambda (str-a str-b pos len)
    (if (>= pos len)
        ""
        (string-append
          (string (string-ref str-a pos))
          (string (string-ref str-b pos))
          (zip-helper str-a str-b (add1 pos) len)))))
```

Question 3

We will start by computing the number of positions in str2 to check. (We don't want to check substrings off the right end of str2.)

```
(define scan-string
  (lambda (str1 str2)
    (scan-helper str1 (string-length str1)
      str2 0
      (- (string-length str2) (string-length str1)))))
(define scan-helper
  (lambda (str1 len1 str2 pos2 len2)
    (if (>= pos2 len2)
        -1
        (if (string=? str1
              (substring str2 pos2 (+ pos2 len1)))
            pos2
            (scan-helper str1 len1 str2 (add1 pos2) len2)))))
```

This takes $O(len2)$ calls to string=?, which can be unacceptable for long strings. Much faster algorithms have been developed, such as the Boyer-Moore algorithm. Look in any reference book under *algorithms* in the bibliography to find out more about string searching.

Question 4

```
(format #t "The values are:  x: ~a  y: ~a  z: ~a~%" x y z)
```
or you could use a begin form with a series of display applications.

Question 5

1. The procedure bound to f in the let calls f, but the f it calls is the one defined at top-level. Remember, the expressions to which the names are bound in a let are evaluated in the enclosing scope.

Question 6

```
( (lambda (a b c)
    ( (lambda (disc)
        (/ (+ (- b) (sqrt disc))
           (* 2 a)))
      (- (* b b) (* 4 (* a c)))))
  4 9 2)
```

Question 7

There are two separate problems with this form. First, we don't know the order in which the bindings for a and b are created; therefore, a might be bound to 7, and b to 3, or the reverse. Second, the value provided for c involves the value of a, which isn't defined yet. As a result, when you run it, one of two things will occur. If a is bound in an enclosing scope, its value will be used; otherwise, an error will be generated.

Question 8

```
(define sum-series
  (lambda (f n)
    (letrec
      ((helper
        (lambda (i acc)
          (if (> i n)
            acc
            (helper (add1 i) (+ acc (f i)))))))
      (helper 0 0))))
```

Notice how we have been able to eliminate f and n as arguments to the helper since, first, they do not change between recursive calls, and, second, the helper lies in the scope of their binding.

Question 9

```
(define string-tail-map
  (lambda (proc str)
    (if (= (string-length str) 0)
      (void)
      (begin
        (proc str)
        (string-tail-map proc
          (substring str 1 (string-length str)))))))
```

This procedure doesn't help us in string scanning. Although the general logic is similar, string-tail-map processes every tail. Scanning, on the other hand, suggests that we stop as soon as we've found a match. It is *possible* to twist string-tail-map in this way, but the result would be neither efficient nor readable.

Answers to Chapter 4 Exercises

Exercise 4-1   a. 1   b. 2   c. 2

Exercise 4-2

```
(define make-pair cons)
(define pair-first car)
(define pair-second cdr)
```

The longer form, (define make-pair (lambda (a d) (cons a d))), isn't wrong, but it is definitely long-winded.

Exercise 4-3   (2 . 4)

Exercise 4-4

```
(module location-polar
  (export make-location-rectangular make-location-polar
    location-x location-y location-rho location-theta)
  (define make-location-rectangular
    (lambda (x y)
      (cons (sqrt (+ (* x x) (* y y))) (atan y x))))
  (define make-location-polar
    (lambda (rho theta) (cons rho theta)))
  (define location-x
    (lambda (loc) (* (car loc) (cos (cdr loc)))))
  (define location-y
```

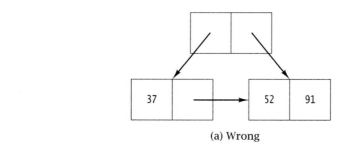

(a) Wrong

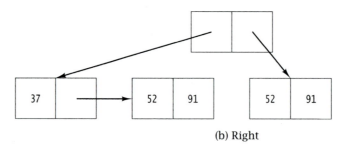

(b) Right

Figure A-4

```
    (lambda (loc) (* (car loc) (sin (cdr loc))))))
    (define location-rho (lambda (loc) (car loc)))
    (define location-theta (lambda (loc) (cdr loc))))
```

We haven't written the display procedures because the previous versions still work. They only use the accessors in the ADT.

Exercise 4-5   There are two ways to diagram this structure, shown in Figure A-4.

Version (a) shows two arrows leading to the same pair, while version (b) shows two different pairs. Either one is satisfactory, according to the rules we've shown so far. In Chapter 5, we'll see why version (b) is the correct way to diagram this structure.

Exercise 4-6

```
(define farther-north
  (lambda (city1 city2)
    (> (city-latitude city1) (city-latitude city2))))
```

Exercise 4-7   We will retain the interface, but store the information differently:

```
(define make-city
  (lambda (name pop lat long)
    (cons pop (cons lat (cons long name)))))
(define city-name (lambda (city) (third-tail city)))
(define city-population (lambda (city) (car city)))
(define city-latitude (lambda (city) (second city)))
(define city-longitude (lambda (city) (third city)))
```

Exercise 4-8

```
(define show-city
  (lambda (city)
    (format #t
      "City ~a at lat: ~a long: ~a has ~a000 people~%"
```

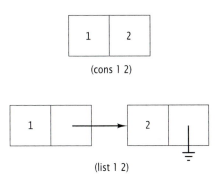

(cons 1 2)

(list 1 2)

Figure A-5

```
(city-name city)
(city-latitude city)
(city-longitude city)
(city-population city))))
```

Exercise 4-9

```
(define make-angle
  (lambda (degrees minutes seconds)
    (cons degrees (cons minutes seconds))))
(define angle-degrees (lambda (angle) (first angle)))
(define angle-minutes (lambda (angle) (second angle)))
(define angle-seconds (lambda (angle) (second-tail angle)))
(define show-angle
  (lambda (angle)
    (format #t " ~a :d ~a :m  seconds :a"
      (angle-degrees angle)
      (angle-minutes angle)
      (angle-seconds angle))))
```

Exercise 4-10
a. 4 (a number);   b. illegal: we cannot apply a symbol; ERROR   c. illegal: Scheme forms must have at least one item within the parentheses. (Some "deviant" Scheme implementations will accept this form; these implementations are incorrect.)

Exercise 4-11
a. b b. 3 c. a d. b e. (quote a)

Exercise 4-12
It takes $O(n)$ operations (cdrs) to determine whether a pair structure with a chain of n conses is a list.
```
(define list?%
  (lambda (ell)
    (if (pair? ell)
      (list?% (cdr ell))
      (null? ell))))
```

Exercise 4-13
(cons 1 2) is a pair containing 1 and 2; (list 1 2) is a pair containing 1 and (2). The box-and-arrow diagrams appear in Figure A-5.

Exercise 4-14
a. (list 1 2 3) b. (list 1 2 4) c. (list (list 1 2) 2 3)

Exercise 4-15
a. (+ 2 2) (a list);   b. (lambda (x) (+ 2 3)) (a list);   c. () (null).   d. '()
This is not null.   e. (1 (2 3))   f. (1 '(2 3)) A quote is not necessary inside a quoted form.   g. 17   h. Illegal: we cannot add the list (* 3 4) to 5.   i. (1.2)
A list containing one element, the number 1.2. The spaces around the dot are

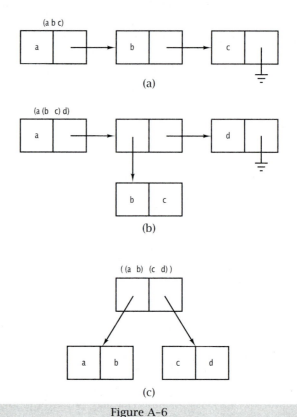

(a)

(b)

(c)

Figure A-6

very important.

Exercise 4-16   The box-and-arrow diagrams appear in Figure A-6.

Exercise 4-17   What should it return if n is invalid? Returning '() is dangerous, because '() might actually be the element at position n in the list. Two possibilities emerge: either return a nonsensical value, or create an error. Here's the former possibility:

```
(define list-ref%
  (lambda (any-list n)
    (if (or (< n 0) (null? any-list))
        'silly-value-for-an-incorrect-use-of-list-ref%
        (if (zero? n)
            (car any-list)
            (list-ref% (cdr any-list) (- n 1))))))
```

Of course, one person's silly value might be the element at position n in another's list! The second possibility reports an error. Some Scheme systems use the procedure error for this purpose. It takes two arguments: a symbol that is the name of the procedure reporting the error, and a string describing what's wrong.

The error-reporting version replaces the fourth line in list-ref% by

```
                              (error 'list-ref% "Invalid argument")
```

By the way, you really ought to check that any-list is a pair, too!

Exercise 4-18   (happyville) or (riverdale 3000 happyville)

Exercise 4-19

```
(define largest-of-list
  (lambda (a-list)
    (if (null? a-list)
      -1
      (max (car a-list)
        (largest-of-list (cdr a-list))))))
```

Exercise 4-20

```
(define length%
  (lambda (any-list)
    (if (null? any-list)
      0
      (if (pair? any-list)
        (add1 (length% (cdr any-list)))
        (error 'length% "Invalid argument")))))
```

Exercise 4-21

```
(define population-list-ref
  (lambda (any-list n)
    (if (zero? n)
      (car (cdr any-list))
      (population-list-ref (cdr (cdr any-list)) (- n 1)))))
```

Exercise 4-22

```
(define population-find
  (lambda (city-name city-list)
    (if (null? city-list)
      ...error...
      (if (symbol-equal? city-name (car city-list))
        (car (cdr city-list))
        (population-find city-name (cdr (cdr city-list)))))))
```

Exercise 4-23   (a (b c) d e)

Exercise 4-24   (x y z)

Exercise 4-25   append% cdrs down its first list argument, consing each element from it onto the result of applying append% to the cdr. So it performs O(m) conses, regardless of how long the second list is.

Exercise 4-26

```
(define largest-population
  (lambda (cities)
    (if (null? cities)
      #f
      (largest-pop-helper (city-population (car cities))
        (city-name (car cities)) (cdr cities)))))
(define largest-pop-helper
  (lambda (pop name cities)
    (if (null? cities)
      name
      (let ((p (city-population (car cities))))
        (if (> p pop)
          (largest-pop-helper p
            (city-name (car cities)) (cdr cities))
          (largest-pop-helper pop name (cdr cities)))))))
```

Exercise 4-27

```
> (append% '(x y) '(z z y))
(x y z z y)
> (append% '(x y z) '())
(x y z)
> (append%  'foo '(bar))
Error in cdr: foo is not a pair.
```

append% assumes its arguments are lists.
(append% '(foo) 'bar) ⇒ (foo . bar)

Exercise 4-28   See the file `airline.scm`.

Exercise 4-29

```
(define flights-for-airline
  (lambda (flight-list carrier)
    (if (null? flight-list)
        '()
        (if (symbol-equal? carrier
              (flight-carrier (car flight-list)))
          (cons (car flight-list)
            (flights-for-airline (cdr flight-list) carrier))
          (flights-for-airline (cdr flight-list) carrier)))))
```

Exercise 4-30   Well, (new-append% '(1 2 3) '(4 5 6)) ⇒ (3 2 1 4 5 6).
Effectively, new-append% is consing the x list onto the beginning of y, but (sadly for Al) the first element in x is the first to be consed onto y, then the second is consed *in front of* the first. Problem 1 at the end of the chapter asks you to fix this.

Exercise 4-31   Applying display-lists-cdr to the car causes the procedure to forget that the pair must begin and end with parentheses:
```
> (badshow (cons 1  (cons (cons 2  3)  4)))
(1    . 2) . 3) . 4) WRONG!
```
Compare this with the correct output:
```
> (display-lists (cons 1 (cons (cons 2  3)  4)))
(1 (2 . 3) . 4)
```

Exercise 4-32

```
(subst  '(wisdom and stupidity are not the same))
  ⇒  (wisdom and wisdom are not the same)
```

Exercise 4-33   a. (map add1 '(2 5 8 9)) ⇒ (3 6 9 10)
b. (map (lambda (x) (cons x 'foo)) '(a b c))
⇒ ((a . foo) (b . foo) (c . foo))

Exercise 4-34

```
(define for-each%
  (lambda (proc x)
    (if (null? x)
      (void)
      (begin
        (proc (car x))
        (for-each% proc (cdr x))))))
```

Exercise 4-35   This answer just follows the general idea of writing a recursive helper to build the results tail-recursively, and then reversing them.
```
(define unzip
  (lambda (l)
    (letrec
      ((help
        (lambda (in out1 out2)
```

```
          (if (null? in)
            (cons (reverse out1) (reverse out2))
            (help (cdr in)
              (cons (car (car in)) out1)
              (cons (car (cdr (car in))) out2))))))
      (help l '() '()))))
```

But what is the structure of the input list? It's a collection of two-element lists. The result we want is a pair whose car is the list of first elements from the lists, and whose cdr is the list of second elements of the lists. Consider:

(map car '((n1 v1) (n2 v2) (n3 v3))) ⇒ (n1 n2 n3)

This suggests a simple form of unzip:

```
(define unzip
  (lambda (l)
    (cons (map car l) (map (lambda (x) (car (cdr x))) l))))
```

Exercise 4-36   A: cons   B: cons   C: cdr   D: cdr

Exercise 4-37   (250 400 225 900)

Exercise 4-38   ((2 3) (8 7) ((2)))

Exercise 4-39

```
(define delete
  (lambda (from lst)
    (if (null? lst)
      '()
      (if (equal? from (car lst))
        (delete from (cdr lst))
        (cons (car lst) (delete from (cdr lst)))))))
```

Exercise 4-40   What if we had used and? and is a special form. Scheme treats special forms differently, and you cannot use them in the same place as procedures.

Exercise 4-41   First we need the filter procedure:

```
(define only
  (lambda (routes airline)
    (filter (lambda (x) (all-on? x  airline)) routes)))
```

Next we write the procedure all-on? that fails and returns #f when the carrier code is not the same as the given airline. The simplest way to write all-on? is to use every?:

```
(define all-on?
  (lambda (route airline)
    (every?
      (lambda (x) (equal? (flight-carrier x) airline))
      route)))
```

It's also worth looking at all?, a specialized version of every? that is written directly as a list procedure, without using reduce-map:

```
(define all?
  (lambda (pred? x)
    (if (null? x)
      #t
      (and (pred? (car x)) (all? pred? (cdr x))))))
(define all-on?
  (lambda (route airline)
    (all? (lambda (x) (equal? (flight-carrier x) airline))
      route)))
```

The definition of all-on? is similar in both cases. What is different? The and form does not continue to evaluate its arguments once one of them has evaluated

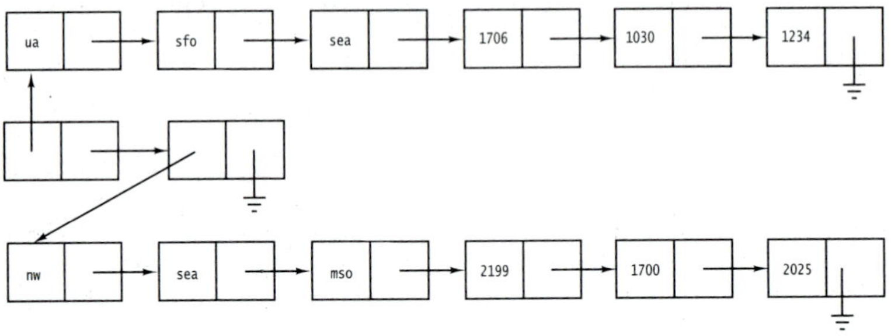

Figure A-7

to #f. every?, being based on reduce-map, will continue to apply the predicate to all elements of the list, so all? is generally more efficient than every?.

Exercise 4-42
Exercise 4-43

```
(reduce (lambda (x y) (+ x (* 2 y))) 5 '(17 22 11)) ⇒ 145
```

```
(define vmember
  (lambda (in . rest)
    (if (null? rest)
        #f
        (let ((res (member (car rest) in)))
          (if res
              res
              (apply vmember in (cdr rest)))))))
```

Exercise 4-44

```
(define map-variadic%
  (lambda (proc . args)
    (if (null? (car args))
        '()
        (cons (apply proc (map% car args))
              (apply map-variadic% proc (map% cdr args))))))
```

The variadic form of map-variadic% binds args to the list of the arguments to proc, each of which is a list. In the example, proc is bound to (lambda (x y) (* x y)) and args to ((2 4 6 8 10) (1 2 3 4 5)). map-variadic% conses the result of applying proc to the first element of the argument lists to the recursive result of map-variadic% with the cdrs of the argument lists.

Exercise 4-45   The diagram appears in Figure A-7.

Exercise 4-46   A simple structure is a list of lists—each sublist is a collection of airports sharing a city. To determine whether air1 and air2 are the same city, find the sublist containing air1. If there is one, check whether air2 is in it. Otherwise, they aren't in the same city.

```
(define airports-in-same-city
  '((sjc oak sfo)))
(define same-city?
  (lambda (air1 air2)
    (or (equal? air1 air2)
        (let ((in (find-first
                     (lambda (x) (member air1 x))
                     airports-in-same-city)))
          (if in
```

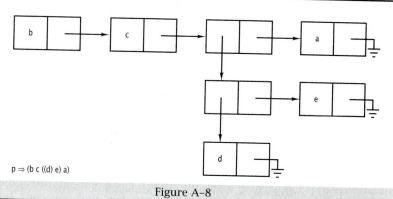

p ⇒ (b c ((d) e) a)

Figure A-8

```
(if (member air2 in) #t #f)
#f)))))
```

Answers to Chapter 4 Self-Assessment Questions

Question 1   a. (b ((a . b) c)) b. (((a 'c) b) (a 'c) b)
or (((a 'c) b) . ((a 'c) b))

Question 2   ((d) e)

Question 3   The diagram appears in Figure A-8.

Question 4   A. cons B. append C. list

Question 5

```
(define odd-reverse
  (lambda (ob)
    (letrec
      ((even
         (lambda (in)
           (if (pair? in) (map odd in) in)))
       (odd
         (lambda (in)
           (if (pair? in) (map even (reverse in)) in))))
      (if (pair? ob)
        (map even (reverse ob))
        ob))))
```

Question 6

```
(define flipper
  (lambda (l)
    (letrec
      ((split
         (lambda (m a b)
           (if (null? m)
             (cons a (reverse b))
             (if (null? (cdr m))
               (cons (cons (car m) a) (reverse b))
               (split (cdr (cdr m)) (cons (car m) a)
                 (cons (car (cdr m)) b))))))
       (merge
```

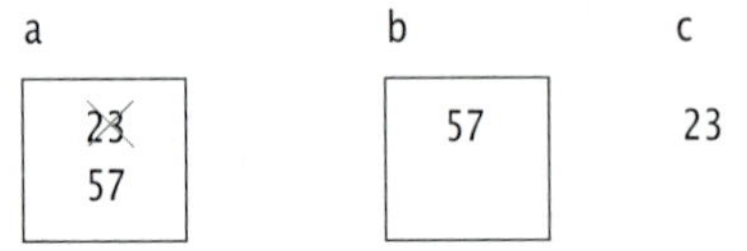

Figure A-9

```
(lambda (a b)
   (if (null? a)
       b
       (if (null? b)
           a
           (cons (car a)
                 (cons (car b) (merge (cdr a) (cdr b)))))))))))
   (let ((them (split l '() '())))
     (merge (car them) (cdr them)))))))
```

Question 7

```
(define reverse-r
   (lambda (l)
     (letrec
       ((help
          (lambda (pos)
            (if (< pos 0)
                '()
                (cons (list-ref l pos) (help (sub1 pos)))))))
       (help (sub1 (length l)))))))
```

The complexity of reverse-r is $O(n^2)$; help is called n times, and list-ref requires $O(n)$ time.

Question 8

```
(define delete
   (lambda (from lst)
     (filter (lambda (x) (not (equal? from x))) lst)))
```

Answers to Chapter 5 Exercises

Exercise 5-1 The first one displays 6, and the second 7, because f uses the contents of the box that is w's value.

Exercise 5-2 You might draw a diagram something like Figure A-9. The diagram shows that the returned value is (57 57 23).

Exercise 5-3 Since they don't agree on the answer, one of them probably thinks that it is 1, whereas the other thinks that the answer is 0. The first programmer is assuming that arguments are evaluated from left to right, whereas the second thinks they are evaluated from right to left.

Both are wrong. Any form whose value depends upon the order of evaluation of procedure arguments has an undefined value. The fact that any given Scheme system will almost certainly produce a specific value is irrelevant. It is computationally far too expensive to check for errors of this sort during evaluation. The answer, therefore, is that this form has no value.

Exercise 5-4 Neither balance-deposit nor balance-withdraw check to ensure that the numbers are not negative. Depositing a large enough negative number could result in an undetected overdraft. Withdrawing a negative number might result in an increase in the customer's balance without any actual money changing

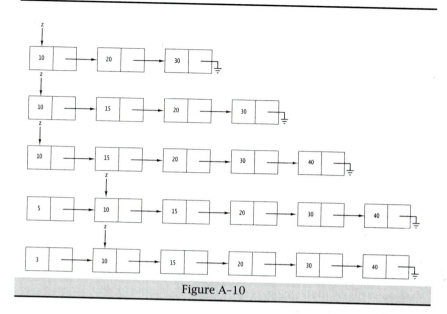

Figure A-10

hands. You might be tempted to fix the problems by adding code to `balance-deposit` and `balance-withdraw`, but that would be wrong. The right place is in `check-number`.

Exercise 5-5

```
(module balance
  (export make-balance balance-amount
    balance-deposit! balance-withdraw!
    balance-transaction-count)
  (define number-of-transactions (make-box 0))
```
`make-balance` and `balance-amount` are unchanged.
```
  (define balance-deposit!
    (lambda (bal amt)
      (check-bal bal)
      (check-number amt)
      (box-set! number-of-transactions
        (add1 (box-ref number-of-transactions)))
      (box-set! bal (+ (box-ref bal) amt))))
```
`balance-withdraw!` is modified similarly.
```
  (define balance-transaction-count
    (lambda ()
      (box-ref number-of-transactions)))
```
The remaining procedures are unchanged.

Exercise 5-6   Because `set-balance` mutates the balance directly, bypassing any error checks. Code that calls `set-balance` directly (often written by programmers who think they are making the program more efficient) would probably introduce new bugs, and might even introduce security holes in the code.

Exercise 5-7   The diagram appears in Figure A-10.

Exercise 5-8

```
(define append!
  (lambda (x y)
```

```
(if (null? x)
    y
    (let ((last (lastcdr x)))
      (set-cdr! last y)
      x))))
```

Exercise 5–9

a. No. The definition of *list* given in Chapter 4 requires us to reach a null list by following the cdrs of the pairs.

b. A circular list, according to the definition given in the text, has the cdr of the last pair containing an arrow to the first pair. This implies that there must be at least one pair.

c.
```
(define circular-list-length
  (lambda (c-list)
    (letrec
      ((helper
         (lambda (current len)
           (if (equal? c-list current)
               len
               (helper (cdr current) (add1 len))))))
      (helper (cdr c-list) 1))))
```
This procedure has a minor bug caused by the use of equal?. This bug is explained in Section 5.2.3.

Exercise 5–10

```
(define structural-equal?%
  (lambda (x y)
    (if (atomic? x)
        (atomic? y)
        (if (string? x)
            (string? y)
            (if (box? x)
                (box? y)
                (and (pair? y)
                     (structural-equal?% (car x) (car y))
                     (structural-equal?% (cdr x) (cdr y))))))))
```

Exercise 5–11

No, because equivalence implies, with mutable data, sharing. For structural equality, we don't even care whether two atomic values have the same type, let alone the same value. It wouldn't be possible to speak of structural equivalence in such a case.

Exercise 5–12

The problem lies in what to do if the key is not found. In this case the program could return null; however, null might be a legitimate value associated with a key (for example, if we're keeping bowling scores, and one player hasn't played any games yet). Another possibility is to halt with an error message, but this is often too brutal. Since assoc *always* returns a pair when it succeeds, and always returns null when it fails, there is never any confusion.

Exercise 5–13

Scheme will complain that higamus is not a pair; assoc% assumes all elements of the list are pairs.

Exercise 5–14

Some error-checking would be useful here, too! Remember to export vend-load from the module.
```
(define vend-load
  (lambda (button name price number)
    (set-car! (list-tail items button)
      (list name price number))))
```

Exercise 5-15

```
(define number-of-customers 0)
(define vend-choose
  (lambda (n)
    (set! number-of-customers
      (remainder (add1 number-of-customers) 50))
    (if (< n (length items))
      (dispense (list-ref items n))
      (display "Tilt!~%"))
    (if (= number-of-customers 0)
      (dispense (list-ref items 0)))))
```

Exercise 5-16

```
(let ((temp a))
  (set! a b)
  (set! b c)
  (set! c temp))
```

Exercise 5-17   We label the frame from the anonymous procedure anon$_0$ by convention, as shown in Figure A-11 (a).

Exercise 5-18   The snapshot is shown in Figure A-11 (b).

Exercise 5-19   `(define k-function (lambda (k) (lambda (x) k)))`

Exercise 5-20 $3f(x)-2g(x)$
```
(combine -
  (combine * f (k-function 3))
  (combine * g (k-function 2)))
```
$4f(x)*g(x)$
```
(combine * (combine * f (k-function 4)) g)
```

Exercise 5-21

```
(define compose
  (lambda (f g) (lambda (x) (f (g x)))))
```

Exercise 5-22   `(define upcase-no-spaces (compose string-upcase no-spaces))`

Exercise 5-23

```
(define remember
  (let
    ((last #f)
     (val #f))
    (lambda (n)
      (if last
        (begin
          (set! val (+ last n))
          (set! last n)
          val)
        (begin
          (set! last n)
          (format #t "First time~%"))))))
```

Exercise 5-24   Look back to the example of `fact` without a helper in Figure 5-22. Like those frames, all the other applications of `fact-helper` connect to the frame named `let`$_0$, just like the frame labeled `fact-helper`$_0$.

Exercise 5-25   The snapshot (Figure A-12) abbreviates names to save space.

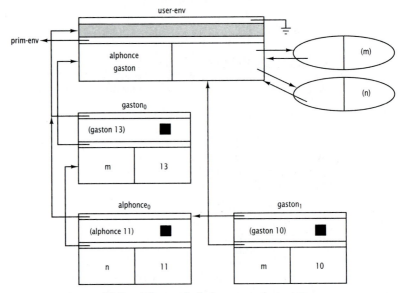

(a) Snapshot for (confusing 4)

(b) Snapshots of alphonce and gaston

Figure A-11

Answers to Chapter 5 Self-Assessment Questions

Question 1   The appearance of the answer will depend upon the Scheme system used. On a typical system, it might look like (6 9 #<box 8>). You might think that the

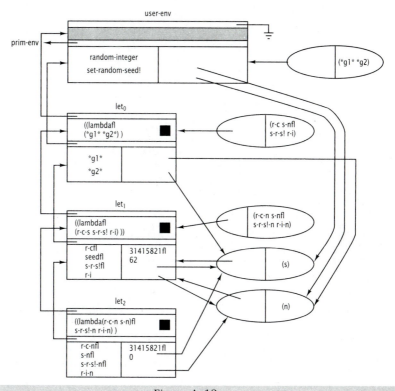

Figure A-12

(box-set! (box-ref c) 8) form would mutate b's box; however, if you draw a picture, you will see that c contains a second box that in turn initially contains 9, and then 8.

Boxes that contain other boxes aren't much use in Scheme, but are absolutely vital in languages such as C and C++.

Question 2   We can represent a box using a pair; the car contains the value in the box, and the cdr isn't used (or contains a special value so that we can implement box? as

```
(define box?
  (lambda (x)
    (and (pair? x) (eqv? (cdr x) '*I-am-a-box*))))
```

This representation wastes a bit of space, but it works.

Question 3   ((5 2) 4)

Question 4   Lists a and b share some memory. Therefore, mutating b mutates a. In fact, a ⇒ (1 2 3 7) afterwards.

Question 5

```
(define delete-odd!
  (lambda (ell)
    (if (null? ell)
        '()
        (if (odd? (car ell))
            (delete-odd! (cdr ell))
```

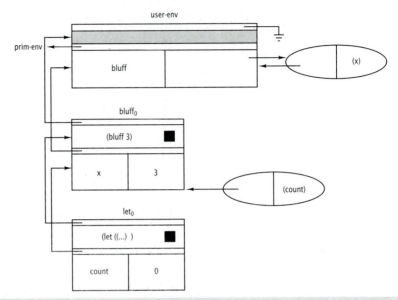

Figure A-13

```
(if (null? (cdr ell))
    ell
    (if (odd? (car (cdr ell)))
        (begin
          (set-cdr! ell
            (delete-odd! (cdr ell)))
          ell)
        (delete-odd! (cdr ell)))))))))
```

Question 6   Naming a functional procedure after a Roman emperor seems peculiar, so our new version, which could have been written in Chapter 2, is named after a somewhat earlier Roman.

```
(define romulus
  (lambda (n)
    (letrec
      ((helper
         (lambda (m x)
           (if (< m n)
               (helper (add1 m)
                 (if (> (remainder m 5) 3)
                     (+ x m)
                     m))
               x))))
      (helper 1 0))))
```

This shorter version demonstrates that mutation doesn't necessarily lead to better programs!

Question 7   (bluff 2) ⇒ 2
(bluff 3) ⇒ 3

Question 8   The snapshot appears in Figure A-13.

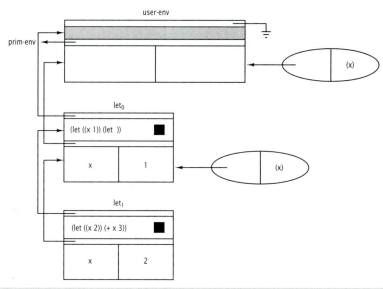

Figure A-14

Question 9

```
(define remember-all
  (let ((inputs '()))
    (lambda (x)
      (set! inputs (cons x inputs))
      inputs)))
```

Question 10

```
(define linear-combination
  (lambda (a b c)
    (lambda (x y z) (+ (* a x) (* b y) (* c z)))))
```

Question 11

```
(define make-sequence
  (lambda (a b)
    (let ((v b))
      (lambda () (set! v (+ v a)) v))))
```

Question 12   The value is 5. The snapshot is in Figure A-14.

Question 13   A letrec should not be used to construct a series of variables, each depending on the previous values. let* is the proper form to use. letrec doesn't guarantee that the forms will be evaluated in the order given!

Answers to Chapter 6 Exercises

Exercise 6-1   Each month the bank sends each customer a statement showing the transactions for the month. This information must therefore be part of the account's state. Therefore we need a message to get the set of transactions or, even better, to map a procedure onto the set of transactions. We also need a message to clear the set of transactions, so that at the beginning of the next month a new set of transactions begins to accumulate.

Exercise 6-2   The state must include the set of course marks (it probably has much additional information, such as the student's name and address, if we are to be able to mail out transcripts). The behavior must include the ability to add a new course, to get the student's marks (as in Exercise 6-1, it is better to map over the course marks), and to compute the student's GPA.

Exercise 6-3

```
((name)
 name)
```

Exercise 6-4

```
((bonus)
 (set! balance (+ balance 5.00))
 balance)
```

Exercise 6-5

```
(define biggest-balance
  (lambda (account-list)
    (letrec
      ((help
        (lambda (x winner win-balance)
          (if (null? x)
              winner
              (if (> ((car x) 'balance) win-balance)
                  (help (cdr x) (car x) ((car x) 'balance))
                  (help (cdr x) winner win-balance))))))
      (if (null? account-list)
          #f
          (help (cdr account-list) (car account-list)
            ((car account-list) 'balance))))))
```

Exercise 6-6   None. Instances of both classes respond to balance.

Exercise 6-7

a. Change the class name to child-account.
b. Add a slot named number-of-withdrawals, initialized to 0.
c. Modify the withdraw method as follows:

```
((withdraw)
 (let
   ((amount (get-argument args 0)))
   (if (> (- balance amount) 0)
       (if (> amount 10)
           (format #t
             "Customer ~a: sorry, withdrawal too large.~%"
             name)
           (if (> number-of-withdrawals 2)
               (format #t
                 "Customer ~a: too many withdrawals.~%"
                 name)
               (begin
                 (set! balance (- balance amount))
                 (set! number-of-withdrawals
                   (add1 number-of-withdrawals))
                 (set! transactions
                   (cons (cons 'withdraw amount)
                     transactions)))))
       (format #t
         "Customer ~a: overdrafts aren't permitted.~%"
         name))
   balance))
```

d. Modify the `clear` method so that it zeros `number-of-withdrawals`.

Exercise 6-8

```
(define-class game-piece
  (class-variables (n 1))
  (class-methods (message . args)
    ((set-n)
     (set! n (get-argument args 0))))
  (constructor-arguments row col)
  (methods (message . args)
    ((ahead)
     (set! row (+ row n)))
    ((diagonal-right)
     (set! col (+ col n))
     (set! row (+ row n)))
    ((diagonal-left)
     (set! col (- col n))
     (set! row (+ row n)))
    ((where)
     (cons row col)))))
```

Did you forget `where`? Since the row and column information is encapsulated, we need some way of getting the position of the piece. (You might argue the same about n).

Exercise 6-9   Add the following clauses to the class definition:

```
(class-variables
  (interest-rate 0.05)
  (maximum-withdrawal 10)
  (maximum-number-of-withdrawals 2))
(class-methods (message . args)
  ((set-rate)
   (set! interest-rate (get-argument args 0)))
  ((set-withdrawal-limits)
   (set! maximum-withdrawal (get-argument args 0))
   (set! maximum-number-of-withdrawals
     (get-argument args 1))))
```

(You might have had two class methods for setting each value separately. Either technique is fine.)

```
((withdraw)
 (let
   ((amount (get-argument args 0)))
   (if (> (- balance amount) 0)
     (if (> amount maximum-withdrawal)
       (format #t
         "Customer ~a: withdrawal too large.~%"
         name)
       (if (> number-of-withdrawals
              maximum-number-of-withdrawals)
         (format #t
           "Customer ~a: too many withdrawals.~%"
           name)
         (begin
           (set! balance (- balance amount))
           (set! number-of-withdrawals
             (add1 number-of-withdrawals))
           (set! transactions
```

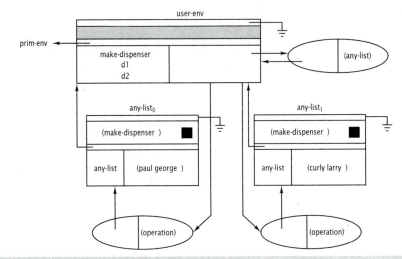

Figure A-15

```
      (cons (cons 'withdraw amount)
        transactions)))))
  (format #t
    "Customer ~a: overdrafts aren't permitted.~%"
    name))
balance))
```

Exercise 6–10   The snapshot appears in Figure A–15.

Exercise 6–11

1. Instances of the class are created by evaluating (dispenser 'make *any-list*) instead of by calling make-dispenser.
2. The only messages understood by the class instances are get and peek. Other messages trigger an error.

Exercise 6–12

```
(define make-location
  (lambda (x y)
    (lambda (message . args)
      (if (eqv? message 'move)
          (begin
            (set! x (+ x (get-argument args 0)))
            (set! y (+ x (get-argument args 1))))
          (if (eqv? message 'distance-from-origin)
              (sqrt (+ (* x x) (* y y))))))))
```

Exercise 6–13   (joel-symbol-equal? 'symb2 'symb2) correctly returns #t. (joel-symbol-equal? 'symb1 'symb2) correctly returns #f. (joel-symbol-equal? 'symb1 'symb2) incorrectly returns #f. (joel-symbol-equal? 'symb2 'symb1) incorrectly returns #t.

This procedure is incorrect, because what it actually does is to check whether its first argument is the symbol symb2. The case form doesn't evaluate symb2 as a key.

Exercise 6–14   It is possible to use case for this purpose; for example,
```
(case my-symbol
```

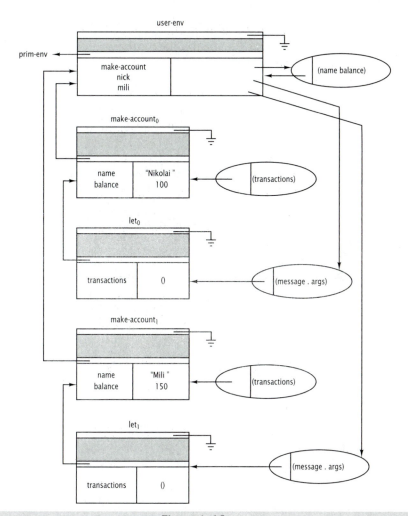

Figure A-16

```
((else) "It was else!")
(else   "It was anything except else"))
```

Keys are enclosed in parentheses, but the else clause starts with the keyword else not enclosed in parentheses.

Exercise 6-15   The snapshot appears in Figure A-16.

Exercise 6-16   device, heater, air conditioning system, lamp; report; schedule; sensor, thermometer, photocell.

An air conditioning system might be one single entity, and would thus seem not to be an appropriate class. On the other hand, it is an external entity, and therefore we should include it.

Exercise 6-17   One-to-one relationships: car has-a steering-wheel, car has-a engine, and wheel has-a tire.

One-to-many relationships: `car` has-a `wheel`, `car` has-a `window`, and `engine` has-a `hose`.

Exercise 6-18   `user` has-a `item`, one-to-many; `shelf` has-a `item`, one-to-many; `item` has-a `shelf`, one-to-one; `magazine` has-a `volume`, one-to-many; `volume` is-a `item`; `book` is-a `item`.

Exercise 6-19   The `delete-event` message creates an event first. Then it calls `remove-from-place` to copy the list of events. When it encounters an event that overlaps, it checks whether the two events are equal.

```
((delete-event)
 (let ((event (create-event)))
   (case (event 'kind)
     ((weekly)
      (let ((day-of-week-pair
             (assv  (event 'day-of-the-week) wevents)))
        (set-cdr! day-of-week-pair
          (remove-from-place event
            (cdr day-of-week-pair)))))
     ((appointment)
      (set! events (remove-from-place event events))))))
;;; remove-from-place checks events, identifying equal
;;; events, and deleting them.
(define remove-from-place
  (lambda (event events)
    (if (null? events)
        (begin
          (display "Could not find ") (event 'print) (newline)
          '())
        (let ((res (e-overlap event (car events))))
          (if (eqv? res 'less)
              (cons event events)
              (if (eqv? res 'grtr)
                  (cons (car events)
                    (remove-from-place event (cdr events)))
                  (if (equal-events? event (car events))
                      (begin
                        (display "Event:") (event 'print)
                        (display " deleted.") (newline)
                        (cdr events))
                      (remove-from-place event
                        (cdr events)))))))))
```

Answers to Chapter 6 Self-Assessment Questions

Question 1

```
(define check-passwords
  (lambda (passwords)
    (lambda (name password)
      (let ((answer (assv name passwords)))
        (if answer
            (let ((rest (cdr answer)))
              (if (> (cdr rest) 2)
                  "No way"
                  (if (eqv? (car rest) password)
                      (begin
                        (set-cdr! rest 0)
```

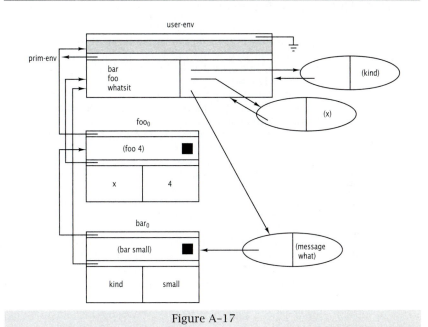

Figure A-17

```
                         "Ok")
                        (begin
                          (set-cdr! rest (add1 (cdr rest)))
                          "Try again"))))
                    "No such name")))))
```

Question 2   The snapshot appears in Figure A-17.

Question 3

```
(define make-ballot-box
  (lambda (ballots)
    (lambda (mess what)
      (case mess
        ((vote)
          (let ((party (assv what ballots)))
            (set-cdr! party (add1 (cdr party)))
            (cdr party)))
        ((tally)
         (if (eqv? what 'all)
           ballots
           (cdr (assv what ballots)))))))))
```

Question 4

```
(define vote-list
  (lambda (parties)
    (if (null? parties)
      '()
      (cons (cons (car parties) 0)
        (vote-list (cdr parties))))))
```

Answers to Chapter 7 Exercises

Exercise 7-1   Here are some possible answers.

1. Expressiveness: If you are familiar with other programming languages, you might say that Scheme lacks arrays and loops. Of course, we get loops via recursion, and arrays (called *vectors*) are part of the language. Formatted output is another lack. (Again, these can be remedied with a good library.)

2. Readability and protection from sloppy mistakes: Some of the names are not well chosen. (No doubt there was a time when you found `lambda` mysterious.) Names like `car` and `cdr` are definitely undesirable. Scheme has some primitives for common combinations of `car` and `cdr`; for example, (cadr x) is shorthand for (car (cdr x)). It's easy to write `cadadr` when you mean `cdadar`, so we don't use them. Parentheses as a way of grouping things are fine (in a correct program, you can just ignore them), but parenthesis errors are hard to track down manually. (Most Scheme systems have elaborate facilities for matching parentheses in the editor, precisely to catch such mistakes.)

3. Orthogonality: you might think that variables and environments ought to be first-class citizens, but they're not. There are good reasons why they should be, and some Scheme systems do make environments first-class. Still, Scheme as we've studied it relegates each of these concepts to second-class status.

Exercise 7-2   Operations: `plus`, `times`, and `divide` take two arguments, and return the appropriate value; `negative` and `sqrt` take one argument; `less` takes two arguments returns a Boolean.

Commands: `variable`, `assign`, `test`, `print`, and `in-sequence`.

One could argue that `program` is a command, though it doesn't really do anything and can only appear once. We would describe `program` more as a barnacle: it attaches itself to the program, and does nothing useful. Many actual programming languages have large numbers of barnacles: little bits of punctuation and keywords that communicate nothing useful to the programmer or to the evaluator.

Exercise 7-3   If we had `remainder`, this would be completely trivial. Unfortunately, we don't. We compute floor(x/17)×17. If this is equal to x, we're fine.

```
(program
    (variable x)
    (assign x ...)
    (test (equal (times (floor (divide x 17)) x) x)
          (print "Number is divisible by 17")
          (print "Number is not divisible by 17")))
```

Exercise 7-4   With `variable` you can introduce variable names without giving them an initial value. As a result, it is easy in a language such as Dream, to write programs that work with variables that are not bound to a value. (This is impossible in Scheme: every form that introduces a variable specifies how it is to be bound to a value.) Some languages offer "help" here, by setting such uninitialized variables to 0. If the programmer had intended the variable to be initialized to, say, 1, it might be difficult to track down the reason why the answer was slightly incorrect!

Exercise 7-5

code:	US-ZIP-code | Can-postal-code | Rur-code
US-zip-code:	main-zip [plus-4]
main-zip:	digit digit digit digit digit
plus-4:	"-" digit digit digit digit
Can-postal-code:	letter digit letter digit letter digit
Rur-code:	"A000" | peasant-letter digit digit digit
digit:	"0" | "1" | "2" | ... | "9"
letter:	"A" | peasant-letter

```
peasant-letter:    "B" | "C" | ... | "Z"
```

Exercise 7-6 a. Valid. b. Valid. c. Invalid. At least one digit must be present. d. Valid, though a bit strange.

Exercise 7-7 It's hard to imagine what (divide (sqrt 4) 3 1) could mean, but it's valid: an expr contains any number of exprs.

Exercise 7-8 You have to look at the family tree upside down for this question to make sense. Each person is the root node of a tree. The only problem is that, assuming we trace everybody's ancestry back to Adam and Eve, everybody who has ever lived is in some way related to them. This means that the 50th generation of offspring from one person almost certainly has some persons in common with the 50th generation of another person.

(Incidentally, some anthropologists trace all of humanity to a few dozen individuals in Africa several million years ago.)

Exercise 7-9

```
("President"
  ("VP Sales"
    ("Sales Dir East")
    ("Sales Dir West")
    ("Sales Dir International")
  ("VP Development"
    ("Dir, Software Division")
    ("Dir, Hardware Division"))))
```

Exercise 7-10 Because a non-null tree, according to our definition, is a list whose car is the item and whose cdr is a list of subtrees. However, c isn't a subtree.

Exercise 7-11

```
(define trav-print
  (lambda (tree)
    (traverse-tree
      (lambda (x) (display x) (newline))
      tree)))
```

Exercise 7-12

```
(define traverse-tree-combine
  (lambda (combiner tree noder null)
    (letrec
      ((traverse-subtree
        (lambda (node-list)
          (if (null? node-list)
            null
            (combiner
              (traverse-tree-combine
                combiner (car node-list) noder null)
              (traverse-subtree (cdr node-list)))))))
      (if (null? tree)
        null
        (combiner (noder (car tree))
          (traverse-subtree (cdr tree)))))))
```

Exercise 7-13

```
call dream-expr-eval: (times 2 (times 3 5))
| call dream-expr-eval: (times 3 5)
| | call dream-expr-eval: 5
| | return from dream-expr-eval: 5
| | call dream-expr-eval: 3
| | return from dream-expr-eval: 3
```

```
| return from dream-expr-eval: 15
| call dream-expr-eval: 2
| return from dream-expr-eval: 2
return from dream-expr-eval: 30
```

Exercise 7-14

```
(define dream-expr-eval
  (lambda (expr)
    (if (expr-constant? expr)
        expr
        (if (expr-variable? expr)
            (variable-value expr)
            (let
              ((op (operator-procedure (expr-op expr)))
               (operands
                 (map dream-expr-eval (expr-args expr))))
              (apply op operands))))))
(define operator-name-list
  (list
    (cons 'plus +)
    (cons 'difference -)
    ...
    (cons 'sqrt sqrt)
    (cons 'negative -)
    (cons 'floor floor)))
```

This version makes it somewhat harder to do error-checking than the version shown in the text. The text version can simply check the length of the list (the code for that isn't shown), but this version needs to keep track of the number of operands each operator expects (perhaps as another item in each entry of operator-name-list).

Exercise 7-15

dream-eval does not check that the first item of the program is the keyword program, which is required, according to the Dream language definition. It can be easily fixed, as follows:

```
(define dream-eval
  (lambda (prog)
    (if (and (pair? prog) (eqv? (car prog) 'program))
        (begin
          (variable-clear)
          (dream-command-sequence (cdr prog)))
        (error "Invalid Dream program"))))
```

Whether it's worth fixing is a different issue. On the one hand, even if the program keyword is misspelled, the meaning of the program will be clear to both the computer and a person. On the other, what if somebody tries to evaluate something that is not a Dream program? A simple error check can prevent a lot of grief!

Exercise 7-16

You might think to try something like this:

```
(define build-increment!
  (lambda (form)
    (if (= (length form) 2)
        (let ((name (car (cdr form))))
          (list 'set! name (list 'add1 name)))
        (begin
          (format #t "Error in build-increment!: ")
          (format #t "incorrect number of arguments.~%")))
    ))
```

It's safe to evaluate (cdr form). If no arguments are given, form will be bound to (increment).

Unfortunately, this form violates the rules of macros, because, in the error case, it returns no form for the evaluator to use. (It returns whatever display returns, which is unspecified.) Therefore, a good way to solve this problem is to use error:

```
(define build-increment!
  (lambda (form)
    (if (or (null? (cdr form))
            (not (null? (cdr (cdr form)))))
        (error 'build-increment!
          "incorrect number of arguments.")
        (let ((name (car (cdr form))))
          (list 'set! name (list 'add1 name))))))
```

This version terminates when it encounters an error so that the evaluator never has to handle an unspecified form.

Exercise 7-17   What happens will depend upon the implementation: it's an error. The variable increment! has not been bound, and therefore has no value. Instead, we placed increment! into the evaluator's table of macros, which, as we've said, has nothing whatsoever to do with variables. Some implementations will report errors such as Unbound variable, or Misuse of macro name. Others might do quite strange things.

Exercise 7-18   As far as the macro is concerned, i is just a symbol. Therefore, Joel gets an error in the form (= x 0), which, for this use of the macro, is (= 'i 0). The primitive = is only defined on numbers, whereas i is a symbol. With macros, we have no way of going from variable names to their values, so we have no way of accessing the value bound to i.

Of course, we could write

```
(define-macro fact
  (lambda (form) (build-fact form)))
(define build-fact
  (lambda (form)
    (list
      'letrec
      '((helper
          (lambda (x)
            (if (= x 0) 1 (* x (helper (sub1 x)))))))
      (list 'helper (car (cdr form))))))
```

but this is cheating. (We're not writing the procedure as a macro, merely writing a macro that writes the procedure.)

Exercise 7-19   In this form, bindings will be bound to ((foo (lambda (x) x))), and body to (foo 3). The first map application yields ((foo #f)), and the second yields ((set! foo (lambda (x) x))). The final form that is evaluated is

```
(let
  ((foo #f))
  (set! foo (lambda (x) x))
  (foo 3))
```

We did not need to use letrec here, since the procedure isn't recursive.

Exercise 7-20   until is the opposite of while, so we can write

```
(define-macro until
  (lambda (form) (build-until form)))
(define build-until
  (lambda (form)
```

```
          (cons 'while%
            (cons (list 'not (car (cdr form)))
              (cdr (cdr form)))))))
```

but this is cheating, and relies on the while% macro to do all the error-checking.

Exercise 7-21

```
(define postage
  (lambda (weight)
    (cond
      ((< weight 30) 15)
      ((and (>= weight 30) (< weight 49)) 17)
      ((and (>= weight 50) (< weight 99)) 22)
      (else (/ weight 4)))))
```

Exercise 7-22

```
(define-macro case%
  (lambda (form) (build-case% form)))
(define build-case%
  (lambda (forms)
    (letrec
      ((handle-test
         (lambda (val test)
           (if (null? test)
             '()
             (cons
               (list 'eqv? val (list 'quote (car test)))
               (handle-test val (cdr test))))))
       (helper
         (lambda (val form)
           (if (null? form)
             '()
             (cons 'if
               (cons
                 (let ((test (car (car form))))
                   (if (eqv? test 'else)
                     #t
                     (cons 'and (handle-test val test))))
                 (cons
                   (cons
                     'begin
                     (cdr (car form)))
                   (if (null? (cdr form))
                     '()
                     (list (helper val (cdr form))))))))))
      (helper (car (cdr forms)) (cdr (cdr forms))))))
```

Exercise 7-23   Using a flag like **procedure** permits the deception. We could design our flag so that no one could type it in, either by using a gensym or by making the flag the result of a cons. In the first case, a gensym is a unique symbol. In the second, no two pairs are equivalent, so Wile E. could not cons a flag that would deceive is-procedure?.

Exercise 7-24   The car of this form is (if foo bar baz). This will not be equivalent to any symbol. Therefore, assv will not find it on the alist.

Exercise 7-25

```
(define-special-form 'let
  (lambda (exp env)
    (let
      ((it (make-two (get-arg exp 1)))
       (eval-arg (lambda (arg) (self-eval arg env))))
      (self-sequence
        (get-rest exp 2)
        (extend-environment
          (car it) (map eval-arg (cdr it)) env)))))
(define make-two
  (lambda (l)
    (cons (map car l)
      (map (lambda (x) (car (cdr x))) l))))
```

Exercise 7-26

```
if { d > 5 } goto 400 &
print { d - 3 } &
goto 500 &
print d &
.....
```

Exercise 7-27   In the worst case, beam-find's helper would have to examine all *n* of the statements.

Exercise 7-28   There are many opportunities for semantic error-checking; for example, do-factor never checks that variable-value has returned a valid value. Then there's syntactic error-checking. Sometimes interpret-command skips elements in the input. In none of these cases does it check to see that proper tokens are in those positions. Also, there's no checking for duplicate line numbers. Overall, a very careless and far-from-production-quality evaluator!

Exercise 7-29   Replace the section on input in interpret-command with

```
((input)
  (beam-inputs (cdr commands)))
```

and include

```
(define beam-inputs
  (lambda (commands)
    (variable-assign (car commands) (read))
    (if (eqv? '! (list-ref commands 1))
      (beam-inputs (list-tail commands 2))
      (list-tail commands 3))))
```

Answers to Chapter 7 Self-Assessment Questions

Question 1

```
command-string:    {command} time-command {command} "S"
command:           time-command | power-command
time-command:      "T" digit {digit}
power-command:     "P" digit
digit:             "0" | "1" | "2" | "3" | "4" |
                   "5" | "6" | "7" | "8" | "9"
```

Question 2   The question doesn't define the tree representation. We'll pick a representation in which leaves are represented as pairs, and nonleaves are represented as a list whose car is the directory name, and whose other elements are the subtrees. We can distinguish the two by asking whether the cdr is a number. You might well have picked a different representation, and written different code.

```
(define delim "\\") ;;; Change this if you don't like DOS.
```

```
(define find-big-files
  (lambda (tree n)
    (letrec
      ((leaf?
        (lambda (node) (number? (cdr node))))
       (helper
        (lambda (t name)
          (if (leaf? t)
            (if (> (cdr t) n)
              (format #t "~a~a~a~%" name delim (car t)))
            (let
              ((myname (car t)))
              (for-each
                (lambda (x)
                  (helper x
                    (string-append name delim myname)))
                (cdr t)))))))
      (helper tree delim))))
```

Question 3

```
(define connect-strings
  (lambda (s1 s2)
    (if (= (string-length s2) 0)
      s1
      (string-append s1 ", " s2))))
(traverse-tree-combine
  connect-strings consolidated (lambda (x) x) "")
```

Question 4

```
(define display-infix
  (lambda (form)
    (if (pair? form)
      (begin
        (display "[")
        (display-infix (car (cdr form)))
        (display (car form))
        (display-infix (car (cdr (cdr form))))
        (display "]"))
      (display form))))
```

Question 5

a. $O(nd)$, where n is the number of variables bound per application, and d is the depth of procedure calls. In most rational programs, n is a very small number, and a good approximation would be $O(d)$. The complexity we measure is worst-case complexity. Most program variables are near the active frame, so the number of frames accessed is generally small. Moreover, Scheme evaluators use specialized techniques to access bindings in the primitive frame.

b. $O(1)$.

Question 6

Any primitive can trivially be written as a special form instead. We could, for example, have a display-special form, as follows:

```
(define-special 'display-special
  (lambda (exp env)
    (show (self-eval (get-arg exp 1) env) env)))
```

However, this is a poor choice. The "normal" use of display-special wouldn't be affected, but we couldn't, for example, write

```
(for-each display-special '(hearts clubs spades diamonds))
```

Procedures are values, and, as such, are first-class citizens. Special forms can only be used in the way that their syntax specifies.

Question 7

```
(define-macro and%
  (lambda (form) (build-and form)))
(define build-and
  (lambda (forms)
    (letrec
      ((helper
         (lambda (forms prev)
           (if (null? forms)
               prev
               (list 'if
                 (car forms)
                 (helper (cdr forms) (car forms))
                 #f)))))
      (helper (cdr forms) #t))))
```

Answers to Chapter 8 Exercises

Exercise 8-1   First, look in the schedule to find that flight 802 is leaving Boston, and then look in the passenger manifest to find that passenger Wilson is on flight 802.

Exercise 8-2   a. columns: item description, number of items desired, stores where that item might be available, suggested price   b. columns: courses taken, year and semester, grade achieved. (Grade-point averages and degrees and diplomas awarded don't quite fit into that framework.)   c. columns: performer name, name of the piece, tape or CD, tape or CD number

Exercise 8-3

a. Students selected

st-no	name	gpa
417	Baker, R.	3.7

b. Students selected-2

st-no	name	gpa

Exercise 8-4   The relational operations are as follows:
1. Join `addresses` and `final-grades` on `st-no`.
2. Select rows with `grade` equal to A from the result of Step 1.
3. Project the result of Step 2 on column `city`.

Exercise 8-5   It doesn't appear that students actually register for courses. Hence a final grade might be submitted for a student who had not paid tuition for a course.

Exercise 8-6   The exact fields will vary, but you should have written something like this:
```
(define accounts
  (make-table
    (cons 'account-no number?) (cons 'name string?)
    (cons 'address string?) (cons 'balance number?)))
```

Exercise 8-7   We could use `string?` to check that the name is valid. We could use `string?` for phone column as well, but that wouldn't help catch many errors. A more sophisticated procedure, which made sure that the phone number consisted of an area code followed by seven digits, would be useful. You might amuse yourself by trying to write one. (You'll need to use some of the string-processing procedures mentioned in Appendix D.)

Exercise 8-8   We need to have three columns: the course, the instructor's name, and a Boolean that tells us whether we've received the marks. We can scan this table and print out the names of all instructors for which the marks-received field was false.

Exercise 8-9   (table-select final-marks 'mark > 85)

Exercise 8-10   Since we build student-averages from students, and since student-no is a key in students, we are certain that there will not be more than one row per student. (If this assumption is violated, all sorts of code will break, so it is a reasonable assumption.)

Contradicting the previous paragraph, no, it isn't good programming style. Whatever can go wrong will go wrong, so it would be much better to put in the check.

Exercise 8-11   First, many possible errors in input to the table ADT consist of type mismatches between the arguments to the procedures and the parameters of the procedures; for example, the car of the pair comprising a column descriptor might not be a symbol. There are other blatant errors—all of these procedures will perform badly (perhaps without complaining) if the table argument is not a table! Another subtle error might occur if a comparison procedure happened to return values other than less-than, equal-to and greater-than. We've stated that the predicate argument to table-select should return a Boolean value, but certainly Scheme won't complain if it doesn't. Selection won't work, however, because a non-Boolean value is never #f! Errors would also occur if one were to assume that secondary arguments are lists (as in rowlist and column-names).

Exercise 8-12   Since there are various algorithms for doing the same task, we want to give our procedure a name that says *what* it does, not *how* it does it; thus, we should have called this procedure sort. We chose not to do so for two reasons: first, many Scheme systems have a sort primitive built in; second, we want to refer to a specific sorting procedure by name.

Exercise 8-13   We're assuming that the values of such columns are the same in both tables, or, at the very least, that if the values differ, we are to take the result from the first column. This is a somewhat dubious assumption, except in the case of the join column, of course.

Exercise 8-14   Recall our suggestion that insertion sorting n items requires around $n^2/2$ comparisons. We have to sort each table separately. The subscriber table has 3×10^6 rows, which means about 4.5×10^{12} comparisons. The long-distance call table has about 15×10^6 rows, which means about 100×10^{12} comparisons. Call the sum 10^{14} comparisons. This will be about 10^8 seconds, which works out to about three years.

The telephone company is not likely to use insertion sort to do its billing.

Exercise 8-15   Insertion sort only takes $O(n)$ comparisons if the original list is already in order. When we join two tables, we get something that is in order, so the sorting operation in table-print is very fast if we print out a table that is the result of a join. Nobody takes the trouble to sort already sorted lists, but it's nice to have fast sorting in this case.

Exercise 8-16   You will want to change layouts so that each column descriptor contains three parts: a column name, a validation procedure, and a format string. For example, the string "~15a" means "write the field in 15 characters", and "~8d" means "write the field as 8 decimal characters". Check your system documentation for format for more details. When you modify the printing code, don't use the layout format for printing the column headers!

Exercise 8-17   We have used some obvious abbreviations in order to save space.

album	label	composer	piece	performer
Surfeit	ABC	Bach	The Unbegun	UWEV Orch.
Surfeit	ABC	Bach	Pervertimento	UWEV Orch.
Surfeit	ABC	Bodobeek	Baroque	UWEV Orch.
Tepidity	SC	Davis	Notes	Chan
Tepidity	SC	Davis	More Notes	Charker
Tepidity	SC	Bodobeek	Scampering	Bodobeek

Exercise 8-18   The 2NF version is as follows:

album	label	piece	performer
Surfeit	ABC	The Unbegun	UWEV Orch.
Surfeit	ABC	Pervertimento	UWEV Orch.
Surfeit	ABC	Baroque	UWEV Orch.
Tepidity	SC	Notes	Chan
Tepidity	SC	More Notes	Charker
Tepidity	SC	Scampering	Bodobeek

piece	composer
The Unbegun	Bach
Pervertimento	Bach
Go For Baroque	Bodobeek
Notes	Davis
More Notes	Davis
Scampering	Bodobeek

Exercise 8-19   The table of composers is already in 3NF, and doesn't need to be shown again. The label is functionally dependent upon the album title.

album	piece	performer
Surfeit	The Unbegun	UWEV Orch.
Surfeit	Pervertimento	UWEV Orch.
Surfeit	Baroque	UWEV Orch.
Tepidity	Notes	Chan
Tepidity	More Notes	Charker
Tepidity	Scampering	Bodobeek

album	label
Surfeit	ABC
Tepidity	SC

Exercise 8-20   The database would be inconsistent if you deleted a row from the table of composers or the table of albums without deleting the corresponding row(s) from the table of pieces. Deleting a row from the table of albums would not do any damage to the other tables.

Answers to Chapter 8 Self-Assessment Questions

Question 1

```
(table-print
  (table-project
    (table-select
      (table-join courses depts 'dept compare-strings)
      'course-name string-equal? "Prin CS I")
    '(dept-name))
  'dept-name compare-strings)
```

Question 2

```
(table-print
  (table-project
    (table-select
      (table-join  cars company 'make compare-strings)
      'model string-equal? "Hog")
    '(name))
  'name compare-strings)
```

Question 3

a. name, number-in-stock, handedness, supplier, type.

b. type and supplier.

c. Two reasons: first, the number changes all the time; second, it is not necessarily unique.

Question 4

```
(make-table
  (cons 'name string?) (cons 'capital string?)
  (cons 'population
    (lambda (x) (and (number? x) (> x 0)))))
```

The only way to prevent an invalid country name from being added is to check for membership in a table of country names. Since this table is supposed to *be* our master table of countries, we appear trapped in an infinite regress.

Question 5

a. $x \leq n$ rows, c columns   b. n rows, $y \leq c$ columns

Question 6

Each entry is unique in its column, because both columns are key columns. Thus, there will only be one row in the output for each key that appears in both columns. The number of rows is $min(m, n)$.

Question 7

We need: a members table, with columns member-number (key), name, address, and phone; a books table, with columns accession-number (key), title, author, and catalog-number; a borrowed table, with columns member-number and accession-number, both of which constitute the key.

Answers to Chapter 9 Exercises

Exercise 9-1

```
(define tlist-append!
  (lambda (t1 t2)
    (if (tlist-empty? t1)
        t2
        (if (tlist-empty? t2)
            t1
            (begin
              (set-cdr! (cdr t1) (car t2))
              (set-cdr! t1 (cdr t2))
              t1)))))
```

Exercise 9-2

```
(define tlist-remove-right!
  (lambda (tlist)
    (if (tlist-empty? tlist)
        (error 'tlist "Attempt to remove from empty tlist")
```

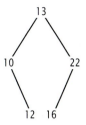

Figure A-18

```
        (let* ((x (cdr tlist))
               (prev (scan-lst (car tlist) x)))
          (set-cdr! tlist prev)
          (set-cdr! prev '())
          (car x)))))
(define scan-lst
  (lambda (lst x)
    (if (null? lst)
        (error 'scan-lst "Ran off list")
        (if (eq? (cdr lst) x)
            lst
            (scan-lst (cdr lst) x)))))
```

Exercise 9-3   Suppose that the program takes 1 hour to run, so that procedure a accounts for a total of 15 minutes, and c accounts for 108 seconds. If we double a's speed, we shave $7\frac{1}{2}$ minutes off the running time of the whole program. If we multiply b's speed by 10, we save about 11 seconds.

Exercise 9-4

a.
```
(search data
  (lambda (x) (> (+ (car x) (cdr x)) 100))
  (lambda (x) x)
  (lambda () 'no-luck))
```
b.
```
(search data
  (lambda (x) (zero? (remainder (cdr x) 3)))
  (lambda (x) x)
  (lambda ()
    (error 'search
      "none is evenly divisible by three")))
```

Exercise 9-5   It's not a BST because the 3 node occurs to the right of the root, which contains 4. The subtree whose root is 6 is a BST, however.

Exercise 9-6   The resulting tree would be, graphically:

and in Scheme:
```
(13 (10 () (12))
    (22 (16) ()))
```

Exercise 9-7

```
(define make-dictionary
  (lambda ()
    (make-box (make-bst))))
(define dictionary-insert
```

```
          (lambda (dict proc)
            (box-set! dict (bst-insert! (box-ref dict) proc))))
        (define dictionary-search
          (lambda (dict item)
            (let ((res (bst-search (box-ref dict) item)))
              (if res
                  res
                  (error 'dictionary-search "Key not found")))))
        (define dictionary-found?
          (lambda (dict key)
            (bst-search (box-ref dict) key)))
        (define dictionary-map
          (lambda (dict proc)
            (bst-traverse (box-ref dict) proc)))
```

Exercise 9-8   4 2 6 1 3 5 7

Exercise 9-9   6 5 4 3 2 1 7 8 9 10 11 or
6 5 7 4 8 3 9 2 10 1 11
Any sequence where the elements on the left subtree occur in decreasing order and those on the right subtree occur in increasing order will do.

Exercise 9-10

```
(define pre-order
  (lambda (tree proc)
    (if (not (bst-empty? tree))
        (begin
          (proc (bst-node-key tree) (bst-node-value tree))
          (pre-order (bst-node-left tree) proc)
          (pre-order (bst-node-right tree) proc)))))
```

The output is
```
My key and value are 7 and seven
My key and value are 5 and five
My key and value are 1 and one
My key and value are 10 and ten
```

Exercise 9-11   Appending the end of the result list creates only n cells, where the input is length n. treesort conses n cells, and then reverse, the tail-recursive version, creates n more, a total of $2n$ cells. But appending to the end of the list examines $n(n-1)/2$ or $O(n^2)$ cells, while treesort only checks n cells during reverse.

Exercise 9-12

```
(define count-false
  (lambda (v)
    (letrec
      ((len (vector-length v))
       (counter
         (lambda (p)
           (if (>= p len)
               0
               (if (vector-ref v p)
                   (counter (add1 p))
                   (add1 (counter (add1 p))))))))
      (counter 0))))
```

Exercise 9-13

```
(define vleft!
  (lambda (vec)
    (letrec
```

```
                ((len-minus-1 (sub1 (vector-length vec)))
                 (left!
                   (lambda (p)
                     (if (< p len-minus-1)
                         (begin
                           (vector-set! vec p
                             (vector-ref vec (add1 p)))
                           (left! (add1 p)))))))
                (if (> (vector-length vec) 0)
                  (let ((first (vector-ref vec 0)))
                    (left! 0)
                    (vector-set! vec
                      (sub1 (vector-length vec)) first)))))))
```

Exercise 9-14

```
      (define deletev
        (lambda (v p)
          (letrec
            ((len (vector-length v))
             (move
               (lambda (i)
                 (if (< i len)
                     (begin
                       (vector-set! v (sub1 i)
                         (vector-ref v i))
                       (move (add1 i)))))))
            (move (add1 p)))))
```

Exercise 9-15   T marks the position of the pivot.
```
          11 3 14 17 23 19 18 21
             <=T      T  >=T
```

Exercise 9-16

```
      (define vector-append
        (lambda (v1 v2)
          (let ((new (make-vector
                       (+ (vector-length v1) (vector-length v2)))))
            (letrec
              ((vector-copy
                 (lambda (from to first past start)
                   (if (< first past)
                       (begin
                         (vector-set! to (+ start first)
                           (vector-ref from first))
                         (vector-copy from to (add1 first)
                                      past start))))))
              (vector-copy v1 new 0 (vector-length v1) 0)
              (vector-copy v2 new 0 (vector-length v2)
                (vector-length v1))
              new))))
```

Exercise 9-17   47 66 24

Exercise 9-18

```
      (define make-stack
        (lambda ()
          (cons (make-vector 100) -1)))
      (define stack-push!
        (lambda (stack item)
```

```
            (set-cdr! stack (add1 (cdr stack)))
            (vector-set! (car stack) (cdr stack) item)))
      (define stack-pop!
        (lambda (stack)
          (if (stack-empty? stack)
            (error 'stack "Attempt to pop from an empty stack")
            (let ((item (vector-ref (car stack) (cdr stack))))
              (set-cdr! stack (sub1 (cdr stack)))
              item))))
      (define stack-empty?
        (lambda (stack)
          (= -1 (cdr stack))))
```

Exercise 9-19

```
      (define reverse-s
        (lambda (lst)
          (letrec
            ((help
               (lambda (coll s)
                 (if (null? coll)
                   (pop-em s)
                   (begin
                     (stack-push! s (car coll))
                     (help (cdr coll) s)))))
             (pop-em
               (lambda (s)
                 (if (stack-empty? s)
                   '()
                   (let ((top (stack-pop! s)))
                     (cons top (pop-em s)))))))
            (help lst (make-stack)))))
```

Exercise 9-20   23 24 47

It is instructive to compare this output with that produced by stacks.

Exercise 9-21   After we execute the first add, the operand stack contains 4 9. We then perform a multiply, giving us 36 on the operand stack. We now push 11 and add, getting 45. Finally, we push 2 and multiply, obtaining 90.

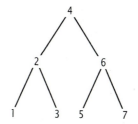

Figure A-19

Answers to Chapter 9 Self-Assessment Questions

Question 1

One such sequence is: 4 2 6 1 3 5 7, and the resulting tree is in Figure A-19.

You can generate the sequence by writing down a well-balanced tree and reading off the nodes in a pre-order traversal.

Question 2

```
(define make-queue
  (lambda ()
    (cons -1 (make-vector 100))))
(define queue-insert!
  (lambda (q item)
    (let
      ((recent (car q))
       (v (cdr q)))
      (if (>= recent 99)
        (error 'queue-insert!
          "Attempt to insert into a full queue")
        (begin
          (let ((new (add1 recent)))
            (vector-set! v new item)
            (set-car! q new)))))))
(define queue-remove!
  (lambda (q)
    (let
      ((recent (car q))
       (v (cdr q)))
      (if (<= recent 0)
        (error 'queue-remove!
          "Attempt to remove from an empty queue")
        (begin
          (letrec
            ((out (vector-ref v 0))
             (move
               (lambda (i)
                 (if (<= i recent)
                   (begin
                     (vector-set! v (sub1 i)
                       (vector-ref v i))
                     (move (add1 i)))))))
            (move 1)
```

```
                 (set-car! q (sub1 recent))
                 out))))))
          (define queue-empty?
            (lambda (queue)
              (<=  (car queue) 0)))
```

Question 3

a.
```
     (define list-of-procedures '())
     (define make-triple
       (lambda (name procedure number)
         (list name procedure number)))
     (define triple-name car)
     (define triple-procedure (lambda (x) (car (cdr x))))
     (define triple-number (lambda (x) (car (cdr (cdr x)))))
     (define triple-increment!
       (lambda (t)
         (set-car! (cdr (cdr t))
           (add1 (triple-number t)))
         (triple-number t)))
     (define enter-procedure
       (lambda (n p l)
         (cons (make-triple n p 0) l)))
     (define find-procedure
       (lambda (n l)
         (let ((r (assv n l)))
           (if r
             (triple-increment! r)
             r))))
```

b. The compare procedure is:
```
     (define compare
       (lambda (triple1 triple2)
         (let ((v1 (triple-number triple1))
               (v2 (triple-number triple2)))
           (if (< v1 v2)
             'less-than
             (if (> v1 v2)
               'greater-than
               'equal-to)))))
```

c. $O(n)$

d. $O(\lg n)$

Question 4 The tree appears in Figure A-20.

Question 5 Any strictly increasing or decreasing sequence of numbers will generate an unbalanced tree where all elements occur as right branches or, respectively, left branches of the tree. The resulting tree search will perform no better than a linear list, since the tree is effectively a linear list.

Question 6

```
     (define vright!
       (lambda (vec)
         (letrec
           ((len (vector-length vec))
            (right!
              (lambda (p)
                (if (> p 0)
                  (begin
```

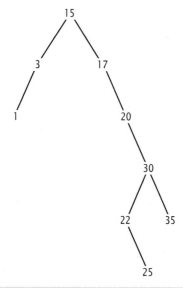

Figure A-20

```
          (vector-set! vec p (vector-ref vec (sub1 p)))
          (right! (sub1 p)))))))
  (if (> len 1)
    (let ((last (vector-ref vec (sub1 len))))
      (right! (sub1 len))
      (vector-set! vec 0 last))))))
```

Answers to Chapter 10 Exercises

Exercise 10–1   We only have to change the first rule (these rules are modular!):

IF the student has CS prerequisites **AND** the student has calculus prerequisites **AND** the student has taken Physics 12, **THEN** the student can take CS128.

Exercise 10–2   a. #t   b. #t; it is not required that ? must match the *same* value in each position. c. error; `simple-match?` will attempt to evaluate (car target). Our matchers don't check whether they are given lists, so that they will be easier to understand. This is, of course, not good programming style.

Exercise 10–3
```
(define simple-match?
  (lambda (pattern target)
    (cond
      ((null? pattern) (null? target))
      ((null? target) #f)
      ((pair? (car pattern))
       (and (pair? (car target)))
       (simple-match? (car pattern) (car target))
       (simple-match? (cdr pattern) (cdr target)))
      ((eqv? (car pattern) '?)
       (simple-match? (cdr pattern) (cdr target)))
      ((equal? (car pattern) (car target))
```

```
                          (simple-match? (cdr pattern) (cdr target)))
                     (else #f))))
```

Compare this with our definition of equal? in Chapter 5.

Exercise 10-4

```
(define select-faculty
  (lambda (students fac)
    (if (null? students)
        '()
        (if (var-match? (list '?x '?y fac '?z)
                        (car students))
            (cons (car students)
              (select-faculty (cdr students) fac))
            (select-faculty (cdr students) fac)))))
(define select-arts
  (lambda (students)
    (select-faculty students 'arts)))
```

Exercise 10-5

The input pattern of m-project-table can include things other than pattern variables, of course. Thus, if we want a phone list for arts students, we can write:
(m-project-table student-list '(?a ?b arts ?c) '(?b ?c))

Exercise 10-6

```
(define m-join-table
  (lambda (in1 in2 patin1 patin2 patout)
    (letrec
      ((join
         (lambda (in1s)
           (if (null? in1s)
               '()
               (append
                 (mapj (lambda (x) (join1 (car in1s) x)) in2)
                 (join (cdr in1s))))))
       (mapj
         (lambda (proc lst)
           (if (null? lst)
               '()
               (let ((v (proc (car lst))))
                 (if (null? v)
                     (mapj proc (cdr lst))
                     (cons v (mapj proc (cdr lst))))))))
       (join1
         (lambda (r1 r2)
           (let
             ((m1 (var-match? patin1 r1))
              (m2 (var-match? patin2 r2)))
             (if (and m1 m2
                      (consistent-alists m1 m2))
                 (substitute-alist
                   (substitute-alist patout m1)
                   m2)
                 '())))))
      (join in1))))
(define consistent-alists
  (lambda (l1 l2)
    (if (null? l1)
        #t
```

```
        (let ((look (assv (car (car 11)) 12)))
          (if (or (not look)
                  (eqv? (cdr look) (cdr (car 11))))
              (consistent-alists (cdr 11) 12)
              #f)))))
```

Exercise 10-7

```
(define question
  (lambda (declare)
    (let ((m (var-match? '(?a ?b ?c ?d) declare)))
      (if (not m)
          (display "Hey, not a sentence")
          (substitute-alist '(?c ?a ?b ?d) m)))))
```

Exercise 10-8   a. (? is here)   b. (?? is ?? here)   c. (?? not ?x this ??)

Exercise 10-9   We will need a sixth table, `timetable`, that contains the times for each section of each course. We'd join `timetable` and `courses` on *two* columns, `course` and `section`. (DBScheme only lets us join on one column; it's conceptually trivial but a fair bit of coding to modify it to handle more than one column.) We would then sort by student number, and scan the resulting table to check for conflicts in each group of rows representing the courses for one student.

Exercise 10-10   (We said go to the library!) Certainly you should look for RSA in a book on encryption, for LZW in a book on data compression or coding, and Ethernet in texts on communication.

Exercise 10-11   a. Valid, but false. The argument is based on a false premise: that eye color matters in discussion of morality.   b. You may agree that the conclusion is true. However, the previous statements are just verbiage, and don't lead to any conclusion at all (though, if spoken in an appropriately enthusiastic way, they may well be able to sway an audience!).

Exercise 10-12   a. student(Bill)   b. forall x, computer(x) implies runs(x, DOS)   c. exists x, computer(x) and runs(x, DOS)   d. forall x, (computer(x) and runs(x, DOS)) implies runs(x, Megacalc)

Exercise 10-13   a. forall y, forall y, (computer(x) andprogram(y)) implies runs(x, y)   b. exists y, program(y) and forall x, computer(x) implies runs(x, y)   c. forall x, computer(x) implies exists y, program(y)) and runs(x, y)   d. exists y, program(y) and forall x, computer(x) implies not runs(x, y)

Exercise 10-14   a. There is a food that no persons likes.   b. All foods are liked by someone. c. Some persons like all foods.

Exercise 10-15   a. ((can-run ?x DOS) (computer ?x))
b. ((can-run ?x MegaCalc) (computer ?x) (can-run ?x DOS))
c. Two rules are needed:
((can-run ?x MegaCalc) (computer ?x) (can-run ?x DOS))
((can-run ?x MegaCalc) (computer ?x) (can-run ?x UNIX))

Exercise 10-16

```
((same-division ?x ?y) (indirectly-supervises ?z ?x)
                       (indirectly-supervises ?z ?y))
((same-division ?x ?y) (indirectly-supervises ?x ?y))
((same-division ?x ?y) (indirectly-supervises ?y ?x))
```

Exercise 10-17   (can-take bill cs100) will fail because the complete list of facts only includes (can-take ?x cs100).

Exercise 10-18   This set of flights won't work for finding the flights between Vancouver and New York. This is because as `backward` searches for all connections between Vancouver and New York (the initial goal). There is no direct flight (the first connect rule), so `backward` tries the second `connect` rule. Eventually that rule binds ?z to newyork, which generates the initial query. Thus, backward loops infinitely.

Exercise 10–19

```
(define phone-of-student
  (lambda (student)
    (table-find students 'student-no = student 'phone)))
```

Exercise 10–20

```
(define student-of-phone
  (lambda (phone)
    (table-find students 'phone
      string-equal? phone 'phone)))
```

Answers to Chapter 10 Self-Assessment Questions

Question 1

```
((?x . sardines))
#f
#f
((?x . program) (?y . computers))
```

Question 2

We assume the predicate knows(*person*, *language*). This problem could also be solved using the predicate knows-Scheme(*person*).

a. forall x, takes(x, CS124) implies knows(x, Scheme).   b. forall x, my-friend(x) implies not knows(x, Scheme).   c. forall x, knows(x, Scheme) implies exists y, knows(x, y) and notequal(y,Scheme).

Question 3

The steps are the following:
1. likes-to-program(Don).
2. published(Don, The-Complexity-of-Megasort, Bitty-Bytes).
3. published(Don, Scheme-is-Fun, Computers-for-Idiots).
4. refereed(Bitty-Bytes).
5. From (2) and (4), publishes(Don).
6. From (1) and (5), computer-scientist(Don).

Step 3 is a dead end; however, we don't know that at the time.

Question 4

The steps are the following:
1. likes-to-program(Don).
2. Try publishes(Don).
3. published(Don, Scheme-is-Fun, Computers-for-Idiots).
4. refereed(Computers-for-Idiots). Failure: dead end.
5. published(Don, The-Complexity-of-Megasort, Bitty-Bytes).
6. refereed(Bitty-Bytes).
7. We can conclude publishes(Don).
8. We can therefore conclude computer-scientist(Don).

Question 5

a	*b*	not a and b
false	false	false
false	true	true
true	false	false
true	true	false

Answers to Chapter 11 Exercises

Exercise 11–1   #x9612 and #xBADFACE, respectively.

Exercise 11–2 $9 = 1 * 8^1 + 1 * 8^0$ is 11 in octal, $65 = 1 * 8^2 + 1 * 8^0$ is 101 in octal, and $128 = 2 * 8^2$ is 200 in octal.

Exercise 11-3

```
(define read-hex-number
  (lambda ()
    (letrec
      ((rdn
        (lambda (x)
          (let ((d (read-hex-digit)))
            (if (< d 0)
                x
                (rdn (+ (* 16 x) d)))))))
      (rdn 0))))
(define read-hex-digit
  (lambda ()
    (let ((ch (read-char)))
      (if (or (char<? ch #\0) (char>? ch #\9))
          (if (or (char<? ch #\A) (char>? ch #\F))
              -1
              (+ 10 (- (char->integer ch)(char->integer #\A))))
          (- (char->integer ch) (char->integer #\0))))))
```

Exercise 11-4   The trick is to recurse on n, rather than the number.
```
(define write-leading
  (lambda (x n)
    (if (> n 0)
        (begin
          (write-leading (quotient x 10) (sub1 n))
          (write-digit (remainder x 10))))))
```

Exercise 11-5   Subtracting a number from all 1's is the one's complement. Therefore the two's complement will be 1 greater.

Exercise 11-6   On a 4-bit machine, zero is represented both by 0000 and 1111.

Exercise 11-7   Any binary number system represents an even number of integers. There is an odd number of integers from $-k$ to k, so the negation of the largest positive integer can't be represented.

Exercise 11-8

a. The instruction is 016043AC or
   0000 0001 0110 0000 0100 0011 1010 1100.
b. The instruction is 89200079 or
   1000 1001 0010 0000 0000 0000 0111 1001.

Exercise 11-9   All values are shown in hexadecimal.
```
00: 004000B0
01: 005000C0
02: 8E600045
03: 02600060
04: 00400090
05: 04000070
06: 004000A0
07: 9D400000
08: A0000000
09: 0000002E
0A: 0000004D
0B: 0000000A
0C: 0000000C
```

The output will be 46 decimal, 2E in hexadecimal.

Exercise 11-10   The first loads the contents of memory location 1 into register 5, while the second loads the value 1 into register 5.

Exercise 11-11

```
        (quo 3 2 9)   ; quotient in r3
        (rem 4 2 9)   ; remainder in r4
        (add 3 4 5)   ; result in r3
```

Exercise 11-12   (sub 5 0 4)

Exercise 11-13

```
; Display (as a character) (min foo bar).
start   (load 8 foo)      ; Get foo.
        (load 9 bar)      : Get bar
        (lss? 7 8 9)      ; Compare with bar.
        (jtrue 8 show)    ; Jump to show if foo<bar.
        (copy 8 9)        ; We will display bar.
show    (outchar 8)       ; Display it.
        (halt)            ; Stop execution.
foo     (dataword 65)     ; Code for #\A.
bar     (dataword 67)     ; Code for #\C.
```

Note that if you change, in the original, lss? to gtr? and jfalse to jtrue, the meaning of the program has changed, but it turns out not to affect the result because if they're equal it doesn't matter which you pick. In some other context, however, it *would* matter.

Exercise 11-14   #x00601002, a load instruction that references memory location #x1000.

Exercise 11-15   When the call instruction transfers control to 100, pcr contains 51. At the jump instruction, pcr contains 51, so the jump instruction calculates an effective address that is the sum of the contents of register 0, which contains 0, and the contents of pcr, which contains 51. The jump instruction sets the PC to its effective address, so the next instruction will come from location 51.

Exercise 11-16

```
(define-symbols (veca . #x1000) (vecb . #x1400))
;;; r3: length, r4: temporary counter and index register
diff        (copy 4 0)              ; Initialize counter.
diff-help   (lss? 5 4 3)
            (jfalse 5 diff-done)    ; if so, done
            (load 6 veca 4)         ; load (vector-ref veca i)
            (load 7 vecb 4)         ; load (vector-ref vecb i)
            (sub 6 6 7)             ; difference
            (store 6 vecc 4)        ; store
            (add 4 4 1)             ; incr i
            (jump 0 diff-help)      ; loop
diff-done   (jump 0 0 pcr)          ; return
```

Exercise 11-17

```
;;; r3: n, r4: result, r2: contains 2
fib         (store pcr 0 sr)    ; push return address
            (add sr sr 1)
            (lss? 5 3 2)        ; if n < 2 then...
            (jtrue 5 fib1-done) ; ... jump to fib1-done.
            (sub 3 3 1)         ;
            (store 3 0 sr)      ; push n-1 onto stack
            (add sr sr 1)
            (call pcr fib)      ; compute F_(n-1) in r4
            (sub sr sr 1)       ; pop n-1 off stack
            (load 3 0 sr)
            (sub 3 3 1)         ; n-2
```

```
                    (store 4 0 sr)          ; push F_(n-1) onto stack
                    (add sr sr 1)
                    (call pcr fib)          ; compute F_(n-2) in r4
                    (sub sr sr 1)           ; pop F_(n-1) into r5
                    (load 5 0 sr)
                    (add 4 5 4)             ; add
                    (sub sr sr 1)           ; pop return address
                    (load pcr 0 sr)
                    (jump 0 0 pcr)
        fib1-done   (copy 4 1)              ; result is 1
                    (sub sr sr 1)           ; pop return address
                    (load pcr 0 sr)
                    (jump 0 0 pcr)          ; return
```

Exercise 11-18

```
        wpn         (store pcr 0 sr)         ; n comes in register 2
                    (add sr sr 1)
                    (eql? 4 2 0)             ; if n = 0 then...
                    (jtrue 4 wpn-done)       ; ... jump to wpn-done.
                    (store 2 0 sr)           ; push 2 onto the stack
                    (add sr sr 1)            ; increment stack pointer
                    (load 3 ten)
                    (quo 2 2 3)
                    (call pcr wpn)
                    (sub sr sr 1)            ; result in 3
                    (load 2 0 sr)            ; pop n off stack
                    (load 3 ten)             ; now in reg2
                    (rem 3 2 3)              ; now in reg2
                    (call pcr write-digit)   ; result in 3
                    (sub sr sr 1)
                    (load pcr 0 sr)
                    (jump 0 0 pcr)
        wpn-done    (sub sr sr 1)
                    (load pcr 0 sr)
                    (jump 0 0 pcr)
        ten         (dataword 10)
```

Exercise 11-19   Whenever a procedure is called, its arguments are stored in the registers. When a recursive procedure calls itself, the arguments, if needed again, are stored on the stack. The growing memory use of a recursive procedure results from storing these values on the stack. Thus the frames in the environment model appear in the registers at first, and then on the stack, if the procedure is not tail-recursive.

Exercise 11-20   You will need *rows*, the number of rows in the image.
```
(define draw-line%-x-y
    (lambda (x y) ;; in (x,y) coordinates
        (basic-draw-line
            current-x (- *rows* current-y) x (- *rows* y))
        (set! current-col x)
        (set! current-row y)))
```

Exercise 11-21

```
display-ratio (quo 5 4 3)            ;; sum in r4, n in r3
              (outnum 5)
              (load 5 dot)
              (outchar 5)
              (rem 5 4 3)
```

```
                        (load 6 hundred)
                        (mpy 5 5 6)
                        (quo 5 5 3)
                        (outnum 5)
                        (jump 0 0 pcr)
           hundred      (dataword 100)
           dot          (dataword 46)  ;#\.
```

Exercise 11-22

```
           add3   (load 3 three)
                  (add 8 2 3)
                  (jump 0 0 pcr)
           three  (dataword 3)
```

Tricky point here: you have to make a dataword to hold the constant 3; writing (add 0 3) would add the contents of *location* 3 to register 0. It is extremely unlikely (literally a 4-billion-to-one chance) that location 3 would happen to contain the number 3.

Exercise 11-23

```
           a-plus-b-plus-one  (add 8 2 3)
                              (add 8 8 1)
                              (jump 0 0 pcr)
```

Exercise 11-24

```
           fact (eql? 2 1)    ;; r2: n, r3: a
                (jtrue 2 done)
                (mpy 3 2 3)
                (sub 2 2 1)
                (jump 0 fact)
           done (copy 8 3)
                (jump 0 0 pcr)
```

Answers to Chapter 11 Self-Assessment Questions

Question 1

```
           > (write-positive-hex-number 26)
           A> (write-positive-hex-number 16)
           >
```

Question 2

```
                        (load 5 p)
                        (jtrue 5 true)
                        (load 5 d)
                        (load 5 two)
                        (add 5 5 6)
                        (jump 0 done)
           true  (load 5 c)
                 (load 6 one)
                 (add 5 5 6)
           done  (halt)
           one   (dataword 1)
           two   (dataword 2)
```

Question 3

```
           while (load 5 i)
                 (gtr? 6 5 0)
                 (jfalse 6 done)
                 (load 6 two)
                 (add 6 5 6)
```

```
               (store 6 j)
               (sub 5 5 one)
               (jmp 0 while)
done     (halt)
two      (dataword 2)
```

This code can be made more efficient by putting the value 2 into register 7 before the while form begins so the load instruction occurs only once.

Question 4

```
cubes      (copy 5 0)  ; result
           (copy 6 1)  ; counter
sum-loop (gtr? 7 6 4)
           (jtrue 7 sum-done)
           (mpy 7 6 6)
           (mpy 7 7 6)
           (add 5 7 5)
           (add 6 6 1)
           (jump 0 sum-loop)
sum-done (jump 0 0 pcr)
```

Question 5   a. 10 b. 5 c. here (jump 0 here)

Question 6   foo must push its return address before calling bar, as well as push z on the stack. Before calling itself, bar must push a and its return address. baz doesn't push any values, because it doesn't call any procedures.

Answers to Chapter 12 Exercises

Exercise 12-1

```
           ;;; args in 2: x, 3: y, result in 3, reg. 1 contains 1
append     (store pcr 0 sr)
           (add sr sr 1)
           (null? 4 2)
           (jtrue 4 append-done)
           (store 2 0 sr)       ; push reg2 onto the stack
           (add sr sr 1)        ; increment stack register
           (cdr 2 2)
           (call pcr append)    ; result in reg3
           (sub sr sr 1)        ; pop x off stack
           (load 2 0 sr)        ; now in reg2
           (car 2 2)            ; (car x)
           (cons 3 2 3)         ; (cons (car x) (append...
           (sub sr sr 1)
           (load pcr 0 sr)
           (jump 0 0 pcr)
append-done (sub sr sr 1)
           (load pcr 0 sr)
           (jump 0 0 pcr)
```

Exercise 12-2

```
               ;;; args in tmp0: list, tmp1:n, result in tmp0
list-ref       (eql? tmp2 tmp1 0)
               (jtrue tmp2 list-ref-done)
               (sub tmp1 tmp1 rone)
               (cdr tmp0 tmp0)
               (jump 0 list-ref)
list-ref-done  (car tmp0 tmp0)
               (jump 0 0 pcr)
```

Exercise 12–3

```
;;; tmp1: target, tmp2: alist, tmp3: result
assv       (null? tmp0 tmp2)      ; End of list?
           (jtrue tmp0 assv-not)
           (copy tmp0 tmp2)       ; Get the first pair...
           (car tmp0 tmp0)        ; ...of the alist.
           (copy tmp3 tmp0)       ; Now get the symbol...
           (car tmp3 tmp3)        ; ...(car) of the pair.
           (eqv? tmp3 tmp3 tmp1)  ; Is this it?
           (jtrue tmp3 assv-in)   ; Jump if so.
           (cdr tmp2 tmp2)        ; Look at next pair.
           (jump 0 assv)          ; Try again.
assv-not   (load tmp3 false)      ; Didn't find it *sigh*.
           (jump 0 0 pcr)
assv-in    (copy tmp3 tmp0)       ; Get value from pair.
           (jump 0 0 pcr)
```

Exercise 12–4   We must get rid of the tag part; otherwise, the wrong memory address will be accessed. The instructions

```
(load 8 tagdivide)
(remainder 5 5 8)
```

(where `tagdivide` is as in the main text) will do the job. We might take the opportunity here to check that we are indeed taking the car or cdr of a pair, by looking at the tag value. Scheme systems in fact do this.

Exercise 12–5   See the code for the imperative evaluator in the Software Package.

Exercise 12–6

```
(define copy-file
  (lambda ()
    (let ((command (program-arguments)))
      (file-copy (car (cdr command))
        (car (cdr (cdr command)))))))
```

Error-checking would be nice, too.

Exercise 12–7

```
(define file-copy
  (lambda (sources destination)
    (let
      ((f2 (channel-open destination #f #t)))
      (letrec
        ((copy
          (lambda (from)
            (let ((ch (channel-read from)))
              (if (eqv? ch 'eof)
                (channel-close from)
                (begin
                  (channel-write f2 ch)
                  (copy))))))
        (open-copy
          (lambda (source)
            (copy (channel-open source #f #f)))))
        (map open-copy sources)
        (channel-close f2)))))
```

Exercise 12–8   We don't, but in that case the length of every file would have to be a multiple of the block size. Early operating systems actually worked this way. As a result, programs either had to check for a special "end-of-file" character, or they would

Exercise 12-9
get a slew of spaces or nulls (or something) at the end of the file.

The subtrees of a tree must be distinct. Therefore, no entry can be in more than one directory.

Practical operating systems often allow this restriction to be violated, or at least bent, which vastly complicates programs that traverse the tree structure (e.g., to back up all current files onto magnetic tape).

Answers to Chapter 12 Self-Assessment Questions

Question 1

```
;;; tmp0: to, tmp1: from, tmp2: in, tmp3: result
subst       (store pcr 0 sr)
            (add sr sr rone)
            (null? tmp3 tmp2)
            (jfalse tmp3 subst-cont)
            (copy tmp3 tmp2)
            (jump 0 subst-done)
subst-cont (pair? tmp3 tmp2)
            (jtrue tmp3 subst-pair)
            (eqv? tmp3 tmp1 tmp2)
            (jtrue tmp3 subst-rep)
            (copy tmp3 tmp2)
            (jump 0 subst-done)
subst-rep  (copy tmp3 tmp tmp0)
            (jump 0 subst-done)
subst-pair (store tmp2 0 sr)      ; push reg2 onto the stack
            (add sr sr rone)       ; increment stack register
            (car tmp2 tmp2)
            (call pcr subst)       ; result in tmp3
            (sub sr sr rone)       ; pop n off stack
            (load tmp2 0 sr)       ; now in reg2
            (store tmp3 0 sr)
            (add sr sr rone)       ; increment stack register
            (cdr tmp2 tmp2)
            (call pcr subst)       ; result in tmp3
            (sub sr sr rone)       ; pop car-result off stack
            (load tmp4 0 sr)       ; now in reg2
            (cons tmp3 tmp4 tmp3)
            (jump 0 subst-done)
subst-done (sub sr sr rone)
            (load pcr 0 sr)
            (jump 0 0 pcr)
```

Question 2

If our translation were very sloppy, then it might not handle tail recursion properly, causing the stack to grow each time we call a procedure. Then even a procedure such as

```
(define doit
  (lambda (n)
    (if (> n 0) (doit (- n 1))))))
```

could overflow the stack if n were large.

Question 3

The advantages can be expressed in one word: efficiency. Register access is fast and compact. The disadvantages are many. Code is no longer modular; bugs in one procedure can easily affect another. Even behavior that is not a bug can cause problems, if, for example, we don't notice that a certain piece of code changes the contents of a particular register. We can certainly run out of registers (though there are actually enough registers for our imperative evaluator).

Question 4   A file is a collection of data on disk (or perhaps on another kind of device). A channel is a program's connection to a file or device, and is thus a program's abstraction of a file.

Appendix B

Scheme Reference Summary

Could we teach taste or genius by rules, they would be no longer taste and genius.
— Sir Joshua Reynolds (1723–92), *Discourses on Art*

This appendix includes a summary of the features of Scheme used in this book. Scheme is defined by a document informally called the *Report*, or $R^n RS$. The current version is known as the *Revised^4 Report on the Algorithmic Language Scheme*, because it is the fourth revision.[1] Many Scheme evaluators provide additional features not described in $R^n RS$.

This appendix does not give complete rules for the language, or for the additional features your Scheme evaluator might provide. If you want to know more, consult $R^n RS$ or the documentation for your Scheme evaluator. We have tried to provide sufficient information to answer most of the questions you might encounter when programming.

Some of the features discussed in this book are not part of standard Scheme, though all Scheme evaluators can be modified (by loading a special file) to support these "extended" features. Extended features are marked in this appendix with the flag [Extension].

B.1 Lexical Rules

Scheme's lexical rules define how a Scheme program may be written on paper or in a computer file.

Upper- and lowercase forms of letters are never distinguished except within character and string constants. For example, Foo is the same identifier as FOO and foo, and #x1AB is the same number as #X1ab. Most Scheme programmers prefer lowercase letters, except for the digits of a hexadecimal number.

B.1.1 Tokens, Whitespace, and Comments   The basic elements of any Scheme program are tokens such as identifiers, numbers, and parentheses.

Whitespace characters are spaces and newlines. Implementations typically provide additional whitespace characters such as tab or page break. Whitespace is used for improved readability and as necessary to separate tokens from each other, but is otherwise insignificant. Whitespace may occur between any two tokens, but not within a token. Whitespace may also occur inside a string, where it is significant; for example, "Hello world " is not the same string as "Helloworld".

A semicolon (;) indicates the start of a comment. The comment continues to the end of the line on which the semicolon appears. Comments are invisible to Scheme, but the end of the line is visible as whitespace. This prevents a comment from appearing in the middle of an identifier or number.

Although it is not required by the language, most Scheme programmers use the number of semicolons on a comment to control how it is to be displayed. "Pretty-printing" programs can use this information to produce more readable code listings.

---

[1] The appendix has been adapted from $R^n RS$.

1A comment beginning with one semicolon is placed to the right of a code line.

2A comment beginning with two semicolons is indented in the same way as a line of code.

3A comment beginning with three or more semicolons is indented to the left margin.

B.1.2 Identifiers   Identifiers are used as names in `define` and `let` forms. The precise rules for identifiers will vary from evaluator to evaluator, but all evaluators treat as an identifier any sequence of letters, digits, and the following characters:

```
+ - . * / < = > ! ? : $ _ & ~   ^
```

provided that the sequence cannot be interpreted as a number.

By convention, Scheme programmers generally separate words in an identifier with minus signs. A Scheme programmwer would normally write `draw-circle` and not `draw_circle`.

The following identifiers are special keywords, and should not be used as variables.

`=>`	`do`	`or`
`and`	`else`	`quasiquote`
`begin`	`if`	`quote`
`case`	`lambda`	`set!`
`cond`	`let`	`unquote`
`define`	`let*`	`unquote-splicing`
`delay`	`letrec`	

The following keywords are not discussed in this appendix; see $R^n RS$ for more information.

`=>`	`delay`	`do`
`quasiquote`	`unquote`	`unquote-splicing`

The following identifiers are [Extension] special keywords, and should not be used as variables.

```
define-macro    define-class    module
```

B.2   Scheme Values and Their Types

The type of a value determines what operations may be performed on that value. Scheme provides the following types:

- Boolean
- character
- number
- procedure
- string
- vector
- null
- symbol
- pair
- port
- box [Extension]
- void [Extension]

Values of these types are known as first-class citizens, meaning that they can be the values of variables (see Section B.4), passed as arguments to procedures, or returned as the result of a procedure.

Strings, vectors, pairs, and boxes are mutable. For each of these types, appropriate mutation primitives are provided.

There are type-checking primitive procedures for each of these types. Only one of these type-checking procedures will return *true* for any given value; for example, it is impossible for a value to be both a number and a vector.[2]

B.3 External representations of Scheme values

The external representation of a Scheme value is a sequence of characters that is converted by `read` into the value, and is produced by applying `display` to the value.

The following kinds of Scheme values have external representations.
- Booleans
- numbers
- characters
- strings
- null
- symbols
- pairs and lists
- vectors

Of these, Booleans, numbers, characters, and strings are self-evaluating—they need not be quoted in a Scheme program. Symbols, null, pairs, lists, and vectors must be quoted in a Scheme program.

B.3.1   True and False   The Boolean values are `#t` for true and `#f` for false. Any Scheme value can be used as a Boolean value for the purpose of a conditional test. All values count as *true* in such a test except for `#f`. We use the word *true* to refer to any Scheme value that counts as *true*, and the word *false* to refer to `#f`.

B.3.2   Numbers   Numbers may be written as integers (e.g., `123`, `-542`), floating-point numbers (e.g., `3.14159`, `-2.718281828`), fractions (e.g., `7/3`), or complex numbers (e.g., `2.6+4.2i`). Not all implementations support fractions and complex numbers.

The range of numbers will depend upon the Scheme evaluator. The better implementations allow as many digits in an integer as memory allows (thousands, for example). More limited evaluators restrict the range to something like $\pm 2^{28}-1$. Floating-point numbers also have a limited precision, often 14 digits, and a limited range, often $\pm 10^{308}$.

Numbers may be written in binary, octal, or hexadecimal, as well as decimal, by using a radix prefix. For example, the decimal number 100 may be written in binary as `#b1100100`, in octal as `#o144`, and in hexadecimal as `#x64`.

Floating-point numbers may be followed by an exponent, a power of 10 used to scale the number. Avogadro's number, 6.023×10^{23}, may be written as `6.023E23`.

Scheme distinguishes between exact and inexact numbers. The precise rules are complex, and designed to support extremely accurate numerical computation. Roughly speaking, integers may be thought of as exact, and floating-point numbers as inexact. Some procedures require exact integers. Rounding a floating-point number to an integer is not sufficient; it is necessary to convert the result to an exact integer, using the primitive `inexact->exact`.

B.3.3   Characters   Characters are written using the prefix `#\`, e.g., `#\A` or `#\(`. Some characters may be written using a name (e.g., `#\space`). Consult your local documentation for a list of the character names that may be used in your evaluator. All evaluators will

---

[2] Some implementations will implement boxes as pairs, and void as a symbol. Thus `pair?` may return `#t` if given a box, and `symbol?` may return `#t` if given void. Older implementations do not distinguish between `#f` and null. On these older implementations, `(null? #f)` ⇒ `#t`.

allow #\space and #\newline.

Upper- and lowercase are distinct in character constants; (char=? #\A #\a) ⇒ #f, though (char-ci=? #\A #\a) ⇒ #t.

Normally, you should follow a character constant by a delimiter character or by whitespace.

B.3.4   Strings   Strings are written with surrounding quotation marks. All characters, including spaces, are significant in a string. Quotation marks and backslash characters in a string must be preceded by a backslash.

```
"Woolamaloo"      "The word \"recursion\" has many meanings."
"c:\\user\\scheme\\lab3.scm"
```

B.3.5   Null   Null is written as (), and must be quoted. (Some Scheme evaluators allow null to be written without quoting, but this is an error on the part of the implementor.)

B.3.6   Symbols   Symbols are written in the same form as identifiers. Symbols must be quoted in Scheme programs.

```
> (eqv? 'foo 'FOO)
#t
> (symbol? (read))
novosibirsk
#t
```

The symbol novosibirsk was not quoted because it was an item of input data, not part of a program.

(gensym)   primitive [Extension]

Returns a newly created symbol each time it is called. Symbols created by this procedure are often called gensyms. Many Scheme evaluators allow you to control the format of the symbols returned by gensym. By default, they generally look like G followed by an integer, e.g., G3728.

B.3.7   Pairs and Lists   Pairs are written in "dotted" notation, and must be quoted. For example, (5 . funf) is the external representation of a pair whose car is the number 5 and whose cdr is the symbol funf. Each of the two components of a pair may be any Scheme value, including another pair. For example,

```
(twas . (brillig . (and . (the . (slithy . (toves . ()))))))
```

is a pair whose car is twas and whose cdr is another pair.

There is no Scheme list type, but read and display, as well as the list-processing procedures such as member and append, treat specially a pair whose cdr is either null or another pair. The above structure can also be written as (twas brillig and the slithy toves).

B.3.8   Vectors   Vectors are written in the form #(...), and must be quoted. The elements of a vector can be any values. For example, #(47 #(call me ishmael) (1 2 3)), is a vector of three elements: a number, another vector, and a list, respectively.

B.4   Variables and Scope

Any identifier that is not a keyword (see Section B.1.2) may be used as a variable. A variable is a binding between an identifier and a memory location (roughly speaking, a box). Variables are not first-class citizens.

The set of bindings currently in effect is called the environment in effect. Some Schemes allow environments to be first-class citizens. The desirability of doing this is a controversial point among Schemers. For the purposes of this book, we do not treat environments as first-class citizens.

Certain Scheme forms (binding forms) allow you to create new variables: `define`, `lambda`, `let`, `let*`, `letrec`, and `do`. Of these, the most fundamental is `lambda`, which can be used to explain all of the other forms.

Scheme uses static scoping to associate an identifier in a program with a specific variable. To each place where a variable is bound in a program, there corresponds a region of the program text within which the binding is effective. The region is the body of the particular binding form that created the variable. To find the binding of a variable name, a Scheme evaluator looks at the innermost region, and then at successively larger regions, until it reaches the global region. The search stops when either a binding is found or the global region is reached. If no binding is found, the identifier is said to be unbound.

B.5   Basic Forms

This section lists the fundamental forms in Scheme.

B.5.1   Variables

variable name   syntax

An expression consisting of an identifier is a variable reference, and is searched for in the environment according to the rules in Section B.4.

B.5.2   Literal Expressions

`(quote` *datum*`)`	syntax
`'`*datum*	syntax
`(quasiquote` *datum*`)`	syntax
`` `datum``	syntax
constant	syntax

`(quote` *datum*`)` evaluates to *datum*, which can be any external representation, as defined in Section B.3; `'`*datum* is an abbreviation for `(quote` *datum*`)`.

Constants for numbers, strings, characters, and Booleans need not be quoted.

It is an error to mutate the value of a literal expression using a procedure such as `set-car!`. Most Scheme evaluators do not display an error message in such a case; programs with this error may malfunction in hard-to-debug ways.

`(quasiquote` *template*`)` specifies a template; its value is like that of a quoted form, except where a comma appears. The expression following the comma is evaluated ("unquoted"), and its value is inserted into the structure. The expression following a comma and an at-sign (@) must evaluate to a list, whose elements are then inserted in place of the expression. `` `datum`` is an abbreviation for `(quasiquote` *datum*`)`.

B.5.3   Procedures

(*procedure argument* ...)   syntax

A form in parentheses that doesn't start with one of the special syntax keywords (or a macro name—see Section B.5.9) is a procedure call, or application. The *operator* form must evaluate to a procedure, which is applied to the arguments. The procedure and the arguments are evaluated in an unspecified order.

(lambda (*name* ...) *form* ...)	syntax
(lambda *rest-name form*) ...	syntax
(lambda (*name* ... *name* . *rest-name*) *form* ...)	syntax

A lambda form creates a procedure with arguments as specified by the *name*s and *rest-name*s. In the first format, the name of each argument is specified, and the number of arguments must match the number of *name*s. In the second format, *rest-name* is bound to a list of the arguments. In the third format, there must be at least as many arguments as *name*s; *rest-name* is bound to a list of the remaining arguments.

Once the arguments have been bound, the *form*s are evaluated in the resulting environment, as for begin.

B.5.4   Sequencing

(begin *form* ...)	syntax

Evaluates the *form*s in order, and returns the value of the last one.

B.5.5   Binding Constructs

(let (*bindings*) *form* ...)	syntax
(let* (*bindings*) *form* ...)	syntax
(letrec (*bindings*) *form* ...)	syntax

For each of these forms, *bindings* is of the form ((*name* *init-form*) ...).

Each of these forms binds each *name* to the value of the corresponding *init-form* as specified by the *bindings*, and evaluates the *form*s as for begin. A let form evaluates the bindings in an unspecified order; let* evaluates the bindings in strict order from left to right. A letrec binds all of the names to an unspecified value, evaluates each *init-form*, and mutates the bindings accordingly.

The *init-form*s in a letrec should all be lambda forms.

B.5.6   Conditionals

(if *condition then-part else-part*)	syntax
(if *condition then-part*)	syntax

An if form is evaluated by evaluating the *condition*. If the result is *true* (see Section B.3.1), the *then-part* is evaluated, and its value returned. If the value is false, the *else-part* is evaluated and its value returned; if no *else-part* is provided, the result is unspecified.

(cond *clause* ...)	syntax

Each *clause* has the format (*condition* *form* ...). The *clause*s are processed in order. The *form*s of the first *clause* whose *condition* evaluates to *true* (see Section B.3.1) are evaluated as for *begin*, and the value of the last *form* is the value of the cond form. The last clause may have a *condition* else, in which case its *form*s are evaluated if no other *condition* was *true*.

If no else clause is given, and none of the *conditions* evaluate to *true*, the result is unspecified.

(case *key-form clause* ...)	syntax

Each *clause* can have the form ((*datum* ...) *form* ...). The *key-form* is evaluated, and the *clause*s processed. The *datum*s in each clause are examined; if any datum is equivalent to the value of *key-form* (see Section B.6.2), the corresponding *form*s are evaluated, as for begin. The condition of the last *clause* may be else; if none of the clauses match the value of *key-form*, the forms of this last clause are evaluated as for begin.

If no else clause is given, and none of the clauses match, the result is unspecified.

(and *form* ...)	syntax

The forms are evaluated from left to right. If any form returns *false* (see Section B.3.1), the result is the value of that form. If all of the forms return *true*, the result is the value of the last form. (and) ⇒ #t.

(or *form* ...)   syntax

The forms are evaluated from left to right. If any form returns *true* (see Section B.3.1), the result is the value of that form. If all of the forms return *false*, the result is the value of the last form. (or) ⇒ #f.

B.5.7 Assignments

(set! *name form*)   syntax

The *form* is evaluated, and the value of the variable *name*, which must be bound, is mutated to this value.

B.5.8 Definitions

(define *name form*)   syntax
(define (*name formals*) *form*)   syntax

The second format of define is equivalent to (define *name* (lambda (*formals*) *body*)), and is provided for programmer convenience. Schemers like to argue about whether using the second format is a good idea. We haven't used the second format in this book, but you may want to use it in your programs.

A define form has one of two different meanings, depending upon whether it is at the top level or not.

B.5.8.1 Top-Level Definitions

A define form at the top level (not enclosed in another form) has the effect of defining the *name* in the environment with the value of *form*. If the name is already bound, the effect of a definition is the same as (set! *name form*). Note: don't use define to simulate set!. This feature is provided only so you can load a file of definitions into a Scheme evaluator several times, correcting mistakes each time.

B.5.8.2 Internal Definitions

The body of a lambda, let, let*, or letrec form (or a define in the second format) may start with one or more internal definitions. These definitions have the same syntax as top-level definitions, but have a different meaning. An internal definition is another way of writing a letrec.

For example,

```
(let ((x 5))
  (define fact
    (lambda (n)
      (if (= n 0) 1 (* n (fact (sub1 n))))))
  (fact x))
```

is equivalent to

```
(let ((x 5))
  (letrec
    ((fact
      (lambda (n)
        (if (= n 0) 1 (* n (fact (sub1 n)))))))
    (fact x)))
```

Whether you use internal definitions is a matter of style.

B.5.9 Macros [Extension]

(define-macro *keyword form*) syntax [Extension]

New kinds of forms may be defined by means of the define-macro form; *keyword* is an identifier that has not been bound as a variable name or a special keyword (see Section B.1.2), and *form* evaluates to a procedure of one argument. The *keyword* is recorded as a macro, with a "transformer" procedure that is the value of *form*.

A define-macro form must always be at the top level; it cannot be nested in another form.

(*keyword datum ...*) syntax [Extension]

A macro call is a form in parentheses, with the first item being the macro name. Succeeding *datum*s are passed as arguments to the macro's "transformer" procedure. The result of that procedure is then evaluated by the Scheme evaluator; the result of that evaluation is the result of the macro call.

$R^n RS$ uses a different—and much more complicated—macro system. Almost all Scheme systems support extensions that in turn can be used to provide define-macro as we've used it.

B.5.10 Modules

(module *export definition*) syntax [Extension]

A module form is evaluated by evaluating the *definition*s. The export clause is in the format (export *name ...*). Any name that appears in the export clause is made public; there must be a corresponding *definition* of that name. Any *definition*s whose names don't appear in the export clause are made private, and cannot be used outside the module.

B.5.11 Classes

(define-class *class-name clause*) syntax [Extension]

The define-class special form creates a class whose name is *class-name*. The *clause*s specify various features of the class:

```
(define-class class-name
  (class-variables bindings)
  (class-methods (message . args)
    ((keyword) form ...)
    ...)
  (constructor-arguments names)
  (slots bindings)
  (methods (message . args)
    ((keyword) form ...)
    ...))
```

See Chapter 6 for a complete description of the define-class form.

B.6 Primitives

This section lists the primtive procedures in Scheme.

B.6.1 Boolean Procedures

(not *obj*) primitive

Returns #t if *obj* is false, and #f otherwise.

(boolean? *obj*) primitive

Returns #t if *obj*'s type is Boolean, and #f otherwise.

B.6.2 Equality

(eq? obj1 obj2)	primitive
(eqv? obj1 obj2)	primitive
(equal? obj1 obj2)	primitive

These three forms return #t if *obj1* and *obj2* are equal, in some sense, and #f otherwise. Roughly speaking, eqv? tests equivalence; it returns #t if *obj1* and *obj2* share storage (i.e., if mutating one mutates the other), and #f otherwise; equal? returns #t if *obj1* and *obj2* display the same, and #f otherwise. The eq? primitive is slightly more fussy than eqv?; numbers can be equivalent without being equal. We have not used eq? in this book.

The equal? primitive can go into a loop if obj1 or obj2 is a circular structure.

B.6.3 Pairs and Lists

(pair? *obj*)   primitive

Returns #t if obj is a pair, and #f otherwise.

(cons *obj1 obj2*)   primitive

Returns a new pair whose car contains *obj1* and whose cdr contains *obj2*.

(car *pair*)   primitive
(cdr *pair*)   primitive

Returns the car or cdr of the *pair*.

(set-car! *pair obj*)   primitive
(set-cdr! *pair obj*)   primitive

Mutates the car or cdr of the *pair* to *obj*.

(null? *obj*)   primitive

Returns #t if *obj* is null, and #f otherwise.

(list? *obj*)   primitive

Returns #t if *obj* is a list, and #f otherwise. Not all pairs are lists; list? returns #t if *obj* satisfies the recursive definition of a list in Chapter 4.

(list *obj ...*)   primitive

Returns a list with one element for each *obj*.

(length *list*)   primitive

Returns the number of pairs in a list.

(append *list ...*)   primitive

Returns a list consisting of the elements of the first *list* followed by the elements of the second *list*, and so on.

(reverse *list ...*)   primitive

Returns a new list consisting of the elements of *list* in reverse order.

(last-pair *list*)   primitive

[Extension]

Returns the last pair of *list*. It is an error when *list* is null.

(list-tail *list k*)   primitive

Returns the pair of *list* obtained by applying cdr to *list k* times.

(list-ref *listk*)   primitive

Equivalent to (car (list-tail *list k*)).

(list-set! *listk v*)   primitive

[Extension]

Equivalent to (set-car! (list-tail *list k*) *v*.

(first *list*)   primitive

[Extension]

Equivalent to (list-ref (list-tail *list* 0) *v*.

The corresponding primitives second up to tenth are also provided.

(first-tail *listk*)   primitive

[Extension]

Equivalent to (list-tail *list 1*)

The corresponding primitives second-tail up to tenth-tail are also provided.

(memq *obj list*)   primitive
(memv *obj list*)   primitive
(member *obj list*)   primitive

These procedures return true if *obj* is a member of *list*, and #f otherwise. The return result is the tail (as with list-tail of *list* whose car is equal to *obj*. memq uses eq? for this test, memv uses eqv?, and member uses equal?.

(assq *obj alist*)   primitive
(assv *obj alist*)   primitive
(assoc *obj alist*)   primitive

An *alist* is a list of items, each of which is a pair. These procedures find the first pair in *alist* whose car is equal to *obj*, and return that pair, or #f if no item matches. assq uses eq? for this test, assv uses eqv?, and assoc uses equal?.

B.6.4 Symbols

(symbol? *obj*)   primitive

Returns #t if *obj* is a symbol, and #f otherwise.

(symbol->string *symbol*)   primitive

Returns the name of *symbol* as a string. It is an error (one not detected by many Scheme evaluators) to mutate this string with string-set!.

(string->symbol *string*)   primitive

Returns the symbol whose name is *string*. It is possible to use string->symbol to create symbols that cannot be read in, for example, (symbol->string "MixedCase"), but this is generally considered bad programming style.

B.6.5 Numbers

(number? *obj*)   primitive
(complex? *obj*)   primitive
(real? *obj*)   primitive
(rational? *obj*)   primitive
(integer? *obj*)   primitive

Each of these returns #t if *obj* is of the specified type, and #f otherwise. Note: (real? 3) $\Rightarrow$ #t, because 3 is a real number, even though it is an integer as well. If you want to find out whether a number x is a noninteger, use (and (real? x) (not (integer? x))).

(exact? *obj*)	primitive
(inexact? *obj*)	primitive

Return #t if *obj* is exact or inexact, respectively, and #f otherwise. Every number will be either exact or inexact. In many but not necessarily all Scheme evaluators, integers are exact, and reals are inexact.

(= *x y z ...*)	primitive
(< *x y z ...*)	primitive
(> *x y z ...*)	primitive
(<= *x y z ...*)	primitive
(>= *x y z ...*)	primitive

These procedures return #t if the specified relation is true, and #f otherwise. When used with more than two arguments, each of these primitives checks whether the arguments are in the specified order. Note: with inexact numbers, equality is a hit-and-miss affair. Because of inaccuracies of representations, on many Scheme evaluators (= 1.0 (* 10.0 0.1)) ⇒ #f.

(zero? *x*)	primitive
(positive? *x*)	primitive
(negative? *x*)	primitive
(odd? *x*)	primitive
(even? *x*)	primitive

These procedures return #t if the specified condition is true, and #f otherwise; odd? and even? are defined only for integers.

(+ *x y z ...*)	primitive
(- *x y z ...*)	primitive
(* *x y z ...*)	primitive
(/ *x y z ...*)	primitive

These procedures return the sum, difference, product, or result of real division of their arguments, respectively.

(- *x*)	primitive
(/ *x*)	primitive

These procedures return the negative or reciprocal of *x*, respectively.

(abs *x*)	primitive

Returns the magnitude (absolute value, for real numbers) of *x*.

(quotient *x y*)	primitive
(remainder *x y*)	primitive
(modulo *x y*)	primitive

These procedures do division on integers, returning an integer result. remainder and modulo return the same result for positive integers, but different results for negative integers (see $R^n RS$).

(gcd *x ...*)	primitive
(lcm *x ...*)	primitive

Return the greatest common divisor or least common multiple of the integer arguments.

(numerator *x*)	primitive
(denominator *x*)	primitive

These procedures convert *x* to a rational number (a fraction), and return the numerator or denominator of that fraction, respectively.

(floor *x*)	primitive

`(ceiling x)`	primitive
`(truncate x)`	primitive
`(round x)`	primitive

These procedures return inexact integers. `floor` finds the largest integer not larger than x; `ceiling` finds the smallest integer not smaller than x; `truncate` throws away any decimal places (it's like `floor` if x is positive, and `ceiling` if x is negative); `round` returns the closest integer.

Note: the results of these procedures are inexact numbers. If an exact value is needed (e.g., for use with vector operations), pass the result to `inexact->exact`.

`(sqrt x)`	primitive
`(exp x)`	primitive
`(expt x y)`	primitive
`(log x)`	primitive
`(sin x)`	primitive
`(cos x)`	primitive
`(tan x)`	primitive
`(asin x)`	primitive
`(acos x)`	primitive
`(atan x)`	primitive
`(atan y x)`	primitive

These are the mathematical functions. They compute square root, exponential (e^x), power (x^y), logarithm ($\log_e x$), power (x^y), sine, cosine, tangent, arcsine, arccos, and arctangent, respectively. The two-argument form of `atan` computes $\arctan(y/x)$, and works correctly even if $x=0$.

`(inexact->exact x)`	primitive
`(exact->inexact x)`	primitive

These procedures return the exact or inexact counterpart of their argument, respectively. They are most useful with the truncation procedures.

`(number->string x base)`	primitive
`(string->number x base)`	primitive

These procedures convert between string and number representations. *base* can be omitted, in which case 10 is assumed. If the input string isn't a valid number, `string->number` returns #f.

B.6.6   Characters

`(char? obj)`	primitive

Returns #t if *obj* is a character, and #f otherwise.

`(char=? c1 c2)`	primitive
`(char<? c1 c2)`	primitive
`(char>? c1 c2)`	primitive
`(char<=? c1 c2)`	primitive
`(char>=? c1 c2)`	primitive

Return #t if the specified condition is true, and #f otherwise. Refer to your Scheme evaluator documentation for precise rules on the comparison order.

`(char-ci=? c1 c2)`	primitive
`(char-ci<? c1 c2)`	primitive
`(char-ci>? c1 c2)`	primitive
`(char-ci<=? c1 c2)`	primitive
`(char-ci>=? c1 c2)`	primitive

These procedures return the result of a "case-independent" comparison. Upper- and lower-case are considered equivalent.

`(char-alphabetic? `*char*`)`	primitive
`(char-numeric? `*char*`)`	primitive
`(char-whitespace? `*char*`)`	primitive
`(char-upper-case? `*letter*`)`	primitive
`(char-lower-case? `*letter*`)`	primitive

These procedures return #t if the specified condition is true, and #f otherwise.

`(char->integer `*char*`)`	primitive
`(integer->char `*x*`)`	primitive

These procedures convert between characters and their numeric codes. See your local documentation for a list of the codes.

`(char-upcase `*char*`)`	primitive
`(char-downcase `*char*`)`	primitive

These procedures convert between the upper- and lowercase versions of a character. If *char* is not a letter, the result is *char*.

B.6.7 Strings

`(string `*obj*`)`   primitive

Returns #t if *obj* is a string, and #f otherwise.

`(make-string `*k* *char*`)`   primitive

Returns a string of *k* characters; *char* is optional. If it is supplied, the string characters will all be *char*. Otherwise, the string characters are unspecified.

`(string `*char* ...`)`   primitive

Returns a string consisting of the character arguments, in the order given.

`(string-length `*string*`)`   primitive

Returns the number of characters in *string*.

`(string-ref `*string* *k*`)`	primitive
`(string-set! `*string* *k* *char*`)`	primitive

Gets or sets the *k*th character of *string*.

`(string=? `*s1* *s2*`)`	primitive
`(string<? `*s1* *s2*`)`	primitive
`(string>? `*s1* *s2*`)`	primitive
`(string<=? `*s1* *s2*`)`	primitive
`(string>=? `*s1* *s2*`)`	primitive
`(string-ci=? `*s1* *s2*`)`	primitive
`(string-ci<? `*s1* *s2*`)`	primitive
`(string-ci>? `*s1* *s2*`)`	primitive
`(string-ci<=? `*s1* *s2*`)`	primitive
`(string-ci>=? `*s1* *s2*`)`	primitive

Returns the result of the specified comparison; *s1* and *s2* are strings. The `-ci` versions ignore case in the strings.

`(substring `*string* *start* *end*`)`   primitive

Returns a new string containing the characters of *string* starting at position *start* and ending before position *end*. (*end* is the position in *string* of the first character that is *not* to appear in the result.)

(string-append *string* ...)   primitive

Returns a string made by appending the characters of each string in turn.

(string->list *string*)   primitive
(list->string *list*)   primitive

These procedures convert between lists of characters and strings.

(string-copy *string*)   primitive

Returns a new string containing the same characters as *string*.

(string-fill *string char*)   primitive

Sets every element of *string* to *char*.

B.6.8   Vectors

(vector? *obj*)   primitive

Returns #t if *obj* is a vector, and #f otherwise.

(make-vector *k fill*)   primitive

Returns a new vector of *k* elements; *fill* is optional. If it is given, each element of the vector is initialized to its value. Otherwise, the elements have unspecified values.

(vector *obj* ...)   primitive

Returns a vector whose elements contain the arguments. Similar to list.

(vector-length *vector*)   primitive

Returns the number of elements in *vector*.

(vector-ref *vector k*)   primitive
(vector-set! *vector k obj*)   primitive

Gets or sets the *k*th element of *vector*.

(vector->list *vector*)   primitive
(list->vector *list*)   primitive

Converts between a list of elements and the corresponding vector.

(vector-fill *vector fill*)   primitive

Sets every element of *vector* to *fill*, and returns an unspecified value.

B.6.9   Boxes [Extension]

(make-box *obj*)   primitive

Returns a newly created box containing *obj*.

(box-ref *box*)   primitive
(box-set! *box obj*)   primitive

Gets or sets the contents of *box*; box-ref returns the contents; box-set! returns an unspecified value.

B.6.10   Procedures and Mapping

(procedure? *obj*)   primitive

Returns #t if *obj* is a procedure, and #f otherwise.

(apply *proc arg-list*)   primitive
(apply *proc arg1* ... *argn arg-list*)   primitive

The first form calls *proc* with the elements of *arg-list* as arguments. The second form is equivalent to (apply *proc* (append (list *arg1* ... *argn*) *arg-list*)).

(map *proc* *list1* ...)   primitive

proc must be a procedure that takes as many arguments as there are *list* arguments to *map*. The *lists* must all have the same length. map applies *proc* to corresponding elements of the *lists*, and returns a list of the results; map operates in an unspecified order, and therefore *proc* must not have any effects.

(for-each *proc* *list1* ...)   primitive

proc must be a procedure that takes as many arguments as there are *list* arguments to *for-each*. The *lists* must all have the same length. for-each applies *proc* to corresponding elements of the *lists*, in order from first to last, and returns an unspecified result.

B.6.11   Input and Output

Many Scheme evaluators provide powerful extensions to Scheme's already fairly sophisticated input/output features. If you wish to do complicated input/output, see your local documentation. The following features are defined by $R^n RS$.

B.6.11.1   Ports   Input and output in Scheme use values called ports, which are abstractions of a file or device. Opening a file or device returns a port, on which read or write operations may be performed. When your program is finished with a port, it should close it.

(call-with-input-file *string* *proc*)   primitive
(call-with-output-file *string* *proc*)   primitive

These procedures do the work of opening and closing the file; *string* gives the name of the file or device (consult your local documentation for rules on filenames),[3] and *proc* is a procedure of one argument that is passed the port. When *proc* returns, the port is automatically closed, and *proc*'s value is the value of call-with-input-file or call-with-output-file.

(input-port? *obj*)   primitive
(input-port? *obj*)   primitive

These procedures return #t if *obj* is an input or output port, respectively, and #f otherwise.

(current-input-port)   primitive
(current-output-port)   primitive

Return the input or output port that the input and output procedures use by default. Any procedure that takes a *port* argument will use the default input or output port if the *port* argument isn't provided.

(with-input-from-file *string* *proc*)   primitive
(with-output-to-file *string* *proc*)   primitive

These procedures call *proc*, which must be a thunk. Before doing so, they mutate the current input or output port so that it refers to the *file* with name *string*. These procedures return the value returned by *proc*, after closing the port and resetting the current input or output port to its prior value.

(open-input-file *string*)   primitive
(open-output-file *string*)   primitive

These procedures return a new port referring to the file named *string*. They don't change the current input or output port. If the file can't be opened, an error is signaled.

(close-input-port *port*)   primitive

---

[3] Some operating systems use the backslash as a filename character. Remember that you must write a backslash as \\ inside a Scheme string.

(`close-output-port` *port*)   primitive

These procedures close the port, and return an unspecified value.

B.6.11.2 Input

(`read` *port*)   primitive

Returns the next input value read from *port*, or the current input port if no argument is given. Any valid Scheme external representation can be read. If no further values are found in the file, an "end-of-file" object is returned.

(`read-char` *port*)   primitive

Returns the next input character read from *port*, or the current input port if no argument is given. If no further characters are found in the file, an "end-of-file" object is returned.

(`peek-char` *port*)   primitive

Returns the input character that would be read by `read-char` from *port*, or the current input port if no argument is given. The port is not updated to the following character. Any number of `peek-char`s without an intervening `read-char` will return the same character. If no further characters are found in the file, an "end-of-file" object is returned.

(`eof-object?` *obj*)   primitive

Returns #t if *obj* is the "end-of-file" object that `read`, `read-char`, and `peek-char` return when no further input is available, and #f otherwise. The exact "end-of-file" object will differ among Scheme evaluators, but it can never be a value that can be read in by `read`.

B.6.11.3　Output

Two kinds of output are available: displaying a value produces output intended for human consumption, whereas writing produces output intended to be read back into a Scheme program.

(write *obj port*)　　　　　　　　　　　　　　　　　　　　primitive

This procedure writes a value out to the *port*, or to the current output port if *port* isn't provided, and returns an unspecified value.

(display *obj port*)　　　　　　　　　　　　　　　　　　　primitive

This procedure displays a value to the *port*, or to the current output port if *port* isn't provided, and returns an unspecified value.

(newline *port*)　　　　　　　　　　　　　　　　　　　　　primitive

This procedure writes #\newline to *port*, or to the current output port if *port* isn't provided, and returns an unspecified value.

(write-char *char port*)　　　　　　　　　　　　　　　　　primitive

This procedure writes *char* to *port*, or to the current output port if *port* isn't provided, and returns an unspecified value.

B.6.11.4　Formatted Output

(format *destination string obj* ...)　　　　　　　　primitive [Extension]

format produces a string, the "output string", that is the external representation of the *obj*s, under control of *string*, which is known as a *format string*. format is too complex to discuss in full here. Instead, we will present the features we have used in the book. Consult your local documentation if you want to understand all of format's features.

destination is a Boolean or an output port.

- If it is #t, the output string is written to the current output port, and the return value is unspecified.
- If it is #f, the output string is returned as the value of format.
- If it is an output port, the output string is written to that port, and the return value is unspecified.

The format string contains ordinary text and "tilde sequences", which specify how the various *obj*s are to be formatted. Ordinary text is appended to the output string, whereas a tilde sequence generally causes an *obj* to be converted into a string and appended to the output string. There are many tilde sequences, but the following are generally sufficient:

- ~*n*a: the converted string is produced as though the corresponding *obj* were displayed, in *n* columns. If *n* is omitted, the minimum number of columns is used.
- ~*n*s: the converted string is produced as though the corresponding *obj* were displayed, in *n* columns. If *n* is omitted, the minimum number of columns is used.
- ~*n*d: the converted string is produced by displaying the corresponding *obj* as a decimal number, in *n* columns. If *n* is omitted, the minimum number of columns is used.
- ~%: a newline is produced. No *obj* is consumed.
- ~~: the character ~ is produced.

For example,

```
> (format #t "Hello, ~a~%" "world")
Hello, world
> (define my-string (format #f "2+2=~3d!" (+ 1 3)))
> my-string
2+2=  4!
```

B.6.12 Graphics [Extension]   Many Scheme systems allow powerful graphics. We have used some very basic graphics procedures in this book. They draw on a 500×500 graphics window, with the origin in the lower left corner. Some of these procedures use a "current point", which is originally (0,0) (the lower left corner of the graphics window).

(draw-clear)   primitive

Erases the graphics window, and returns the current point to the origin. Returns an unspecified value.

(draw-move *x y*)   primitive

Sets the current point to (*x,y*), and returns an unspecified value.

(draw-line *x y*)   primitive

Draws from the current point to (*x,y*), and sets the current point to (*x,y*). Returns an unspecified value.

(draw-text *string*)   primitive

Displays *string* at the current point, and does not change the current point.

B.6.13   System features

(eval *value*)   primitive

Treats *value* as a Scheme form, and evaluates it. If *value* is self-evaluating (e.g., a number, character, string, boolean, or null), the value is *value*. If *value* is a symbol or pair, eval treats it as the representation of a Scheme form, and evaluates that form.

The only variables that can be used in a list passed to eval are either those bound in the form, or variables in the global environment.

(load *string*)   primitive

Reads forms from the file whose name is *string*, and evaluates each one.

(error *symbol value* ...)   primitive

Generates and reports an error to the user. *symbol* is by convention the name of the procedure or module in which the error was detected, and the *value*s are either strings describing the error or the values that caused the problem.

Many Scheme systems allow the programmer to "catch" calls to error, in order to provide custom error-handling. See your system documentation for more information.

(trace *proc* ...)   primitive

Upon evaluation of proc, Scheme prints the argument to the procedure, and the returned value of the procedure on exit. More than one procedure may be specified. Format of the output will vary in different systems.

(trace *proc* ...)   primitive

Stops tracing of proc.

Appendix C

Gleam Reference Manual

Now there is one outstandingly important fact regarding Spaceship Earth, and that is that no instruction book came with it.
— Buckminster Fuller, *Operating Manual for Spaceship Earth*

Gleam is a simple hypothetical computer used to explain the ideas of programming at the machine level. A simulator that implements the fundamental elements of Gleam and gap, an assembler, translates assembler code into Gleam's machine language. Like many machines, Gleam has a small set of instructions that access memory. Most of its instructions perform computations using values in registers and leave the result in a register. Chapters 11 and 12 describe programming techniques for Gleam and Gleam/2, an extended version of Gleam that provides list processing and tagged data. This appendix collects the specifications of the instructions for Gleam and Gleam/2, and shows how to use the assembler and Gleam simulator.

Chapters 11 and 12 describe advanced features of the Gleam machine structure, including a graphics frame buffer and device registers. The simulator described here only implements the set of instructions described here, applied to memory values, and does not include the advanced features.

Gleam machine-language instructions have two formats. The first is for instructions that include the address of a memory location, and the second is for instructions that only compute values in the registers. Figure 11-10 shows the structure of the two formats. Here we will use the instruction syntax of gap, the assembler for Gleam, to describe the instructions. The first item of an instruction is always an opcode, and the second is always a register number. The two formats differ in the third and fourth elements of the instructions. In the memory-reference instructions, which include the load and store instructions and the various jump instructions, the third item in the instruction is a memory address, and the fourth is the number of an index register, a register whose contents are included in the calculation of the memory address. Memory instructions have the form

```
(instruction  register memory-address index-register)
```

If the fourth element of the instruction is omitted, it's assumed to be 0, so many instructions are in the form

```
(instruction  register memory-address)
```

The second type of instruction, the register instruction, has the form

```
(instruction  dest-reg source-reg1 source-reg2)
```

The inputs are in registers source-reg1 and source-reg2; the result ends up in dest-reg. If any elements of the instruction are omitted, they are assumed to be zero. Only trailing elements may be omitted.

C.1 Address Calculation

Each time any memory-reference instruction is executed, the machine calculates an *effective address*, or *EA*. The effective address is normally the number of the cell to be affected by this instruction, though some types of instructions use it differently. Indeed, some instructions simply ignore the effective address altogether. Nonetheless, it is always computed.

Two values from the instruction are used in computing the EA: the address part and the index part. The address part is an integer from 0 to 65,535 ($2^{16}-1$); the index part is an integer from 0 to 15. The EA is calculated as follows:

1. If the index is 0, the EA is the same as the address.

2. If the index isn't 0, the EA is computed by adding the contents of the index register to the address. This calculation is done in the Memory-Address Register, so neither the index register nor the memory location is modified during the computation.

In the description of the operation of Gleam instructions, we mean the effective address whenever we refer to the address.

C.2 Gleam Memory Access Instructions

This section describes each of the instructions provided by the Gleam CPU. Each entry provides a brief description, an example of the instruction, and a description of errors that can occur. The gap assembler determines some errors (described in the section on the assembler), but others can occur when the program is run. In theory, Gleam only checks for arithmetic errors, such as divide by zero, and integer overflow, when the value is less than -2^{31} or greater than $2^{31}-12$. Gleam/2 also tests whether the operands to instructions are the right type. The simulator tests all instructions for such errors.

Gleam uses only numeric values. Therefore, the result of comparison operations are coded as 0 for *false*, and anything nonzero for *true*.

load   Transfer a memory value to a register.
Description   Copy the contents of a specific memory cell into the specified register. The register is changed to contain the new value; the memory cell is unchanged.
Errors   Memory error: the address given doesn't exist on the computer.

store   Transfer the contents of a register to memory.
Description   Copy the contents of a register into a memory cell. The memory cell is changed to contain the new value; the register is unchanged.
Errors   Memory error: the address given doesn't exist on the computer.

jtrue   If a register contains *true*, jump to another program cell.
Description   Examine the contents of the specified register. If it does not contain 0, then the program counter is set to the specified address. Otherwise, the program counter is incremented by 1.
Errors   Memory error: the address given doesn't exist on the computer.

jfalse   If a register contains *false*, jump to another program cell.
Description   Examine the contents of the specified register. If the register contains 0, then the program counter is set to the specified address. Otherwise, the program counter is incremented by 1.
Errors   Memory error: the address given doesn't exist on the computer.

jump   Unconditionally jump to another program cell.
Description   Set the program counter to the memory address. The register is unused, and is conventionally 0.
Errors   Memory error: the address given doesn't exist on the computer.

call   Call a procedure.

gap Code	Op Code	Type	Operation Performed
load	#x00	MRI	Transfer a memory value to the CPU.
store	#x01	MRI	Transfer a CPU value to memory.
jtrue	#x02	MRI	If a register contains *true*, jump to specified location.
jfalse	#x03	MRI	If a register contains *false*, jump to specified location.
jump	#x04	MRI	Unconditionally jump to specified location.
call	#x05	MRI	Call a procedure.
copy	#x86	Reg	Transfer a value from one CPU register to another.
add	#x87	Reg	Compute the sum of two values.
sub	#x88	Reg	Compute the difference of two values.
mpy	#x89	Reg	Compute the product of two values.
quo	#x8A	Reg	Compute the quotient of two values.
rem	#x8B	Reg	Compute the remainder of two values.
lss?	#x8C	Reg	Test one value to see whether it's less than another.
gtr?	#x8D	Reg	Test one value to see whether it's greater than another.
eql?	#x8E	Reg	Test two values to see whether they're equal
and	#x90	Reg	Set each bit of destination to and of sources.
or	#x91	Reg	Set each bit of destination to or of sources.
not	#x92	Reg	Set each bit of destination to inverse of source bit.
inchar	#x9c	Reg	Read a single character.
outchar	#x9d	Reg	Write a single character.
innum	#x9e	Reg	Read a decimal integer.
outnum	#x9f	Reg	Write a decimal integer.
halt	#xa0	Reg	Stop the computer.

(b) Register instructions

Figure C-1   Gleam instruction summary

Description   Deposit the address of the next instruction into the register and then do an unconditional jump to the address given by the effective address.
Errors   `Memory error`: the address given doesn't exist on the computer.

C.3   Gleam **Register instructions**

`copy`   Copy contents of source-reg1 into dest-register.
Description   Copy the contents of one register into another. The register from which the value is to be copied is placed into the "address" part of the instruction. The index-register portion of the instruction is ignored.
Errors   None.

`add`   Compute the sum of two values.
Description   Add the contents of the two source registers, and leave the result in the destination register.
Errors   `Arithmetic error`: one of the operands is not an integer. `Overflow`: result is outside the range of integer values.

`sub`   Compute the difference of two values.
Description   Subtract the contents of the second source register from the contents of the first source register, and leave the result in the destination register.
Errors   `Arithmetic error`: one of the operands is not an integer. `Overflow`: result is outside the range of integer values.

`mpy`   Compute the product of two values.
Description   Multiply the contents of the two source registers, and leave the result in the destination register.
Errors   `Arithmetic error`: one of the operands is not an integer. `Overflow`: result is outside the range of integer values.

`quo`   Compute the quotient of two values.
Description   Divide the contents of the first source register by those of the second source register, and place the quotient in the destination register (the remainder is discarded), like `quotient` in Scheme.
Errors   `Arithmetic error`: one of the operands is not an integer. `Division by zero`.

`rem`   Compute the remainder of two values.
Description   Divide the contents of the first source register by those of the second source register, and place the remainder in the destination register (the quotient is discarded), like `remainder` in Scheme.
Errors   `Arithmetic error`: one of the operands is not an integer. `Division by zero`.

Note that the remainder in a division is only defined if both operands are positive. Various Gleam computers are free to give different answers if one or both operand(s) is/are negative, or even to halt with an error.[1]

---

[1] For those interested in matters mathematical, the problem is that there are actually several different remainder functions, including the remainder and the modulus. Most computer designers don't care too much about this, and therefore give different answers. In fact, a prominent computer scientist in Britain once sent an "arithmetic test" to some of his colleagues, asking them to tell him the answers to various problems involving remainders of negative operands. They didn't agree. If eminent computer scientists and mathematicians don't agree, it's no surprise that computer programmers don't, either.

lss?   Test one value to see whether it's less than another.
Description   Compare the value in the first source register with the value in the second source register. The destination register is set to 1 if the first source register's contents are less than those of the second source register, and 0 otherwise.
Errors   Arithmetic error: one of the operands is not an integer.

gtr?   Test one value to see whether it's less than another.
Description   Compare the value in the first source register with the value in the second source register. The destination register is set to 1 if the first source register's contents are greater than those of the second source register, and 0 otherwise.
Errors   Arithmetic error: one of the operands is not an integer.

eql?   Test one value to see whether it's equal to another.
Description   Compare the value in the first source register with the value in the second source register. The destination register is set to 1 if the first source register's contents are equal, arithmetically, to those of the second source register, and 0 otherwise.
Errors   Arithmetic error: one of the operands is not an integer.

and   Set each bit of destination to bitwise and of sources.
Description   Compare the value in the first source register with the value in the second source register, bit by bit. Each bit in the destination register is set to the bitwise and of the corresponding bits in the first source register and the second source register.
Errors   None.

or   Set each bit of destination to bitwise or of sources.
Description   Compare the value in the first source register with the value in the second source register, bit by bit. Each bit in the destination register is set to the bitwise or of the corresponding bits in the first source register and the second source register.
Errors   None.

not   Set each bit of destination to bitwise not of source register 1.
Description   Each bit in the destination register is set to the bitwise not of the corresponding bit in the first source register.
Errors   None.

inchar   Read a character.
Description   Read a single character from input and places its numeric code into the destination register. Ignores both source registers.
Errors   None.

outchar   Write a character.
Description   Write a single character, specified by its numeric code, from the destination register to output. Ignores both source registers.
Errors   Register contains a value less than 0 or greater than 255.

innum   Read a number.
Description   Read a single number from input, and place it into the destination register. Ignores both source registers.
Errors   Input contains characters not interpretable as a number.

outnum   Write a number.
Description   Write a single number from the destination register to output. Ignores both source registers.
Errors   Register contains a non-numeric value.

halt   Stop the computer.
Description   Cause Gleam to halt.
Errors   Halted, though you might not consider this an error!

C.4   Gleam/2 **Instructions**

cons   Make a new pair.
Description   Create a new pair in the destination register; the car of the pair is given by the first source register, and the cdr is given by the second source register.
Errors   None.

car   Take the car of a register.
Description   Take the car of the first source register and put it into the destination register. Ignores the second source register.
Errors   `Pair error`: operand isn't a pair.

cdr   Take the cdr of a register.
Description   Take the cdr of the source register, and put it into the destination register. Ignores the second source register.
Errors   `Pair error`: operand isn't a pair.

setcar   Mutate the car of a pair.
Description   Mutate the car of the pair in the destination register to be the contents of the first source register. Ignores the second source register.
Errors   `Pair error`: operand isn't a pair.

setcdr   Mutate the cdr of a pair.
Description   Mutate the cdr of the pair in the destination register to be the contents of the first source register. Ignores the second source register.
Errors   `Pair error`: operand isn't a pair.

boolean?   Ask whether a value is a Boolean.
Description   Test the first source register to see whether it contains a Boolean, and load 1 into the destination register if so; otherwise, load 0 into the register. Ignores the second source register.
Errors   None.

symbol?   Ask whether a value is a symbol.
Description   Test the first source register to see whether it contains a symbol, and load 1 into the destination register if so; otherwise, load 0 into the register. Ignores the second source register.
Errors   None.

number?   Ask whether a value is a number.
Description   Test the first source register to see whether it contains a number, and load 1 into the destination register if so; otherwise, load 0 into the register. Ignores the second source register.
Errors   None.

char?   Ask whether a value is a character.
Description   Test the first source register to see whether it contains a character, and load 1 into the destination register if so; otherwise, load 0 into the register. This instruction ignores the second source register.
Errors   None.

string?   Ask whether a value is a string.
Description   Test the first source register to see whether it contains a string, and load 1 into the destination register if so; otherwise, load 0 into the register. Ignores the second source register.
Errors   None.

pair?   Ask whether a value is a pair.

Description   Test the first source register to see whether it contains a pair, and load 1 into the destination register if so; otherwise, load 0 into the register. Ignores the second source register.

Errors   None.

null?   Ask whether a value is null.

Description   Test the first source register to see whether it contains null, and load 1 into the destination register if so; otherwise, load 0 into the register. Ignores the second source register.

Errors   None.

eqv?   Ask whether two value are equivalent.

Description   Compare the contents of the first source register and the second source register. Load 1 into the destination register if they are equivalent, and 0 otherwise. This instruction operates as eqv? does in Scheme.

Errors   None.

read   Read a Scheme value from input.

Description   As with read in Scheme, the read instruction reads a Scheme value and returns it in the destination register. The value read can be a character (using #\ . . . notation), number, string, Boolean, or symbol, or it can be a list.

Errors   None.

display   Write a Scheme value to output.

Description   As with display in Scheme, this procedure writes a single Scheme value to output. The value is in the register.

Errors   None.

C.5   Gleam **Assembly Language:** gap

The assembler for Gleam is gap. Programs in gap are written in list notation. Items are either symbols or lists; a symbol is taken as a name for the current location, whereas a list is either a machine instruction or a special assembly-language operation.

There are two special assembly-language operations:

- (define-symbols *defn...*) allows you to define names for use in a Gleam program. Each *defn* is a pair whose car is a name to be defined, and whose cdr is a value. Defined names can be used as register numbers, as addresses, or as dataword values.

  Examples:

  ```
          (define-symbols
            (tmp0 . 0)
            (newline-char . 10))
          ...
          (load tmp0 foo)
  nl-char (dataword newline-char)
  ```

- (dataword *value*) places the value in the next word; *value* can be any Scheme value, or a name which has been defined by define-symbols. To create a dataword whose contents are a symbol, quote it.

  Examples: assume the symbols defined above are still in effect:

  ```
          (dataword 0)
          (dataword 'foobar)
          (dataword newline-char)
  ```

The assembler checks some errors. It can determine when the register is out of range and will report the error and continue. It also checks the memory address against `memory-size`, a variable set to the size of the memory used in the emulator. Different Gleam machines may have different memory sizes, so you can change the value from the default of 8192 (the value is deliberately small so the simulator can run on small PCs).

Bibliography

ABELSON, H., AND G. J. SUSSMAN, WITH J. SUSSMAN *Structure and Interpretation of Computer Programs*. McGraw-Hill, 1985.

AHO. A, R. SETHI. AND J. D. ULLMAN *Compilers: principles, techniques, tools* Addison-Wesley, 1986.

BENTLEY, J. *Programming Pearls*. Addison-Wesley, 1989.

BENTLEY, J. *More Programming Pearls*. Addison-Wesley, 1990.

BOOCH, G. *Object-Oriented Analysis and Design, With Applications*, 2nd ed. Benjamin/Cummings, 1994.

BROOKS, F. P. *The Mythical Man-Month: Essays on Software Engineering*. Addison-Wesley, 1975.

PAULSON, L. C. *ML for the Working Programmer*. Cambridge University Press, 1991.

CORMEN, T.H. , C. E. LEISERSON, AND R. L. RIVEST *Introduction to Algorithms*. MIT Press, 1992.

CLOCKSIN, W., AND C. S. MELLISH *Programming in Prolog*, 3rd ed. Springer Verlag, 1987.

COPI, I. M. *Introduction to Logic*, 7th ed. Macmillan, 1986.

DATE, C. J. *An Introduction to Database Systems*, Vol. 1, 5th ed., Addison-Wesley, 1991.

DATE, C. J. *Database: A Primer*. Addison-Wesley, 1983.

DECKER, R., AND S. HIRSHFIELD *The Analytical Engine*. Wadsworth, 1990.

DREYFUSS, H. L. *What Computers Still Can't Do*. MIT Press, 1992.

EISENBERG, M. *Programming in Scheme*. Scientific Press, 1988.

ELIASON, A. L. *Systems Development: Application, Design, and Implementation*. Little, Brown, and Co., 1987.

FEIGENBAUM, E., AND J. FELDMAN (EDS.) *Computers and Thought*. McGraw-Hill, 1963.

FISCHER, C. N., AND R. J. LEBLANC *Crafting a Compiler*. Benjamin/Cummings, 1988.

FOLEY, J. D., A. VAN DAM, S. K. FEINER, AND J. F. HUGHES *Computer Graphics Principles and Practice*. Addison-Wesley, 1990.

FRIEDMAN, D., AND M. FELLEISEN *The Little Lisper*. MIT Press, 1987.

FRIEDMAN, D., M. WAND, AND C. HAYNES *Essentials of Programming Languages*. MIT Press, 1992.

GOLDSTINE, H. *The Computer from Pascal to von Neumann*. Princeton, 1972.

HEADINGTON, M. R., AND D. D. RILEY *Data Abstraction and Structures Using C++*. D. C. Heath, 1994.

HENNESSY, J. L., AND D. A. PATTERSON *Machine Organization: Basic Principles*. Morgan Kaufmann, 1992.

HILL JR., F. S. *Computer Graphics*. MacMillan, 1990.

HODGES, A. *Alan Turing: The Enigma*. Burnett Books, 1983.

HOFSTADTER, D. R. *Gödel, Escher and Bach: An Eternal Golden Braid*. Basic Books, 1979.

KNUTH, D. E. *Fundamental Algorithms*, Vol. 1 of *The Art of Computer Programming*. Addison-Wesley, 1973.

KNUTH, D. E. *Seminumerical Algorithms*, Vol. 2 of *The Art of Computer Programming*. Addison-Wesley, 1981.

KNUTH, D. E. *Sorting and Searching*, Vol. 3 of *The Art of Computer Programming*. Addison-Wesley, 1973.

KORTH, H. F., AND A. SILBERSCHATZ *Database system concepts*. McGraw-Hill, 1986.

KRETZMANN, N. *Elements of Formal Logic*. Bobbs-Merrill, 1965.

KRUSE, R., B. P. LEUNG, AND C. TONDO *et al. Introduction to Data Structures using C++*. Prentice-Hall, 1993.

LANGER, S. K. *An Introduction to Symbolic Logic*. 3rd ed. Dover, 1967.

LIPPMAN, S. *C++ Primer*, 2nd ed. Addison-Wesley, 1993.

MAIER, D., AND D. WARREN *Computing with Logic: Logic Programming with Prolog*. Benjamin/Cummings, 1988.

MINSKY, M. L. *Computation: Finite and Infinite Machines*. Prentice-Hall, 1967.

MINSKY, M. L. *The Society of Mind*. Simon and Schuster, 1986.

POLYA, G. *How to Solve It*. Doubleday, 1957.

POWERS, M. J., D. R. ADAMS, AND H. D. MILLS *Computer Information Systems Development: Analysis and Design*. South-Western Publishing Co, 1984.

RANDELL, B. (ED.) *The Origins of Digital Computers*. Springer-Verlag, 1982.

RAYMOND, E. S. (ED.) *The New Hacker's Dictionary*. MIT Press, 1991.

ROSENBERG, R. S. *The Social Impact of Computers*. Academic Press, 1992.

SEDGWICK, R. *Algorithms in C*. Addison-Wesley, 1990.

SHAFER, D., AND D. A. RITZ *Practical Smalltalk: using Smalltalk/V*. Springer-Verlag, 1991.

SPRINGER, G., AND D. P. FRIEDMAN *Scheme and the Art of Programming*. MIT Press, 1990.

STALLINGS, W., *Computer Organization and Architecture: Principles of Structure and Function*. Macmillan, 1993.

TANENBAUM, A. *Computer Networks*, 2nd ed. Prentice-Hall, 1989.

TANENBAUM, A. *Modern Operating Systems*. Prentice-Hall, 1992.

TANENBAUM, A. *Structured Computer Organization*, 3rd ed. Prentice-Hall, 1989.

TANIMOTO, S. *The Elements of Artificial Intelligence Using Common Lisp* W. H. Freeman, 1990.

TUFTE, E. R. *The Visual Display of Quantitative Information* Graphics Press, 1983.

ULLMAN, J. D. *Principles of Database Systems*, Computer Science Press, 1980.

WARD, S. A., AND R. J. HALSTEAD *Computation Structures*. MIT Press, 1993.

WHITTEN, J. L., L. D. BENTLEY, AND T. I. HO *Systems Analysis and Design Methods* Times-Mirror/Mosby College Publishing, 1986.

WINSTON, P. H. *Artificial Intelligence*. Addison-Wesley, 1991.

Glossary

1NF   See **First Normal Form**. (p. 451)

2NF   See **Second Normal Form**. (p. 452)

3NF   See **Third Normal Form**. (p. 453)

abstract data type (ADT)   A programmer-defined data type whose interface specifies the values and operations of the data type, but not the underlying implementation. (p. 153)

abstraction   The fundamental technique of program design, in which we identify a unit of code that has a clearly defined **interface**, by suppressing all irrelevant detail about the **implementation**. Once we have done this correctly, the implementation of the code can be done independently of the **client** code. (p. 35)

abstraction barrier   An interface that hides internal structure. (p. 150)

accessor   A procedure in an ADT that returns a value from the ADT. (p. 154)

accumulator   A parameter used by a tail-recursive procedure to build up the result during recursion. The accumulator is returned as the value in the base case. (p. 92)

action   A specification of the computation performed based on successful rule matching. (p. 526)

address   A number that specifies a **cell** in a computer's **memory**. (p. 592)

algorithm   A series of steps that transform input to output. (p. 5)

alist   See association list. (p. 249)

allocate   Find a free section of memory, mark it used, and return its address. (p. 651)

analog   A representation that shares physical properties with what it represents. Usually used to mean a continuously varying quantity, such as voltage or pressure, used to represent a continuous computational value. (p. 578)

anonymous procedure   A procedure used without being bound to a name. (p. 265)

application   A Scheme **form** in which a **procedure** is applied to **arguments**, yielding a result. In common computing parlance, "application" has a second, separate, meaning, equivalent to "program". (p. 21)

architecture   The programmer's view of a hardware or software system. In a system of many components, the architecture will be the collection of **interfaces** of these components. (p. 590)

argument   A value provided as input to a function or procedure. (p. 18)

array   A generalized **vector**, in which a number of index values are used to identify a specific element. (p. 491)

artificial intelligence   The study of how computation can perform functions normally deemed "intelligent". (p. 525)

assembler   A program that converts assembly language to the machine language of a particular machine. (p. 600)

assembly language   A programming language designed to be easy to translate into **machine language**. Assembly language programs are much more readable than their machine language counterparts, but must pay attention to all of the details of the machine. (p. 11)

assignment   Changing the value of a variable using `set!` (p. 252)

association list   A list structure whose elements are pairs, whose cars are unique within the list and serve as keys for their cdr values. (p. 249)

atomic   Values that can't be broken down into smaller parts. (p. 244)

audit trail   A record of the changes that have been made in a database. (p. 424)

automaton   A device that can perform the processing specified by an algorithm (*pl.,* **automata**. (p. 5)

axioms   Statements that are taken as given. (p. 544)

Backus-Naur Form   A notation for expressing the syntax of programming languages. The version here is called Extended BNF (EBNF). (p. 353)

backward chaining   A proof method that starts with the conclusion and works backward to the assumptions. (p. 552)

base case   A case, in recursion, for which the value is known. (p. 64)

base register   An index register containing the address of the first location in a region of memory. (p. 609)

batch processing   A way of allocating processing resource by running user programs to completion, one at a time, in order of priority. Compare **interactive**. (p. 414)

behavior   In **object-oriented programming**, the set of **messages** to which an object responds. (p. 305)

big-oh notation   A mathematical function f is said to be "on the order of $g(x)$"—we write $f(x)$ is $O(g(x))$—if we can approximate f by g when x is large. (p. 85)

binary digits   Symbolic data items represented as 0 and 1. (p. 579)

binary search tree   A tree with two subtrees labeled "left" and "right". The keys of nodes in the left subtree are less than the key of the root and the keys of nodes in the right subtree are greater than the root key. (p. 472)

binding   An association between a **name** and a **value** (up to Chapter 5), or a name and a location (after Chapter 5). Names are **bound** to values/locations. (p. 30)

bisection   A method for finding roots (or searching for data) in which the area to be searched is split in two. Depending upon a single comparison, one of the two ranges is then searched recursively. (p. 70)

bitblt   An operation that copies some or all bits in a source bitmap into the corresponding bits of the destination. (p. 626)

bitmap   A data structure that represents a raster graphics image. (p. 621)

bits   See **binary digits**. (p. 579)

black-box testing   Testing a program using cases determined by its specification, not its implementation. (p. 95)

block   A collection of data written and read as a unit on a disk. (p. 440)

body   The form that is evaluated when a **procedure** is applied. The body may consist of more than one form; see **implicit begin**. (p. 25)

bootstrap   A program, stored in a fixed area, loaded by the hardware when the machine is switched on. Most bootstrap programs do nothing more than read the operating system into memory. The term comes from the phrase "lifting oneself by one's own bootstraps": we have to have a program in memory to read in another program. (p. 678)

bound   See **binding**. (p. 30)

box   A value that can contain another Scheme value. (p. 233)

box-and-arrow   A diagramming method for showing a list structure: each pair is shown as two boxes containing the car and cdr; items that do not fit in a box are drawn outside the box connected by an arrow. (p. 173)

BST   See **binary search tree**. (p. 472)

buffer   A temporary holding place for data as it passes between external storage and internal program space (p. 440)

bug   An error in a program. Sometimes a fault in a piece of equipment. (p. 5)

CAD   See **computer-assisted design**. (p. 507)

call   To apply a **procedure** to its **arguments**. (p. 60)

calling frame   The frame in which a procedure was called. (p. 259)

captured frame   A frame in the chain of frames connected by static links from a procedure returned as a value. (p. 272)

car   The first of the two boxes in a **pair**. (p. 168)

cardinality   In a **containment** relationship, the number of objects that are part of an object's state. (p. 329)

cdr   The second of the two boxes in a **pair**. (p. 168)

cell   An element of memory that can hold a single value. (p. 440)

central processing unit (CPU)   The component of a computer that fetches program **instructions** and carries them out. (p. 10)

character   A Scheme data type to represent keyboard input, including alphabetic, numeric and control characters. (p. 110)

cipher   A method of encrypting text by replacing individual characters. (p. 116)

circular list   A list structure in which a sequence of cdrs returns to an element in it. (p. 244)

class   In **object-oriented programming**, a group of objects that all have the same set of **instance variables** (with, generally, different values), and the same set of **methods**. (p. 306)

class libraries   An integrated set of classes, in an object-oriented language, that provide a unified set of abstractions. (p. 647)

class method   In **object-oriented programming** a method that acts on behalf of the whole class, rather than a specific object. (p. 313)

class variable   In **object-oriented programming**, a variable that can be accessed by all instances of a given class. (p. 313)

client The user of a procedure, module, or program. A client is only concerned with the **interface**, but not the **implementation**, of the code. (p. 27)

code Generically, any piece of a program, or anything written in a programming language (p. 16)

There are two definitions!A method of encrypting text by replacing words. (p. 116)

cohesive (Of procedures) Concise, and serving a single purpose. (p. 120)

column The values in a table of a property for all individuals. (p. 415)

command A form whose purpose is primarily to produce an effect. (p. 126)

comments Text entered in a program file that is not interpreted as Scheme code but as comments to the reader of the program (a human). (p. 68)

comparator A procedure that returns one of three symbols, `less-than`, `equal-to`, or `greater-than`, depending on the values of its arguments. (p. 426)

compiler A program that translate programs from one language into another. (p. 369)

complexity A measure of a program's efficiency, ignoring factors such as computer and programming language. (p. 81)

composite Composed of simpler parts. (p. 244)

compress Use a more space-efficient representation for a large amount of data. (p. 507)

computation The use of systematic methods for finding results for algebraic or symbolic problems. Some people use "computation" as a synonym for "computer science". (p. 3)

computer-assisted design (CAD) The use of computers for developing designs in engineering, architecture, and manufacturing. (p. 507)

conclusion A statement derived by means of rules and proof. (p. 544)

concurrent tasks Tasks performed at the same time. (p. 290)

conditional A special form that makes a decision. This book discusses three types of conditional forms: `if`, `case`, and `cond`. (p. 40)

cons To make a **pair** whose **car** and **cdr** have specified values. (p. 169)

constructor The procedure in an ADT that creates a value of the data type. (p. 153)

containment A relationship between two **objects**, in which one object has a second object as part of its state. (p. 329)

context switch A change of control between two processes, necessitating storage of program context. (p. 682)

contradiction A logical formula that is false regardless of the truth values of its variables. (p. 547)

control characters Non-printing characters whose function is to specify control in communications. (p. 113)

conversion procedures Procedures that map a value of one data type into a corresponding value in another data type. (p. 112)

correctness (Of an algorithm) Does what the specification requires. (p. 8)

cross-compile To compile code on one machine for evaluation on another type of machine. (p. 660)

cross-matching   Joining tables that are not related. (p. 420)

cybernetic device   An **automaton** that controls its environment in response to data read from the environment. (p. 9)

data   A representation of information suitable for use in an algorithm. (p. 5)

data abstraction   Program design using an abstract interface to data that hides the implementation. (p. 153)

database   A large collection of data accessed via a general interface. Normally, the term is reserved for collections of **persistent** data. (p. 411)

database description   A description of the information in a database and its organization. (p. 413)

database design   Determining the relationships among the data in a database. (p. 237)

database layer   A collections of procedures that manage data, providing an abstraction layer. (p. 412)

database management system   A set of procedures implementing a general database abstraction. (p. 413)

data dictionary   A list of all of the columns in any tables in the database, along with a specification of each one. (p. 454)

data structure   The organization and representation of information in a computer to facilitate an algorithm. (p. 168)

DBMS   See **database management system**. (p. 413)

debug   Identify the error in a program that produces incorrect results, and determine how to correct the error. (p. 33)

debugger   A program that helps a programmer examine the state of a user program to locate bugs. (p. 395)

decode cycle   The operation cycle in which the CU determines the components of an instruction. (p. 597)

decomposition   Designing code by breaking large problems down into smaller, more manageable portions that can be understood on their own. (p. 35)

definition   Creating a **binding** in the top-level **environment**. (p. 29)

delegation   A technique for implementing specialization in which an object of the generalized class is kept as an instance variable of the corresponding object of the specialized class (p. 333)

delimiter   A marker that identifies the beginning and ending of a group. (p. 203)

destination register   The register where the result is stored in a Gleam instruction. (p. 598)

destructive   A data operation that mutates the data in a structure. (p. 241)

device dependence   Reliance, in a program, on particular device characteristics. (p. 673)

device interface   A procedure responsible for interacting with a device. (p. 656)

device registers   Registers in a device concerned with its state. (p. 656)

digital   Representation using symbolic components termed digits. (p. 578)

directory   A structure recording the names and locations of files. (p. 674)

discrete event simulation Simulation where the state is modeled as passing through a set of events occurring at discrete clock ticks. (p. 512)

dispenser A procedure that encapsulates a list and delivers one item at a time, with two operations: `get` the next element, and `peek` at the next element. (p. 317)

divide and conquer A recursion technique in which the problem is divided, conquered (solved), and the solutions of the subproblems are combined. (p. 75)

dot notation Scheme's notation for printing a pair. Scheme prints a parenthesis, followed by the car of the pair, a period (the dot), then the cdr of the pair. (p. 170)

driver A procedure that abstracts a device interface by providing the programmer with a set of problem-oriented procedures that operate the device. (p. 658)

droid A "worker" that is used to evaluate a procedure in the **Droid Model**. Droids remember the argument values given to a procedure and the recipient of the result. (p. 59)

droid diagram A graphical depiction of the relation among procedure applications, using the Droid Model. (p. 60)

Droid Model A model of evaluating Scheme forms that is based upon Ҭһҽ Ʀսӏҽѕ but focuses on how procedures are called. (p. 59)

dynamic link The connection between a frame and the frame to which the frame's value is returned. (p. 259)

effect A change in the computer system. (p. 125)

effective address The memory address formed by adding the contents of the index register to the address field of the instruction. (p. 608)

Egyptian peasant method A multiplication method that operates by doubling and halving. Unlike the repetitive addition algorithm, Egyptian peasant multiplication takes only logarithmic time. (p. 83)

embed Place a `let` form inside a **scope**, either to make the bindings in the enclosing scope available to the embedded forms, or to hide the embedded names. (p. 143)

embedded computer A computer built into a device. (p. 580)

emulator A procedure for performing operations as if the service was part of the computer. (p. 646)

environment Initially, the collection of built-in and user-defined **bindings**. After Chapter 5, it includes the bindings contained in the current **frame** and all other frames that are parents of the current frame. (p. 32)

environment model A computational model of Scheme based on frames and procedure application. (p. 258)

equality Two values are equal if they print the same way. Scheme makes a distinction between identity, checked by `eq?`, **equivalence**, checked by `eqv?`, and **equality**, checked by `equal?`. We do not make that distinction in this book. (p. 245)

equivalent Indistinguishable by the operations of Scheme. See also **equality** and **identity**. (p. 245)

evaluate To compute the result of a **form** in a program. (p. 16)

evaluator A program that reads a second program and carries out the operations specified by that program. (p. 4)

executable file   A file containing program code in machine language. (p. 672)

execute   The operation cycle in which the CU performs the specified instruction. (p. 597)

existential quantification   Stating that a property applies to at least one individual. (p. 548)

exponential complexity   Complexity of an algorithm that increases by a multiplicative factor for each additional unit of input. (p. 88)

export   Make a name visible to the rest of the program. (p. 150)

Extended Backus-Naur Form   A simplification of Backus-Naur Form. (p. 353)

external entity   In **object-oriented design,** a device or person that provides data to the system or receives data from the system. (p. 328)

fact   A statement that is declared to be true. (p. 524)

factory   A procedure whose result is a procedure. (p. 271)

feasible   (Of an algorithm) Each step can in fact be carried out. (p. 8)

fetch   The operation cycle in which the CU gets the instruction from memory. (p. 597)

fetch/decode/execute loop   Essential iteration of the CU. (p. 597)

field   The value at the intersection of a row and column in a table. (p. 415)

FIFO   "First-in/first/out". A policy for managing **time-ordered structures** in which the earliest item inserted is the first one to be retrieved. (p. 498)

file   A persistent collection of data on external storage. (p. 674)

file server   A server that maintains a collections of files. (p. 680)

filtering   Producing a list by selecting elements from another list using a predicate. (p. 213)

finding classes   The first major step in **object-oriented design,** identifying the **classes** that are needed in a specific problem. (p. 326)

finite   (Of an algorithm) Doesn't go on forever, but terminates with an answer. (p. 9)

first-class citizens   Values that can be bound to variables, passed as arguments, and returned as the values of procedures. (p. 133)

first-in-first-out   A policy in which the first item to enter a **time-ordered** structure is the first to be removed. (p. 498)

First Normal Form   An organization in database design where each is a simple piece of data. (p. 451)

floating point   A kind of number that contains a decimal point. The decimal point can "float" through the number, rather than being in a fixed place. (p. 70)

font   A collection of character images in a particular style. This book is set in a collection of fonts known as Lucida Bright. Fonts may be either bitmapped (as in Chapter 11) or outline (as in good-quality commercial fonts). (p. 626)

form   A unit of Scheme code that can be entered into an evaluator. (p. 16)

format string   A string that specifies both literal output and how to display the printed representation of a set of values that follow. (p. 128)

forward chaining   A proof method that starts with the original information and works forward to the conclusion. (p. 552)

frame   A structure created on procedure application, containing bindings and static and dynamic information regarding the procedure (p. 258)

frame buffer   A data structure in memory that represents an image to be drawn on a graphics display. In a raster graphics display, the frame buffer will be a two-dimensional array of **pixels.** (p. 622)

free list   A Scheme system data structure that records the free pairs in the heap. (p. 651)

free name   Name not bound in the current scope. (p. 262)

free pair   A pair on the heap that is not used. (p. 651)

functionally dependent   (Of database columns) one column's values are determined by another's. (p. 452)

garbage collection   The process of determining the unused pairs in the heap and putting them on the free list. (p. 653)

garbage collector   The procedure that performs **garbage collection.** (p. 653)

general-purpose computer   A computer that is meant to run user programs. (p. 580)

general register   One of the registers in the Register Unit, used to hold data during a computation. (p. 595)

generated symbol   A unique symbol generated by Scheme. (p. 377)

gensym   See **generated symbol.** (p. 377)

glass-box testing   Testing a program based on the internal structure of the program. (p. 95)

global variable   A variable defined in the user frame. (p. 259)

glyph   An elementary value that a computer can manipulate. See also **bit.** (p. 578)

graphics accelerator   A hardware device that performs graphics algorithms such as line drawing and **bitblting** at high speed. (p. 646)

graphic user interface   A way of using computers that allows users to manipulate items directly on the screen, often using icons, dialog boxes, and controls such as scroll bars (p. 301)

GUI   See **graphic user interface.** (p. 301)

hardware   Tangible pieces of computing equipment, such as computers, monitors, keyboards, and so on. Often, the word "hardware" is used specifically to refer to the computer, in opposition to **software.** (p. 4)

heap   A section of memory dedicated to holding pairs. (p. 651)

helper   A procedure that does a task on behalf of another procedure, and is not intended to be called by a **client.** (p. 34)

hexadecimal   A representation of numbers using base 16. (p. 582)

hot view   A table that is dynamically constructed to represent a subset of the data in a table. (p. 421)

identity   Two objects are identical if mutating one mutates the other. See also **equivalent** and **equal.** (p. 245)

image   See **raster image.** (p. 506)

immutable   Values whose state cannot be changed. (p. 233)

imperative evaluator A Scheme evaluator written directly in Gleam instructions. (p. 660)

implementation The aspect of a procedure, module, or program that specifies how the code operates, including the **algorithms** and **data structures**. (p. 27)

implication The logical connective expressing "*a implies b*". (p. 546)

implicit begin The body of a procedure is evaluated in order as if it were enclosed in a begin form. (p. 129)

improper list A chain of pairs not terminated by null. (p. 186)

index register In a Gleam memory-reference instruction, a register whose contents are added to the source address to form the effective address. (p. 598)

individual A single identifiable object. (p. 547)

indivisible task A task whose action must be processed completely before working on another. (p. 290)

inductive definition A definition that begins from a base case and describes how to build the defined object by simple steps, starting from the base case. (p. 186)

inference engine A program that implements a proof method. (p. 558)

infinite loop (See infinite loop.) (p. 64)

infinite recursion, infinite loop A loop in which the base case is never reached, and hence which never terminates. (p. 64)

inheritance Accessing the methods of a generalized class from a specialized class, without creating a generalized object as in delegation. (p. 332)

in-order A method of **traversing** a tree in which the left subtree is visited before the root, and the right subtree is visited after the root. (p. 479)

input Data that is entered into a computer from the outside world. (p. 10)

insertion sort Sorting by inserting new items in the correct place in a sorted collection. (p. 441)

instance An **object** is an instance of its **class**. (p. 306)

instance variable A variable that is part of the state of an **object**. There are two kinds of instance variables: **constructor arguments** and **slots**. (p. 307)

instantiate To create a new **instance** of a **class**. (p. 306)

instruction A pattern of bits stored in its memory that the CPU will interpret as a command to perform an operation. (p. 597)

instruction register Register in the CU holding the current instruction. (p. 597)

instruction set The collection of basic operations of a computer. (p. 597)

interactive A system is interactive if it responds immediately to a user request. Compare **batch-processing**. (p. 14)

interface The aspect of a procedure, module, or program that specifies how the code is used by **clients**. (p. 27)

interpret Evaluate a program by computing the value or effect of each element. (p. 364)

interrupt A machine operation, caused by an event, that halts program control and transfers control to a handler for the event. (p. 657)

invocation   To apply a procedure to its arguments. (p. 60)

iteration   A program structure where a body of code is repeatedly evaluated. (p. 93)

join   A **relational operation** that produces a new table from two existing fields that have a column in common. (p. 422)

key   A value that uniquely identifies a particular element of a collection such as a dictionary, `table`, alist, or BST. (p. 248)

knapsack   The problem of finding a maximum size subset of a collection of objects of differing size. (p. 89)

`lambda` **form**   A Scheme form that specifies the **interface (parameters)** and **implementation (body)** of a procedure. (p. 25)

`lambda` **over** `lambda`   A `lambda` form whose body is a `lambda` form. (p. 277)

language   (*i*) A *natural language* such as English or French; (*ii*) a *programming language* such as Scheme. Programming languages are systems of writing instructions for a computer, and owe more to algebra than to natural languages. (p. 5)

last-in-first-out   A policy in which the last item to enter a **time-ordered** structure is the first to be removed. (p. 498)

layout   Description of the columns in a table. (p. 417)

leaf node   An element in a tree structure having no descendants. (p. 359)

legacy code   Programs written using obsolete tools and design techniques, but that are still useful. (p. 303)

`let` **over** `lambda`   A `let` form whose body is a `lambda` form. (p. 276)

lexical   A type of scoping also known as static scoping. (p. 144)

library   A collection of useful procedures that is provided to the programmer as a package. Library procedures are designed to perform tasks that occur frequently. (p. 127)

LIFO   "Last-in/first out". A policy for managing **time-ordered structures** in which the most recently inserted item is the first one to be retrieved. (p. 498)

limit   In calculus, a sequence reaches a limit when the difference between successive terms becomes so small that it doesn't matter. (p. 72)

list   A Scheme abstract data type, using pairs, that can contain an indefinite number of items, implemented as null or a chain of pairs whose last cdr is null. (p. 185)

logic   The study of reasoning and proof. Modern logic draws from philosophy, mathematics, and computer science. (p. 544)

logical structure   The logical relations among elements of a database. (p. 412)

logic programming   Programming by specification using logic. (p. 552)

loop   A programming structure that specifies operations be repeated. In this book, the overwhelming majority of loops are done via **recursion**. (p. 57)

machine abstraction   A set of operations that constitute an abstract computational device. (p. 642)

machine language   The programming language directly processed by a computer. (p. 11)

macro   A programmer-defined special form. A form whose first element is a name defined as a macro is processed by the macro builder procedure, and the resulting structure is processed as if it were the input form. (p. 373)

mapping   Applying a procedure to all elements of a list. (p. 208)

masking   Altering the value of a bit by performing bitwise operations. (p. 630)

match   A correspondence between a pattern and a target. (p. 526)

mathematical function   A rule in mathematics for computing an answer from some input values. (p. 18)

mathematical induction   A proof technique for proving propositions referring to the integers. (p. 551)

mechanism   A set of specific techniques by which a program achieves its ends, as distinguished from **policy**. (p. 506)

memory   (also *storage*) The part of a computer that contains storage devices for holding information during the execution of a program. (p. 10)

Memory Address Register   Memory unit register holding the number of the memory cell accessed. (p. 595)

Memory Data Register   Memory unit register holding the value to be transferred to or from memory. (p. 595)

memory-mapped input/output   Input/output accomplished by storing data in reserved locations. The storage operation instead causes input/output to devices. (p. 656)

memory-reference instructions   A Gleam instruction involving transfer of data to or from memory. (p. 598)

merge   Unite two ordered collections, preserving the order. (p. 414)

message   A request that is made to an **object**. (p. 304)

method   The procedure that the object uses to carry out the request of a method. (p. 305)

MIPS   Millions of Instructions executed Per Second. A measure of computer speed. Because this measurement depends upon the particular kinds of instructions a computer can execute, MIPS figures are susceptible to exaggeration or distortion. As a result, many cynics claim "MIPS" stands for "meaningless indicator of processor speed". (p. 80)

module   A collection of definitions serving a common purpose in which internal definitions can be hidden. (p. 150)

multiway recursion   A form of recursion in which each level triggers more than one recursive call. See also **tree recursion**. (p. 79)

mutable   (Of a value) able to be changed. (p. 233)

mutation   The process of changing a value's state. (p. 233)

mutator   A procedure that changes a value's state. (p. 233)

mutual recursion   Two procedures that call each other exhibit mutual recursion. (p. 129)

name   An element of a Scheme program that can be bound to a value. (p. 256)

narrative method   A method of **finding classes** that operates by examining a description of the system to be built, and using the nouns as the names of possible classes. (p. 326)

nine's-complement A representation of decimal numbers in which the negation of a number is represented by subtracting digits from 9. (p. 587)

node An element in a tree structure. (p. 359)

normal forms A set of organizing rules for database design. (p. 451)

normalizing Ensuring that a database satisfies certain organizational rules. (p. 451)

null The Scheme value representing the empty list. (p. 185)

null string A string of zero length containing no characters. (p. 114)

numeral The written representation of a number. (p. 21)

object A value in an object-oriented program. Objects respond to **messages** sent to them by client code, by applying an appropriate **method**. An object encapsulates its state. (p. 304)

object-based design A variety of **object-oriented design** in which the resulting program is not intended to be written in an object-oriented language. In object-based design, we attempt to minimize the use of **polymorphism** and **specialization**. Object-based design is being superseded as more and more languages acquire object-oriented features. (p. 334)

object-oriented design A program design technique that organizes the program around classes and their relationships. (p. 324)

object program A translated version of a program in executable form. (p. 369)

octal A representation of numbers using base 8. (p. 582)

one's-complement A representation of binary numbers in which the negation of a number is represented by subtracting digits from 1. (p. 588)

one-to-many containment A **containment** in which each object contains, as the value of a specific instance variable, a collection of other objects. (p. 329)

one-to-one containment A **containment** in which each object contains, as the value of a specific instance variable, a single object. (p. 329)

opcode The numeric code representing an instruction in the machine. (p. 598)

open To prepare a file for access. (p. 674)

operating system A collection of programs that implement important computer resource management functions. (p. 671)

operation A computation implemented by a computer. (p. 597)

orthogonal By analogy with linear algebra, having a small set of independent features that can be combined to express all necessary operations. (p. 349)

output Data that is sent by a computer to the outside world. (p. 10)

pair A representation of two values as a single value. (p. 168)

parallel computation A programming style in which more than one computation is active at the same time. (p. 81)

parameter A name that acts as a placeholder for an **argument** in a lambda form. (p. 25)

parent frame The frame in which a procedure was created. (p. 259)

partition A division of a collection into a collection of groups that, between them, contain all of the elements in the original collection. Quicksort partitions all of the "small" elements (those less than the **pivot**) into one group, and all of the "large" ones into the other. (p. 485)

password   An identifier known only to the user. (p. 456)

pattern   A representation of the structure of a class of items, including constant and variable elements. (p. 526)

pattern variables   Variable elements in a pattern that act as wild cards, matching anything. Two different items cannot match one pattern variable. (p. 527)

persistent data   Data that exists beyond the life of the program that created it. (p. 440)

physical structure   The physical, as opposed to logical, structure of the data. (p. 412)

pipeline   Overlap the components of an operation to speed up its operation. (p. 659)

pivot   In Quicksort, a value from the original collection that is used to determine whether any other value is "small" or "large". (p. 486)

pixels   A picture element on a raster device. (p. 506)

placemarker   A value that holds the address of a control point to which a program can return. (p. 663)

plausible   (Of data) seems reasonable. Data can be **valid** without being plausible, but not the reverse. (p. 424)

policy   A set of general rules by which the program operates, as distinguished from **mechanism**. (p. 505)

polymorphism   The ability of a **procedure** to accept arguments of different types, or of different kinds of **objects** to respond to the same messages. (p. 312)

pop   Remove the top item from a **push-down stack**. (p. 501)

portable   Of code, able to be run on any implementation of the source language. (p. 247)

position   The number of an item in a string, list, or vector, counting from zero. (p. 114)

precedence   Ordering of operators in expressions. Those with highest precedence are grouped first, and then grouping occurs in order of decreasing precedence. (p. 399)

predicate   A procedure—user-defined or primitive—that returns a Boolean result. By convention, the names of predicates end with a question mark. (p. 42)

predicate logic   Logic allowing not only propositions but also properties referring to individuals, as well as quantifiers. (p. 547)

premise   An assumed fact or rule. (p. 544)

primitive   Something that can't be defined in terms of something simpler. In Scheme, primitive generally means "primitive procedure", one of the **procedures** that are built in to the Scheme **evaluator**. (p. 21)

primitive data type (PDT)   The interface to a Scheme primitive. (p. 168)

privacy   Protection in a **database** to ensure that only those authorized to see certain data can actually see that data (p. 420)

private   Hidden within a scope, as in a `let` or `module` (p. 150)

procedure   A Scheme value obtained by evaluating a `lambda` form (p. 26)

process   The execution of a program. (p. 682)

profiler   A program that keeps track of the amount of time spent in each procedure of a program. (p. 469)

program A set of instructions which tells a computer how to transform input data into the desired outputs. (p. 4)

program counter (PC) Register in the CU that holds the address of the current instruction. (p. 597)

programming in the large Programming large software systems, usually performed by groups of people. (p. 139)

programming in the small The process of programming a small number of procedures, by a single programmer. (p. 139)

projection A **relational operator** that produces a new table by extracting one or more columns from an original table. (p. 419)

prolog A sequence of instructions executed at the beginning of a procedure. (p. 610)

prompt Ask the user for a specific kind of input. (p. 16)

prompting Output that notifies the program user that the program is ready to read input. (p. 126)

proof A careful argument that demonstrates a conclusion. Proof is used to show that a program works correctly. (p. 95)

proof method A technique for constructing correct proofs. (p. 552)

proof rule A means of deriving conclusions. (p. 544)

proposition A statement to which one can attribute truth or falsity. (p. 545)

propositional logic Logic using only individual symbols standing for propositions and logical connectives. (p. 545)

protocol A set of rules followed by communicating programs. (p. 680)

protocol family A group of protocols intended to work together. (p. 680)

prove To derive by means of logical rules. (p. 544)

pseudocode An **algorithm** notation that is intended for human rather than computer consumption, omitting detail. The book uses two forms of pseudocode: structured English and a Scheme-like notation. (p. 6)

pseudorandom sequence A sequence of values which has been generated by an algorithm, but in which the next value can't be determined from the previous ones without performing the steps of the algorithm. Pseudorandom sequence have the same statistical properties as genuinely random ones produced, e.g., by flipping a coin. (p. 277)

push To put an item into a **push-down stack**. (p. 501)

push-down stack A **time-ordered** structure that follows a **LIFO** policy. (p. 501)

quantification In logic, a way of describing the set of individuals to which a formula applies. (p. 548)

query optimization Reorganizing a query to speed its computation. (p. 449)

quote A special form that tells the evaluator not to evaluate the following form. (p. 179)

RAM See **random access memory**. (p. 594)

random access Of storage devices such as memory and disks, indicates that any item without accessing other items. Contrast with **sequential retrieval**. (p. 594)

random access memory   A memory device in which any item can be accessed without accessing other items. (p. 594)

random sequence   A sequence of values in which the next value cannot be predicted from the previous ones. (p. 277)

raster   See **raster device**. (p. 506)

raster device   A two-dimensional display device whose elements form a grid that is accessed in order from top left to bottom right, stepping along horizontal rows. (p. 506)

raster graphics   Graphics on raster displays. (p. 621)

raster image   A two-dimensional collection of brightness values, to be displayed on a raster device. (p. 506)

reading   Inputting Scheme values from an external source. (p. 124)

read only memory   Random access memory that only allows read operations. (p. 595)

real-time   Able to perform computation in a fixed, small amount of time, usually to meet strict interaction demands, such as controlling machinery. (p. 655)

record structure   A data structure describing a collection of simpler pieces of information. (p. 415)

recursion   A programming technique for **loops** that is based upon a procedure calling itself with a simpler argument. Recursive procedures are generally divided into a **base case** and a **recursion step**. From the Latin words meaning "running again". (p. 63)

recursion step   Applying a recursive procedure to reduce the problem to a simpler case, finally leading to the **base case**. (p. 64)

recursive definition   A definition that describes an object in terms of a base object or a simpler object that of the same type. (p. 188)

recursive descent   A method of processing expressions by translating the **EBNF** specifications into a programming language. (p. 401)

reduction   Computing a function that depends on all members of a list (p. 215)

referential integrity   A condition in databases requiring that all referenced rows must exist. (p. 454)

register conventions   Programming conventions that specify the symbolic names and the contents of registers. (p. 647)

register instructions   A Gleam instruction only involving data in registers. (p. 598)

relation   A tabular representation of information. Each row contains information about an individual. Each column contains a particular kind of information about a set of individuals. (p. 418)

relational operations   The operations of our relational model for combining tables. The relational operations are **selection, projection**, and **join**. (p. 418)

repl   Short for "read-eval-print" loop. Scheme's master control loop that repeatedly reads forms from the user, evaluates them, and displays the result. (p. 205)

representation   The internal structure that corresponds to some information. (p. 151)

resume point   The location in the program at which control resumes when an application completes. (p. 259)

return address   The memory address to which control returns on completion of a procedure. (p. 608)

reusability   The quality of code that allows a component—a procedure, module, or class, for example—to be used in many different programs. (p. 303)

ROM   See **read only memory**. (p. 595)

root node   An element in a tree structure having no ancestor. (p. 359)

row   A record in a table describing the values of the properties of an individual. (p. 415)

rule   A conclusion together with the conditions that must be true to make the conclusion true. (p. 524)

ruleset   A data structure representing a collection of rules. (p. 554)

run time   During the execution of a program. (p. 369)

scope   The region in the text of the program where the **binding** of a **variable** is known, either the body of a `let` form or a `lambda` form. (p. 141)

Second Normal Form   An organization in database design where no column is functionally dependent on just one part of the key. (p. 452)

security   Protection in a **database** to ensure that unauthorized changes are not performed on the data. (p. 420)

seed   A value that is used as the first element of a **pseudorandom sequence**. (p. 277)

selection   A **relational operation** that creates a new table from an existing table by choosing only those rows that satisfy a specific criterion. (p. 419)

self-modifying code   Code in a machine-language program that creates and executes new instructions as it proceeds. Scheme systems that provide `eval` primitives lead to similar coding practices. This practice is generally frowned upon, because it leads to unreadable programs. (p. 607)

semantics   The set of rules that define the meaning of programs—i.e. what the program actually computes—in a language. (p. 13)

sentinel   A special data value chosen to signal the end of input. (p. 124)

sequencing   Evaluating a set of forms in the order written. (p. 127)

sequential retrieval   Retrieving an element in a structure by sequentially passing through all elements from the beginning (or end) until the desired element is found. (p. 481)

server   A program or machine that provides a service. (p. 456)

service   A function of common utility in a computer system. (p. 150)

shadowing   A variable shadows all other variables of the same name that occur higher in the chain of frames connected by static links. (p. 262)

shared storage   Two values share storage when they occupy the same portion of memory. Mutating one value mutates the other. (p. 246)

shared variable   A variable used in an inner `let` or `lambda` that occurs in an enclosing scope. The value of the variable must be the same in both scopes. (p. 147)

shell   A program that reads operating system commands and executes them. (p. 671)

side effects   Effects produced by a program that are not the direct effect intended by the program. (p. 125)

simulation   Computing the state of a system by modeling the relations among its components and their behavior over time. (p. 512)

slot   One of the **instance variables** of an **object**. In `define-class` a slot is an instance variable that isn't one of the constructor arguments. (p. 310)

snapshot   A diagram of the frames, variables bindings, and procedures in the Scheme environment during a computation. (p. 259)

software   Computer programs in a collective sense. See also **hardware**. (p. 4)

software engineering   The process and techniques of developing programs, managing code and communication among programmers. (p. 139)

sort   Arrange in a specified order. (p. 414)

source program   A program in the language being interpreted or translated. (p. 369)

source register   A registers that provides input in Gleam register instructions. (p. 598)

special form   A form that starts with a keyword known to Scheme. Special forms are not treated as procedure applications, but are evaluated according to a specific rule for each type of special form. See also **macro**. (p. 30)

specialization   A relationship between **classes** in which one class has the state and behavior of a second. (p. 331)

specification   A statement of the inputs, outputs, assumptions and the relation between the inputs and outputs of a program. (p. 50)

specification language   A language for describing the input/output relation of a program. (p. 551)

stack   See **push-down stack**. (p. 501)

state   Time-varying properties of an entity. (p. 232)

static link   The connection between a frame and the parent frame of the procedure applied to create the frame. (p. 259)

static scoping   Determining the **scope** of a **variable** by examining the text of the program, independent of the execution of the program. (p. 144)

static type checking   Certain languages associate types with names. In these languages, static type checking detects errors in assigning values of the wrong type to names or elements of data structures. (p. 369)

stepwise refinement   A problem-solving method in which we start with a simplified version of a procedure, leaving many of the details as **stubs**. Once we have this version working, we can implement the stubs. (p. 221)

storage-mapping function   A mathematical function that relates a position in a two-dimensional grid to a position in a one-dimensional vector used to store the grid in memory. (p. 622)

stored program   Of computers, refers to the concept of putting the program into memory rather than "hard-wiring" it into the computer. (p. 592)

string   A data type representing a fixed-length sequence of characters. (p. 114)

string recursion   Recursion based on incrementing a current position in a structure with a fixed length, such as a string. (p. 115)

structured analysis   A method of problem-solving in which the operations of a business or other organization are broken down into a set of tasks, and each of those tasks broken down into subtasks hierarchically. Contrast with **object-oriented design**. (p. 304)

stub procedure   A procedure that performs no computation, returning a value of the expected kind, used in program development and later replaced. (p. 121)

sublist   A list that is part of another list. (p. 193)

substitution   Replacing a **form** with its **value**. (p. 20)

substring recursion   Processing strings by handling the first character and then passing (substring str 1 len) to the recursive call. (p. 118)

subsystem   A set of procedures that have a common function. (p. 149)

subtree   A tree whose root node is a node in another tree. (p. 359)

swap   Exchange the value of two variables. (p. 255)

syllogisms   A form of reasoning that starts with two assumed premises and leads to a conclusion. (p. 544)

syntactic abstraction   Creating new special forms to express common program elements simply. (p. 375)

syntactic sugar   A syntactic construct that adds expressiveness without increasing functionality. (p. 379)

syntax   The set of rules that define what is grammatical in a programming language. (p. 13)

systems analysis   Analyzing the type of information and the relations among its constituents in a data processing system. (p. 237)

table   A database representation of properties of a set of individuals. (p. 415)

tag   A collection of bits that identifies the type of value in a cell. (p. 650)

tail call   A procedure call as the last operation of a procedure. (p. 612)

tail recursion   Recursion where the recursion step is the last step in the procedure. (p. 92)

target   The structure compared against the pattern. (p. 527)

tautology   A formula that is true regardless of the truth values of its variables. (p. 547)

temporary variable   A variable used to hold a value for a short period of time. (p. 255)

ten's-complement   A representation of decimal numbers in which the negation of a number is represented by subtracting digits from 10. (p. 587)

termination test   The test in an recursion that finds whether the recursion is at the base case. (p. 98)

test   Verify the **correctness** of a program by checking its behavior with various input values. (p. 33)

test case   A program input (together with the output) used to determine whether the code works properly. (p. 95)

theorem   A statement derived from axioms by rules of argument or proof. (p. 544)

Third Normal Form   An organization in database design where no nonkey field depends on a field other than the key. (p. 453)

thunks   Procedures without arguments, usually given as arguments, meant to delay evaluation of the body. (p. 136)

time-ordered structure   A data structure whose contents reflect the sequence in which values were inserted. (p. 498)

tlist   A list together with an additional pair whose car and cdr contain the first and last pairs of the list. (p. 466)

top-down programming   Programming that begins with the problem specification and progressively expands a simple solution, filling in details. (p. 120)

top level   The top level of a list is the set of elements contained in the cars of all the cells in a direct line from the cell at the beginning of the list and all the cdrs until the end of the list. (p. 190)

toy language   A language designed as a vehicle for studying one or more aspects of programming languages rather than for any useful programming purpose. (p. 350)

trace   Display the arguments and return value of a procedure each time it is called. Most Scheme systems provide a `trace` special form to cause trace output to be produced each time a procedure is called or returns. (p. 66)

transform   To alter the value of data in a systematic way, such as scaling. (p. 135)

translate   Create an equivalent program in a different language. (p. 364)

traverse   Visit all of the nodes of a tree structure. (p. 361)

tree   A structure in which each element has only one ancestor and zero or more descendants. (p. 359)

tree recursion   A form of recursion in which each recursion generates, like a tree, more than one recursive call. Recursive procedures on trees are necessarily tree-recursive. (p. 361)

truth table   A table showing the truth value of a formula under all assignments of truth values to its variables. (p. 546)

truth value   A value describing the truth of a statement or proposition, usually *true* or *false*. (p. 546)

two-dimensional array   An array structure indexed by row and column. (p. 622)

two's-complement   A representation of binary numbers in which the negation of a number is represented by subtracting digits from two. (p. 587)

type   A specific kind of data. Many Scheme procedures and special forms require operands to be of a specific type. The built-in Scheme types studied in this book are: numbers, Booleans, procedures, void, pairs, symbols, null, strings, characters, and vectors. See also **abstract data type**. (p. 41)

type check   Check the validity of data on input. (p. 437)

unification   A generalized matching method for handling patterns and targets both containing pattern variables. (p. 565)

unimplemented instruction exception   A technique in hardware that recognizes nonexistent instructions and transfers control to a handler that can perform the required operations. (p. 646)

universal quantification   Stating that a formula applies to all individuals. (p. 548)

user interface   The portion of a company system that reads data from a user and communicates information to a user. (p. 288)

user interface object   An **object** whose state and behavior are concerned with interacting with the user. In a **GUI**, windows, dialogs, message boxes, and so on are all connected to user interface objects. (p. 307)

valid   (Of a chain of reasoning) connected by correct application of proof rules to the assumptions. (p. 544)

validity   (Of data) correct according to certain well-defined rules. (p. 424)

value   A piece of datum that a Scheme program can process. (p. 17)

variable   A binding of a name to a value. (p. 256)

variadic   (Of a procedure) taking a variable number of arguments. (p. 217)

vector   A collection of items, like a list, but stored in such a way that we can access any item in the vector in constant time. (p. 491)

vector graphics   Graphics performed on a display by specifying line segments (vectors) swept out on the display. (p. 621)

virtual machine   A computer simulation of a machine other than the physical machine, to allow the programmer to write programs as if she were using a real machine. (p. 643)

void   A special non-printing value. (p. 126)

wild card   A pattern element that can match anything. (p. 526)

wordsize   The size of a standard collection of bits treated as a unit by a computer, usually the same size as an instruction. (p. 581)

Index

F

H

halt (Gleam instruction), 777
halve, 83
Handwriting recognition, 584
Hard problems, 88
Harneck, Sheldon, 526
Hash tables, 649*n*
Heap, 651, 653
Helper, 73
Hennessy, John L., 684
Hexadecimal radix, 757
Hickson, W. E., 69
Hiding, code, 140
Hirshfield, Stuart, 51
Hoare, C. A. R., 485
Hodges, Andrew, 51
Hollerith, Herman, 15
Holmes, Sherlock, 29
Hopper, Grace Murray, 5, 15, 49
Hot view, 421
HP-PA (Hewlett-Packard Corp.), 592
Hume, David, 167

I

IBM Corporation, 14, 15, 113*n*, 137, 680
IBM Personal Computer, 39
Ice cream and object-oriented languages, 332*n*
Identity, 305245, 305
if (special form), 40, 43, 48, 127, 196, 380, 760
If rule, 46, 47
"if ...then ..." (logic), 546*n*
Image processing, 506, 584
Immutable values, 233, 247
Imperative programming, 231
Imperative evaluator, 660
Implementations, 27
Implication, 546
Implicit begin, 129
Improper lists, 186
inchar (Gleam instruction), 598, 648, 656, 677, 777
Inclusive "or", 41
Indexing (databases), 446, 481, 491
Index registers, 608
Individuals, 547

Indivisible tasks, 290
Induction, 551
Inductive definitions, 186
Inexact number (data type), 757
inexact->exact (primitive), 70, 766
inexact? (primitive), 765
Inference engines, 558
Infinite loops, 64, 813
Information, 8
Ingerman, Peter Z., 136*n*
Ingres, J. A. D., 618
Inheritance, 332
Initialization rule, 47
innum (Gleam instruction), 598, 777
In-order traversal, 479
Input, 123–25, 136
Input devices, 10, 110*n*, 584
Input/Output Unit, 593
Input/output,
    memory-mapped, 656
    numeric, 583–86
input-port? (primitive), 769
Insertion in lists, 241
Insertion sort, 441
    compared with Quicksort, 488
Instance of class, 306
Instance variables, 307, 310, 319, 329
Instructions,
    Gleam, 597–604, 648–650
    unimplemented machine, 646
Integer (data type), 70, 757
integer->char (primitive), 112, 767
integer? (primitive), 70, 764
Integrated circuits, 646
Integrity, referential, 454
interest, 96
Interfaces, 27
International codes, 113
Interpreters, 364, 364–68
    versus compilers, 382
Interrupts, 657, 683
Invariant, 493
Inventory management, 498–506
IOU, 593
Irrational numbers, 72
ISWIM, 347
Item (data type), 499
Iteration, 93

T

Colophon

We also thank Betty Dexter for the extreme effort she put into setting this report in TEX, and Donald Knuth for designing the program that caused her troubles. — *Revised[4] Report on the Algorithmic Language Scheme*

. . . the sturdiness of the original Lucida and Lucida Math fonts is not as important as formerly. Users of those early designs today seem to choose them more for their "look" than for their intended low-res applications, since I see them on American potato chip packaging, frankfurter labels, and French chocolate advertising, all of which is high res, and, come to think of it, high calorie. — Charles Bigelow

This book was typeset by the authors in Lucida Bright, a font family designed by Charles Bigelow and Kris Holmes in the early 1980s, based upon their original Lucida fonts, which were originally designed to reproduce well on low-resolution devices such as early 300 dpi laser printers. Lucida Bright has become popular for scientific and mathematical copy because of its readability at smaller sizes, and its harmonious mathematical and typewriter fonts.

The interior book design was done by Mona Pompili, the project manager, incorporating some of the authors' ideas.

The authors used the Epsilon and GNU Emacs text editors to enter the original text. Draft illustrations were prepared by the authors, and final versions produced by TTP International (Surrey, England), using Adobe Illustrator. The authors typeset the book using two versions of TEX—the standard UNIX version, and a PC version developed by Y&Y Software (Concord, Massachusetts). A specially tuned version of Lucida Bright, also developed by Y&Y, was used.

The authors provided the printers with PostScript files containing the entire text, except for the image at the beginning of each chapter, which was superimposed by the printers, because it was too large to be processed in any other way. Network technology has not yet reached enough of the participants in the publication process to transport such files electronically; Federal Express was used instead.

These files were printed on an Escher-Grad EG8000 by R. R. Donnelley and Sons Company (Harrisonburg, Virginia).